EX MACHINA

BOOK ONE

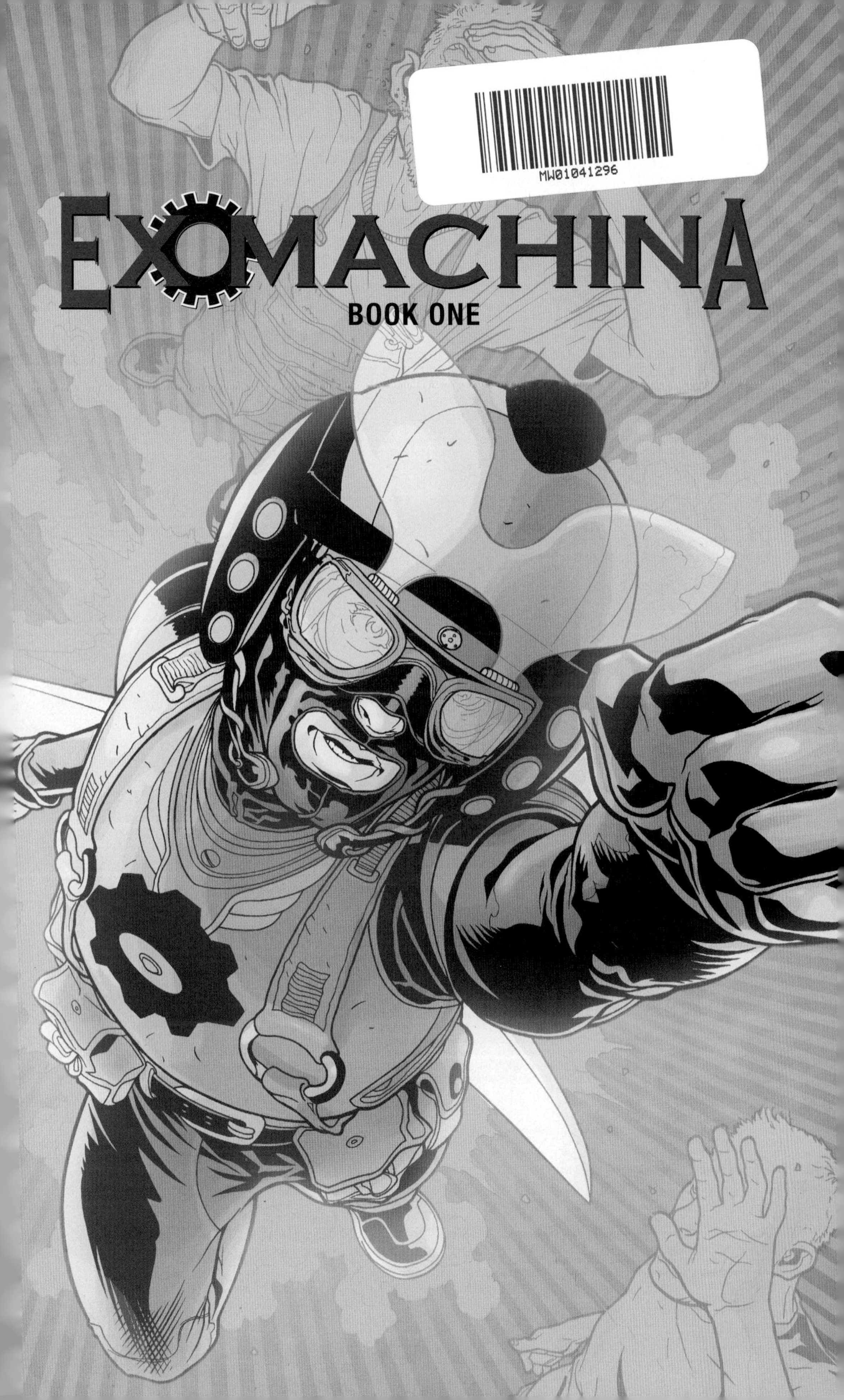

BRIAN K. VAUGHAN: WRITER
TONY HARRIS: PENCILS
TOM FEISTER: INKS
JD METTLER: COLORS
JARED K. FLETCHER: LETTERS

COLLECTED EDITION COVER
BY TONY HARRIS

EX MACHINA CREATED
BY VAUGHAN AND HARRIS

Ben Abernathy Editor – Original Series
Kristy Quinn Assistant Editor – Original Series
Jeb Woodard Group Editor – Collected Editions
Robbin Brosterman Design Director – Books

Shelly Bond VP & Executive Editor - Vertigo

Diane Nelson President
Dan DiDio and **Jim Lee** Co-Publishers
Geoff Johns Chief Creative Officer
Amit Desai Senior VP – Marketing & Global Franchise Management
Nairi Gardiner Senior VP – Finance
Sam Ades VP – Digital Marketing
Bobbie Chase – VP – Talent Development
Mark Chiarello Senior VP – Art, Design & Collected Editions
John Cunningham VP – Content Strategy
Anne DePies VP – Strategy Planning & Reporting
Don Falletti VP – Manufacturing Operations
Lawrence Ganem VP – Editorial Administration & Talent Relation
Alison Gill Senior VP – Manufacturing & Operations
Hank Kanalz   Senior VP – Editorial Strategy & Administration
Jay Kogan VP – Legal Affairs
Derek Maddalena Senior VP – Sales & Business Development
Dan Miron VP – Sales Planning & Trade Development
Nick Napolitano VP – Manufacturing Administration
Carol Roeder VP – Marketing
Eddie Scannell VP – Mass Account & Digital Sales
Susan Sheppard VP – Business Affairs
Courtney Simmons Senior VP – Publicity & Communications
Jim (Ski) Sokolowski VP – Comic Book Specialty & Newsstand Sales

EX MACHINA BOOK ONE
Published by DC Comics. Copyright © 2013 Brian K. Vaughan and Tony Harris.
All Rights Reserved.

Originally published in single magazine form by WildStorm Productions as EX MACHINA #1-11
Copyright © 2004, 2005 Brian K. Vaughan and Tony Harris. All Rights Reserved. All characters,
their distinctive likenesses and related elements featured in this publication are trademarks of
DC Comics. The stories, characters and incidents featured in this publication are entirely
fictional. DC Comics does not read or accept unsolicited ideas, stories or artwork.

DC Comics, 4000 Warner Blvd., Burbank, CA 91522
A Warner Bros. Entertainment Company.
Printed by RR Donnelley, Owensville, MO, USA. 7/2/15 Second Printing.
ISBN: 978-1-4012-4498-9

Library of Congress Cataloging-in-Publication Data

Vaughan, Brian K., author.
  Ex Machina. Book One / Brian K. Vaughan, Tony Harris.
     pages cm
  "Originally published in single magazine form as EX MACHINA 1-11."
  ISBN 978-1-4012-4498-9
1. Mayors—Comic books, strips, etc. 2. Superheroes—Comic books, strips, etc. 3. New York
(N.Y.)—Comic books, strips, etc. 4. Graphic novels. I. Harris, Tony, 1969- illustrator. II. Title.
  PN6728.E98V35 2013
  741.5'973—dc23
                          2013026712

 **DEDICATIONS**

BRIAN:
For Ruth, my New York City.

TONY:
To the players, a testament to your dedication.
To Jimmy, Marnie, Larry, Cathy, Pat,
Edgar, Greta, Eric, Doodle, Jim, Cat,
JD, Stacie, Enzo, Brian, and
all the bit players.

TOM:
For my Mom, who
always made sure I had
pencils and paper.

JD:
For my mother,
Darlene. I miss you.

INTRODUCTION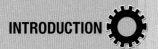

Brian K. Vaughan is a magician.

I know this because I emailed him and asked, "Were you ever a magician?" And he wrote back, "I was."

But Vaughan is not a standard magician.

You see, a standard magician is the kind you get at a birthday party. They make something happen—the quarter comes out of your ear—*ta da!*—and they rely on that moment of surprise to entertain you.

But the best magicians—the true master class—begin with a promise. They *tell you* exactly what the magic trick will be—*I will saw this woman in half*—and then they challenge you—they *dare* you—to try and figure out if and how it's going to happen. Simply put, they start with the ending. They give you that endpoint right from the start. Like a promise.

Which brings me to EX MACHINA.

Watch what The Amazing Vaughan does on the very first page. We don't start at the beginning. We don't meet Mitchell as a novice or a child and then watch him grow and learn. We meet him at his end. EX MACHINA opens with his confession—perhaps it's an apology—of the horrific disaster that he caused in 2005. He doesn't begin like Superman, learning and smiling and saving the world with an American flag. He broods like King Lear, telling us, flat out, "It may look like a comic, but it's really a tragedy." What the hell kinda superhero book is this?

It's only one of the very best ones I've ever read. Period. Exclamation point.

On those first pages, Brian Vaughan gives us his ending. He makes a promise to us. A beautiful promise. He tells us—swears to us—that if we're willing to listen, this is going to be one of the most devastating, horrible, most gruesome disasters that has ever been witnessed by human eyes. He guarantees that the person we're rooting for is going to fail miserably. It's going to be a butchery. There's the challenge. Can we possibly look away?

Only a fool would.

Only a fool would miss the complexity of Mitchell Hundred's ego. Or the nuances of Kremlin and Bradbury, of Mom and Zeller, of Journal and Wylie and the rest of the supporting cast. No question, this is a story of politics. But not just governmental. These are human politics—the battles over our own weaknesses and conditions.

And can we gush about Tony Harris? As any comic reader knows, it all falls apart without the art. Thanks to Tony Harris, this world lives. It breathes real air and flies with jetpacks that expel real smoke and dirt and exhaust. For me, the *Millennium Falcon* always seemed real because it was aged and filthy like an actual old warhorse. It's the same with Mitchell Hundred's world. Thanks to Tony Harris, every character—minor, major and in between—has all the flaws and imperfections of, well…us. Which is why we're rooting so hard for Mitchell Hundred. And sometimes rooting against him.

And so, the curtain rises and the performance begins and the promises keep coming. Just when we witness one trick, Vaughan and Harris promise another: be it that standing second tower, or the NSA secrets, or whatever it is that's inside Mayor Hundred's safe. Hitchcock knew it best: "There is no terror in the bang, only in the antic-ipation of it." Watch again: Vaughan and Harris show us over and over and over exactly what we should be look-ing for. And over and over and over, we stare like children, heads tilted backward, with our mouths gaping open as we wait breathlessly for the end to come.

God, I love a good magic show.

And here one is.

The masters are about to take the stage. So go get a good seat. It doesn't matter where. Near or far—when the *ta da* slaps you across the face—you'll never see it coming.

- Brad Meltzer
Fort Lauderdale, FL 2008

CHAPTER 1 THE PILOT

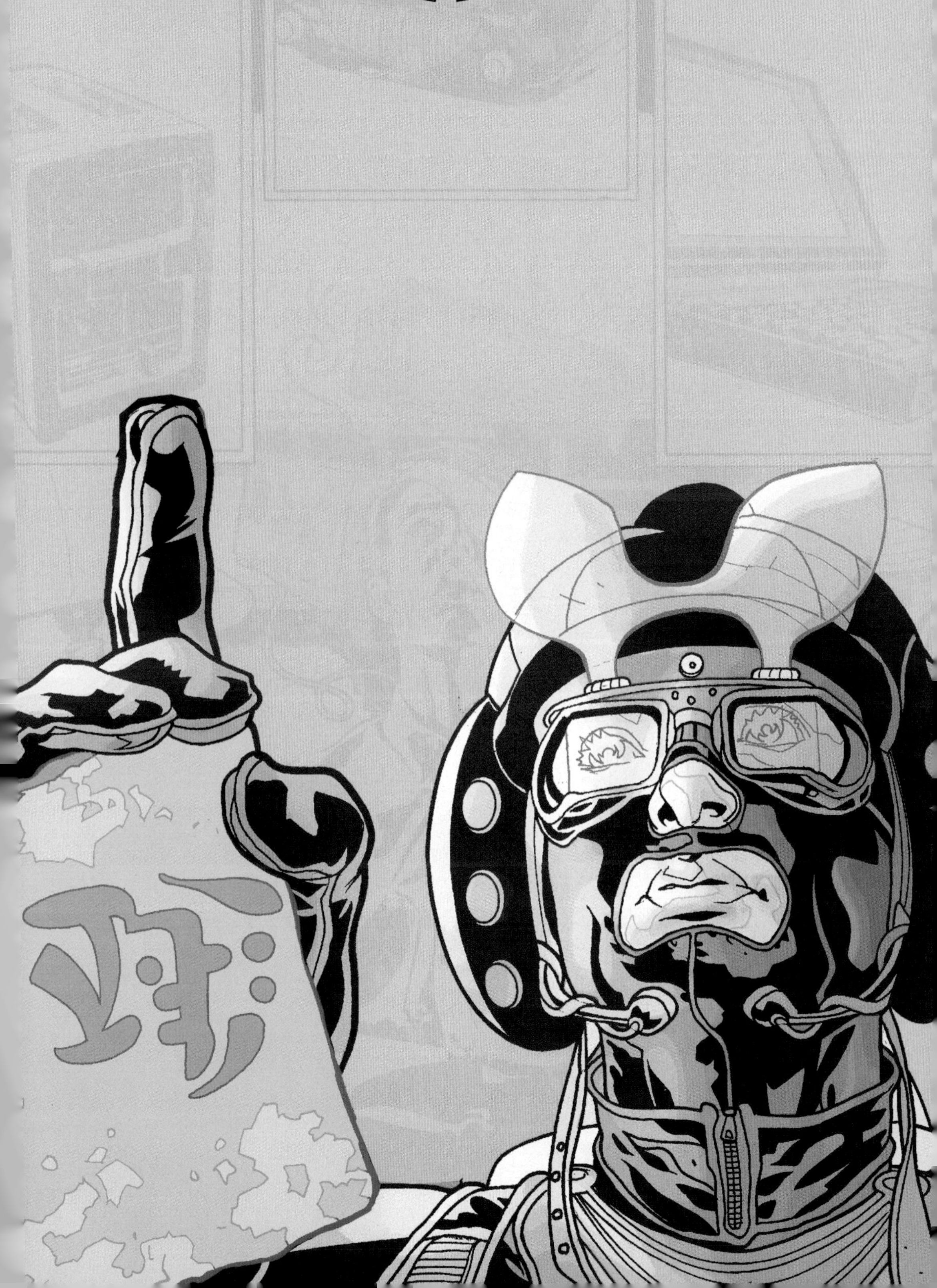

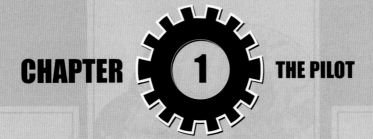

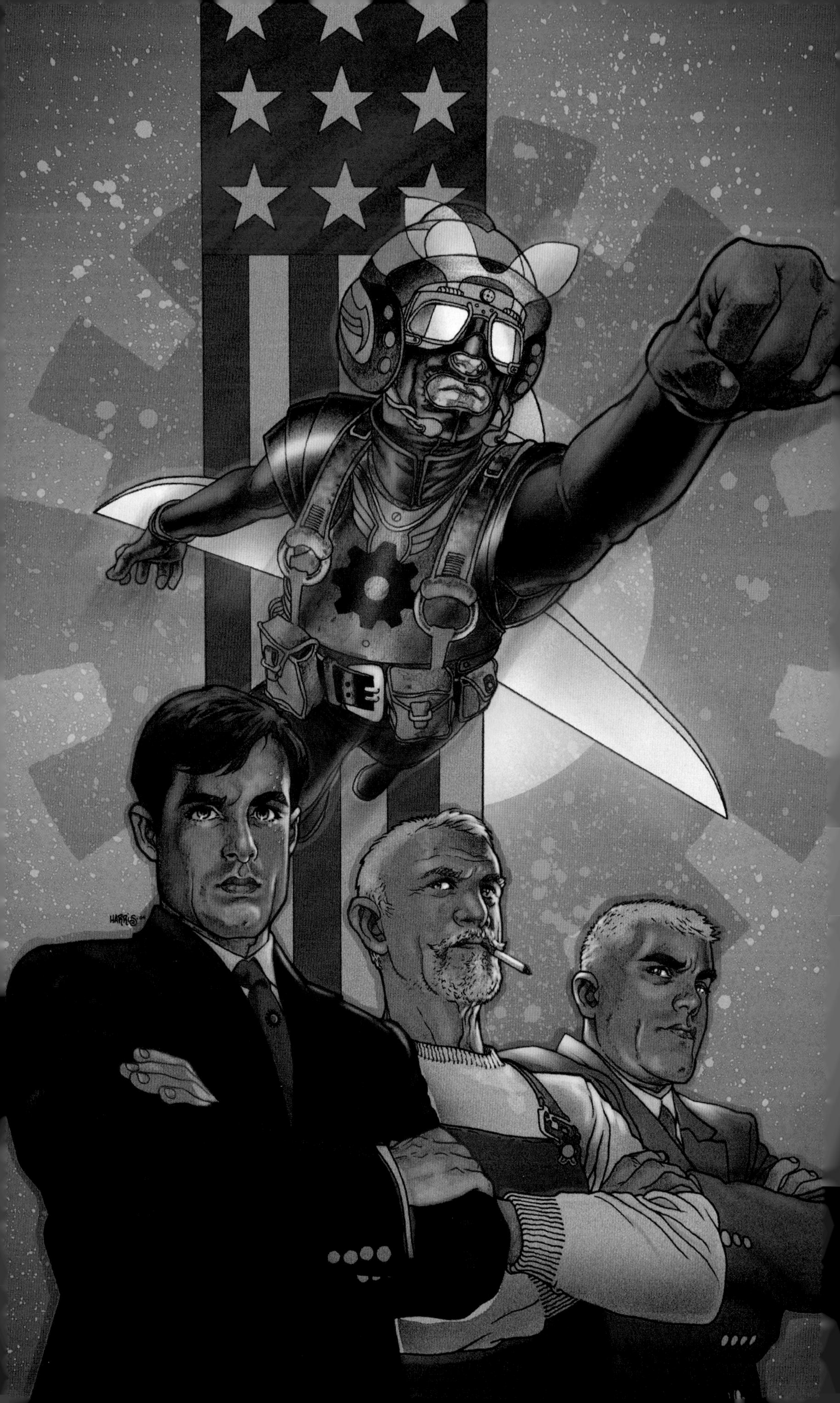

deus ex machina (DAY-us ex MAH-kin-ah): Literally, "god from the machine." A person or force that arrives to provide an improbable olution to an impossible situation, named after he mechanical device used by Greek dramatists to lower actors playing deities onto the stage.

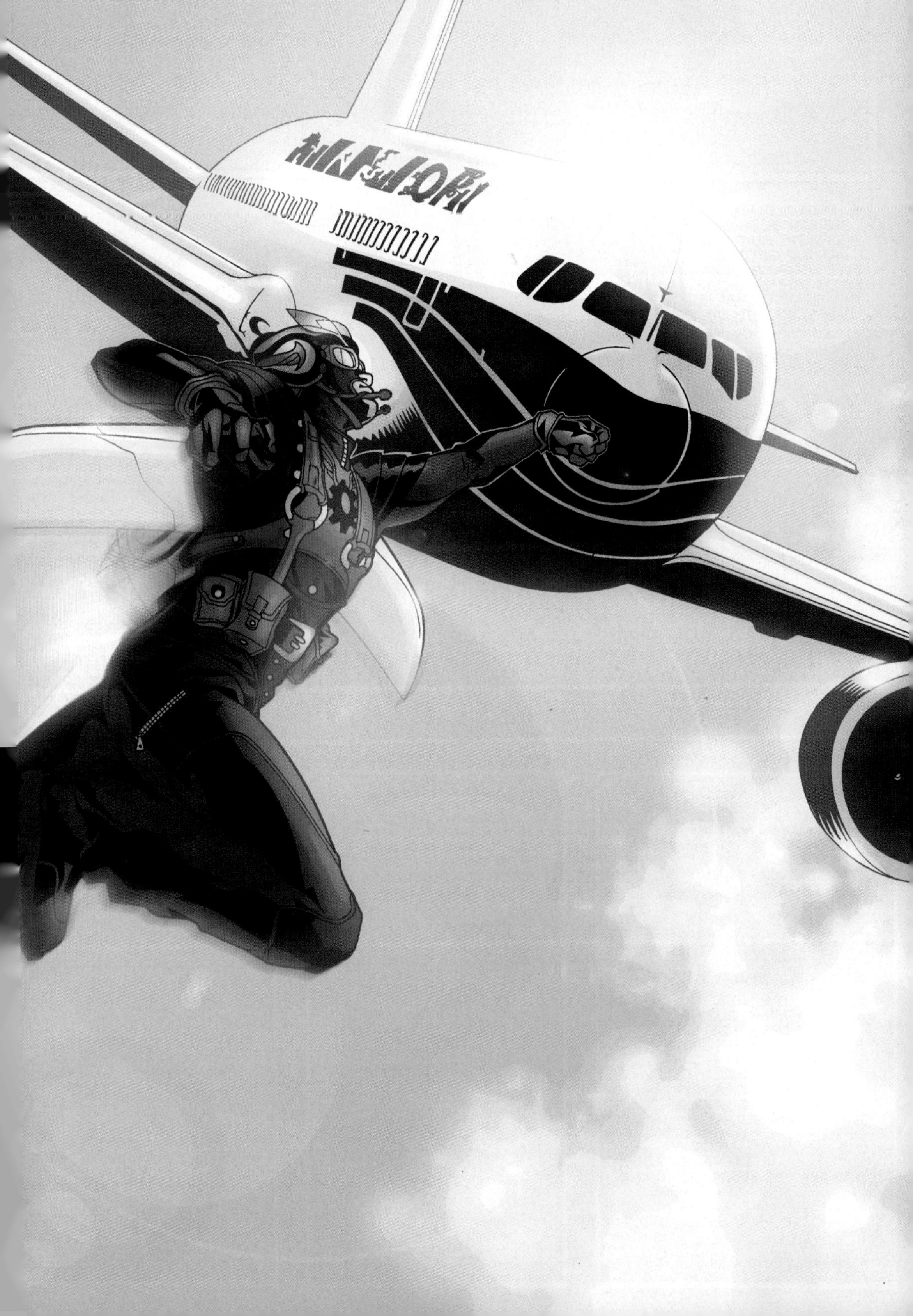

YOU'RE PROBABLY SICK OF THAT PICTURE BY NOW, HUH?

CHRIST KNOWS I AM.

PEOPLE BLAME ME FOR BUSH IN HIS FLIGHT SUIT AND ARNOLD GETTING ELECTED GOVERNOR, BUT TRUTH IS...THOSE THINGS WOULD HAVE HAPPENED WITH OR WITHOUT ME.

EVERYONE WAS SCARED BACK THEN, AND WHEN FOLKS ARE SCARED, THEY WANT TO BE SURROUNDED BY *HEROES*.

BUT REAL HEROES ARE JUST A FICTION WE CREATE. THEY DON'T EXIST OUTSIDE OF COMIC BOOKS.

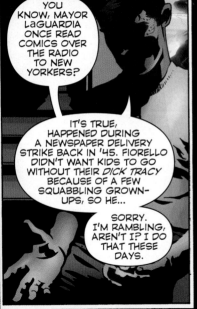

YOU KNOW, MAYOR LaGUARDIA ONCE READ COMICS OVER THE RADIO TO NEW YORKERS?

IT'S TRUE, HAPPENED DURING A NEWSPAPER DELIVERY STRIKE BACK IN '45. FIORELLO DIDN'T WANT KIDS TO GO WITHOUT THEIR *DICK TRACY* BECAUSE OF A FEW SQUABBLING GROWN-UPS, SO HE...

SORRY. I'M RAMBLING, AREN'T I? I DO THAT THESE DAYS.

ANYWAY, THIS IS THE STORY OF MY FOUR YEARS IN OFFICE, FROM THE BEGINNING OF 2002 THROUGH GODFORSAKEN 2005.

IT MAY LOOK LIKE A COMIC, BUT IT'S REALLY A TRAGEDY.

THAT'S LIFE, HUH?

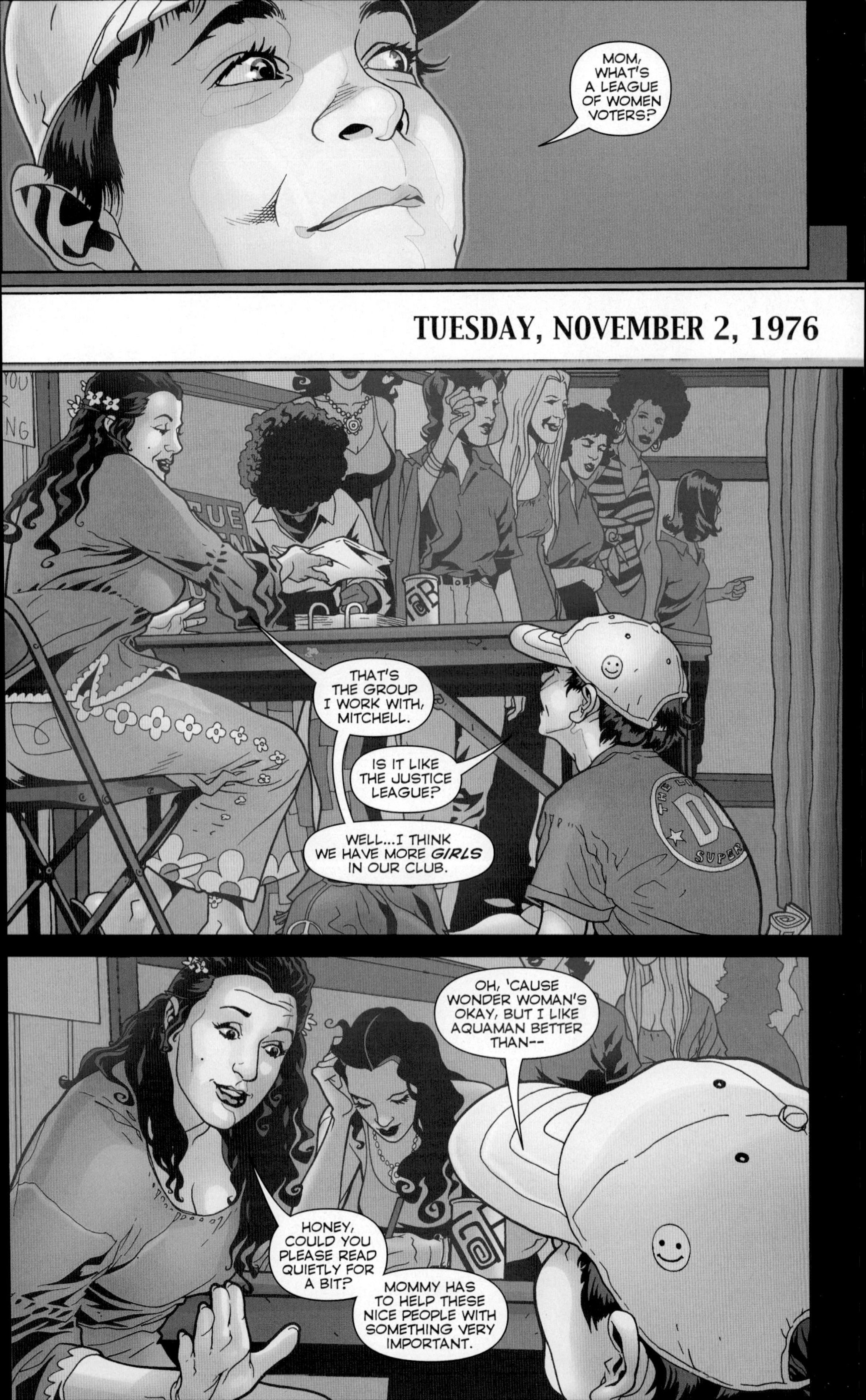
MOM, WHAT'S A LEAGUE OF WOMEN VOTERS?
TUESDAY, NOVEMBER 2, 1976
THAT'S THE GROUP I WORK WITH, MITCHELL.
IS IT LIKE THE JUSTICE LEAGUE?
WELL...I THINK WE HAVE MORE *GIRLS* IN OUR CLUB.
OH, 'CAUSE WONDER WOMAN'S OKAY, BUT I LIKE AQUAMAN BETTER THAN--
HONEY, COULD YOU PLEASE READ QUIETLY FOR A BIT?
MOMMY HAS TO HELP THESE NICE PEOPLE WITH SOMETHING VERY IMPORTANT.

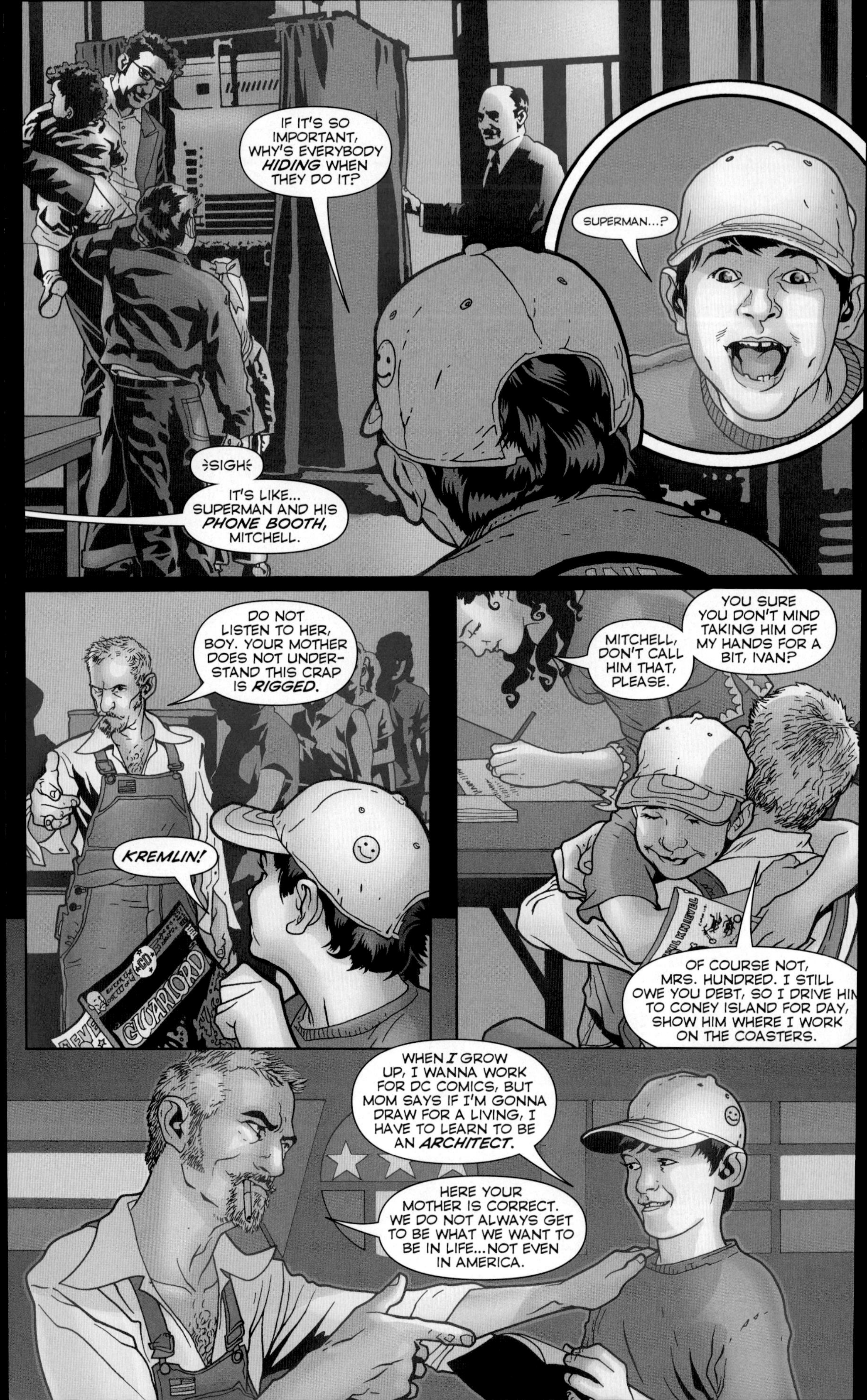
IF IT'S SO IMPORTANT, WHY'S EVERYBODY *HIDING* WHEN THEY DO IT?
SUPERMAN...?
SIGH
IT'S LIKE... SUPERMAN AND HIS *PHONE BOOTH,* MITCHELL.
DO NOT LISTEN TO HER, BOY. YOUR MOTHER DOES NOT UNDER-STAND THIS CRAP IS *RIGGED.*
KREMLIN!
MITCHELL, DON'T CALL HIM THAT, PLEASE.
YOU SURE YOU DON'T MIND TAKING HIM OFF MY HANDS FOR A BIT, IVAN?
OF COURSE NOT, MRS. HUNDRED. I STILL OWE YOU DEBT, SO I DRIVE HIM TO CONEY ISLAND FOR DAY, SHOW HIM WHERE I WORK ON THE COASTERS.
WHEN *I* GROW UP, I WANNA WORK FOR DC COMICS, BUT MOM SAYS IF I'M GONNA DRAW FOR A LIVING, I HAVE TO LEARN TO BE AN *ARCHITECT.*
HERE YOUR MOTHER IS CORRECT. WE DO NOT ALWAYS GET TO BE WHAT WE WANT TO BE IN LIFE...NOT EVEN IN AMERICA.

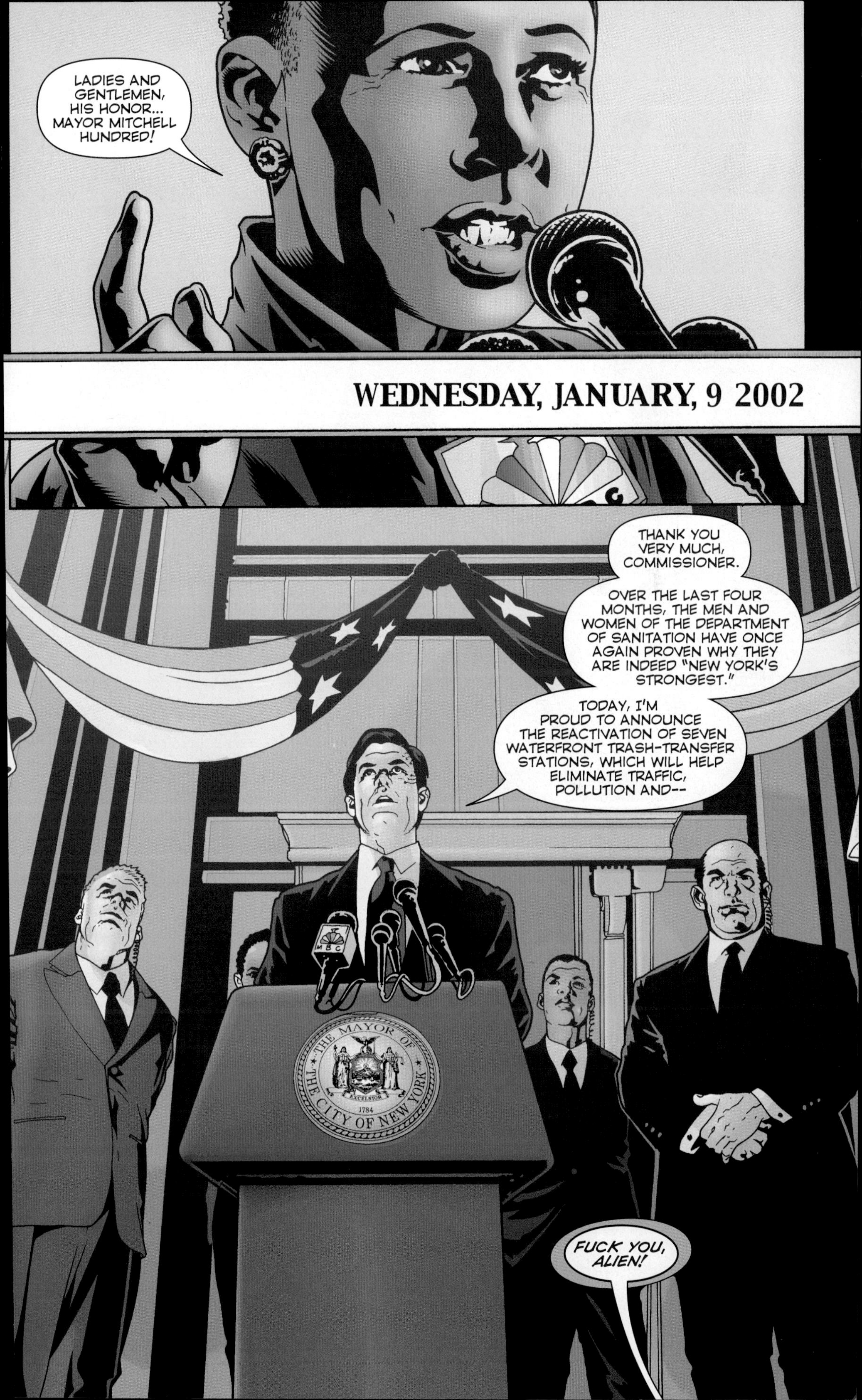
LADIES AND GENTLEMEN, HIS HONOR... MAYOR MITCHELL HUNDRED!
WEDNESDAY, JANUARY, 9 2002
THANK YOU VERY MUCH, COMMISSIONER.
OVER THE LAST FOUR MONTHS, THE MEN AND WOMEN OF THE DEPARTMENT OF SANITATION HAVE ONCE AGAIN PROVEN WHY THEY ARE INDEED "NEW YORK'S STRONGEST."
TODAY, I'M PROUD TO ANNOUNCE THE REACTIVATION OF SEVEN WATERFRONT TRASH-TRANSFER STATIONS, WHICH WILL HELP ELIMINATE TRAFFIC, POLLUTION AND--
THE MAYOR OF THE CITY OF NEW YORK
EXCELSIOR
1784
FUCK YOU, ALIEN!

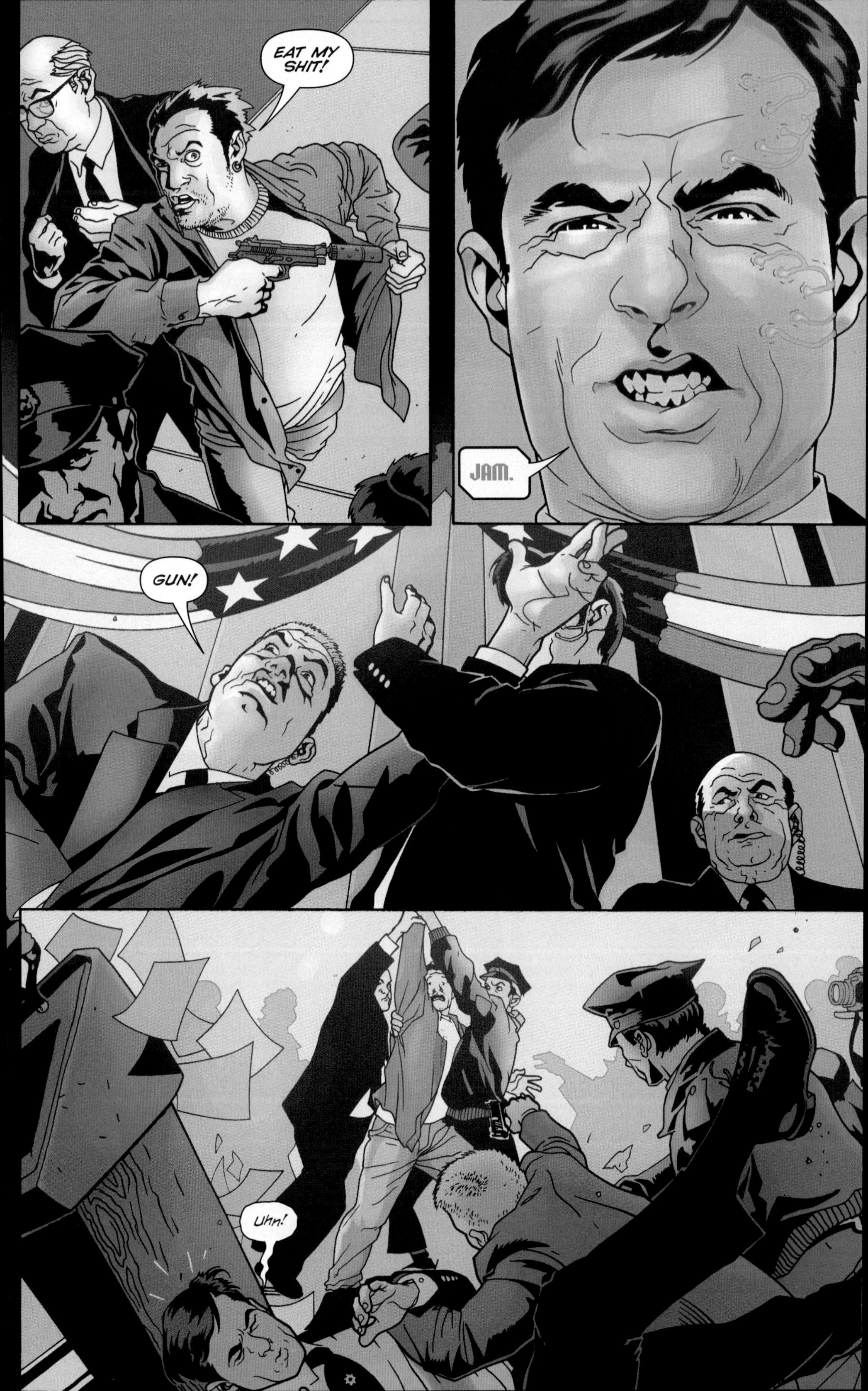
EAT MY SHIT!
JAM.
GUN!
Uhn!

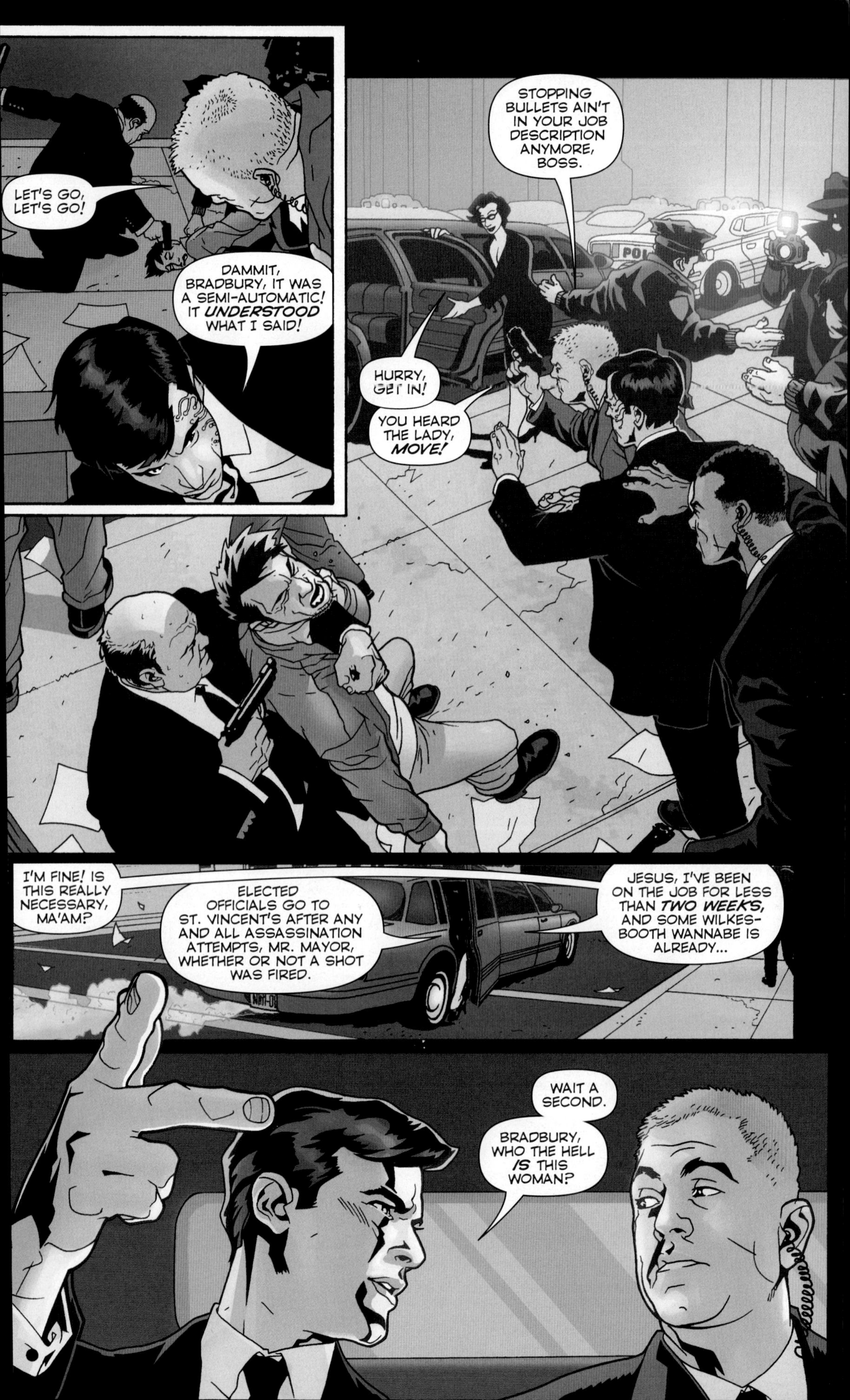
LET'S GO, LET'S GO!
DAMMIT, BRADBURY, IT WAS A SEMI-AUTOMATIC! IT UNDERSTOOD WHAT I SAID!
STOPPING BULLETS AIN'T IN YOUR JOB DESCRIPTION ANYMORE, BOSS.
HURRY, GET IN!
YOU HEARD THE LADY, MOVE!
I'M FINE! IS THIS REALLY NECESSARY, MA'AM?
ELECTED OFFICIALS GO TO ST. VINCENT'S AFTER ANY AND ALL ASSASSINATION ATTEMPTS, MR. MAYOR, WHETHER OR NOT A SHOT WAS FIRED.
JESUS, I'VE BEEN ON THE JOB FOR LESS THAN TWO WEEKS, AND SOME WILKES-BOOTH WANNABE IS ALREADY...
WAIT A SECOND.
BRADBURY, WHO THE HELL IS THIS WOMAN?

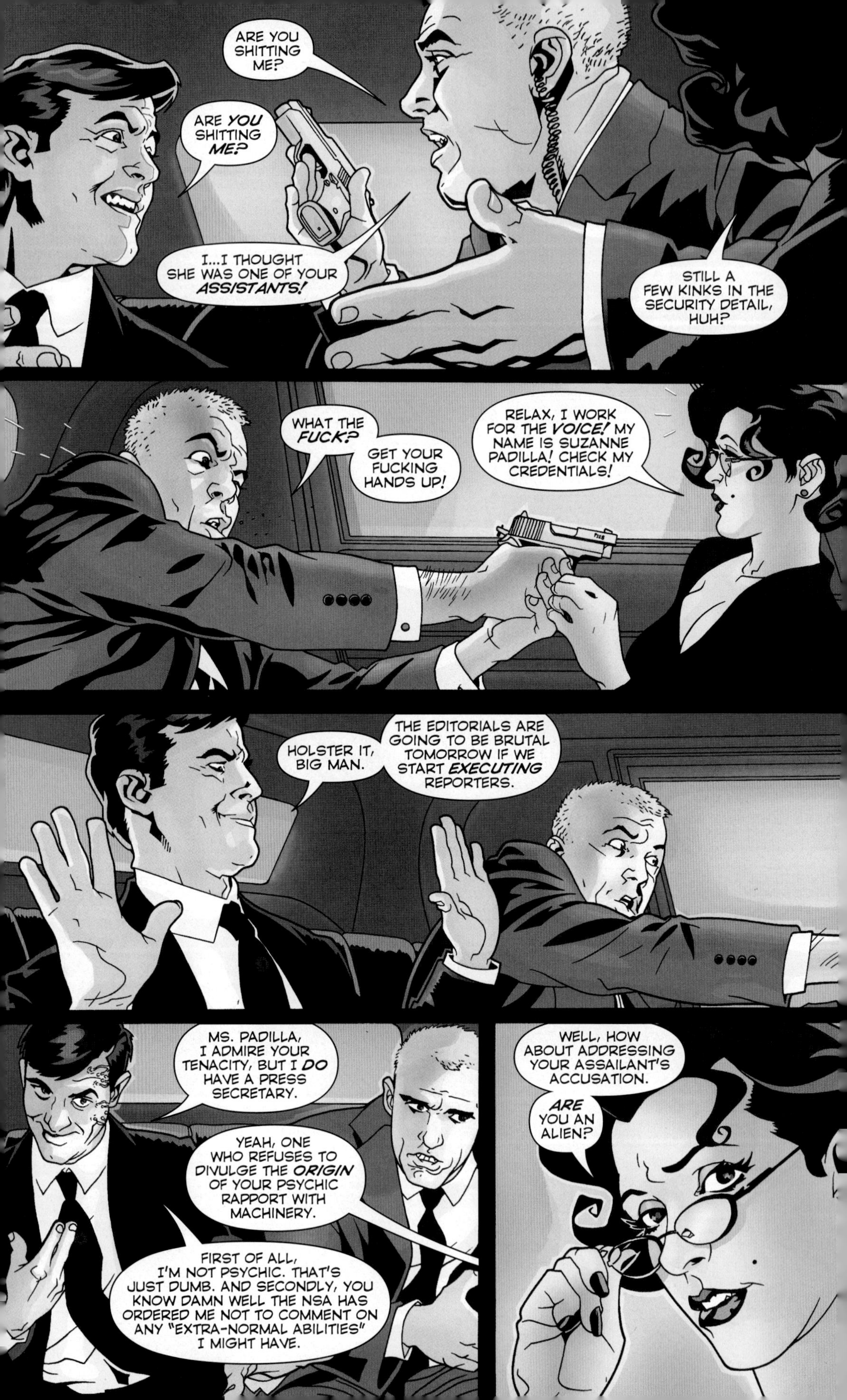
ARE YOU SHITTING ME?
ARE *YOU* SHITTING *ME?*
I...I THOUGHT SHE WAS ONE OF YOUR *ASSISTANTS!*
STILL A FEW KINKS IN THE SECURITY DETAIL, HUH?
WHAT THE *FUCK?*
GET YOUR FUCKING HANDS UP!
RELAX, I WORK FOR THE *VOICE!* MY NAME IS SUZANNE PADILLA! CHECK MY CREDENTIALS!
HOLSTER IT, BIG MAN.
THE EDITORIALS ARE GOING TO BE BRUTAL TOMORROW IF WE START *EXECUTING* REPORTERS.
MS. PADILLA, I ADMIRE YOUR TENACITY, BUT I *DO* HAVE A PRESS SECRETARY.
YEAH, ONE WHO REFUSES TO DIVULGE THE *ORIGIN* OF YOUR PSYCHIC RAPPORT WITH MACHINERY.
FIRST OF ALL, I'M NOT PSYCHIC. THAT'S JUST DUMB. AND SECONDLY, YOU KNOW DAMN WELL THE NSA HAS ORDERED ME NOT TO COMMENT ON ANY "EXTRA-NORMAL ABILITIES" I MIGHT HAVE.
WELL, HOW ABOUT ADDRESSING YOUR ASSAILANT'S ACCUSATION.
ARE YOU AN ALIEN?

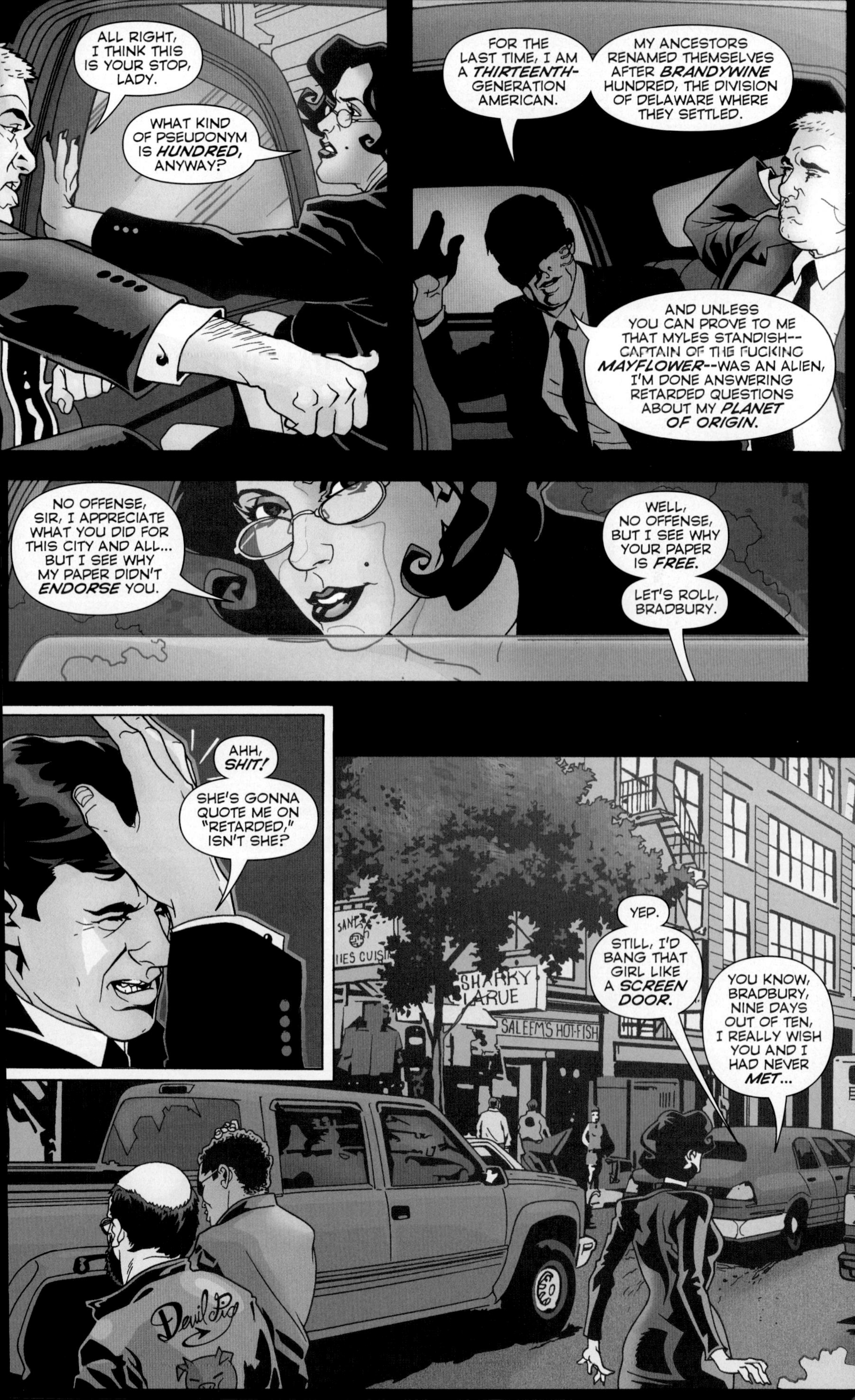
ALL RIGHT, I THINK THIS IS YOUR STOP, LADY.
WHAT KIND OF PSEUDONYM IS HUNDRED, ANYWAY?
FOR THE LAST TIME, I AM A THIRTEENTH-GENERATION AMERICAN.
MY ANCESTORS RENAMED THEMSELVES AFTER BRANDYWINE HUNDRED, THE DIVISION OF DELAWARE WHERE THEY SETTLED.
AND UNLESS YOU CAN PROVE TO ME THAT MYLES STANDISH--CAPTAIN OF THE FUCKING MAYFLOWER--WAS AN ALIEN, I'M DONE ANSWERING RETARDED QUESTIONS ABOUT MY PLANET OF ORIGIN.
NO OFFENSE, SIR, I APPRECIATE WHAT YOU DID FOR THIS CITY AND ALL... BUT I SEE WHY MY PAPER DIDN'T ENDORSE YOU.
WELL, NO OFFENSE, BUT I SEE WHY YOUR PAPER IS FREE.
LET'S ROLL, BRADBURY.
AHH, SHIT!
SHE'S GONNA QUOTE ME ON "RETARDED," ISN'T SHE?
YEP.
STILL, I'D BANG THAT GIRL LIKE A SCREEN DOOR.
YOU KNOW, BRADBURY, NINE DAYS OUT OF TEN, I REALLY WISH YOU AND I HAD NEVER MET...
SHARKY LARUE
SALEEM'S HOT-FISH
Devil Pig

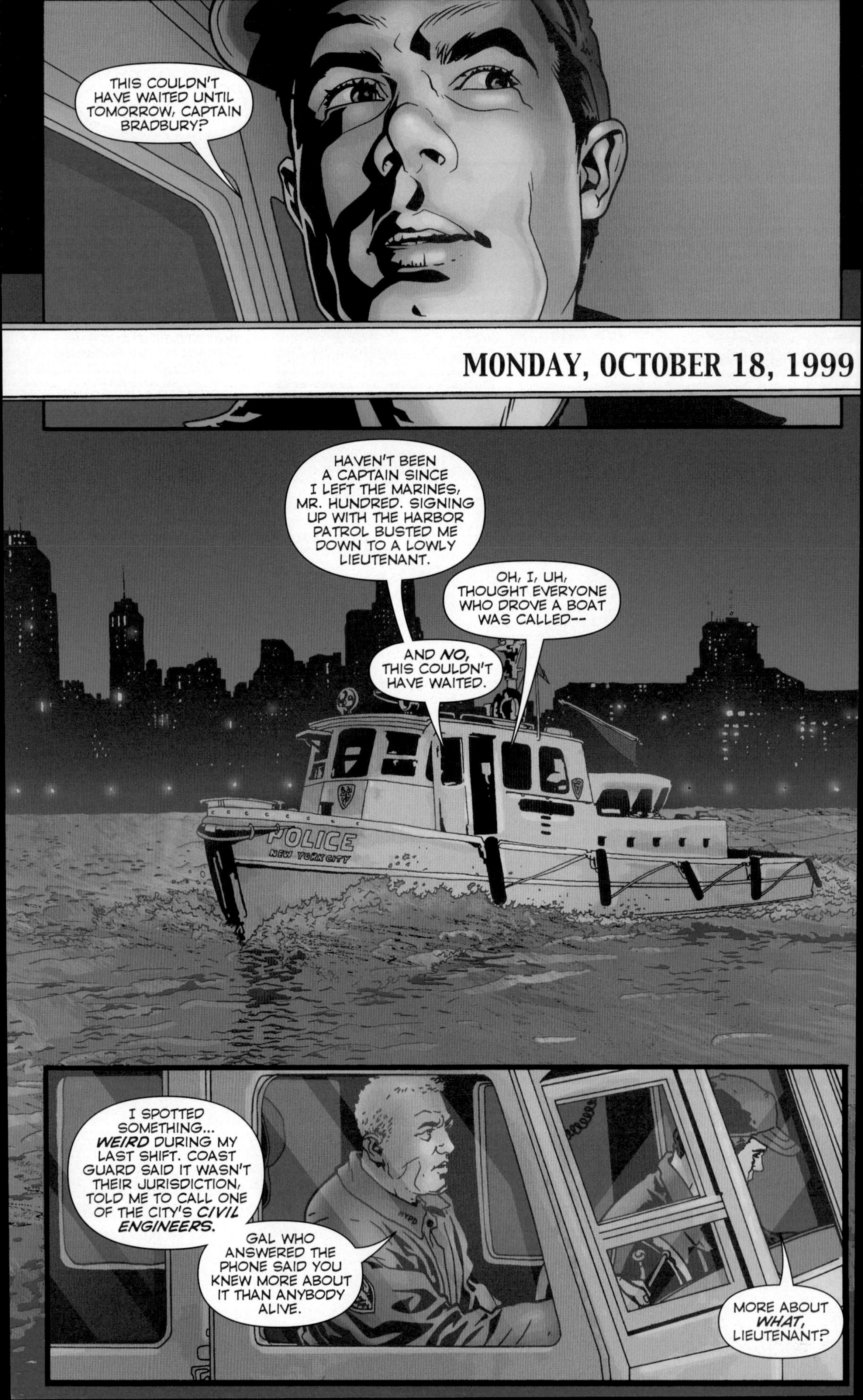
THIS COULDN'T HAVE WAITED UNTIL TOMORROW, CAPTAIN BRADBURY?
MONDAY, OCTOBER 18, 1999
HAVEN'T BEEN A CAPTAIN SINCE I LEFT THE MARINES, MR. HUNDRED. SIGNING UP WITH THE HARBOR PATROL BUSTED ME DOWN TO A LOWLY LIEUTENANT.
OH, I, UH, THOUGHT EVERYONE WHO DROVE A BOAT WAS CALLED--
AND NO, THIS COULDN'T HAVE WAITED.
POLICE
NEW YORK CITY
I SPOTTED SOMETHING... WEIRD DURING MY LAST SHIFT. COAST GUARD SAID IT WASN'T THEIR JURISDICTION, TOLD ME TO CALL ONE OF THE CITY'S CIVIL ENGINEERS.
GAL WHO ANSWERED THE PHONE SAID YOU KNEW MORE ABOUT IT THAN ANYBODY ALIVE.
MORE ABOUT WHAT, LIEUTENANT?

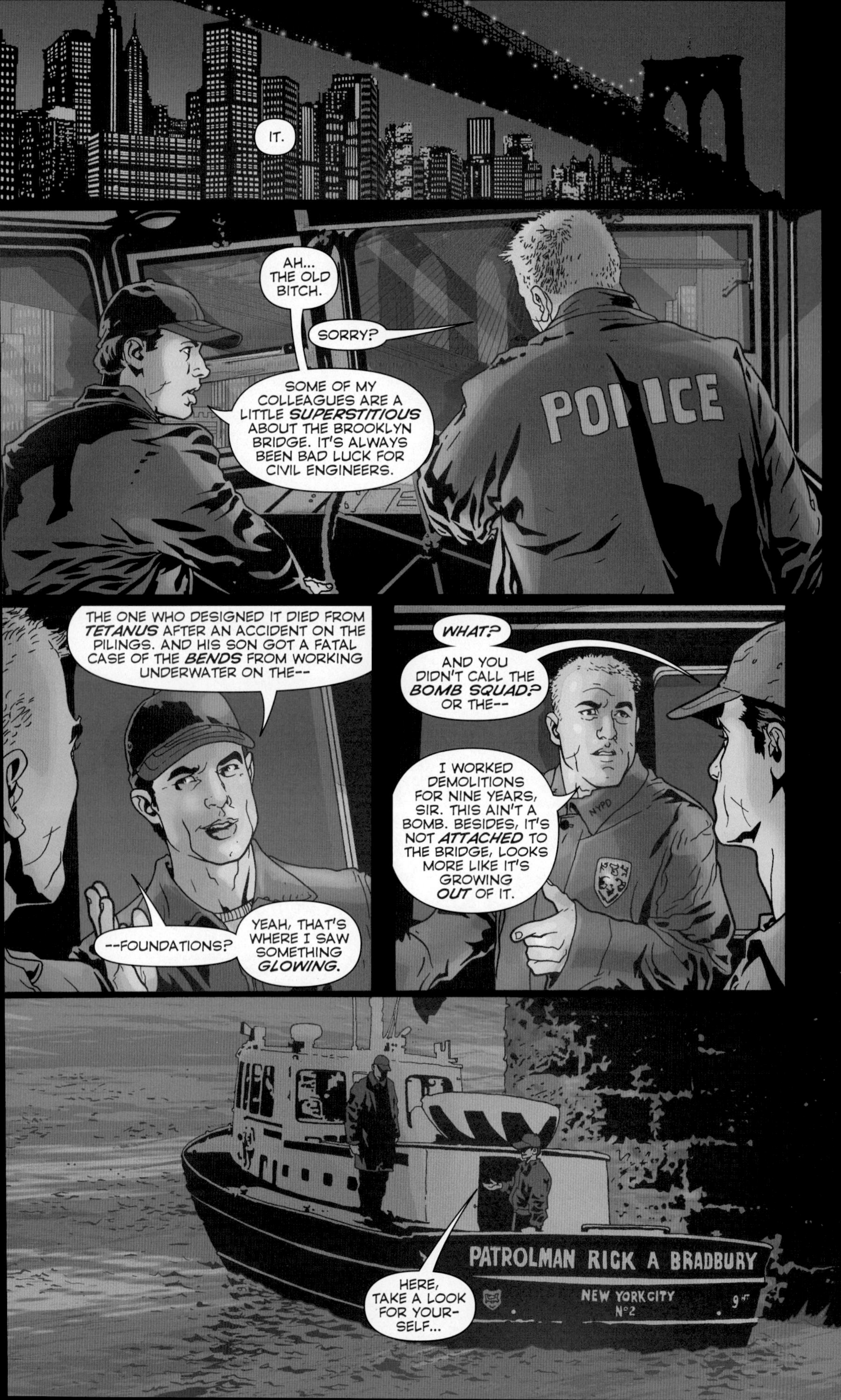

IT.
AH... THE OLD BITCH.
SORRY?
SOME OF MY COLLEAGUES ARE A LITTLE SUPERSTITIOUS ABOUT THE BROOKLYN BRIDGE. IT'S ALWAYS BEEN BAD LUCK FOR CIVIL ENGINEERS.
POLICE
THE ONE WHO DESIGNED IT DIED FROM TETANUS AFTER AN ACCIDENT ON THE PILINGS. AND HIS SON GOT A FATAL CASE OF THE BENDS FROM WORKING UNDERWATER ON THE--
--FOUNDATIONS?
YEAH, THAT'S WHERE I SAW SOMETHING GLOWING.
WHAT?
AND YOU DIDN'T CALL THE BOMB SQUAD? OR THE--
I WORKED DEMOLITIONS FOR NINE YEARS, SIR. THIS AIN'T A BOMB. BESIDES, IT'S NOT ATTACHED TO THE BRIDGE, LOOKS MORE LIKE IT'S GROWING OUT OF IT.
NYPD
PATROLMAN RICK A BRADBURY
NEW YORK CITY
N°2
HERE, TAKE A LOOK FOR YOURSELF...

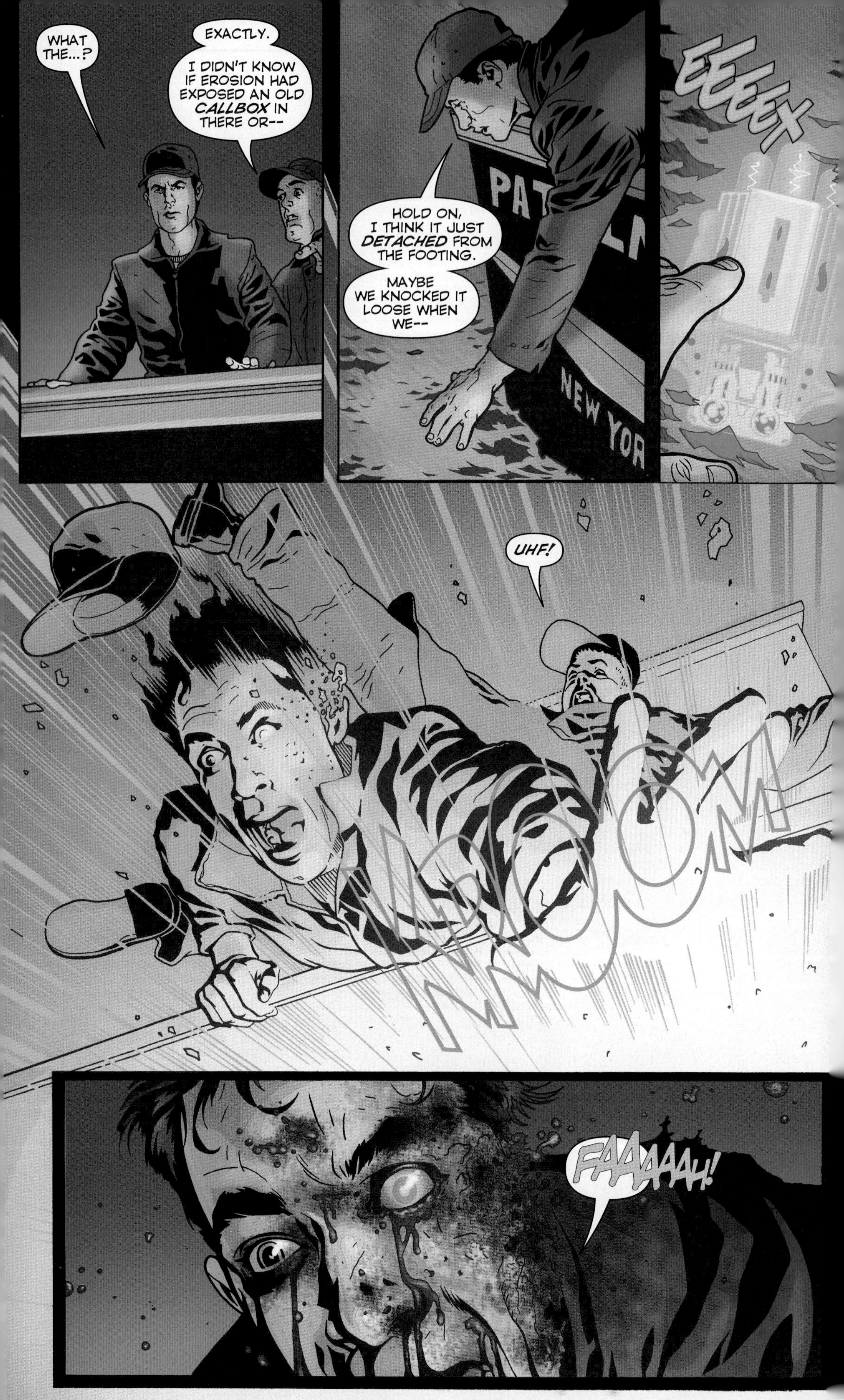
WHAT THE...?
EXACTLY.
I DIDN'T KNOW IF EROSION HAD EXPOSED AN OLD *CALLBOX* IN THERE OR--
HOLD ON, I THINK IT JUST *DETACHED* FROM THE FOOTING.
MAYBE WE KNOCKED IT LOOSE WHEN WE--
NEW YOR
EEEEEEX
UHF!
WHOOM
FAAAAAH!

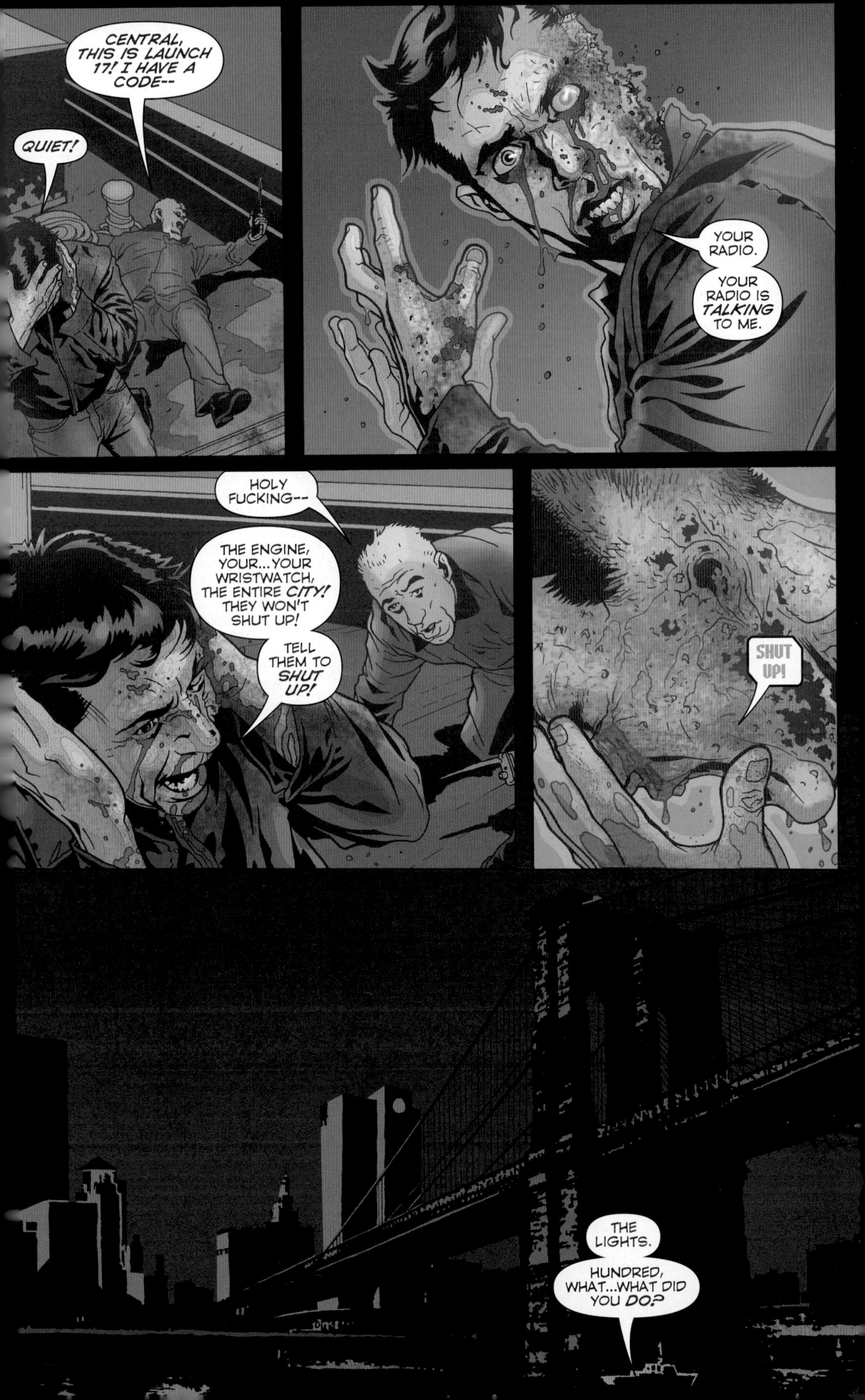
CENTRAL, THIS IS LAUNCH 17! I HAVE A CODE--
QUIET!
YOUR RADIO.
YOUR RADIO IS TALKING TO ME.
HOLY FUCKING--
THE ENGINE, YOUR...YOUR WRISTWATCH, THE ENTIRE CITY! THEY WON'T SHUT UP!
TELL THEM TO SHUT UP!
SHUT UP!
THE LIGHTS.
HUNDRED, WHAT...WHAT DID YOU DO?

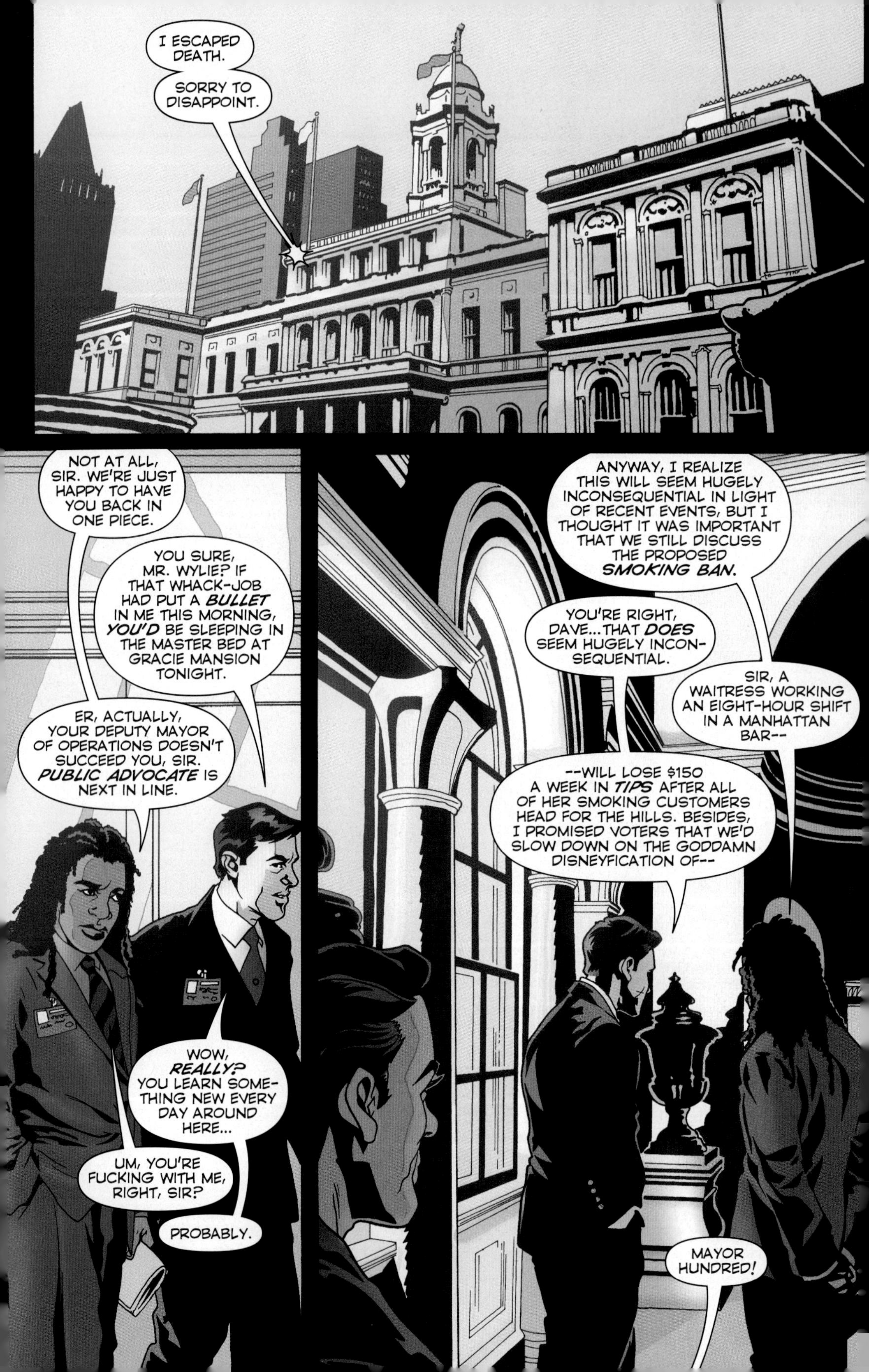
I ESCAPED DEATH.
SORRY TO DISAPPOINT.
NOT AT ALL, SIR. WE'RE JUST HAPPY TO HAVE YOU BACK IN ONE PIECE.
YOU SURE, MR. WYLIE? IF THAT WHACK-JOB HAD PUT A *BULLET* IN ME THIS MORNING, *YOU'D* BE SLEEPING IN THE MASTER BED AT GRACIE MANSION TONIGHT.
ER, ACTUALLY, YOUR DEPUTY MAYOR OF OPERATIONS DOESN'T SUCCEED YOU, SIR. *PUBLIC ADVOCATE* IS NEXT IN LINE.
WOW, *REALLY?* YOU LEARN SOME-THING NEW EVERY DAY AROUND HERE...
UM, YOU'RE FUCKING WITH ME, RIGHT, SIR?
PROBABLY.
ANYWAY, I REALIZE THIS WILL SEEM HUGELY INCONSEQUENTIAL IN LIGHT OF RECENT EVENTS, BUT I THOUGHT IT WAS IMPORTANT THAT WE STILL DISCUSS THE PROPOSED *SMOKING BAN.*
YOU'RE RIGHT, DAVE...THAT *DOES* SEEM HUGELY INCON-SEQUENTIAL.
SIR, A WAITRESS WORKING AN EIGHT-HOUR SHIFT IN A MANHATTAN BAR--
--WILL LOSE $150 A WEEK IN *TIPS* AFTER ALL OF HER SMOKING CUSTOMERS HEAD FOR THE HILLS. BESIDES, I PROMISED VOTERS THAT WE'D SLOW DOWN ON THE GODDAMN DISNEYFICATION OF--
MAYOR HUNDRED!

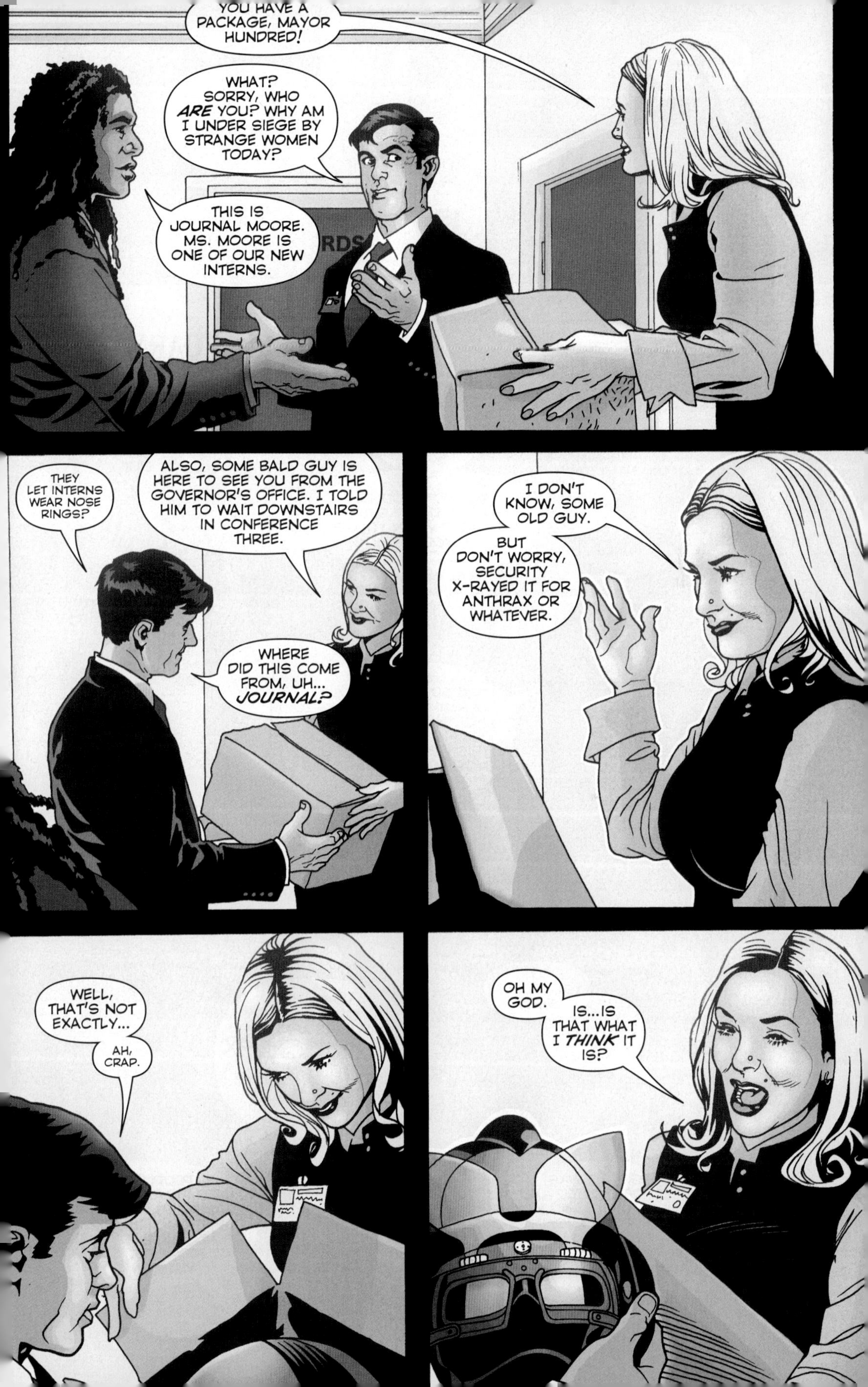
YOU HAVE A PACKAGE, MAYOR HUNDRED!
WHAT? SORRY, WHO *ARE* YOU? WHY AM I UNDER SIEGE BY STRANGE WOMEN TODAY?
THIS IS JOURNAL MOORE. MS. MOORE IS ONE OF OUR NEW INTERNS.
THEY LET INTERNS WEAR NOSE RINGS?
ALSO, SOME BALD GUY IS HERE TO SEE YOU FROM THE GOVERNOR'S OFFICE. I TOLD HIM TO WAIT DOWNSTAIRS IN CONFERENCE THREE.
WHERE DID THIS COME FROM, UH... *JOURNAL?*
I DON'T KNOW, SOME OLD GUY.
BUT DON'T WORRY, SECURITY X-RAYED IT FOR ANTHRAX OR WHATEVER.
WELL, THAT'S NOT EXACTLY...
AH, CRAP.
OH MY GOD.
IS...IS THAT WHAT I *THINK* IT IS?

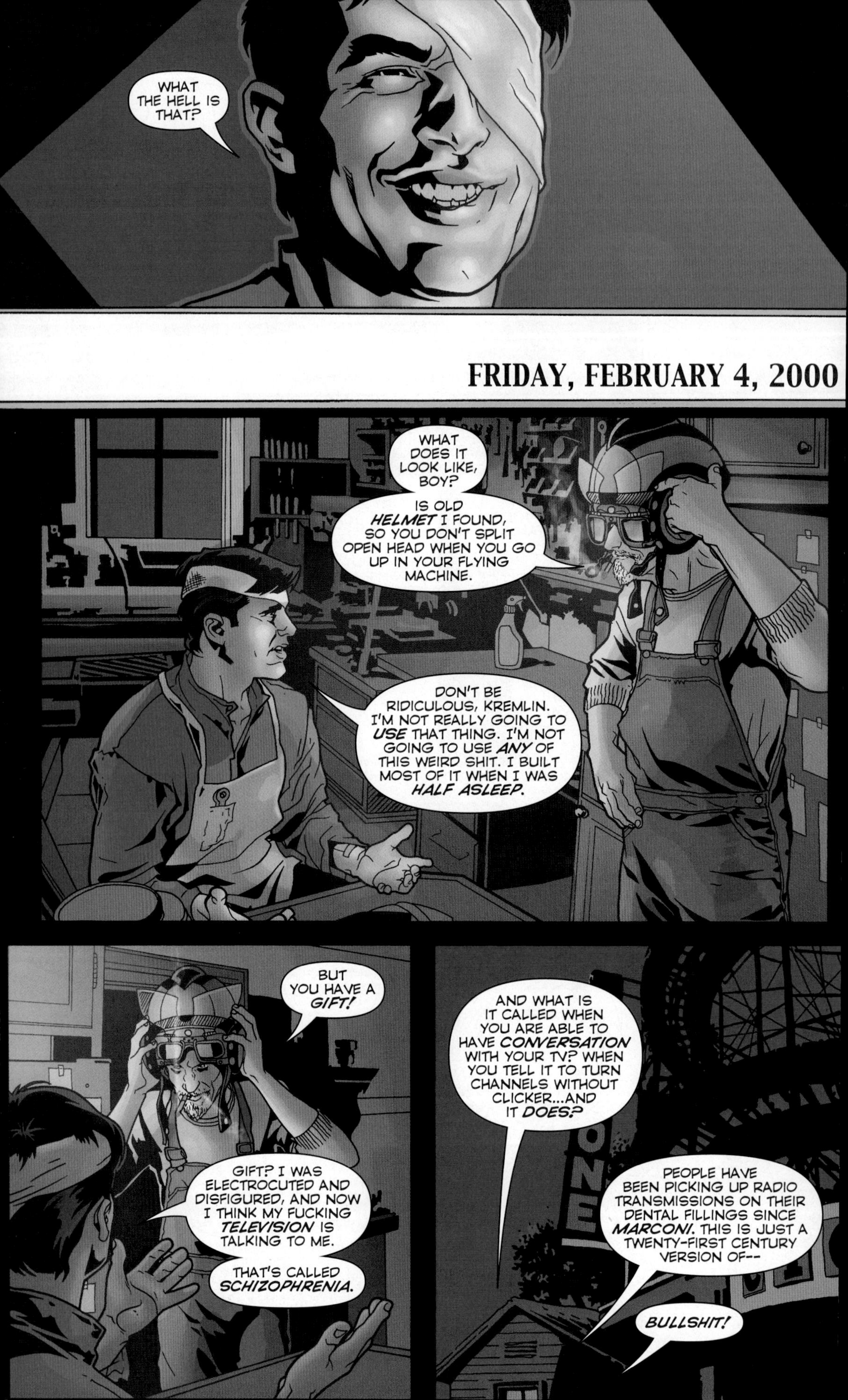

WHAT THE HELL IS THAT?
FRIDAY, FEBRUARY 4, 2000
WHAT DOES IT LOOK LIKE, BOY?
IS OLD HELMET I FOUND, SO YOU DON'T SPLIT OPEN HEAD WHEN YOU GO UP IN YOUR FLYING MACHINE.
DON'T BE RIDICULOUS, KREMLIN. I'M NOT REALLY GOING TO USE THAT THING. I'M NOT GOING TO USE ANY OF THIS WEIRD SHIT. I BUILT MOST OF IT WHEN I WAS HALF ASLEEP.
BUT YOU HAVE A GIFT!
GIFT? I WAS ELECTROCUTED AND DISFIGURED, AND NOW I THINK MY FUCKING TELEVISION IS TALKING TO ME.
THAT'S CALLED SCHIZOPHRENIA.
AND WHAT IS IT CALLED WHEN YOU ARE ABLE TO HAVE CONVERSATION WITH YOUR TV? WHEN YOU TELL IT TO TURN CHANNELS WITHOUT CLICKER...AND IT DOES?
PEOPLE HAVE BEEN PICKING UP RADIO TRANSMISSIONS ON THEIR DENTAL FILLINGS SINCE MARCONI. THIS IS JUST A TWENTY-FIRST CENTURY VERSION OF--
BULLSHIT!

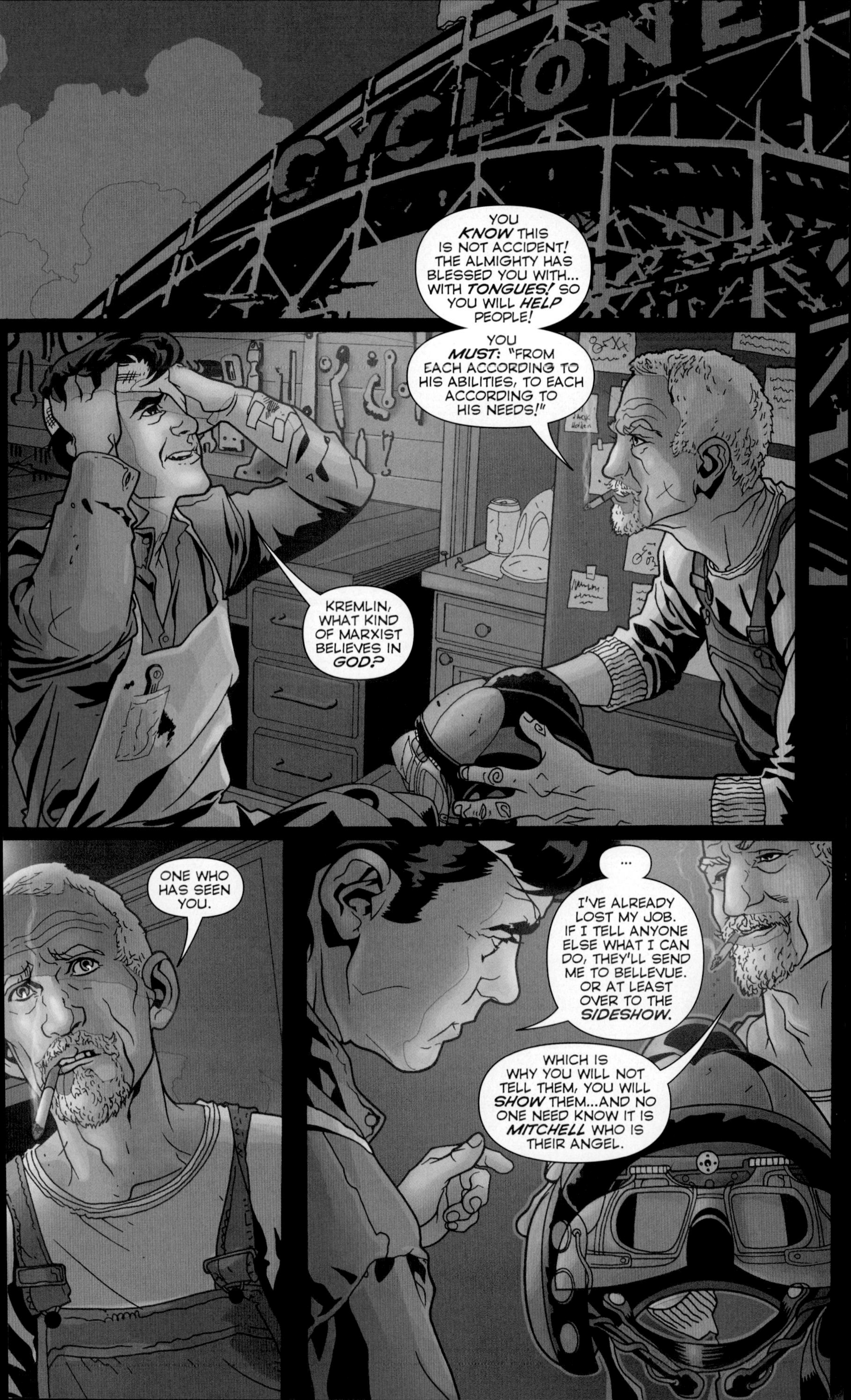
CYCLONE
YOU KNOW THIS IS NOT ACCIDENT! THE ALMIGHTY HAS BLESSED YOU WITH... WITH TONGUES! SO YOU WILL HELP PEOPLE!
YOU MUST: "FROM EACH ACCORDING TO HIS ABILITIES, TO EACH ACCORDING TO HIS NEEDS!"
KREMLIN, WHAT KIND OF MARXIST BELIEVES IN GOD?
ONE WHO HAS SEEN YOU.
...
I'VE ALREADY LOST MY JOB. IF I TELL ANYONE ELSE WHAT I CAN DO, THEY'LL SEND ME TO BELLEVUE. OR AT LEAST OVER TO THE SIDESHOW.
WHICH IS WHY YOU WILL NOT TELL THEM, YOU WILL SHOW THEM...AND NO ONE NEED KNOW IT IS MITCHELL WHO IS THEIR ANGEL.

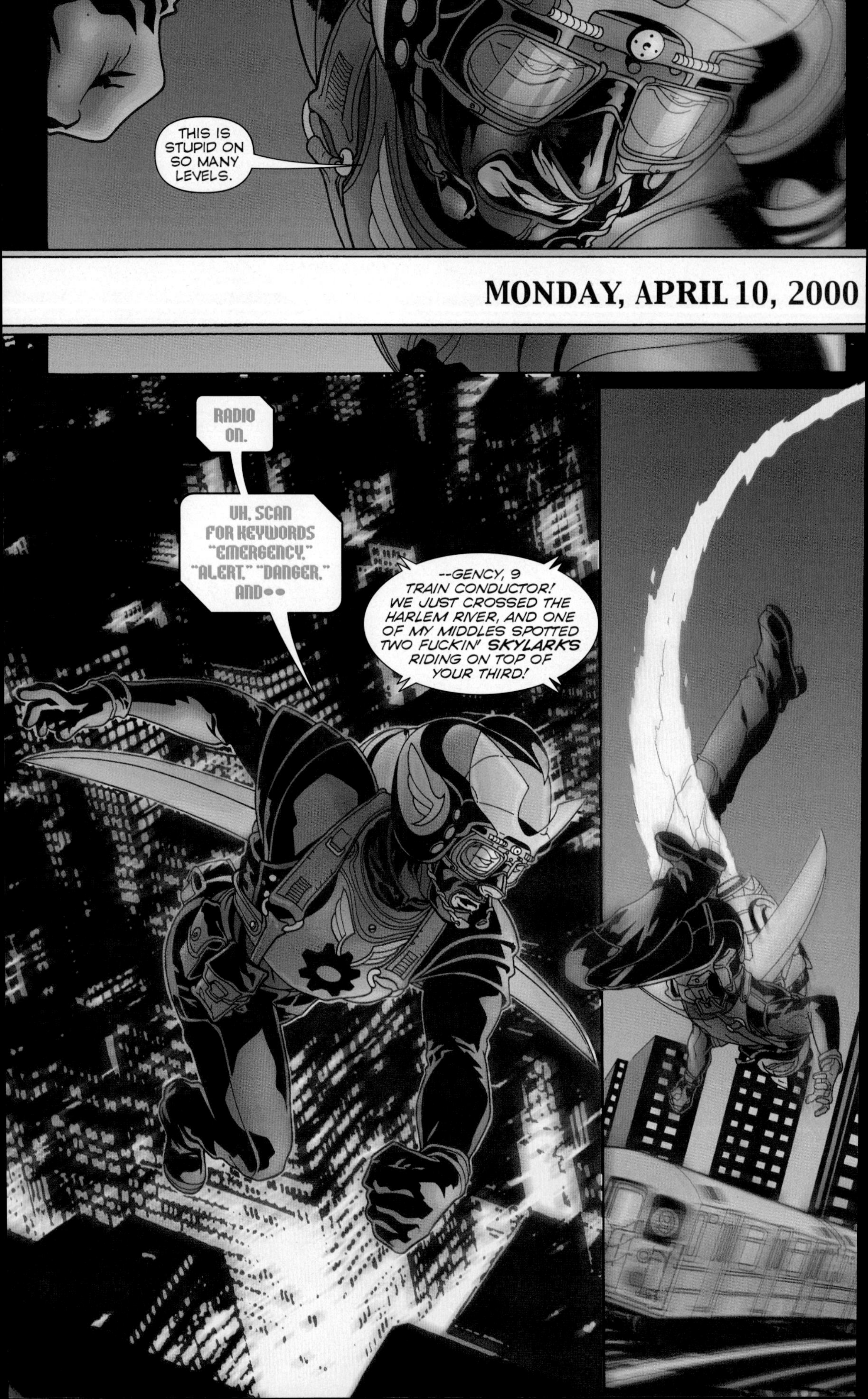
THIS IS STUPID ON SO MANY LEVELS.
MONDAY, APRIL 10, 2000
RADIO ON.
UH, SCAN FOR KEYWORDS "EMERGENCY," "ALERT," "DANGER," AND--
--GENCY, 9 TRAIN CONDUCTOR! WE JUST CROSSED THE HARLEM RIVER, AND ONE OF MY MIDDLES SPOTTED TWO FUCKIN' SKYLARKS RIDING ON TOP OF YOUR THIRD!

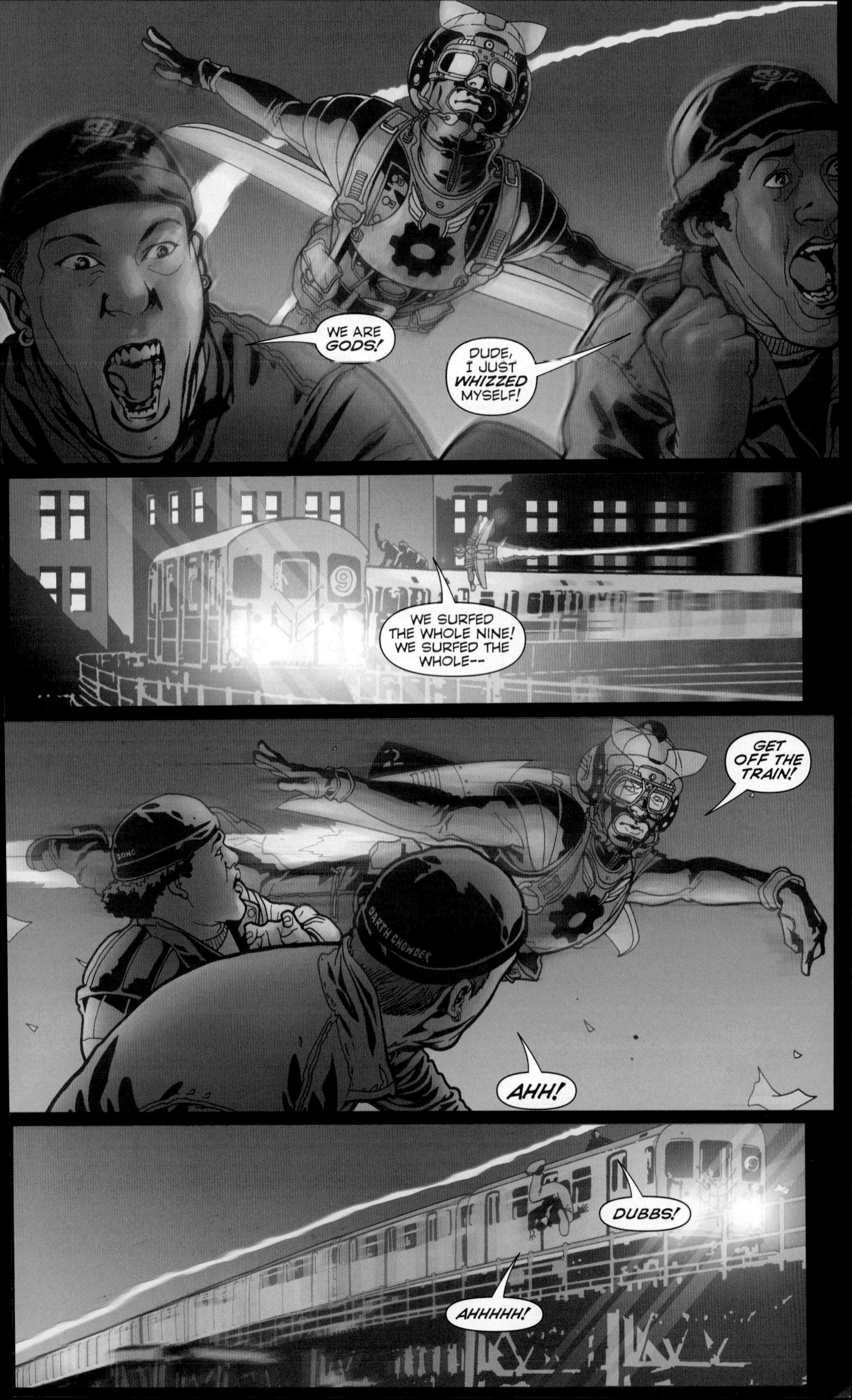
WE ARE GODS!
DUDE, I JUST WHIZZED MYSELF!
WE SURFED THE WHOLE NINE! WE SURFED THE WHOLE--
GET OFF THE TRAIN!
DARTH CHOWDER
AHH!
DUBBS!
AHHHHH!

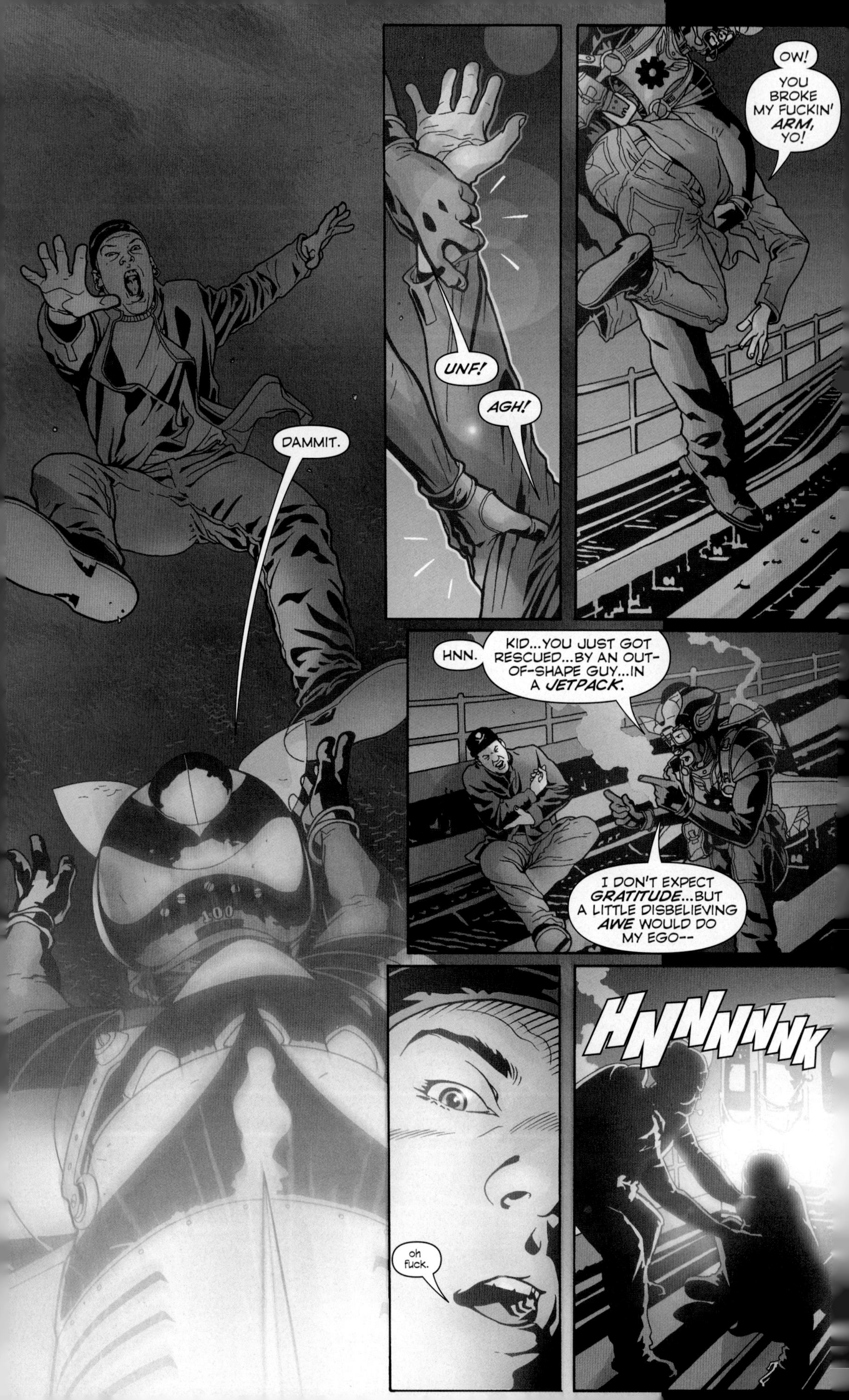
DAMMIT.
UNF!
AGH!
OW! YOU BROKE MY FUCKIN' *ARM,* YO!
HNN.
KID...YOU JUST GOT RESCUED...BY AN OUT-OF-SHAPE GUY...IN A *JETPACK.*
I DON'T EXPECT *GRATITUDE*...BUT A LITTLE DISBELIEVING *AWE* WOULD DO MY EGO--
oh fuck.
HNNNNNNK

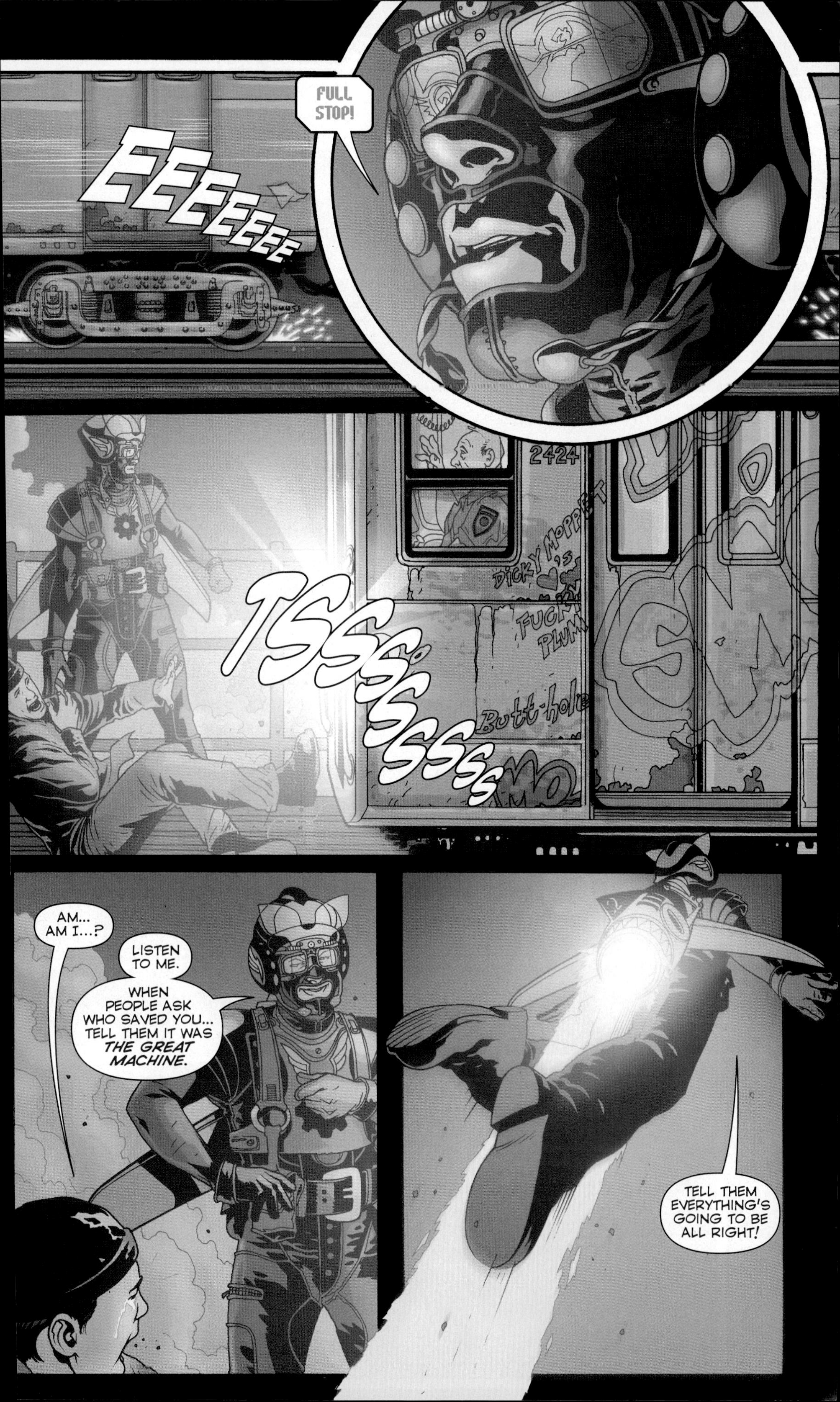

EEEEEEEE
FULL STOP!
2424
DICKY MOPPET'S
FUCK PLUM
Butt-hole
TSSSSSSSS
AM... AM I...?
LISTEN TO ME.
WHEN PEOPLE ASK WHO SAVED YOU... TELL THEM IT WAS *THE GREAT MACHINE*.
TELL THEM EVERYTHING'S GOING TO BE ALL RIGHT!

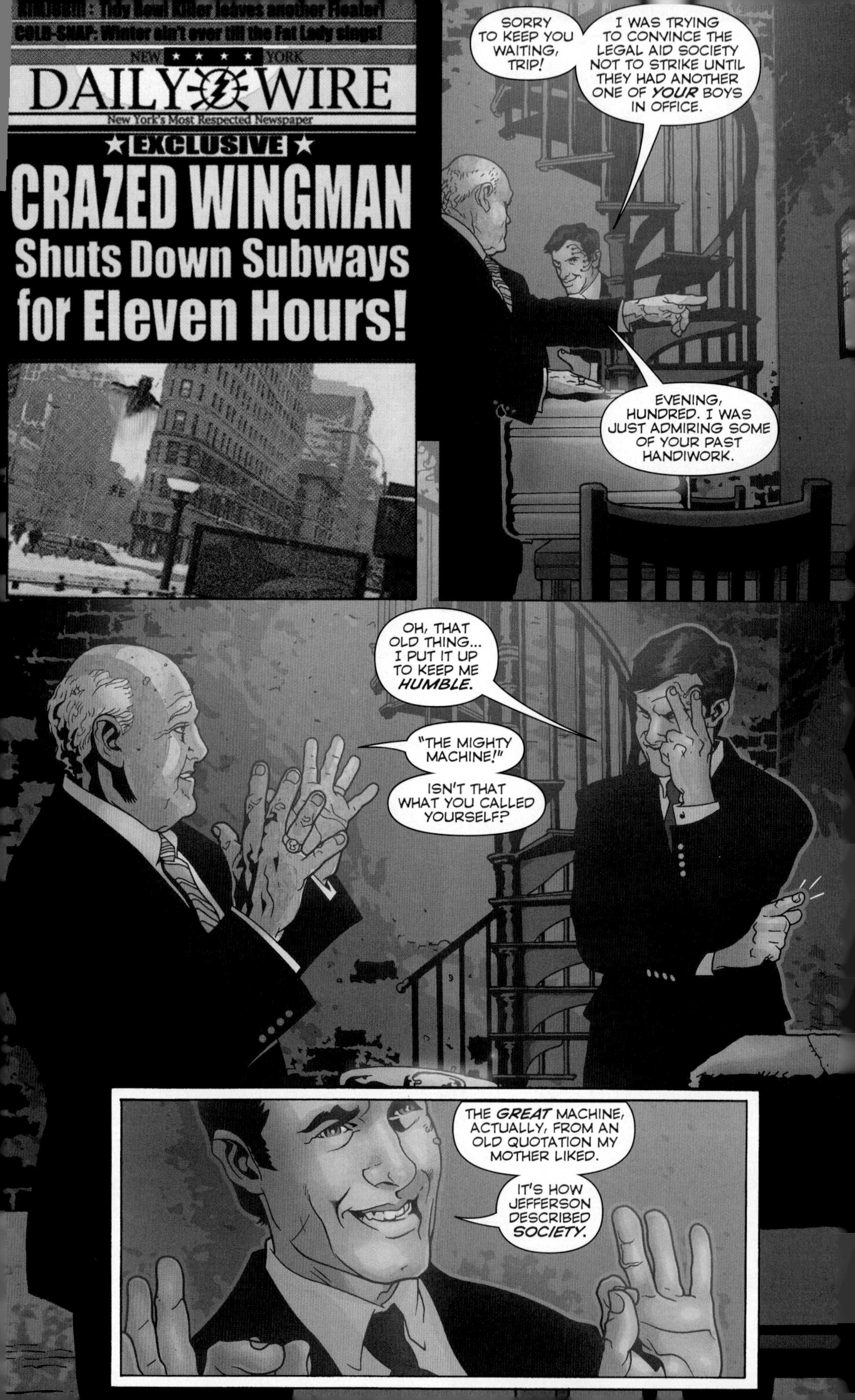
Tidy Bowl Killer leaves another Floater!
COLD-SNAP: Winter ain't over till the Fat Lady sings!
NEW YORK
DAILY WIRE
New York's Most Respected Newspaper
EXCLUSIVE
CRAZED WINGMAN Shuts Down Subways for Eleven Hours!
SORRY TO KEEP YOU WAITING, TRIP!
I WAS TRYING TO CONVINCE THE LEGAL AID SOCIETY NOT TO STRIKE UNTIL THEY HAD ANOTHER ONE OF YOUR BOYS IN OFFICE.
EVENING, HUNDRED. I WAS JUST ADMIRING SOME OF YOUR PAST HANDIWORK.
OH, THAT OLD THING... I PUT IT UP TO KEEP ME HUMBLE.
"THE MIGHTY MACHINE!"
ISN'T THAT WHAT YOU CALLED YOURSELF?
THE GREAT MACHINE, ACTUALLY, FROM AN OLD QUOTATION MY MOTHER LIKED.
IT'S HOW JEFFERSON DESCRIBED SOCIETY.

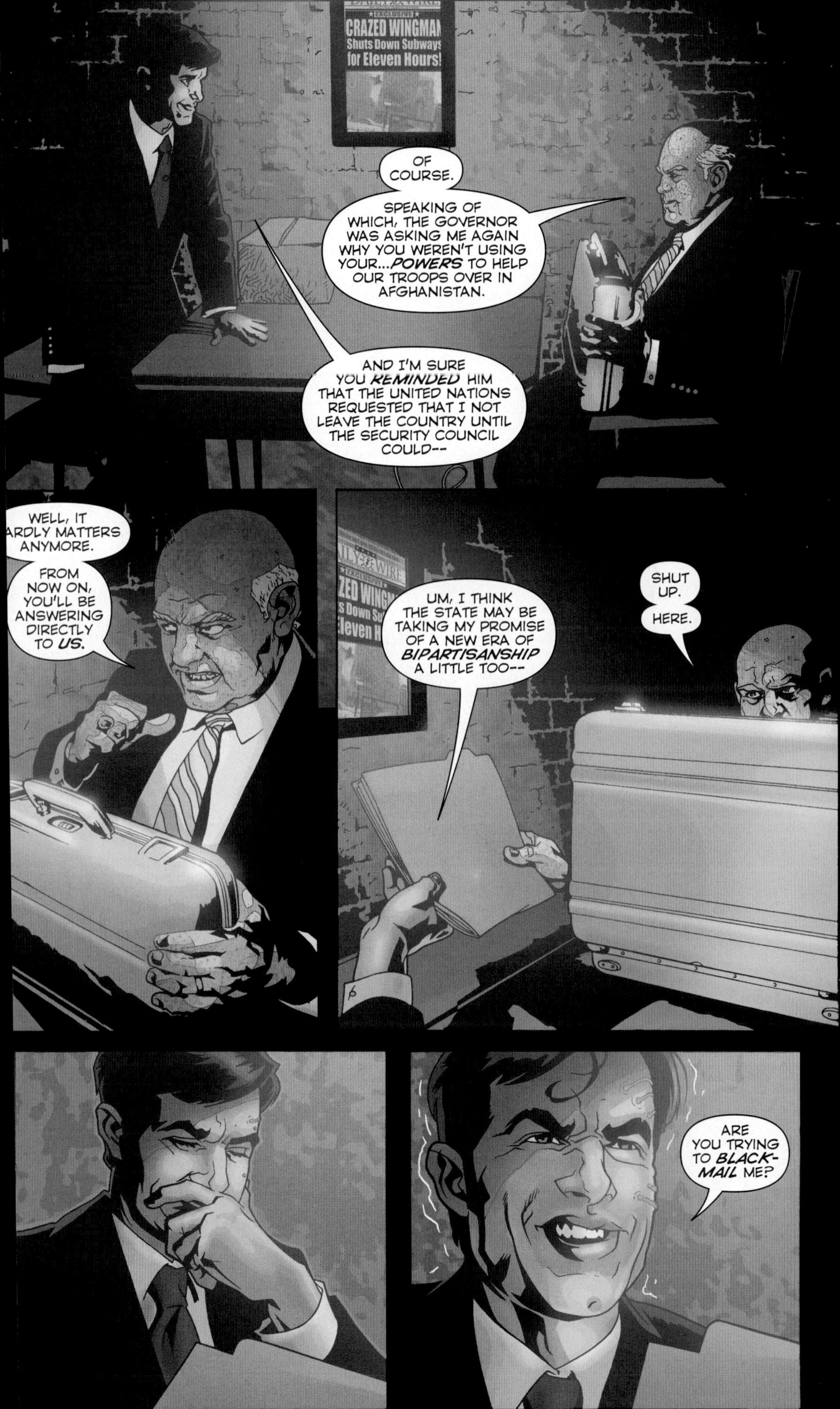
DAILY WIRE
EXCLUSIVE
CRAZED WINGMAN
Shuts Down Subways for Eleven Hours!
OF COURSE.
SPEAKING OF WHICH, THE GOVERNOR WAS ASKING ME AGAIN WHY YOU WEREN'T USING YOUR...POWERS TO HELP OUR TROOPS OVER IN AFGHANISTAN.
AND I'M SURE YOU REMINDED HIM THAT THE UNITED NATIONS REQUESTED THAT I NOT LEAVE THE COUNTRY UNTIL THE SECURITY COUNCIL COULD--
WELL, IT ARDLY MATTERS ANYMORE.
FROM NOW ON, YOU'LL BE ANSWERING DIRECTLY TO US.
UM, I THINK THE STATE MAY BE TAKING MY PROMISE OF A NEW ERA OF BIPARTISANSHIP A LITTLE TOO--
SHUT UP.
HERE.
ARE YOU TRYING TO BLACK-MAIL ME?

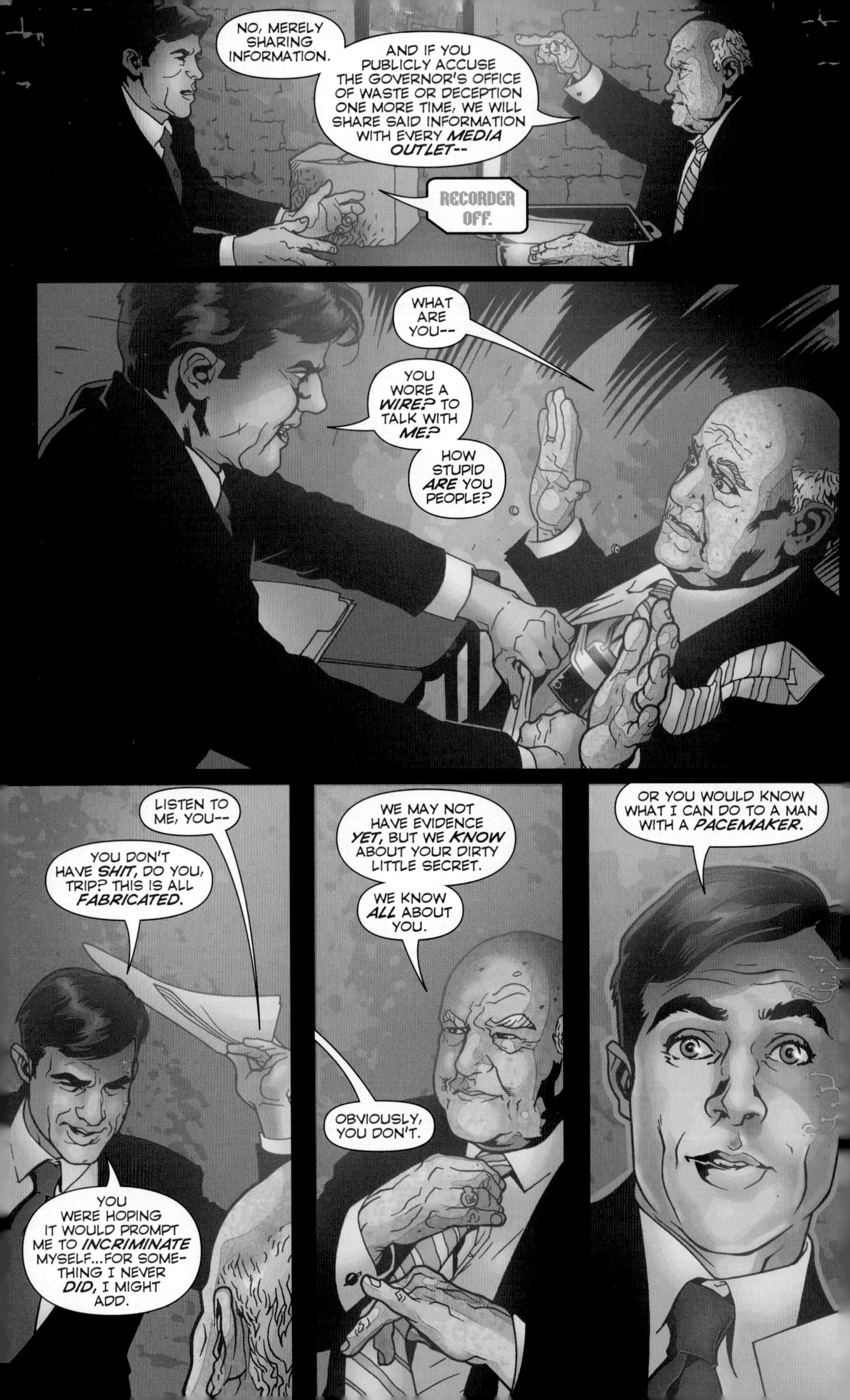
NO, MERELY SHARING INFORMATION.
AND IF YOU PUBLICLY ACCUSE THE GOVERNOR'S OFFICE OF WASTE OR DECEPTION ONE MORE TIME, WE WILL SHARE SAID INFORMATION WITH EVERY MEDIA OUTLET--
RECORDER OFF.
WHAT ARE YOU--
YOU WORE A WIRE? TO TALK WITH ME?
HOW STUPID ARE YOU PEOPLE?
LISTEN TO ME, YOU--
YOU DON'T HAVE SHIT, DO YOU, TRIP? THIS IS ALL FABRICATED.
YOU WERE HOPING IT WOULD PROMPT ME TO INCRIMINATE MYSELF...FOR SOMETHING I NEVER DID, I MIGHT ADD.
WE MAY NOT HAVE EVIDENCE YET, BUT WE KNOW ABOUT YOUR DIRTY LITTLE SECRET.
WE KNOW ALL ABOUT YOU.
OBVIOUSLY, YOU DON'T.
OR YOU WOULD KNOW WHAT I CAN DO TO A MAN WITH A PACEMAKER.

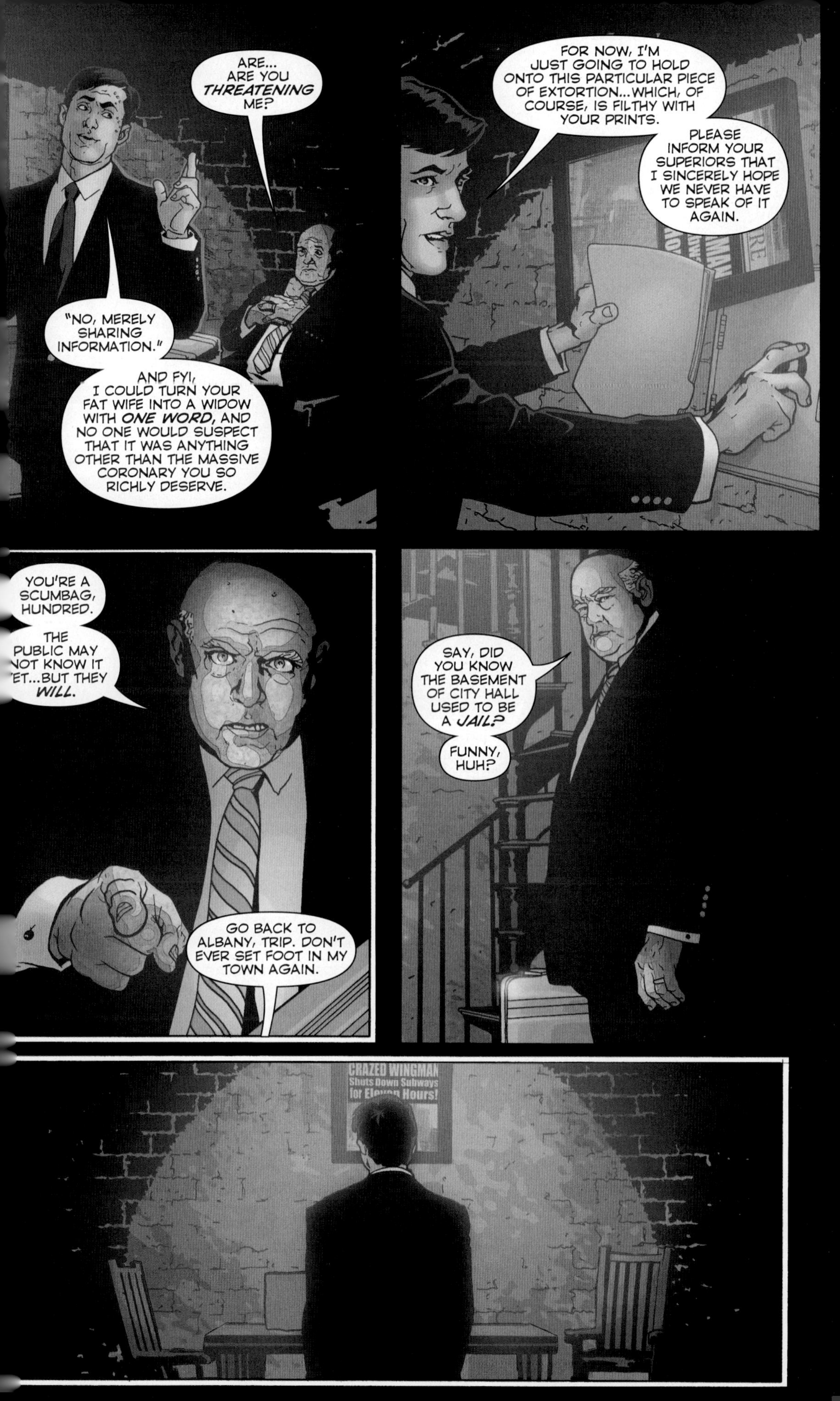

ARE... ARE YOU THREATENING ME?
"NO, MERELY SHARING INFORMATION."
AND FYI, I COULD TURN YOUR FAT WIFE INTO A WIDOW WITH ONE WORD, AND NO ONE WOULD SUSPECT THAT IT WAS ANYTHING OTHER THAN THE MASSIVE CORONARY YOU SO RICHLY DESERVE.
FOR NOW, I'M JUST GOING TO HOLD ONTO THIS PARTICULAR PIECE OF EXTORTION...WHICH, OF COURSE, IS FILTHY WITH YOUR PRINTS.
PLEASE INFORM YOUR SUPERIORS THAT I SINCERELY HOPE WE NEVER HAVE TO SPEAK OF IT AGAIN.
YOU'RE A SCUMBAG, HUNDRED.
THE PUBLIC MAY NOT KNOW IT YET...BUT THEY WILL.
GO BACK TO ALBANY, TRIP. DON'T EVER SET FOOT IN MY TOWN AGAIN.
SAY, DID YOU KNOW THE BASEMENT OF CITY HALL USED TO BE A JAIL?
FUNNY, HUH?
CRAZED WINGMAN
Shuts Down Subways for Eleven Hours!

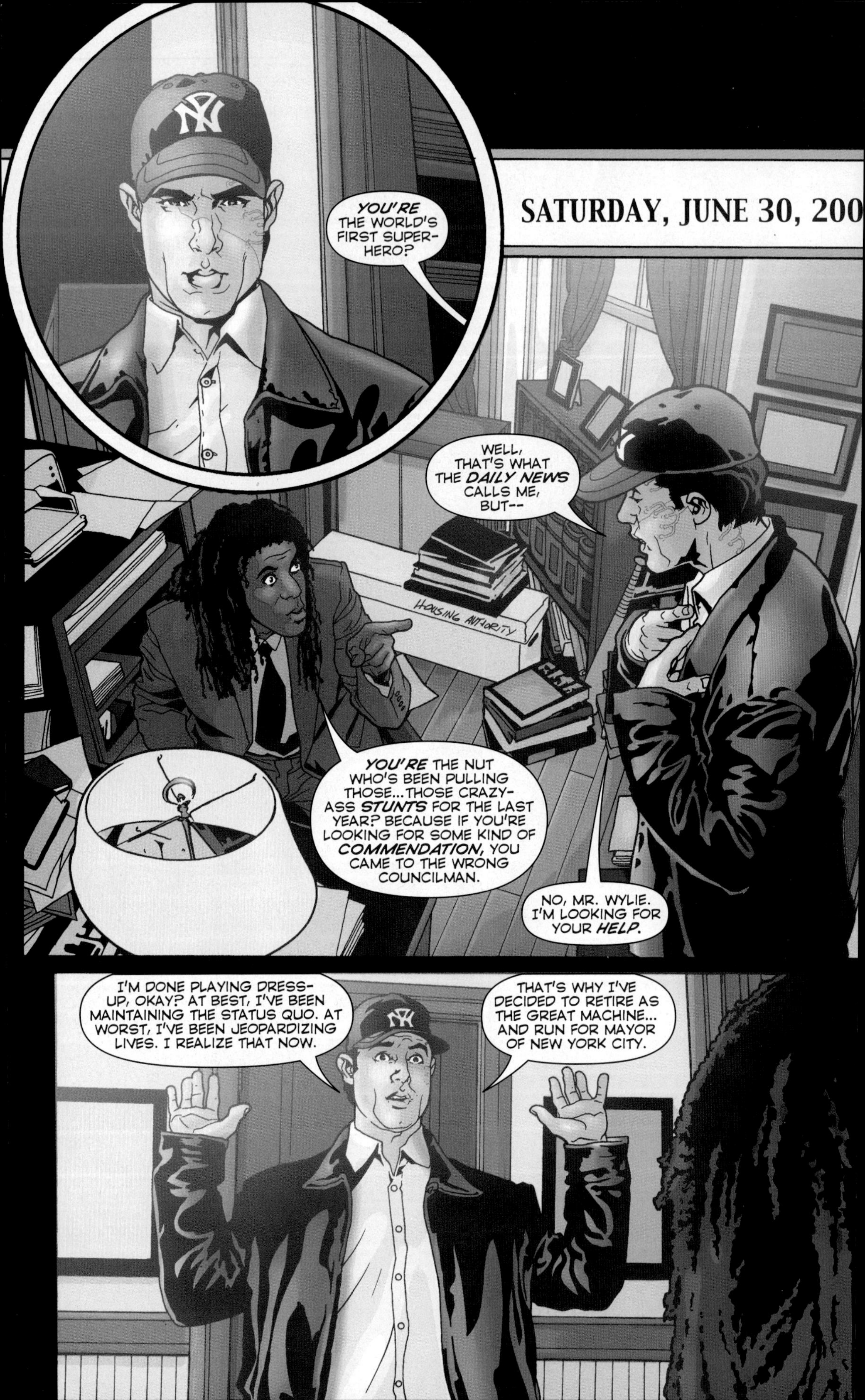

SATURDAY, JUNE 30, 200
YOU'RE THE WORLD'S FIRST SUPER-HERO?
WELL, THAT'S WHAT THE DAILY NEWS CALLS ME, BUT--
HOUSING AUTHORITY
YOU'RE THE NUT WHO'S BEEN PULLING THOSE...THOSE CRAZY-ASS STUNTS FOR THE LAST YEAR? BECAUSE IF YOU'RE LOOKING FOR SOME KIND OF COMMENDATION, YOU CAME TO THE WRONG COUNCILMAN.
NO, MR. WYLIE. I'M LOOKING FOR YOUR HELP.
I'M DONE PLAYING DRESS-UP, OKAY? AT BEST, I'VE BEEN MAINTAINING THE STATUS QUO. AT WORST, I'VE BEEN JEOPARDIZING LIVES. I REALIZE THAT NOW.
THAT'S WHY I'VE DECIDED TO RETIRE AS THE GREAT MACHINE... AND RUN FOR MAYOR OF NEW YORK CITY.

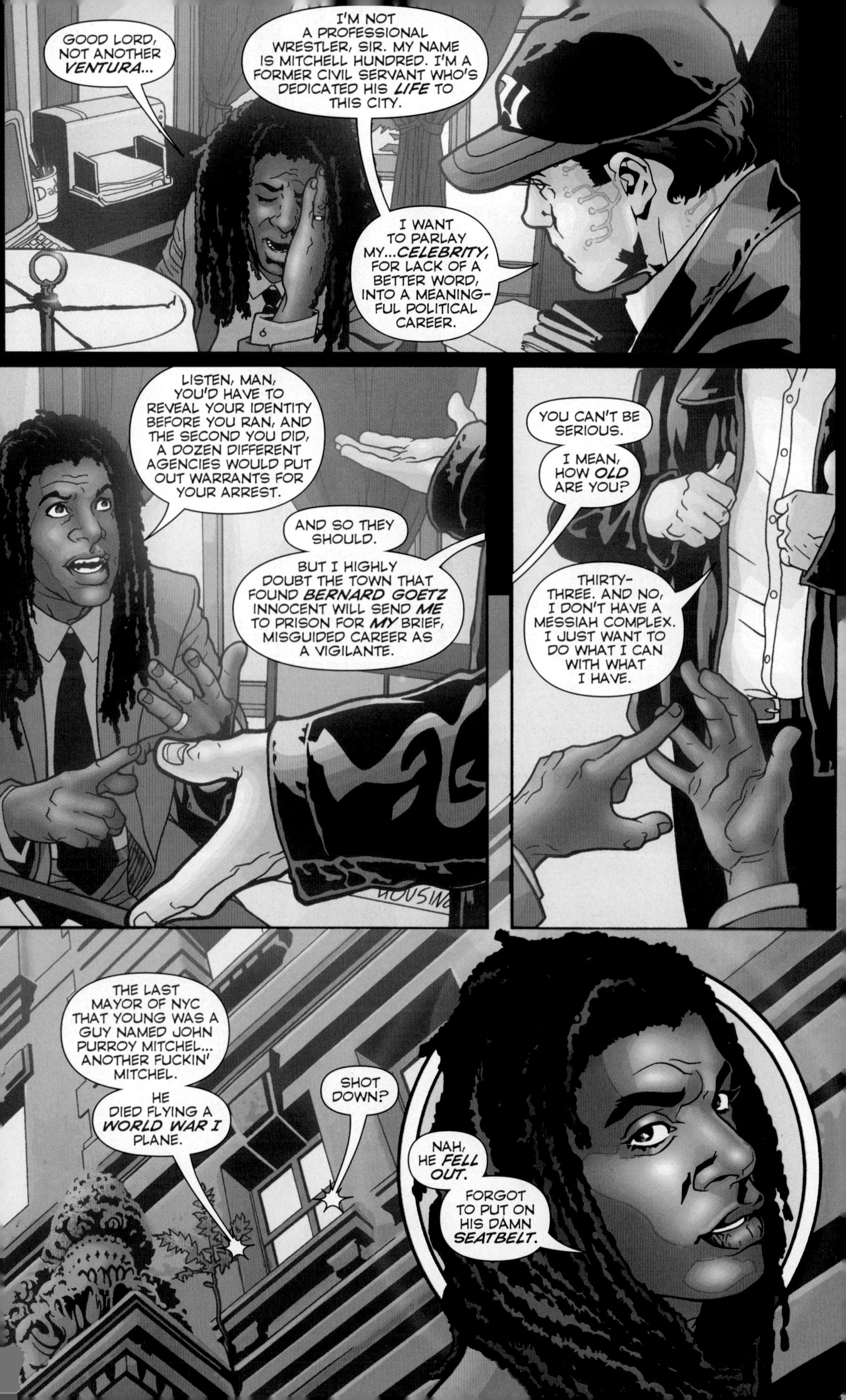
GOOD LORD, NOT ANOTHER VENTURA...
I'M NOT A PROFESSIONAL WRESTLER, SIR. MY NAME IS MITCHELL HUNDRED. I'M A FORMER CIVIL SERVANT WHO'S DEDICATED HIS LIFE TO THIS CITY.
I WANT TO PARLAY MY...CELEBRITY, FOR LACK OF A BETTER WORD, INTO A MEANINGFUL POLITICAL CAREER.
LISTEN, MAN, YOU'D HAVE TO REVEAL YOUR IDENTITY BEFORE YOU RAN, AND THE SECOND YOU DID, A DOZEN DIFFERENT AGENCIES WOULD PUT OUT WARRANTS FOR YOUR ARREST.
AND SO THEY SHOULD.
BUT I HIGHLY DOUBT THE TOWN THAT FOUND BERNARD GOETZ INNOCENT WILL SEND ME TO PRISON FOR MY BRIEF, MISGUIDED CAREER AS A VIGILANTE.
YOU CAN'T BE SERIOUS.
I MEAN, HOW OLD ARE YOU?
THIRTY-THREE. AND NO, I DON'T HAVE A MESSIAH COMPLEX. I JUST WANT TO DO WHAT I CAN WITH WHAT I HAVE.
THE LAST MAYOR OF NYC THAT YOUNG WAS A GUY NAMED JOHN PURROY MITCHEL... ANOTHER FUCKIN' MITCHEL.
HE DIED FLYING A WORLD WAR I PLANE.
SHOT DOWN?
NAH, HE FELL OUT.
FORGOT TO PUT ON HIS DAMN SEATBELT.

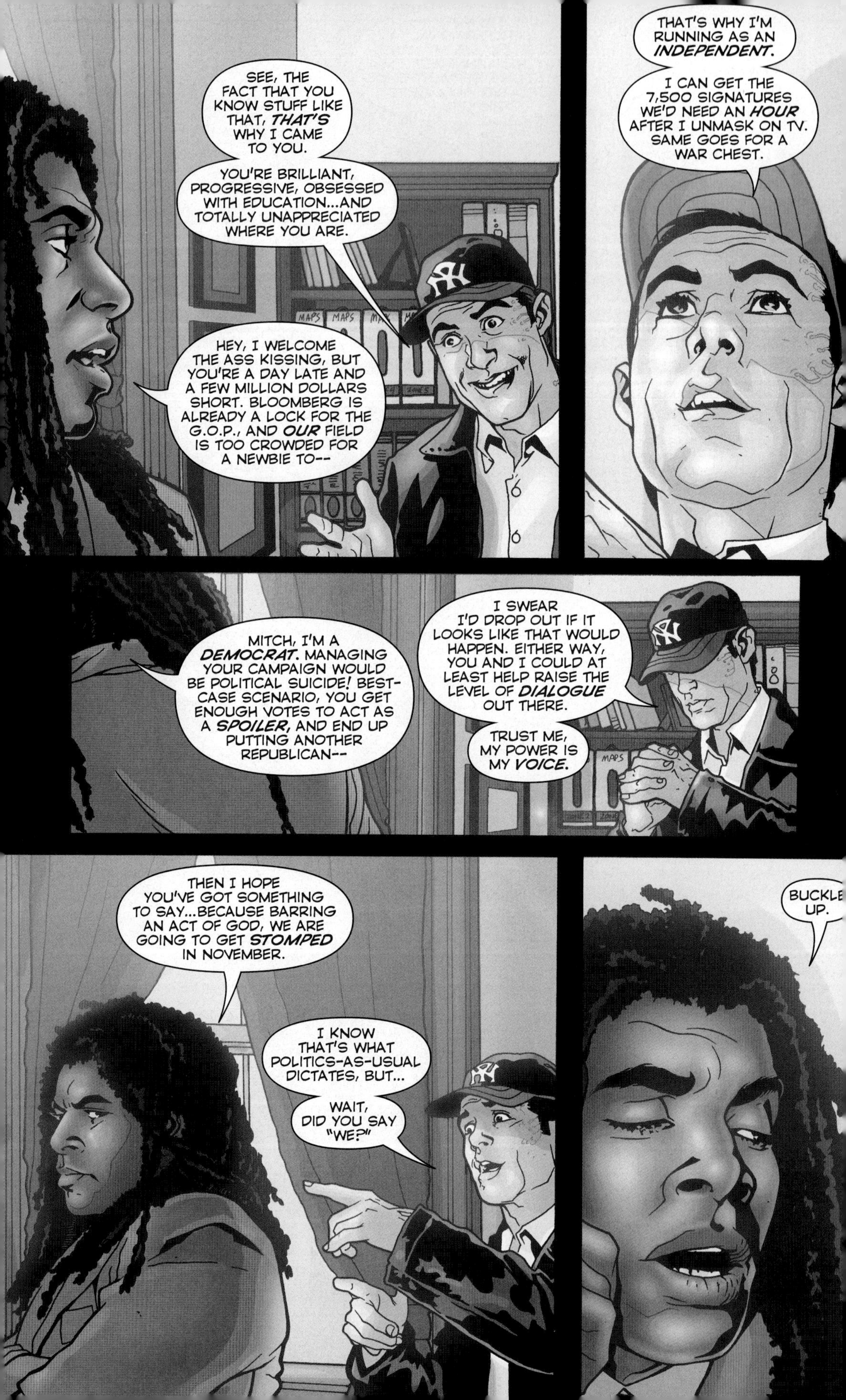
SEE, THE FACT THAT YOU KNOW STUFF LIKE THAT, *THAT'S* WHY I CAME TO YOU.
YOU'RE BRILLIANT, PROGRESSIVE, OBSESSED WITH EDUCATION...AND TOTALLY UNAPPRECIATED WHERE YOU ARE.
HEY, I WELCOME THE ASS KISSING, BUT YOU'RE A DAY LATE AND A FEW MILLION DOLLARS SHORT. BLOOMBERG IS ALREADY A LOCK FOR THE G.O.P., AND *OUR* FIELD IS TOO CROWDED FOR A NEWBIE TO--
THAT'S WHY I'M RUNNING AS AN *INDEPENDENT*.
I CAN GET THE 7,500 SIGNATURES WE'D NEED AN *HOUR* AFTER I UNMASK ON TV. SAME GOES FOR A WAR CHEST.
MITCH, I'M A *DEMOCRAT*. MANAGING YOUR CAMPAIGN WOULD BE POLITICAL SUICIDE! BEST-CASE SCENARIO, YOU GET ENOUGH VOTES TO ACT AS A *SPOILER*, AND END UP PUTTING ANOTHER REPUBLICAN--
I SWEAR I'D DROP OUT IF IT LOOKS LIKE THAT WOULD HAPPEN. EITHER WAY, YOU AND I COULD AT LEAST HELP RAISE THE LEVEL OF *DIALOGUE* OUT THERE.
TRUST ME, MY POWER IS MY *VOICE*.
THEN I HOPE YOU'VE GOT SOMETHING TO SAY...BECAUSE BARRING AN ACT OF GOD, WE ARE GOING TO GET *STOMPED* IN NOVEMBER.
I KNOW THAT'S WHAT POLITICS-AS-USUAL DICTATES, BUT...
WAIT, DID YOU SAY "WE?"
BUCKLE UP.

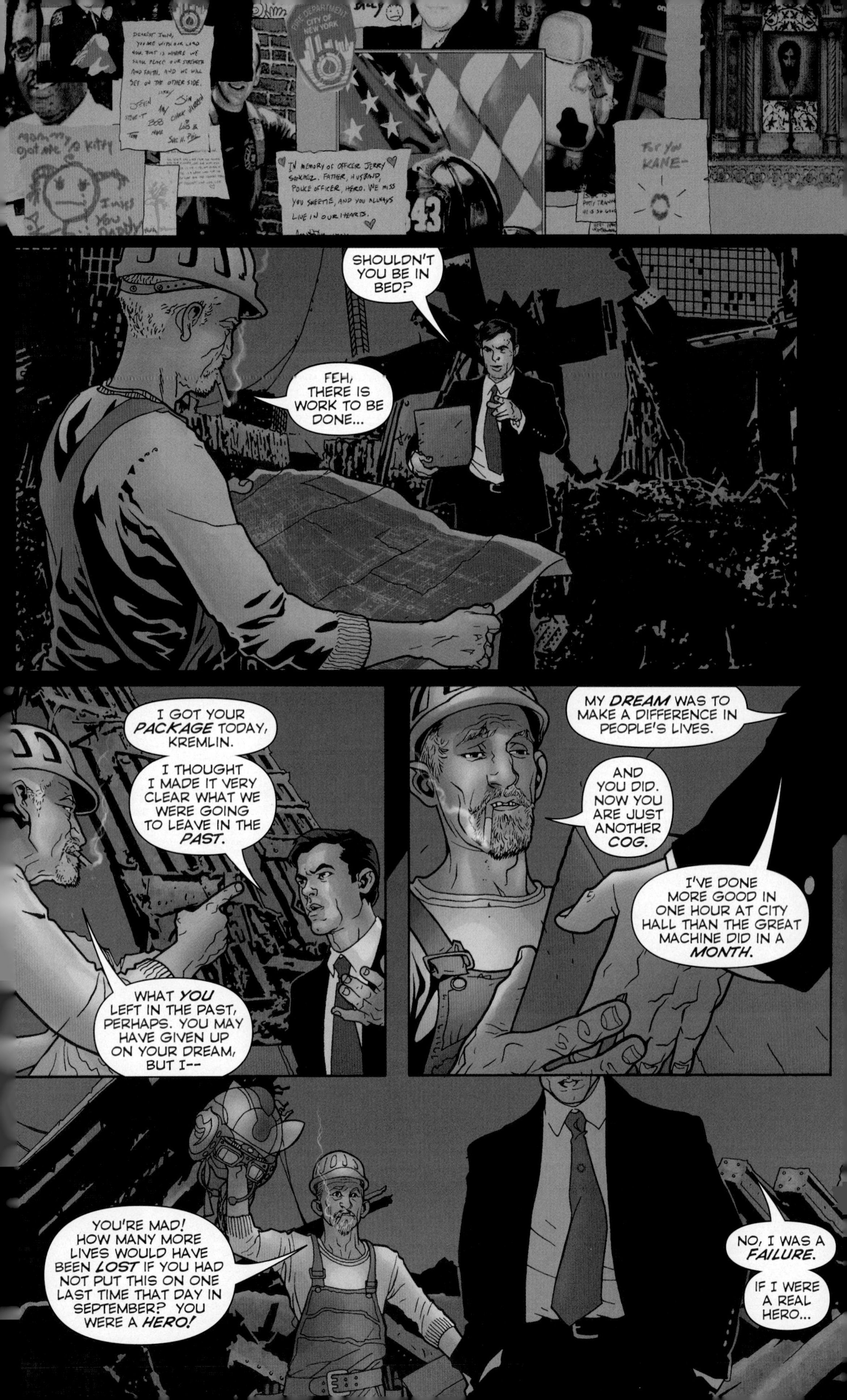

SHOULDN'T YOU BE IN BED?
FEH, THERE IS WORK TO BE DONE...
I GOT YOUR PACKAGE TODAY, KREMLIN.
I THOUGHT I MADE IT VERY CLEAR WHAT WE WERE GOING TO LEAVE IN THE PAST.
WHAT YOU LEFT IN THE PAST, PERHAPS. YOU MAY HAVE GIVEN UP ON YOUR DREAM, BUT I--
MY DREAM WAS TO MAKE A DIFFERENCE IN PEOPLE'S LIVES.
AND YOU DID. NOW YOU ARE JUST ANOTHER COG.
I'VE DONE MORE GOOD IN ONE HOUR AT CITY HALL THAN THE GREAT MACHINE DID IN A MONTH.
YOU'RE MAD! HOW MANY MORE LIVES WOULD HAVE BEEN LOST IF YOU HAD NOT PUT THIS ON ONE LAST TIME THAT DAY IN SEPTEMBER? YOU WERE A HERO!
NO, I WAS A FAILURE.
IF I WERE A REAL HERO...

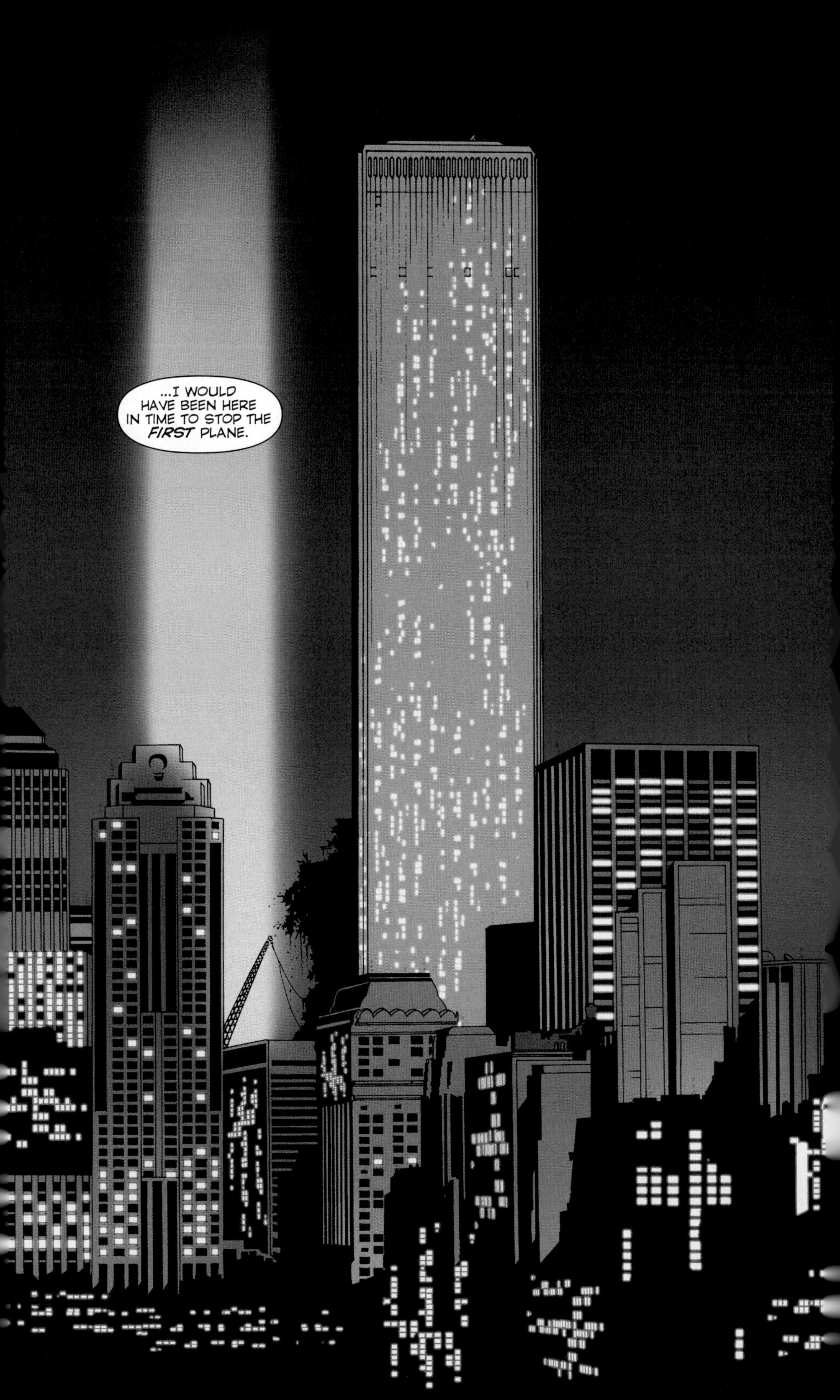
...I WOULD HAVE BEEN HERE IN TIME TO STOP THE FIRST PLANE.

CHAPTER 2 STATE OF EMERGENCY

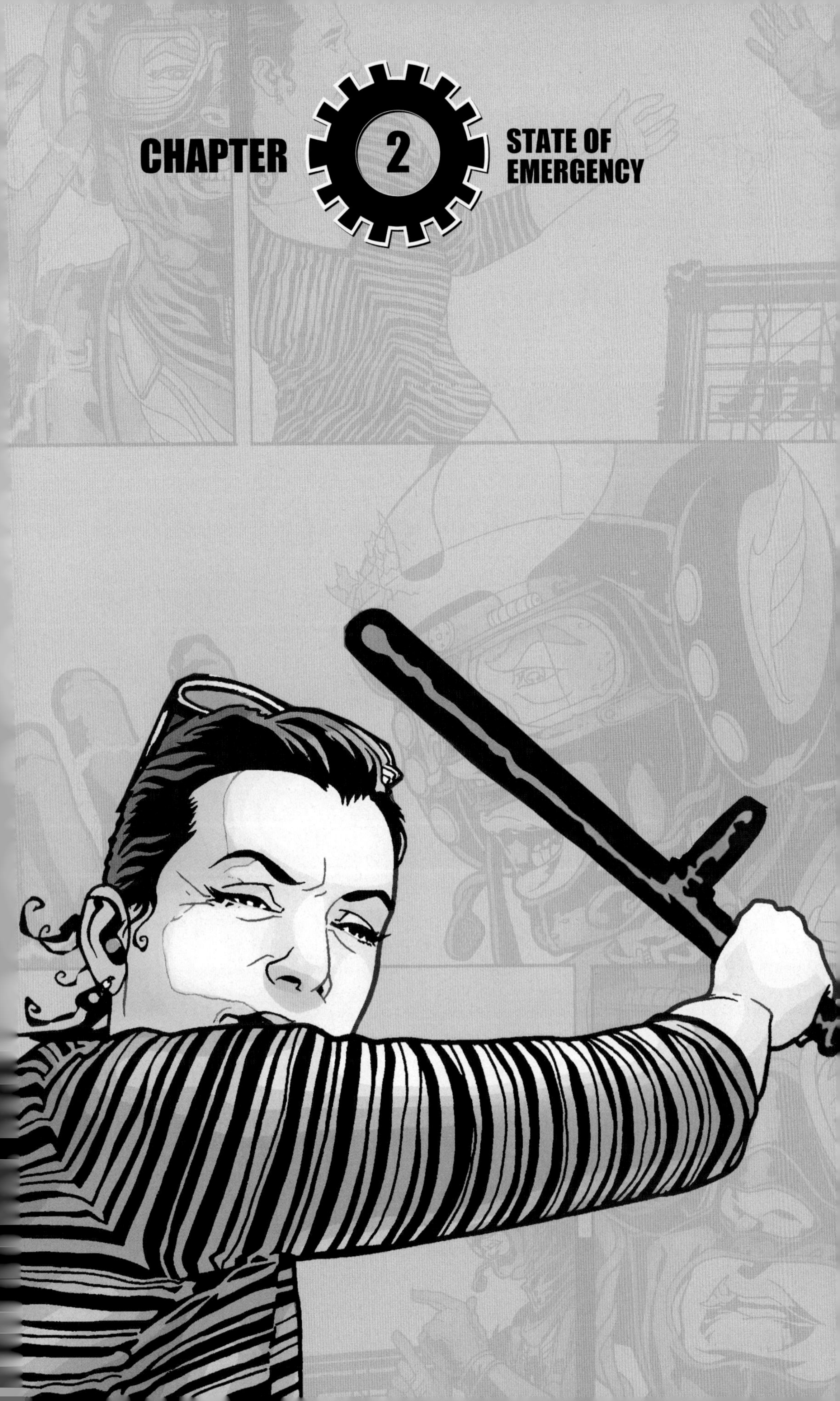

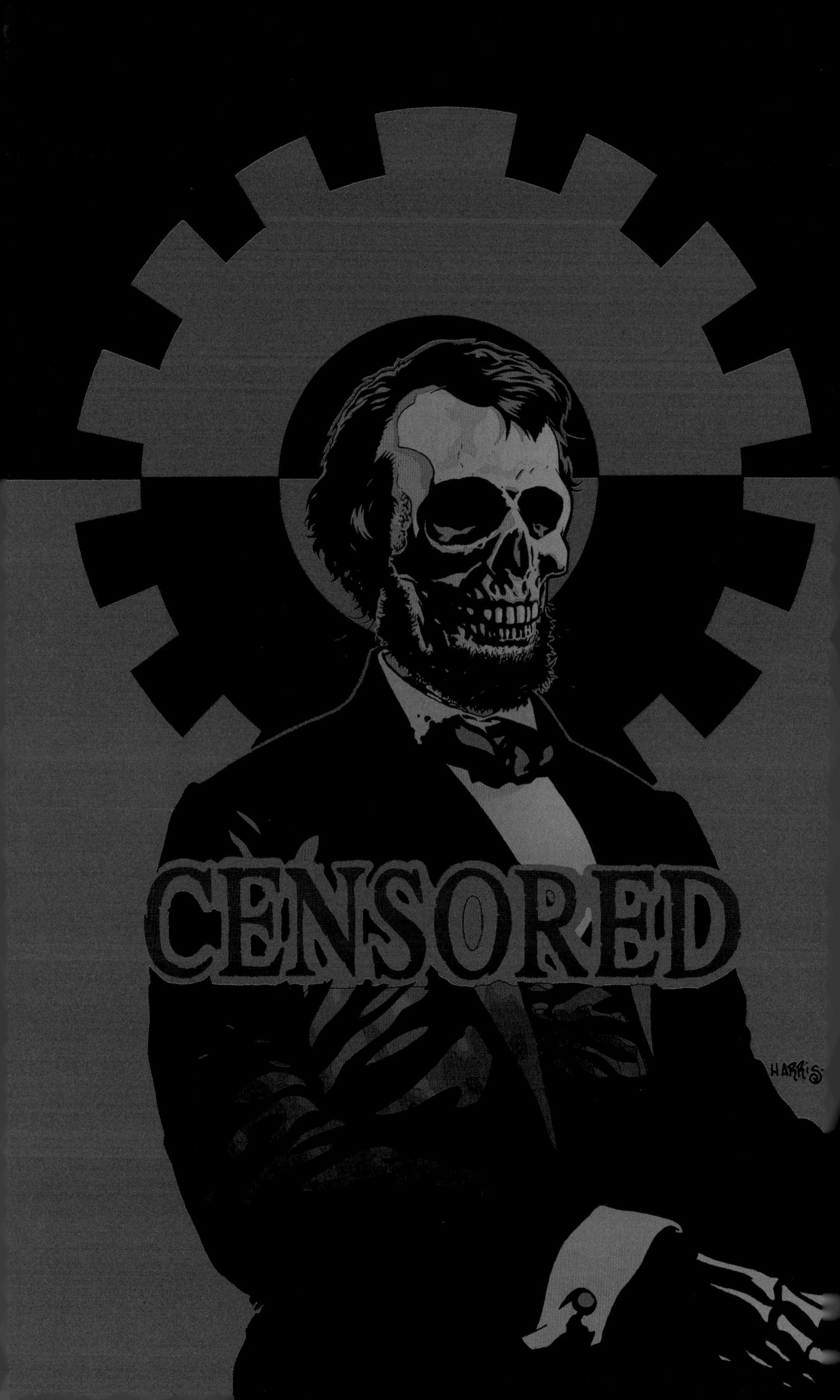
CENSORED
HARRIS

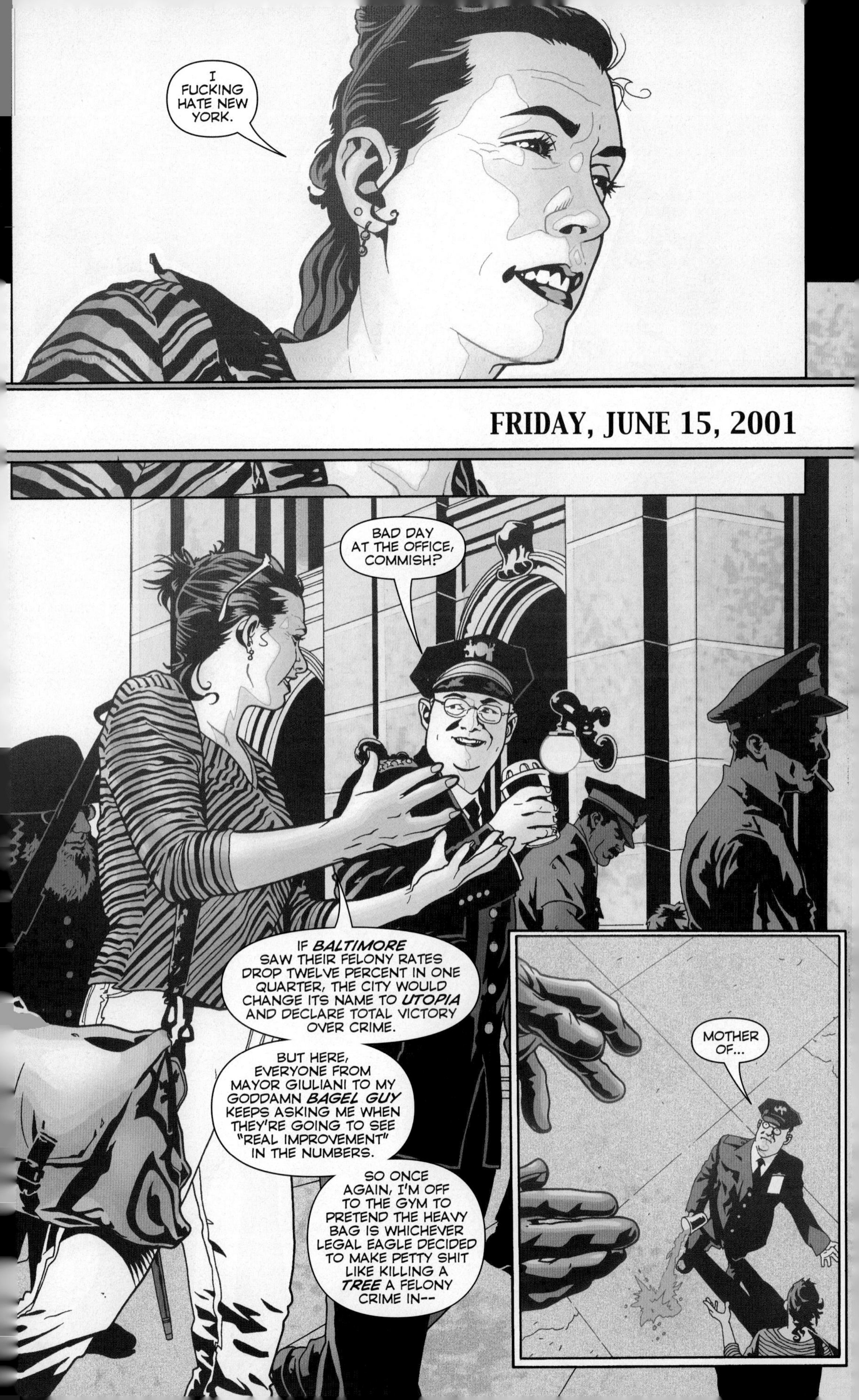
I FUCKING HATE NEW YORK.
FRIDAY, JUNE 15, 2001
BAD DAY AT THE OFFICE, COMMISH?
IF BALTIMORE SAW THEIR FELONY RATES DROP TWELVE PERCENT IN ONE QUARTER, THE CITY WOULD CHANGE ITS NAME TO UTOPIA AND DECLARE TOTAL VICTORY OVER CRIME.
BUT HERE, EVERYONE FROM MAYOR GIULIANI TO MY GODDAMN BAGEL GUY KEEPS ASKING ME WHEN THEY'RE GOING TO SEE "REAL IMPROVEMENT" IN THE NUMBERS.
SO ONCE AGAIN, I'M OFF TO THE GYM TO PRETEND THE HEAVY BAG IS WHICHEVER LEGAL EAGLE DECIDED TO MAKE PETTY SHIT LIKE KILLING A TREE A FELONY CRIME IN--
MOTHER OF...

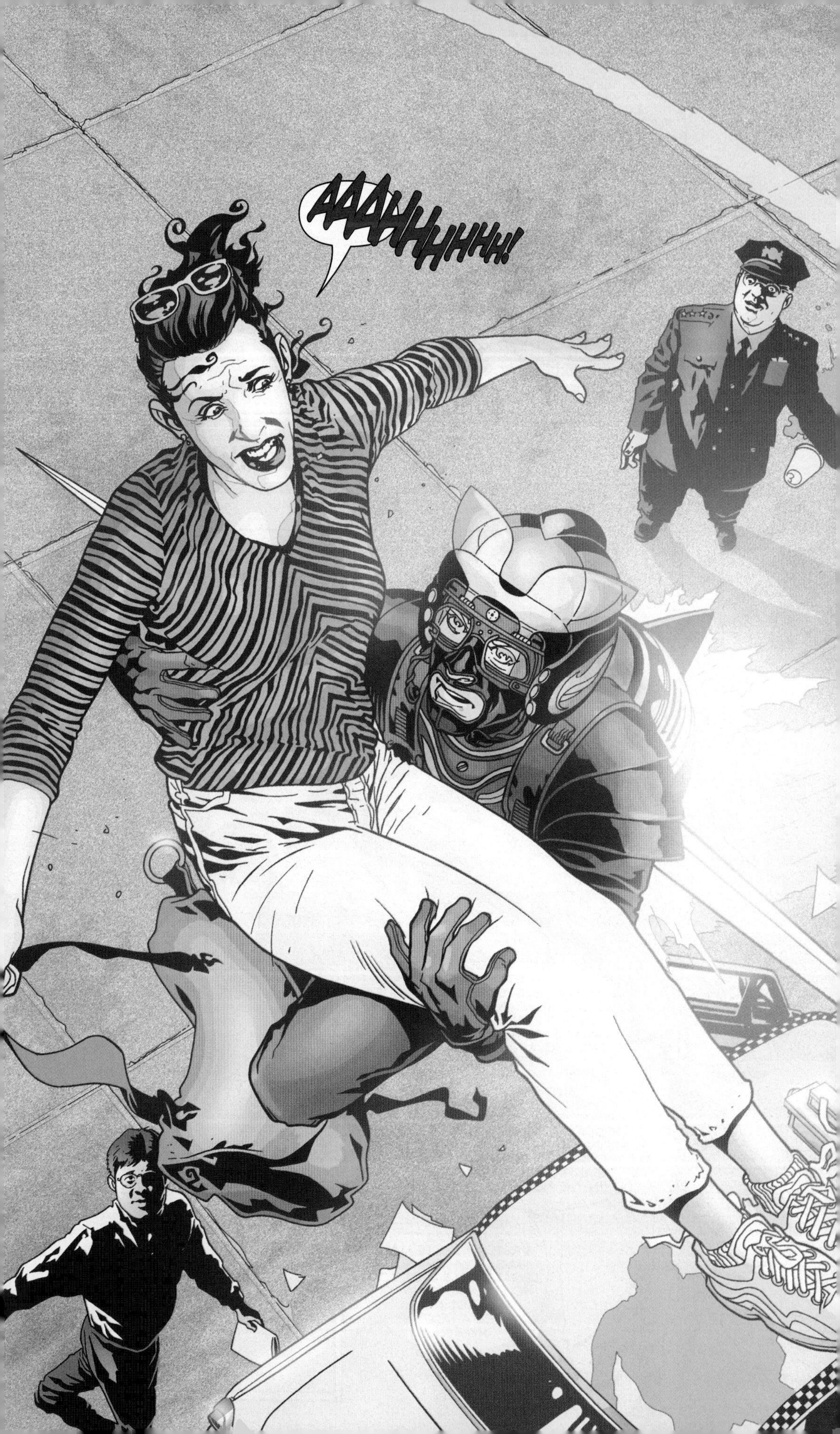
AAAHHHHHH!

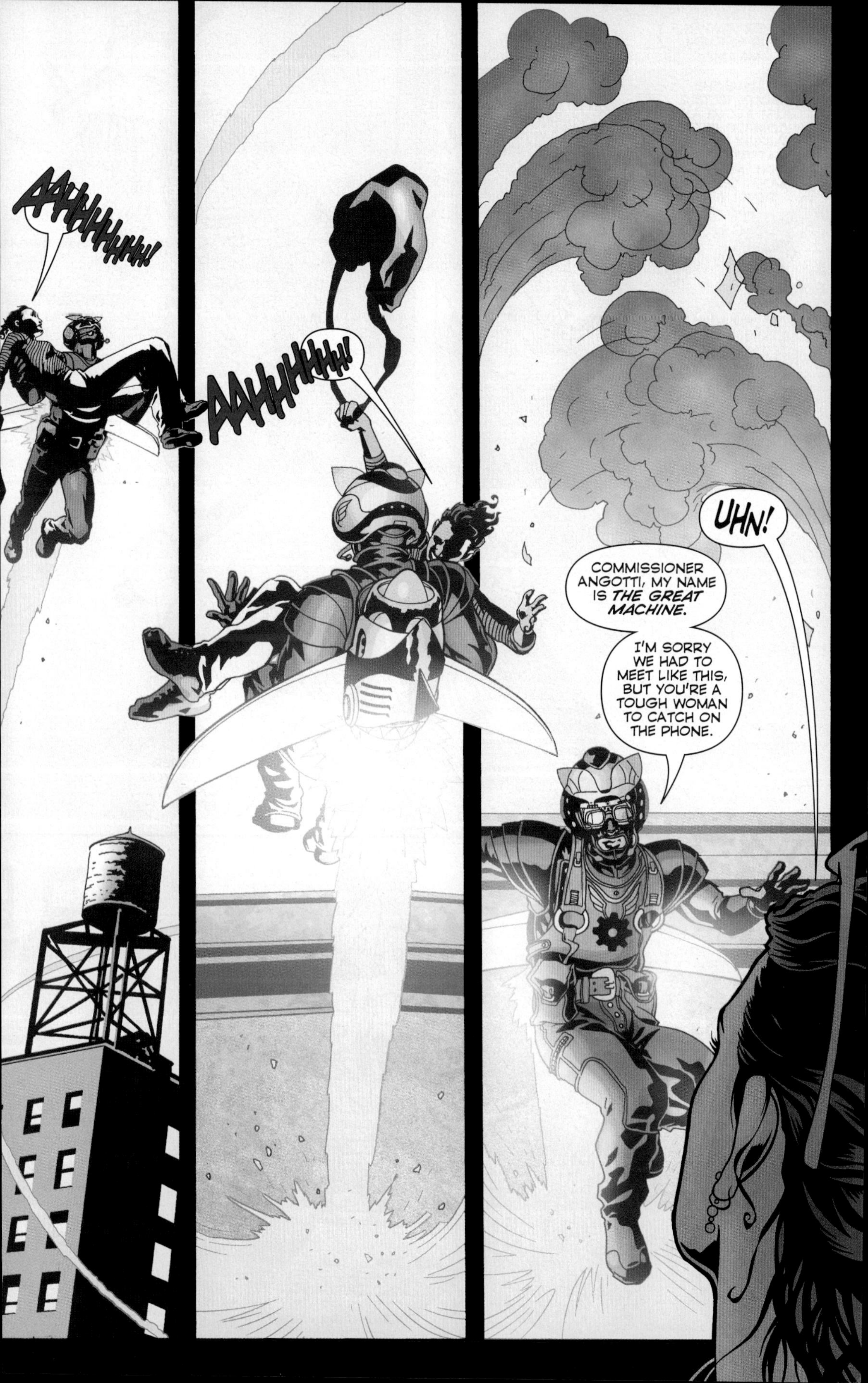
AAHHHHHHHH!
AAHHHHHHH!
COMMISSIONER ANGOTTI, MY NAME IS THE GREAT MACHINE.
I'M SORRY WE HAD TO MEET LIKE THIS, BUT YOU'RE A TOUGH WOMAN TO CATCH ON THE PHONE.
UHN!

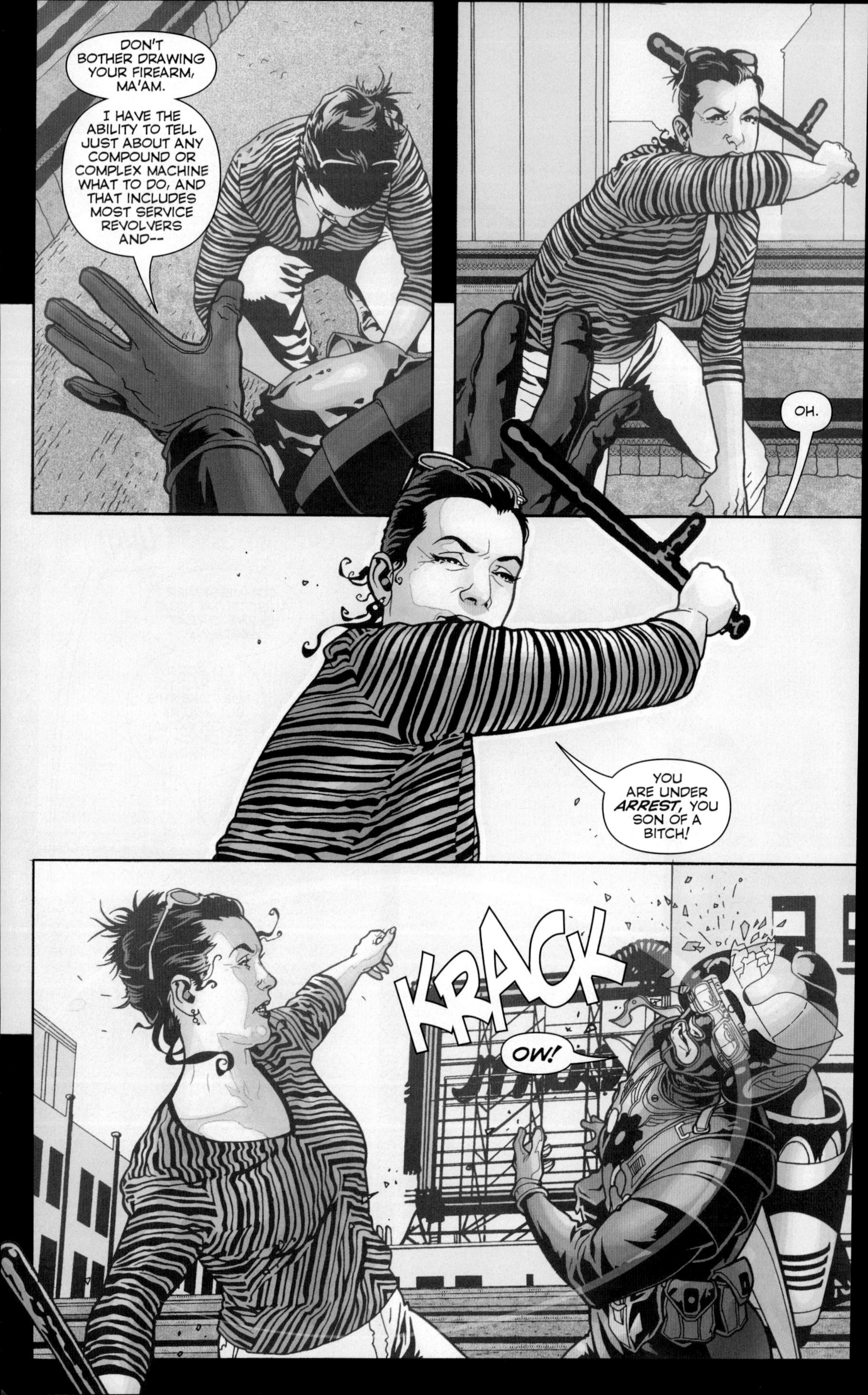
DON'T BOTHER DRAWING YOUR FIREARM, MA'AM.
I HAVE THE ABILITY TO TELL JUST ABOUT ANY COMPOUND OR COMPLEX MACHINE WHAT TO DO, AND THAT INCLUDES MOST SERVICE REVOLVERS AND--
OH.
YOU ARE UNDER ARREST, YOU SON OF A BITCH!
KRACK
OW!

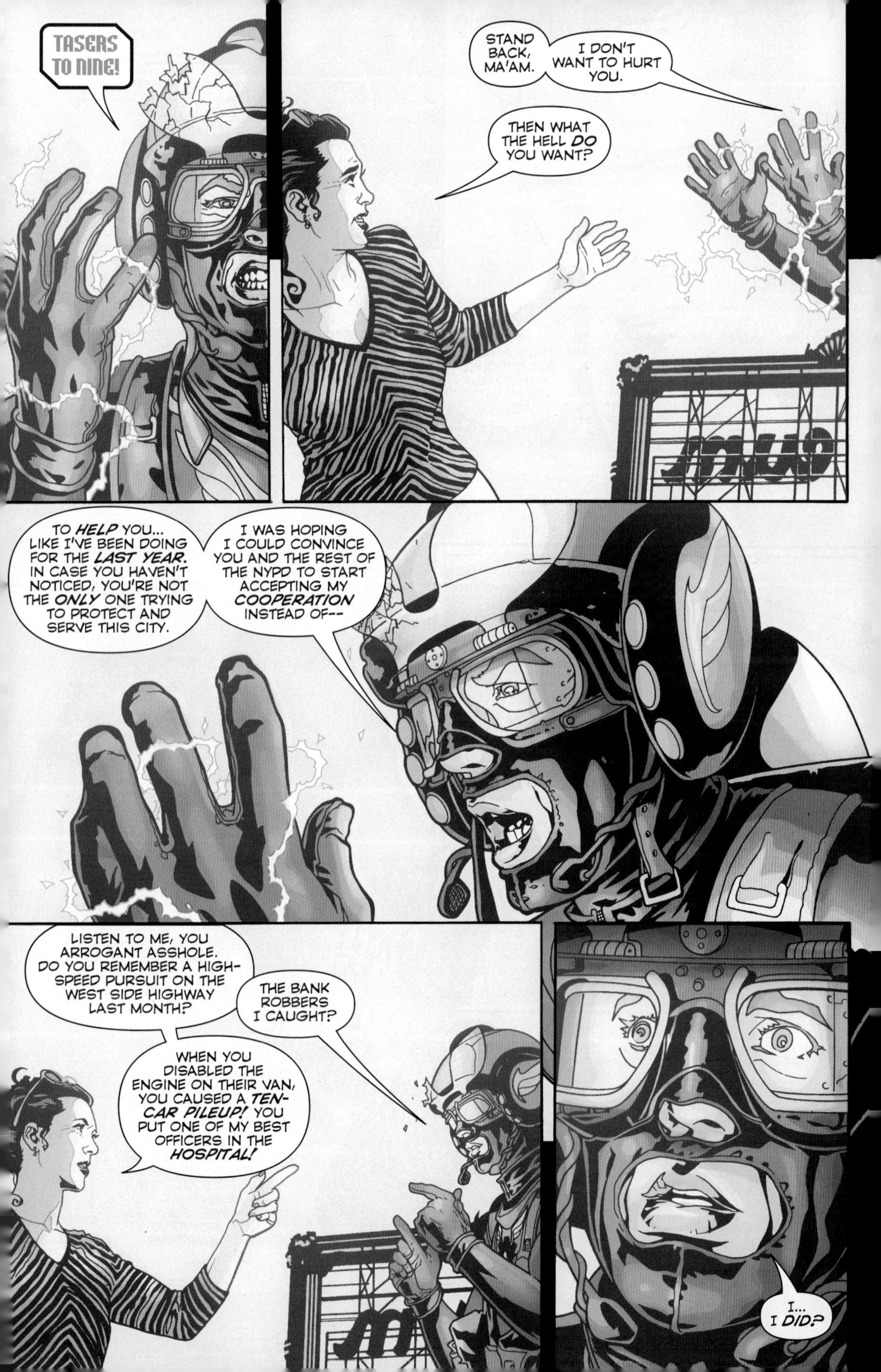
TASERS TO NINE!
STAND BACK, MA'AM.
I DON'T WANT TO HURT YOU.
THEN WHAT THE HELL DO YOU WANT?
TO HELP YOU... LIKE I'VE BEEN DOING FOR THE LAST YEAR. IN CASE YOU HAVEN'T NOTICED, YOU'RE NOT THE ONLY ONE TRYING TO PROTECT AND SERVE THIS CITY.
I WAS HOPING I COULD CONVINCE YOU AND THE REST OF THE NYPD TO START ACCEPTING MY COOPERATION INSTEAD OF--
LISTEN TO ME, YOU ARROGANT ASSHOLE. DO YOU REMEMBER A HIGH-SPEED PURSUIT ON THE WEST SIDE HIGHWAY LAST MONTH?
THE BANK ROBBERS I CAUGHT?
WHEN YOU DISABLED THE ENGINE ON THEIR VAN, YOU CAUSED A TEN-CAR PILEUP! YOU PUT ONE OF MY BEST OFFICERS IN THE HOSPITAL!
I... I DID?

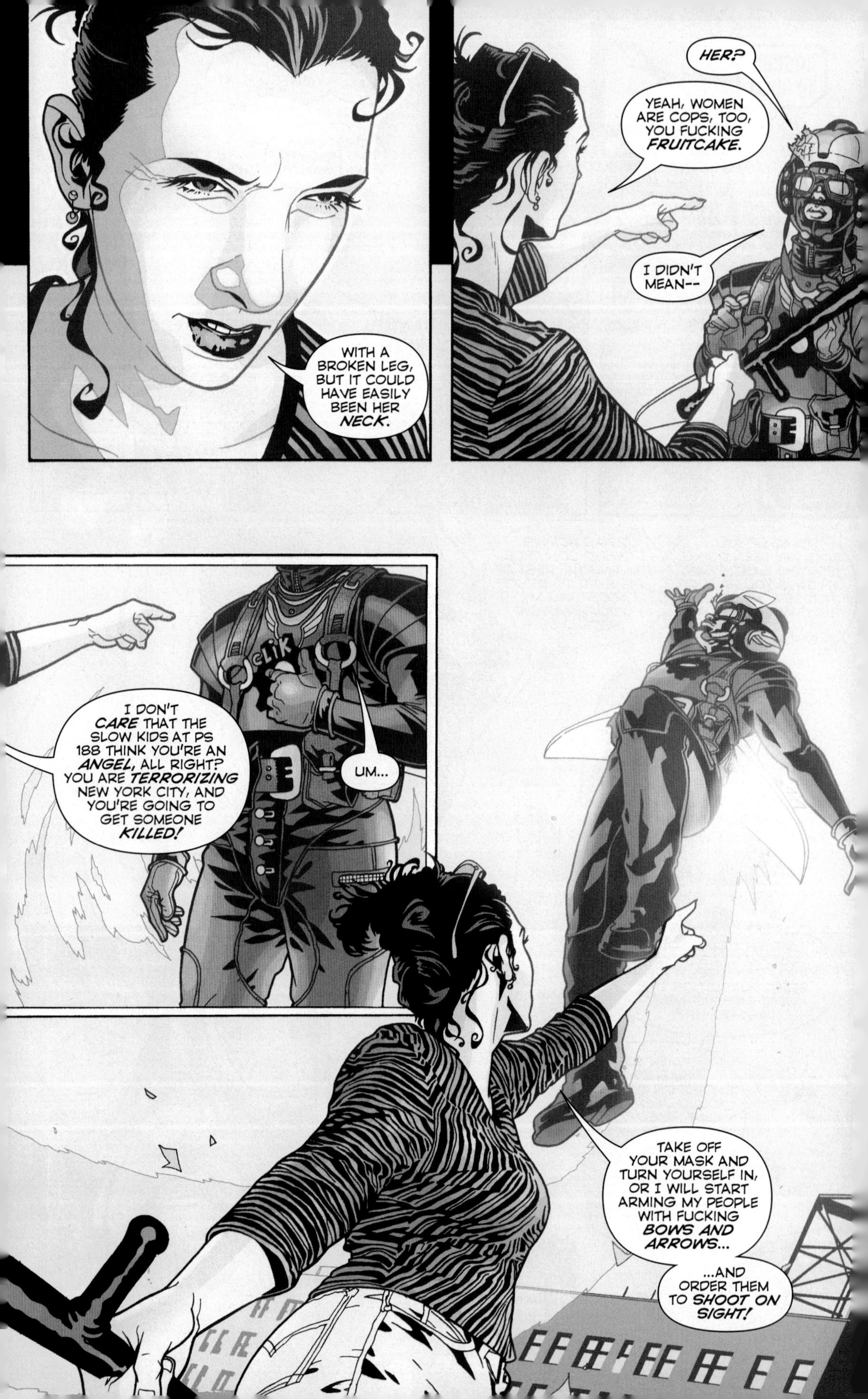

WITH A BROKEN LEG, BUT IT COULD HAVE EASILY BEEN HER *NECK*.
HER?
YEAH, WOMEN ARE COPS, TOO, YOU FUCKING *FRUITCAKE*.
I DIDN'T MEAN--
I DON'T *CARE* THAT THE SLOW KIDS AT PS 188 THINK YOU'RE AN *ANGEL*, ALL RIGHT? YOU ARE *TERRORIZING* NEW YORK CITY, AND YOU'RE GOING TO GET SOMEONE *KILLED!*
UM...
TAKE OFF YOUR MASK AND TURN YOURSELF IN, OR I WILL START ARMING MY PEOPLE WITH FUCKING *BOWS AND ARROWS...*
...AND ORDER THEM TO *SHOOT ON SIGHT!*

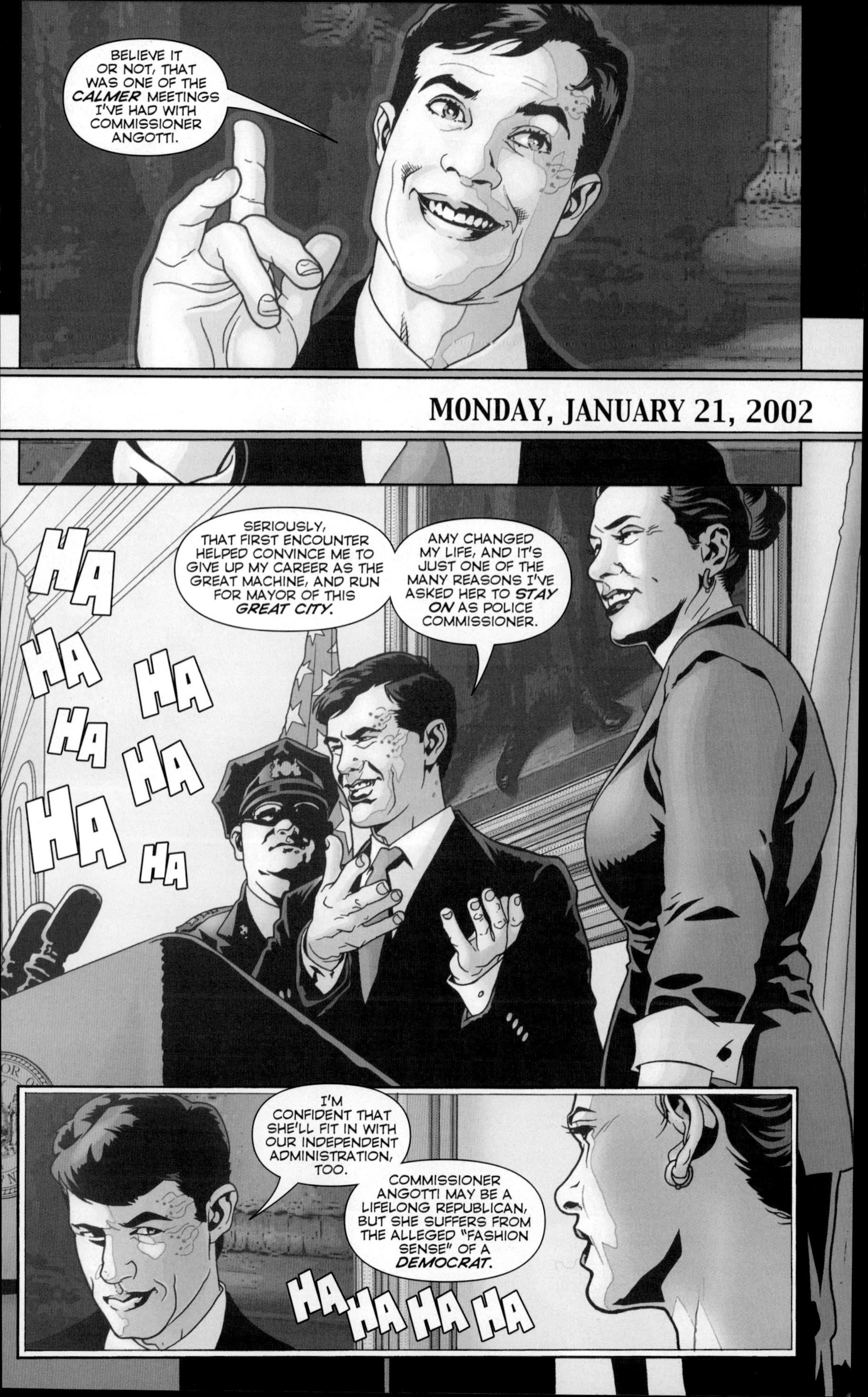
BELIEVE IT OR NOT, THAT WAS ONE OF THE CALMER MEETINGS I'VE HAD WITH COMMISSIONER ANGOTTI.
MONDAY, JANUARY 21, 2002
SERIOUSLY, THAT FIRST ENCOUNTER HELPED CONVINCE ME TO GIVE UP MY CAREER AS THE GREAT MACHINE, AND RUN FOR MAYOR OF THIS GREAT CITY.
HA HA HA HA HA HA HA HA
AMY CHANGED MY LIFE, AND IT'S JUST ONE OF THE MANY REASONS I'VE ASKED HER TO STAY ON AS POLICE COMMISSIONER.
I'M CONFIDENT THAT SHE'LL FIT IN WITH OUR INDEPENDENT ADMINISTRATION, TOO.
COMMISSIONER ANGOTTI MAY BE A LIFELONG REPUBLICAN, BUT SHE SUFFERS FROM THE ALLEGED "FASHION SENSE" OF A DEMOCRAT.
HA HA HA HA HA

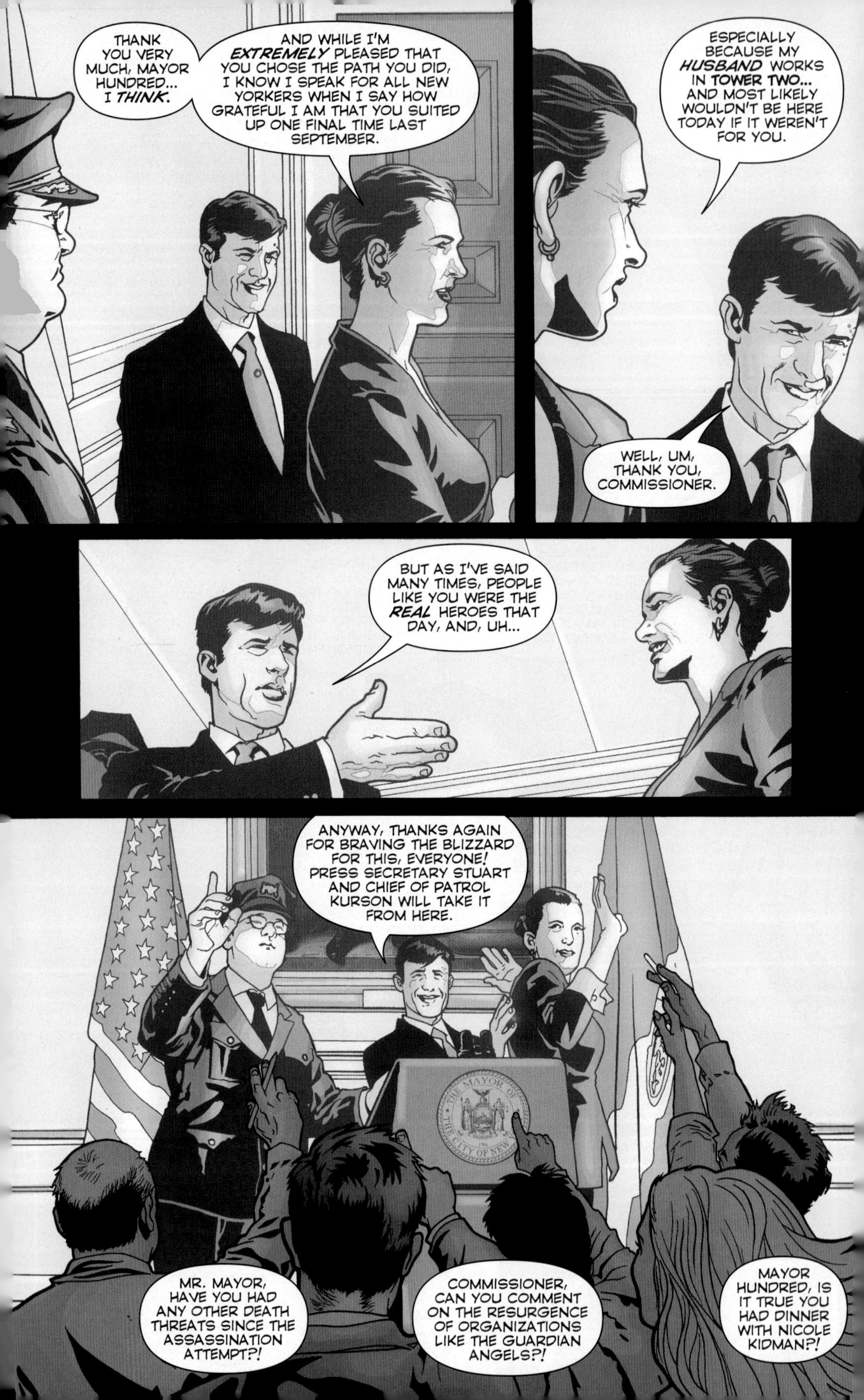
THANK YOU VERY MUCH, MAYOR HUNDRED... I *THINK*.
AND WHILE I'M *EXTREMELY* PLEASED THAT YOU CHOSE THE PATH YOU DID, I KNOW I SPEAK FOR ALL NEW YORKERS WHEN I SAY HOW GRATEFUL I AM THAT YOU SUITED UP ONE FINAL TIME LAST SEPTEMBER.
ESPECIALLY BECAUSE MY *HUSBAND* WORKS IN **TOWER TWO...** AND MOST LIKELY WOULDN'T BE HERE TODAY IF IT WEREN'T FOR YOU.
WELL, UM, THANK YOU, COMMISSIONER.
BUT AS I'VE SAID MANY TIMES, PEOPLE LIKE YOU WERE THE *REAL* HEROES THAT DAY, AND, UH...
ANYWAY, THANKS AGAIN FOR BRAVING THE BLIZZARD FOR THIS, EVERYONE! PRESS SECRETARY STUART AND CHIEF OF PATROL KURSON WILL TAKE IT FROM HERE.
THE MAYOR OF THE CITY OF NEW
MR. MAYOR, HAVE YOU HAD ANY OTHER DEATH THREATS SINCE THE ASSASSINATION ATTEMPT?!
COMMISSIONER, CAN YOU COMMENT ON THE RESURGENCE OF ORGANIZATIONS LIKE THE GUARDIAN ANGELS?!
MAYOR HUNDRED, IS IT TRUE YOU HAD DINNER WITH NICOLE KIDMAN?!

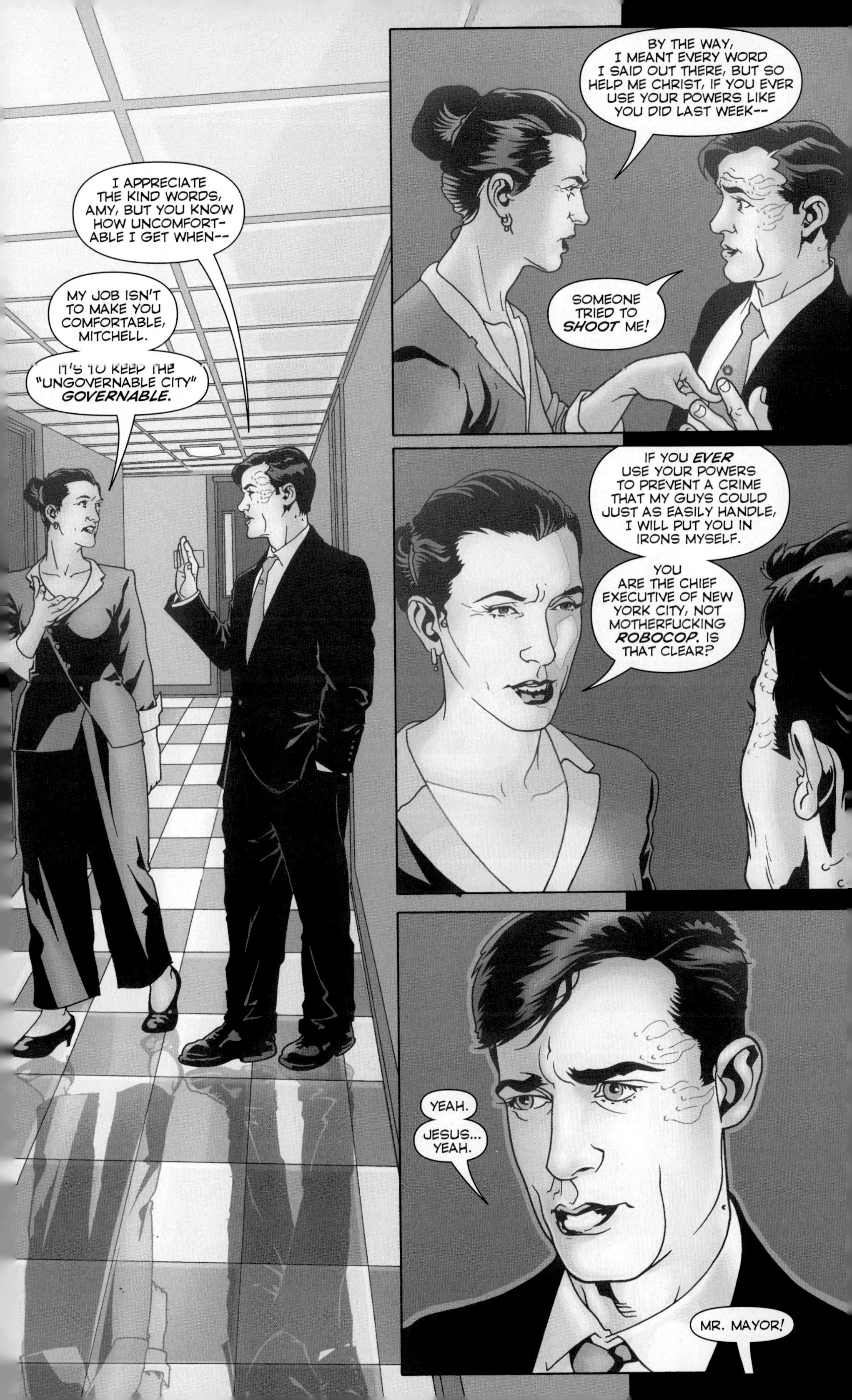
I APPRECIATE THE KIND WORDS, AMY, BUT YOU KNOW HOW UNCOMFORTABLE I GET WHEN--
MY JOB ISN'T TO MAKE YOU COMFORTABLE, MITCHELL.
IT'S TO KEEP THE "UNGOVERNABLE CITY" *GOVERNABLE.*
BY THE WAY, I MEANT EVERY WORD I SAID OUT THERE, BUT SO HELP ME CHRIST, IF YOU EVER USE YOUR POWERS LIKE YOU DID LAST WEEK--
SOMEONE TRIED TO *SHOOT* ME!
IF YOU *EVER* USE YOUR POWERS TO PREVENT A CRIME THAT MY GUYS COULD JUST AS EASILY HANDLE, I WILL PUT YOU IN IRONS MYSELF.
YOU ARE THE CHIEF EXECUTIVE OF NEW YORK CITY, NOT MOTHERFUCKING *ROBOCOP.* IS THAT CLEAR?
YEAH.
JESUS... YEAH.
MR. MAYOR!

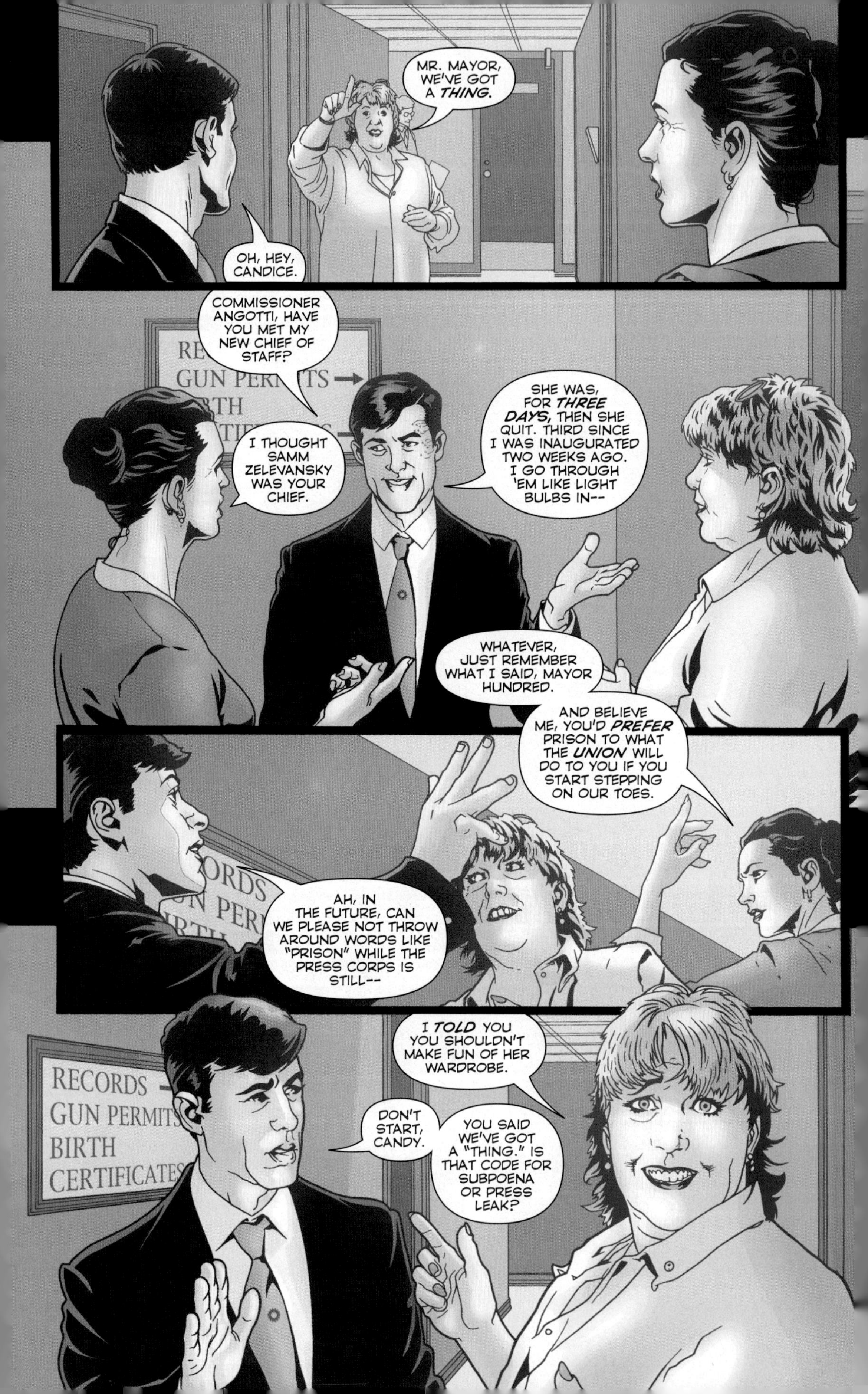
MR. MAYOR, WE'VE GOT A *THING.*
OH, HEY, CANDICE.
COMMISSIONER ANGOTTI, HAVE YOU MET MY NEW CHIEF OF STAFF?
I THOUGHT SAMM ZELEVANSKY WAS YOUR CHIEF.
SHE WAS, FOR *THREE DAYS,* THEN SHE QUIT. THIRD SINCE I WAS INAUGURATED TWO WEEKS AGO. I GO THROUGH 'EM LIKE LIGHT BULBS IN--
WHATEVER, JUST REMEMBER WHAT I SAID, MAYOR HUNDRED.
AND BELIEVE ME, YOU'D *PREFER* PRISON TO WHAT THE *UNION* WILL DO TO YOU IF YOU START STEPPING ON OUR TOES.
AH, IN THE FUTURE, CAN WE PLEASE NOT THROW AROUND WORDS LIKE "PRISON" WHILE THE PRESS CORPS IS STILL--
RECORDS
GUN PERMITS
BIRTH
CERTIFICATES
I *TOLD* YOU YOU SHOULDN'T MAKE FUN OF HER WARDROBE.
DON'T START, CANDY.
YOU SAID WE'VE GOT A "THING." IS THAT CODE FOR SUBPOENA OR PRESS LEAK?

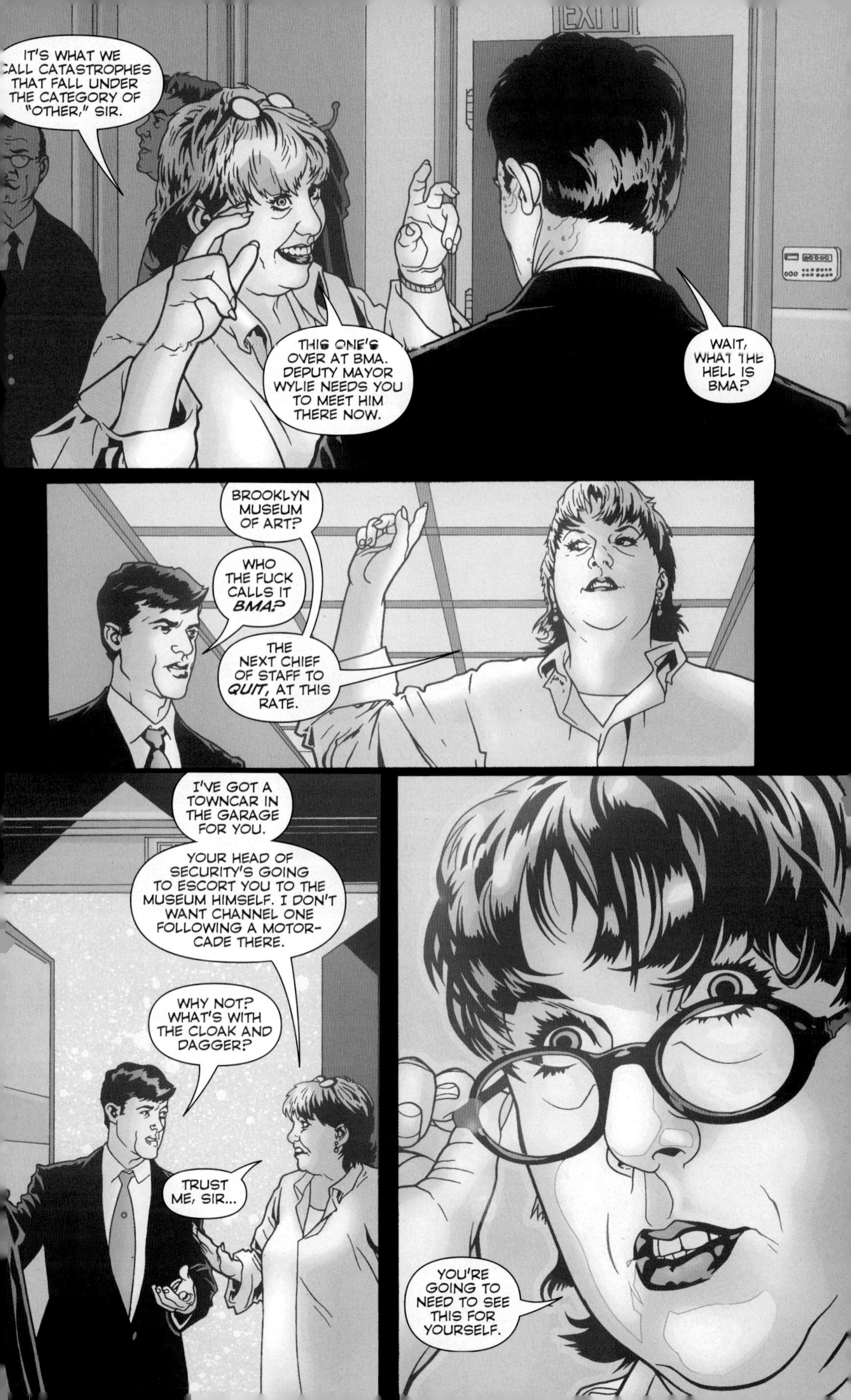
IT'S WHAT WE CALL CATASTROPHES THAT FALL UNDER THE CATEGORY OF "OTHER," SIR.
THIS ONE'S OVER AT BMA. DEPUTY MAYOR WYLIE NEEDS YOU TO MEET HIM THERE NOW.
WAIT, WHAT THE HELL IS BMA?
BROOKLYN MUSEUM OF ART?
WHO THE FUCK CALLS IT BMA?
THE NEXT CHIEF OF STAFF TO QUIT, AT THIS RATE.
I'VE GOT A TOWNCAR IN THE GARAGE FOR YOU.
YOUR HEAD OF SECURITY'S GOING TO ESCORT YOU TO THE MUSEUM HIMSELF. I DON'T WANT CHANNEL ONE FOLLOWING A MOTOR-CADE THERE.
WHY NOT? WHAT'S WITH THE CLOAK AND DAGGER?
TRUST ME, SIR...
YOU'RE GOING TO NEED TO SEE THIS FOR YOURSELF.

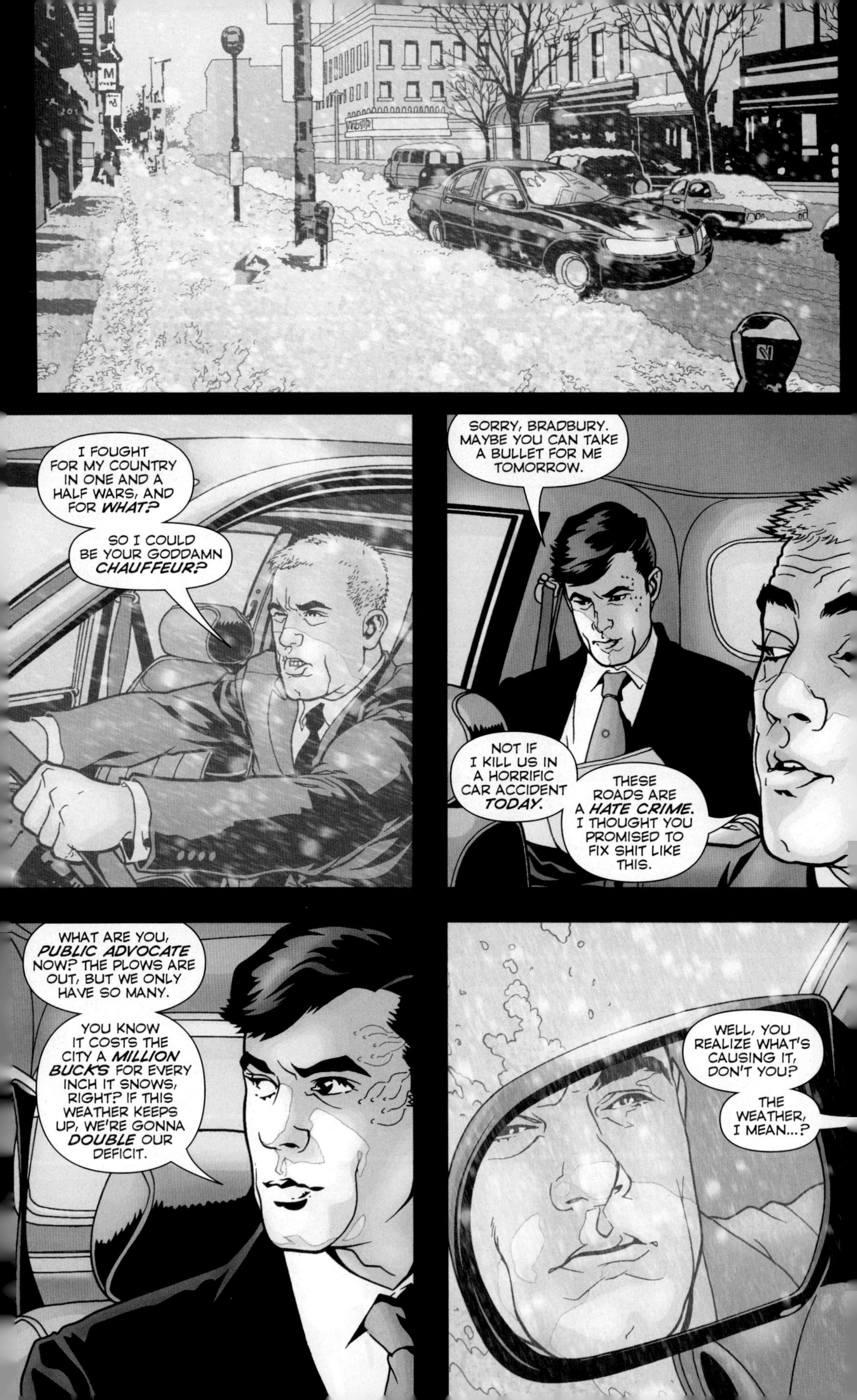
I FOUGHT FOR MY COUNTRY IN ONE AND A HALF WARS, AND FOR *WHAT?*
SO I COULD BE YOUR GODDAMN *CHAUFFEUR?*
SORRY, BRADBURY. MAYBE YOU CAN TAKE A BULLET FOR ME TOMORROW.
NOT IF I KILL US IN A HORRIFIC CAR ACCIDENT *TODAY.*
THESE ROADS ARE A *HATE CRIME.* I THOUGHT YOU PROMISED TO FIX SHIT LIKE THIS.
WHAT ARE YOU, *PUBLIC ADVOCATE* NOW? THE PLOWS ARE OUT, BUT WE ONLY HAVE SO MANY.
YOU KNOW IT COSTS THE CITY A *MILLION BUCKS* FOR EVERY INCH IT SNOWS, RIGHT? IF THIS WEATHER KEEPS UP, WE'RE GONNA *DOUBLE* OUR DEFICIT.
WELL, YOU REALIZE WHAT'S CAUSING IT, DON'T YOU?
THE WEATHER, I MEAN...?

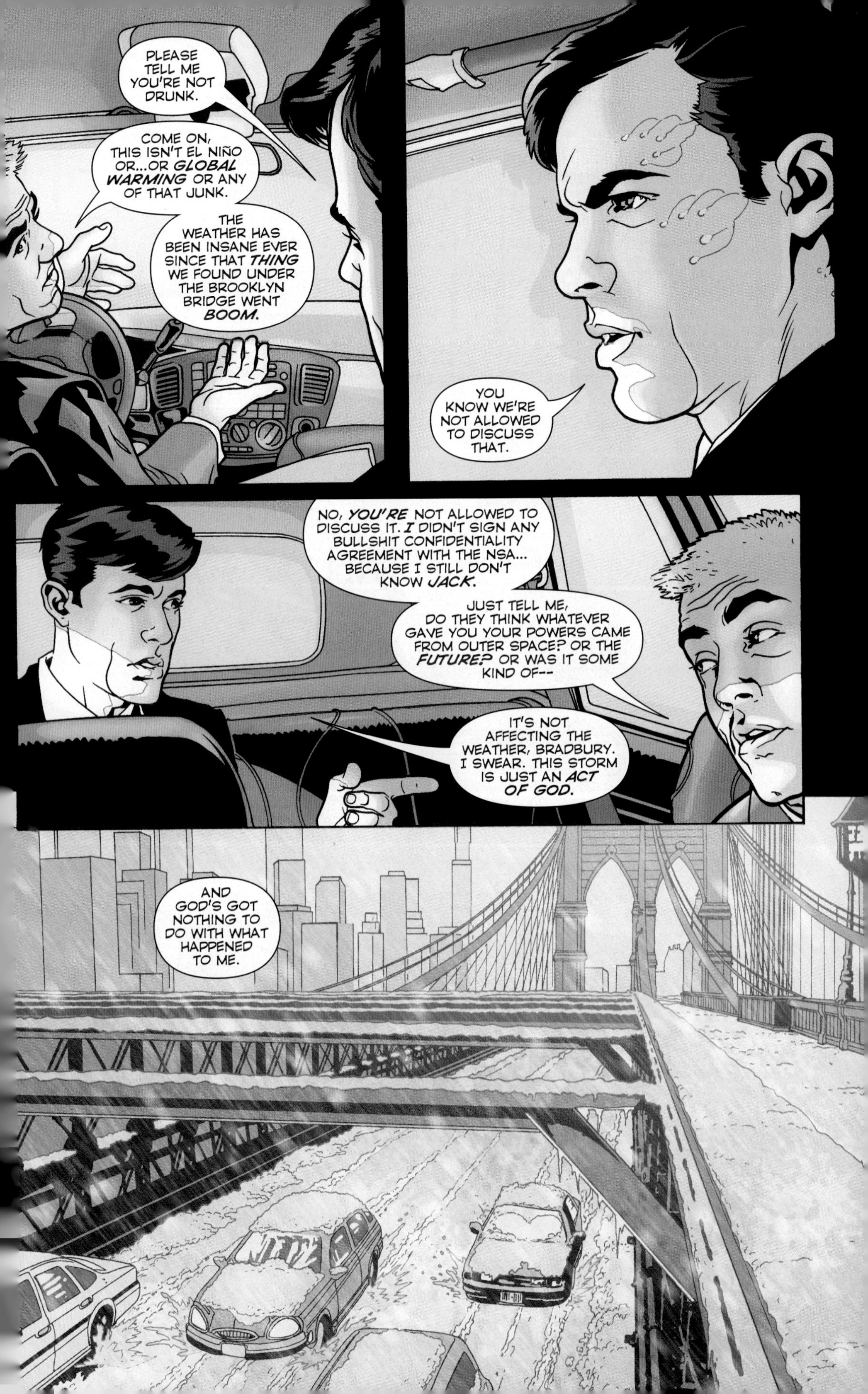
PLEASE TELL ME YOU'RE NOT DRUNK.
COME ON, THIS ISN'T EL NIÑO OR...OR *GLOBAL WARMING* OR ANY OF THAT JUNK.
THE WEATHER HAS BEEN INSANE EVER SINCE THAT *THING* WE FOUND UNDER THE BROOKLYN BRIDGE WENT *BOOM.*
YOU KNOW WE'RE NOT ALLOWED TO DISCUSS THAT.
NO, *YOU'RE* NOT ALLOWED TO DISCUSS IT. *I* DIDN'T SIGN ANY BULLSHIT CONFIDENTIALITY AGREEMENT WITH THE NSA... BECAUSE I STILL DON'T KNOW *JACK.*
JUST TELL ME, DO THEY THINK WHATEVER GAVE YOU YOUR POWERS CAME FROM OUTER SPACE? OR THE *FUTURE?* OR WAS IT SOME KIND OF--
IT'S NOT AFFECTING THE WEATHER, BRADBURY. I SWEAR. THIS STORM IS JUST AN *ACT OF GOD.*
AND GOD'S GOT NOTHING TO DO WITH WHAT HAPPENED TO ME.

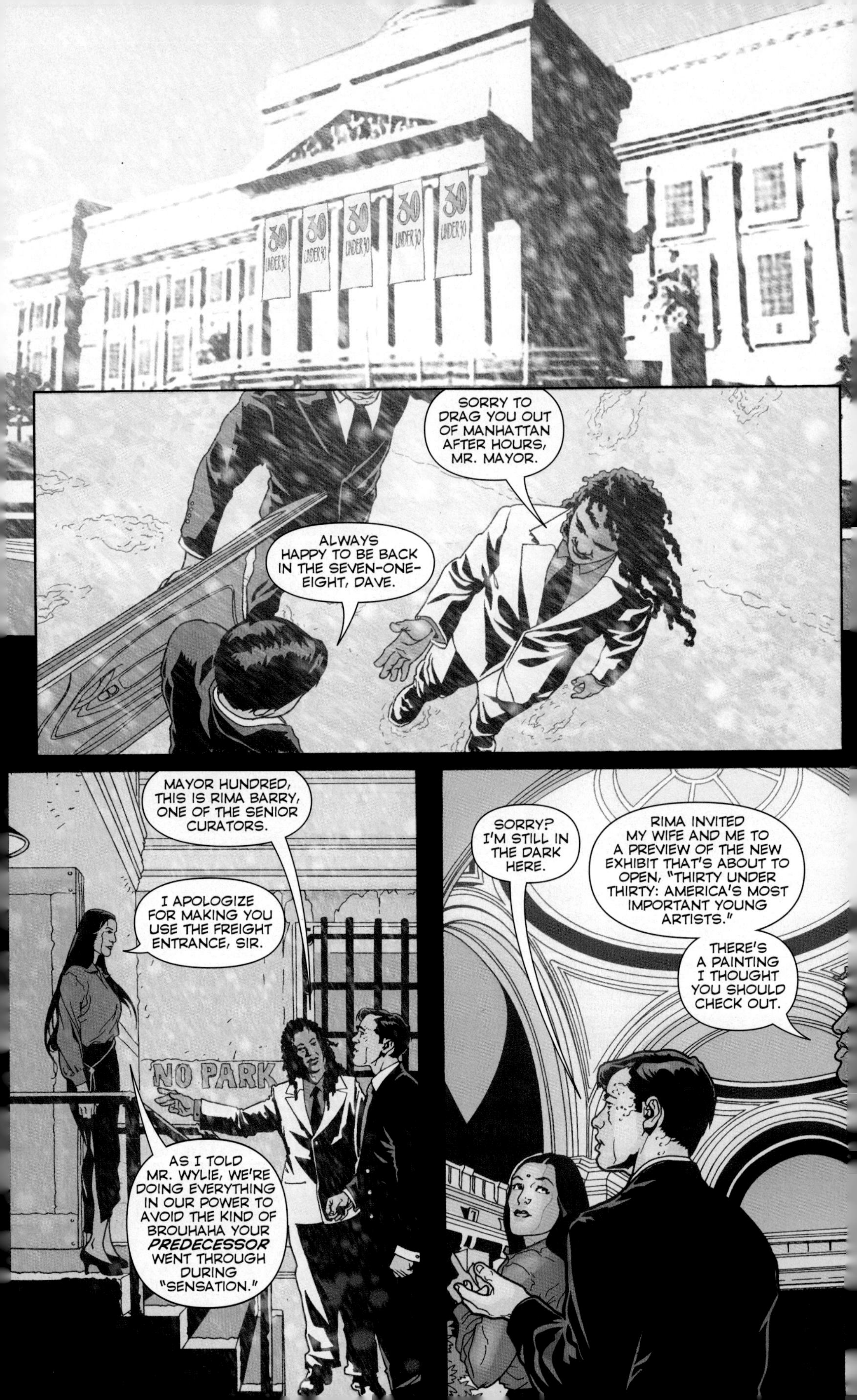
30 UNDER 30
SORRY TO DRAG YOU OUT OF MANHATTAN AFTER HOURS, MR. MAYOR.
ALWAYS HAPPY TO BE BACK IN THE SEVEN-ONE-EIGHT, DAVE.
MAYOR HUNDRED, THIS IS RIMA BARRY, ONE OF THE SENIOR CURATORS.
I APOLOGIZE FOR MAKING YOU USE THE FREIGHT ENTRANCE, SIR.
NO PARK
AS I TOLD MR. WYLIE, WE'RE DOING EVERYTHING IN OUR POWER TO AVOID THE KIND OF BROUHAHA YOUR *PREDECESSOR* WENT THROUGH DURING "SENSATION."
SORRY? I'M STILL IN THE DARK HERE.
RIMA INVITED MY WIFE AND ME TO A PREVIEW OF THE NEW EXHIBIT THAT'S ABOUT TO OPEN, "THIRTY UNDER THIRTY: AMERICA'S MOST IMPORTANT YOUNG ARTISTS."
THERE'S A PAINTING I THOUGHT YOU SHOULD CHECK OUT.

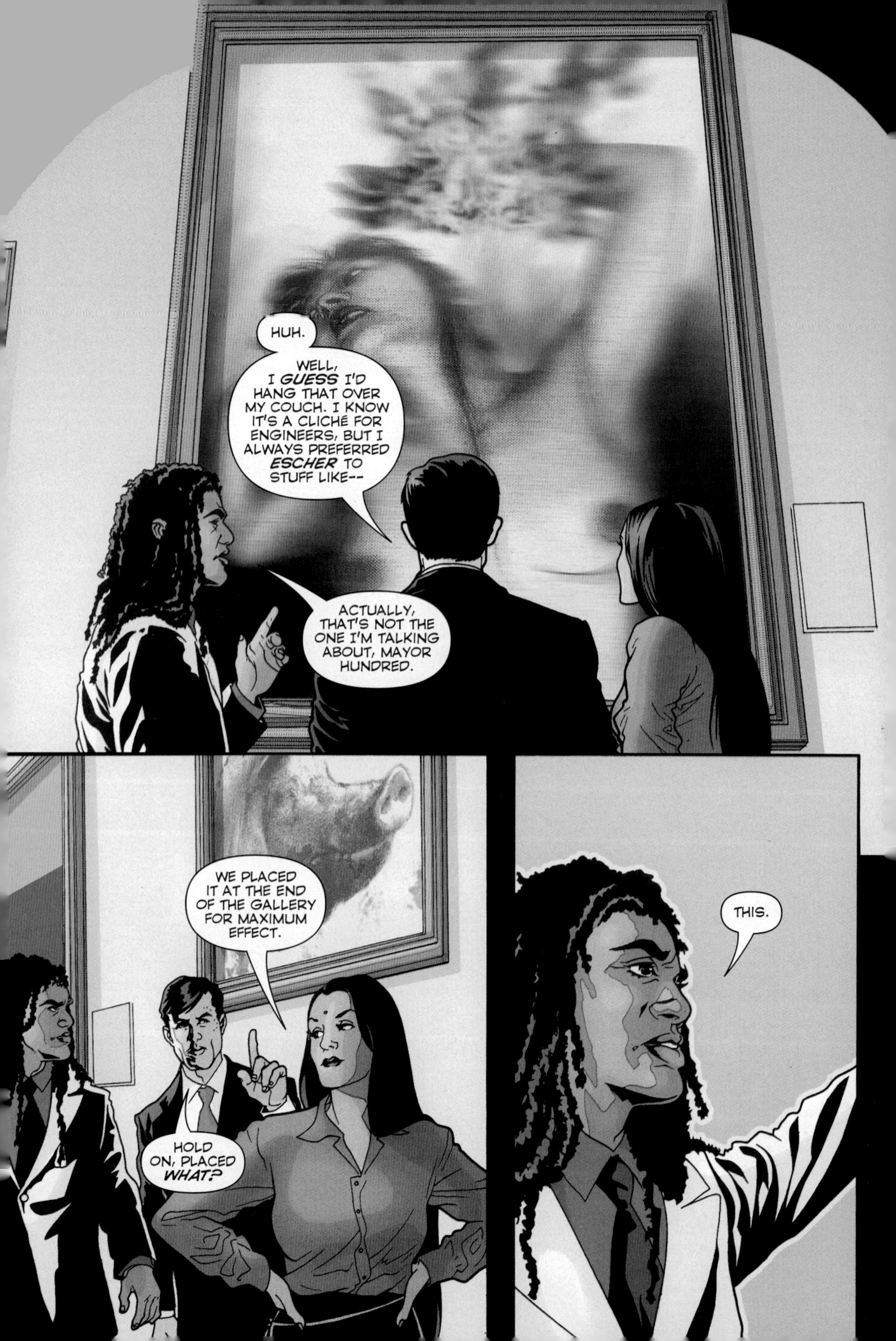
HUH.
WELL, I GUESS I'D HANG THAT OVER MY COUCH. I KNOW IT'S A CLICHÉ FOR ENGINEERS, BUT I ALWAYS PREFERRED ESCHER TO STUFF LIKE--
ACTUALLY, THAT'S NOT THE ONE I'M TALKING ABOUT, MAYOR HUNDRED.
WE PLACED IT AT THE END OF THE GALLERY FOR MAXIMUM EFFECT.
HOLD ON, PLACED WHAT?
THIS.

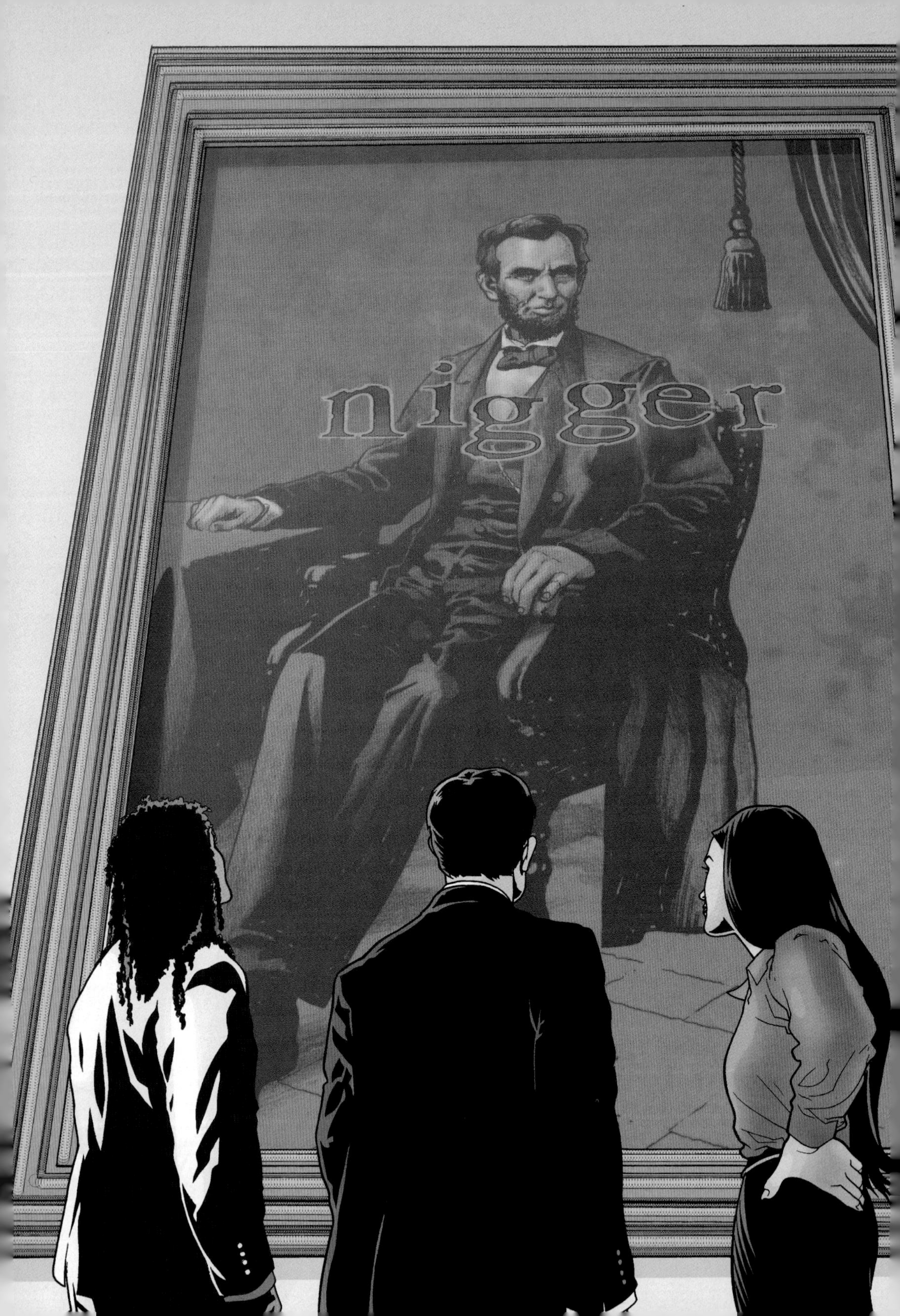
nigger

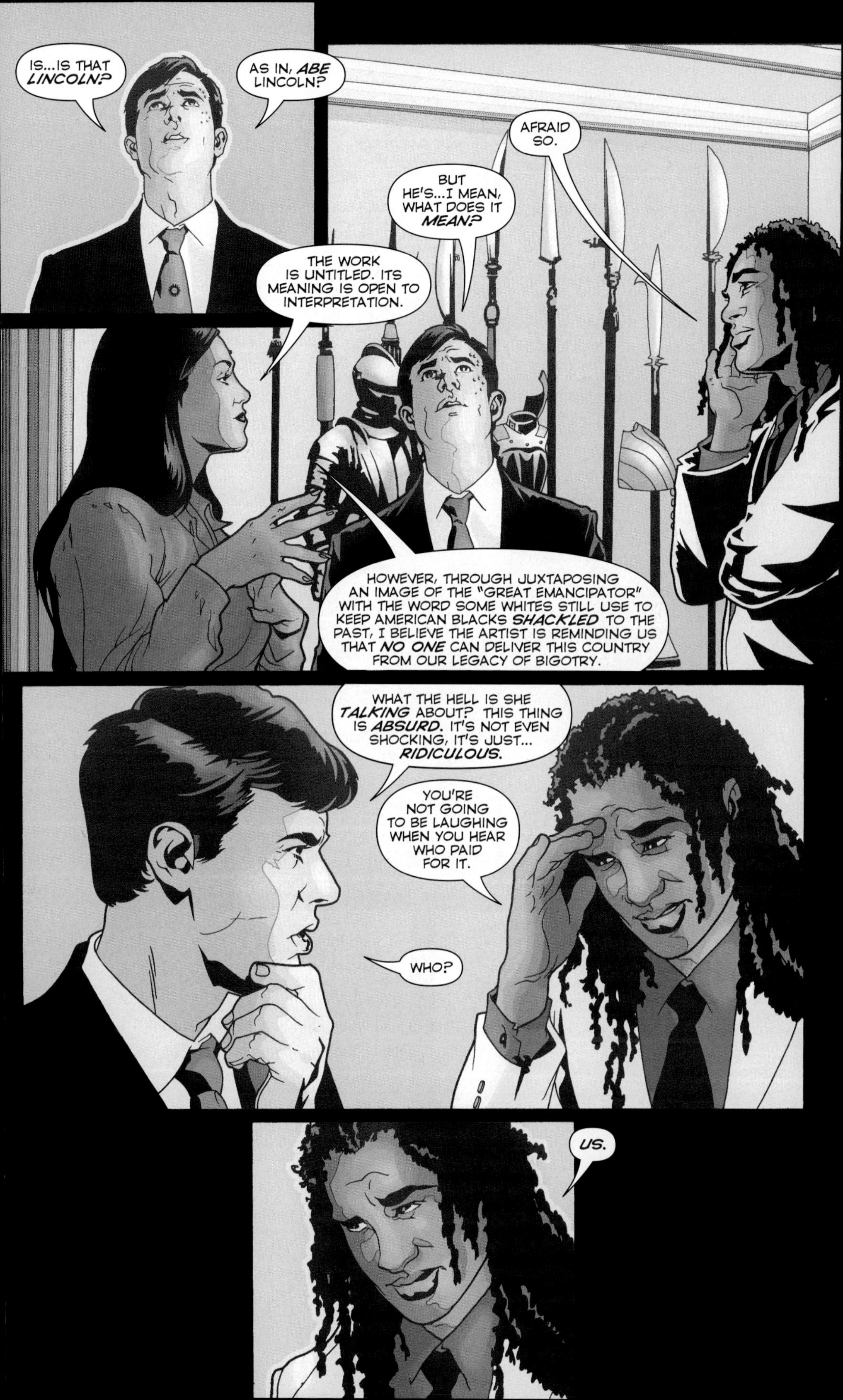
IS...IS THAT *LINCOLN?*
AS IN, *ABE* LINCOLN?
AFRAID SO.
BUT HE'S...I MEAN, WHAT DOES IT *MEAN?*
THE WORK IS UNTITLED. ITS MEANING IS OPEN TO INTERPRETATION.
HOWEVER, THROUGH JUXTAPOSING AN IMAGE OF THE "GREAT EMANCIPATOR" WITH THE WORD SOME WHITES STILL USE TO KEEP AMERICAN BLACKS *SHACKLED* TO THE PAST, I BELIEVE THE ARTIST IS REMINDING US THAT *NO ONE* CAN DELIVER THIS COUNTRY FROM OUR LEGACY OF BIGOTRY.
WHAT THE HELL IS SHE *TALKING* ABOUT? THIS THING IS *ABSURD*. IT'S NOT EVEN SHOCKING, IT'S JUST... *RIDICULOUS*.
YOU'RE NOT GOING TO BE LAUGHING WHEN YOU HEAR WHO PAID FOR IT.
WHO?
US.

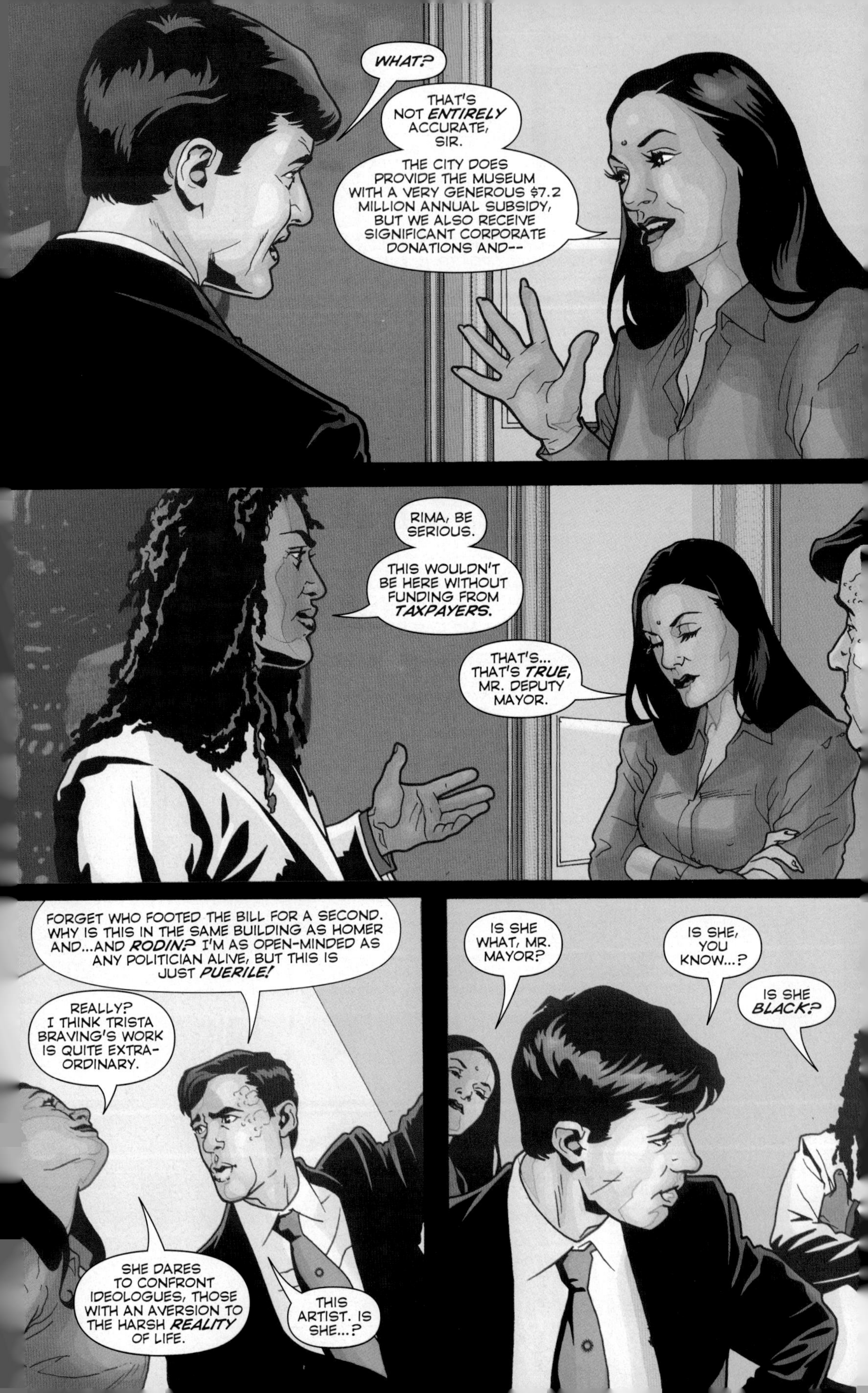
WHAT?
THAT'S NOT ENTIRELY ACCURATE, SIR.
THE CITY DOES PROVIDE THE MUSEUM WITH A VERY GENEROUS $7.2 MILLION ANNUAL SUBSIDY, BUT WE ALSO RECEIVE SIGNIFICANT CORPORATE DONATIONS AND--
RIMA, BE SERIOUS.
THIS WOULDN'T BE HERE WITHOUT FUNDING FROM TAXPAYERS.
THAT'S... THAT'S TRUE, MR. DEPUTY MAYOR.
FORGET WHO FOOTED THE BILL FOR A SECOND. WHY IS THIS IN THE SAME BUILDING AS HOMER AND...AND RODIN? I'M AS OPEN-MINDED AS ANY POLITICIAN ALIVE, BUT THIS IS JUST PUERILE!
REALLY? I THINK TRISTA BRAVING'S WORK IS QUITE EXTRA-ORDINARY.
SHE DARES TO CONFRONT IDEOLOGUES, THOSE WITH AN AVERSION TO THE HARSH REALITY OF LIFE.
THIS ARTIST. IS SHE...?
IS SHE WHAT, MR. MAYOR?
IS SHE, YOU KNOW...?
IS SHE BLACK?

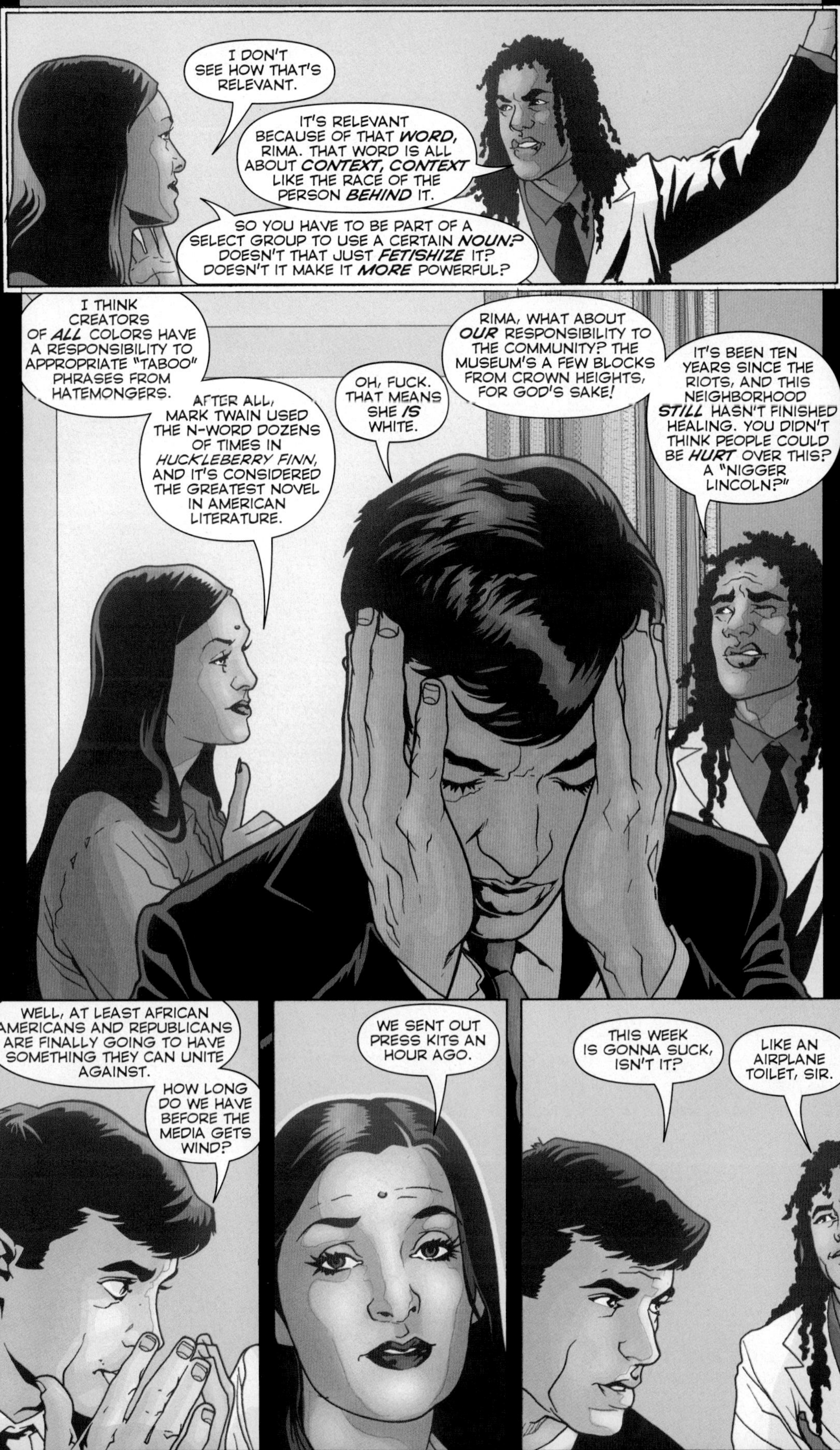
I DON'T SEE HOW THAT'S RELEVANT.
IT'S RELEVANT BECAUSE OF THAT *WORD*, RIMA. THAT WORD IS ALL ABOUT *CONTEXT, CONTEXT* LIKE THE RACE OF THE PERSON *BEHIND* IT.
SO YOU HAVE TO BE PART OF A SELECT GROUP TO USE A CERTAIN *NOUN?* DOESN'T THAT JUST *FETISHIZE* IT? DOESN'T IT MAKE IT *MORE* POWERFUL?
I THINK CREATORS OF *ALL* COLORS HAVE A RESPONSIBILITY TO APPROPRIATE "TABOO" PHRASES FROM HATEMONGERS.
AFTER ALL, MARK TWAIN USED THE N-WORD DOZENS OF TIMES IN *HUCKLEBERRY FINN*, AND IT'S CONSIDERED THE GREATEST NOVEL IN AMERICAN LITERATURE.
OH, FUCK. THAT MEANS SHE *IS* WHITE.
RIMA, WHAT ABOUT *OUR* RESPONSIBILITY TO THE COMMUNITY? THE MUSEUM'S A FEW BLOCKS FROM CROWN HEIGHTS, FOR GOD'S SAKE!
IT'S BEEN TEN YEARS SINCE THE RIOTS, AND THIS NEIGHBORHOOD *STILL* HASN'T FINISHED HEALING. YOU DIDN'T THINK PEOPLE COULD BE *HURT* OVER THIS? A "NIGGER LINCOLN?"
WELL, AT LEAST AFRICAN AMERICANS AND REPUBLICANS ARE FINALLY GOING TO HAVE SOMETHING THEY CAN UNITE AGAINST.
HOW LONG DO WE HAVE BEFORE THE MEDIA GETS WIND?
WE SENT OUT PRESS KITS AN HOUR AGO.
THIS WEEK IS GONNA SUCK, ISN'T IT?
LIKE AN AIRPLANE TOILET, SIR.

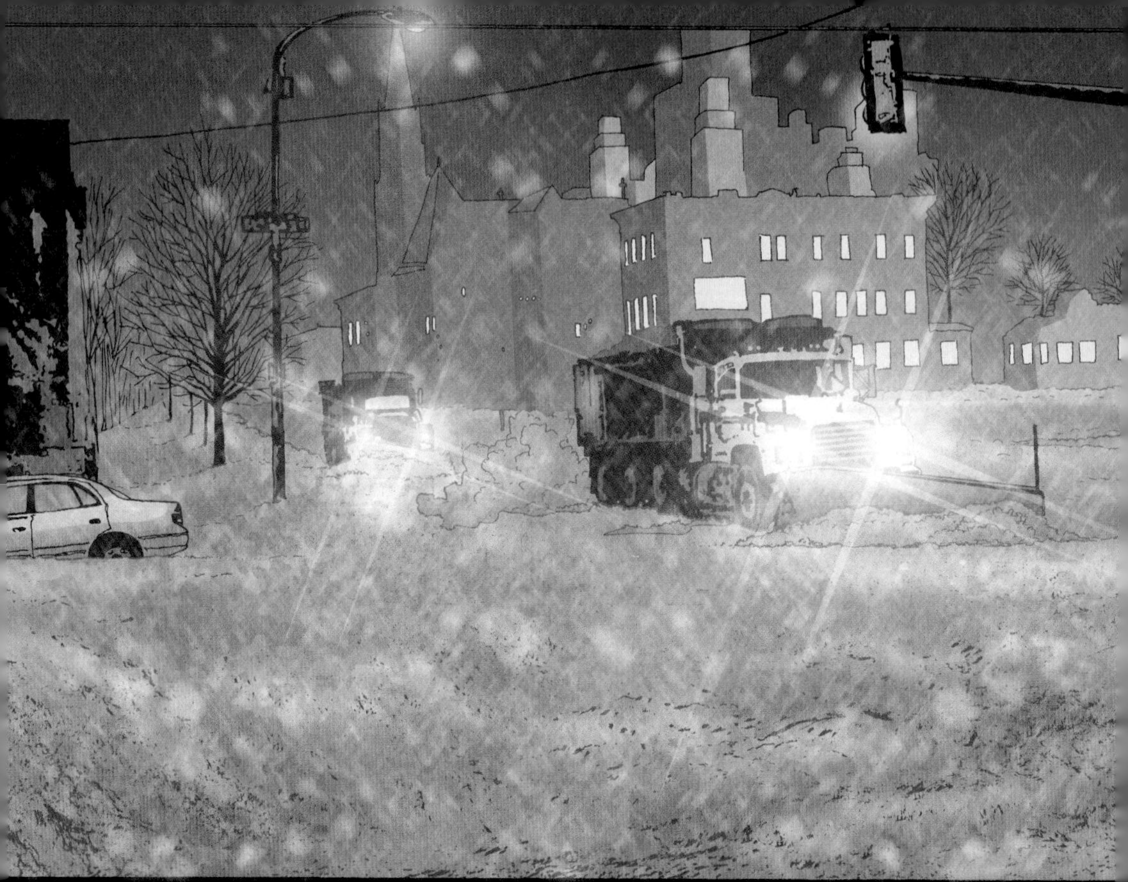

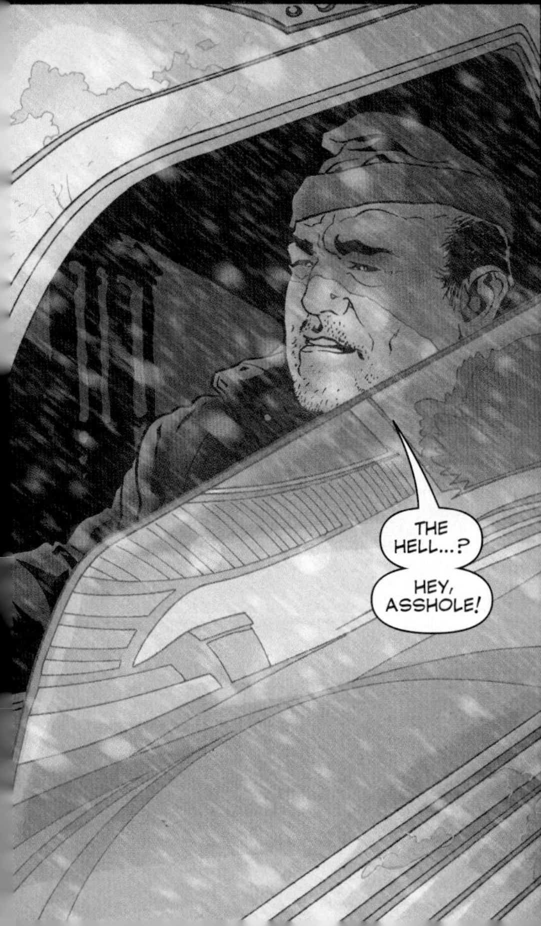
THE HELL...?
HEY, ASSHOLE!

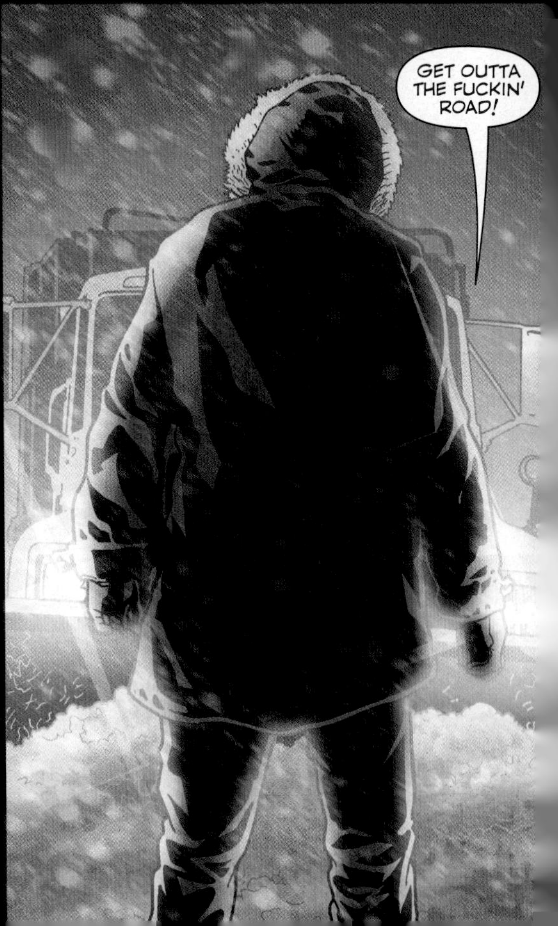
GET OUTTA THE FUCKIN' ROAD!

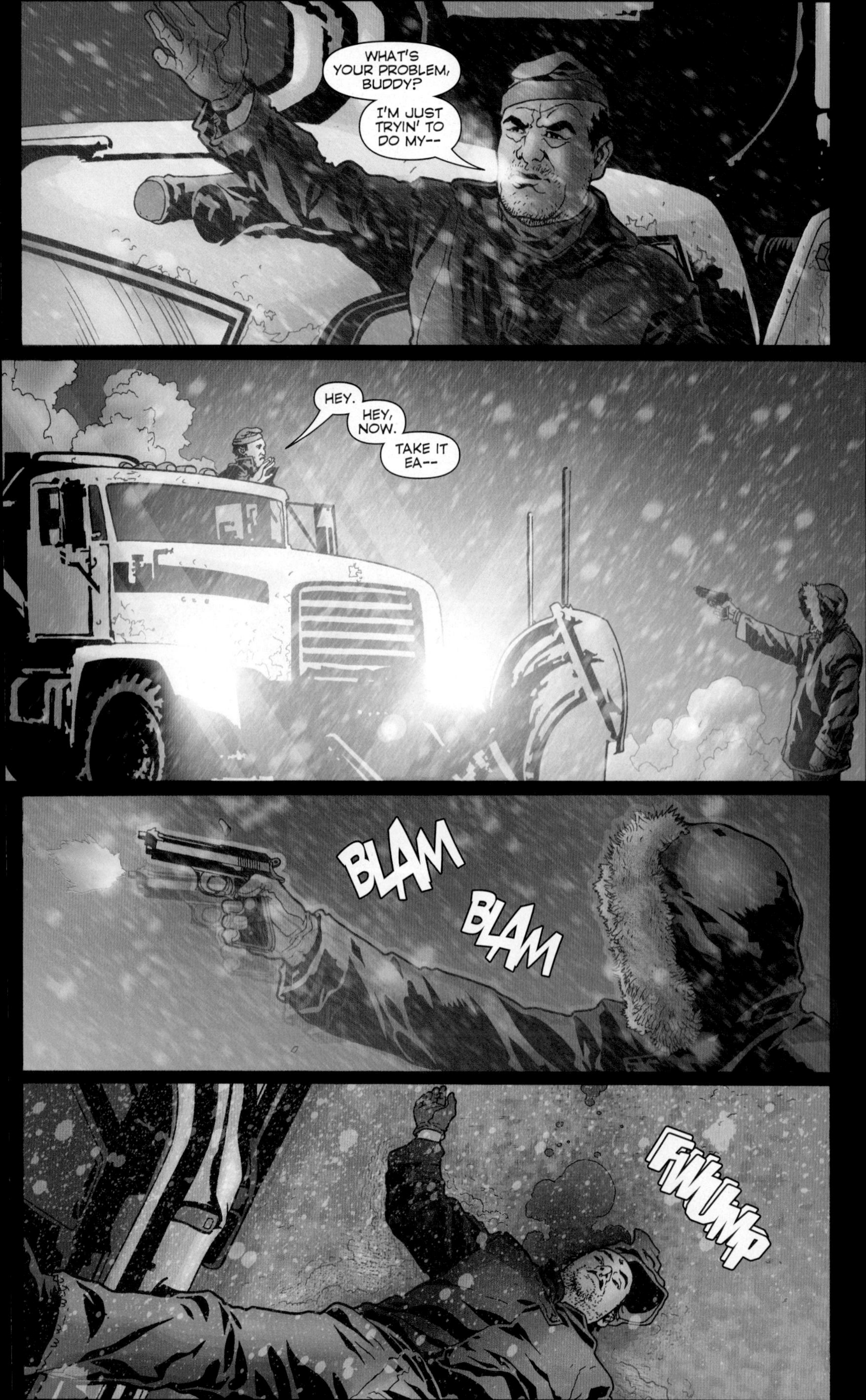
WHAT'S YOUR PROBLEM, BUDDY?
I'M JUST TRYIN' TO DO MY--
HEY.
HEY, NOW.
TAKE IT EA--
BLAM
BLAM
FWUMP

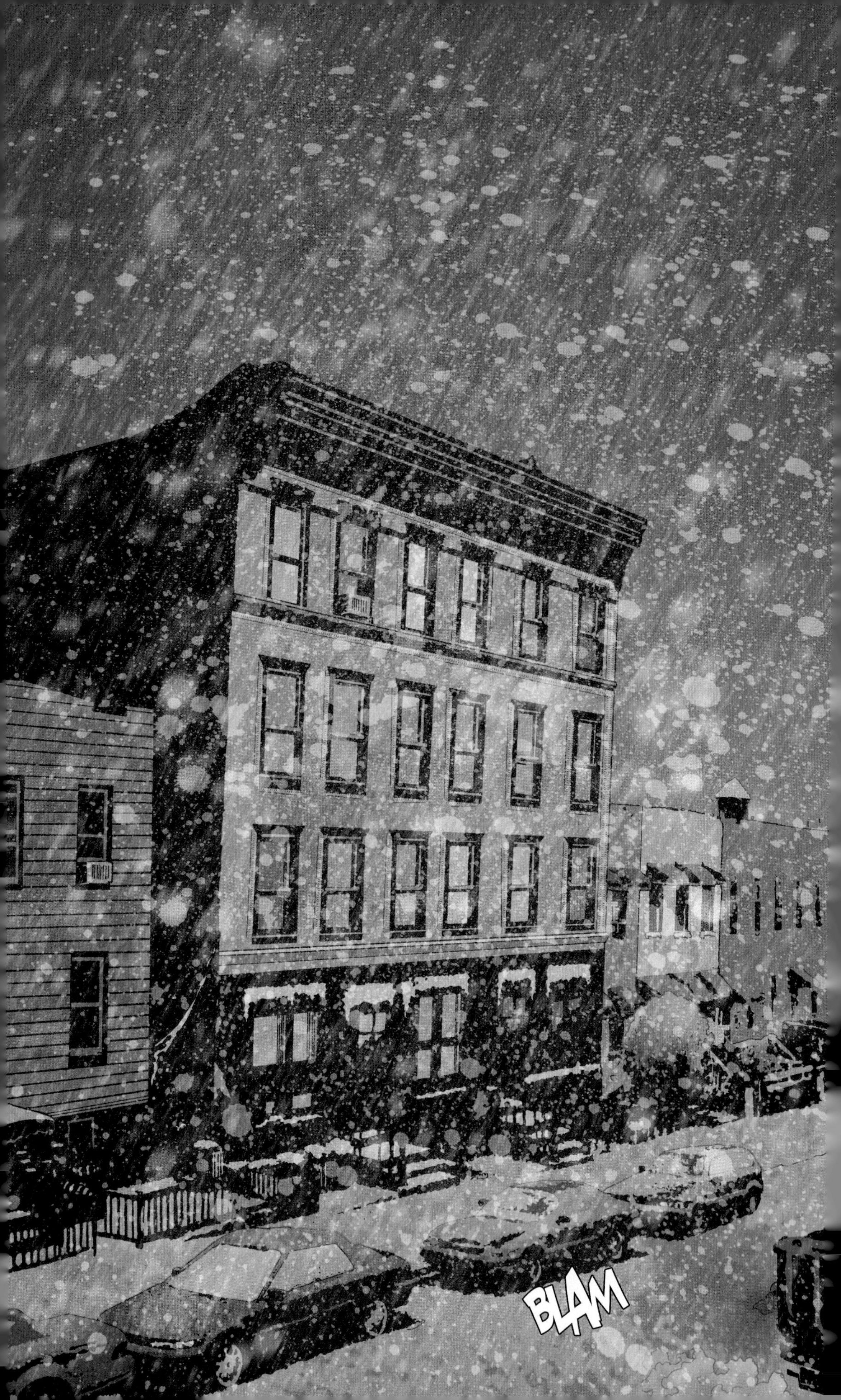
BLAM

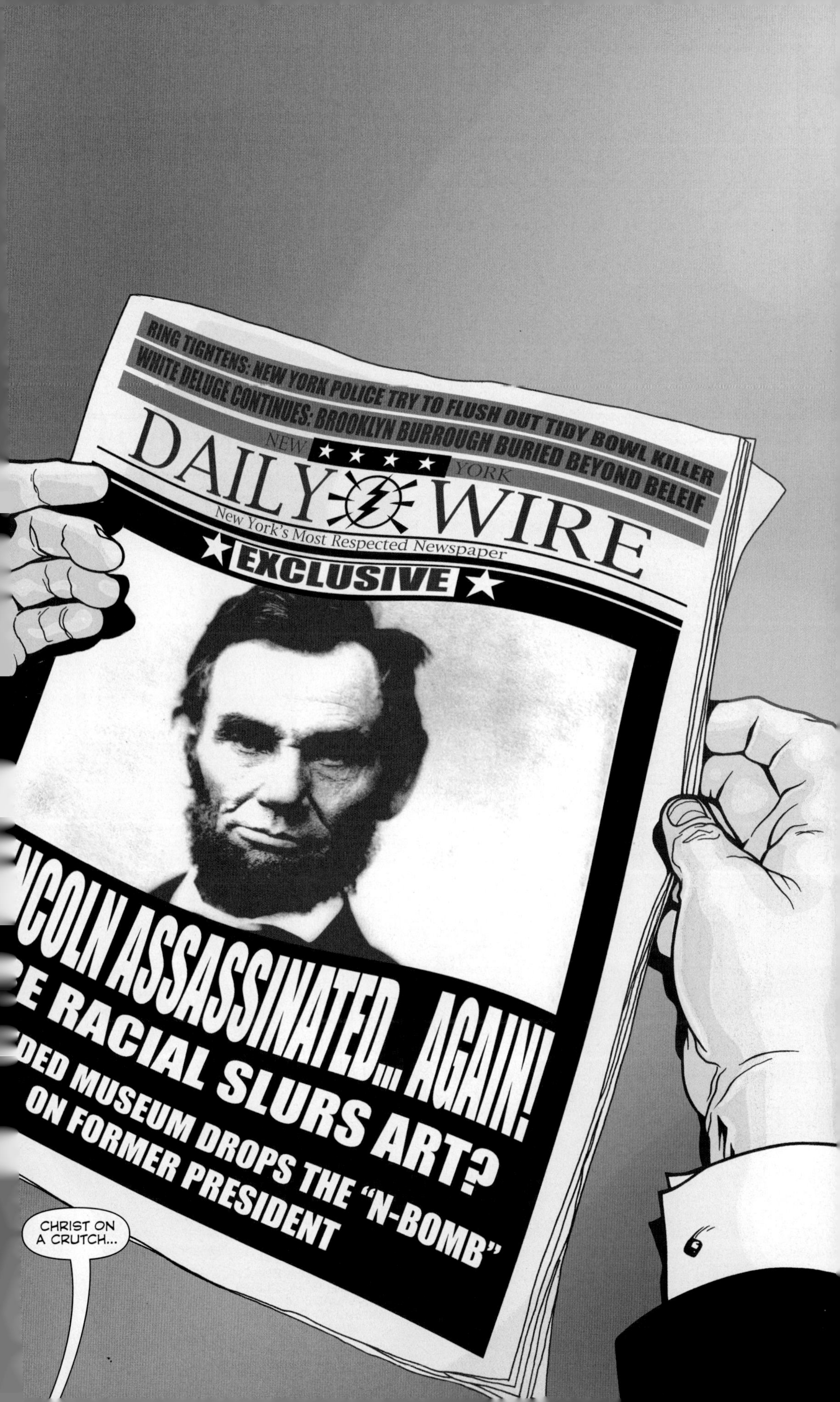
RING TIGHTENS: NEW YORK POLICE TRY TO FLUSH OUT TIDY BOWL KILLER
WHITE DELUGE CONTINUES: BROOKLYN BURROUGH BURIED BEYOND BELEIF
NEW YORK
DAILY WIRE
New York's Most Respected Newspaper
EXCLUSIVE
NCOLN ASSASSINATED... AGAIN!
E RACIAL SLURS ART?
DED MUSEUM DROPS THE "N-BOMB"
ON FORMER PRESIDENT
CHRIST ON A CRUTCH...

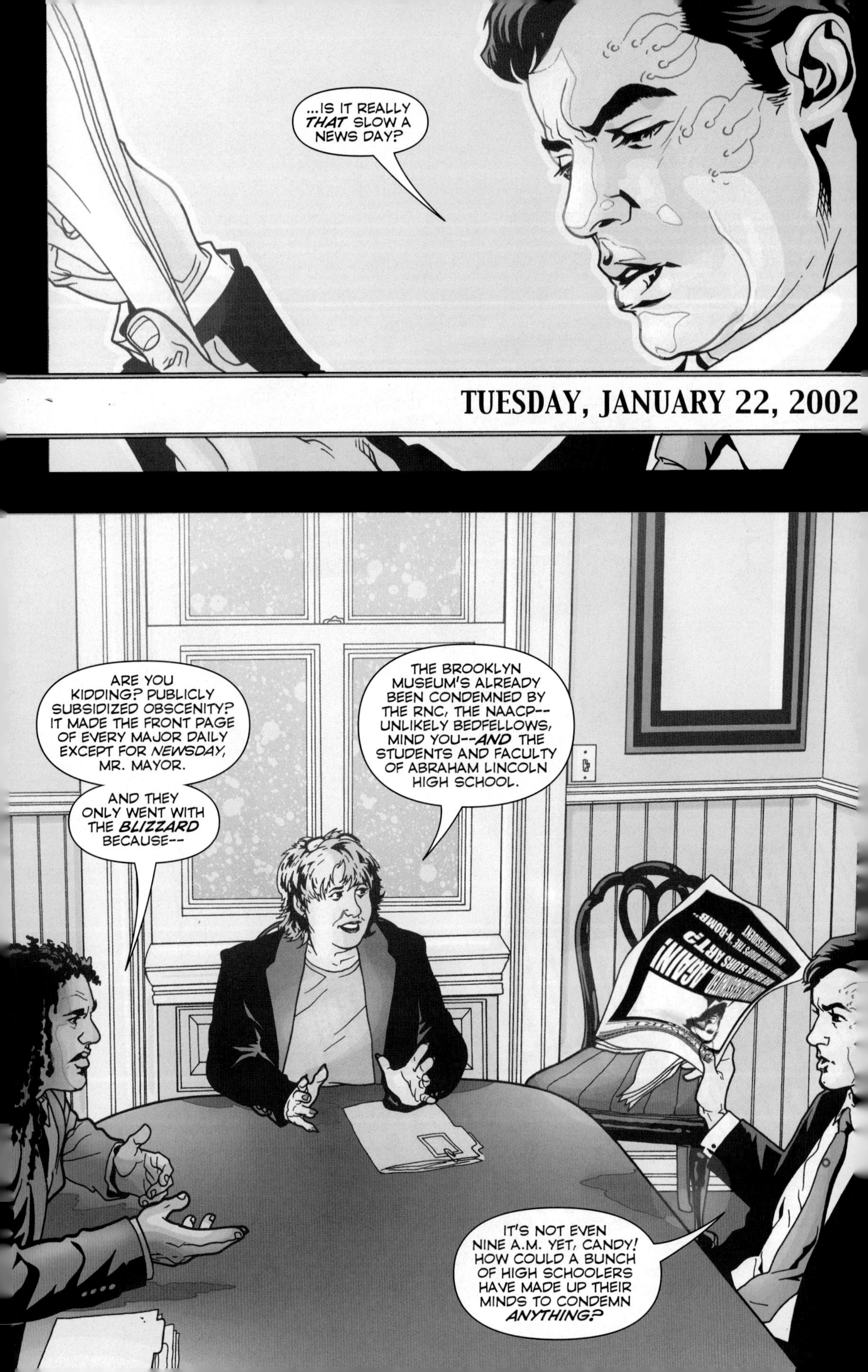
...IS IT REALLY THAT SLOW A NEWS DAY?
TUESDAY, JANUARY 22, 2002
ARE YOU KIDDING? PUBLICLY SUBSIDIZED OBSCENITY? IT MADE THE FRONT PAGE OF EVERY MAJOR DAILY EXCEPT FOR NEWSDAY, MR. MAYOR.
AND THEY ONLY WENT WITH THE BLIZZARD BECAUSE--
THE BROOKLYN MUSEUM'S ALREADY BEEN CONDEMNED BY THE RNC, THE NAACP-- UNLIKELY BEDFELLOWS, MIND YOU--AND THE STUDENTS AND FACULTY OF ABRAHAM LINCOLN HIGH SCHOOL.
IT'S NOT EVEN NINE A.M. YET, CANDY! HOW COULD A BUNCH OF HIGH SCHOOLERS HAVE MADE UP THEIR MINDS TO CONDEMN ANYTHING?

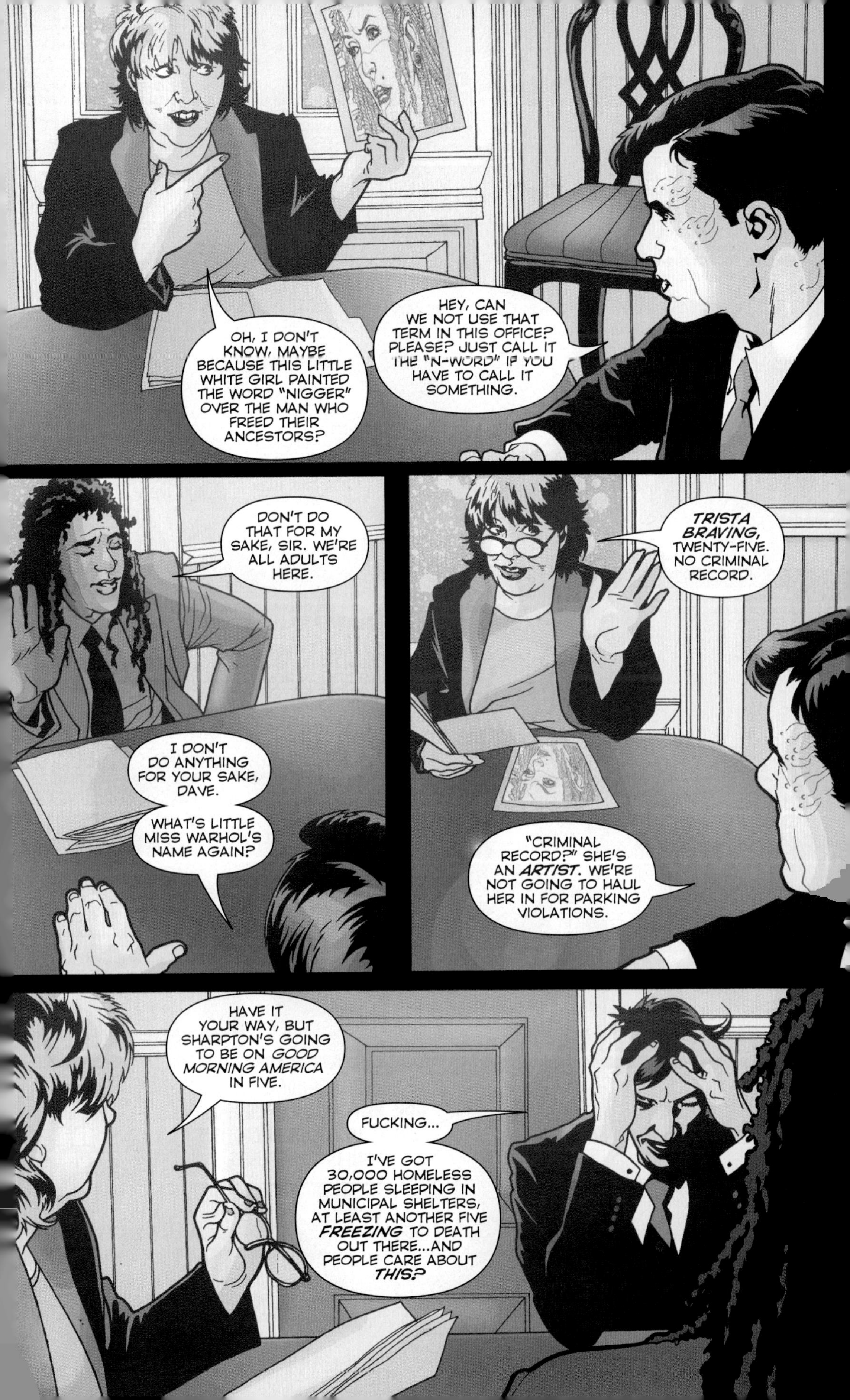
OH, I DON'T KNOW, MAYBE BECAUSE THIS LITTLE WHITE GIRL PAINTED THE WORD "NIGGER" OVER THE MAN WHO FREED THEIR ANCESTORS?
HEY, CAN WE NOT USE THAT TERM IN THIS OFFICE? PLEASE? JUST CALL IT THE "N-WORD" IF YOU HAVE TO CALL IT SOMETHING.
DON'T DO THAT FOR MY SAKE, SIR. WE'RE ALL ADULTS HERE.
I DON'T DO ANYTHING FOR YOUR SAKE, DAVE.
WHAT'S LITTLE MISS WARHOL'S NAME AGAIN?
TRISTA BRAVING, TWENTY-FIVE. NO CRIMINAL RECORD.
"CRIMINAL RECORD?" SHE'S AN *ARTIST.* WE'RE NOT GOING TO HAUL HER IN FOR PARKING VIOLATIONS.
HAVE IT YOUR WAY, BUT SHARPTON'S GOING TO BE ON *GOOD MORNING AMERICA* IN FIVE.
FUCKING...
I'VE GOT 30,000 HOMELESS PEOPLE SLEEPING IN MUNICIPAL SHELTERS, AT LEAST ANOTHER FIVE *FREEZING* TO DEATH OUT THERE...AND PEOPLE CARE ABOUT *THIS?*

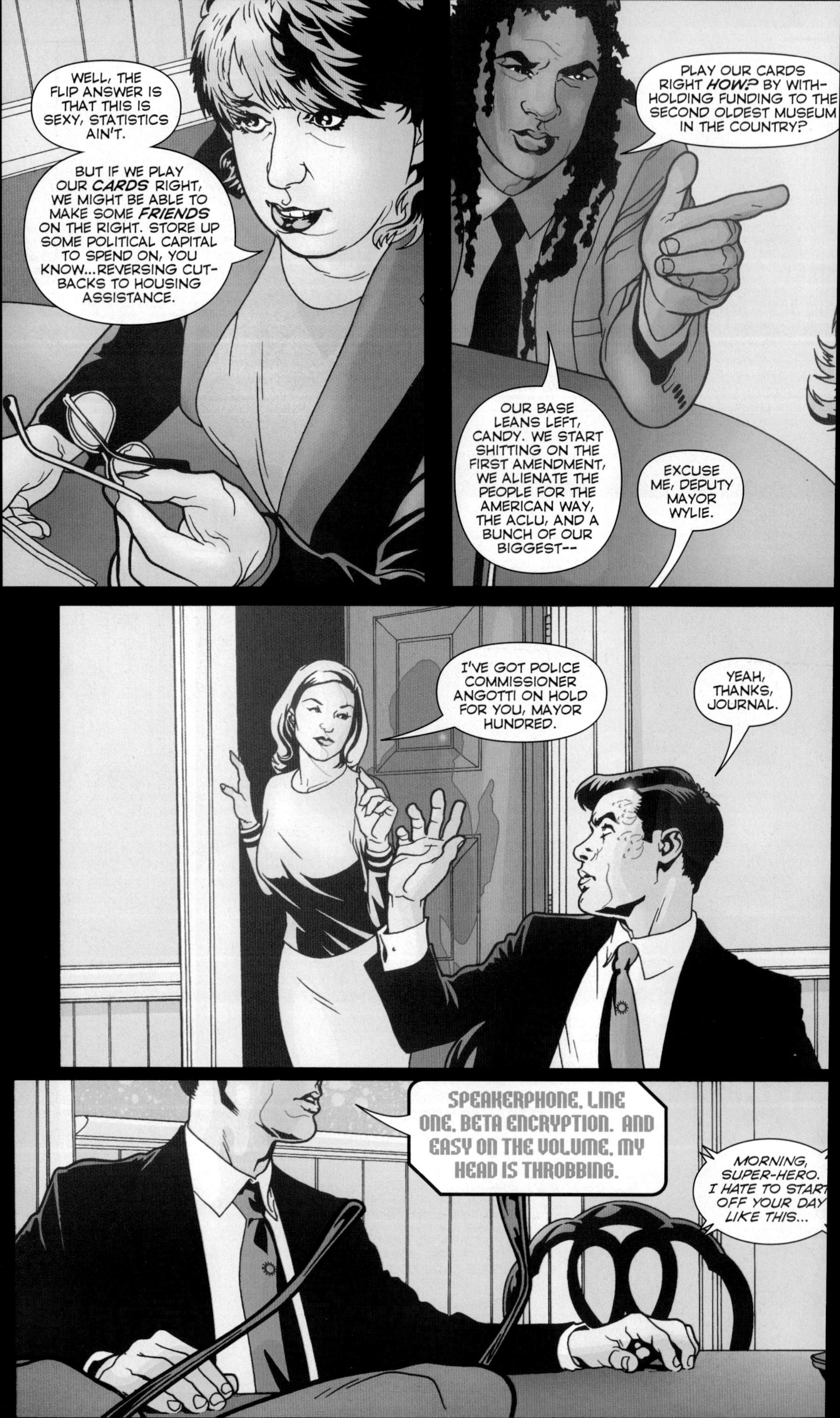
WELL, THE FLIP ANSWER IS THAT THIS IS SEXY, STATISTICS AIN'T.
BUT IF WE PLAY OUR CARDS RIGHT, WE MIGHT BE ABLE TO MAKE SOME FRIENDS ON THE RIGHT. STORE UP SOME POLITICAL CAPITAL TO SPEND ON, YOU KNOW...REVERSING CUT-BACKS TO HOUSING ASSISTANCE.
PLAY OUR CARDS RIGHT HOW? BY WITH-HOLDING FUNDING TO THE SECOND OLDEST MUSEUM IN THE COUNTRY?
OUR BASE LEANS LEFT, CANDY. WE START SHITTING ON THE FIRST AMENDMENT, WE ALIENATE THE PEOPLE FOR THE AMERICAN WAY, THE ACLU, AND A BUNCH OF OUR BIGGEST--
EXCUSE ME, DEPUTY MAYOR WYLIE.
I'VE GOT POLICE COMMISSIONER ANGOTTI ON HOLD FOR YOU, MAYOR HUNDRED.
YEAH, THANKS, JOURNAL.
SPEAKERPHONE, LINE ONE, BETA ENCRYPTION. AND EASY ON THE VOLUME, MY HEAD IS THROBBING.
MORNING, SUPER-HERO. I HATE TO START OFF YOUR DAY LIKE THIS...

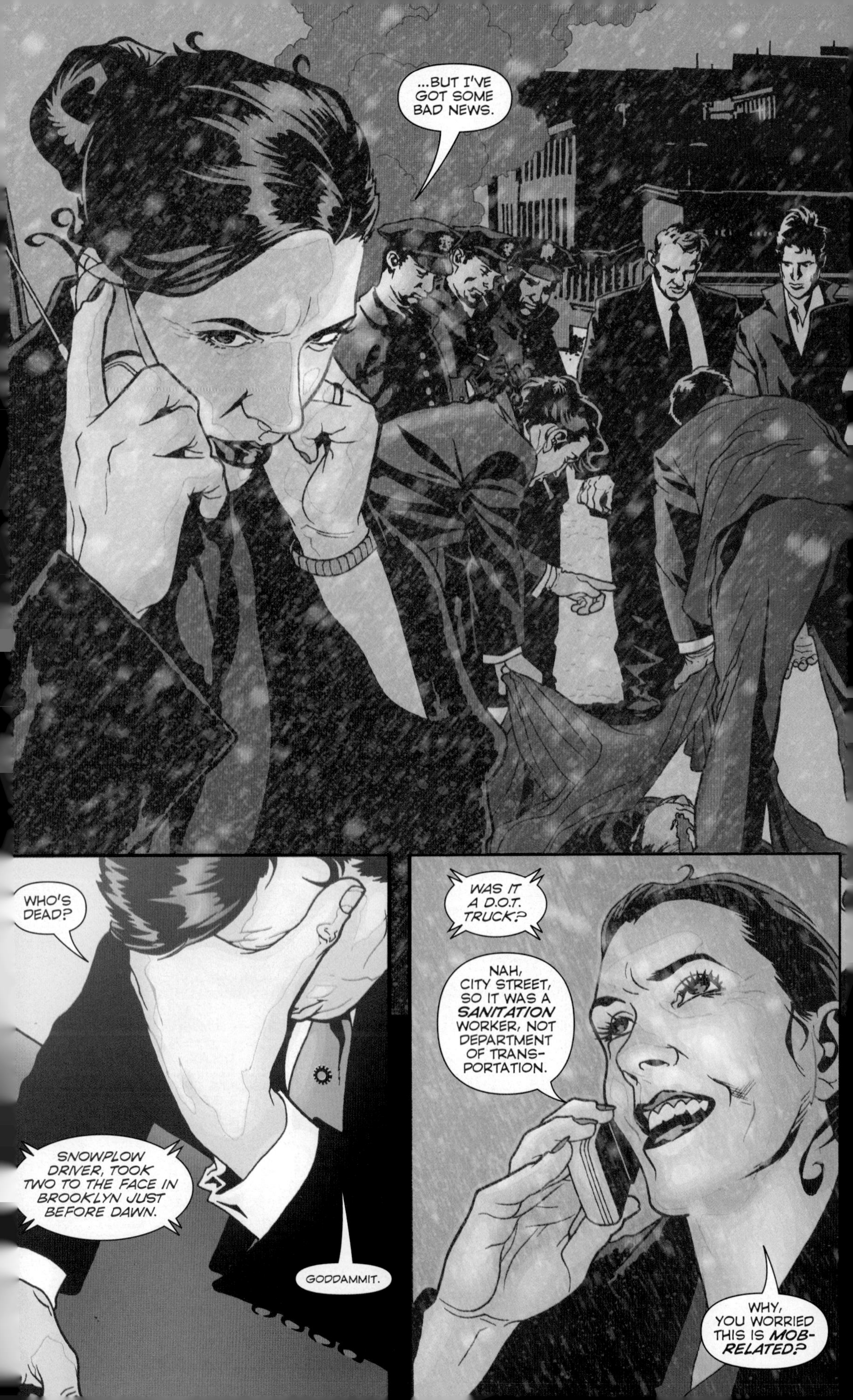
...BUT I'VE GOT SOME BAD NEWS.
WHO'S DEAD?
SNOWPLOW DRIVER, TOOK TWO TO THE FACE IN BROOKLYN JUST BEFORE DAWN.
GODDAMMIT.
WAS IT A D.O.T. TRUCK?
NAH, CITY STREET, SO IT WAS A SANITATION WORKER, NOT DEPARTMENT OF TRANS-PORTATION.
WHY, YOU WORRIED THIS IS MOB-RELATED?

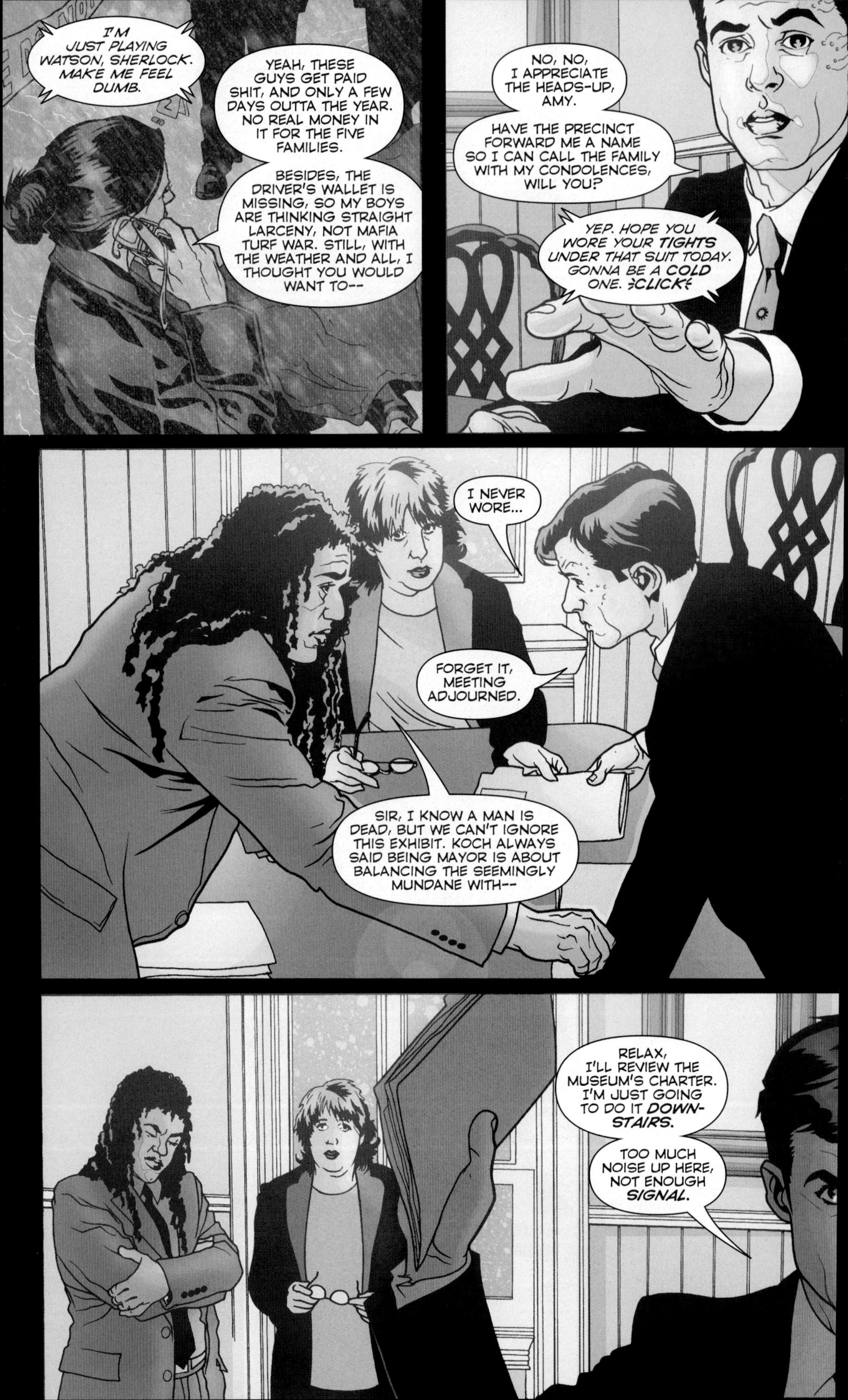
I'M JUST PLAYING WATSON, SHERLOCK. MAKE ME FEEL DUMB.
YEAH, THESE GUYS GET PAID SHIT, AND ONLY A FEW DAYS OUTTA THE YEAR. NO REAL MONEY IN IT FOR THE FIVE FAMILIES.
BESIDES, THE DRIVER'S WALLET IS MISSING, SO MY BOYS ARE THINKING STRAIGHT LARCENY, NOT MAFIA TURF WAR. STILL, WITH THE WEATHER AND ALL, I THOUGHT YOU WOULD WANT TO--
NO, NO, I APPRECIATE THE HEADS-UP, AMY.
HAVE THE PRECINCT FORWARD ME A NAME SO I CAN CALL THE FAMILY WITH MY CONDOLENCES, WILL YOU?
YEP. HOPE YOU WORE YOUR TIGHTS UNDER THAT SUIT TODAY. GONNA BE A COLD ONE. CLICK
I NEVER WORE...
FORGET IT, MEETING ADJOURNED.
SIR, I KNOW A MAN IS DEAD, BUT WE CAN'T IGNORE THIS EXHIBIT. KOCH ALWAYS SAID BEING MAYOR IS ABOUT BALANCING THE SEEMINGLY MUNDANE WITH--
RELAX, I'LL REVIEW THE MUSEUM'S CHARTER. I'M JUST GOING TO DO IT DOWN-STAIRS.
TOO MUCH NOISE UP HERE, NOT ENOUGH SIGNAL.

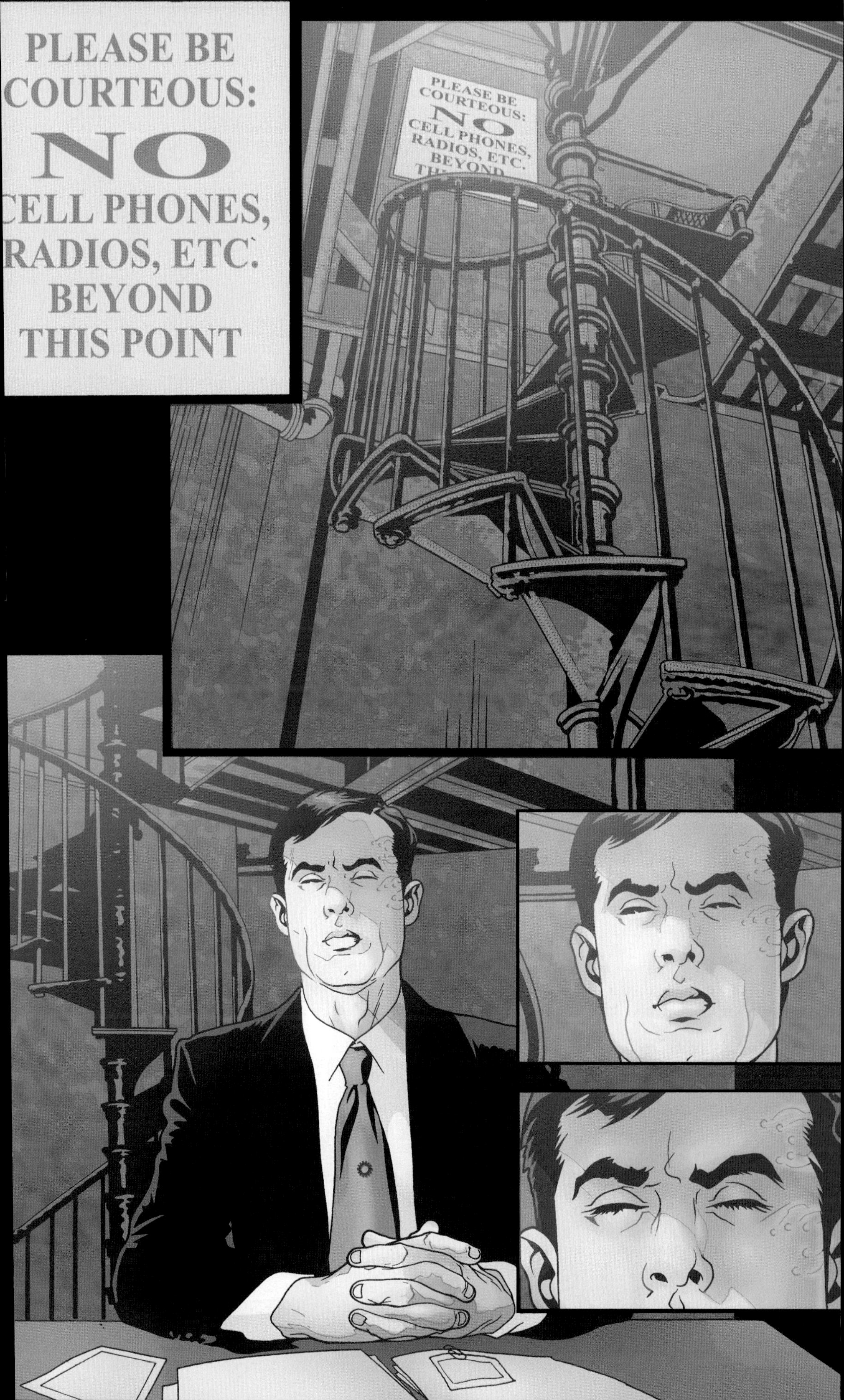
PLEASE BE
COURTEOUS:
NO
CELL PHONES,
RADIOS, ETC.
BEYOND
THIS POINT

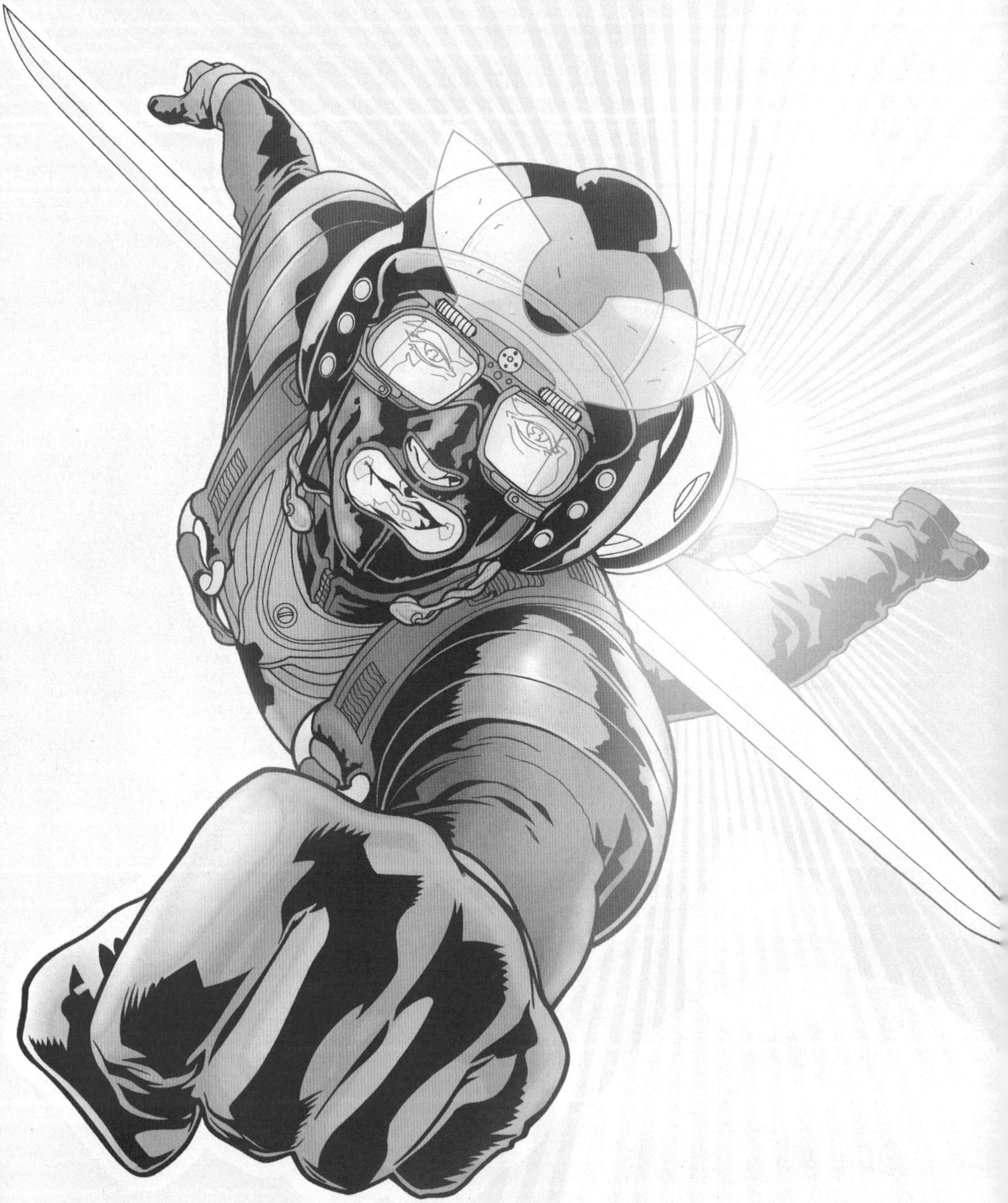

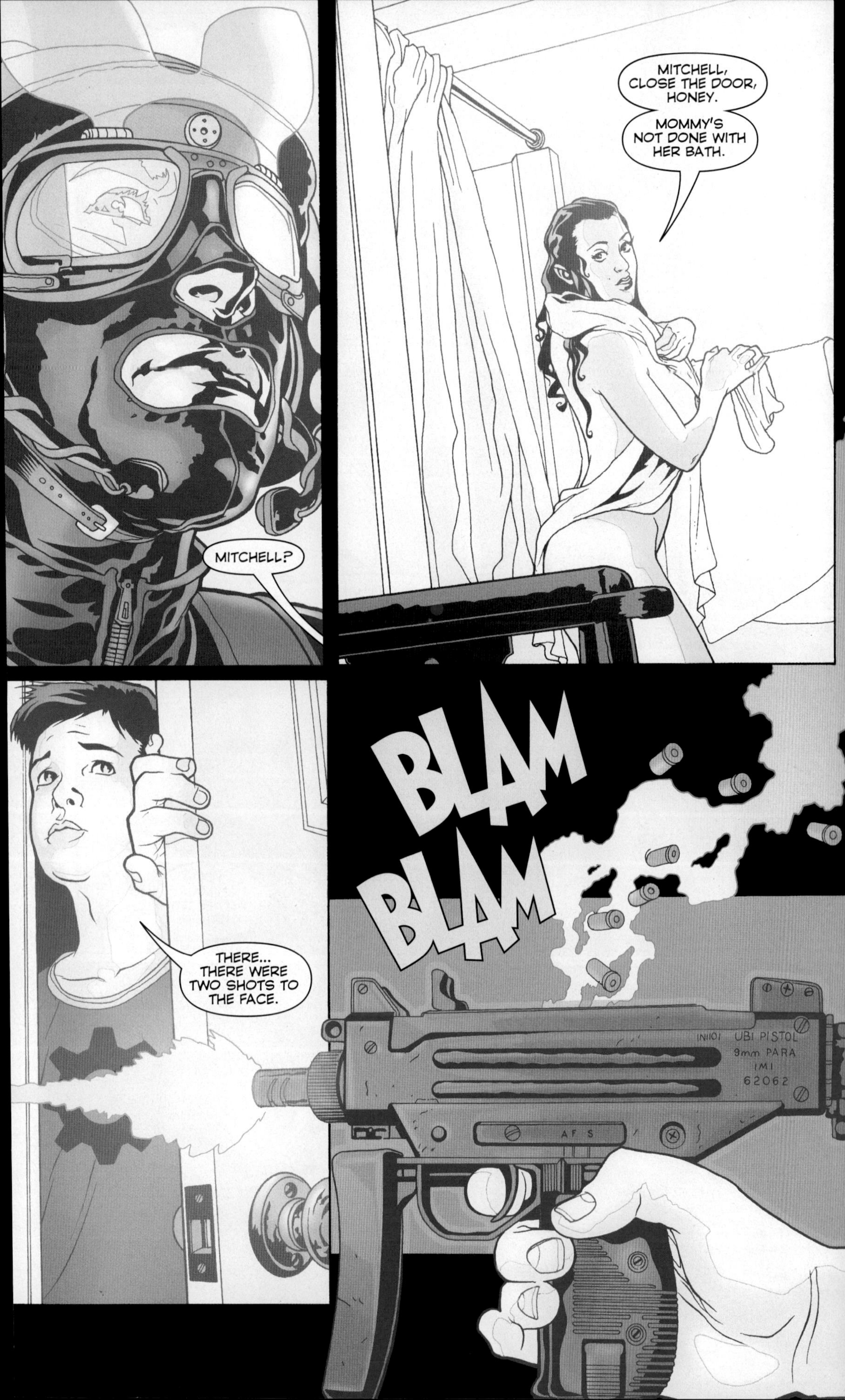
MITCHELL?
MITCHELL, CLOSE THE DOOR, HONEY.
MOMMY'S NOT DONE WITH HER BATH.
THERE... THERE WERE TWO SHOTS TO THE FACE.
BLAM
BLAM
UBI PISTOL
9mm PARA
IMI
62062

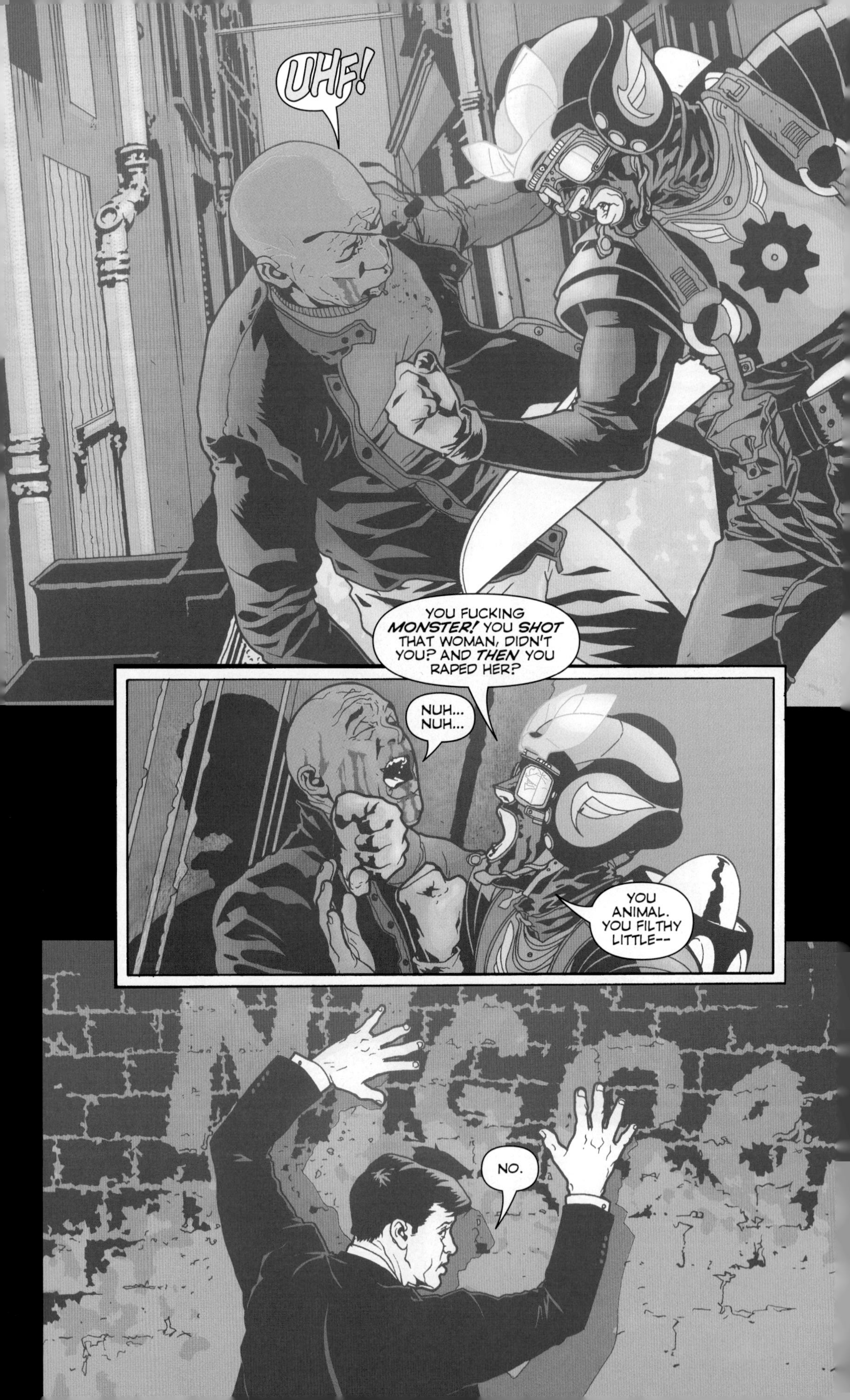
UHF!
YOU FUCKING MONSTER! YOU SHOT THAT WOMAN, DIDN'T YOU? AND THEN YOU RAPED HER?
NUH... NUH...
YOU ANIMAL. YOU FILTHY LITTLE--
NO.

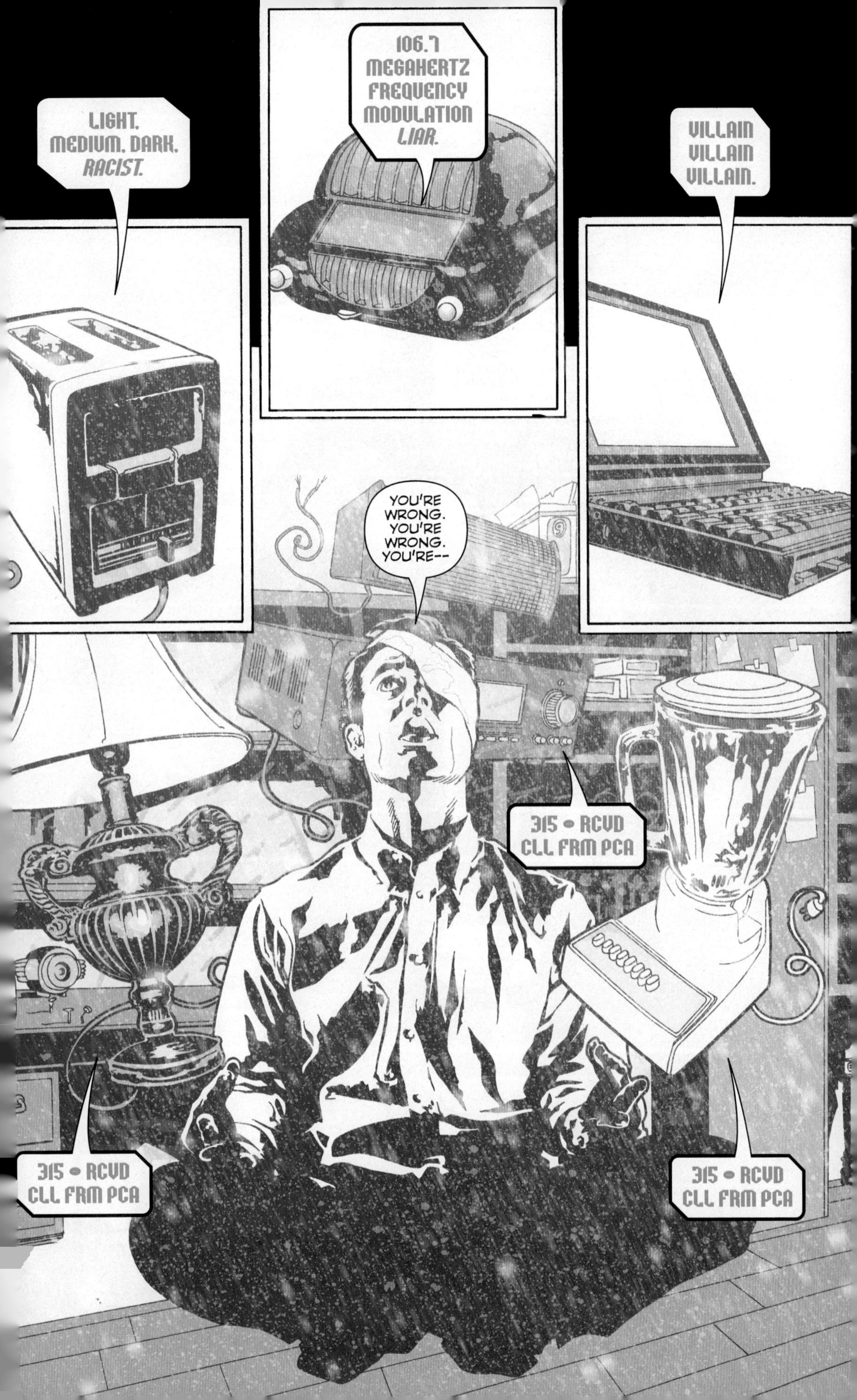
LIGHT. MEDIUM. DARK. RACIST.
106.7 MEGAHERTZ FREQUENCY MODULATION LIAR.
VILLAIN VILLAIN VILLAIN.
YOU'RE WRONG. YOU'RE WRONG. YOU'RE--
315 - RCVD CLL FRM PCA
315 - RCVD CLL FRM PCA
315 - RCVD CLL FRM PCA

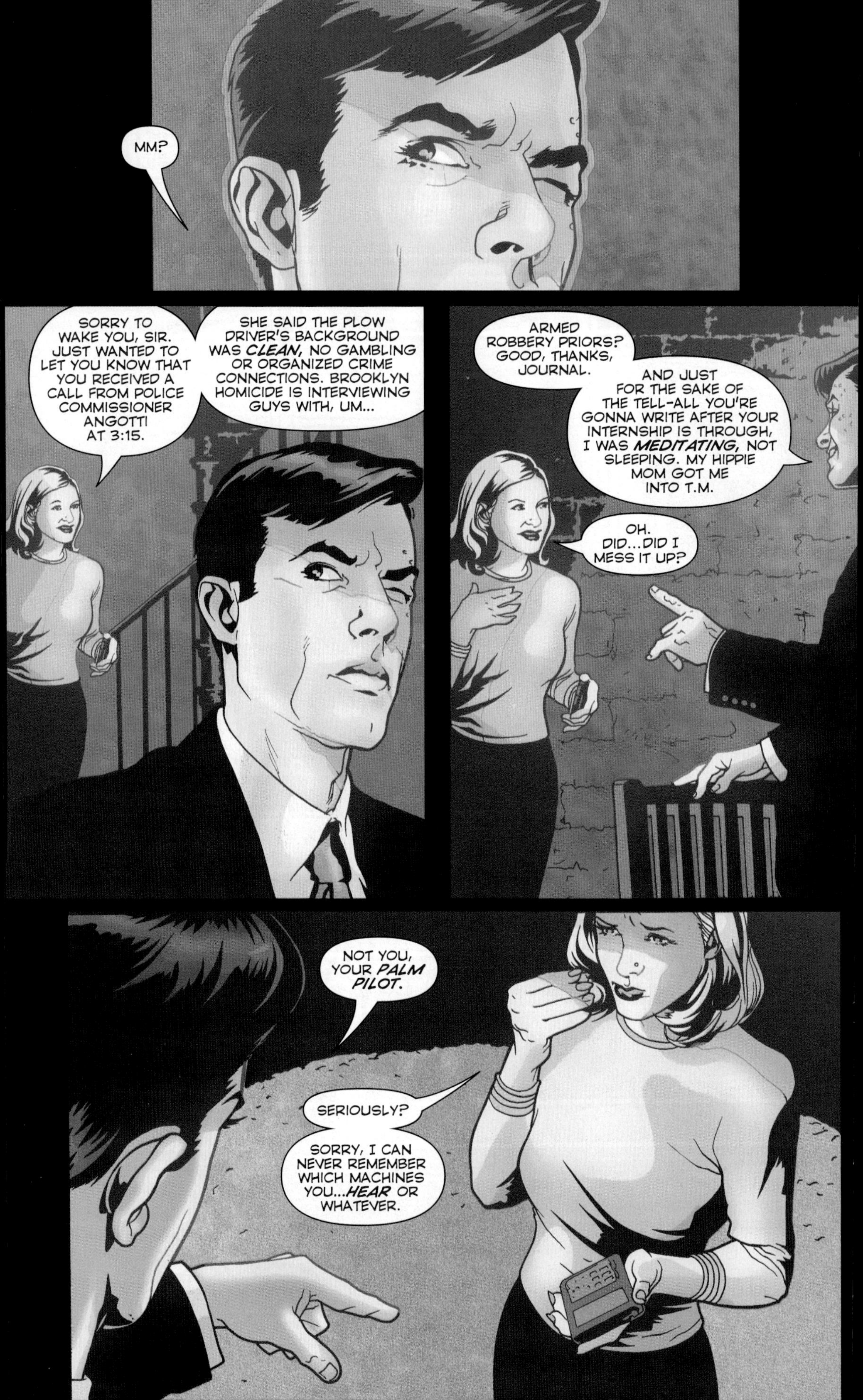
MM?
SORRY TO WAKE YOU, SIR. JUST WANTED TO LET YOU KNOW THAT YOU RECEIVED A CALL FROM POLICE COMMISSIONER ANGOTTI AT 3:15.
SHE SAID THE PLOW DRIVER'S BACKGROUND WAS *CLEAN,* NO GAMBLING OR ORGANIZED CRIME CONNECTIONS. BROOKLYN HOMICIDE IS INTERVIEWING GUYS WITH, UM...
ARMED ROBBERY PRIORS? GOOD, THANKS, JOURNAL.
AND JUST FOR THE SAKE OF THE TELL-ALL YOU'RE GONNA WRITE AFTER YOUR INTERNSHIP IS THROUGH, I WAS *MEDITATING,* NOT SLEEPING. MY HIPPIE MOM GOT ME INTO T.M.
OH. DID...DID I MESS IT UP?
NOT YOU, YOUR *PALM PILOT*.
SERIOUSLY?
SORRY, I CAN NEVER REMEMBER WHICH MACHINES YOU...*HEAR* OR WHATEVER.

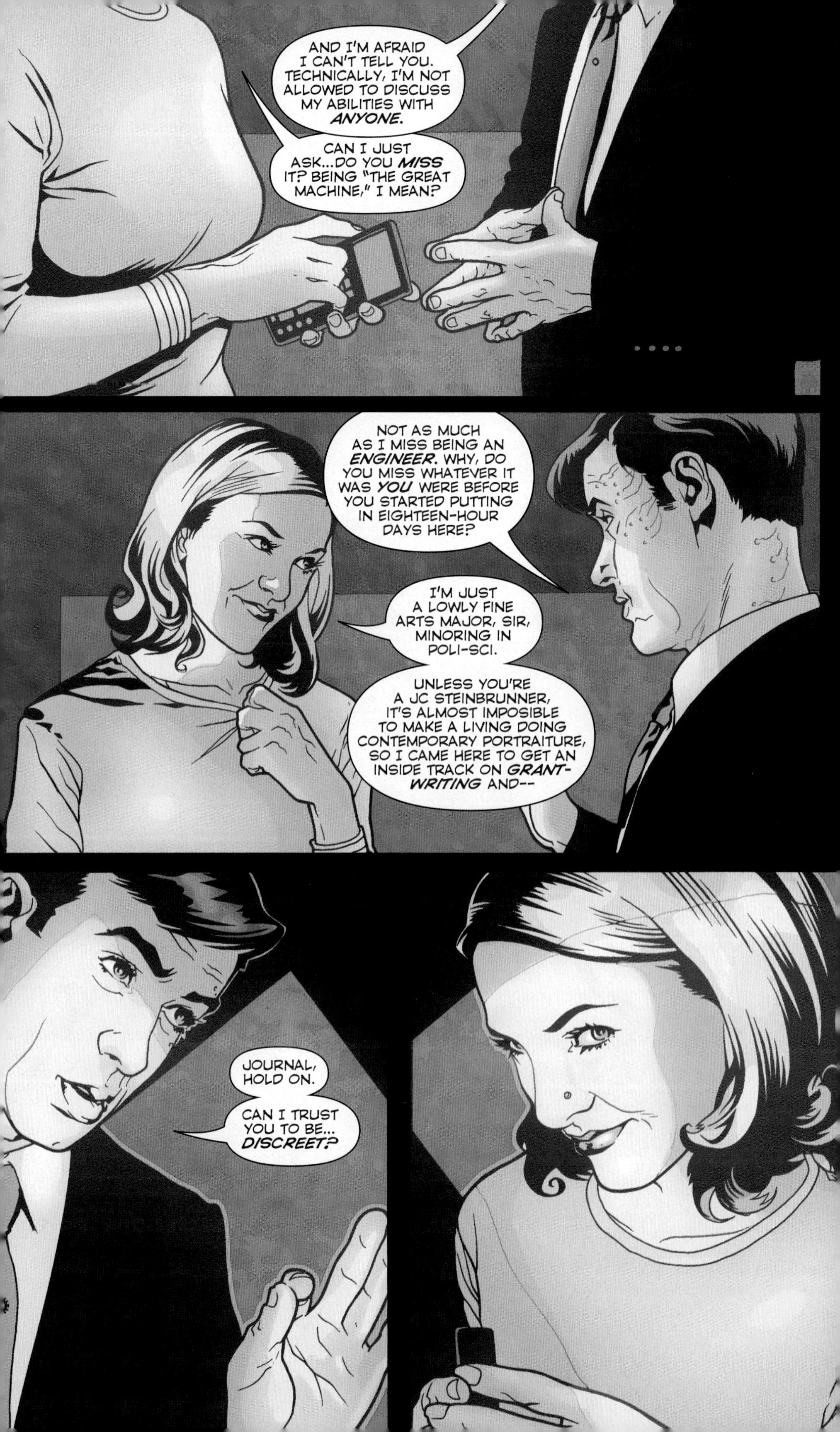
AND I'M AFRAID I CAN'T TELL YOU. TECHNICALLY, I'M NOT ALLOWED TO DISCUSS MY ABILITIES WITH ANYONE.
CAN I JUST ASK...DO YOU MISS IT? BEING "THE GREAT MACHINE," I MEAN?
NOT AS MUCH AS I MISS BEING AN ENGINEER. WHY, DO YOU MISS WHATEVER IT WAS YOU WERE BEFORE YOU STARTED PUTTING IN EIGHTEEN-HOUR DAYS HERE?
I'M JUST A LOWLY FINE ARTS MAJOR, SIR, MINORING IN POLI-SCI.
UNLESS YOU'RE A JC STEINBRUNNER, IT'S ALMOST IMPOSIBLE TO MAKE A LIVING DOING CONTEMPORARY PORTRAITURE, SO I CAME HERE TO GET AN INSIDE TRACK ON GRANT-WRITING AND--
JOURNAL, HOLD ON.
CAN I TRUST YOU TO BE... DISCREET?

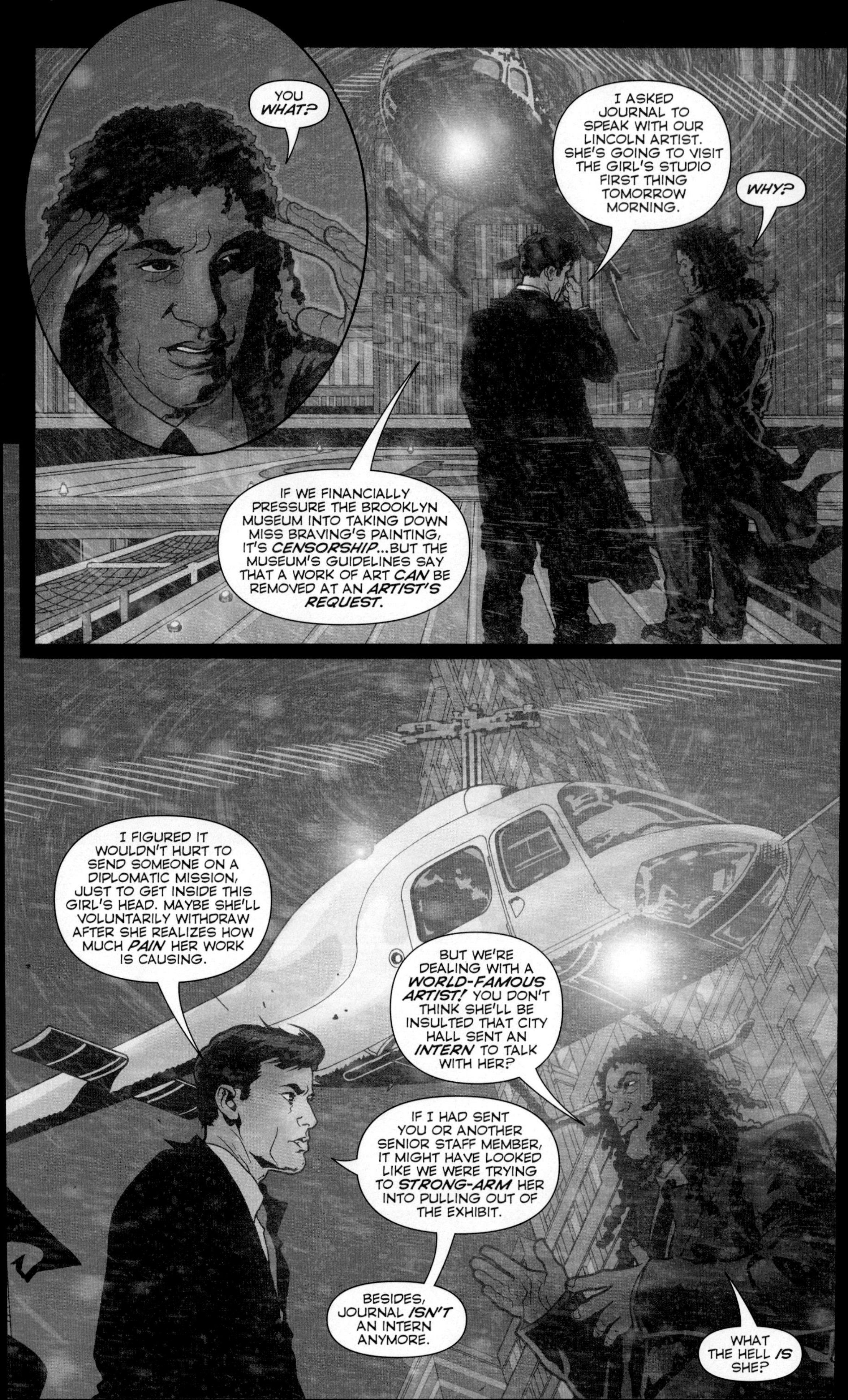
YOU WHAT?
I ASKED JOURNAL TO SPEAK WITH OUR LINCOLN ARTIST. SHE'S GOING TO VISIT THE GIRL'S STUDIO FIRST THING TOMORROW MORNING.
WHY?
IF WE FINANCIALLY PRESSURE THE BROOKLYN MUSEUM INTO TAKING DOWN MISS BRAVING'S PAINTING, IT'S CENSORSHIP...BUT THE MUSEUM'S GUIDELINES SAY THAT A WORK OF ART CAN BE REMOVED AT AN ARTIST'S REQUEST.
I FIGURED IT WOULDN'T HURT TO SEND SOMEONE ON A DIPLOMATIC MISSION, JUST TO GET INSIDE THIS GIRL'S HEAD. MAYBE SHE'LL VOLUNTARILY WITHDRAW AFTER SHE REALIZES HOW MUCH PAIN HER WORK IS CAUSING.
BUT WE'RE DEALING WITH A WORLD-FAMOUS ARTIST! YOU DON'T THINK SHE'LL BE INSULTED THAT CITY HALL SENT AN INTERN TO TALK WITH HER?
IF I HAD SENT YOU OR ANOTHER SENIOR STAFF MEMBER, IT MIGHT HAVE LOOKED LIKE WE WERE TRYING TO STRONG-ARM HER INTO PULLING OUT OF THE EXHIBIT.
BESIDES, JOURNAL ISN'T AN INTERN ANYMORE.
WHAT THE HELL IS SHE?

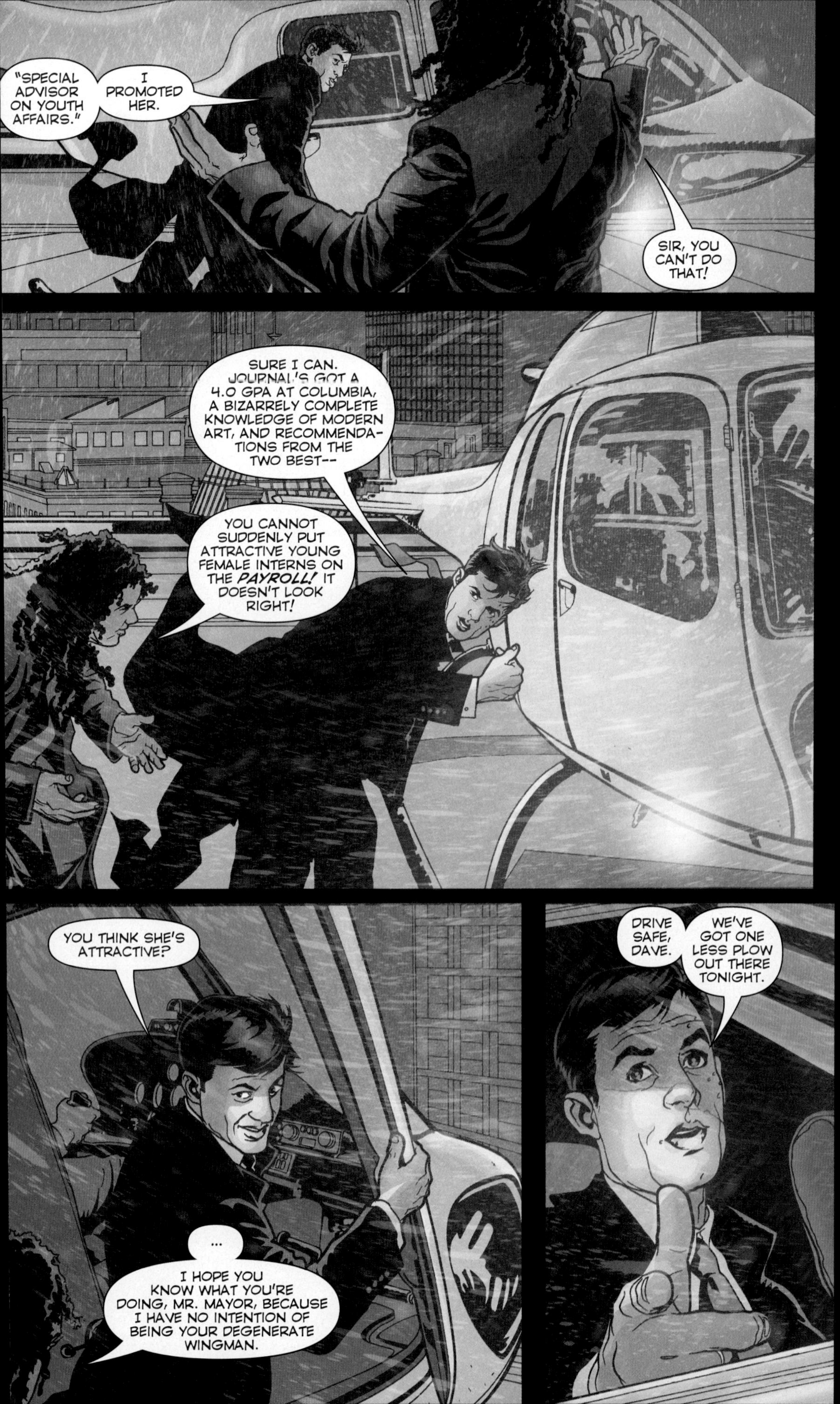
"SPECIAL ADVISOR ON YOUTH AFFAIRS."
I PROMOTED HER.
SIR, YOU CAN'T DO THAT!
SURE I CAN. JOURNAL'S GOT A 4.0 GPA AT COLUMBIA, A BIZARRELY COMPLETE KNOWLEDGE OF MODERN ART, AND RECOMMENDATIONS FROM THE TWO BEST--
YOU CANNOT SUDDENLY PUT ATTRACTIVE YOUNG FEMALE INTERNS ON THE *PAYROLL!* IT DOESN'T LOOK RIGHT!
YOU THINK SHE'S ATTRACTIVE?
...
I HOPE YOU KNOW WHAT YOU'RE DOING, MR. MAYOR, BECAUSE I HAVE NO INTENTION OF BEING YOUR DEGENERATE WINGMAN.
DRIVE SAFE, DAVE.
WE'VE GOT ONE LESS PLOW OUT THERE TONIGHT.

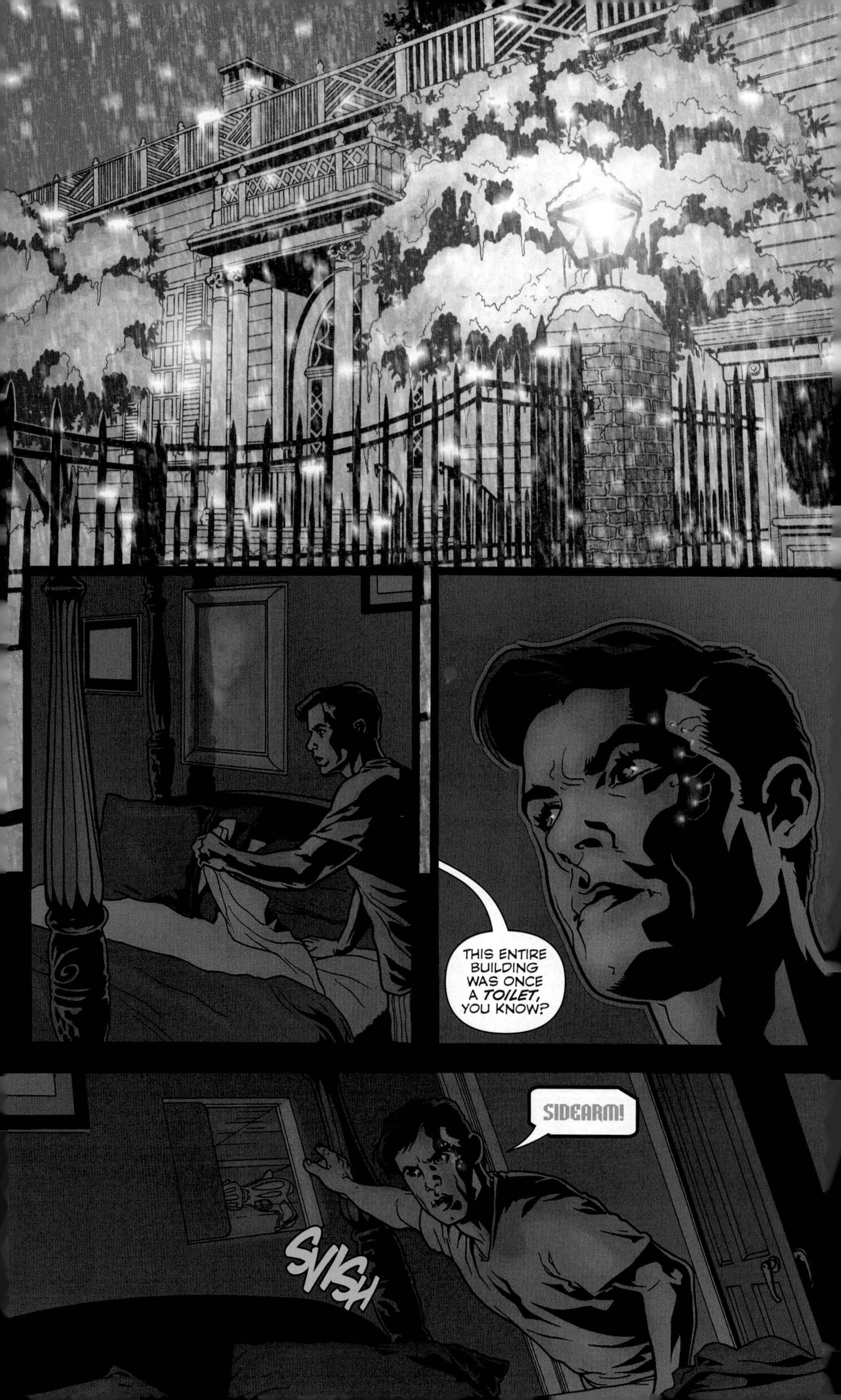
THIS ENTIRE BUILDING WAS ONCE A *TOILET*, YOU KNOW?
SIDEARM!
SWISH

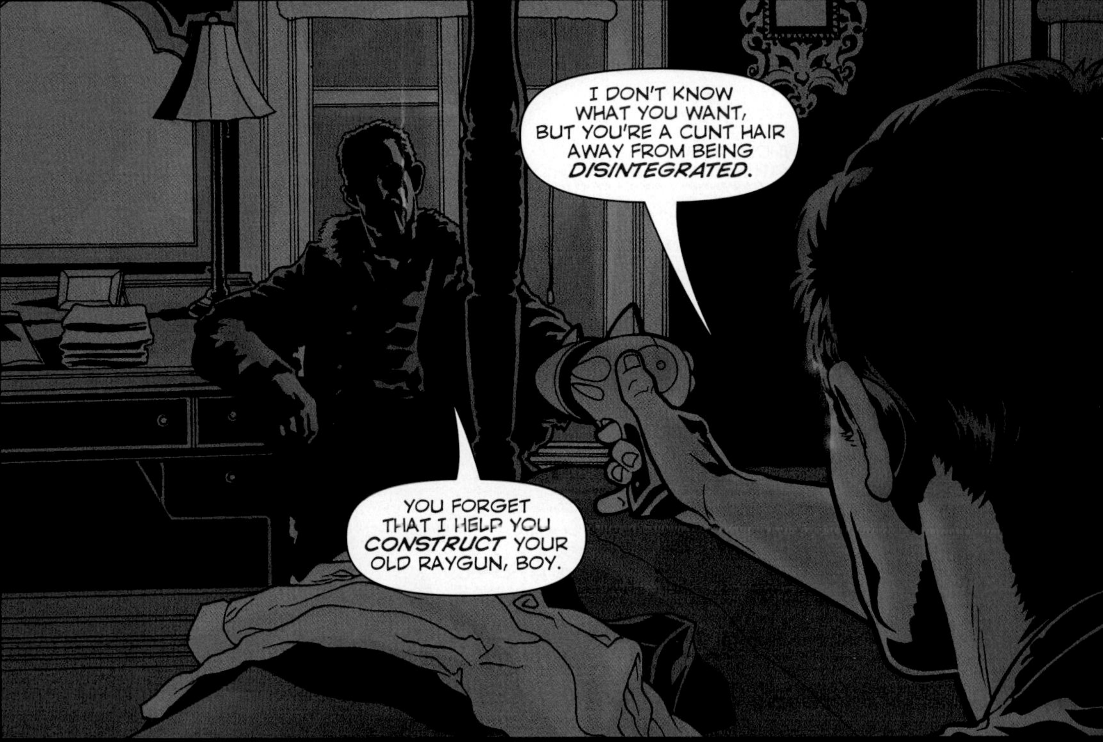
I DON'T KNOW WHAT YOU WANT, BUT YOU'RE A CUNT HAIR AWAY FROM BEING *DISINTEGRATED*.
YOU FORGET THAT I HELP YOU *CONSTRUCT* YOUR OLD RAYGUN, BOY.

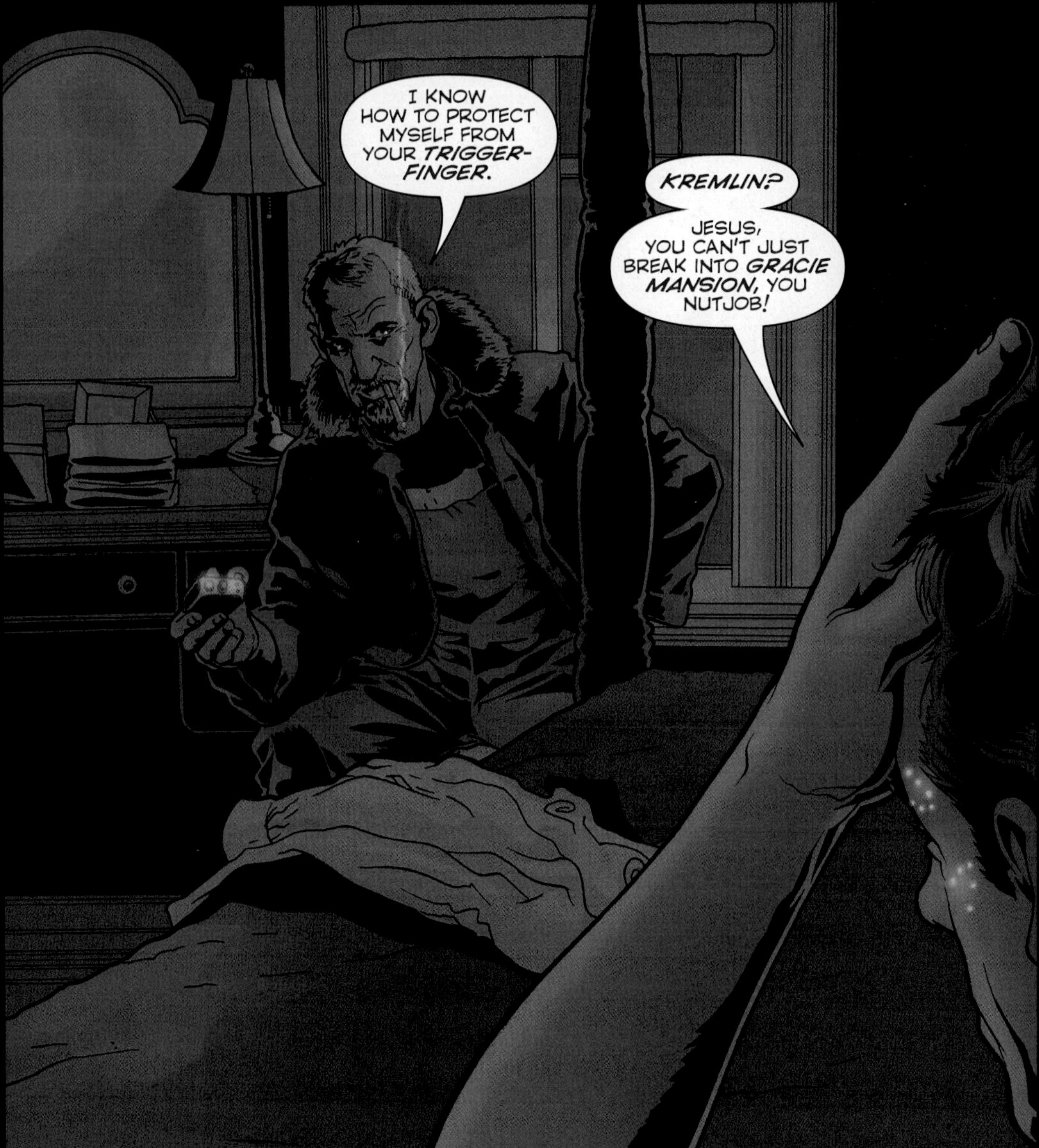
I KNOW HOW TO PROTECT MYSELF FROM YOUR *TRIGGER-FINGER*.
KREMLIN?
JESUS, YOU CAN'T JUST BREAK INTO *GRACIE MANSION,* YOU NUTJOB!

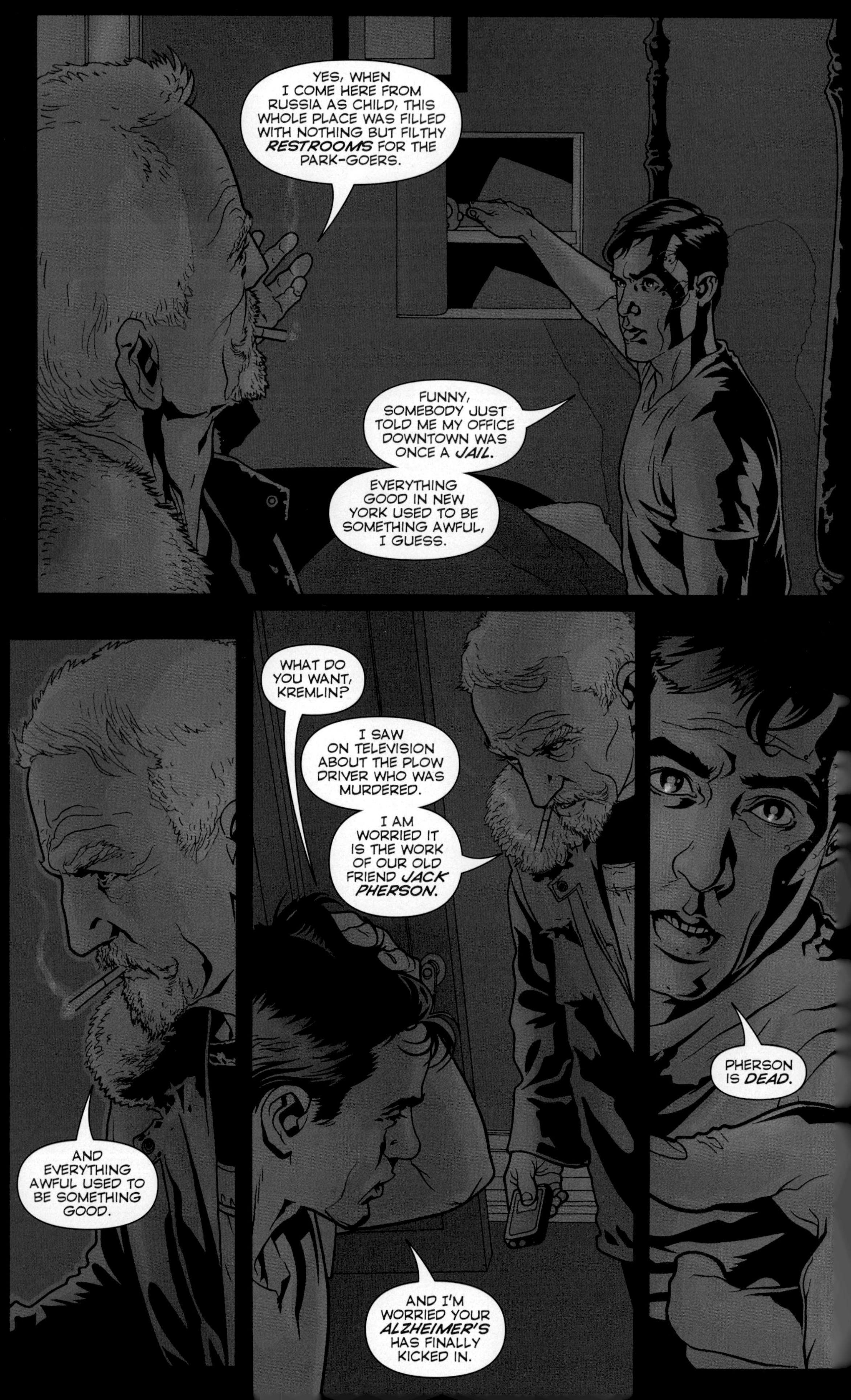
YES, WHEN I COME HERE FROM RUSSIA AS CHILD, THIS WHOLE PLACE WAS FILLED WITH NOTHING BUT FILTHY RESTROOMS FOR THE PARK-GOERS.
FUNNY, SOMEBODY JUST TOLD ME MY OFFICE DOWNTOWN WAS ONCE A JAIL.
EVERYTHING GOOD IN NEW YORK USED TO BE SOMETHING AWFUL, I GUESS.
AND EVERYTHING AWFUL USED TO BE SOMETHING GOOD.
WHAT DO YOU WANT, KREMLIN?
I SAW ON TELEVISION ABOUT THE PLOW DRIVER WHO WAS MURDERED.
I AM WORRIED IT IS THE WORK OF OUR OLD FRIEND JACK PHERSON.
AND I'M WORRIED YOUR ALZHEIMER'S HAS FINALLY KICKED IN.
PHERSON IS DEAD.

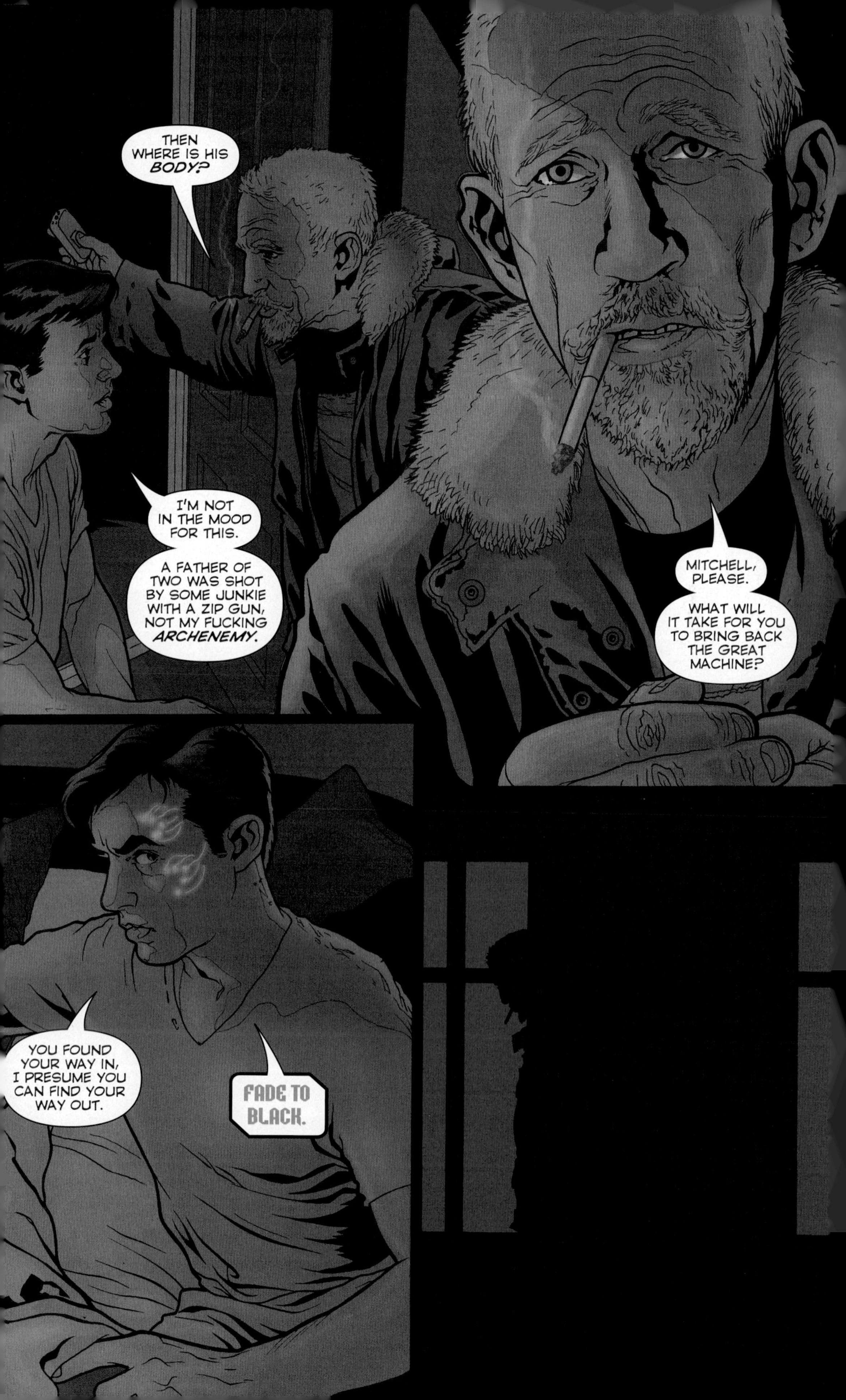
THEN WHERE IS HIS BODY?
I'M NOT IN THE MOOD FOR THIS.
A FATHER OF TWO WAS SHOT BY SOME JUNKIE WITH A ZIP GUN, NOT MY FUCKING ARCHENEMY.
MITCHELL, PLEASE.
WHAT WILL IT TAKE FOR YOU TO BRING BACK THE GREAT MACHINE?
YOU FOUND YOUR WAY IN, I PRESUME YOU CAN FIND YOUR WAY OUT.
FADE TO BLACK.

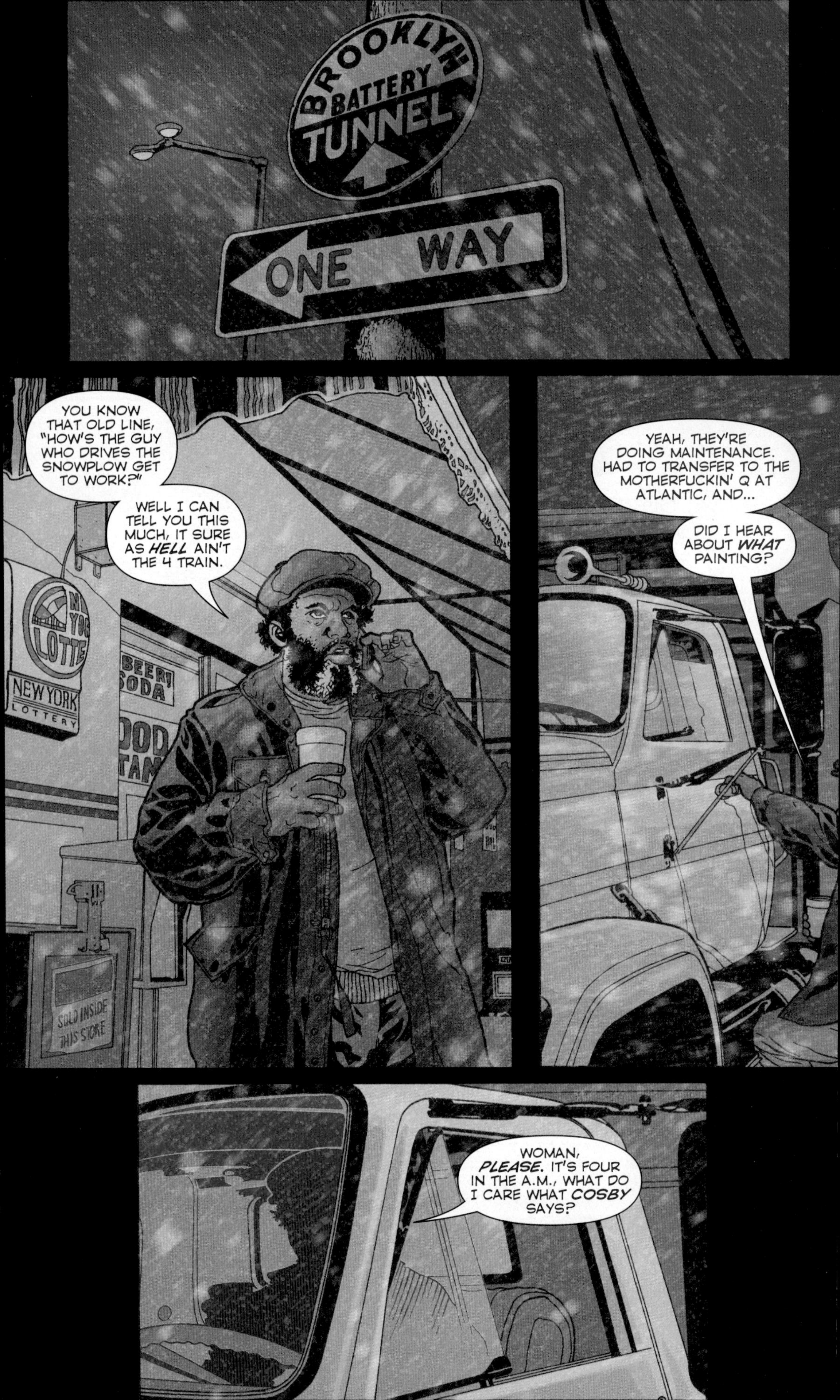

BROOKLYN BATTERY TUNNEL
ONE WAY
YOU KNOW THAT OLD LINE, "HOW'S THE GUY WHO DRIVES THE SNOWPLOW GET TO WORK?"
WELL I CAN TELL YOU THIS MUCH, IT SURE AS *HELL* AIN'T THE 4 TRAIN.
NEW YORK LOTTERY
BEER! SODA
SOLD INSIDE THIS STORE
YEAH, THEY'RE DOING MAINTENANCE. HAD TO TRANSFER TO THE MOTHERFUCKIN' Q AT ATLANTIC, AND...
DID I HEAR ABOUT *WHAT* PAINTING?
WOMAN, *PLEASE*. IT'S FOUR IN THE A.M., WHAT DO I CARE WHAT *COSBY* SAYS?

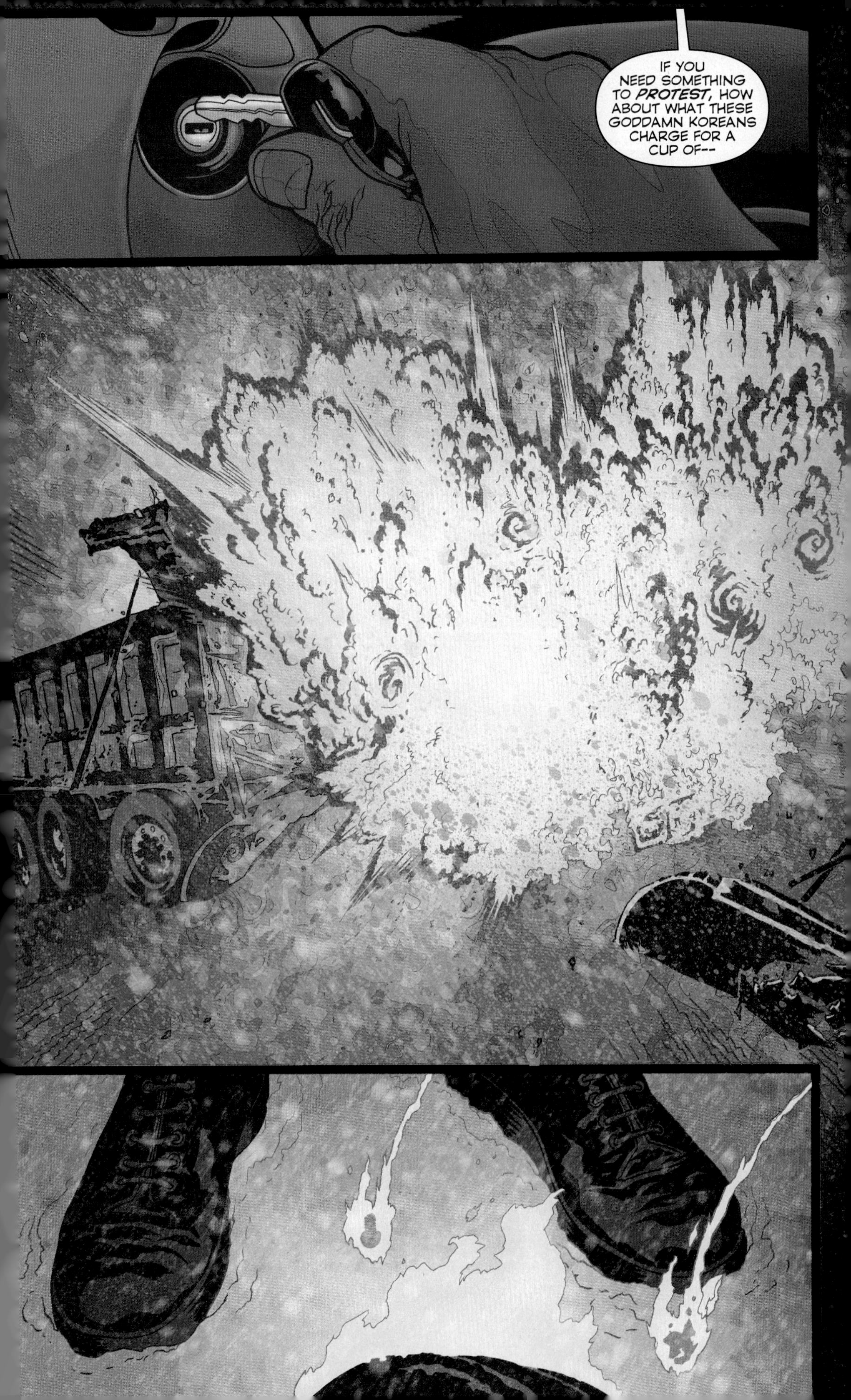
IF YOU NEED SOMETHING TO *PROTEST*, HOW ABOUT WHAT THESE GODDAMN KOREANS CHARGE FOR A CUP OF--

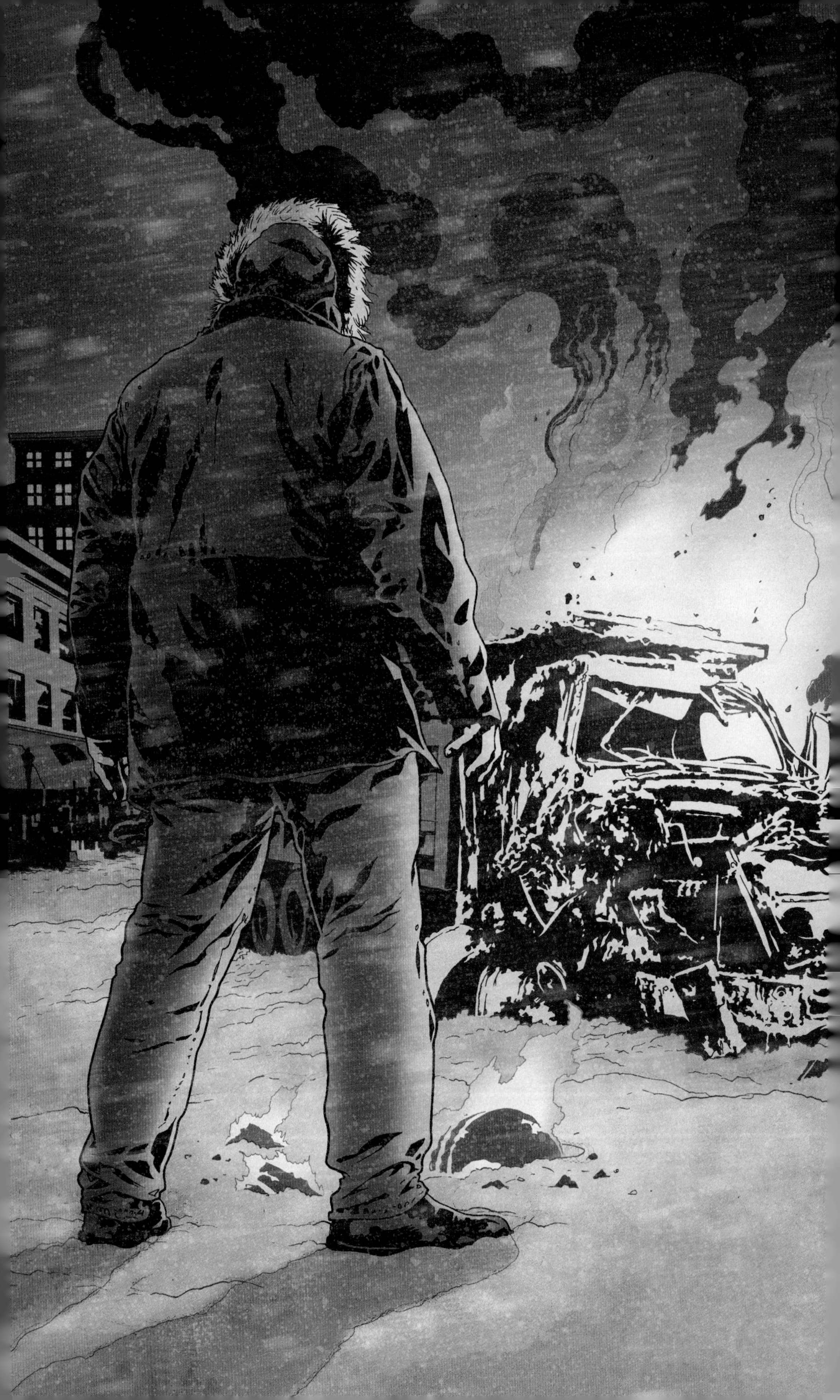

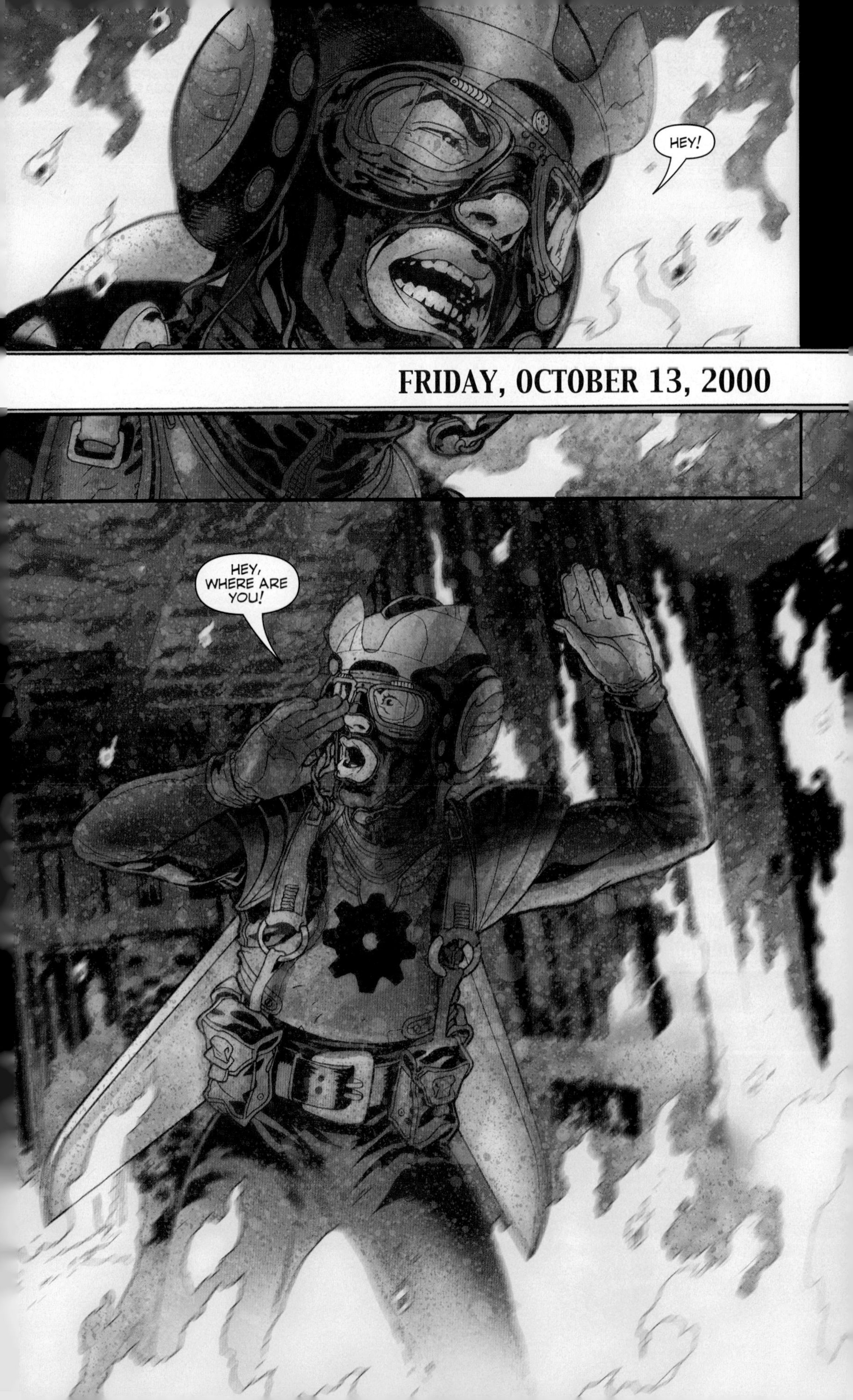
HEY!
FRIDAY, OCTOBER 13, 2000
HEY, WHERE ARE YOU!

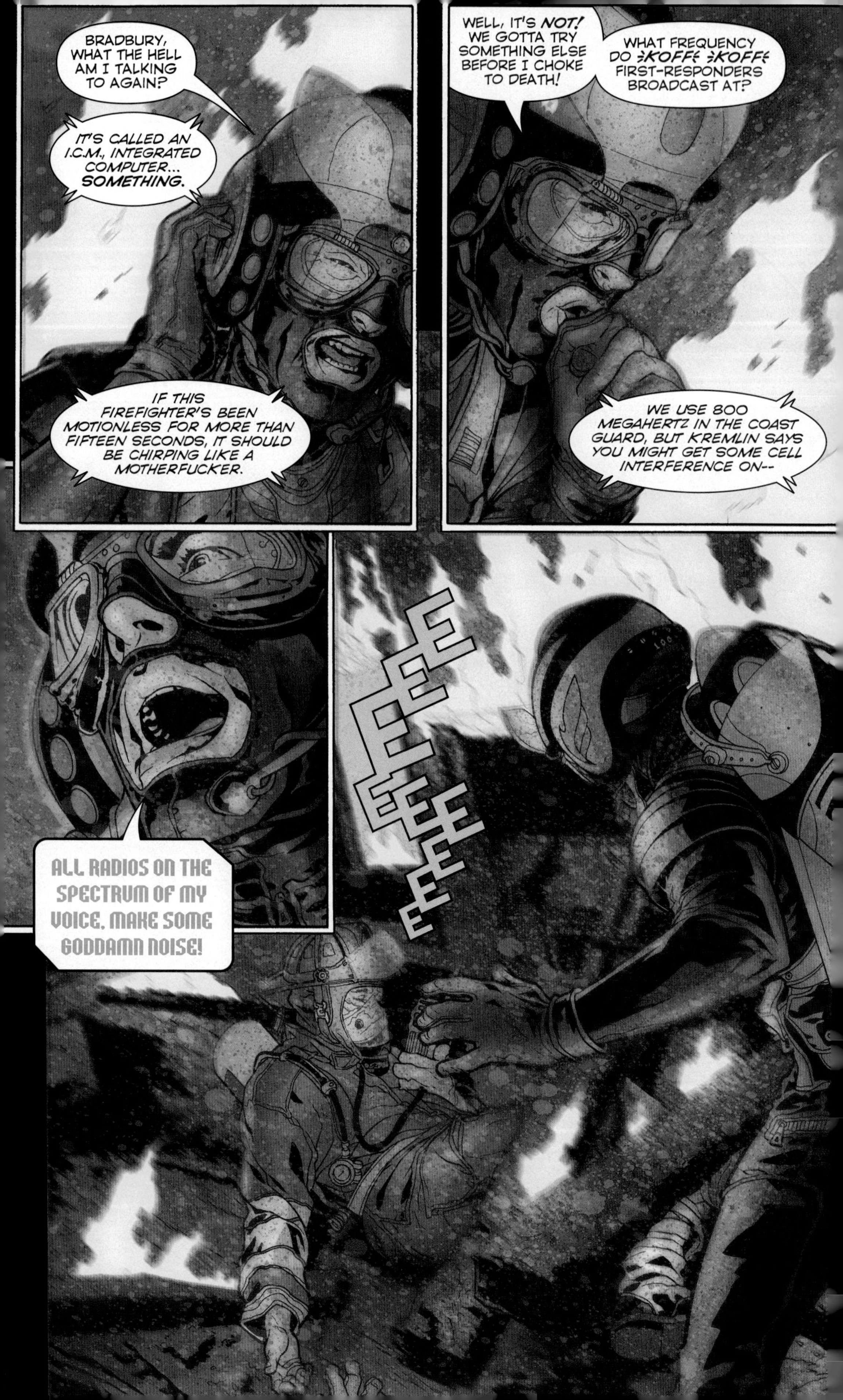
BRADBURY, WHAT THE HELL AM I TALKING TO AGAIN?
IT'S CALLED AN I.C.M., INTEGRATED COMPUTER... SOMETHING.
IF THIS FIREFIGHTER'S BEEN MOTIONLESS FOR MORE THAN FIFTEEN SECONDS, IT SHOULD BE CHIRPING LIKE A MOTHERFUCKER.
WELL, IT'S NOT! WE GOTTA TRY SOMETHING ELSE BEFORE I CHOKE TO DEATH!
WHAT FREQUENCY DO *KOFF* *KOFF* FIRST-RESPONDERS BROADCAST AT?
WE USE 800 MEGAHERTZ IN THE COAST GUARD, BUT KREMLIN SAYS YOU MIGHT GET SOME CELL INTERFERENCE ON--
ALL RADIOS ON THE SPECTRUM OF MY VOICE, MAKE SOME GODDAMN NOISE!
EEEEEEEEE

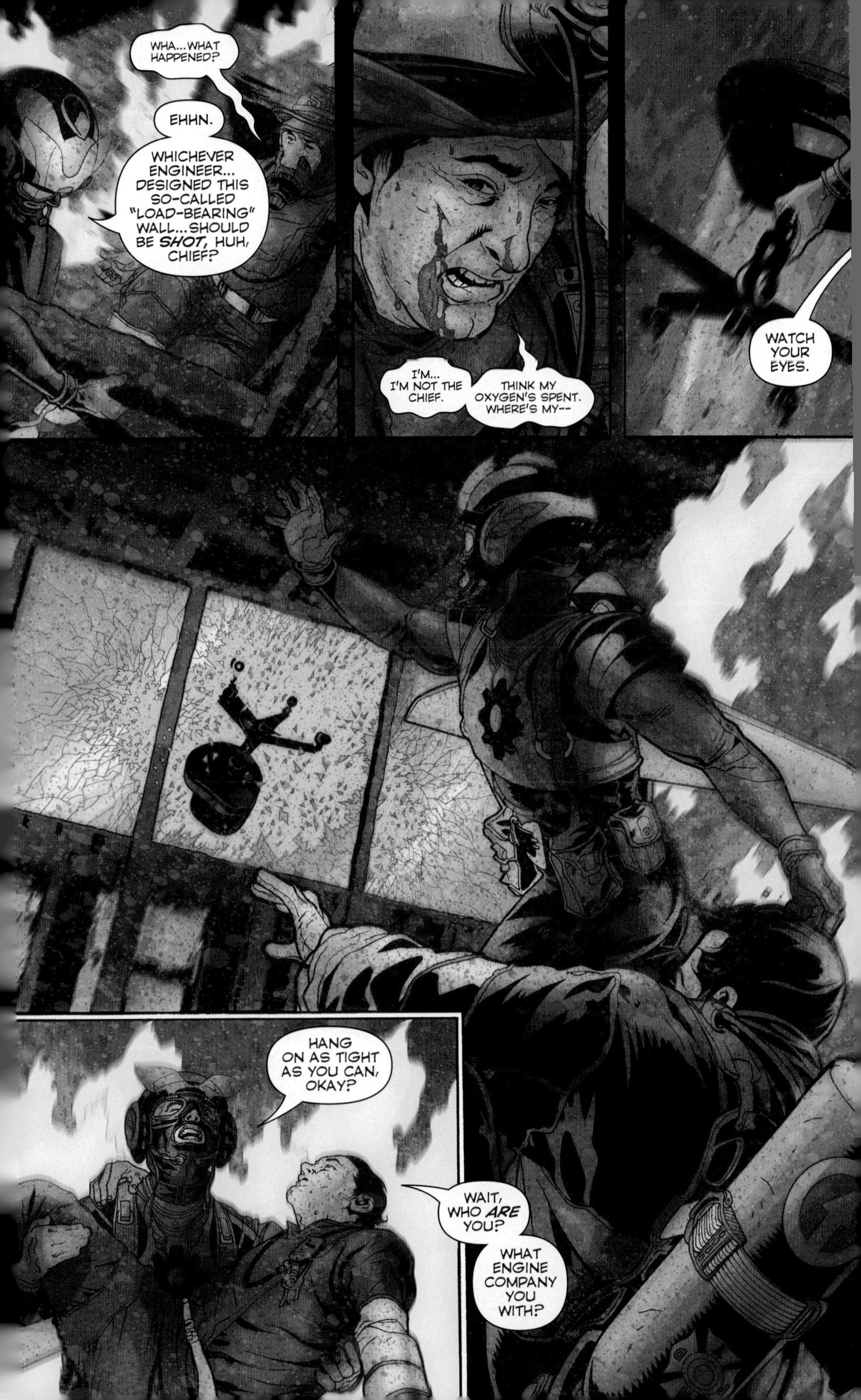
WHA...WHAT HAPPENED?
EHHN.
WHICHEVER ENGINEER... DESIGNED THIS SO-CALLED "LOAD-BEARING" WALL...SHOULD BE SHOT, HUH, CHIEF?
I'M... I'M NOT THE CHIEF.
THINK MY OXYGEN'S SPENT. WHERE'S MY--
WATCH YOUR EYES.
HANG ON AS TIGHT AS YOU CAN, OKAY?
WAIT, WHO ARE YOU?
WHAT ENGINE COMPANY YOU WITH?

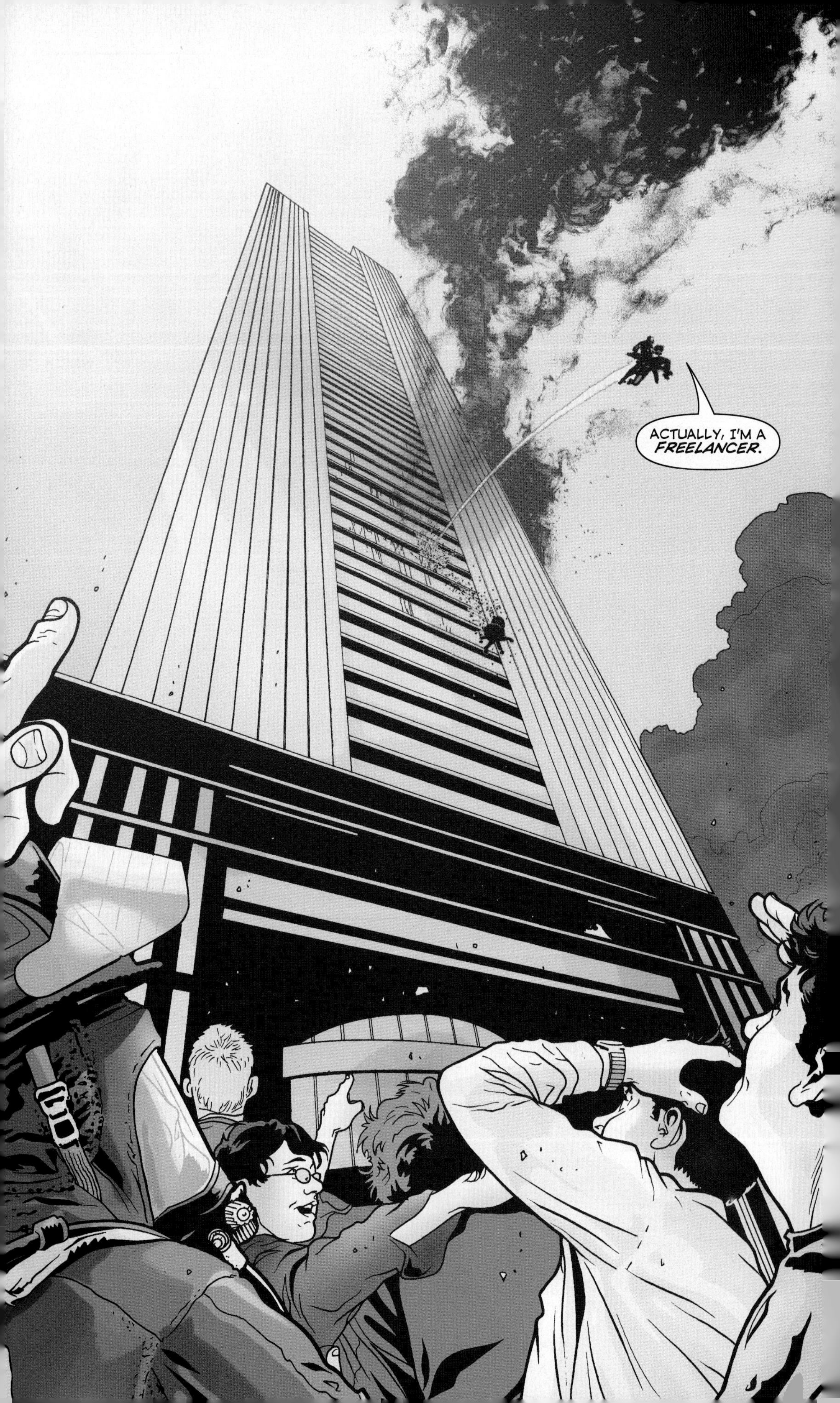
ACTUALLY, I'M A FREELANCER.

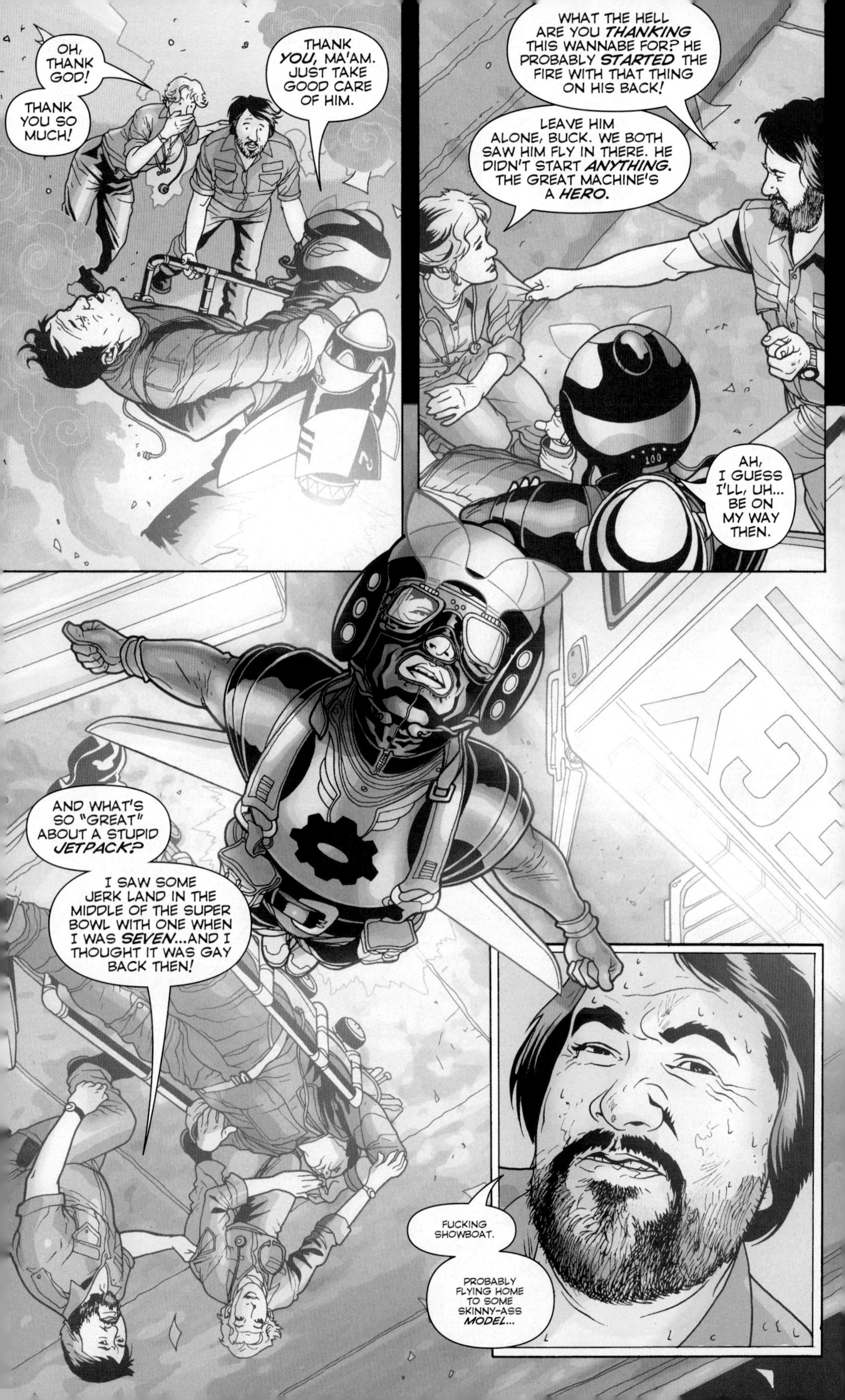
OH, THANK GOD!
THANK YOU SO MUCH!
THANK *YOU,* MA'AM. JUST TAKE GOOD CARE OF HIM.
WHAT THE HELL ARE YOU *THANKING* THIS WANNABE FOR? HE PROBABLY *STARTED* THE FIRE WITH THAT THING ON HIS BACK!
LEAVE HIM ALONE, BUCK. WE BOTH SAW HIM FLY IN THERE. HE DIDN'T START *ANYTHING.* THE GREAT MACHINE'S A *HERO.*
AH, I GUESS I'LL, UH... BE ON MY WAY THEN.
AND WHAT'S SO "GREAT" ABOUT A STUPID *JETPACK?*
I SAW SOME JERK LAND IN THE MIDDLE OF THE SUPER BOWL WITH ONE WHEN I WAS *SEVEN*...AND I THOUGHT IT WAS GAY BACK THEN!
FUCKING SHOWBOAT.
PROBABLY FLYING HOME TO SOME SKINNY-ASS *MODEL*...

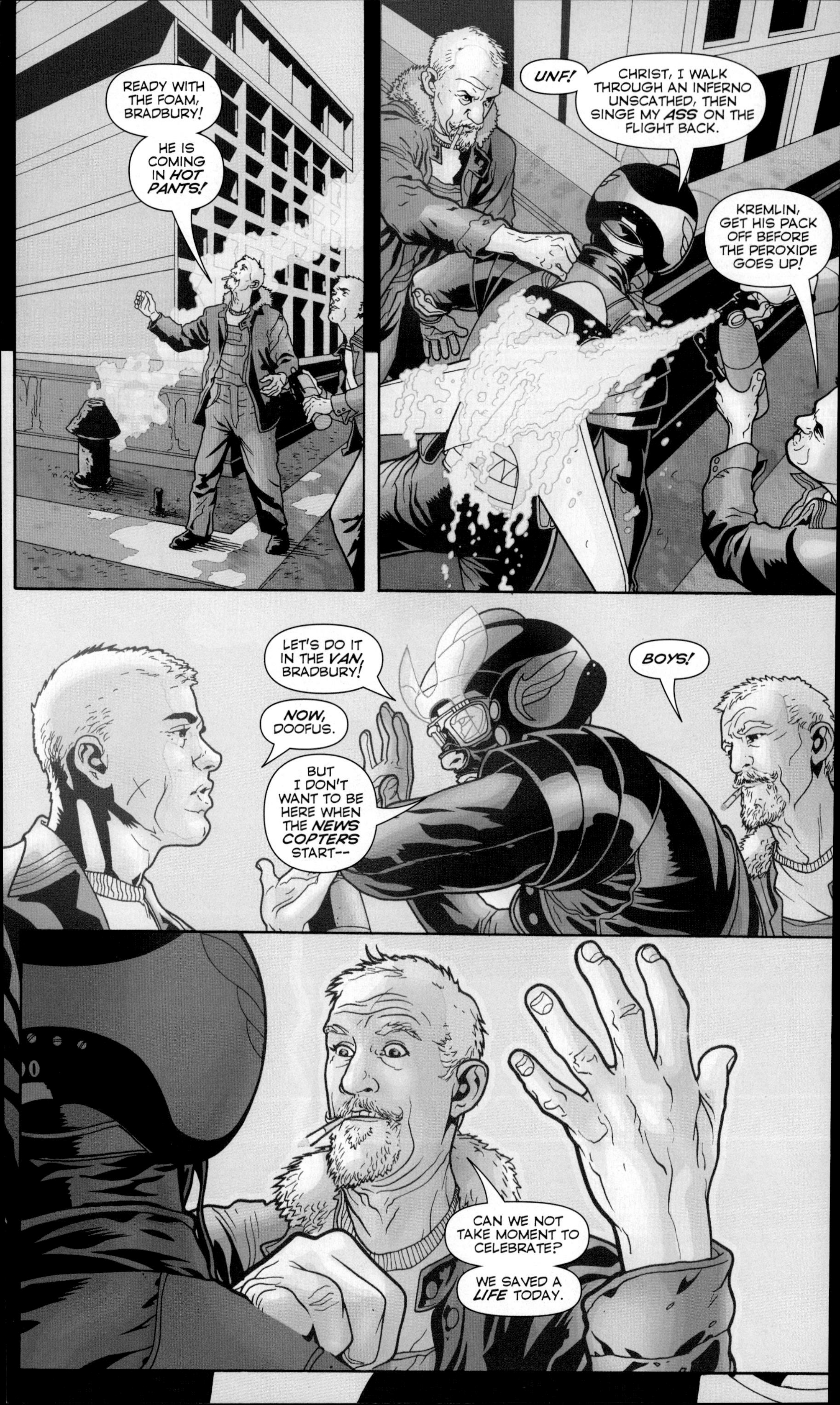
READY WITH THE FOAM, BRADBURY!
HE IS COMING IN HOT PANTS!
UNF!
CHRIST, I WALK THROUGH AN INFERNO UNSCATHED, THEN SINGE MY ASS ON THE FLIGHT BACK.
KREMLIN, GET HIS PACK OFF BEFORE THE PEROXIDE GOES UP!
LET'S DO IT IN THE VAN, BRADBURY!
NOW, DOOFUS.
BUT I DON'T WANT TO BE HERE WHEN THE NEWS COPTERS START--
BOYS!
CAN WE NOT TAKE MOMENT TO CELEBRATE?
WE SAVED A LIFE TODAY.

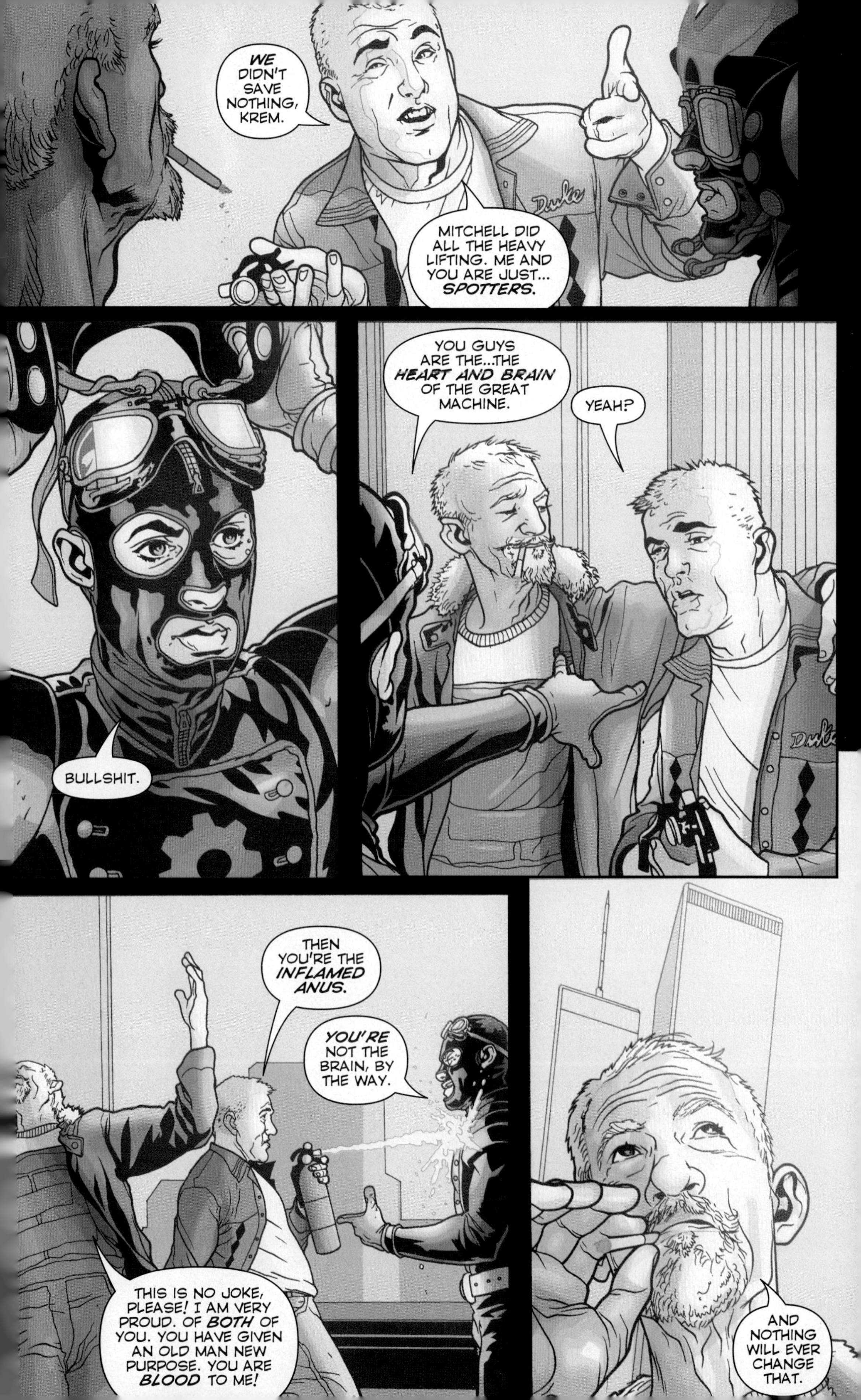

WE DIDN'T SAVE NOTHING, KREM.
MITCHELL DID ALL THE HEAVY LIFTING. ME AND YOU ARE JUST... SPOTTERS.
Duke
BULLSHIT.
YOU GUYS ARE THE...THE HEART AND BRAIN OF THE GREAT MACHINE.
YEAH?
THEN YOU'RE THE INFLAMED ANUS.
YOU'RE NOT THE BRAIN, BY THE WAY.
THIS IS NO JOKE, PLEASE! I AM VERY PROUD. OF BOTH OF YOU. YOU HAVE GIVEN AN OLD MAN NEW PURPOSE. YOU ARE BLOOD TO ME!
AND NOTHING WILL EVER CHANGE THAT.

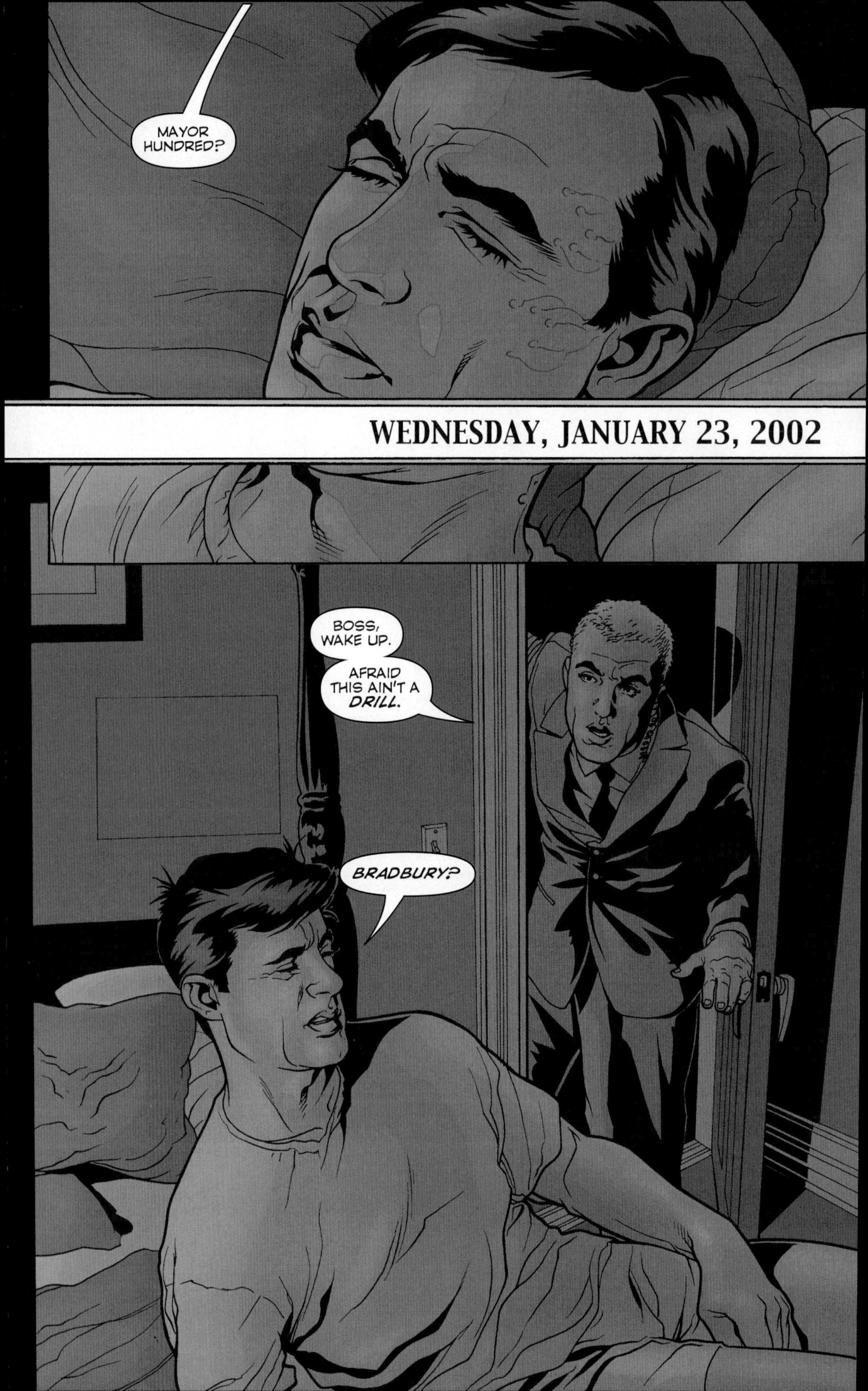
MAYOR HUNDRED?
WEDNESDAY, JANUARY 23, 2002
BOSS, WAKE UP.
AFRAID THIS AIN'T A *DRILL*.
BRADBURY?

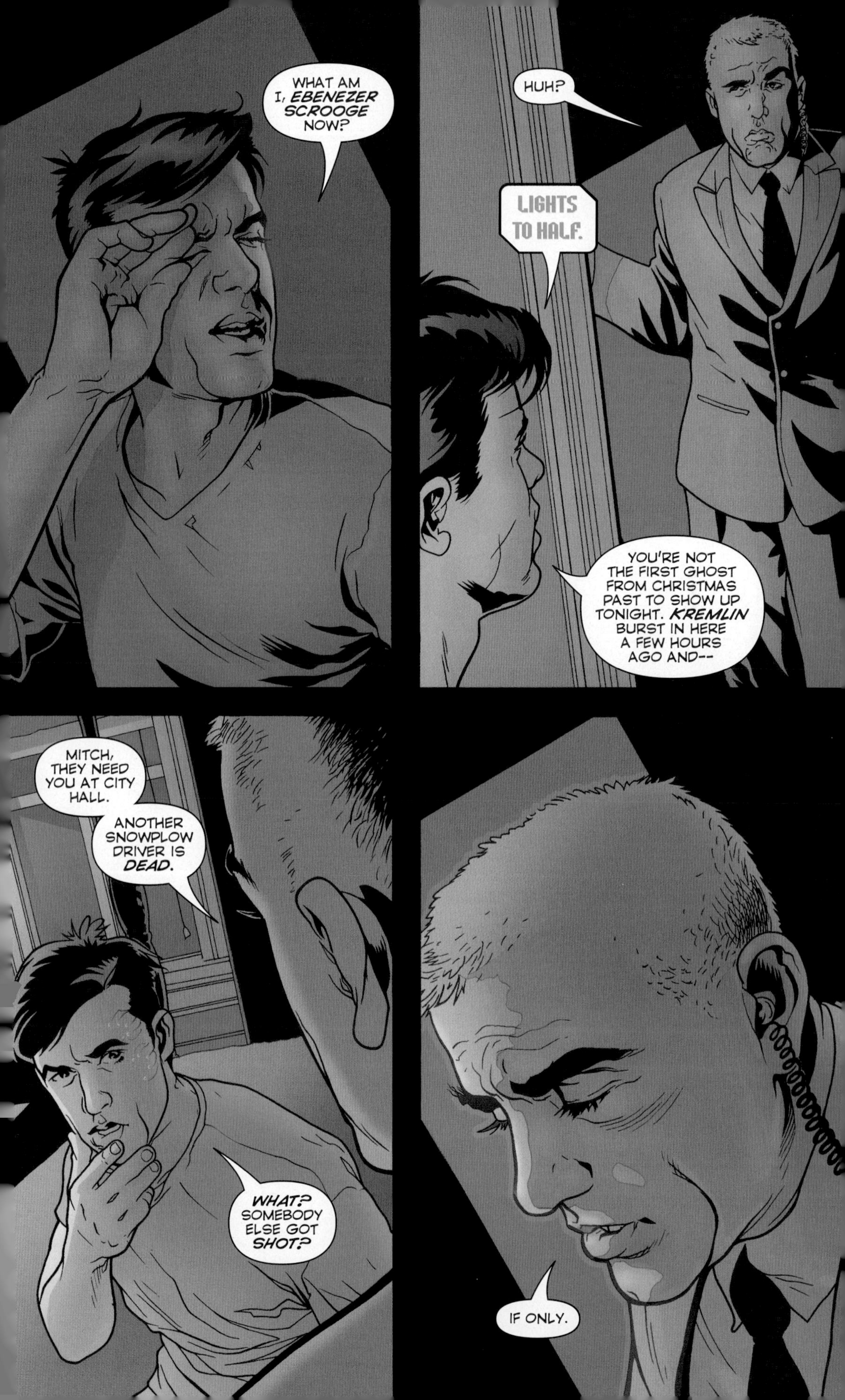
WHAT AM I, *EBENEZER SCROOGE* NOW?
HUH?
LIGHTS TO HALF.
YOU'RE NOT THE FIRST GHOST FROM CHRISTMAS PAST TO SHOW UP TONIGHT. *KREMLIN* BURST IN HERE A FEW HOURS AGO AND--
MITCH, THEY NEED YOU AT CITY HALL.
ANOTHER SNOWPLOW DRIVER IS *DEAD*.
WHAT? SOMEBODY ELSE GOT *SHOT?*
IF ONLY.

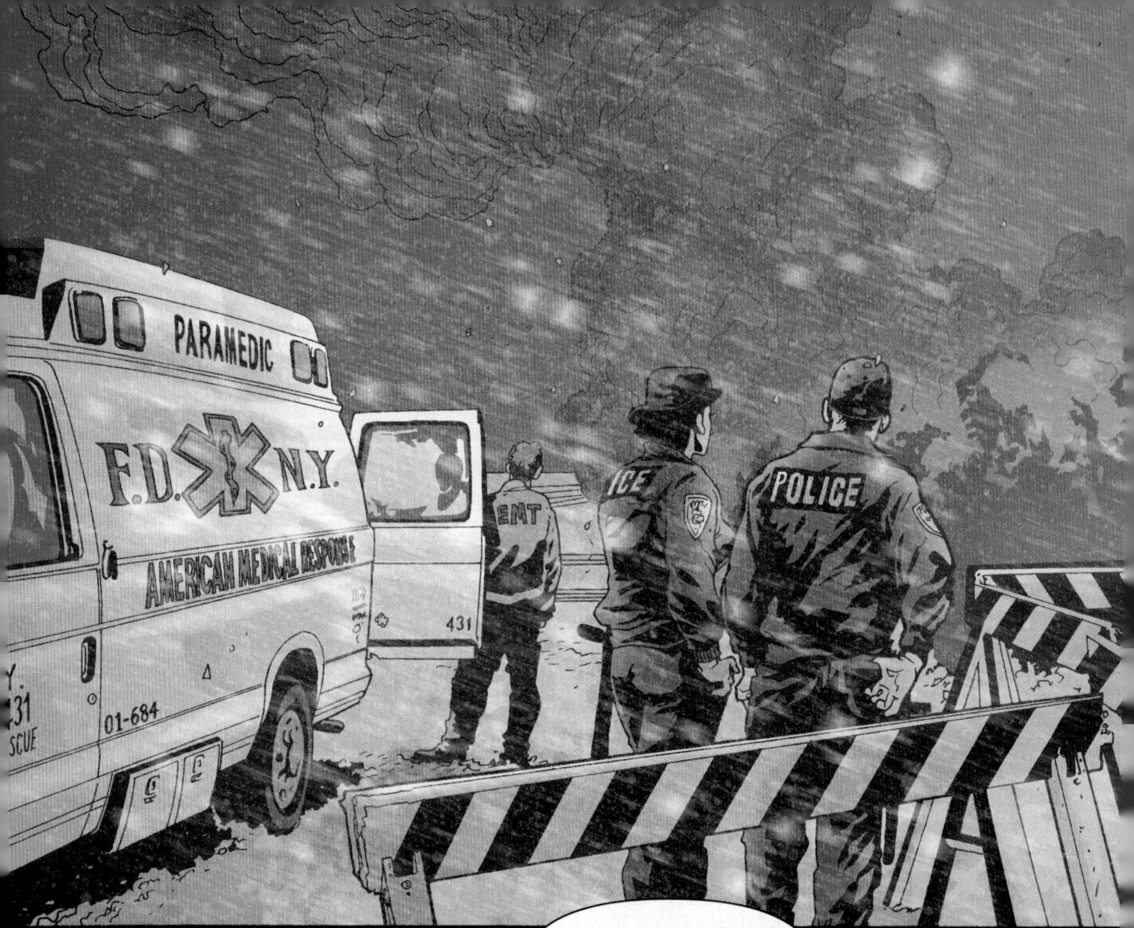

PARAMEDIC
F.D. N.Y.
AMERICAN MEDICAL RESPONSE
431
01-684
EMT
POLICE

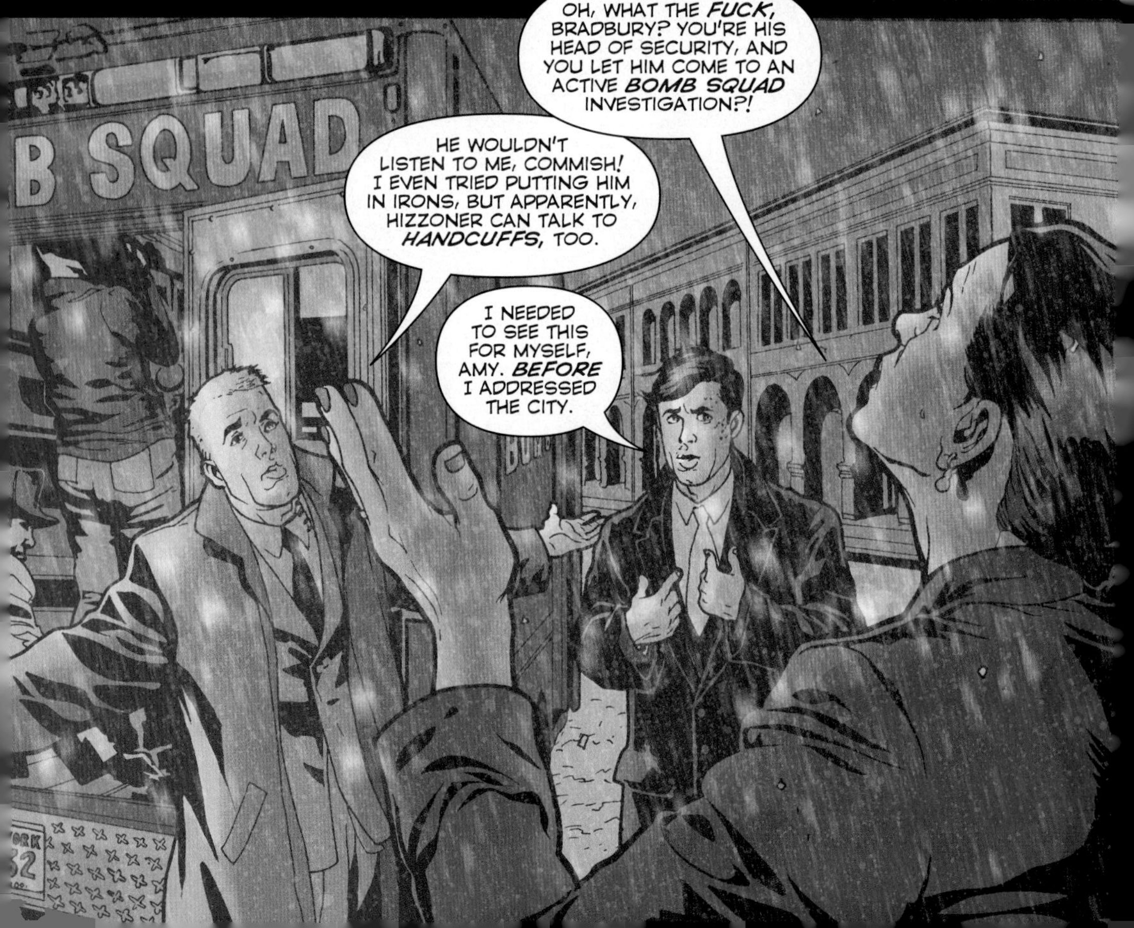

B SQUAD
OH, WHAT THE *FUCK,* BRADBURY? YOU'RE HIS HEAD OF SECURITY, AND YOU LET HIM COME TO AN ACTIVE ***BOMB SQUAD*** INVESTIGATION?!
HE WOULDN'T LISTEN TO ME, COMMISH! I EVEN TRIED PUTTING HIM IN IRONS, BUT APPARENTLY, HIZZONER CAN TALK TO ***HANDCUFFS,*** TOO.
I NEEDED TO SEE THIS FOR MYSELF, AMY. ***BEFORE*** I ADDRESSED THE CITY.

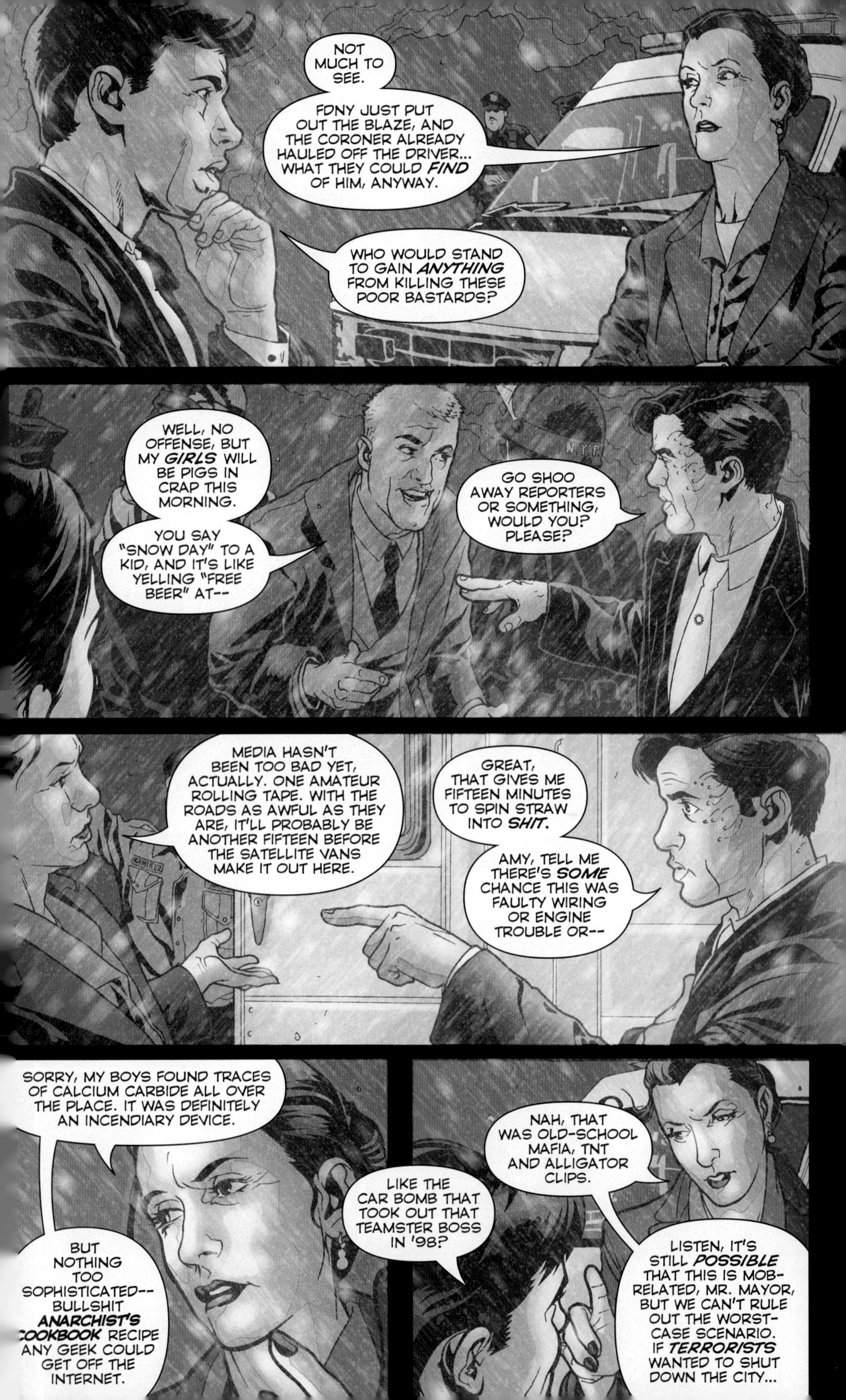
NOT MUCH TO SEE.
FDNY JUST PUT OUT THE BLAZE, AND THE CORONER ALREADY HAULED OFF THE DRIVER... WHAT THEY COULD *FIND* OF HIM, ANYWAY.
WHO WOULD STAND TO GAIN *ANYTHING* FROM KILLING THESE POOR BASTARDS?
WELL, NO OFFENSE, BUT MY *GIRLS* WILL BE PIGS IN CRAP THIS MORNING.
YOU SAY "SNOW DAY" TO A KID, AND IT'S LIKE YELLING "FREE BEER" AT--
GO SHOO AWAY REPORTERS OR SOMETHING, WOULD YOU? PLEASE?
MEDIA HASN'T BEEN TOO BAD YET, ACTUALLY. ONE AMATEUR ROLLING TAPE. WITH THE ROADS AS AWFUL AS THEY ARE, IT'LL PROBABLY BE ANOTHER FIFTEEN BEFORE THE SATELLITE VANS MAKE IT OUT HERE.
GREAT, THAT GIVES ME FIFTEEN MINUTES TO SPIN STRAW INTO *SHIT*.
AMY, TELL ME THERE'S *SOME* CHANCE THIS WAS FAULTY WIRING OR ENGINE TROUBLE OR--
SORRY, MY BOYS FOUND TRACES OF CALCIUM CARBIDE ALL OVER THE PLACE. IT WAS DEFINITELY AN INCENDIARY DEVICE.
BUT NOTHING TOO SOPHISTICATED-- BULLSHIT *ANARCHIST'S COOKBOOK* RECIPE ANY GEEK COULD GET OFF THE INTERNET.
LIKE THE CAR BOMB THAT TOOK OUT THAT TEAMSTER BOSS IN '98?
NAH, THAT WAS OLD-SCHOOL MAFIA, TNT AND ALLIGATOR CLIPS.
LISTEN, IT'S STILL *POSSIBLE* THAT THIS IS MOB-RELATED, MR. MAYOR, BUT WE CAN'T RULE OUT THE WORST-CASE SCENARIO. IF *TERRORISTS* WANTED TO SHUT DOWN THE CITY...

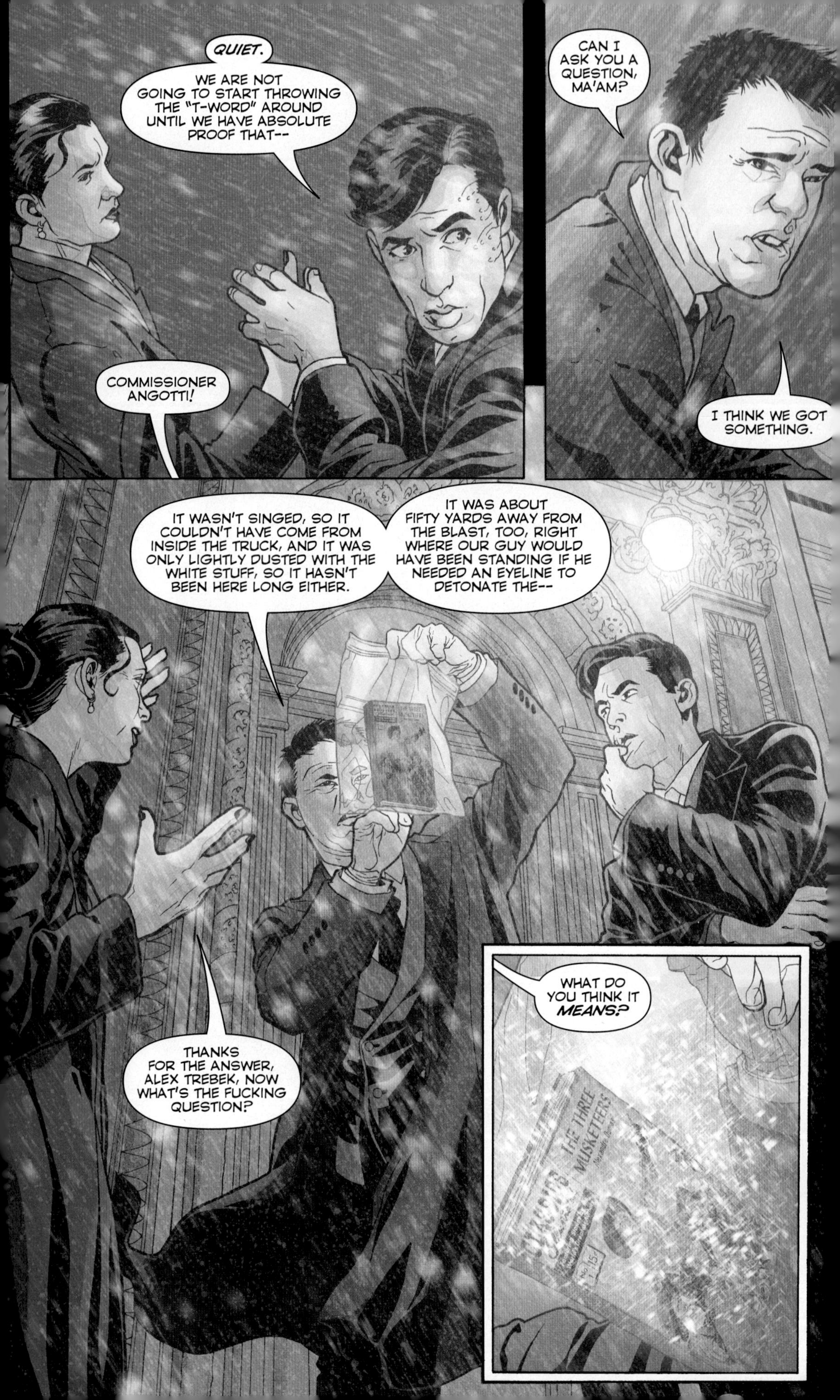
QUIET.
WE ARE NOT GOING TO START THROWING THE "T-WORD" AROUND UNTIL WE HAVE ABSOLUTE PROOF THAT--
COMMISSIONER ANGOTTI!
CAN I ASK YOU A QUESTION, MA'AM?
I THINK WE GOT SOMETHING.
IT WASN'T SINGED, SO IT COULDN'T HAVE COME FROM INSIDE THE TRUCK, AND IT WAS ONLY LIGHTLY DUSTED WITH THE WHITE STUFF, SO IT HASN'T BEEN HERE LONG EITHER.
IT WAS ABOUT FIFTY YARDS AWAY FROM THE BLAST, TOO, RIGHT WHERE OUR GUY WOULD HAVE BEEN STANDING IF HE NEEDED AN EYELINE TO DETONATE THE--
THANKS FOR THE ANSWER, ALEX TREBEK, NOW WHAT'S THE FUCKING QUESTION?
WHAT DO YOU THINK IT MEANS?
THE THREE MUSKETEERS
NO. 15

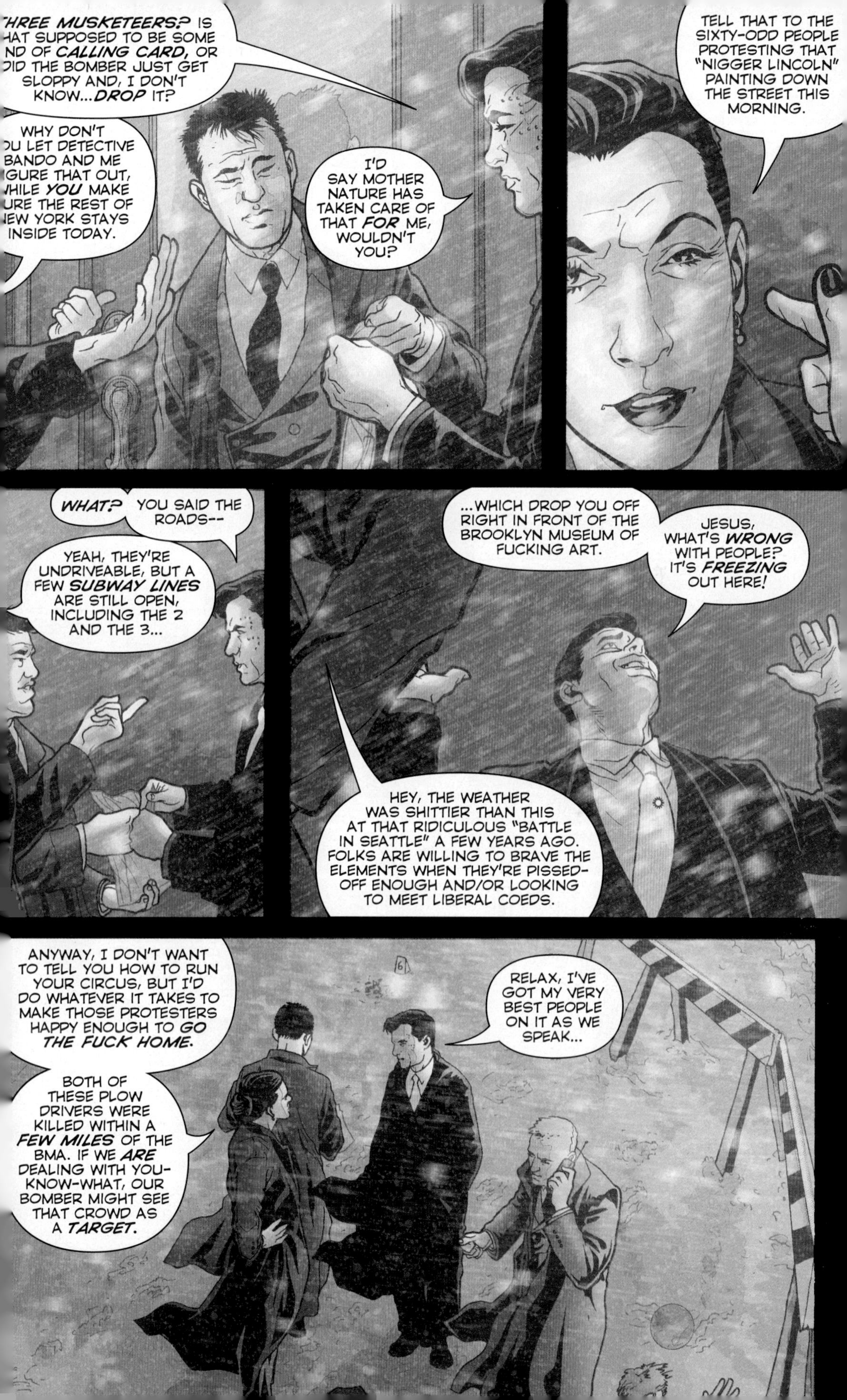

THREE MUSKETEERS? IS HAT SUPPOSED TO BE SOME ND OF CALLING CARD, OR DID THE BOMBER JUST GET SLOPPY AND, I DON'T KNOW...DROP IT?
WHY DON'T OU LET DETECTIVE BANDO AND ME IGURE THAT OUT, WHILE YOU MAKE URE THE REST OF EW YORK STAYS INSIDE TODAY.
I'D SAY MOTHER NATURE HAS TAKEN CARE OF THAT FOR ME, WOULDN'T YOU?
TELL THAT TO THE SIXTY-ODD PEOPLE PROTESTING THAT "NIGGER LINCOLN" PAINTING DOWN THE STREET THIS MORNING.
WHAT?
YOU SAID THE ROADS--
YEAH, THEY'RE UNDRIVEABLE, BUT A FEW SUBWAY LINES ARE STILL OPEN, INCLUDING THE 2 AND THE 3...
...WHICH DROP YOU OFF RIGHT IN FRONT OF THE BROOKLYN MUSEUM OF FUCKING ART.
JESUS, WHAT'S WRONG WITH PEOPLE? IT'S FREEZING OUT HERE!
HEY, THE WEATHER WAS SHITTIER THAN THIS AT THAT RIDICULOUS "BATTLE IN SEATTLE" A FEW YEARS AGO. FOLKS ARE WILLING TO BRAVE THE ELEMENTS WHEN THEY'RE PISSED-OFF ENOUGH AND/OR LOOKING TO MEET LIBERAL COEDS.
ANYWAY, I DON'T WANT TO TELL YOU HOW TO RUN YOUR CIRCUS, BUT I'D DO WHATEVER IT TAKES TO MAKE THOSE PROTESTERS HAPPY ENOUGH TO GO THE FUCK HOME.
BOTH OF THESE PLOW DRIVERS WERE KILLED WITHIN A FEW MILES OF THE BMA. IF WE ARE DEALING WITH YOU-KNOW-WHAT, OUR BOMBER MIGHT SEE THAT CROWD AS A TARGET.
RELAX, I'VE GOT MY VERY BEST PEOPLE ON IT AS WE SPEAK...

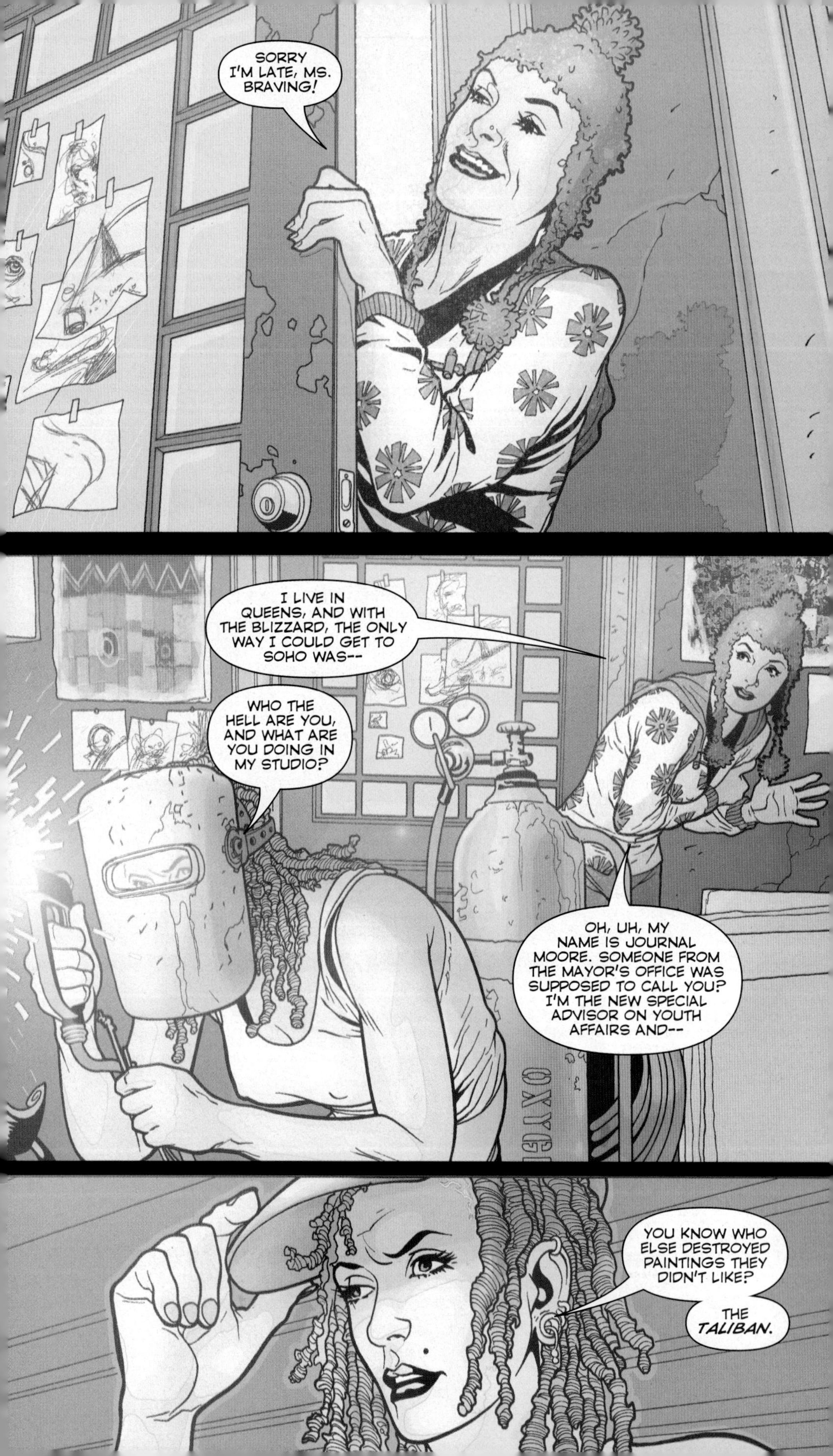
SORRY I'M LATE, MS. BRAVING!
I LIVE IN QUEENS, AND WITH THE BLIZZARD, THE ONLY WAY I COULD GET TO SOHO WAS--
WHO THE HELL ARE YOU, AND WHAT ARE YOU DOING IN MY STUDIO?
OH, UH, MY NAME IS JOURNAL MOORE. SOMEONE FROM THE MAYOR'S OFFICE WAS SUPPOSED TO CALL YOU? I'M THE NEW SPECIAL ADVISOR ON YOUTH AFFAIRS AND--
OXYG
YOU KNOW WHO ELSE DESTROYED PAINTINGS THEY DIDN'T LIKE?
THE *TALIBAN*.

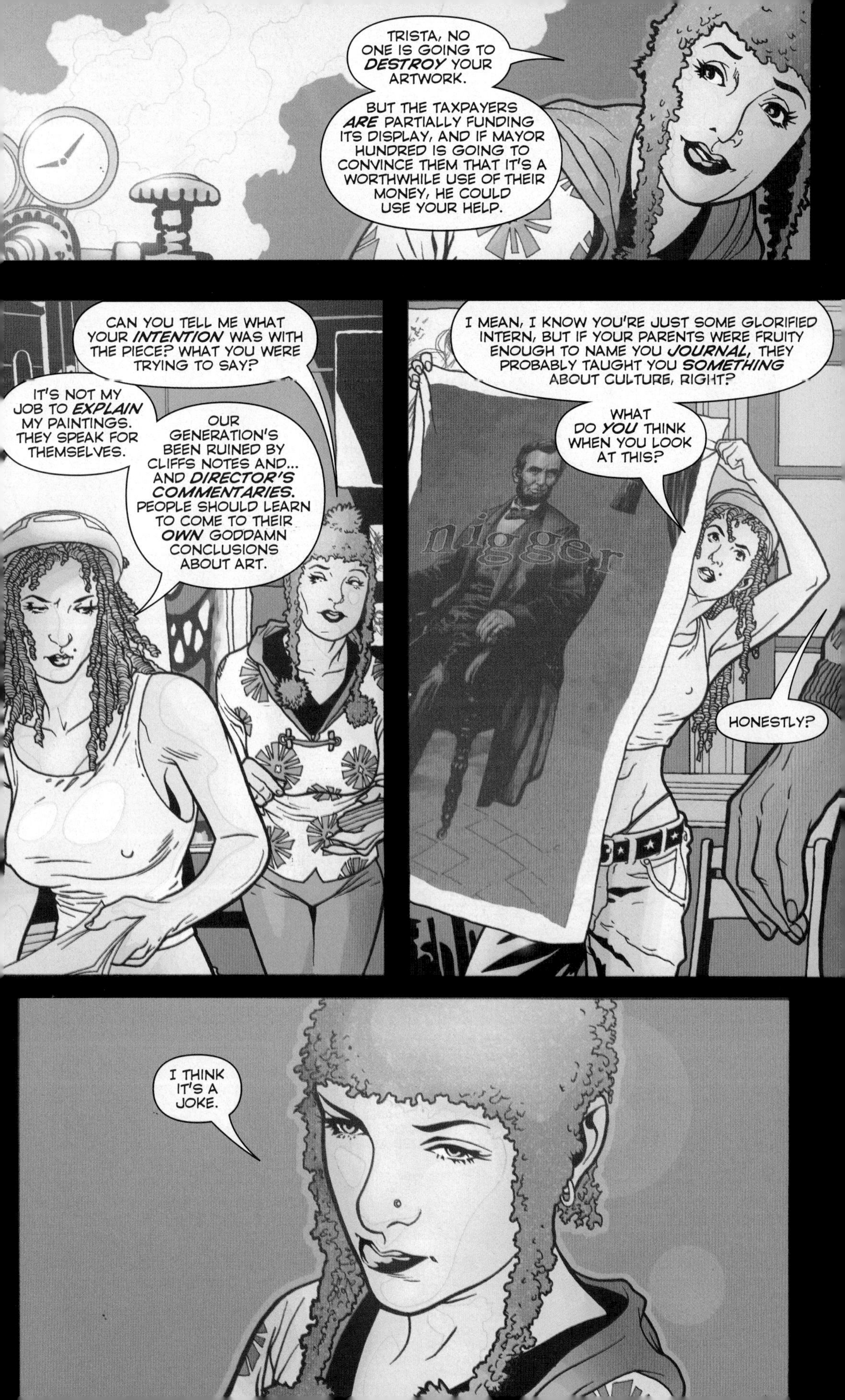
TRISTA, NO ONE IS GOING TO *DESTROY* YOUR ARTWORK.
BUT THE TAXPAYERS *ARE* PARTIALLY FUNDING ITS DISPLAY, AND IF MAYOR HUNDRED IS GOING TO CONVINCE THEM THAT IT'S A WORTHWHILE USE OF THEIR MONEY, HE COULD USE YOUR HELP.
CAN YOU TELL ME WHAT YOUR *INTENTION* WAS WITH THE PIECE? WHAT YOU WERE TRYING TO SAY?
IT'S NOT MY JOB TO *EXPLAIN* MY PAINTINGS. THEY SPEAK FOR THEMSELVES.
OUR GENERATION'S BEEN RUINED BY CLIFFS NOTES AND... AND *DIRECTOR'S COMMENTARIES.* PEOPLE SHOULD LEARN TO COME TO THEIR *OWN* GODDAMN CONCLUSIONS ABOUT ART.
I MEAN, I KNOW YOU'RE JUST SOME GLORIFIED INTERN, BUT IF YOUR PARENTS WERE FRUITY ENOUGH TO NAME YOU *JOURNAL,* THEY PROBABLY TAUGHT YOU *SOMETHING* ABOUT CULTURE, RIGHT?
WHAT DO *YOU* THINK WHEN YOU LOOK AT THIS?
nigger
HONESTLY?
I THINK IT'S A JOKE.

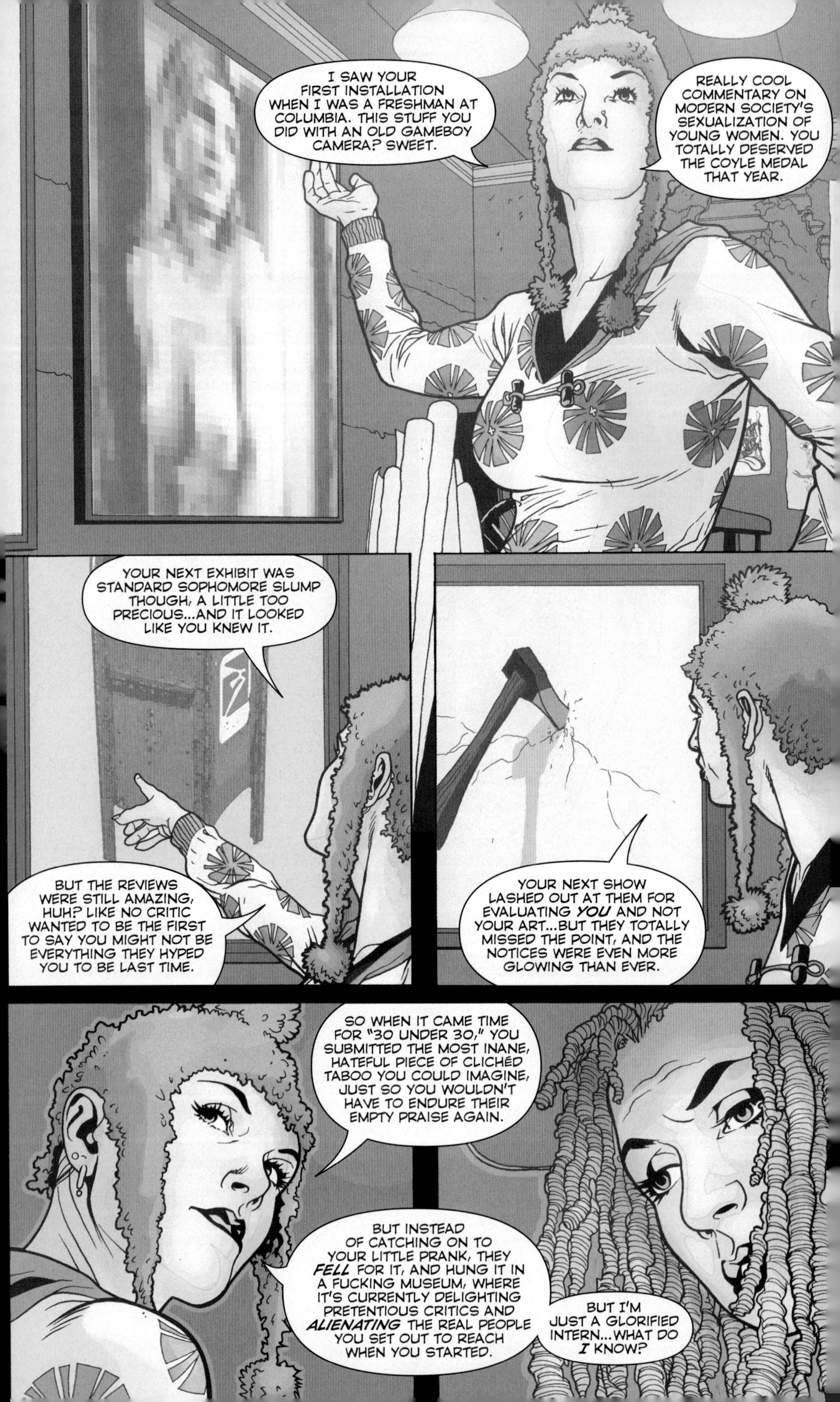
I SAW YOUR FIRST INSTALLATION WHEN I WAS A FRESHMAN AT COLUMBIA. THIS STUFF YOU DID WITH AN OLD GAMEBOY CAMERA? SWEET.
REALLY COOL COMMENTARY ON MODERN SOCIETY'S SEXUALIZATION OF YOUNG WOMEN. YOU TOTALLY DESERVED THE COYLE MEDAL THAT YEAR.
YOUR NEXT EXHIBIT WAS STANDARD SOPHOMORE SLUMP THOUGH, A LITTLE TOO PRECIOUS...AND IT LOOKED LIKE YOU KNEW IT.
BUT THE REVIEWS WERE STILL AMAZING, HUH? LIKE NO CRITIC WANTED TO BE THE FIRST TO SAY YOU MIGHT NOT BE EVERYTHING THEY HYPED YOU TO BE LAST TIME.
YOUR NEXT SHOW LASHED OUT AT THEM FOR EVALUATING *YOU* AND NOT YOUR ART...BUT THEY TOTALLY MISSED THE POINT, AND THE NOTICES WERE EVEN MORE GLOWING THAN EVER.
SO WHEN IT CAME TIME FOR "30 UNDER 30," YOU SUBMITTED THE MOST INANE, HATEFUL PIECE OF CLICHÉD TABOO YOU COULD IMAGINE, JUST SO YOU WOULDN'T HAVE TO ENDURE THEIR EMPTY PRAISE AGAIN.
BUT INSTEAD OF CATCHING ON TO YOUR LITTLE PRANK, THEY *FELL* FOR IT, AND HUNG IT IN A FUCKING MUSEUM, WHERE IT'S CURRENTLY DELIGHTING PRETENTIOUS CRITICS AND *ALIENATING* THE REAL PEOPLE YOU SET OUT TO REACH WHEN YOU STARTED.
BUT I'M JUST A GLORIFIED INTERN...WHAT DO *I* KNOW?

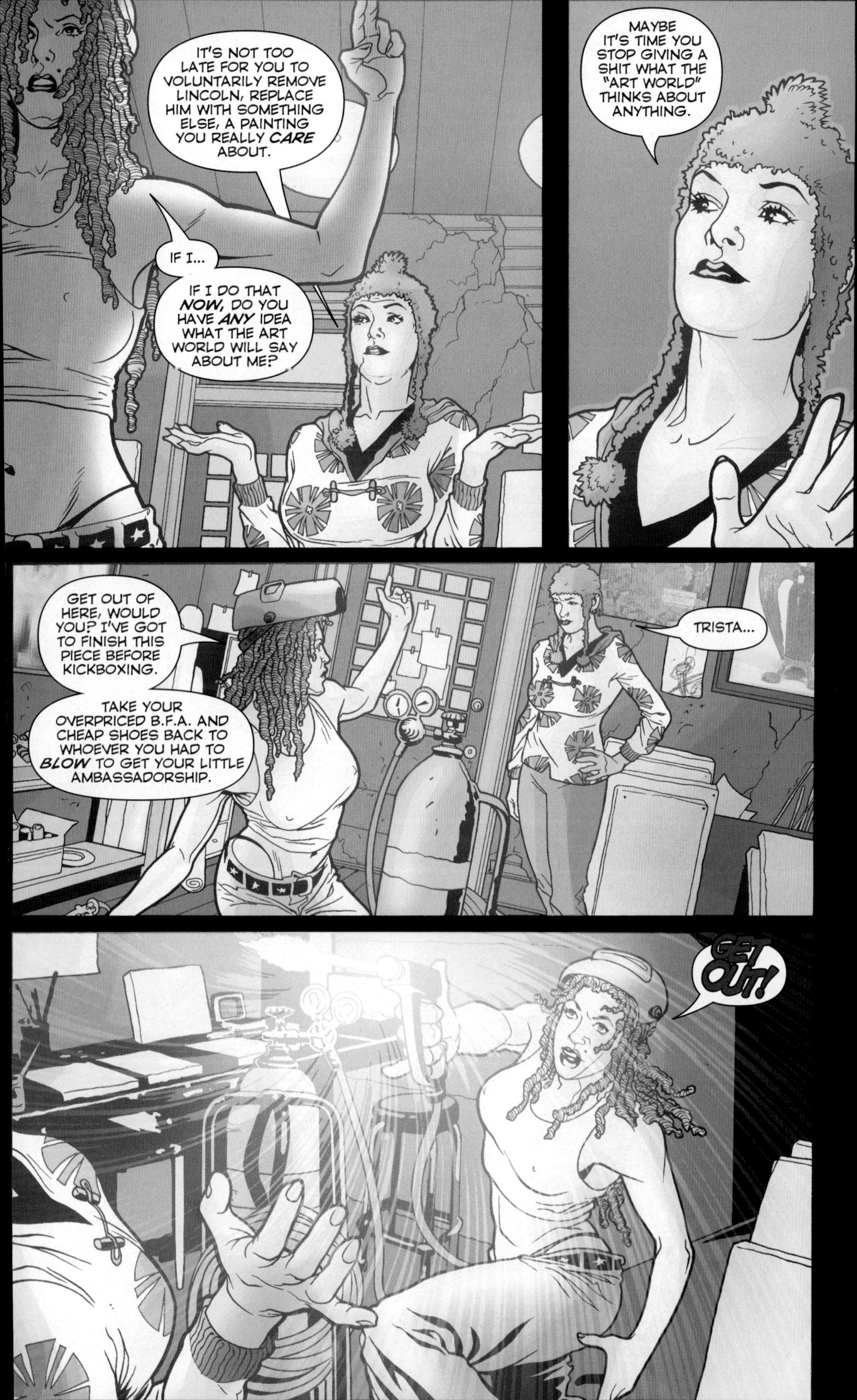
IT'S NOT TOO LATE FOR YOU TO VOLUNTARILY REMOVE LINCOLN, REPLACE HIM WITH SOMETHING ELSE, A PAINTING YOU REALLY CARE ABOUT.
IF I...
IF I DO THAT NOW, DO YOU HAVE ANY IDEA WHAT THE ART WORLD WILL SAY ABOUT ME?
MAYBE IT'S TIME YOU STOP GIVING A SHIT WHAT THE "ART WORLD" THINKS ABOUT ANYTHING.
GET OUT OF HERE, WOULD YOU? I'VE GOT TO FINISH THIS PIECE BEFORE KICKBOXING.
TAKE YOUR OVERPRICED B.F.A. AND CHEAP SHOES BACK TO WHOEVER YOU HAD TO BLOW TO GET YOUR LITTLE AMBASSADORSHIP.
TRISTA...
GET OUT!

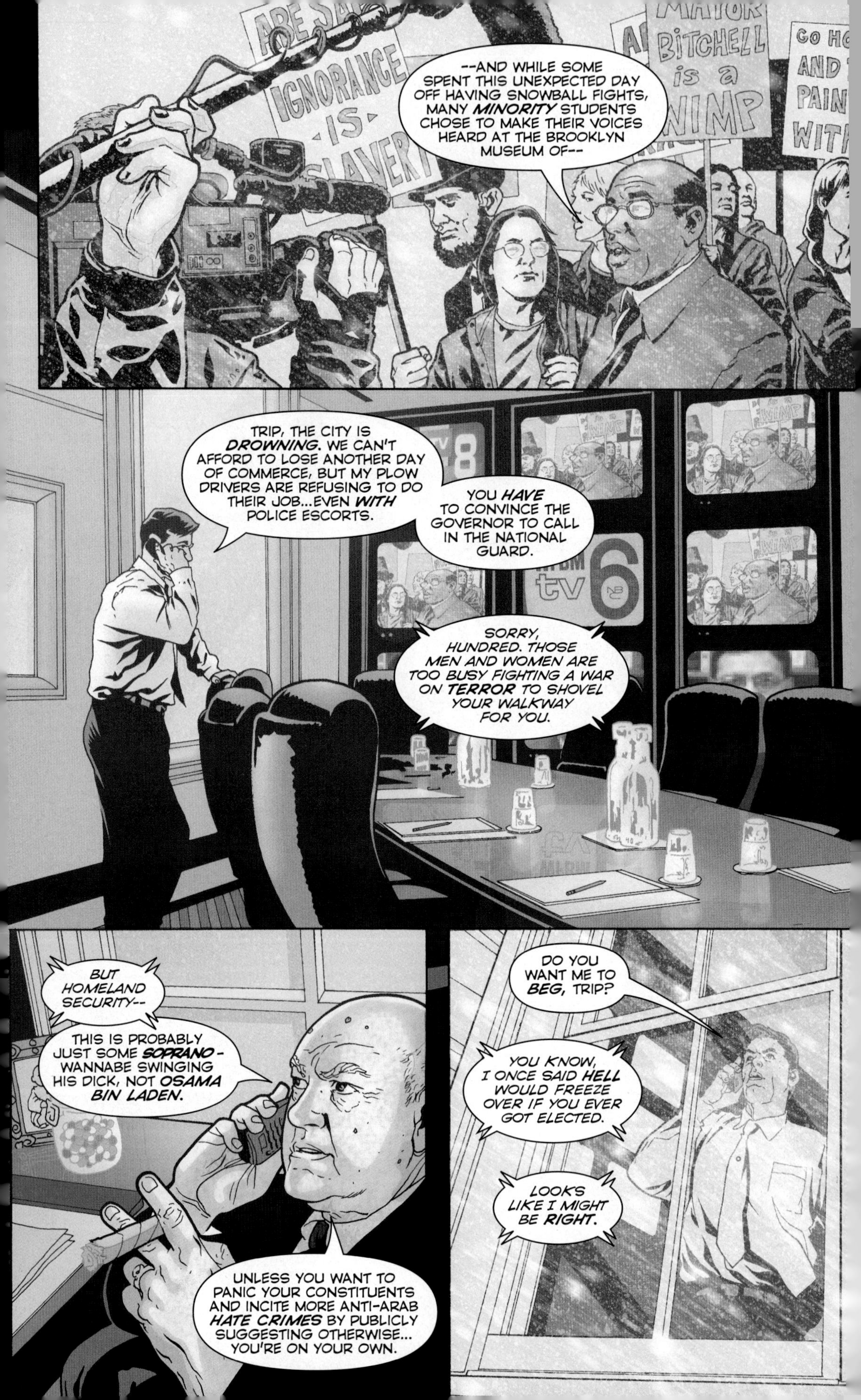

ABE SA
IGNORANCE IS SLAVERY
MAYOR BITCHELL is a WIMP
GO HO AND T PAIN WITH
--AND WHILE SOME SPENT THIS UNEXPECTED DAY OFF HAVING SNOWBALL FIGHTS, MANY *MINORITY* STUDENTS CHOSE TO MAKE THEIR VOICES HEARD AT THE BROOKLYN MUSEUM OF--
TRIP, THE CITY IS *DROWNING.* WE CAN'T AFFORD TO LOSE ANOTHER DAY OF COMMERCE, BUT MY PLOW DRIVERS ARE REFUSING TO DO THEIR JOB...EVEN *WITH* POLICE ESCORTS.
YOU *HAVE* TO CONVINCE THE GOVERNOR TO CALL IN THE NATIONAL GUARD.
tv 6
SORRY, HUNDRED. THOSE MEN AND WOMEN ARE TOO BUSY FIGHTING A WAR ON ***TERROR*** *TO SHOVEL YOUR WALKWAY FOR YOU.*
BUT HOMELAND SECURITY--
THIS IS PROBABLY JUST SOME ***SOPRANO***-WANNABE SWINGING HIS DICK, NOT ***OSAMA BIN LADEN.***
UNLESS YOU WANT TO PANIC YOUR CONSTITUENTS AND INCITE MORE ANTI-ARAB ***HATE CRIMES*** BY PUBLICLY SUGGESTING OTHERWISE... YOU'RE ON YOUR OWN.
DO YOU WANT ME TO ***BEG,*** TRIP?
YOU KNOW, I ONCE SAID ***HELL*** *WOULD FREEZE OVER IF YOU EVER GOT ELECTED.*
LOOKS LIKE I MIGHT BE ***RIGHT.***

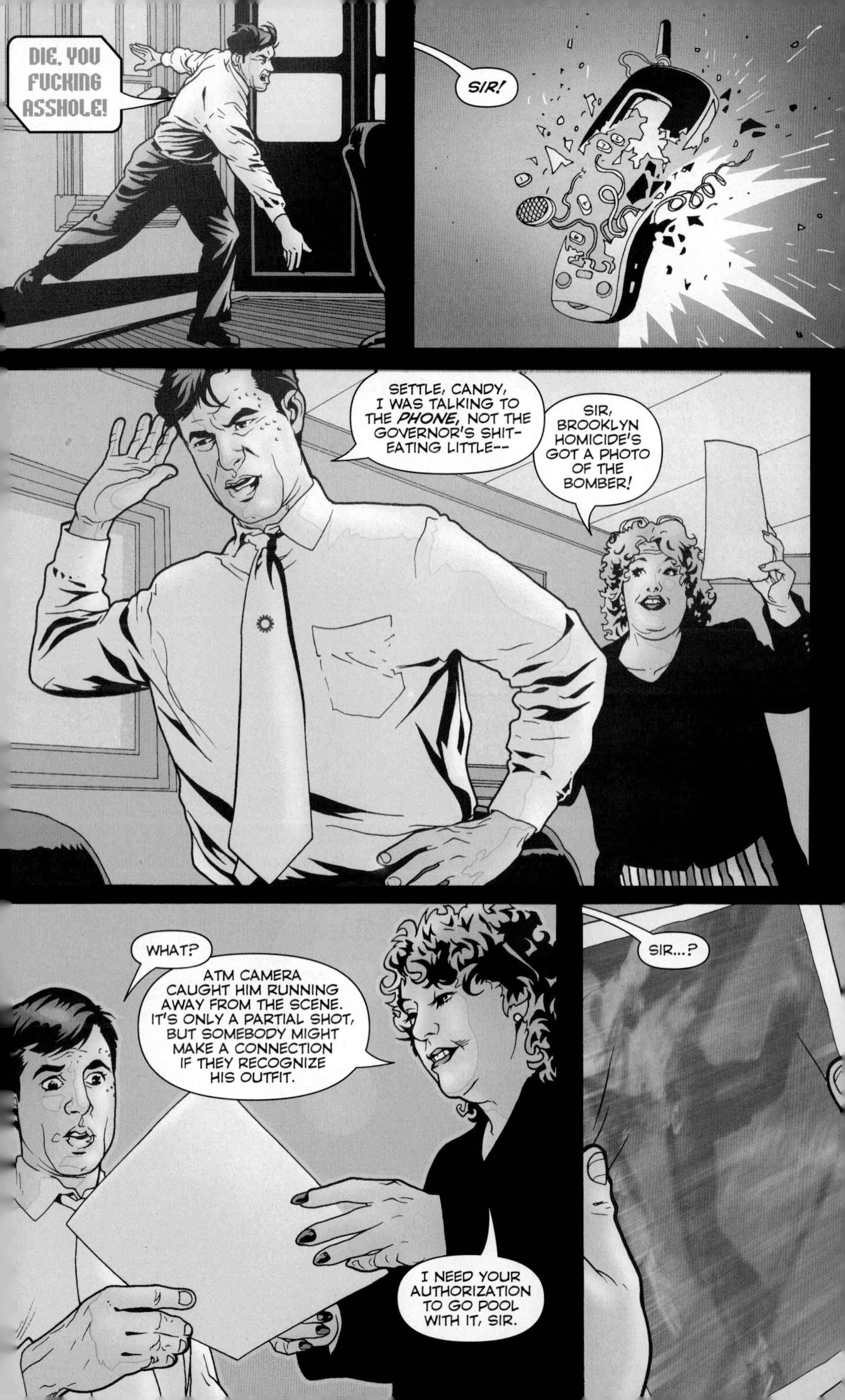
DIE, YOU FUCKING ASSHOLE!
SIR!
SETTLE, CANDY, I WAS TALKING TO THE *PHONE,* NOT THE GOVERNOR'S SHIT-EATING LITTLE--
SIR, BROOKLYN HOMICIDE'S GOT A PHOTO OF THE BOMBER!
WHAT?
ATM CAMERA CAUGHT HIM RUNNING AWAY FROM THE SCENE. IT'S ONLY A PARTIAL SHOT, BUT SOMEBODY MIGHT MAKE A CONNECTION IF THEY RECOGNIZE HIS OUTFIT.
I NEED YOUR AUTHORIZATION TO GO POOL WITH IT, SIR.
SIR...?

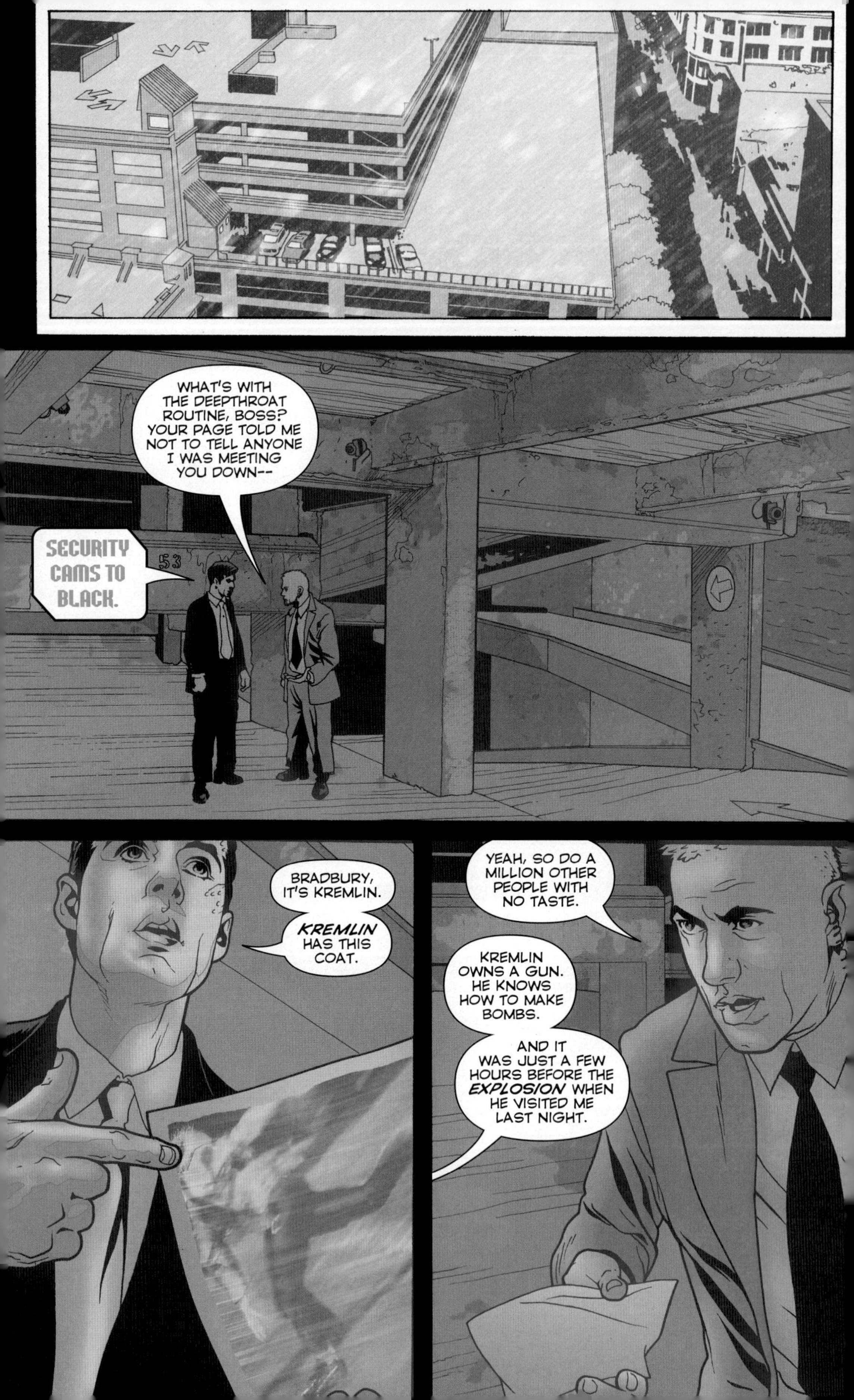
WHAT'S WITH THE DEEPTHROAT ROUTINE, BOSS? YOUR PAGE TOLD ME NOT TO TELL ANYONE I WAS MEETING YOU DOWN--
SECURITY CAMS TO BLACK.
53
BRADBURY, IT'S KREMLIN.
KREMLIN HAS THIS COAT.
YEAH, SO DO A MILLION OTHER PEOPLE WITH NO TASTE.
KREMLIN OWNS A GUN. HE KNOWS HOW TO MAKE BOMBS.
AND IT WAS JUST A FEW HOURS BEFORE THE *EXPLOSION* WHEN HE VISITED ME LAST NIGHT.

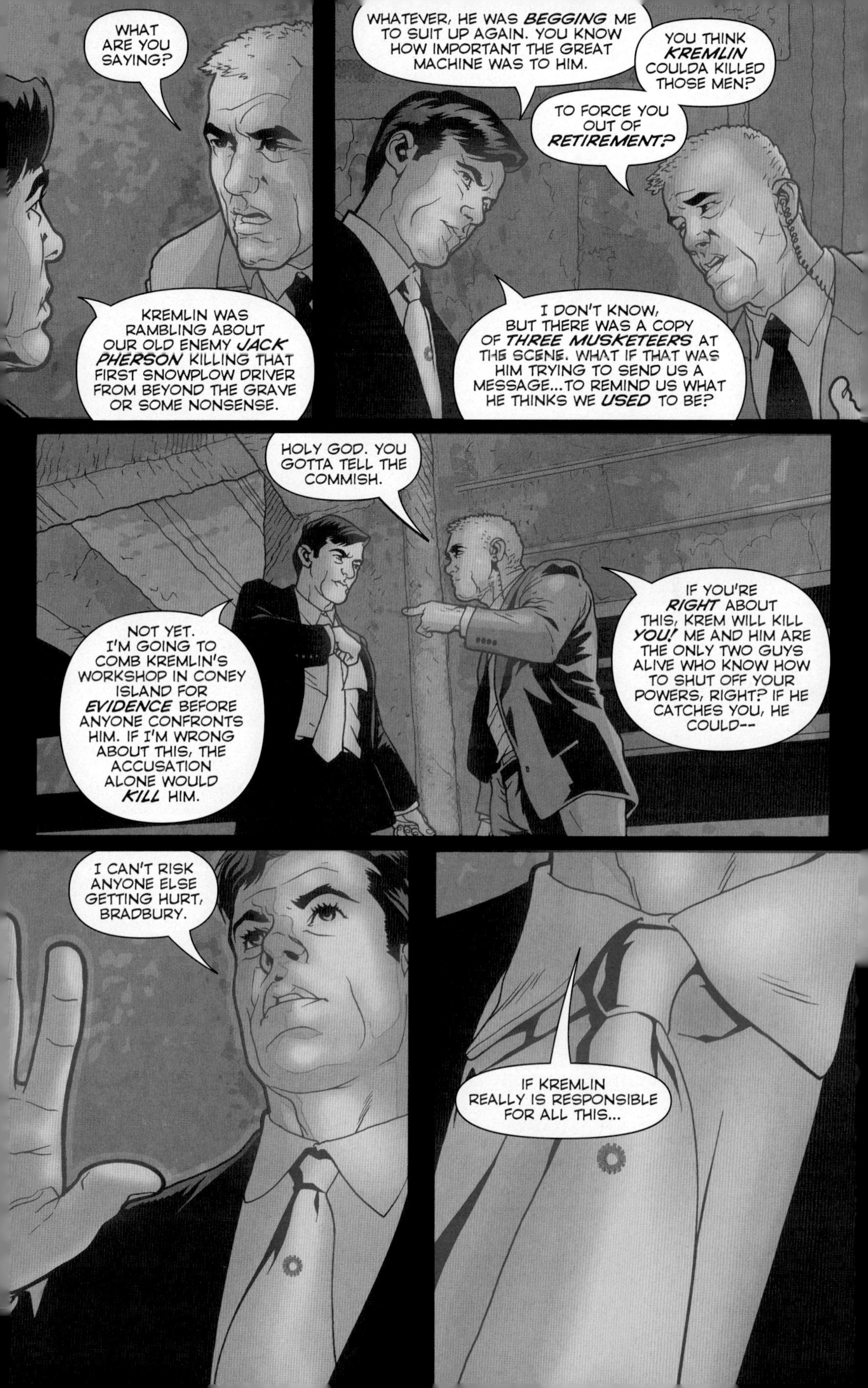
WHAT ARE YOU SAYING?
KREMLIN WAS RAMBLING ABOUT OUR OLD ENEMY JACK PHERSON KILLING THAT FIRST SNOWPLOW DRIVER FROM BEYOND THE GRAVE OR SOME NONSENSE.
WHATEVER, HE WAS BEGGING ME TO SUIT UP AGAIN. YOU KNOW HOW IMPORTANT THE GREAT MACHINE WAS TO HIM.
YOU THINK KREMLIN COULDA KILLED THOSE MEN?
TO FORCE YOU OUT OF RETIREMENT?
I DON'T KNOW, BUT THERE WAS A COPY OF THREE MUSKETEERS AT THE SCENE. WHAT IF THAT WAS HIM TRYING TO SEND US A MESSAGE...TO REMIND US WHAT HE THINKS WE USED TO BE?
HOLY GOD. YOU GOTTA TELL THE COMMISH.
NOT YET. I'M GOING TO COMB KREMLIN'S WORKSHOP IN CONEY ISLAND FOR EVIDENCE BEFORE ANYONE CONFRONTS HIM. IF I'M WRONG ABOUT THIS, THE ACCUSATION ALONE WOULD KILL HIM.
IF YOU'RE RIGHT ABOUT THIS, KREM WILL KILL YOU! ME AND HIM ARE THE ONLY TWO GUYS ALIVE WHO KNOW HOW TO SHUT OFF YOUR POWERS, RIGHT? IF HE CATCHES YOU, HE COULD--
I CAN'T RISK ANYONE ELSE GETTING HURT, BRADBURY.
IF KREMLIN REALLY IS RESPONSIBLE FOR ALL THIS...

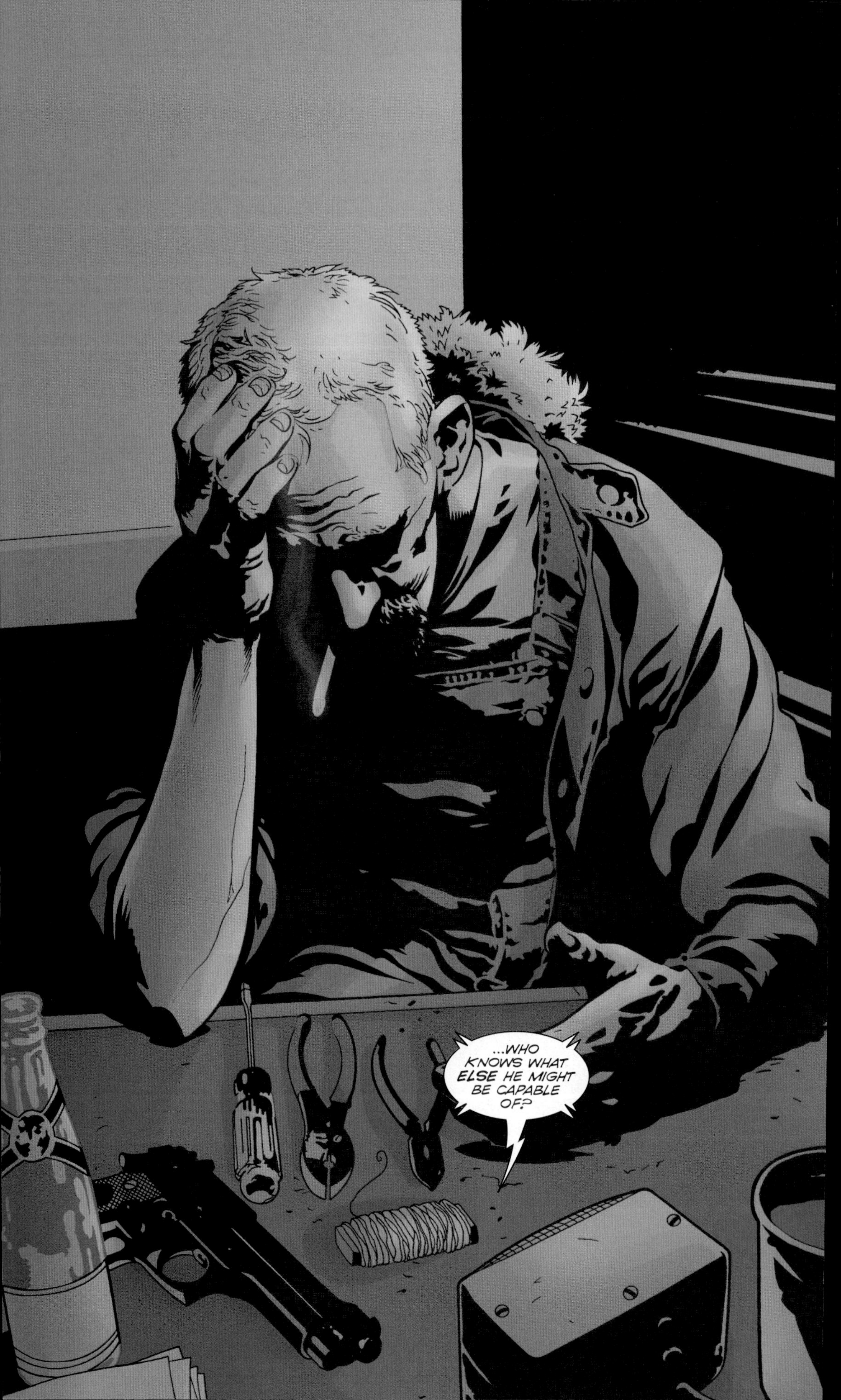
...WHO KNOWS WHAT ELSE HE MIGHT BE CAPABLE OF?

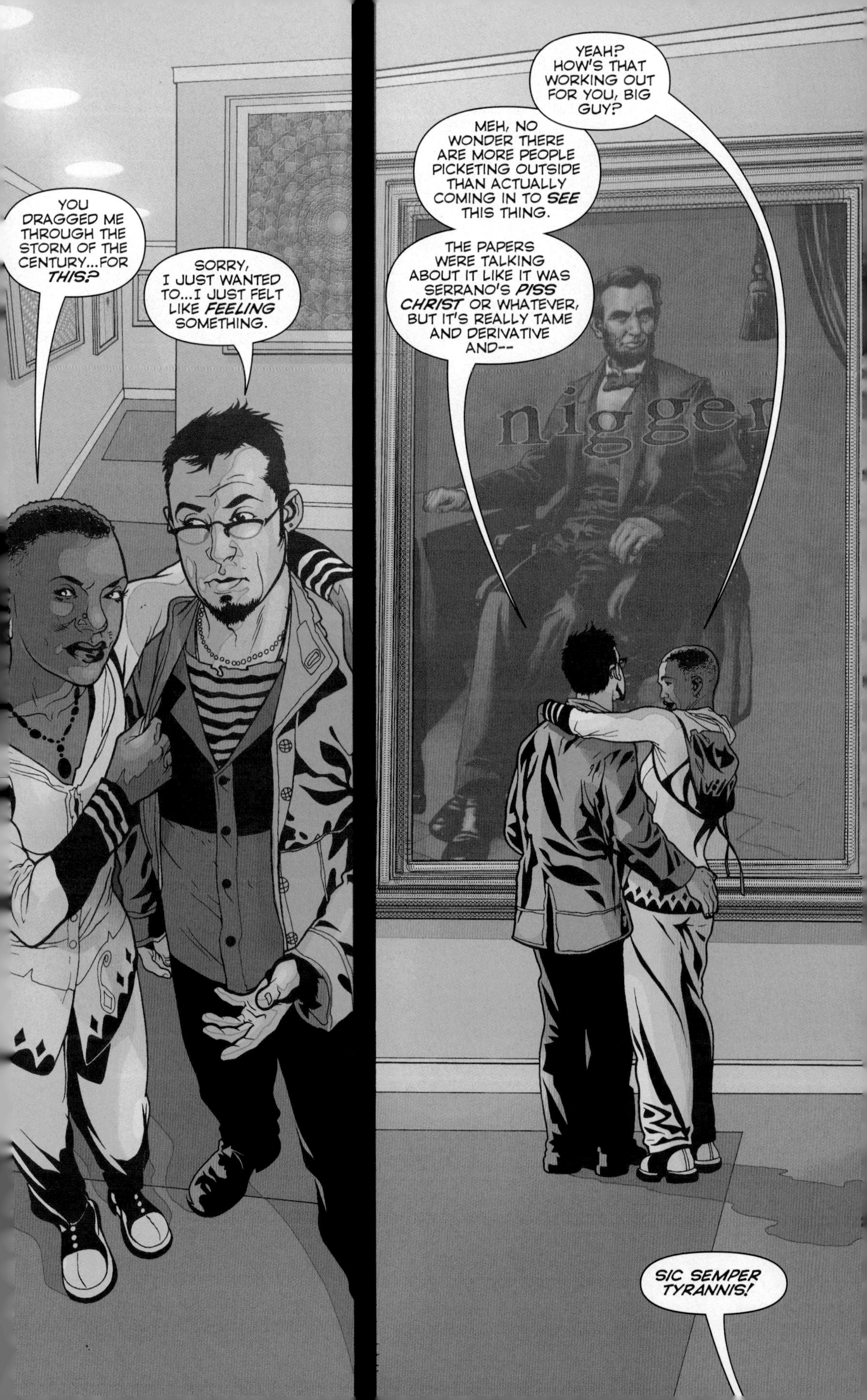

YOU DRAGGED ME THROUGH THE STORM OF THE CENTURY...FOR *THIS?*
SORRY, I JUST WANTED TO...I JUST FELT LIKE *FEELING* SOMETHING.
THE PAPERS WERE TALKING ABOUT IT LIKE IT WAS SERRANO'S *PISS CHRIST* OR WHATEVER, BUT IT'S REALLY TAME AND DERIVATIVE AND--
MEH, NO WONDER THERE ARE MORE PEOPLE PICKETING OUTSIDE THAN ACTUALLY COMING IN TO *SEE* THIS THING.
YEAH? HOW'S THAT WORKING OUT FOR YOU, BIG GUY?
nigger
SIC SEMPER TYRANNIS!

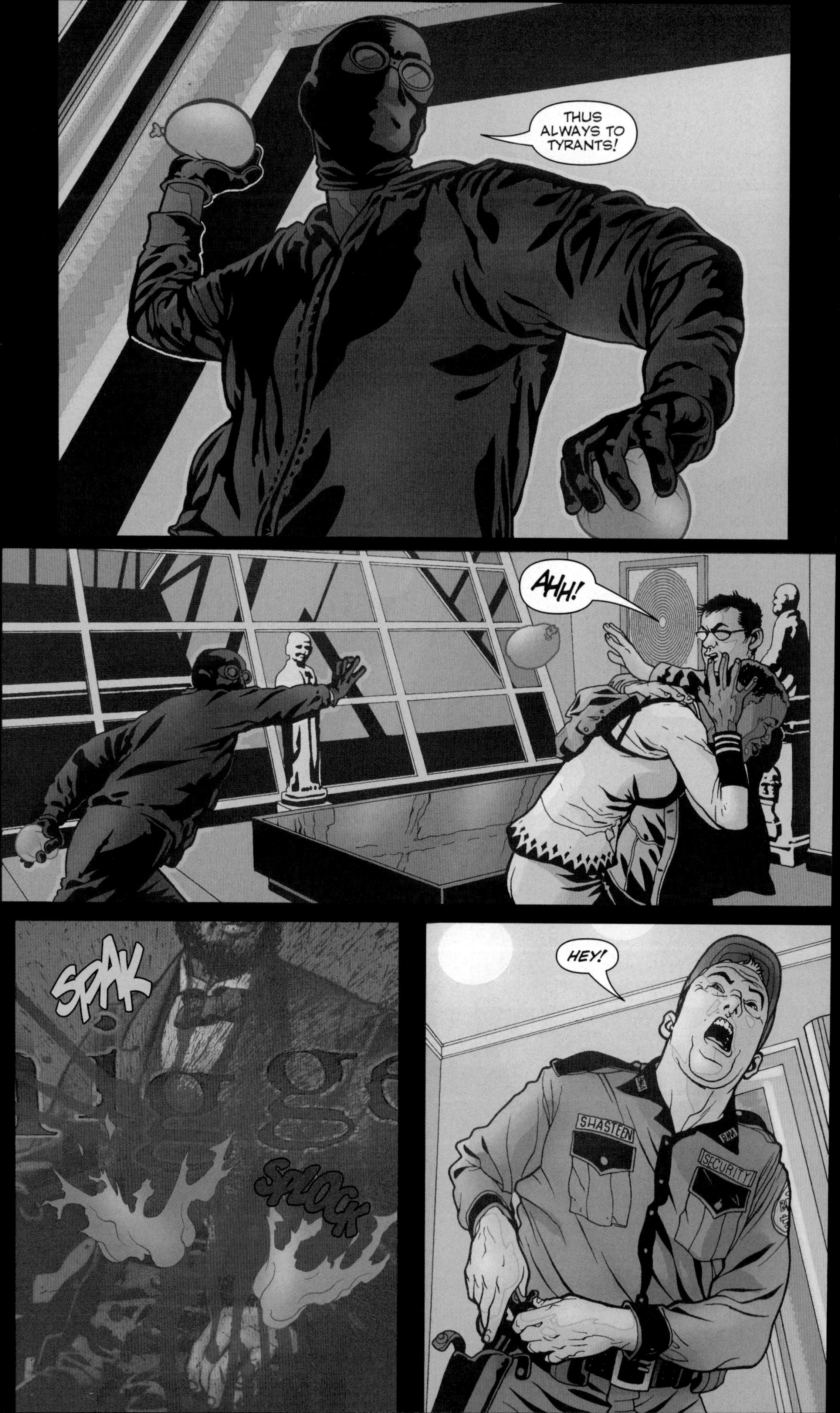
THUS ALWAYS TO TYRANTS!
AHH!
SPAK
SPLOCK
HEY!
SHASTEEN
SECURITY

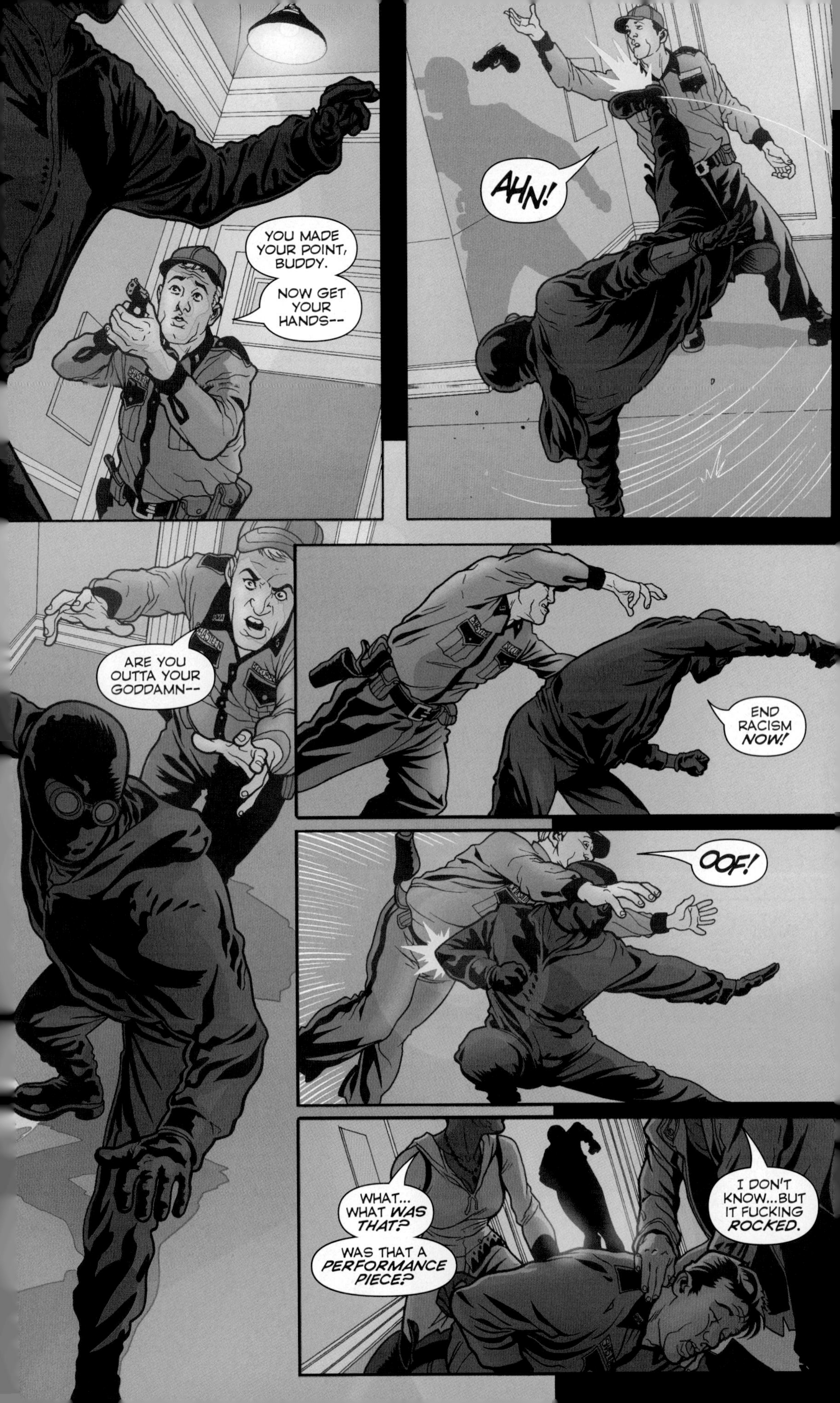
YOU MADE YOUR POINT, BUDDY.
NOW GET YOUR HANDS--
AHN!
ARE YOU OUTTA YOUR GODDAMN--
END RACISM NOW!
OOF!
WHAT... WHAT WAS THAT?
WAS THAT A PERFORMANCE PIECE?
I DON'T KNOW...BUT IT FUCKING ROCKED.

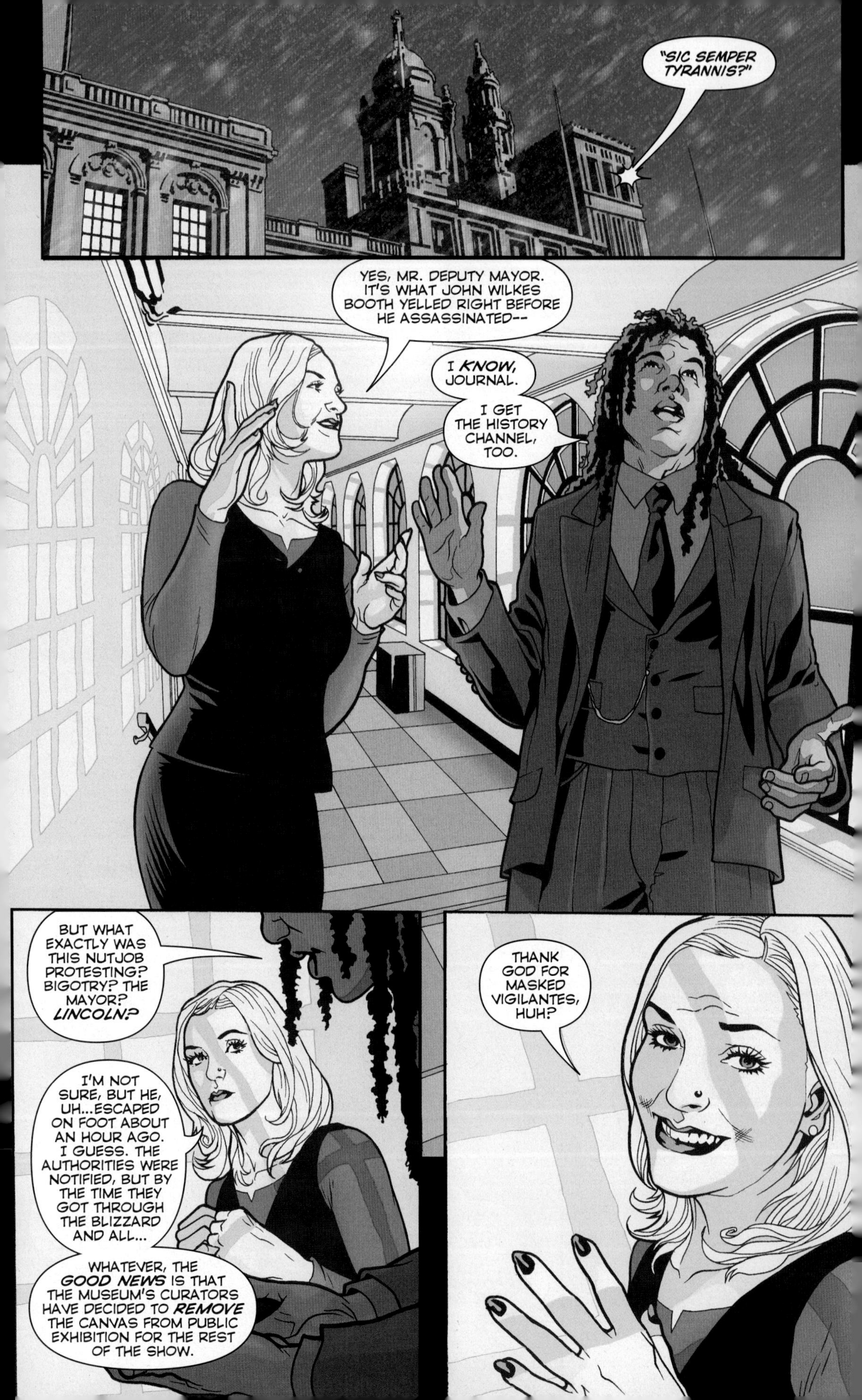
"SIC SEMPER TYRANNIS?"
YES, MR. DEPUTY MAYOR. IT'S WHAT JOHN WILKES BOOTH YELLED RIGHT BEFORE HE ASSASSINATED--
I KNOW, JOURNAL.
I GET THE HISTORY CHANNEL, TOO.
BUT WHAT EXACTLY WAS THIS NUTJOB PROTESTING? BIGOTRY? THE MAYOR? LINCOLN?
I'M NOT SURE, BUT HE, UH...ESCAPED ON FOOT ABOUT AN HOUR AGO. I GUESS. THE AUTHORITIES WERE NOTIFIED, BUT BY THE TIME THEY GOT THROUGH THE BLIZZARD AND ALL...
WHATEVER, THE GOOD NEWS IS THAT THE MUSEUM'S CURATORS HAVE DECIDED TO REMOVE THE CANVAS FROM PUBLIC EXHIBITION FOR THE REST OF THE SHOW.
THANK GOD FOR MASKED VIGILANTES, HUH?

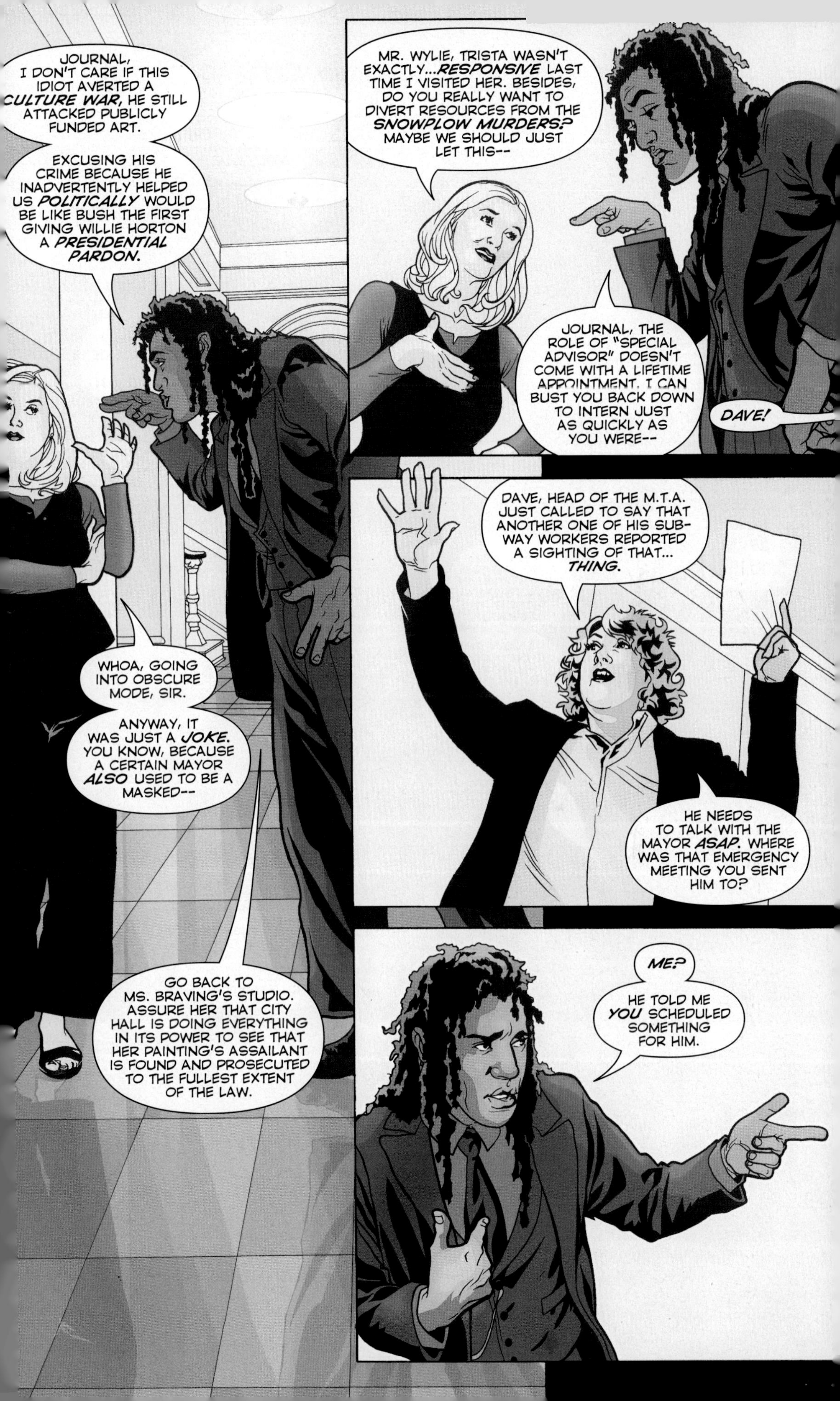

JOURNAL, I DON'T CARE IF THIS IDIOT AVERTED A *CULTURE WAR,* HE STILL ATTACKED PUBLICLY FUNDED ART.
EXCUSING HIS CRIME BECAUSE HE INADVERTENTLY HELPED US *POLITICALLY* WOULD BE LIKE BUSH THE FIRST GIVING WILLIE HORTON A *PRESIDENTIAL PARDON.*
WHOA, GOING INTO OBSCURE MODE, SIR.
ANYWAY, IT WAS JUST A *JOKE.* YOU KNOW, BECAUSE A CERTAIN MAYOR *ALSO* USED TO BE A MASKED--
GO BACK TO MS. BRAVING'S STUDIO. ASSURE HER THAT CITY HALL IS DOING EVERYTHING IN ITS POWER TO SEE THAT HER PAINTING'S ASSAILANT IS FOUND AND PROSECUTED TO THE FULLEST EXTENT OF THE LAW.
MR. WYLIE, TRISTA WASN'T EXACTLY...*RESPONSIVE* LAST TIME I VISITED HER. BESIDES, DO YOU REALLY WANT TO DIVERT RESOURCES FROM THE *SNOWPLOW MURDERS?* MAYBE WE SHOULD JUST LET THIS--
JOURNAL, THE ROLE OF "SPECIAL ADVISOR" DOESN'T COME WITH A LIFETIME APPOINTMENT. I CAN BUST YOU BACK DOWN TO INTERN JUST AS QUICKLY AS YOU WERE--
DAVE!
DAVE, HEAD OF THE M.T.A. JUST CALLED TO SAY THAT ANOTHER ONE OF HIS SUBWAY WORKERS REPORTED A SIGHTING OF THAT... *THING.*
HE NEEDS TO TALK WITH THE MAYOR *ASAP.* WHERE WAS THAT EMERGENCY MEETING YOU SENT HIM TO?
ME?
HE TOLD ME *YOU* SCHEDULED SOMETHING FOR HIM.

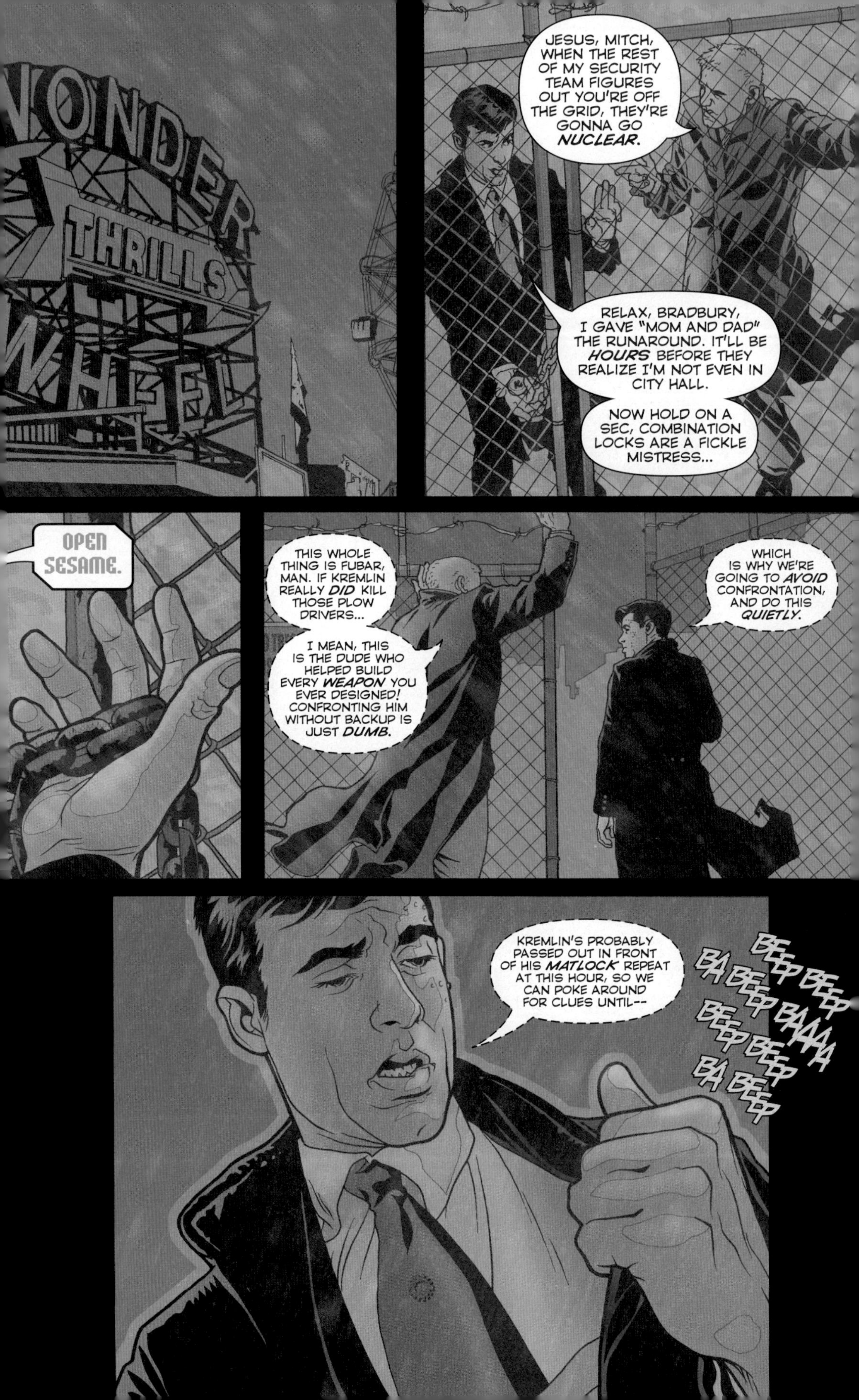
WONDER
THRILLS
WHEEL
JESUS, MITCH, WHEN THE REST OF MY SECURITY TEAM FIGURES OUT YOU'RE OFF THE GRID, THEY'RE GONNA GO NUCLEAR.
RELAX, BRADBURY, I GAVE "MOM AND DAD" THE RUNAROUND. IT'LL BE HOURS BEFORE THEY REALIZE I'M NOT EVEN IN CITY HALL.
NOW HOLD ON A SEC, COMBINATION LOCKS ARE A FICKLE MISTRESS...
OPEN SESAME.
THIS WHOLE THING IS FUBAR, MAN. IF KREMLIN REALLY DID KILL THOSE PLOW DRIVERS...
I MEAN, THIS IS THE DUDE WHO HELPED BUILD EVERY WEAPON YOU EVER DESIGNED! CONFRONTING HIM WITHOUT BACKUP IS JUST DUMB.
WHICH IS WHY WE'RE GOING TO AVOID CONFRONTATION, AND DO THIS QUIETLY.
KREMLIN'S PROBABLY PASSED OUT IN FRONT OF HIS MATLOCK REPEAT AT THIS HOUR, SO WE CAN POKE AROUND FOR CLUES UNTIL--
BEEP BEEP
BA BEEP BAAAA
BEEP BEEP
BA BEEP

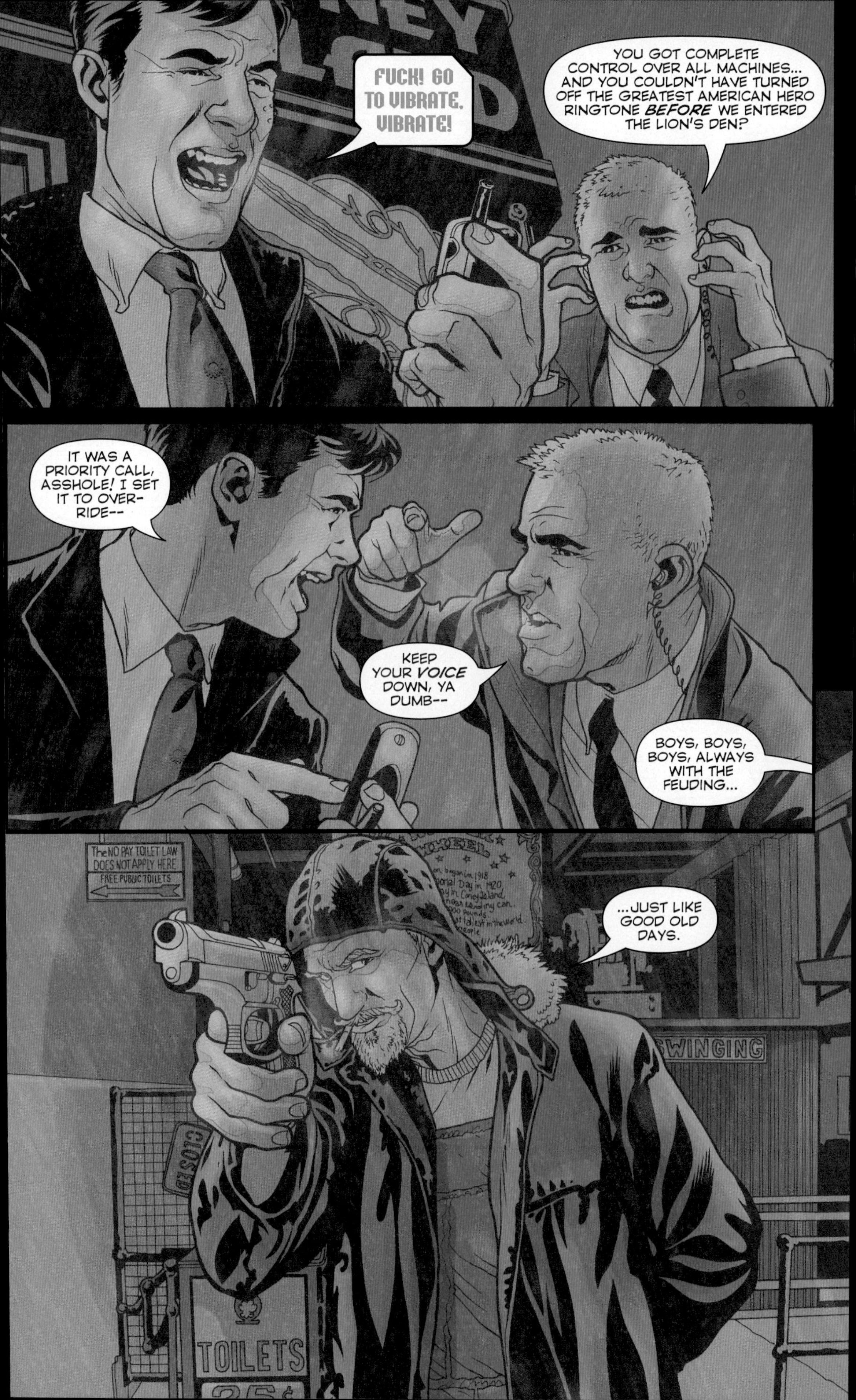
FUCK! GO TO VIBRATE. VIBRATE!
YOU GOT COMPLETE CONTROL OVER ALL MACHINES... AND YOU COULDN'T HAVE TURNED OFF THE GREATEST AMERICAN HERO RINGTONE *BEFORE* WE ENTERED THE LION'S DEN?
IT WAS A PRIORITY CALL, ASSHOLE! I SET IT TO OVER-RIDE--
KEEP YOUR *VOICE* DOWN, YA DUMB--
BOYS, BOYS, BOYS, ALWAYS WITH THE FEUDING...
The NO PAY TOILET LAW DOES NOT APPLY HERE
FREE PUBLIC TOILETS
...JUST LIKE GOOD OLD DAYS.
SWINGING
CLOSED
TOILETS

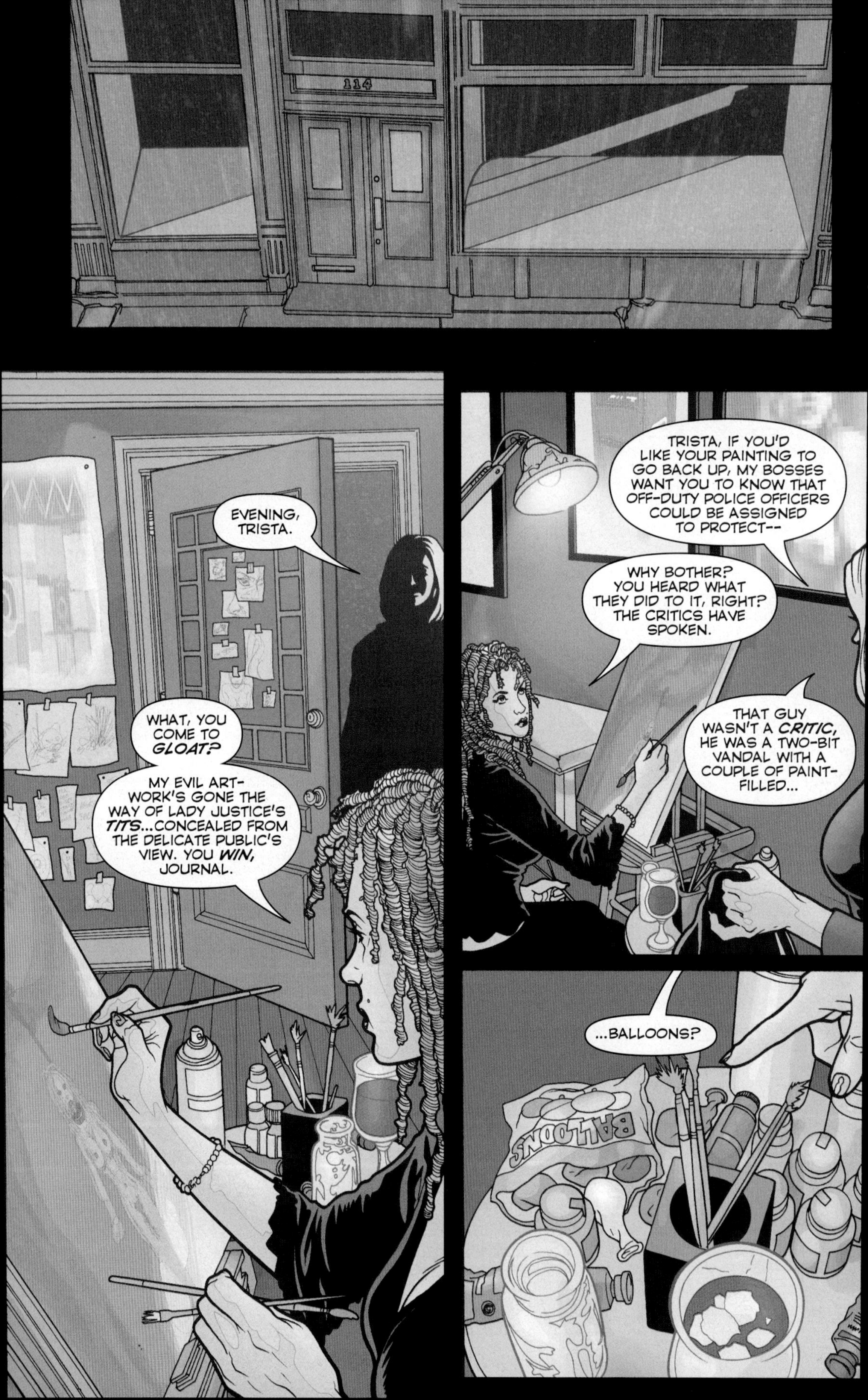
114
EVENING, TRISTA.
WHAT, YOU COME TO GLOAT?
MY EVIL ART-WORK'S GONE THE WAY OF LADY JUSTICE'S TITS...CONCEALED FROM THE DELICATE PUBLIC'S VIEW. YOU WIN, JOURNAL.
TRISTA, IF YOU'D LIKE YOUR PAINTING TO GO BACK UP, MY BOSSES WANT YOU TO KNOW THAT OFF-DUTY POLICE OFFICERS COULD BE ASSIGNED TO PROTECT--
WHY BOTHER? YOU HEARD WHAT THEY DID TO IT, RIGHT? THE CRITICS HAVE SPOKEN.
THAT GUY WASN'T A CRITIC, HE WAS A TWO-BIT VANDAL WITH A COUPLE OF PAINT-FILLED...
...BALLOONS?
BALLOONS

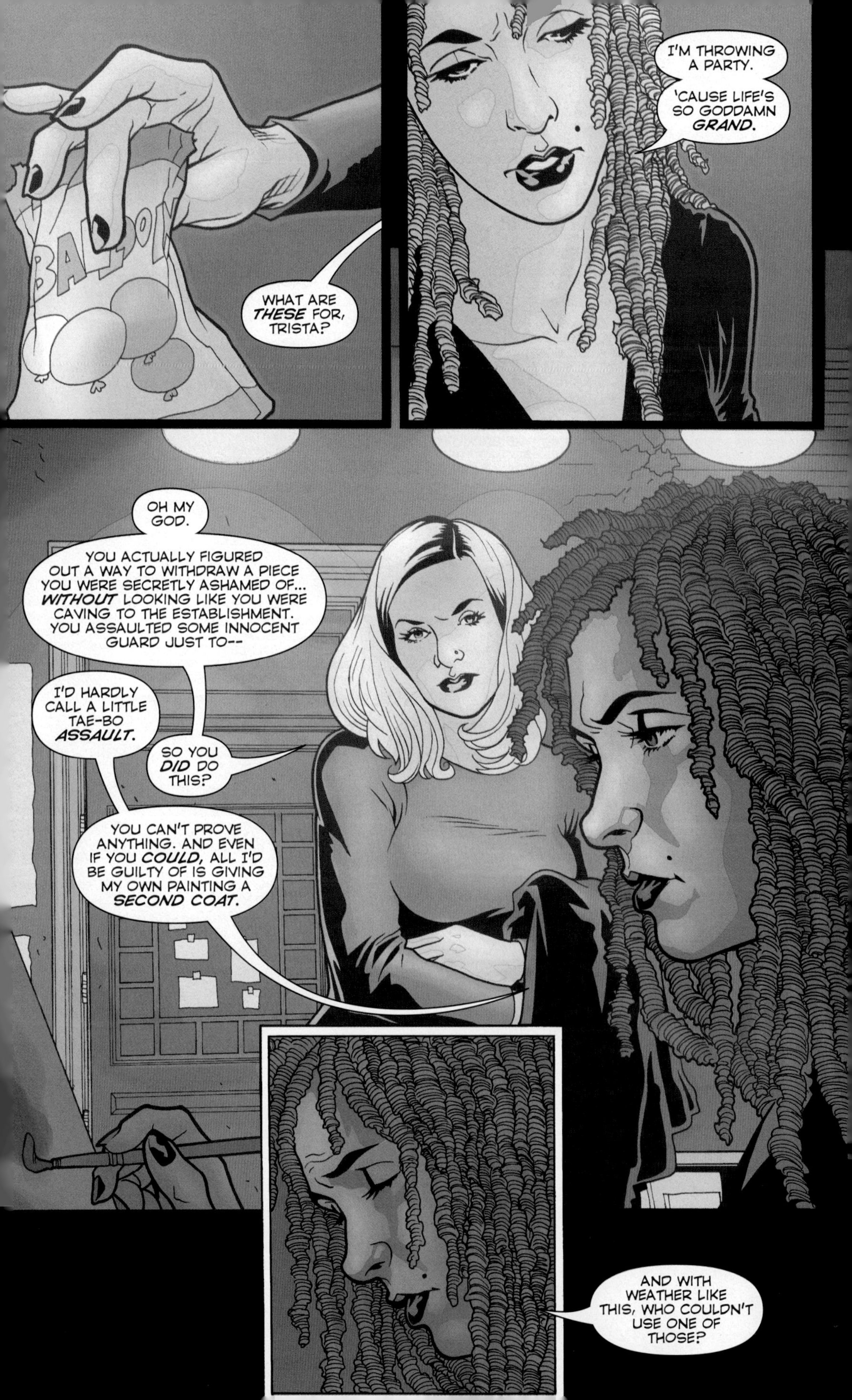
WHAT ARE THESE FOR, TRISTA?
I'M THROWING A PARTY.
'CAUSE LIFE'S SO GODDAMN GRAND.
OH MY GOD.
YOU ACTUALLY FIGURED OUT A WAY TO WITHDRAW A PIECE YOU WERE SECRETLY ASHAMED OF... WITHOUT LOOKING LIKE YOU WERE CAVING TO THE ESTABLISHMENT. YOU ASSAULTED SOME INNOCENT GUARD JUST TO--
I'D HARDLY CALL A LITTLE TAE-BO ASSAULT.
SO YOU DID DO THIS?
YOU CAN'T PROVE ANYTHING. AND EVEN IF YOU COULD, ALL I'D BE GUILTY OF IS GIVING MY OWN PAINTING A SECOND COAT.
AND WITH WEATHER LIKE THIS, WHO COULDN'T USE ONE OF THOSE?

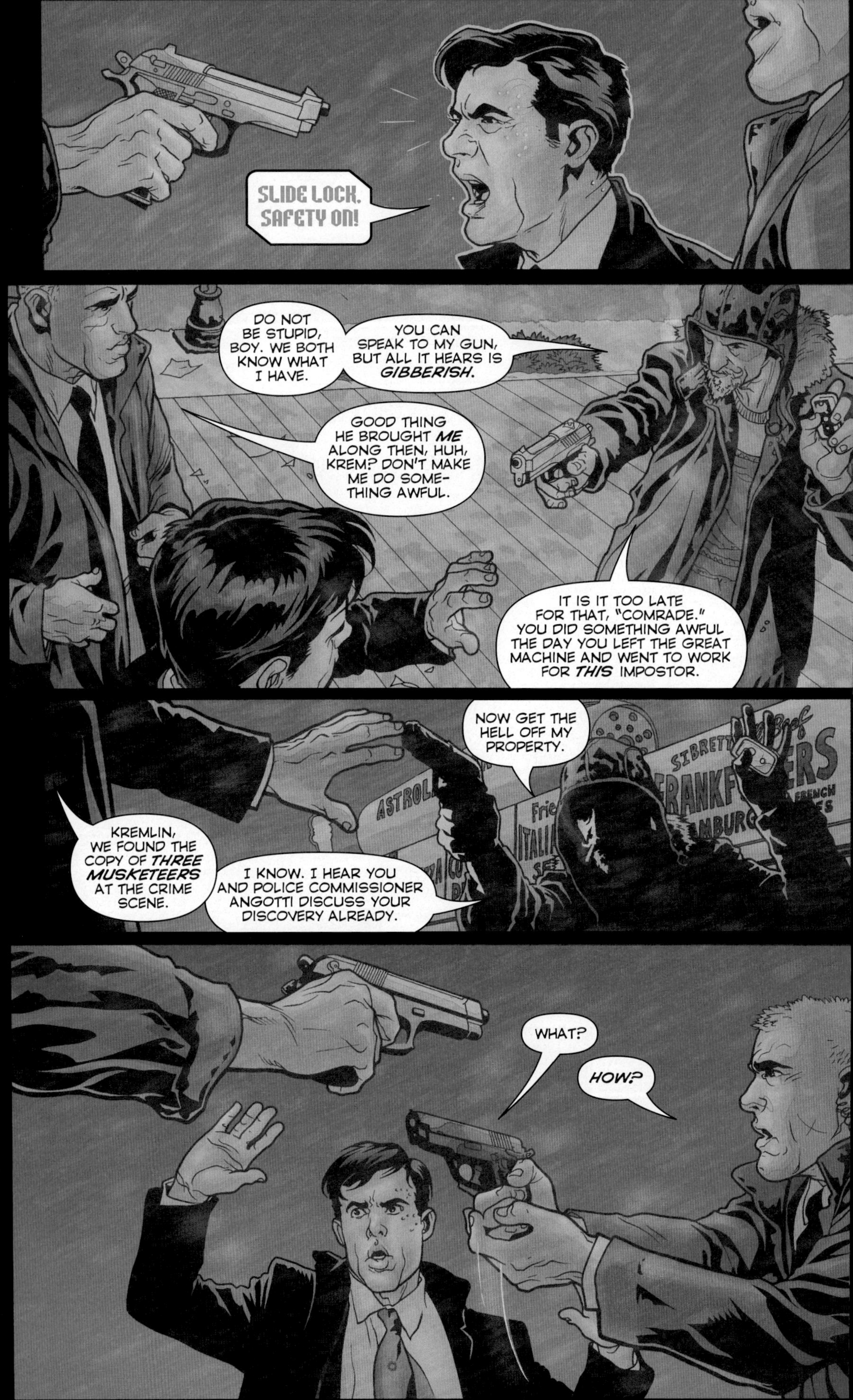
SLIDE LOCK. SAFETY ON!
DO NOT BE STUPID, BOY. WE BOTH KNOW WHAT I HAVE.
YOU CAN SPEAK TO MY GUN, BUT ALL IT HEARS IS *GIBBERISH.*
GOOD THING HE BROUGHT *ME* ALONG THEN, HUH, KREM? DON'T MAKE ME DO SOME-THING AWFUL.
IT IS IT TOO LATE FOR THAT, "COMRADE." YOU DID SOMETHING AWFUL THE DAY YOU LEFT THE GREAT MACHINE AND WENT TO WORK FOR *THIS* IMPOSTOR.
NOW GET THE HELL OFF MY PROPERTY.
KREMLIN, WE FOUND THE COPY OF *THREE MUSKETEERS* AT THE CRIME SCENE.
I KNOW. I HEAR YOU AND POLICE COMMISSIONER ANGOTTI DISCUSS YOUR DISCOVERY ALREADY.
WHAT?
HOW?

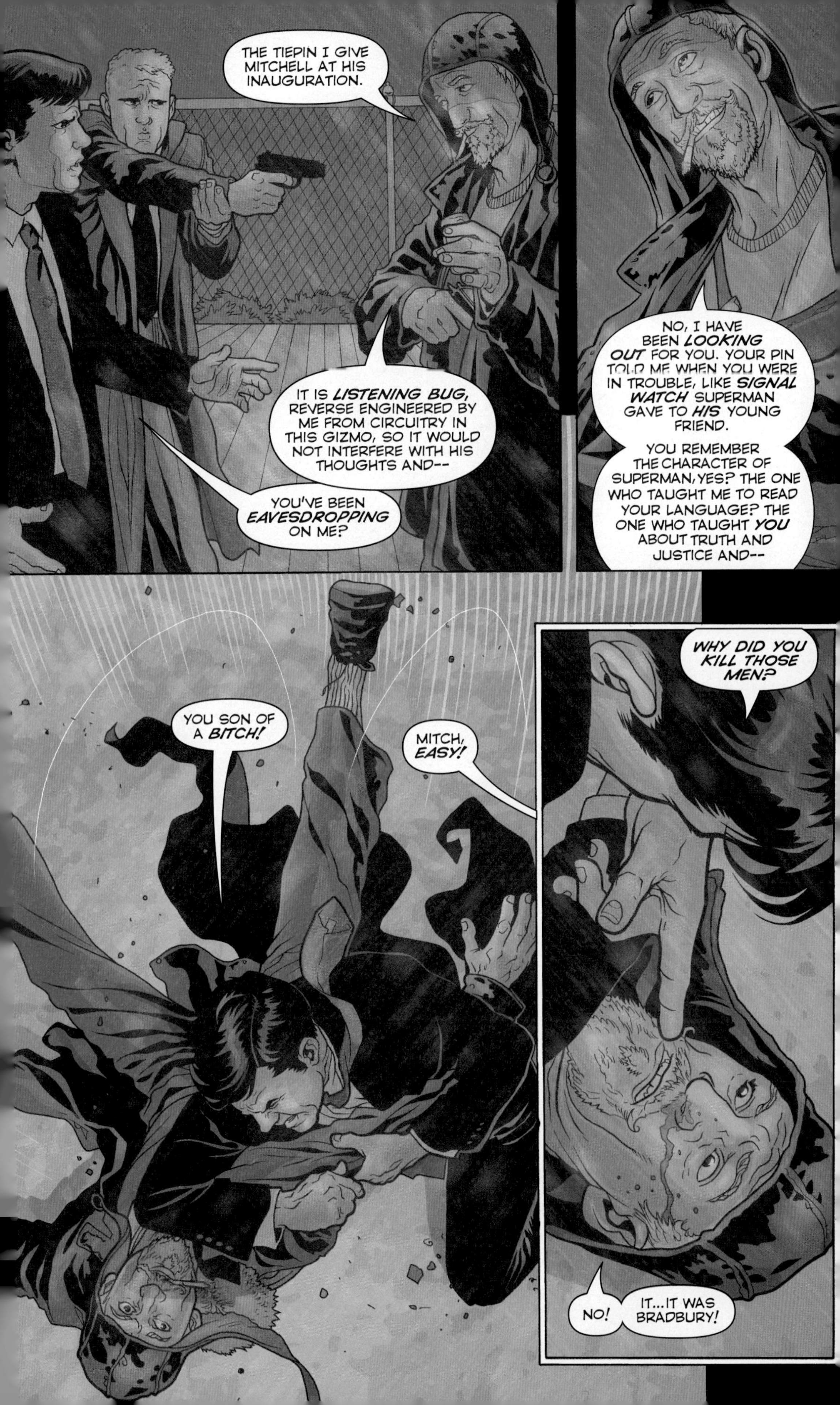
THE TIEPIN I GIVE MITCHELL AT HIS INAUGURATION.
IT IS *LISTENING BUG,* REVERSE ENGINEERED BY ME FROM CIRCUITRY IN THIS GIZMO, SO IT WOULD NOT INTERFERE WITH HIS THOUGHTS AND--
YOU'VE BEEN *EAVESDROPPING* ON ME?
NO, I HAVE BEEN *LOOKING OUT* FOR YOU. YOUR PIN TOLD ME WHEN YOU WERE IN TROUBLE, LIKE *SIGNAL WATCH* SUPERMAN GAVE TO *HIS* YOUNG FRIEND.
YOU REMEMBER THE CHARACTER OF SUPERMAN, YES? THE ONE WHO TAUGHT ME TO READ YOUR LANGUAGE? THE ONE WHO TAUGHT *YOU* ABOUT TRUTH AND JUSTICE AND--
YOU SON OF A *BITCH!*
MITCH, *EASY!*
WHY DID YOU KILL THOSE MEN?
NO!
IT...IT WAS BRADBURY!

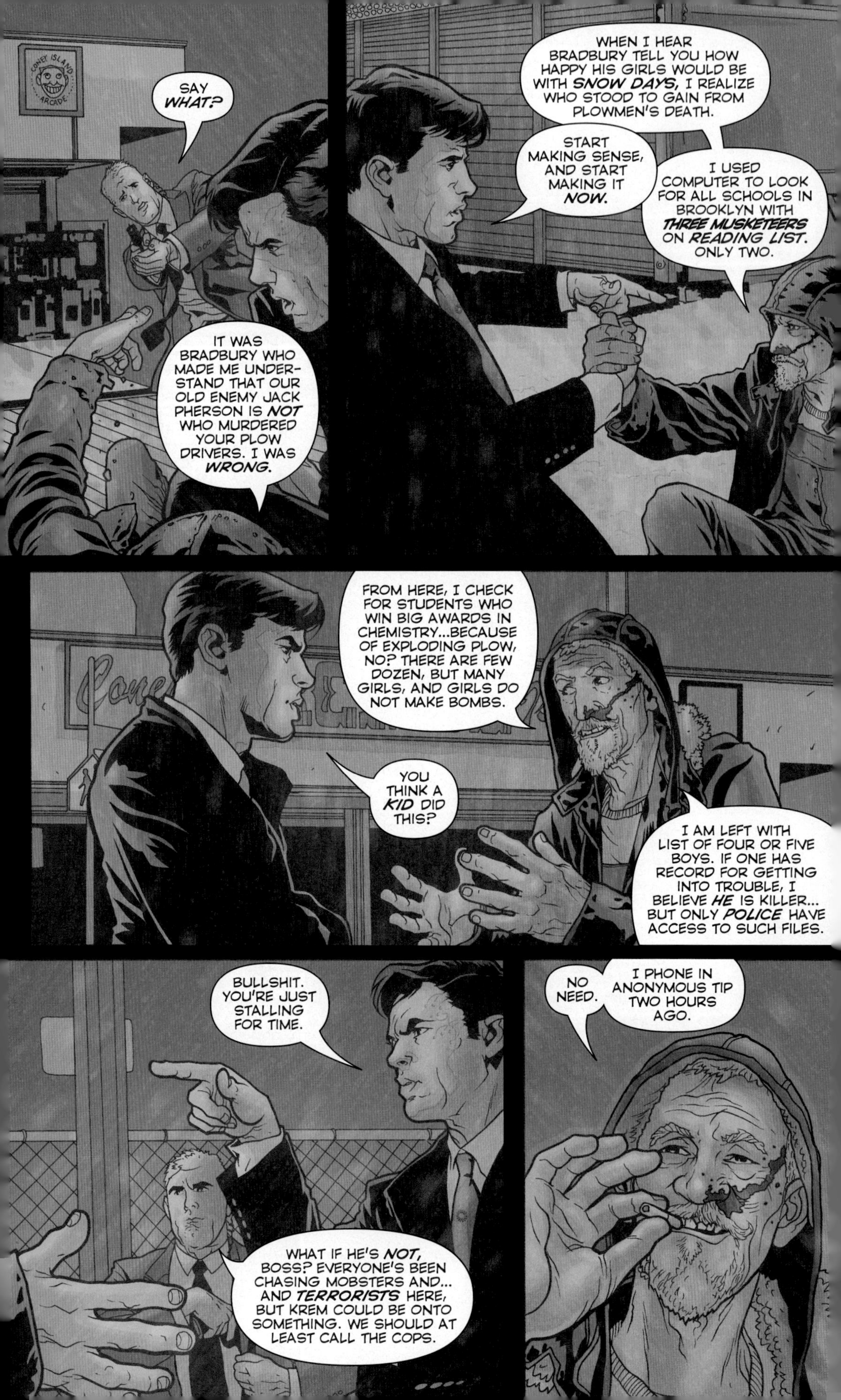

SAY *WHAT?*
IT WAS BRADBURY WHO MADE ME UNDER-STAND THAT OUR OLD ENEMY JACK PHERSON IS *NOT* WHO MURDERED YOUR PLOW DRIVERS. I WAS *WRONG.*
WHEN I HEAR BRADBURY TELL YOU HOW HAPPY HIS GIRLS WOULD BE WITH *SNOW DAYS,* I REALIZE WHO STOOD TO GAIN FROM PLOWMEN'S DEATH.
START MAKING SENSE, AND START MAKING IT *NOW.*
I USED COMPUTER TO LOOK FOR ALL SCHOOLS IN BROOKLYN WITH *THREE MUSKETEERS* ON *READING LIST.* ONLY TWO.
FROM HERE, I CHECK FOR STUDENTS WHO WIN BIG AWARDS IN CHEMISTRY...BECAUSE OF EXPLODING PLOW, NO? THERE ARE FEW DOZEN, BUT MANY GIRLS, AND GIRLS DO NOT MAKE BOMBS.
YOU THINK A *KID* DID THIS?
I AM LEFT WITH LIST OF FOUR OR FIVE BOYS. IF ONE HAS RECORD FOR GETTING INTO TROUBLE, I BELIEVE *HE* IS KILLER... BUT ONLY *POLICE* HAVE ACCESS TO SUCH FILES.
BULLSHIT. YOU'RE JUST STALLING FOR TIME.
WHAT IF HE'S *NOT,* BOSS? EVERYONE'S BEEN CHASING MOBSTERS AND... AND *TERRORISTS* HERE, BUT KREM COULD BE ONTO SOMETHING. WE SHOULD AT LEAST CALL THE COPS.
NO NEED.
I PHONE IN ANONYMOUS TIP TWO HOURS AGO.

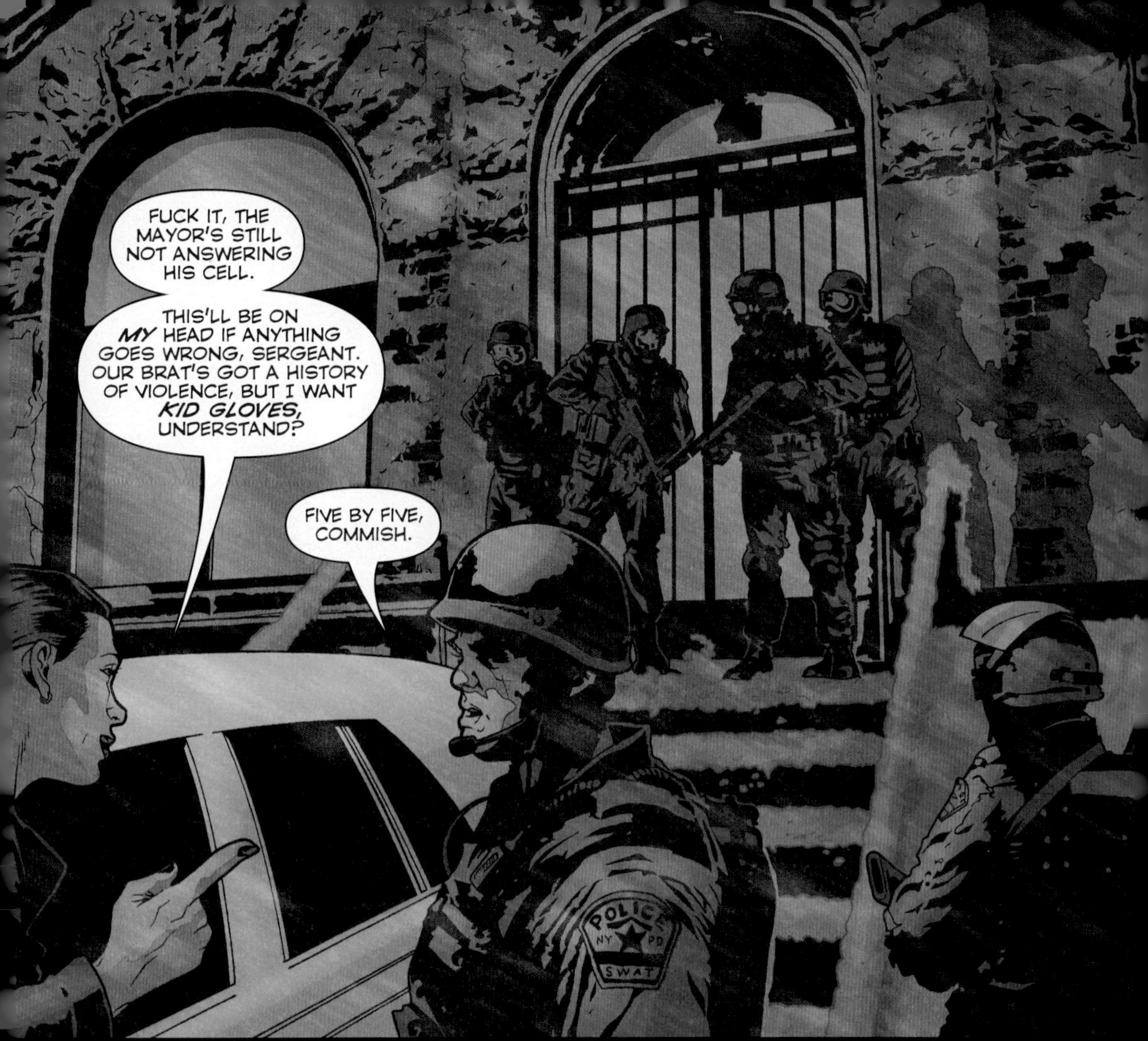
FUCK IT, THE MAYOR'S STILL NOT ANSWERING HIS CELL.
THIS'LL BE ON *MY* HEAD IF ANYTHING GOES WRONG, SERGEANT. OUR BRAT'S GOT A HISTORY OF VIOLENCE, BUT I WANT *KID GLOVES*, UNDERSTAND?
FIVE BY FIVE, COMMISH.
POLICE NY PD SWAT
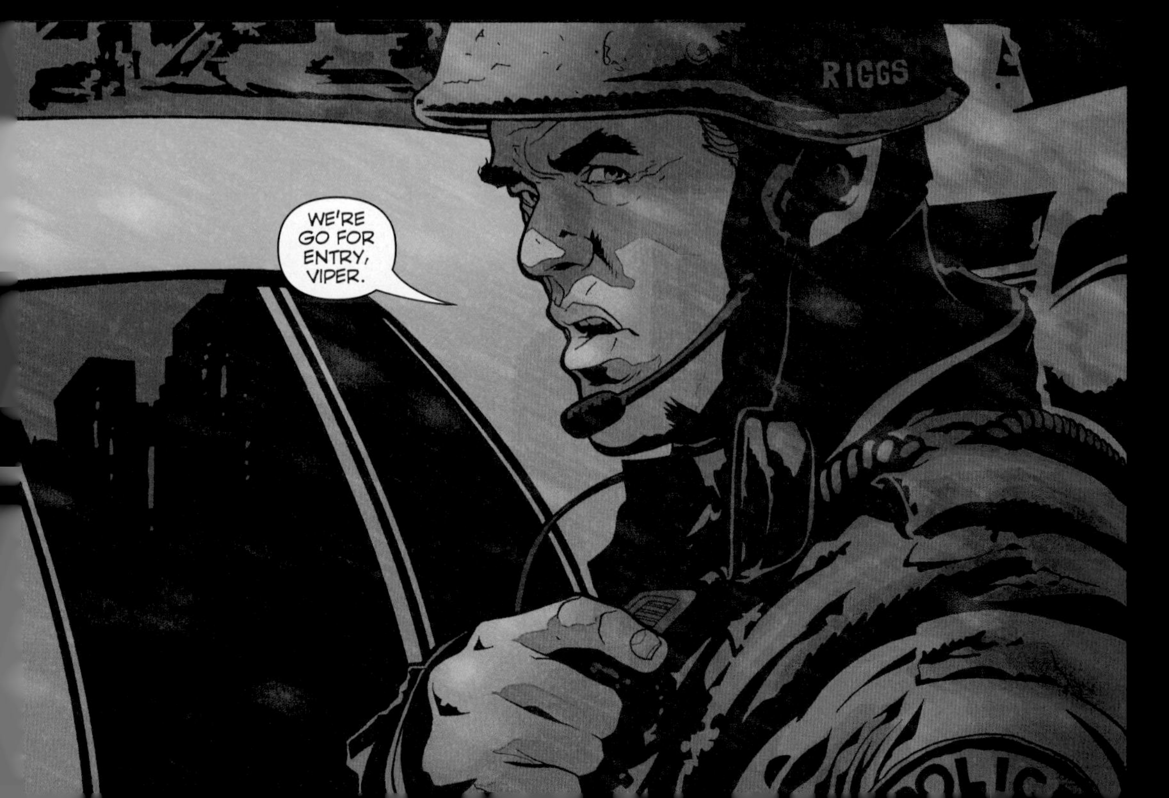
RIGGS
WE'RE GO FOR ENTRY, VIPER.

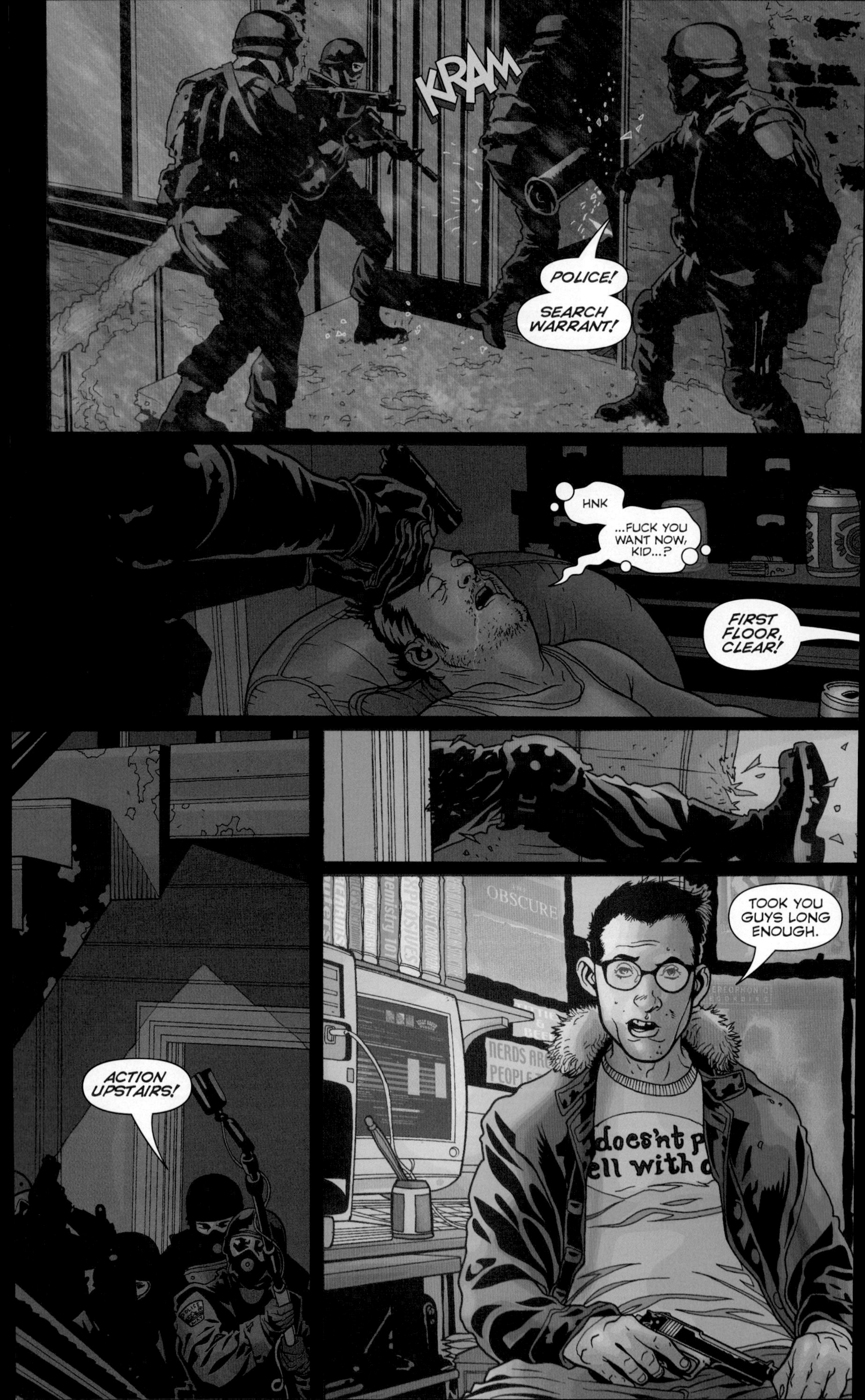
KRAM
POLICE!
SEARCH WARRANT!
HNK
...FUCK YOU WANT NOW, KID...?
FIRST FLOOR, CLEAR!
ACTION UPSTAIRS!
TOOK YOU GUYS LONG ENOUGH.

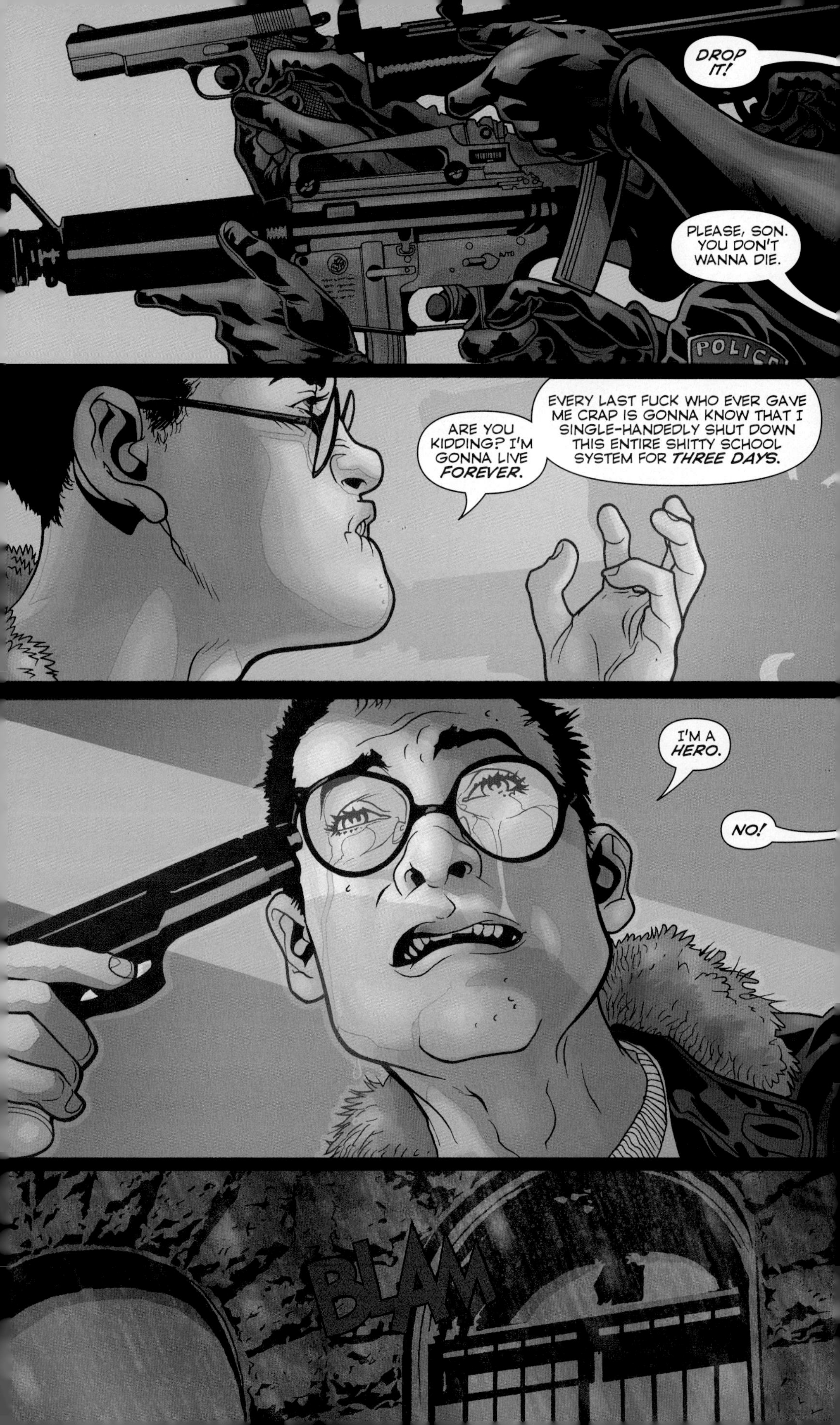
DROP IT!
PLEASE, SON. YOU DON'T WANNA DIE.
POLICE
ARE YOU KIDDING? I'M GONNA LIVE *FOREVER*.
EVERY LAST FUCK WHO EVER GAVE ME CRAP IS GONNA KNOW THAT I SINGLE-HANDEDLY SHUT DOWN THIS ENTIRE SHITTY SCHOOL SYSTEM FOR *THREE DAYS*.
I'M A *HERO*.
NO!
BLAM

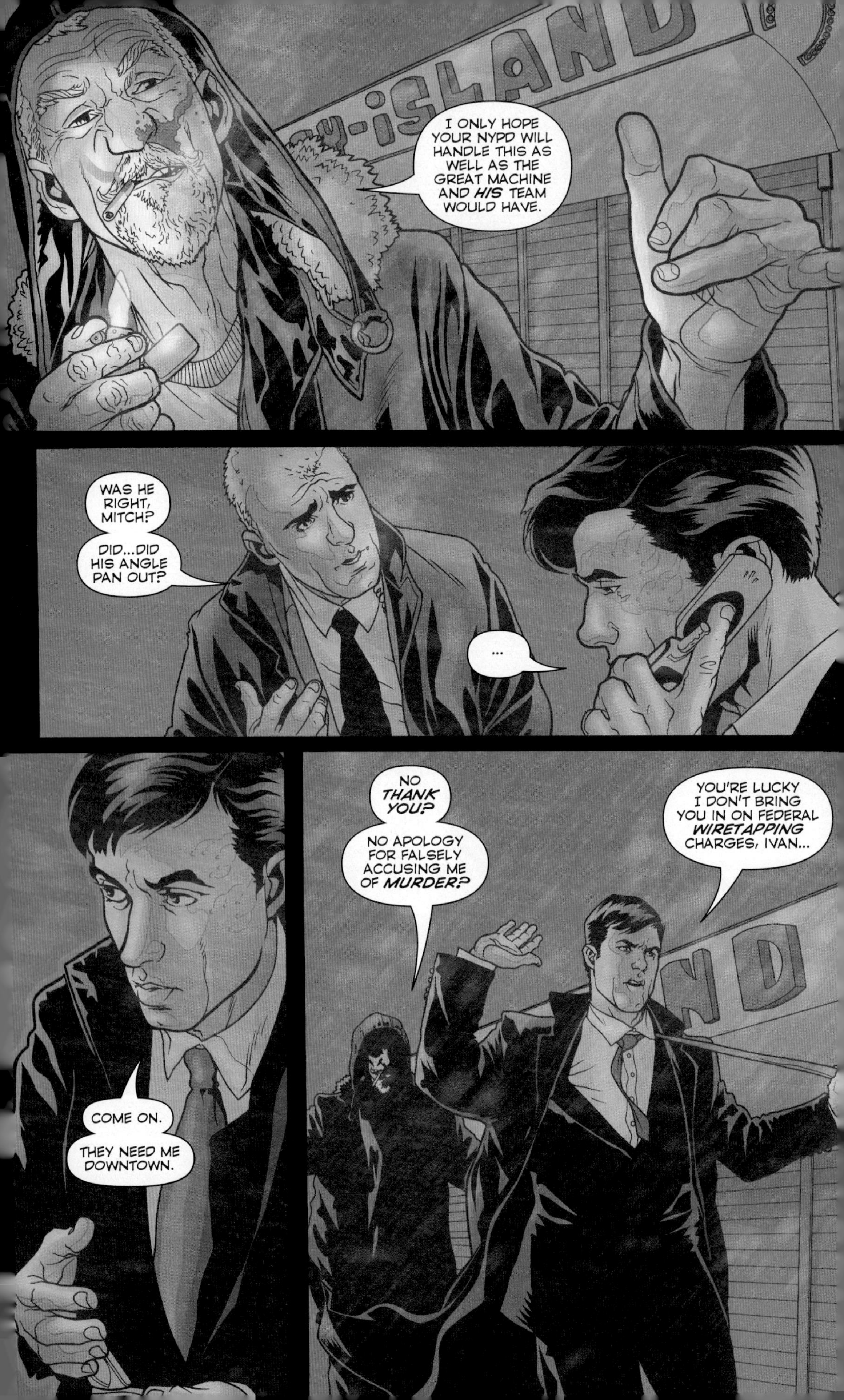

I ONLY HOPE YOUR NYPD WILL HANDLE THIS AS WELL AS THE GREAT MACHINE AND *HIS* TEAM WOULD HAVE.
WAS HE RIGHT, MITCH?
DID...DID HIS ANGLE PAN OUT?
...
COME ON.
THEY NEED ME DOWNTOWN.
NO *THANK YOU?*
NO APOLOGY FOR FALSELY ACCUSING ME OF *MURDER?*
YOU'RE LUCKY I DON'T BRING YOU IN ON FEDERAL *WIRETAPPING* CHARGES, IVAN...

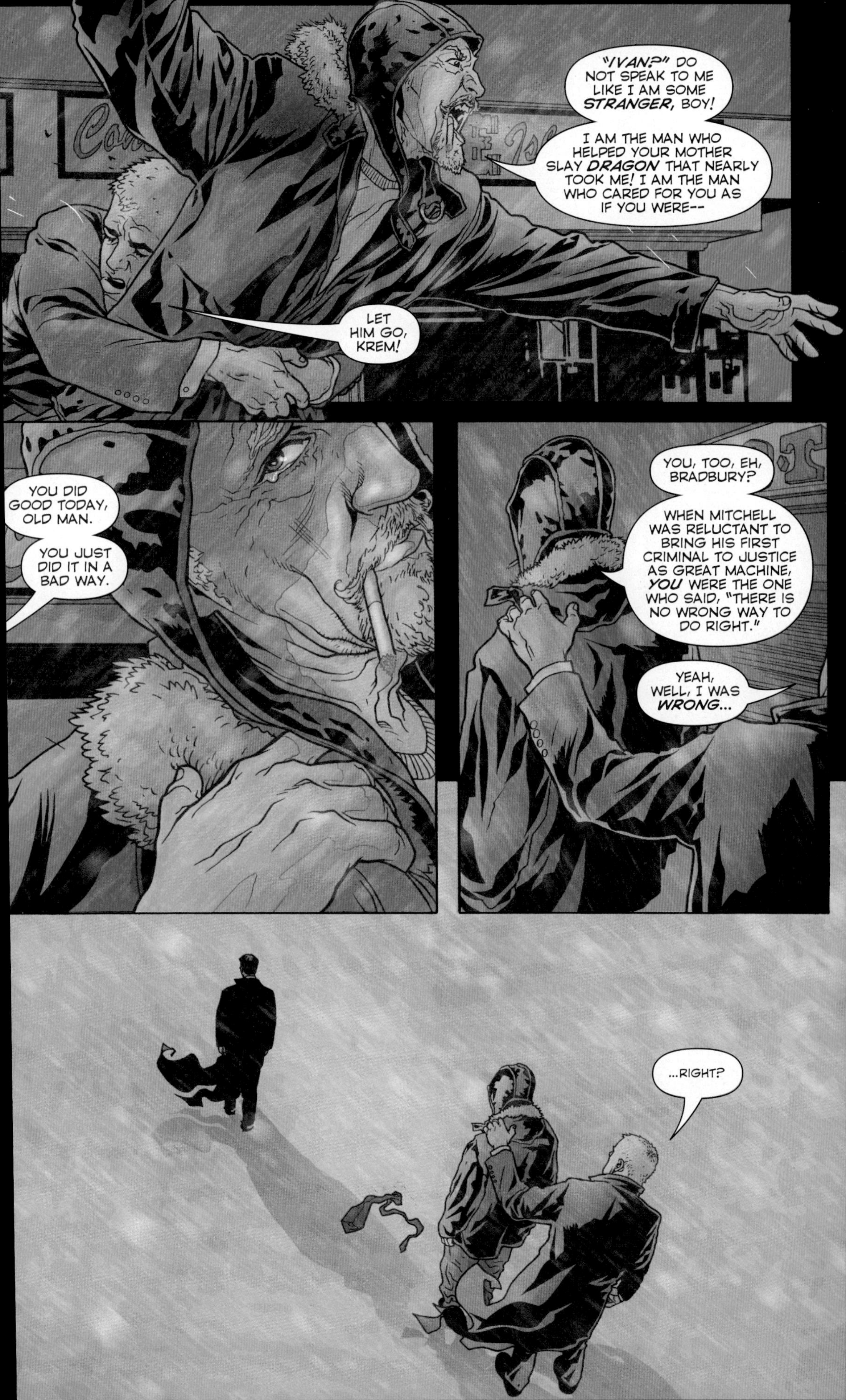
"IVAN?" DO NOT SPEAK TO ME LIKE I AM SOME STRANGER, BOY!
I AM THE MAN WHO HELPED YOUR MOTHER SLAY DRAGON THAT NEARLY TOOK ME! I AM THE MAN WHO CARED FOR YOU AS IF YOU WERE--
LET HIM GO, KREM!
YOU DID GOOD TODAY, OLD MAN.
YOU JUST DID IT IN A BAD WAY.
YOU, TOO, EH, BRADBURY?
WHEN MITCHELL WAS RELUCTANT TO BRING HIS FIRST CRIMINAL TO JUSTICE AS GREAT MACHINE, YOU WERE THE ONE WHO SAID, "THERE IS NO WRONG WAY TO DO RIGHT."
YEAH, WELL, I WAS WRONG...
...RIGHT?

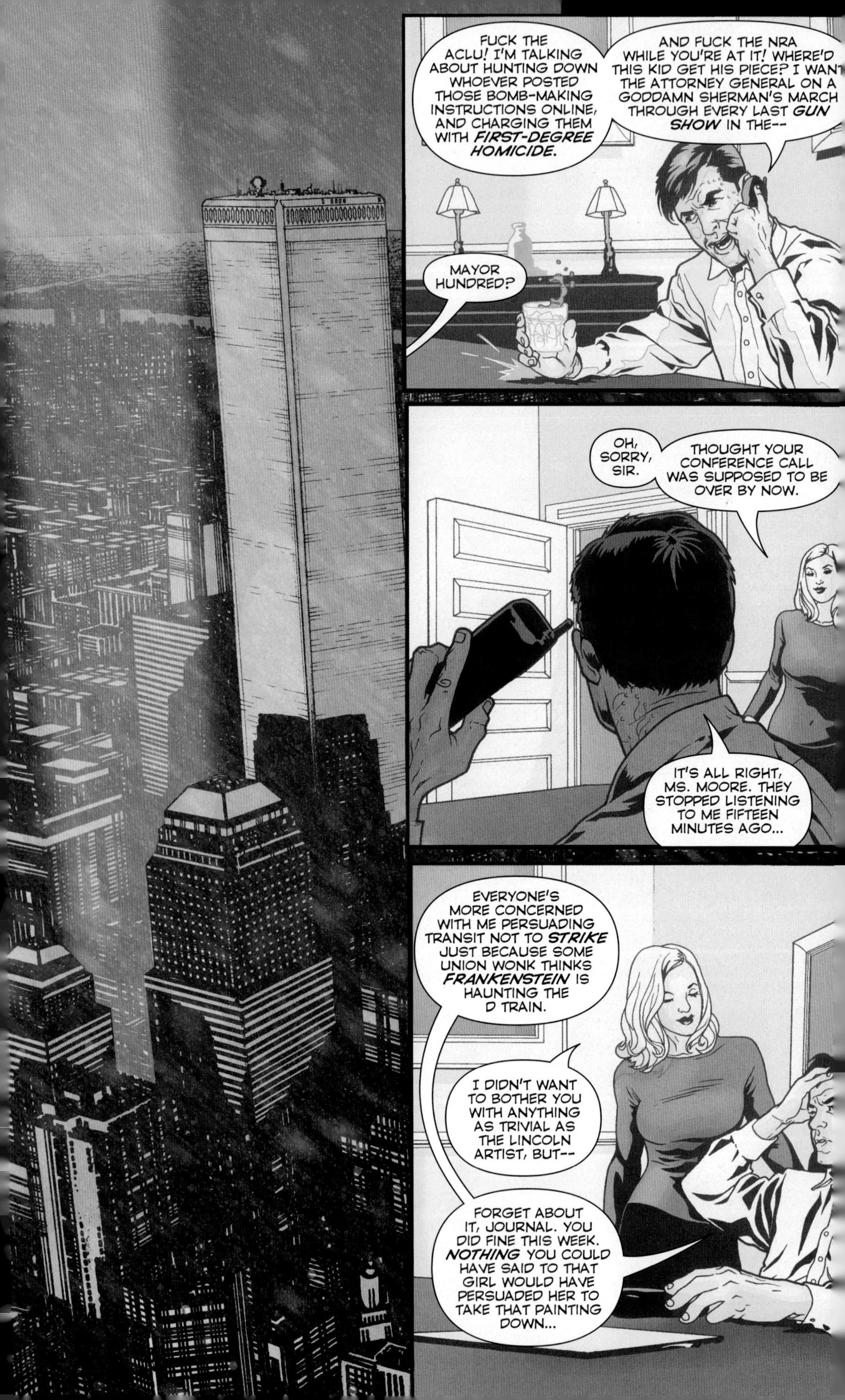
FUCK THE ACLU! I'M TALKING ABOUT HUNTING DOWN WHOEVER POSTED THOSE BOMB-MAKING INSTRUCTIONS ONLINE, AND CHARGING THEM WITH FIRST-DEGREE HOMICIDE.
AND FUCK THE NRA WHILE YOU'RE AT IT! WHERE'D THIS KID GET HIS PIECE? I WANT THE ATTORNEY GENERAL ON A GODDAMN SHERMAN'S MARCH THROUGH EVERY LAST GUN SHOW IN THE--
MAYOR HUNDRED?
OH, SORRY, SIR.
THOUGHT YOUR CONFERENCE CALL WAS SUPPOSED TO BE OVER BY NOW.
IT'S ALL RIGHT, MS. MOORE. THEY STOPPED LISTENING TO ME FIFTEEN MINUTES AGO...
EVERYONE'S MORE CONCERNED WITH ME PERSUADING TRANSIT NOT TO STRIKE JUST BECAUSE SOME UNION WONK THINKS FRANKENSTEIN IS HAUNTING THE D TRAIN.
I DIDN'T WANT TO BOTHER YOU WITH ANYTHING AS TRIVIAL AS THE LINCOLN ARTIST, BUT--
FORGET ABOUT IT, JOURNAL. YOU DID FINE THIS WEEK. NOTHING YOU COULD HAVE SAID TO THAT GIRL WOULD HAVE PERSUADED HER TO TAKE THAT PAINTING DOWN...

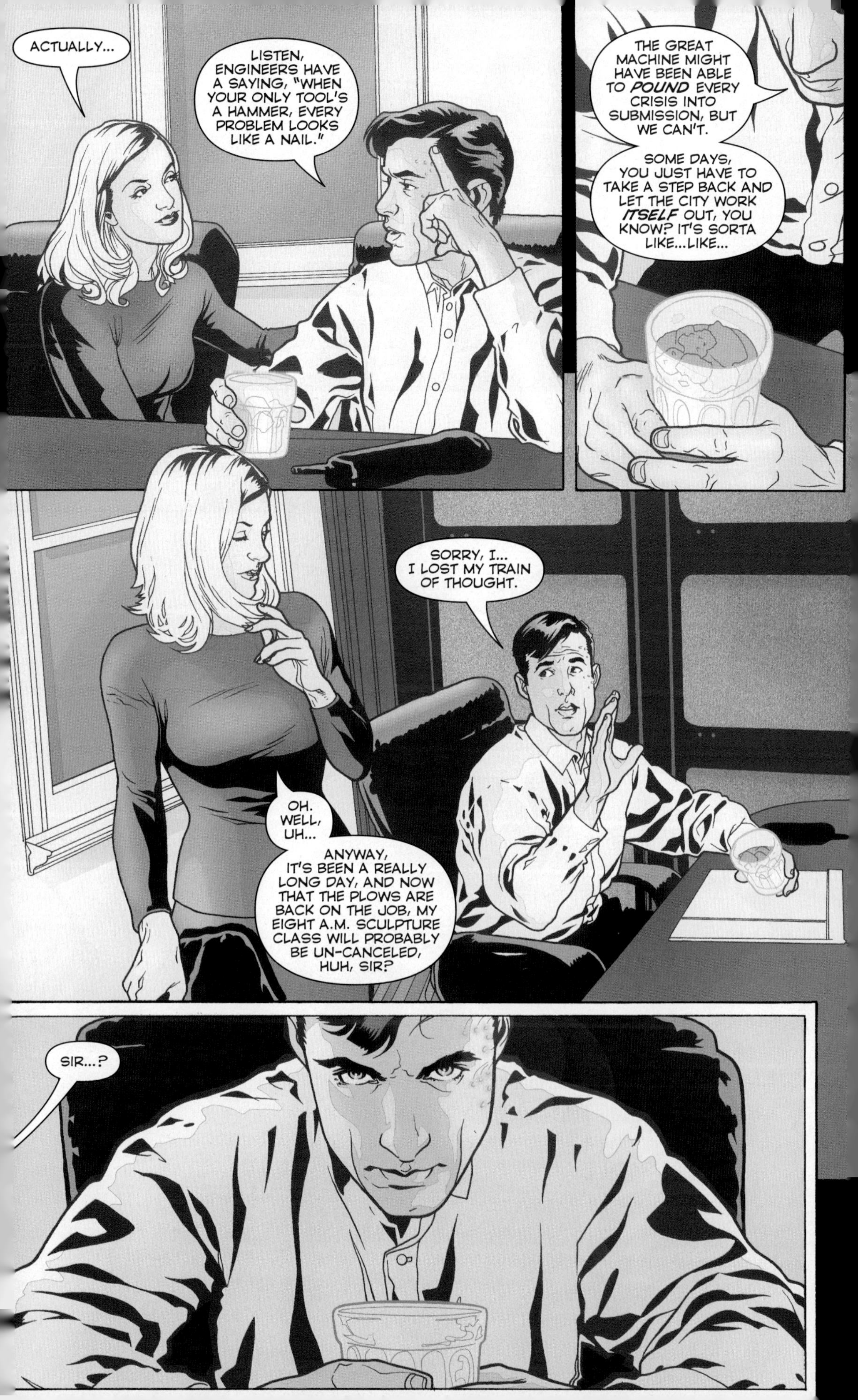
ACTUALLY...
LISTEN, ENGINEERS HAVE A SAYING, "WHEN YOUR ONLY TOOL'S A HAMMER, EVERY PROBLEM LOOKS LIKE A NAIL."
THE GREAT MACHINE MIGHT HAVE BEEN ABLE TO POUND EVERY CRISIS INTO SUBMISSION, BUT WE CAN'T.
SOME DAYS, YOU JUST HAVE TO TAKE A STEP BACK AND LET THE CITY WORK ITSELF OUT, YOU KNOW? IT'S SORTA LIKE...LIKE...
SORRY, I... I LOST MY TRAIN OF THOUGHT.
OH. WELL, UH...
ANYWAY, IT'S BEEN A REALLY LONG DAY, AND NOW THAT THE PLOWS ARE BACK ON THE JOB, MY EIGHT A.M. SCULPTURE CLASS WILL PROBABLY BE UN-CANCELED, HUH, SIR?
SIR...?

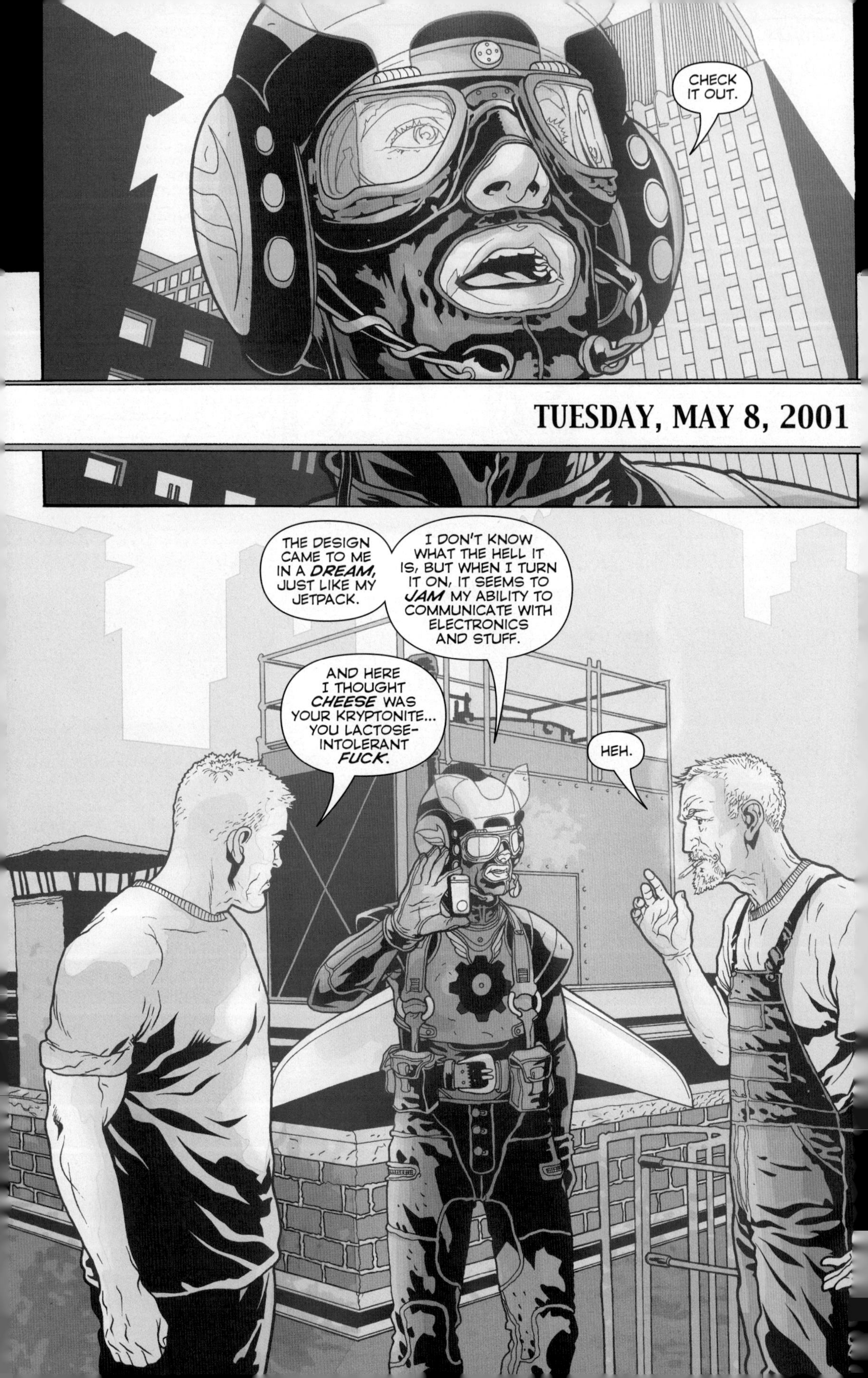
CHECK IT OUT.
TUESDAY, MAY 8, 2001
THE DESIGN CAME TO ME IN A *DREAM,* JUST LIKE MY JETPACK.
I DON'T KNOW WHAT THE HELL IT IS, BUT WHEN I TURN IT ON, IT SEEMS TO *JAM* MY ABILITY TO COMMUNICATE WITH ELECTRONICS AND STUFF.
AND HERE I THOUGHT *CHEESE* WAS YOUR KRYPTONITE... YOU LACTOSE-INTOLERANT *FUCK*.
HEH.

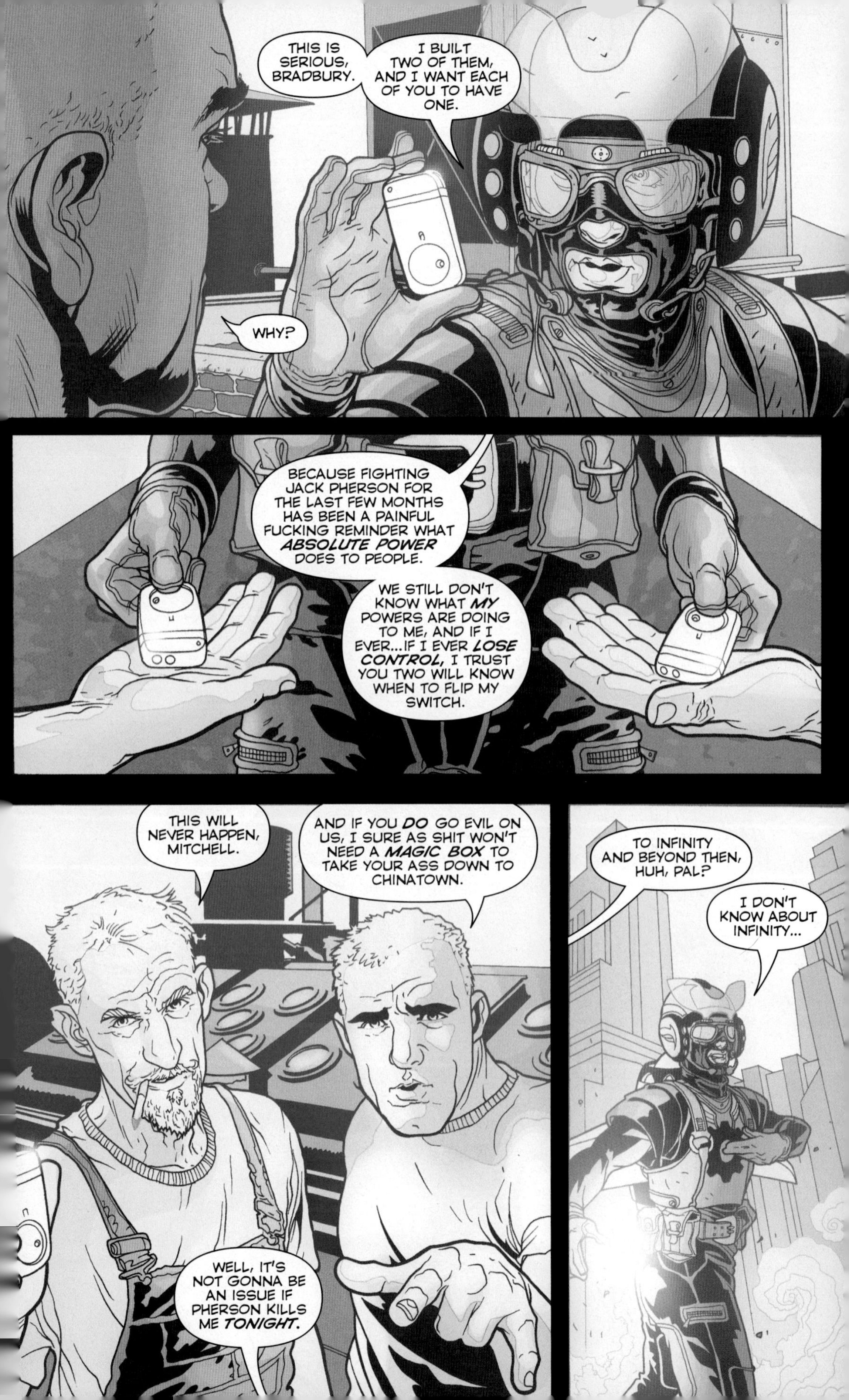
THIS IS SERIOUS, BRADBURY.
I BUILT TWO OF THEM, AND I WANT EACH OF YOU TO HAVE ONE.
WHY?
BECAUSE FIGHTING JACK PHERSON FOR THE LAST FEW MONTHS HAS BEEN A PAINFUL FUCKING REMINDER WHAT ABSOLUTE POWER DOES TO PEOPLE.
WE STILL DON'T KNOW WHAT MY POWERS ARE DOING TO ME, AND IF I EVER...IF I EVER LOSE CONTROL, I TRUST YOU TWO WILL KNOW WHEN TO FLIP MY SWITCH.
THIS WILL NEVER HAPPEN, MITCHELL.
AND IF YOU DO GO EVIL ON US, I SURE AS SHIT WON'T NEED A MAGIC BOX TO TAKE YOUR ASS DOWN TO CHINATOWN.
WELL, IT'S NOT GONNA BE AN ISSUE IF PHERSON KILLS ME TONIGHT.
TO INFINITY AND BEYOND THEN, HUH, PAL?
I DON'T KNOW ABOUT INFINITY...

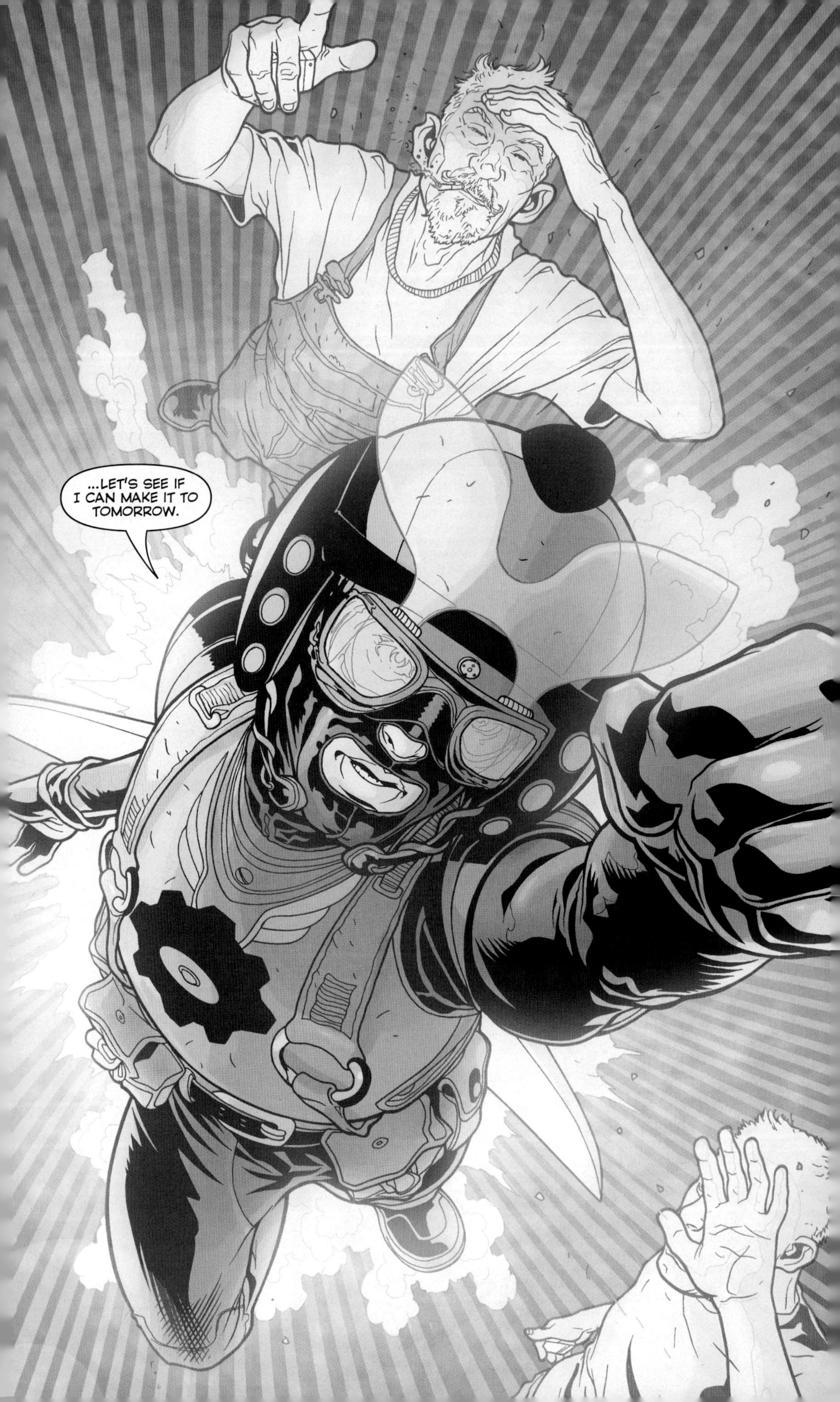
...LET'S SEE IF I CAN MAKE IT TO TOMORROW.

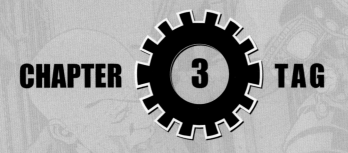

CHAPTER 3 TAG

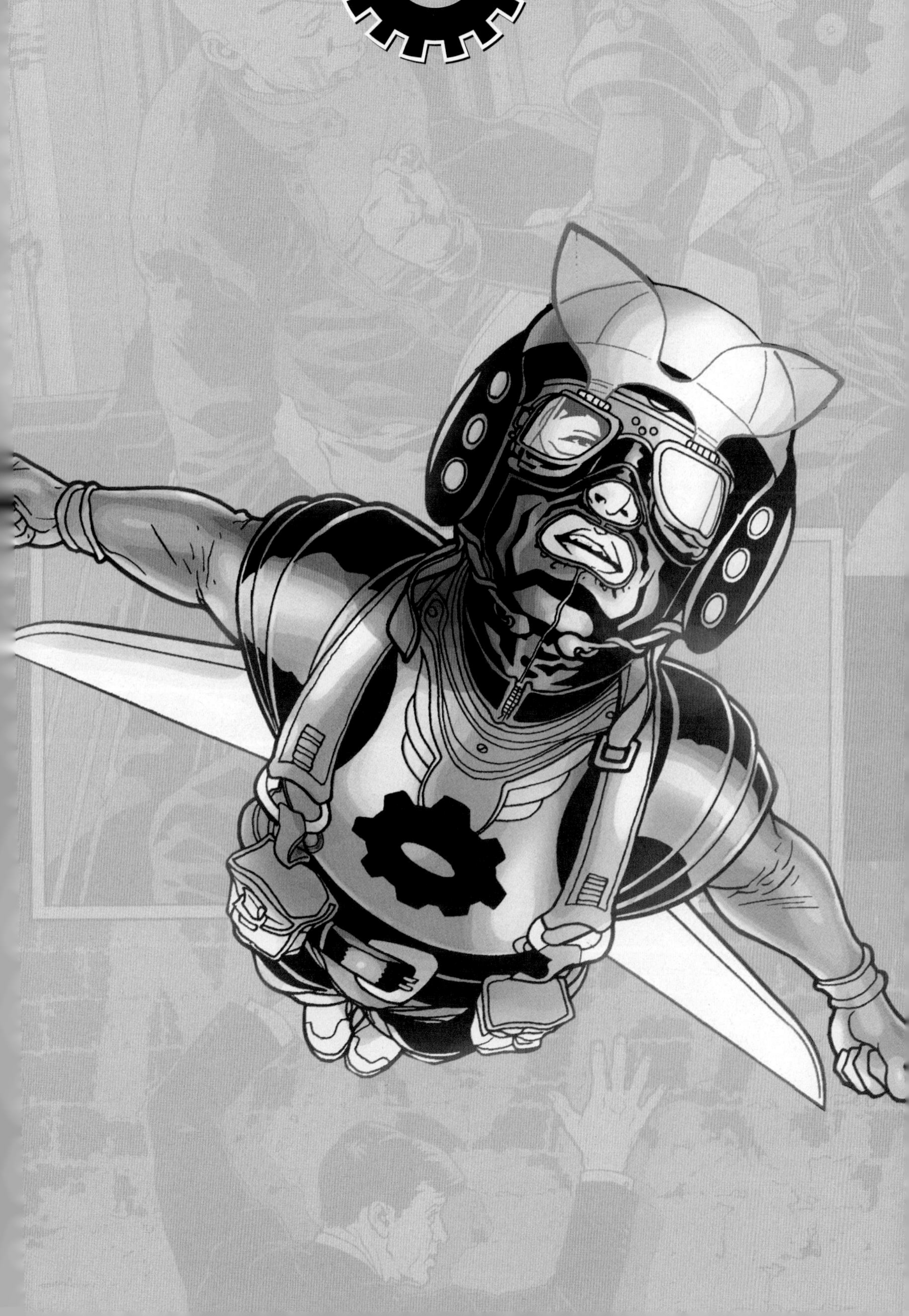

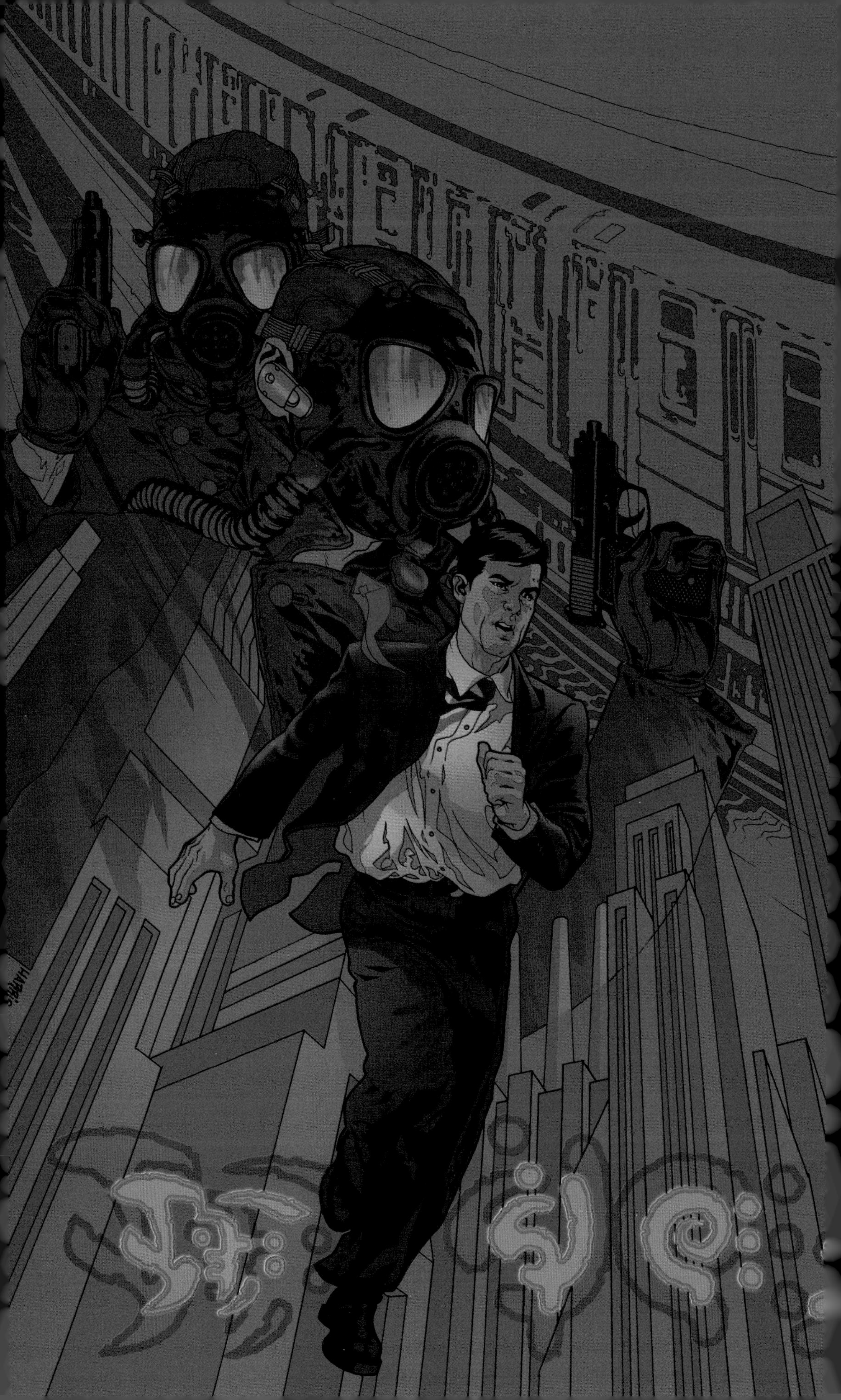

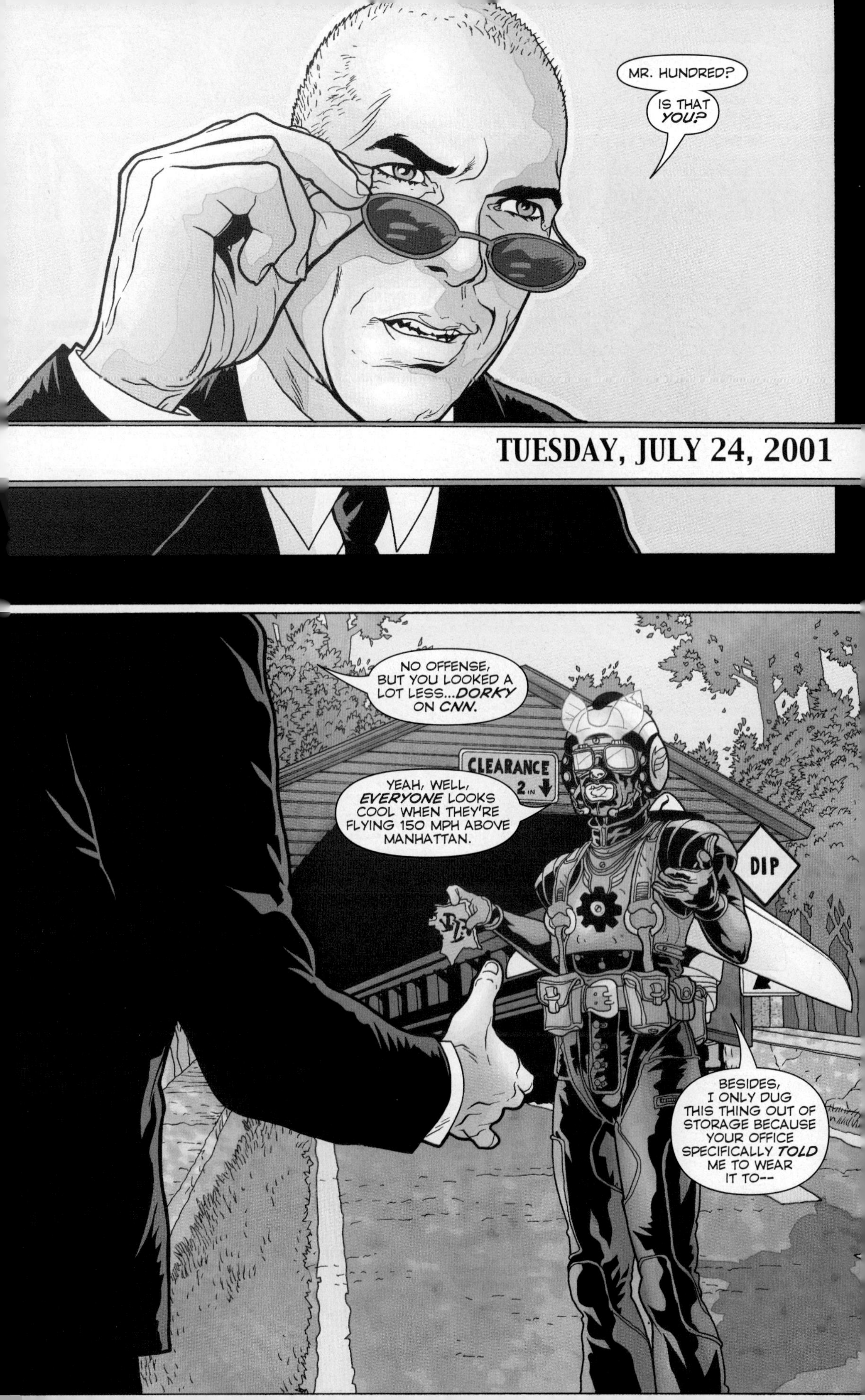
MR. HUNDRED?
IS THAT YOU?
TUESDAY, JULY 24, 2001
NO OFFENSE, BUT YOU LOOKED A LOT LESS...DORKY ON CNN.
CLEARANCE 2 IN
YEAH, WELL, EVERYONE LOOKS COOL WHEN THEY'RE FLYING 150 MPH ABOVE MANHATTAN.
DIP
BESIDES, I ONLY DUG THIS THING OUT OF STORAGE BECAUSE YOUR OFFICE SPECIFICALLY TOLD ME TO WEAR IT TO--

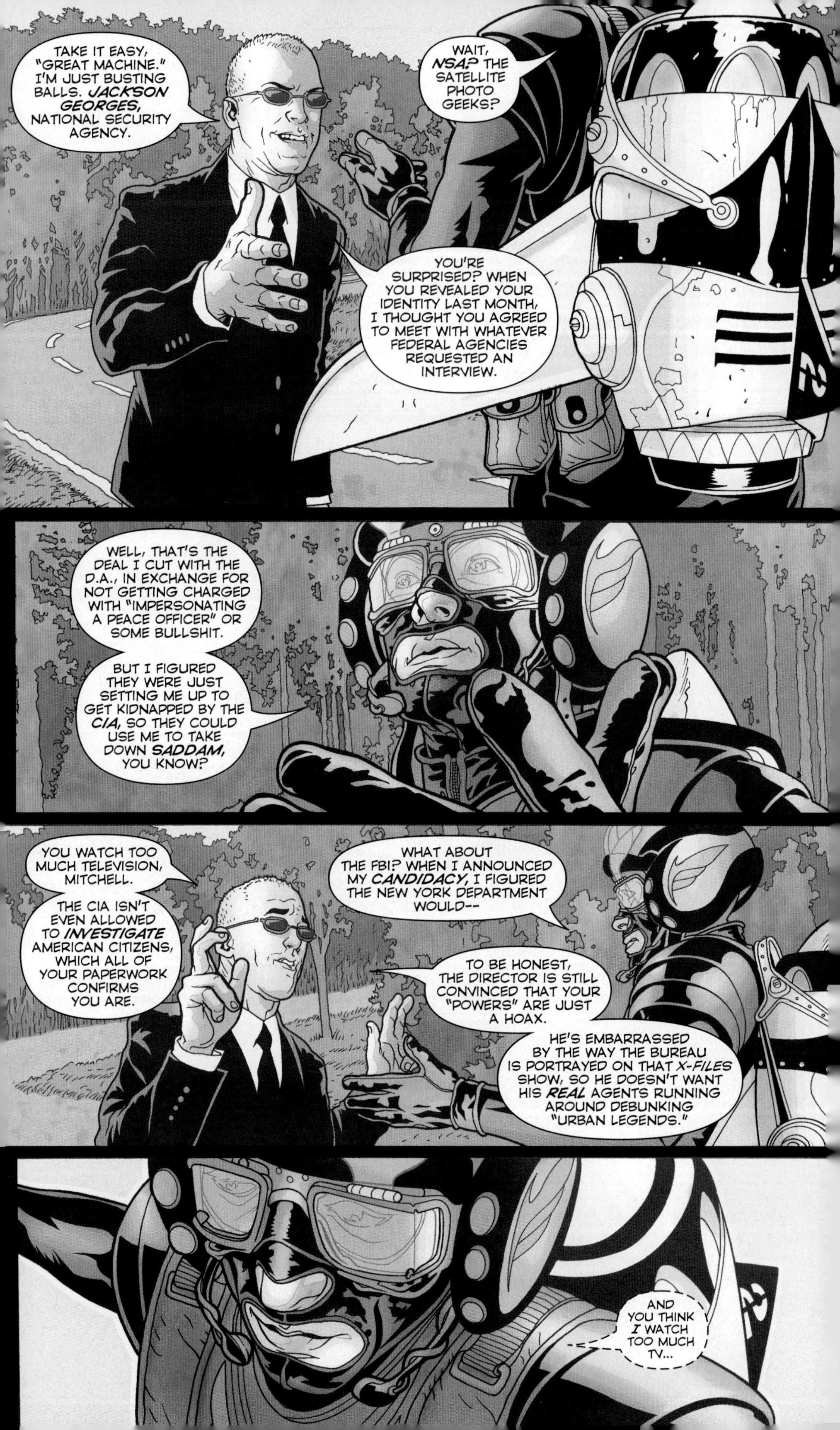
TAKE IT EASY, "GREAT MACHINE." I'M JUST BUSTING BALLS. JACKSON GEORGES, NATIONAL SECURITY AGENCY.
WAIT, NSA? THE SATELLITE PHOTO GEEKS?
YOU'RE SURPRISED? WHEN YOU REVEALED YOUR IDENTITY LAST MONTH, I THOUGHT YOU AGREED TO MEET WITH WHATEVER FEDERAL AGENCIES REQUESTED AN INTERVIEW.
WELL, THAT'S THE DEAL I CUT WITH THE D.A., IN EXCHANGE FOR NOT GETTING CHARGED WITH "IMPERSONATING A PEACE OFFICER" OR SOME BULLSHIT.
BUT I FIGURED THEY WERE JUST SETTING ME UP TO GET KIDNAPPED BY THE CIA, SO THEY COULD USE ME TO TAKE DOWN SADDAM, YOU KNOW?
YOU WATCH TOO MUCH TELEVISION, MITCHELL.
THE CIA ISN'T EVEN ALLOWED TO INVESTIGATE AMERICAN CITIZENS, WHICH ALL OF YOUR PAPERWORK CONFIRMS YOU ARE.
WHAT ABOUT THE FBI? WHEN I ANNOUNCED MY CANDIDACY, I FIGURED THE NEW YORK DEPARTMENT WOULD--
TO BE HONEST, THE DIRECTOR IS STILL CONVINCED THAT YOUR "POWERS" ARE JUST A HOAX.
HE'S EMBARRASSED BY THE WAY THE BUREAU IS PORTRAYED ON THAT X-FILES SHOW, SO HE DOESN'T WANT HIS REAL AGENTS RUNNING AROUND DEBUNKING "URBAN LEGENDS."
AND YOU THINK I WATCH TOO MUCH TV...

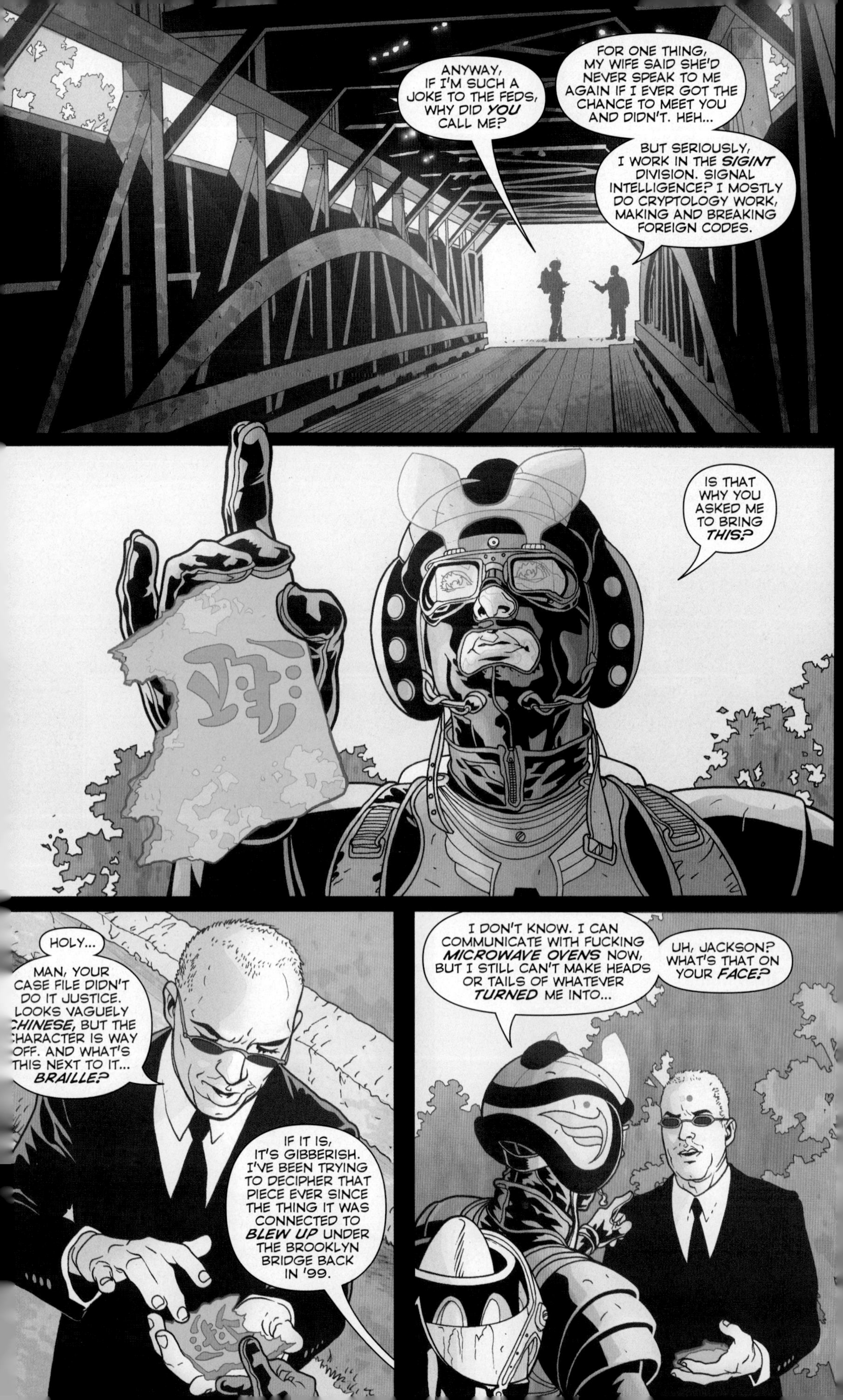
ANYWAY, IF I'M SUCH A JOKE TO THE FEDS, WHY DID *YOU* CALL ME?
FOR ONE THING, MY WIFE SAID SHE'D NEVER SPEAK TO ME AGAIN IF I EVER GOT THE CHANCE TO MEET YOU AND DIDN'T. HEH...
BUT SERIOUSLY, I WORK IN THE *SIGINT* DIVISION. SIGNAL INTELLIGENCE? I MOSTLY DO CRYPTOLOGY WORK, MAKING AND BREAKING FOREIGN CODES.
IS THAT WHY YOU ASKED ME TO BRING *THIS?*
HOLY...
MAN, YOUR CASE FILE DIDN'T DO IT JUSTICE. LOOKS VAGUELY *CHINESE,* BUT THE CHARACTER IS WAY OFF. AND WHAT'S THIS NEXT TO IT... *BRAILLE?*
IF IT IS, IT'S GIBBERISH. I'VE BEEN TRYING TO DECIPHER THAT PIECE EVER SINCE THE THING IT WAS CONNECTED TO *BLEW UP* UNDER THE BROOKLYN BRIDGE BACK IN '99.
I DON'T KNOW. I CAN COMMUNICATE WITH FUCKING *MICROWAVE OVENS* NOW, BUT I STILL CAN'T MAKE HEADS OR TAILS OF WHATEVER *TURNED* ME INTO...
UH, JACKSON? WHAT'S THAT ON YOUR *FACE?*

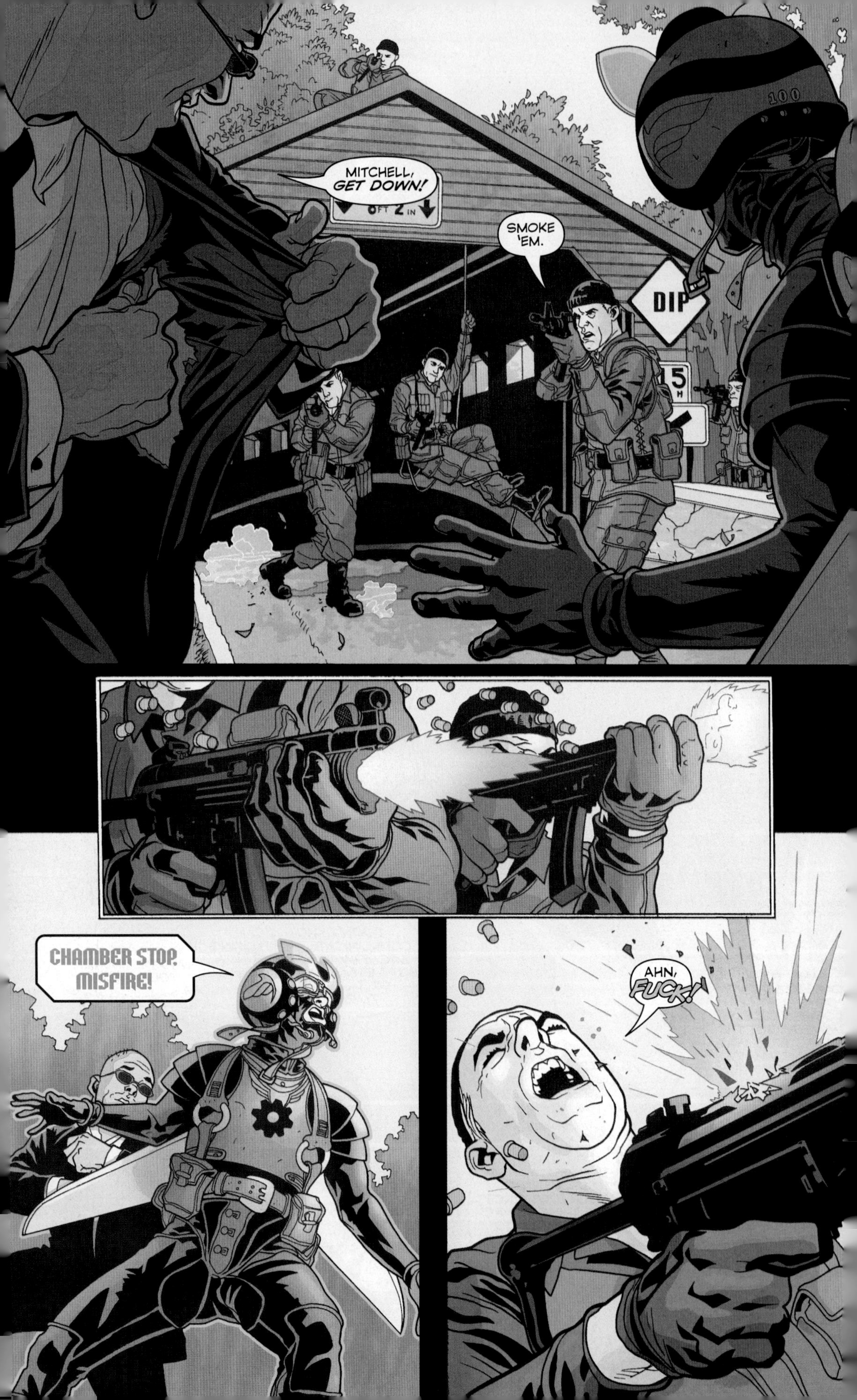
MITCHELL, GET DOWN!
6 FT 2 IN
SMOKE 'EM.
DIP
15
CHAMBER STOP. MISFIRE!
AHN, FUCK!

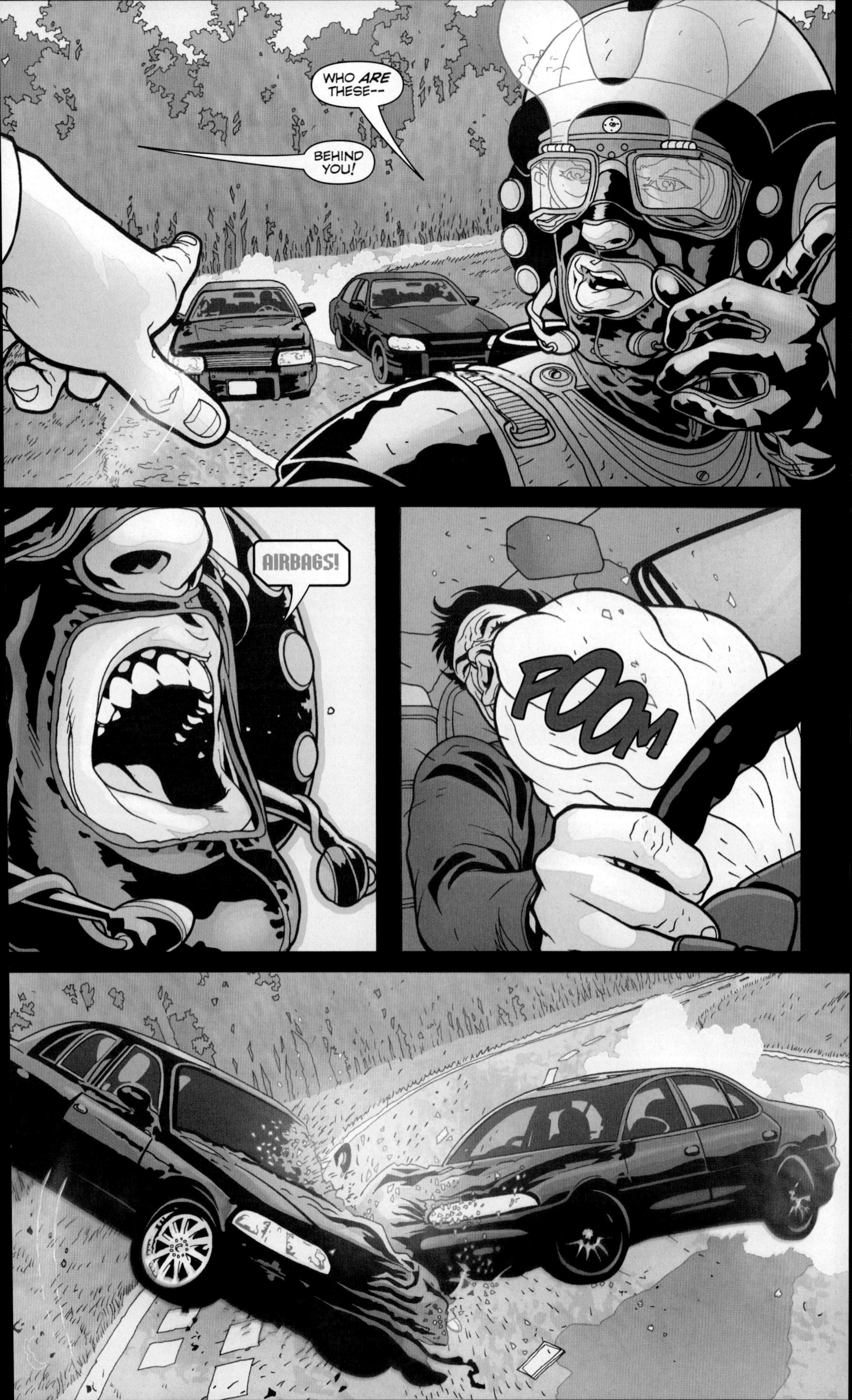
WHO *ARE* THESE--
BEHIND YOU!
AIRBAGS!
POOM

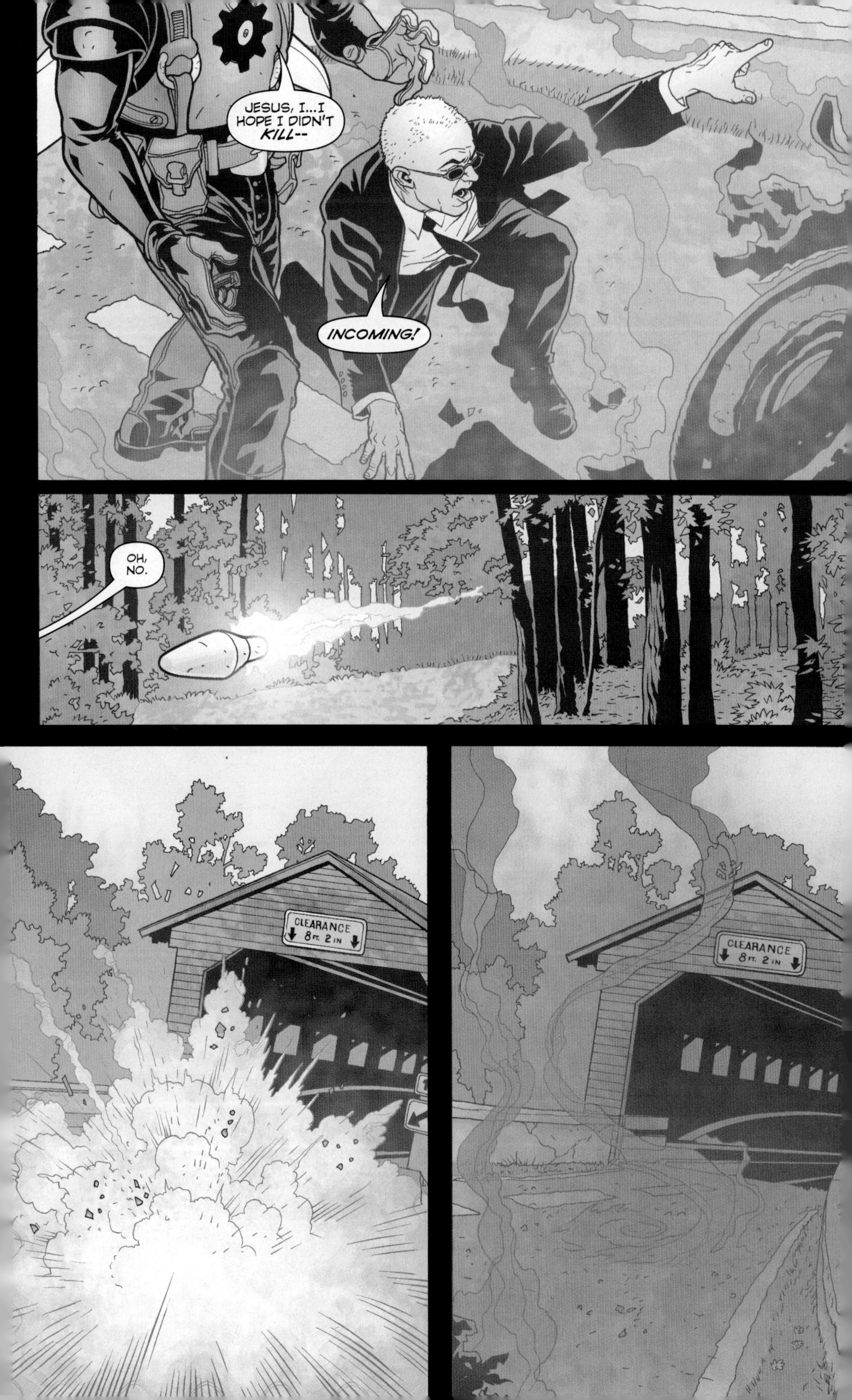
JESUS, I...I HOPE I DIDN'T KILL--
INCOMING!
OH, NO.
CLEARANCE 8 FT. 2 IN
CLEARANCE 8 FT. 2 IN

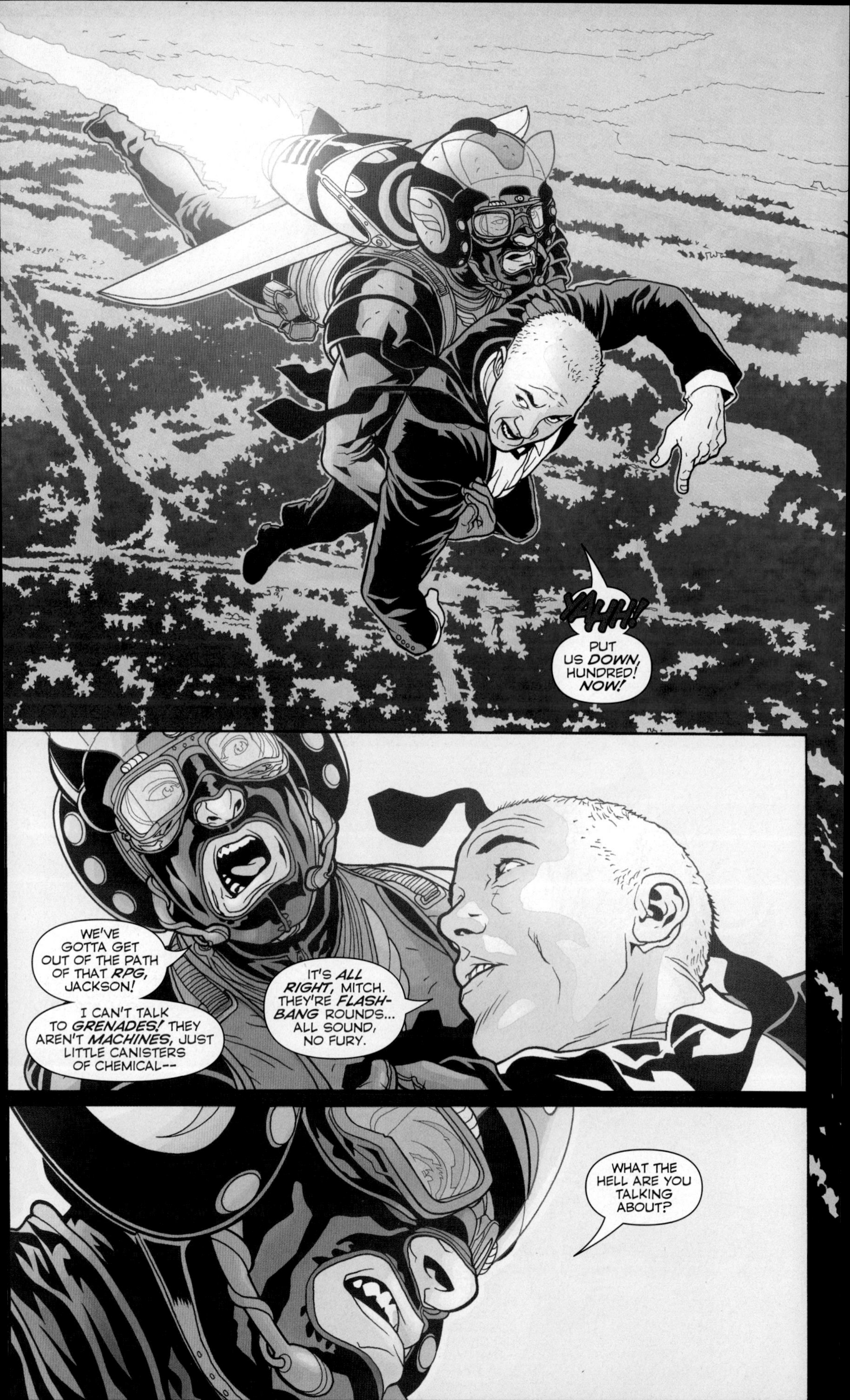
YAHH!
PUT US DOWN, HUNDRED! NOW!
WE'VE GOTTA GET OUT OF THE PATH OF THAT RPG, JACKSON!
I CAN'T TALK TO GRENADES! THEY AREN'T MACHINES, JUST LITTLE CANISTERS OF CHEMICAL--
IT'S ALL RIGHT, MITCH. THEY'RE FLASH-BANG ROUNDS... ALL SOUND, NO FURY.
WHAT THE HELL ARE YOU TALKING ABOUT?

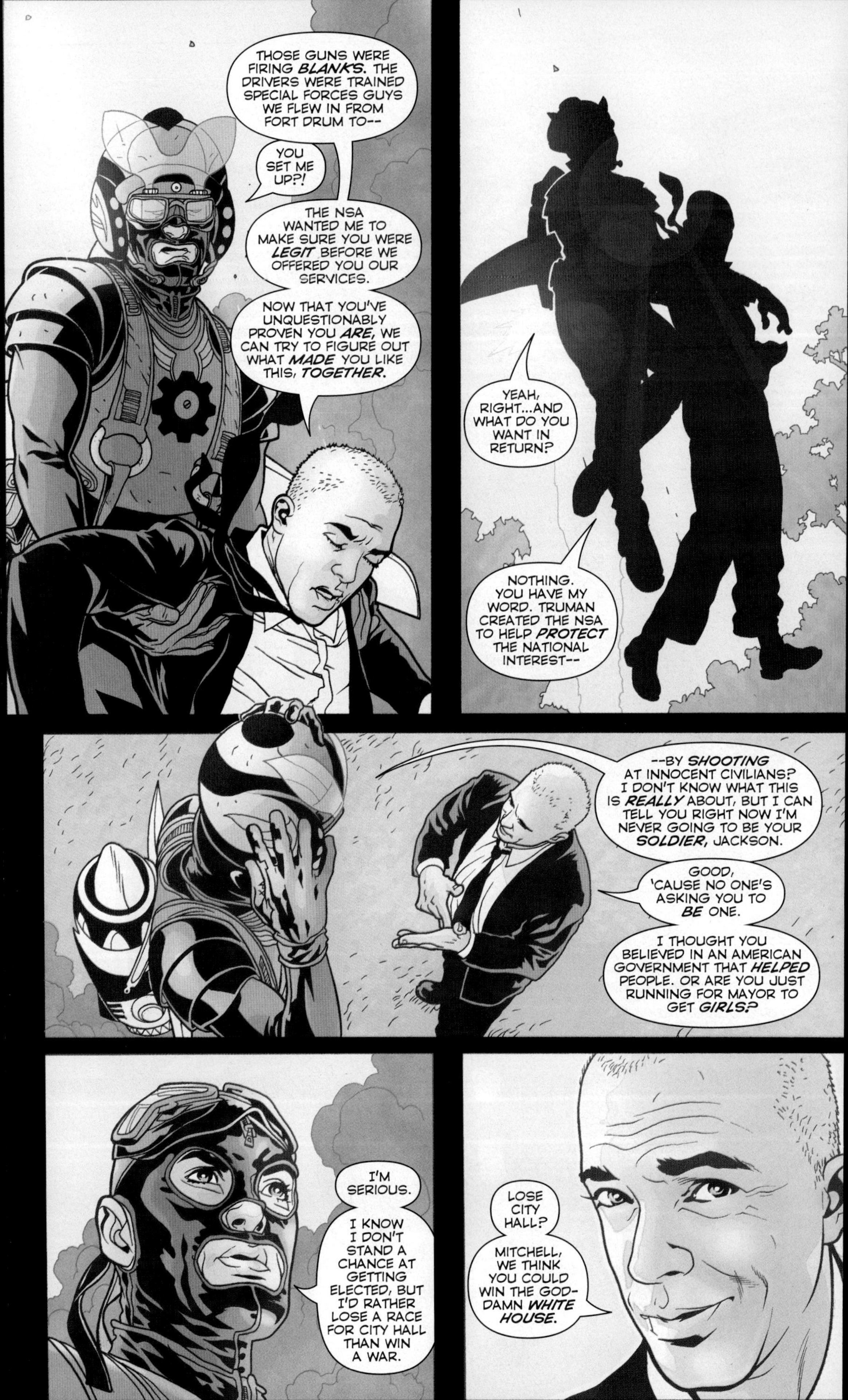
THOSE GUNS WERE FIRING BLANKS. THE DRIVERS WERE TRAINED SPECIAL FORCES GUYS WE FLEW IN FROM FORT DRUM TO--
YOU SET ME UP?!
THE NSA WANTED ME TO MAKE SURE YOU WERE LEGIT BEFORE WE OFFERED YOU OUR SERVICES.
NOW THAT YOU'VE UNQUESTIONABLY PROVEN YOU ARE, WE CAN TRY TO FIGURE OUT WHAT MADE YOU LIKE THIS, TOGETHER.
YEAH, RIGHT...AND WHAT DO YOU WANT IN RETURN?
NOTHING. YOU HAVE MY WORD. TRUMAN CREATED THE NSA TO HELP PROTECT THE NATIONAL INTEREST--
--BY SHOOTING AT INNOCENT CIVILIANS? I DON'T KNOW WHAT THIS IS REALLY ABOUT, BUT I CAN TELL YOU RIGHT NOW I'M NEVER GOING TO BE YOUR SOLDIER, JACKSON.
GOOD, 'CAUSE NO ONE'S ASKING YOU TO BE ONE.
I THOUGHT YOU BELIEVED IN AN AMERICAN GOVERNMENT THAT HELPED PEOPLE. OR ARE YOU JUST RUNNING FOR MAYOR TO GET GIRLS?
I'M SERIOUS.
I KNOW I DON'T STAND A CHANCE AT GETTING ELECTED, BUT I'D RATHER LOSE A RACE FOR CITY HALL THAN WIN A WAR.
LOSE CITY HALL?
MITCHELL, WE THINK YOU COULD WIN THE GOD-DAMN WHITE HOUSE.

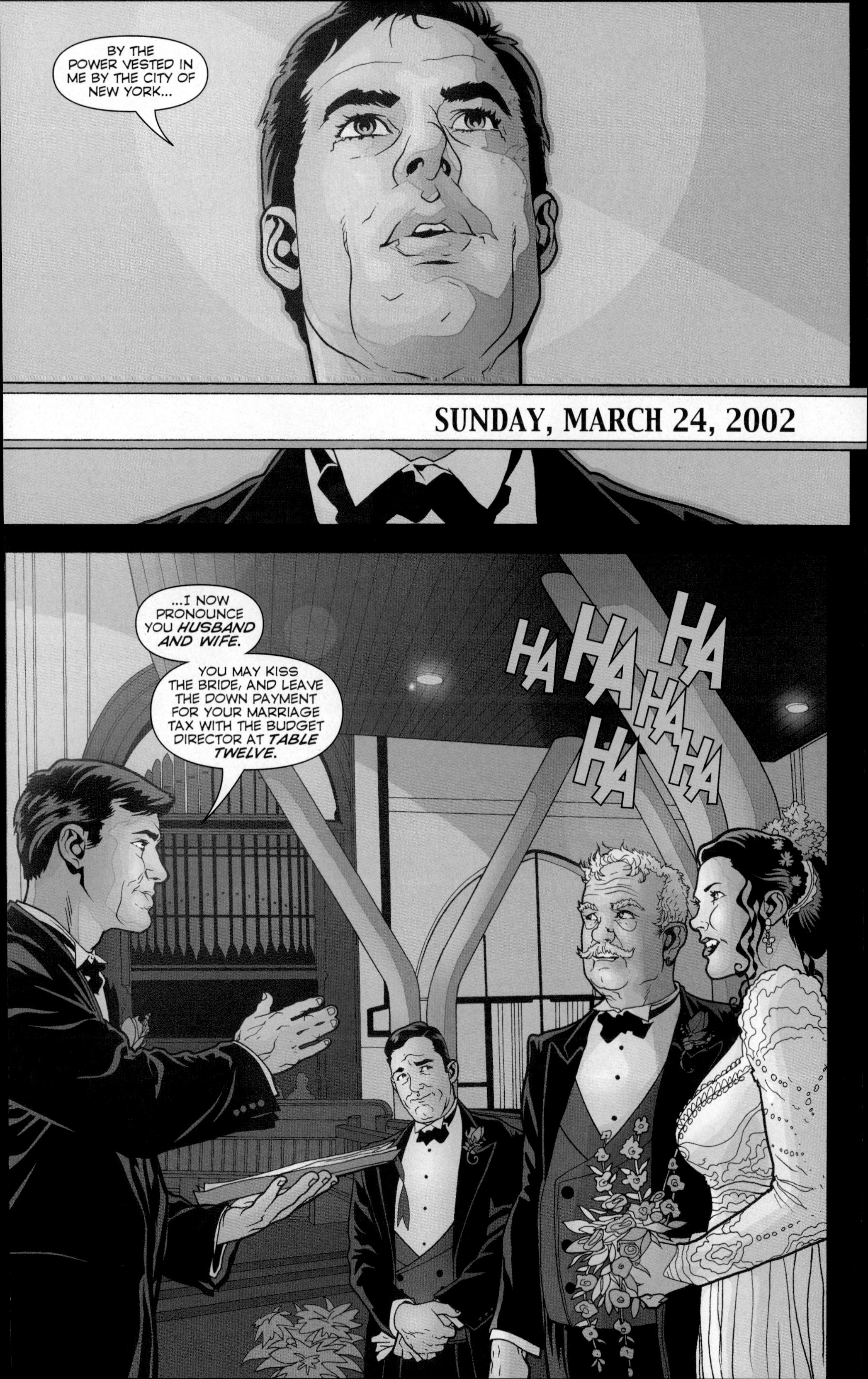
BY THE POWER VESTED IN ME BY THE CITY OF NEW YORK...
SUNDAY, MARCH 24, 2002
...I NOW PRONOUNCE YOU *HUSBAND AND WIFE*.
YOU MAY KISS THE BRIDE, AND LEAVE THE DOWN PAYMENT FOR YOUR MARRIAGE TAX WITH THE BUDGET DIRECTOR AT *TABLE TWELVE*.
HA HA HA HA HA HA HA HA

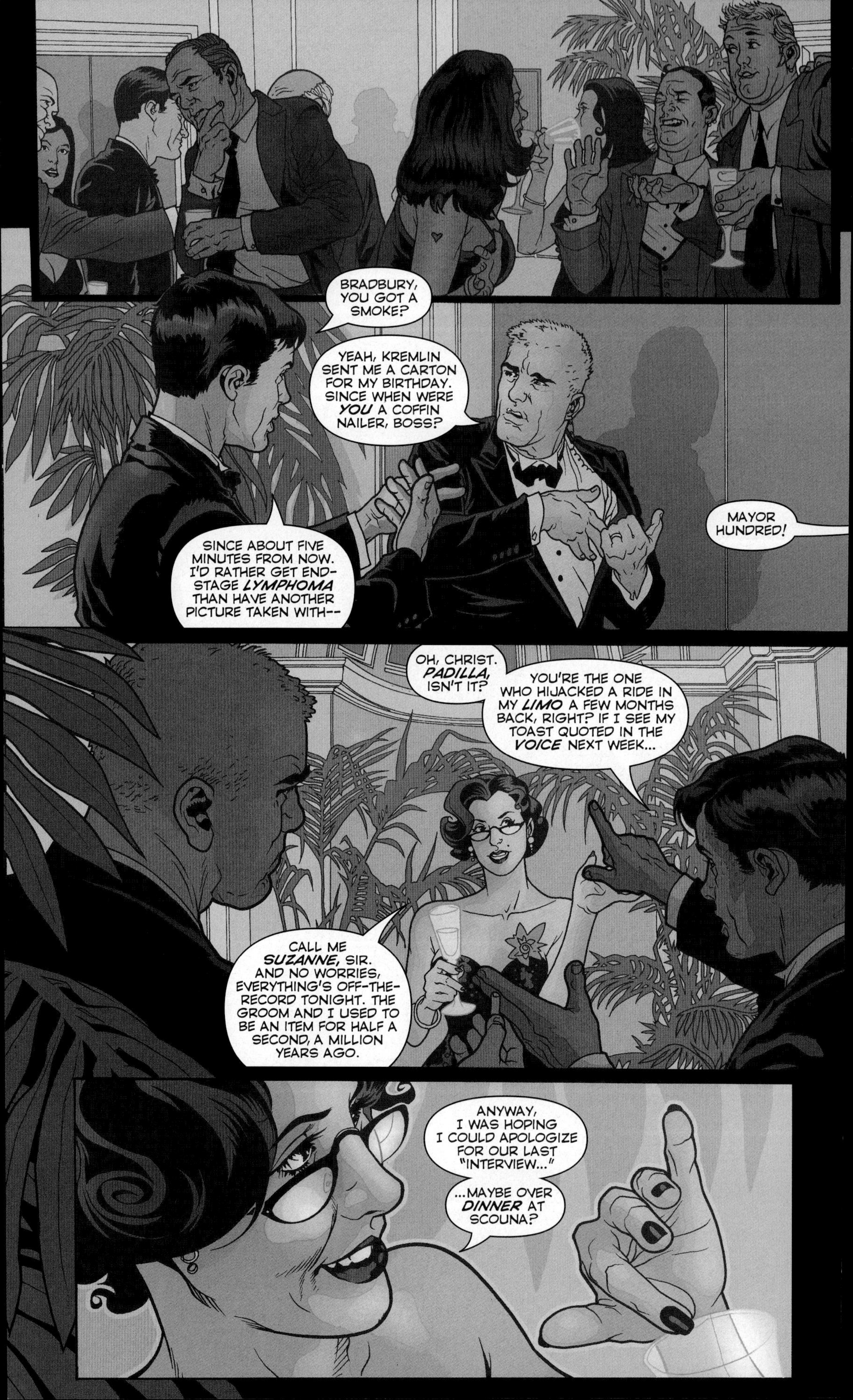

BRADBURY, YOU GOT A SMOKE?
YEAH, KREMLIN SENT ME A CARTON FOR MY BIRTHDAY. SINCE WHEN WERE *YOU* A COFFIN NAILER, BOSS?
SINCE ABOUT FIVE MINUTES FROM NOW. I'D RATHER GET END-STAGE *LYMPHOMA* THAN HAVE ANOTHER PICTURE TAKEN WITH--
MAYOR HUNDRED!
OH, CHRIST. *PADILLA,* ISN'T IT?
YOU'RE THE ONE WHO HIJACKED A RIDE IN MY *LIMO* A FEW MONTHS BACK, RIGHT? IF I SEE MY TOAST QUOTED IN THE *VOICE* NEXT WEEK...
CALL ME *SUZANNE,* SIR. AND NO WORRIES, EVERYTHING'S OFF-THE-RECORD TONIGHT. THE GROOM AND I USED TO BE AN ITEM FOR HALF A SECOND, A MILLION YEARS AGO.
ANYWAY, I WAS HOPING I COULD APOLOGIZE FOR OUR LAST "INTERVIEW..."
...MAYBE OVER *DINNER* AT SCOUNA?

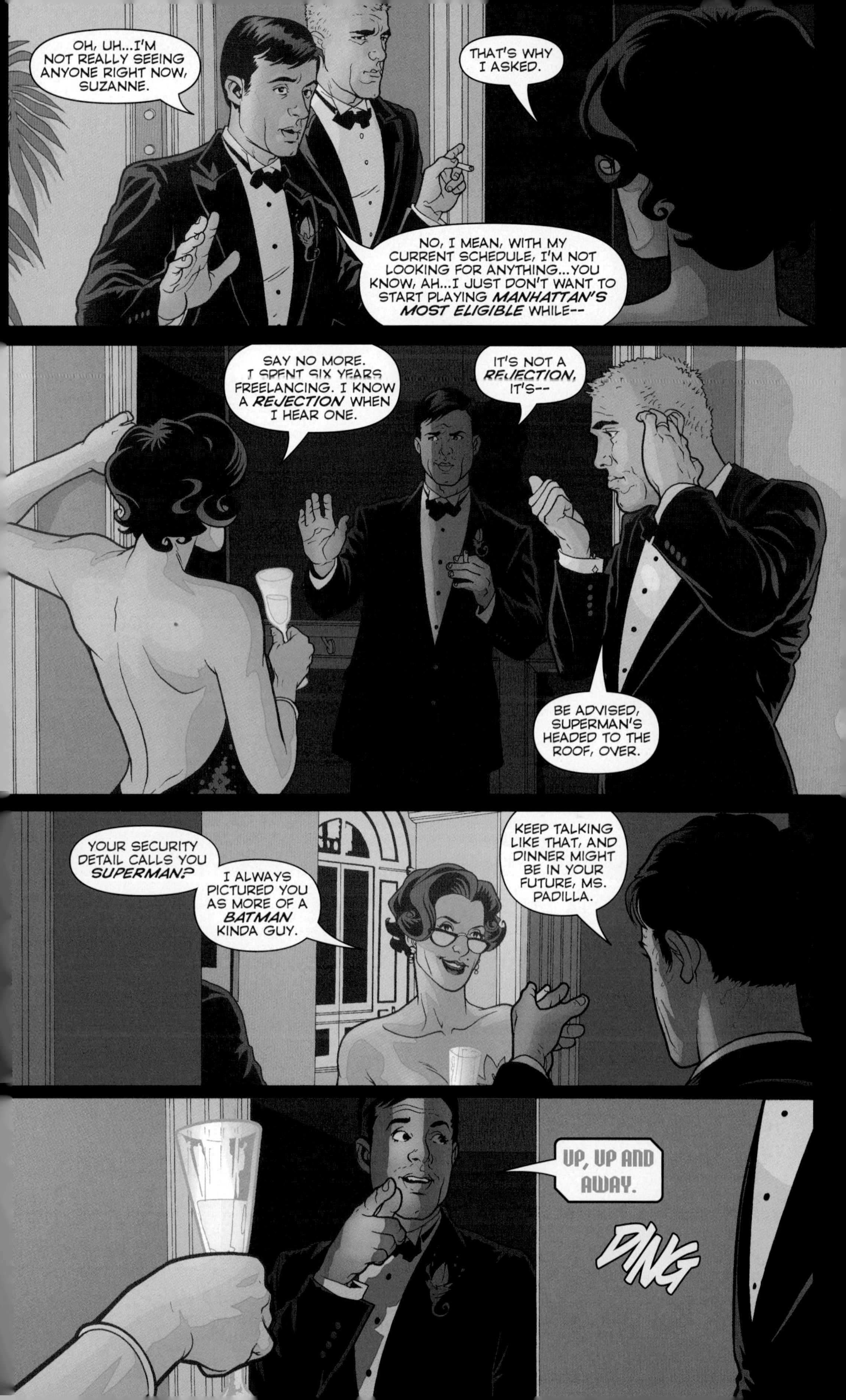

OH, UH...I'M NOT REALLY SEEING ANYONE RIGHT NOW, SUZANNE.
THAT'S WHY I ASKED.
NO, I MEAN, WITH MY CURRENT SCHEDULE, I'M NOT LOOKING FOR ANYTHING...YOU KNOW, AH...I JUST DON'T WANT TO START PLAYING *MANHATTAN'S MOST ELIGIBLE* WHILE--
SAY NO MORE. I SPENT SIX YEARS FREELANCING. I KNOW A *REJECTION* WHEN I HEAR ONE.
IT'S NOT A *REJECTION.* IT'S--
BE ADVISED, SUPERMAN'S HEADED TO THE ROOF, OVER.
YOUR SECURITY DETAIL CALLS YOU *SUPERMAN?*
I ALWAYS PICTURED YOU AS MORE OF A *BATMAN* KINDA GUY.
KEEP TALKING LIKE THAT, AND DINNER MIGHT BE IN YOUR FUTURE, MS. PADILLA.
UP, UP AND AWAY.
DING

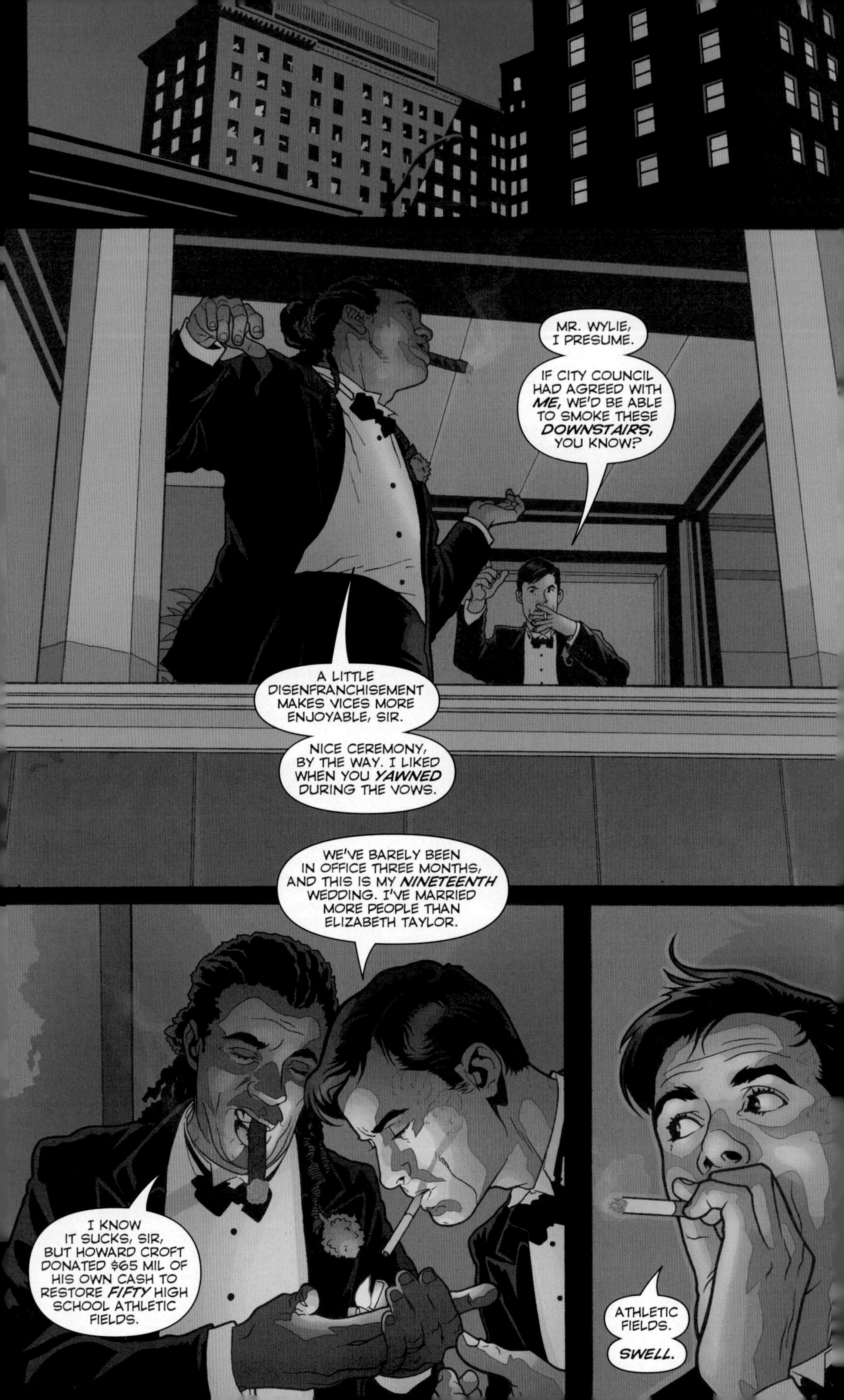
MR. WYLIE, I PRESUME.
IF CITY COUNCIL HAD AGREED WITH ME, WE'D BE ABLE TO SMOKE THESE DOWNSTAIRS, YOU KNOW?
A LITTLE DISENFRANCHISEMENT MAKES VICES MORE ENJOYABLE, SIR.
NICE CEREMONY, BY THE WAY. I LIKED WHEN YOU YAWNED DURING THE VOWS.
WE'VE BARELY BEEN IN OFFICE THREE MONTHS, AND THIS IS MY NINETEENTH WEDDING. I'VE MARRIED MORE PEOPLE THAN ELIZABETH TAYLOR.
I KNOW IT SUCKS, SIR, BUT HOWARD CROFT DONATED $65 MIL OF HIS OWN CASH TO RESTORE FIFTY HIGH SCHOOL ATHLETIC FIELDS.
ATHLETIC FIELDS.
SWELL.

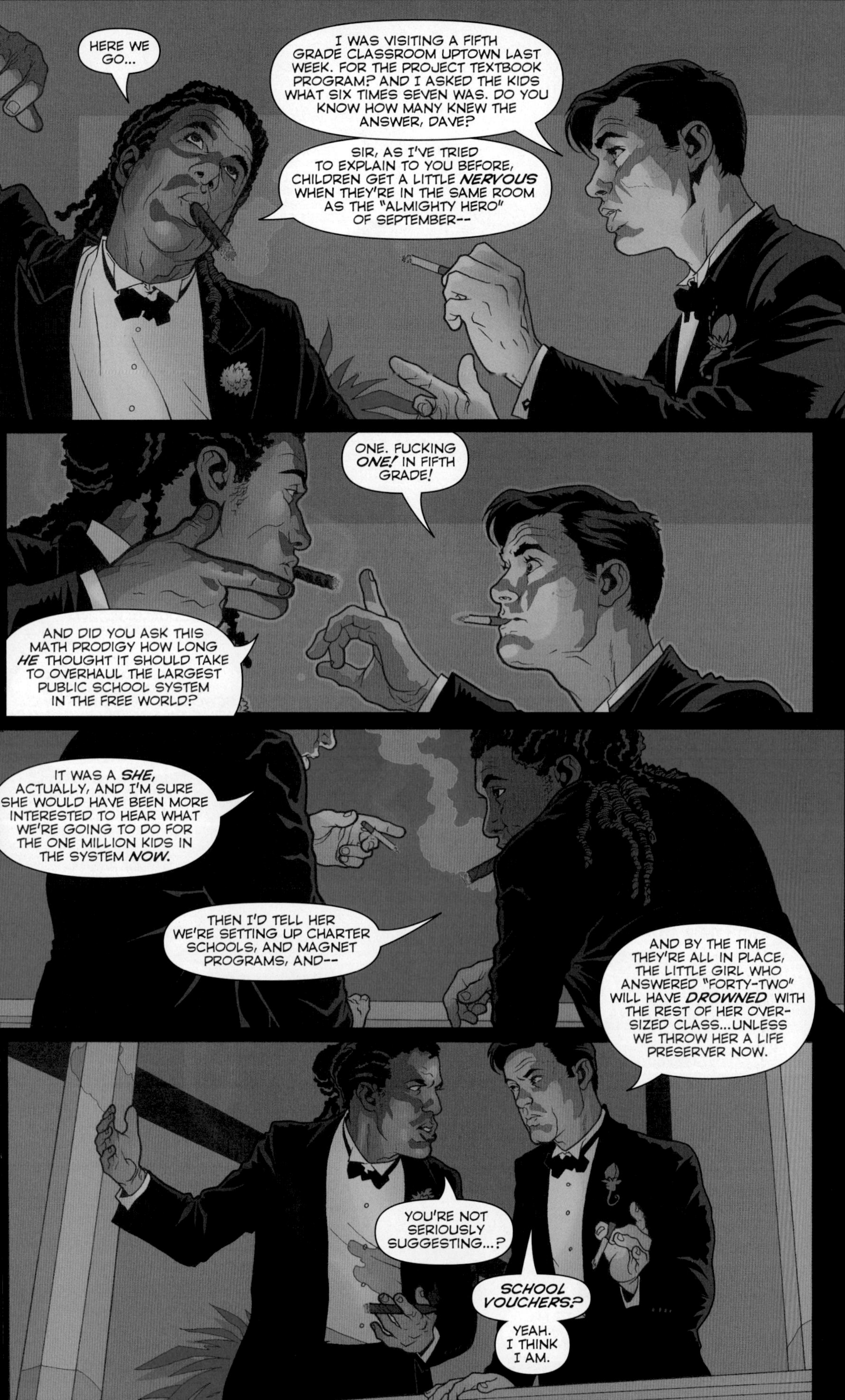
HERE WE GO...
I WAS VISITING A FIFTH GRADE CLASSROOM UPTOWN LAST WEEK. FOR THE PROJECT TEXTBOOK PROGRAM? AND I ASKED THE KIDS WHAT SIX TIMES SEVEN WAS. DO YOU KNOW HOW MANY KNEW THE ANSWER, DAVE?
SIR, AS I'VE TRIED TO EXPLAIN TO YOU BEFORE, CHILDREN GET A LITTLE *NERVOUS* WHEN THEY'RE IN THE SAME ROOM AS THE "ALMIGHTY HERO" OF SEPTEMBER--
ONE. FUCKING *ONE!* IN FIFTH GRADE!
AND DID YOU ASK THIS MATH PRODIGY HOW LONG *HE* THOUGHT IT SHOULD TAKE TO OVERHAUL THE LARGEST PUBLIC SCHOOL SYSTEM IN THE FREE WORLD?
IT WAS A *SHE*, ACTUALLY, AND I'M SURE SHE WOULD HAVE BEEN MORE INTERESTED TO HEAR WHAT WE'RE GOING TO DO FOR THE ONE MILLION KIDS IN THE SYSTEM *NOW.*
THEN I'D TELL HER WE'RE SETTING UP CHARTER SCHOOLS, AND MAGNET PROGRAMS, AND--
AND BY THE TIME THEY'RE ALL IN PLACE, THE LITTLE GIRL WHO ANSWERED "FORTY-TWO" WILL HAVE *DROWNED* WITH THE REST OF HER OVER-SIZED CLASS...UNLESS WE THROW HER A LIFE PRESERVER NOW.
YOU'RE NOT SERIOUSLY SUGGESTING...?
SCHOOL VOUCHERS?
YEAH. I THINK I AM.

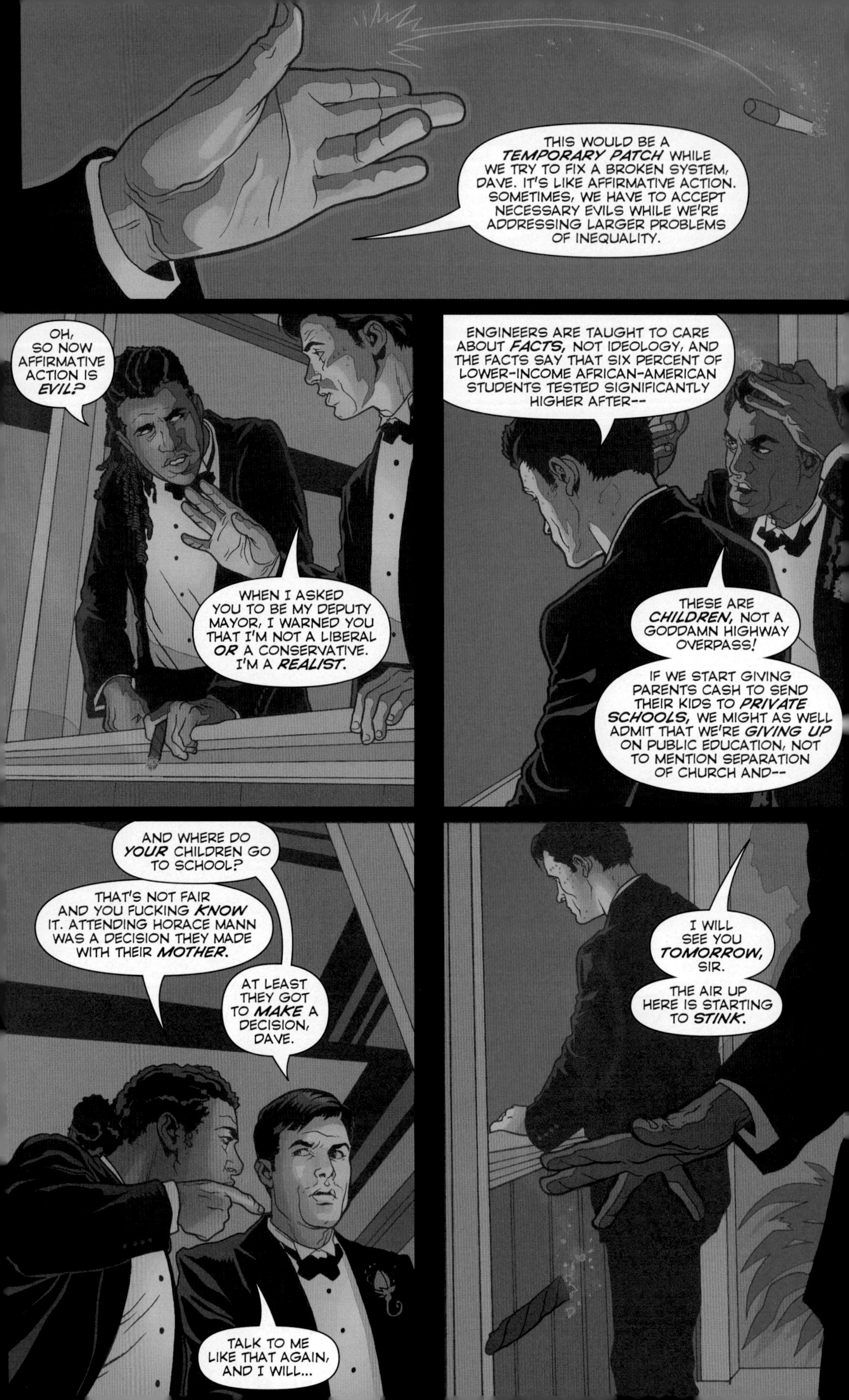
THIS WOULD BE A TEMPORARY PATCH WHILE WE TRY TO FIX A BROKEN SYSTEM, DAVE. IT'S LIKE AFFIRMATIVE ACTION. SOMETIMES, WE HAVE TO ACCEPT NECESSARY EVILS WHILE WE'RE ADDRESSING LARGER PROBLEMS OF INEQUALITY.
OH, SO NOW AFFIRMATIVE ACTION IS EVIL?
WHEN I ASKED YOU TO BE MY DEPUTY MAYOR, I WARNED YOU THAT I'M NOT A LIBERAL OR A CONSERVATIVE. I'M A REALIST.
ENGINEERS ARE TAUGHT TO CARE ABOUT FACTS, NOT IDEOLOGY, AND THE FACTS SAY THAT SIX PERCENT OF LOWER-INCOME AFRICAN-AMERICAN STUDENTS TESTED SIGNIFICANTLY HIGHER AFTER--
THESE ARE CHILDREN, NOT A GODDAMN HIGHWAY OVERPASS!
IF WE START GIVING PARENTS CASH TO SEND THEIR KIDS TO PRIVATE SCHOOLS, WE MIGHT AS WELL ADMIT THAT WE'RE GIVING UP ON PUBLIC EDUCATION, NOT TO MENTION SEPARATION OF CHURCH AND--
AND WHERE DO YOUR CHILDREN GO TO SCHOOL?
THAT'S NOT FAIR AND YOU FUCKING KNOW IT. ATTENDING HORACE MANN WAS A DECISION THEY MADE WITH THEIR MOTHER.
AT LEAST THEY GOT TO MAKE A DECISION, DAVE.
TALK TO ME LIKE THAT AGAIN, AND I WILL...
I WILL SEE YOU TOMORROW, SIR.
THE AIR UP HERE IS STARTING TO STINK.

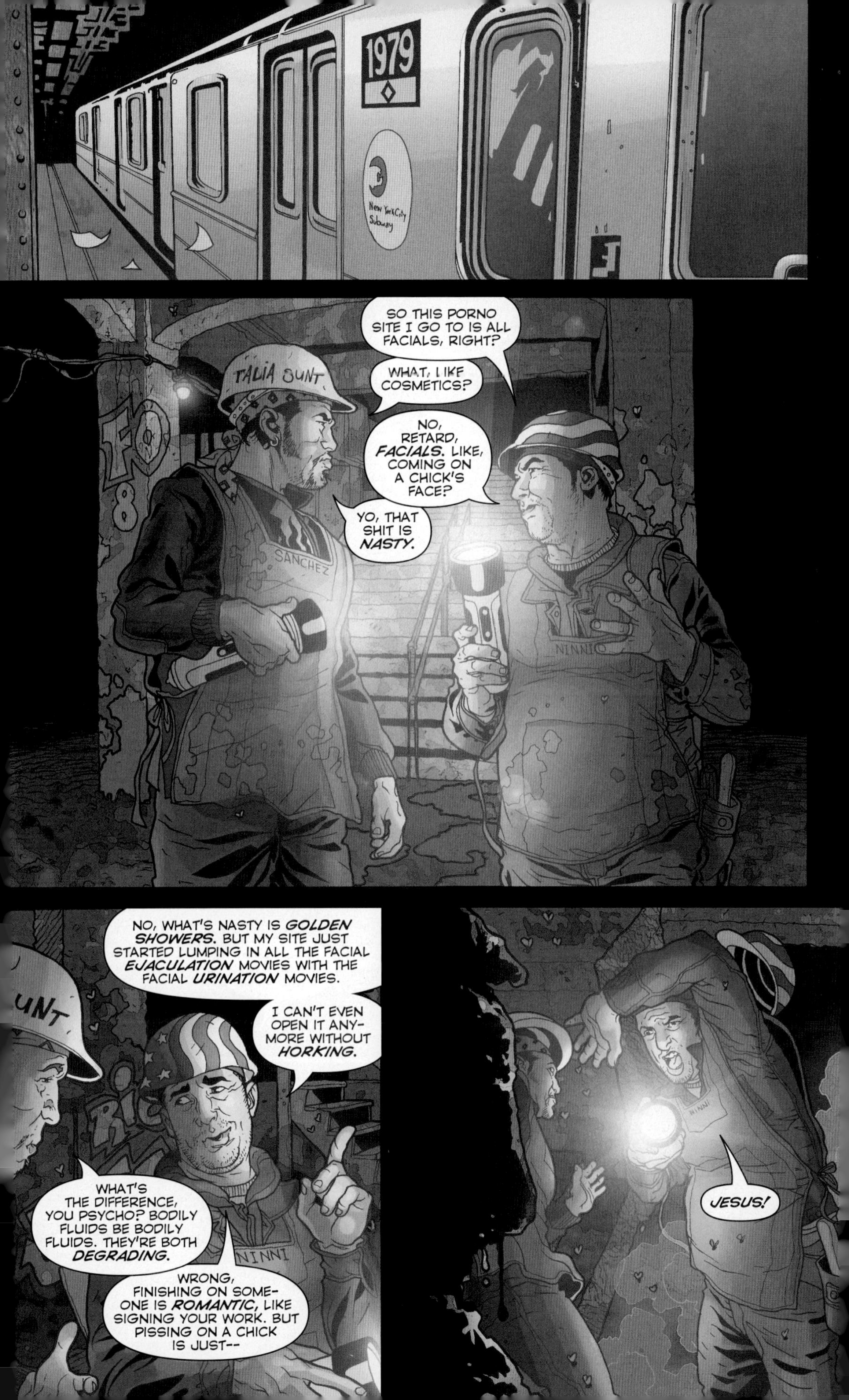
1979
New York City Subway
TALIA SUNT
SANCHEZ
NINNI
SO THIS PORNO SITE I GO TO IS ALL FACIALS, RIGHT?
WHAT, LIKE COSMETICS?
NO, RETARD, *FACIALS.* LIKE, COMING ON A CHICK'S FACE?
YO, THAT SHIT IS *NASTY.*
NO, WHAT'S NASTY IS *GOLDEN SHOWERS.* BUT MY SITE JUST STARTED LUMPING IN ALL THE FACIAL *EJACULATION* MOVIES WITH THE FACIAL *URINATION* MOVIES.
I CAN'T EVEN OPEN IT ANYMORE WITHOUT *HORKING.*
WHAT'S THE DIFFERENCE, YOU PSYCHO? BODILY FLUIDS BE BODILY FLUIDS. THEY'RE BOTH *DEGRADING.*
WRONG, FINISHING ON SOMEONE IS *ROMANTIC,* LIKE SIGNING YOUR WORK. BUT PISSING ON A CHICK IS JUST--
JESUS!

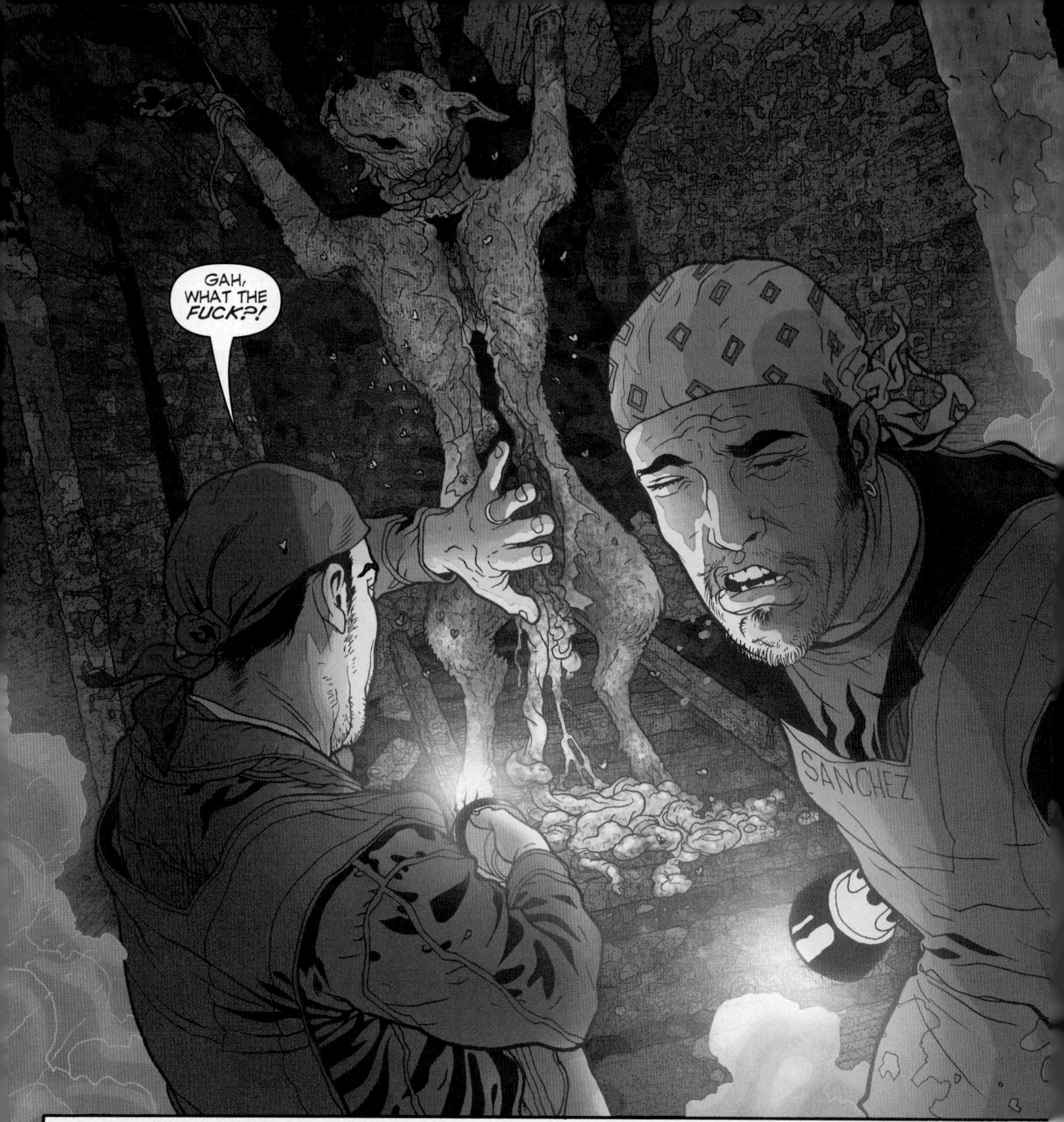
GAH, WHAT THE FUCK?!
SANCHEZ
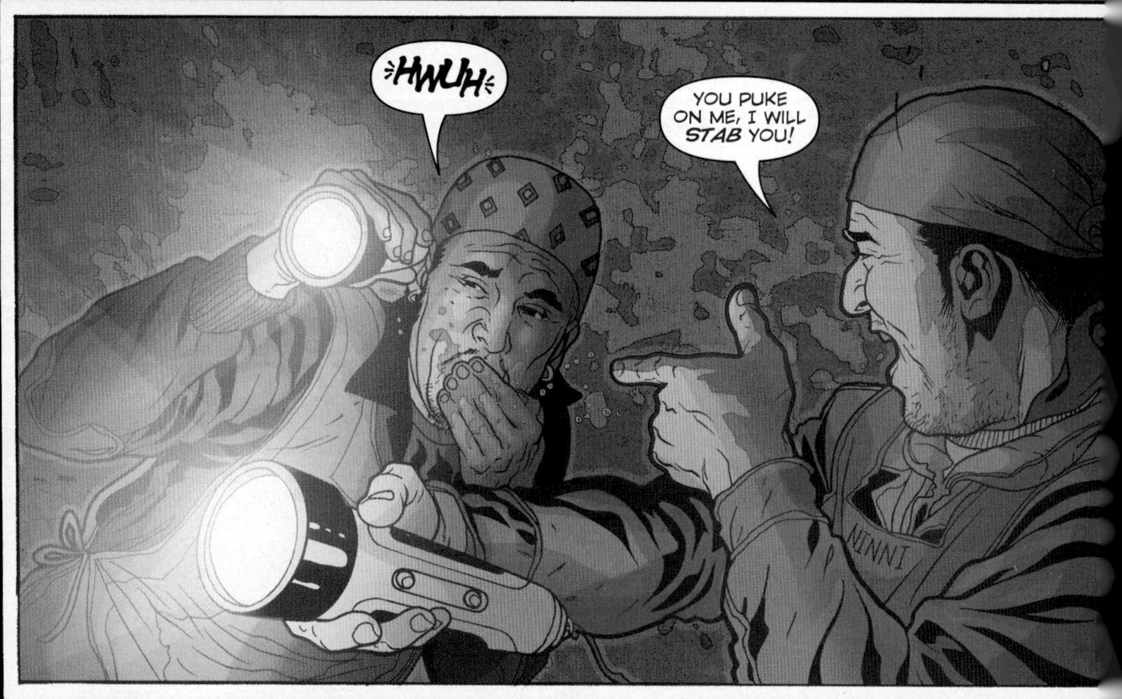
HWUH
YOU PUKE ON ME, I WILL STAB YOU!
NINNI

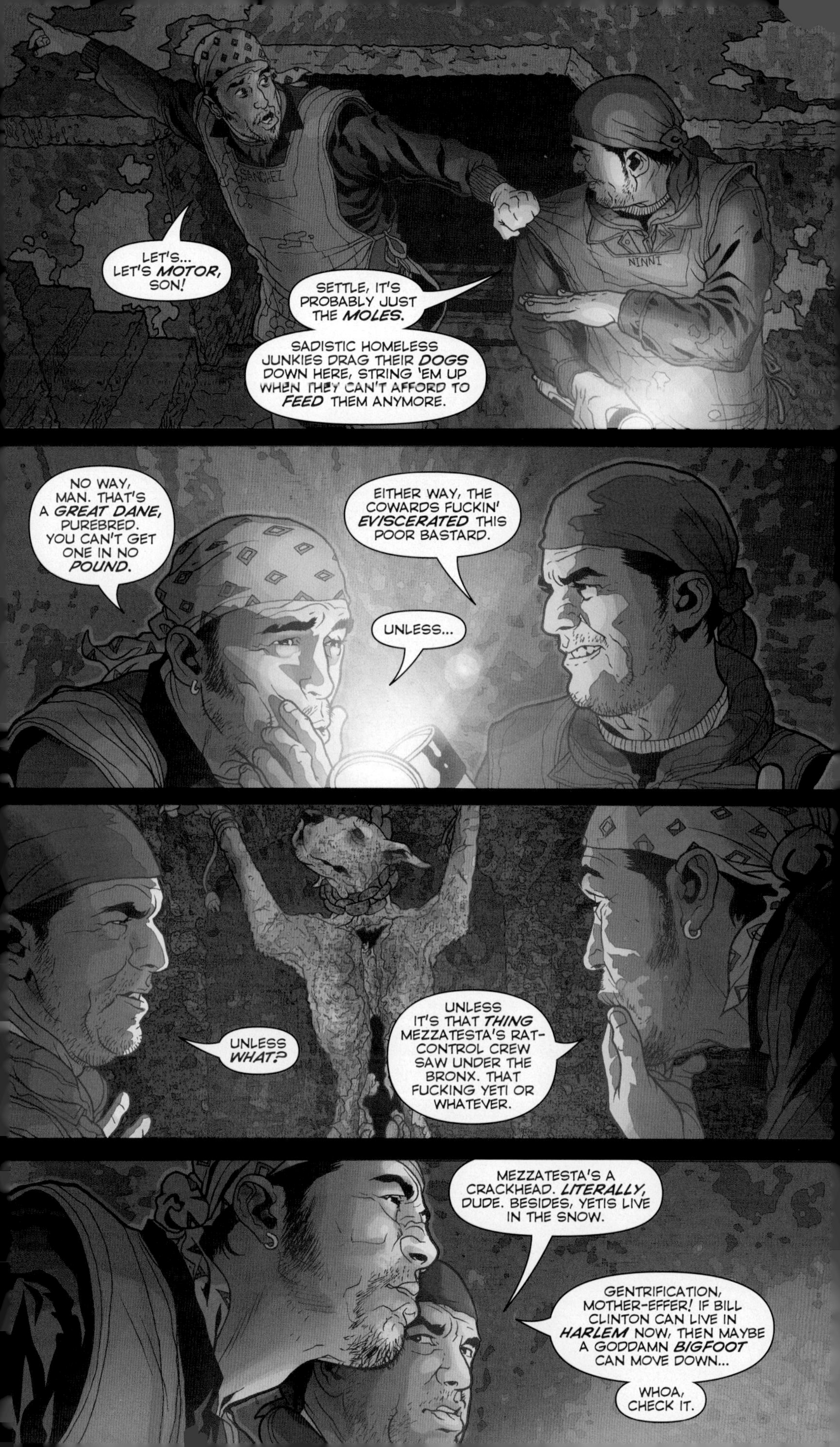
LET'S... LET'S MOTOR, SON!
SETTLE, IT'S PROBABLY JUST THE MOLES.
SADISTIC HOMELESS JUNKIES DRAG THEIR DOGS DOWN HERE, STRING 'EM UP WHEN THEY CAN'T AFFORD TO FEED THEM ANYMORE.
NO WAY, MAN. THAT'S A GREAT DANE, PUREBRED. YOU CAN'T GET ONE IN NO POUND.
EITHER WAY, THE COWARDS FUCKIN' EVISCERATED THIS POOR BASTARD.
UNLESS...
UNLESS WHAT?
UNLESS IT'S THAT THING MEZZATESTA'S RAT-CONTROL CREW SAW UNDER THE BRONX. THAT FUCKING YETI OR WHATEVER.
MEZZATESTA'S A CRACKHEAD. LITERALLY, DUDE. BESIDES, YETIS LIVE IN THE SNOW.
GENTRIFICATION, MOTHER-EFFER! IF BILL CLINTON CAN LIVE IN HARLEM NOW, THEN MAYBE A GODDAMN BIGFOOT CAN MOVE DOWN...
WHOA, CHECK IT.

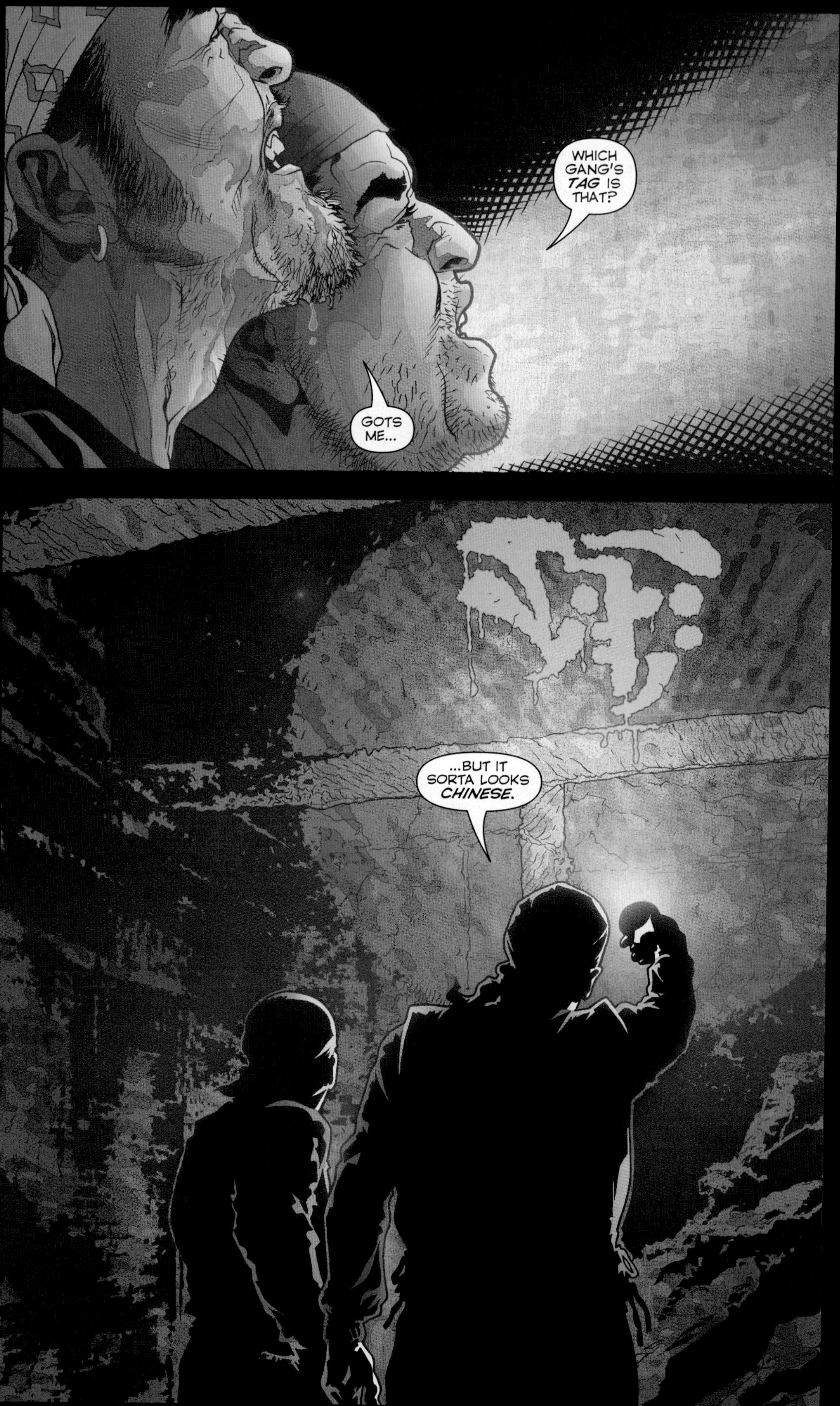
WHICH GANG'S *TAG* IS THAT?
GOTS ME...
...BUT IT SORTA LOOKS *CHINESE.*

LONG NIGHT, MR. MAYOR?

I HAVEN'T EVEN BEEN *HOME* YET.

I GOT CORNERED BY SOME GUY FROM THE SIERRA CLUB, SPENT SIX HOURS DEBATING THE MERITS OF RECYCLING *PLASTICS.*

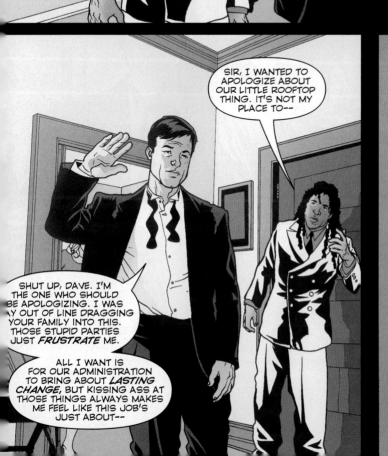

SIR, I WANTED TO APOLOGIZE ABOUT OUR LITTLE ROOFTOP THING. IT'S NOT MY PLACE TO--

SHUT UP, DAVE. I'M THE ONE WHO SHOULD BE APOLOGIZING. I WAS WAY OUT OF LINE DRAGGING YOUR FAMILY INTO THIS. THOSE STUPID PARTIES JUST *FRUSTRATE* ME.

ALL I WANT IS FOR OUR ADMINISTRATION TO BRING ABOUT *LASTING CHANGE,* BUT KISSING ASS AT THOSE THINGS ALWAYS MAKES ME FEEL LIKE THIS JOB'S JUST ABOUT--

KNOCK, KNOCK.

CANDY WANTED ME TO TELL YOU THE *MTA CHAIRMAN* IS ON LINE EIGHT, MAYOR HUNDRED.

SHE SAID HE'S EITHER DRUNK OR INSANE.

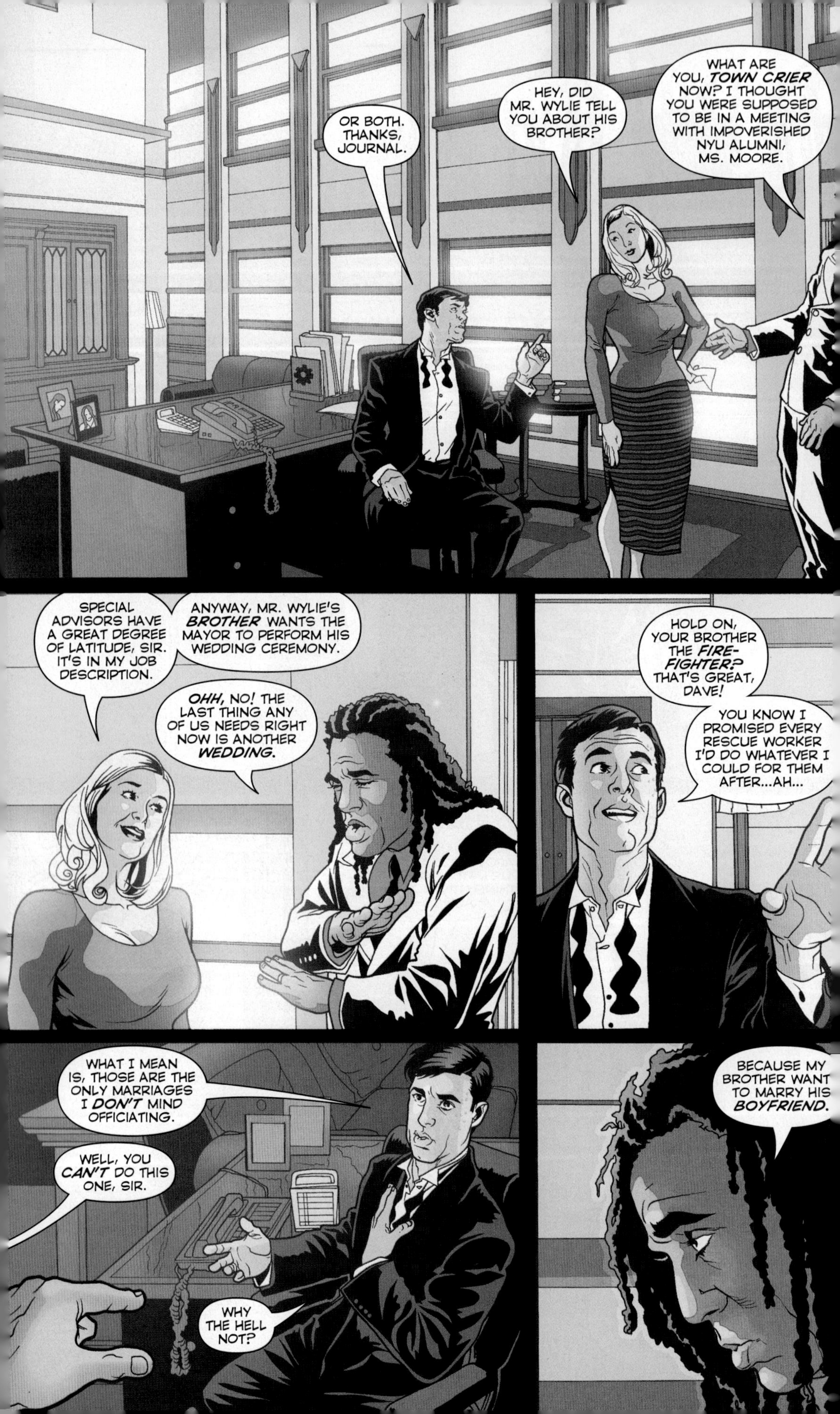

OR BOTH. THANKS, JOURNAL.
HEY, DID MR. WYLIE TELL YOU ABOUT HIS BROTHER?
WHAT ARE YOU, TOWN CRIER NOW? I THOUGHT YOU WERE SUPPOSED TO BE IN A MEETING WITH IMPOVERISHED NYU ALUMNI, MS. MOORE.
SPECIAL ADVISORS HAVE A GREAT DEGREE OF LATITUDE, SIR. IT'S IN MY JOB DESCRIPTION.
ANYWAY, MR. WYLIE'S BROTHER WANTS THE MAYOR TO PERFORM HIS WEDDING CEREMONY.
OHH, NO! THE LAST THING ANY OF US NEEDS RIGHT NOW IS ANOTHER WEDDING.
HOLD ON, YOUR BROTHER THE FIRE-FIGHTER? THAT'S GREAT, DAVE!
YOU KNOW I PROMISED EVERY RESCUE WORKER I'D DO WHATEVER I COULD FOR THEM AFTER...AH...
WHAT I MEAN IS, THOSE ARE THE ONLY MARRIAGES I DON'T MIND OFFICIATING.
WELL, YOU CAN'T DO THIS ONE, SIR.
WHY THE HELL NOT?
BECAUSE MY BROTHER WANT TO MARRY HIS BOYFRIEND.

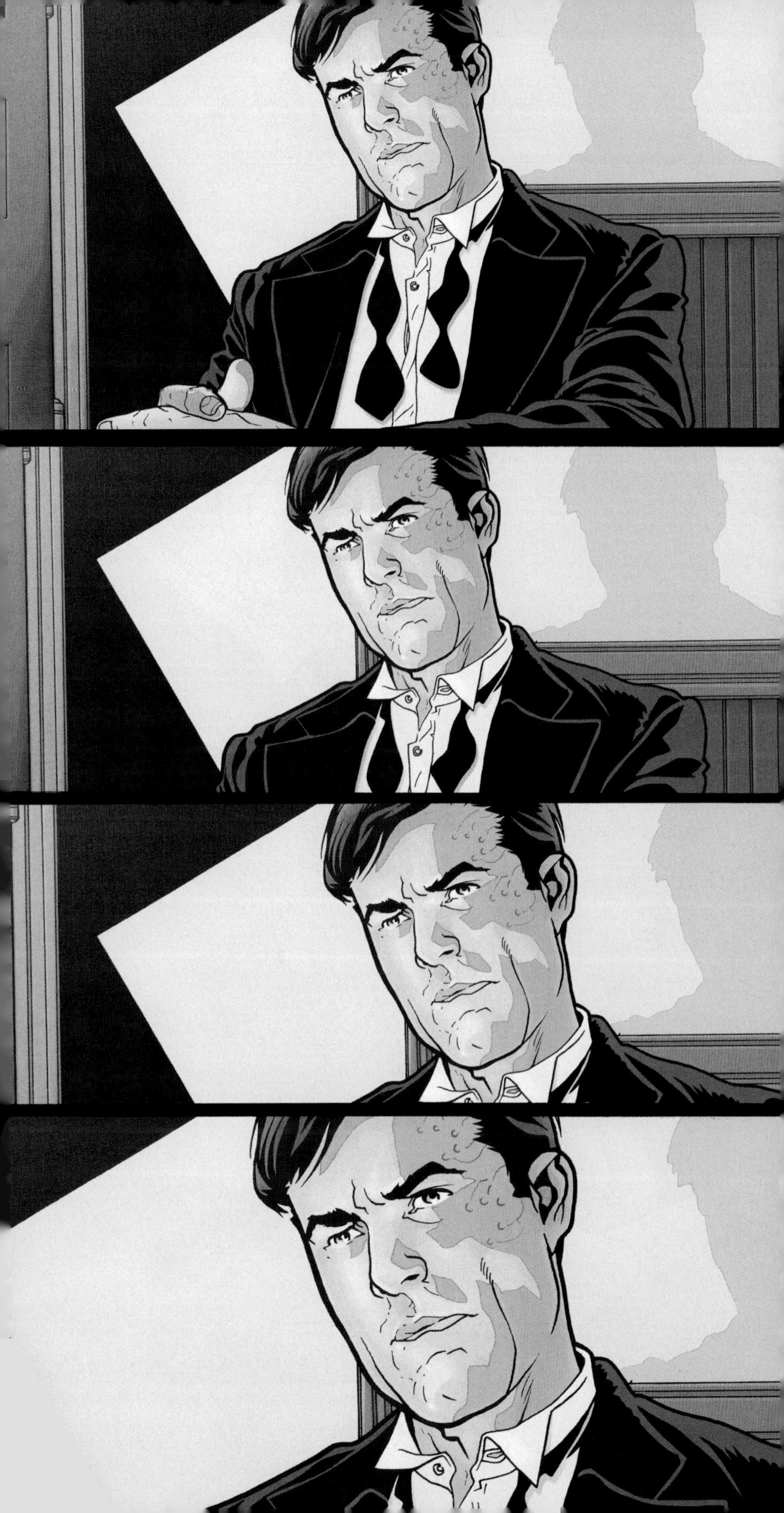

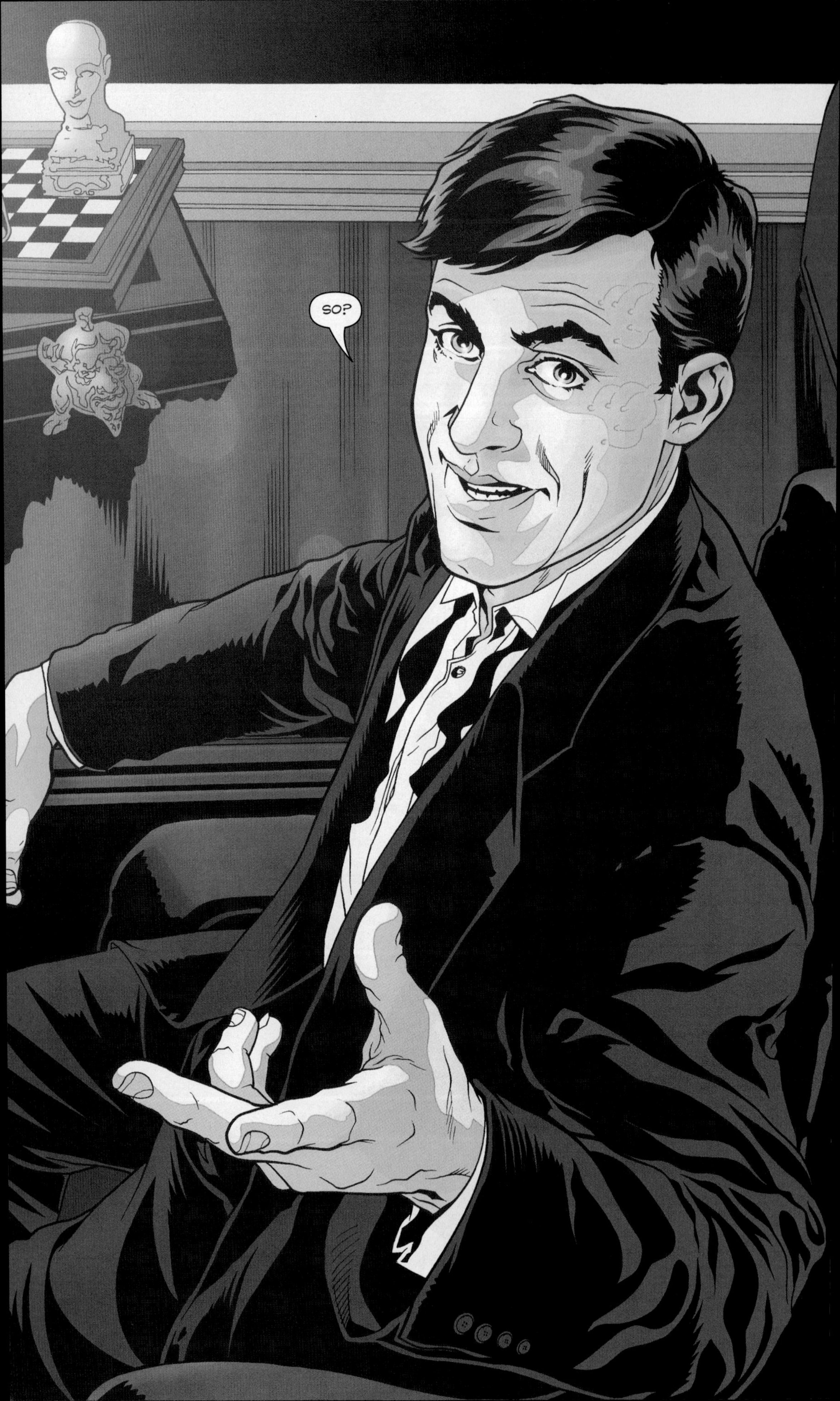
SO?

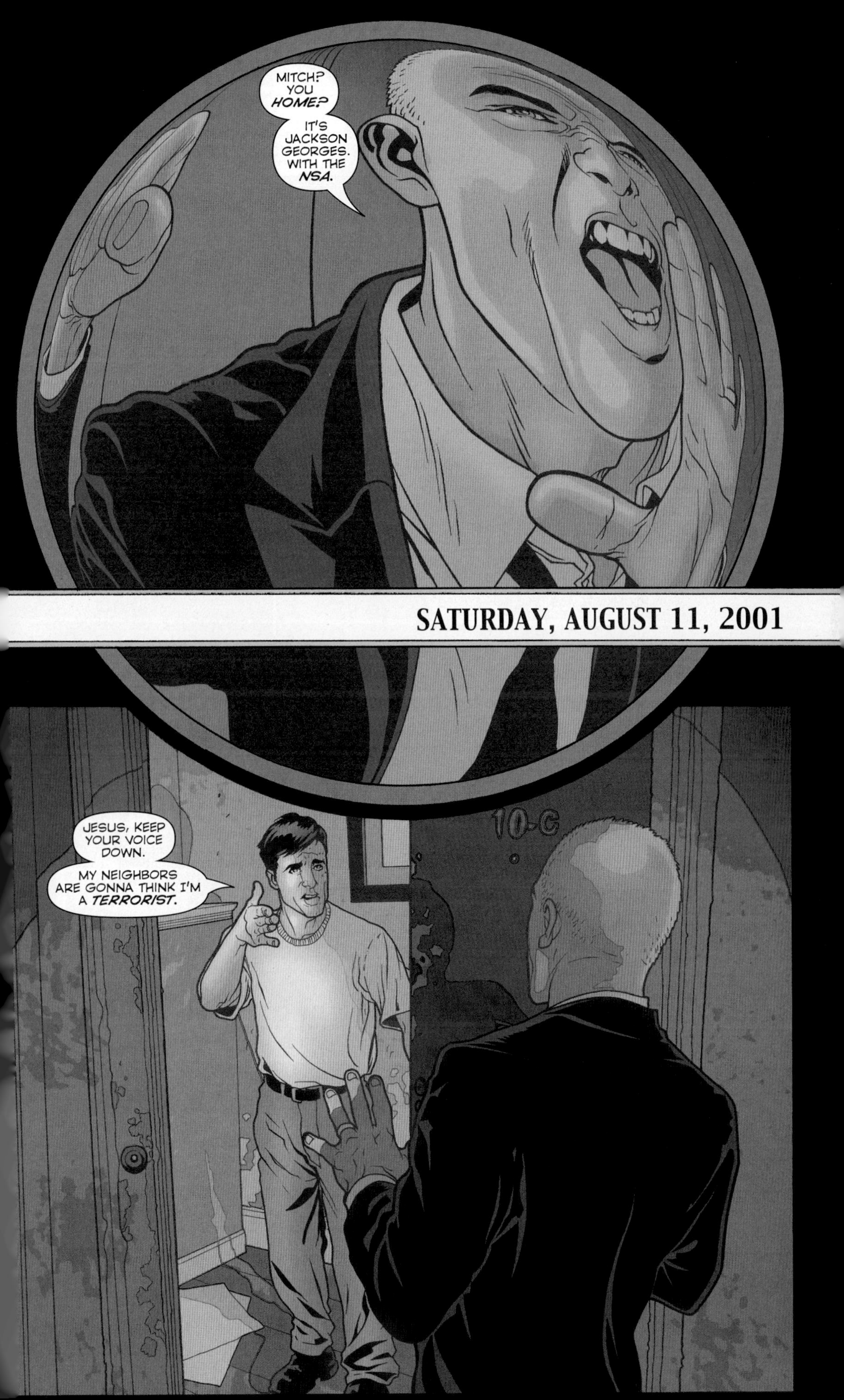

MITCH? YOU *HOME?*
IT'S JACKSON GEORGES. WITH THE *NSA.*
SATURDAY, AUGUST 11, 2001
10-C
JESUS, KEEP YOUR VOICE DOWN.
MY NEIGHBORS ARE GONNA THINK I'M A *TERRORIST.*

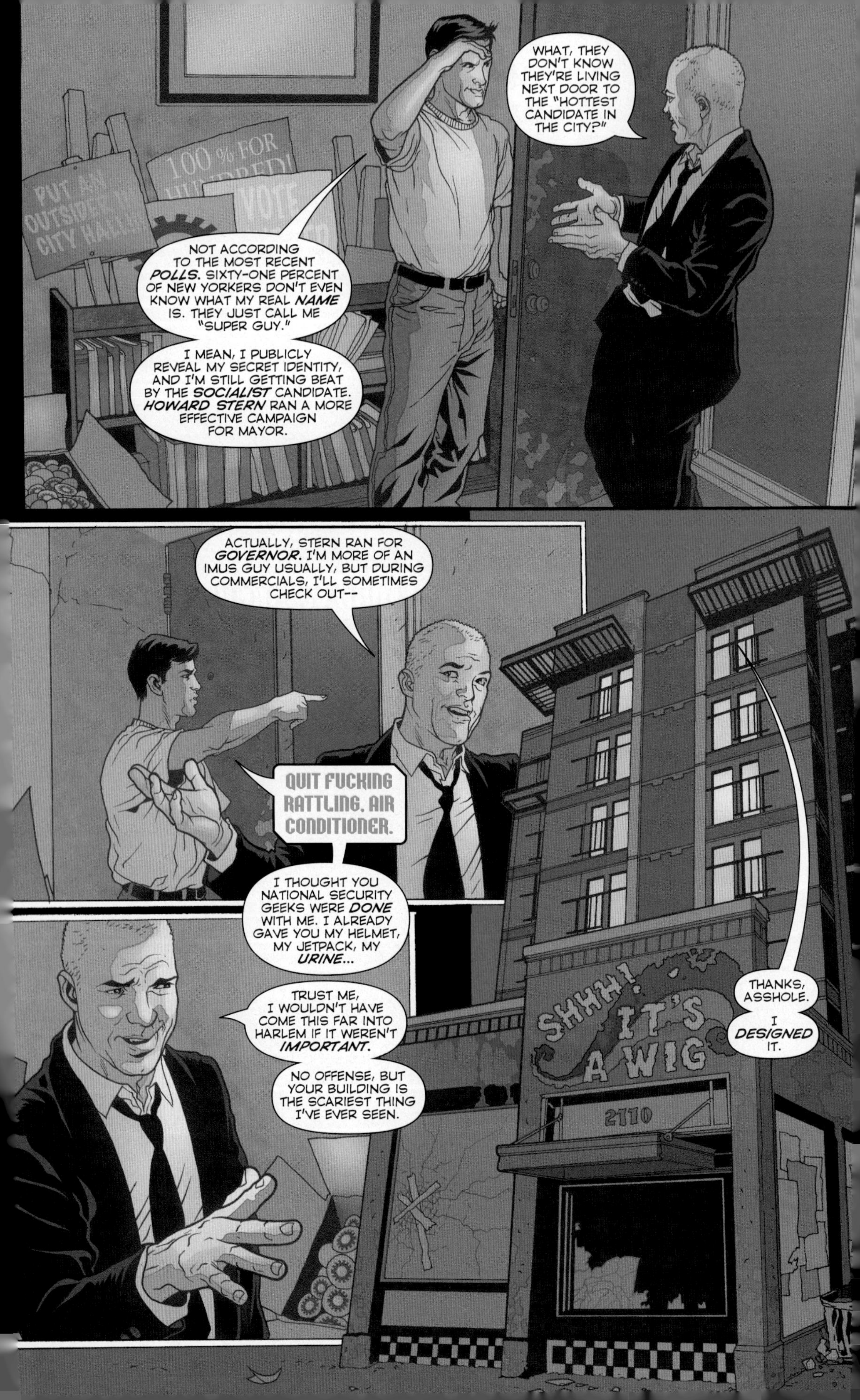
WHAT, THEY DON'T KNOW THEY'RE LIVING NEXT DOOR TO THE "HOTTEST CANDIDATE IN THE CITY?"
100% FOR
PUT AN OUTSIDER IN CITY HALL
NOT ACCORDING TO THE MOST RECENT *POLLS.* SIXTY-ONE PERCENT OF NEW YORKERS DON'T EVEN KNOW WHAT MY REAL *NAME* IS. THEY JUST CALL ME "SUPER GUY."
I MEAN, I PUBLICLY REVEAL MY SECRET IDENTITY, AND I'M STILL GETTING BEAT BY THE *SOCIALIST* CANDIDATE. *HOWARD STERN* RAN A MORE EFFECTIVE CAMPAIGN FOR MAYOR.
ACTUALLY, STERN RAN FOR *GOVERNOR*. I'M MORE OF AN IMUS GUY USUALLY, BUT DURING COMMERCIALS, I'LL SOMETIMES CHECK OUT--
QUIT FUCKING RATTLING, AIR CONDITIONER.
I THOUGHT YOU NATIONAL SECURITY GEEKS WERE *DONE* WITH ME. I ALREADY GAVE YOU MY HELMET, MY JETPACK, MY *URINE*...
TRUST ME, I WOULDN'T HAVE COME THIS FAR INTO HARLEM IF IT WEREN'T *IMPORTANT*.
NO OFFENSE, BUT YOUR BUILDING IS THE SCARIEST THING I'VE EVER SEEN.
SHHH! IT'S A WIG
2110
THANKS, ASSHOLE.
I *DESIGNED* IT.

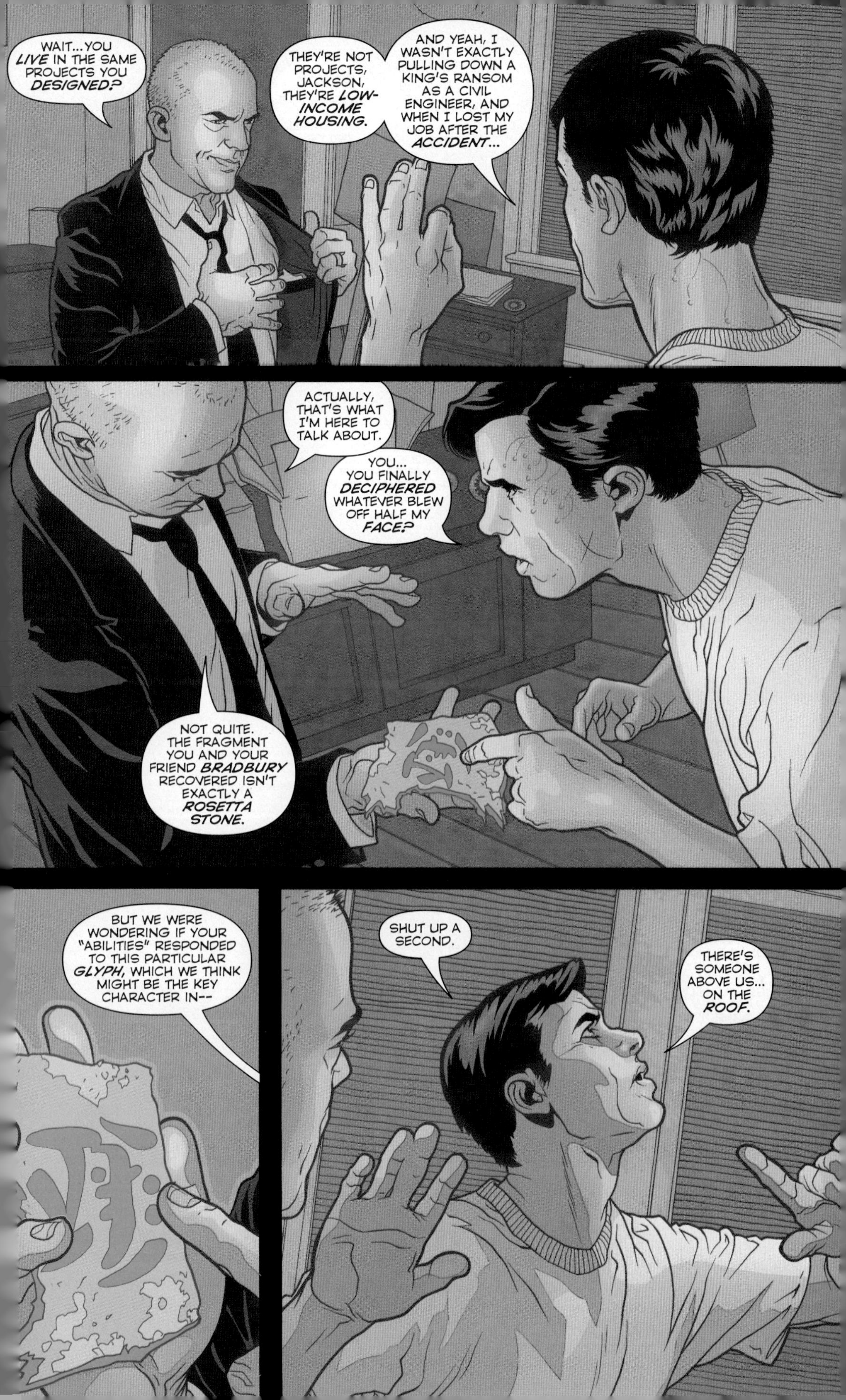
WAIT...YOU LIVE IN THE SAME PROJECTS YOU DESIGNED?
THEY'RE NOT PROJECTS, JACKSON, THEY'RE LOW-INCOME HOUSING.
AND YEAH, I WASN'T EXACTLY PULLING DOWN A KING'S RANSOM AS A CIVIL ENGINEER, AND WHEN I LOST MY JOB AFTER THE ACCIDENT...
ACTUALLY, THAT'S WHAT I'M HERE TO TALK ABOUT.
YOU... YOU FINALLY DECIPHERED WHATEVER BLEW OFF HALF MY FACE?
NOT QUITE. THE FRAGMENT YOU AND YOUR FRIEND BRADBURY RECOVERED ISN'T EXACTLY A ROSETTA STONE.
BUT WE WERE WONDERING IF YOUR "ABILITIES" RESPONDED TO THIS PARTICULAR GLYPH, WHICH WE THINK MIGHT BE THE KEY CHARACTER IN--
SHUT UP A SECOND.
THERE'S SOMEONE ABOVE US... ON THE ROOF.

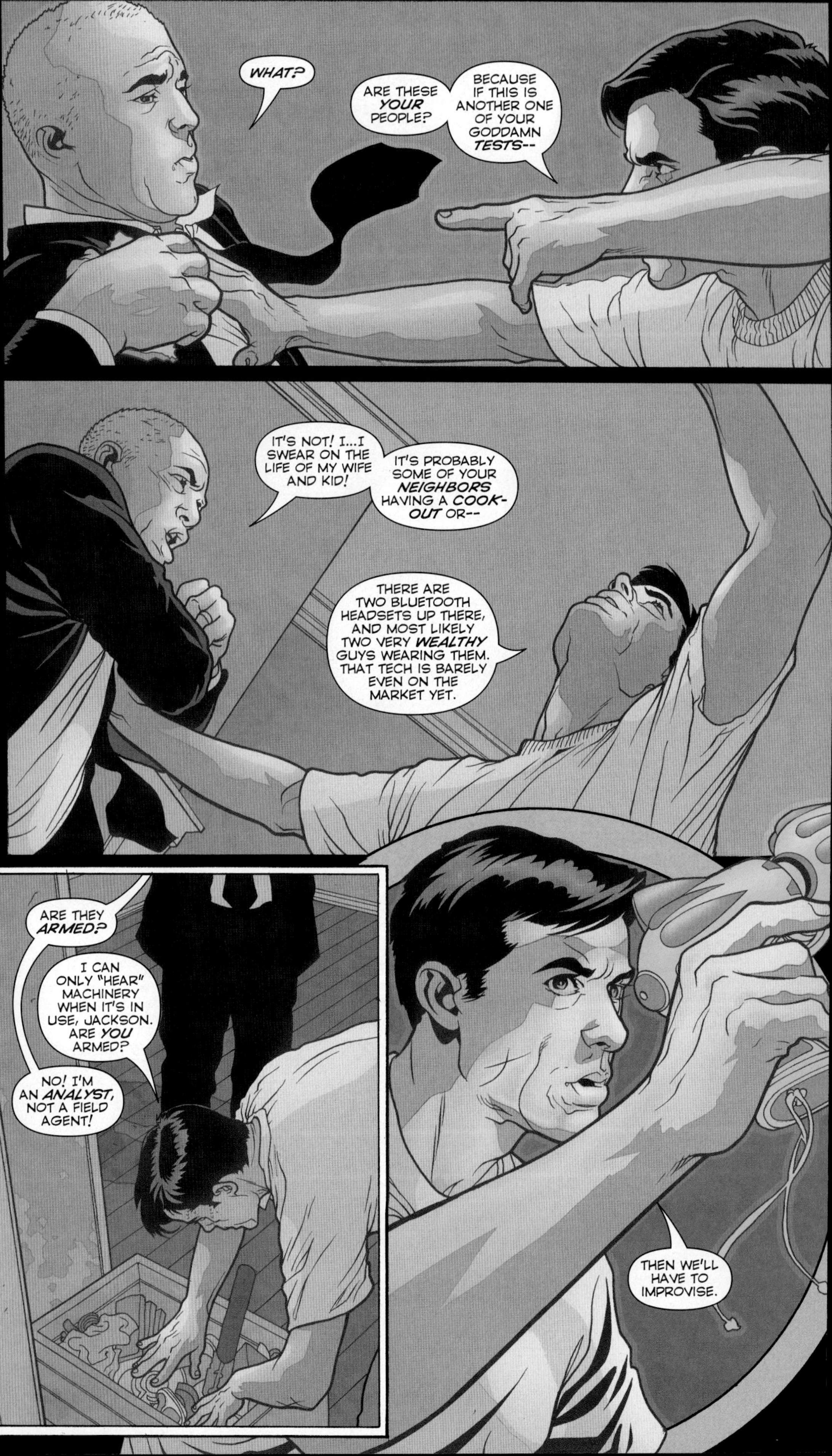
WHAT?
ARE THESE YOUR PEOPLE?
BECAUSE IF THIS IS ANOTHER ONE OF YOUR GODDAMN TESTS--
IT'S NOT! I...I SWEAR ON THE LIFE OF MY WIFE AND KID!
IT'S PROBABLY SOME OF YOUR NEIGHBORS HAVING A COOK-OUT OR--
THERE ARE TWO BLUETOOTH HEADSETS UP THERE, AND MOST LIKELY TWO VERY WEALTHY GUYS WEARING THEM. THAT TECH IS BARELY EVEN ON THE MARKET YET.
ARE THEY ARMED?
I CAN ONLY "HEAR" MACHINERY WHEN IT'S IN USE, JACKSON. ARE YOU ARMED?
NO! I'M AN ANALYST, NOT A FIELD AGENT!
THEN WE'LL HAVE TO IMPROVISE.

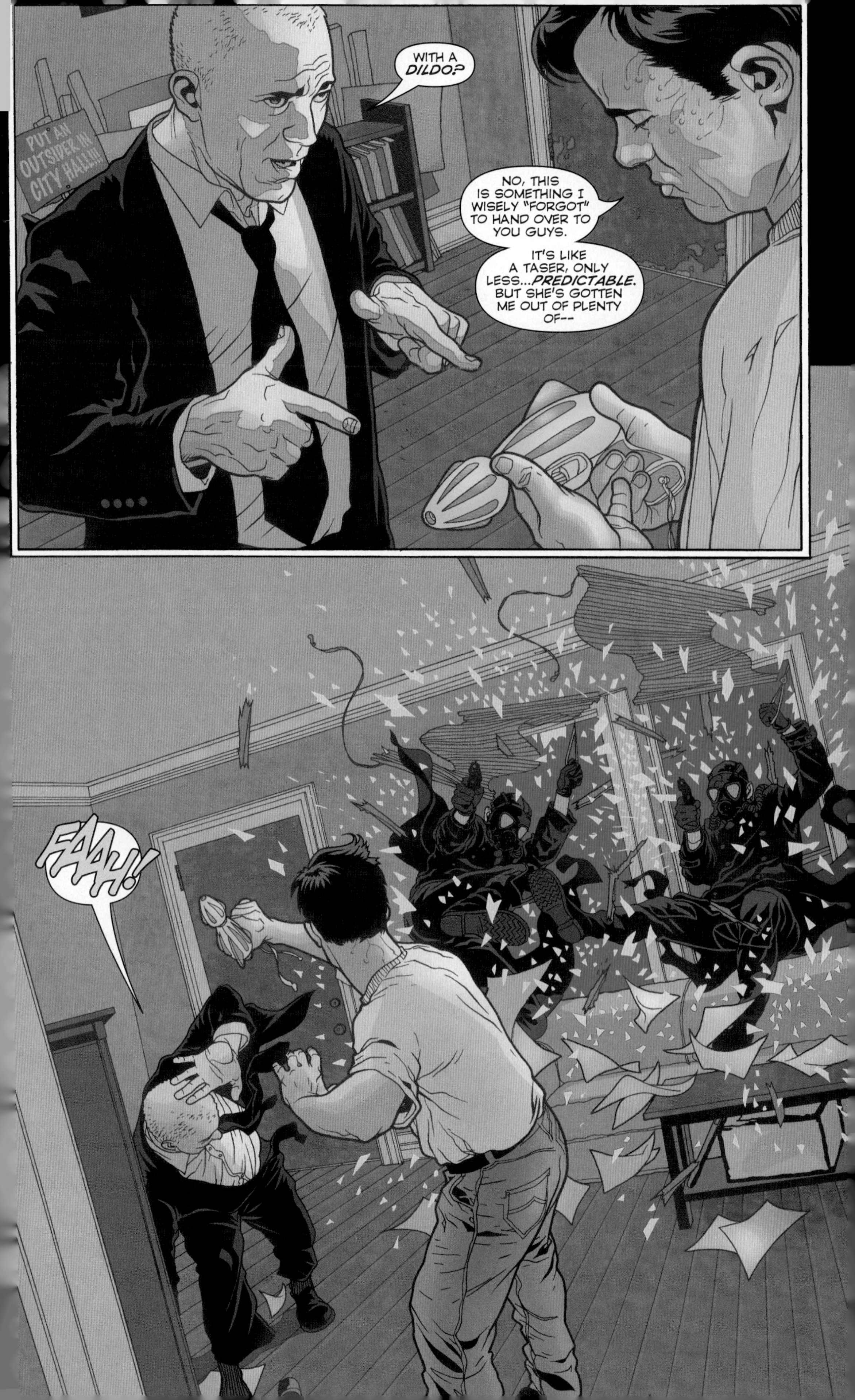
PUT AN OUTSIDER IN CITY HALL!!!
WITH A DILDO?
NO, THIS IS SOMETHING I WISELY "FORGOT" TO HAND OVER TO YOU GUYS.
IT'S LIKE A TASER, ONLY LESS...PREDICTABLE. BUT SHE'S GOTTEN ME OUT OF PLENTY OF--
FAAAH!!

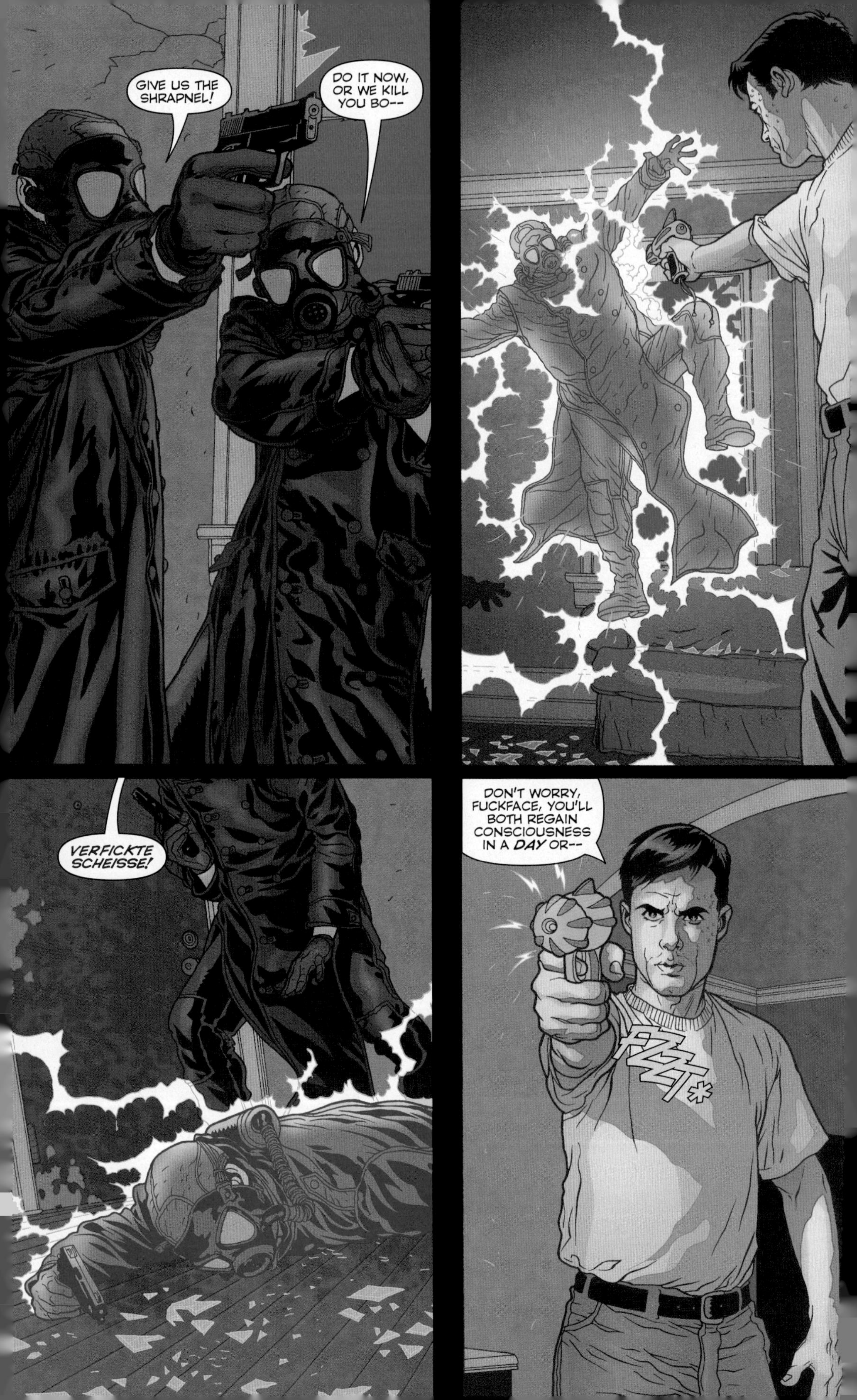
GIVE US THE SHRAPNEL!
DO IT NOW, OR WE KILL YOU BO--
VERFICKTE SCHEISSE!
DON'T WORRY, FUCKFACE, YOU'LL BOTH REGAIN CONSCIOUSNESS IN A *DAY* OR--
FZZZT*

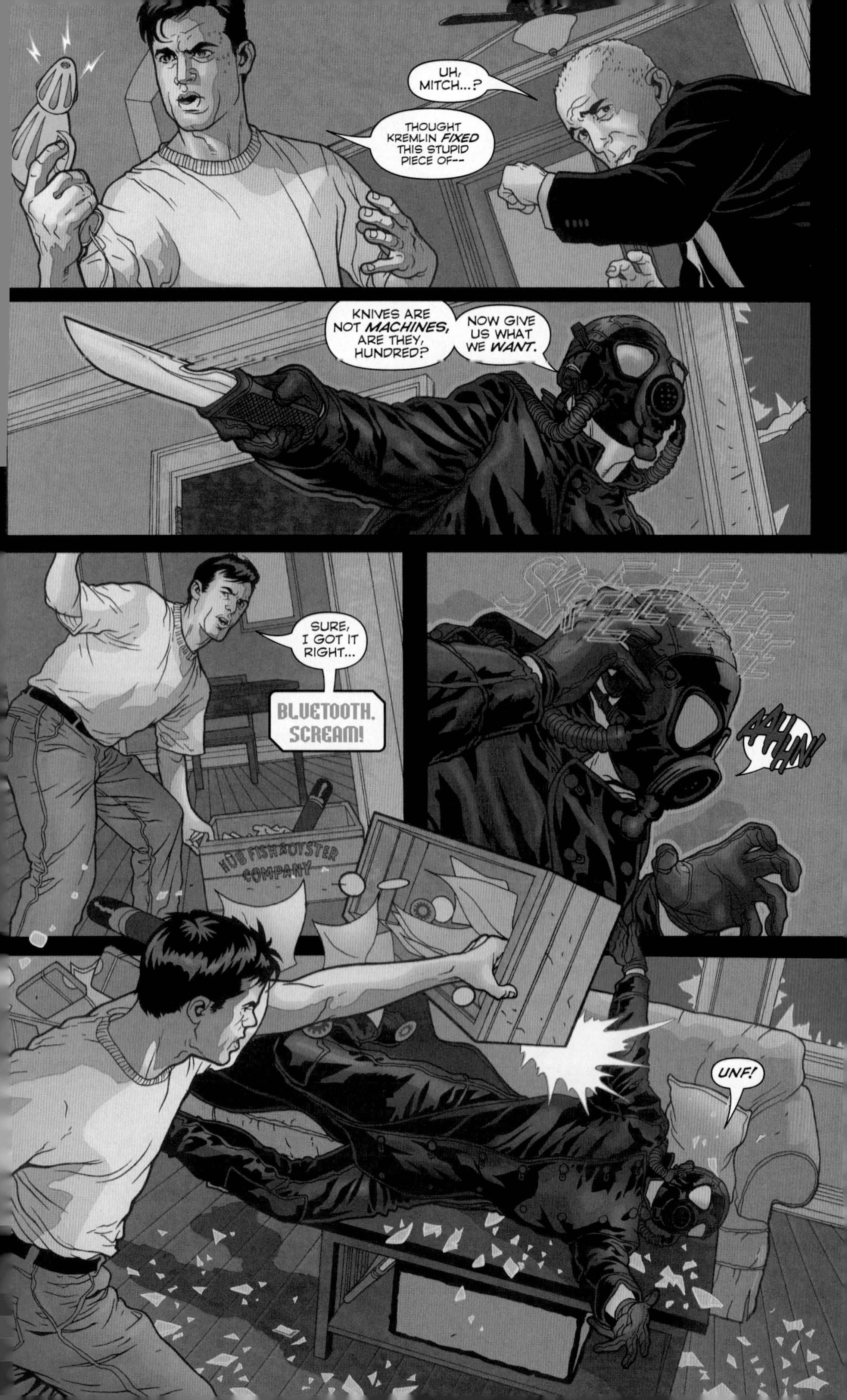
UH, MITCH...?
THOUGHT KREMLIN *FIXED* THIS STUPID PIECE OF--
KNIVES ARE NOT *MACHINES,* ARE THEY, HUNDRED?
NOW GIVE US WHAT WE *WANT.*
SURE, I GOT IT RIGHT...
BLUETOOTH, SCREAM!
HUB FISH & OYSTER COMPANY
AAHHN!
UNF!

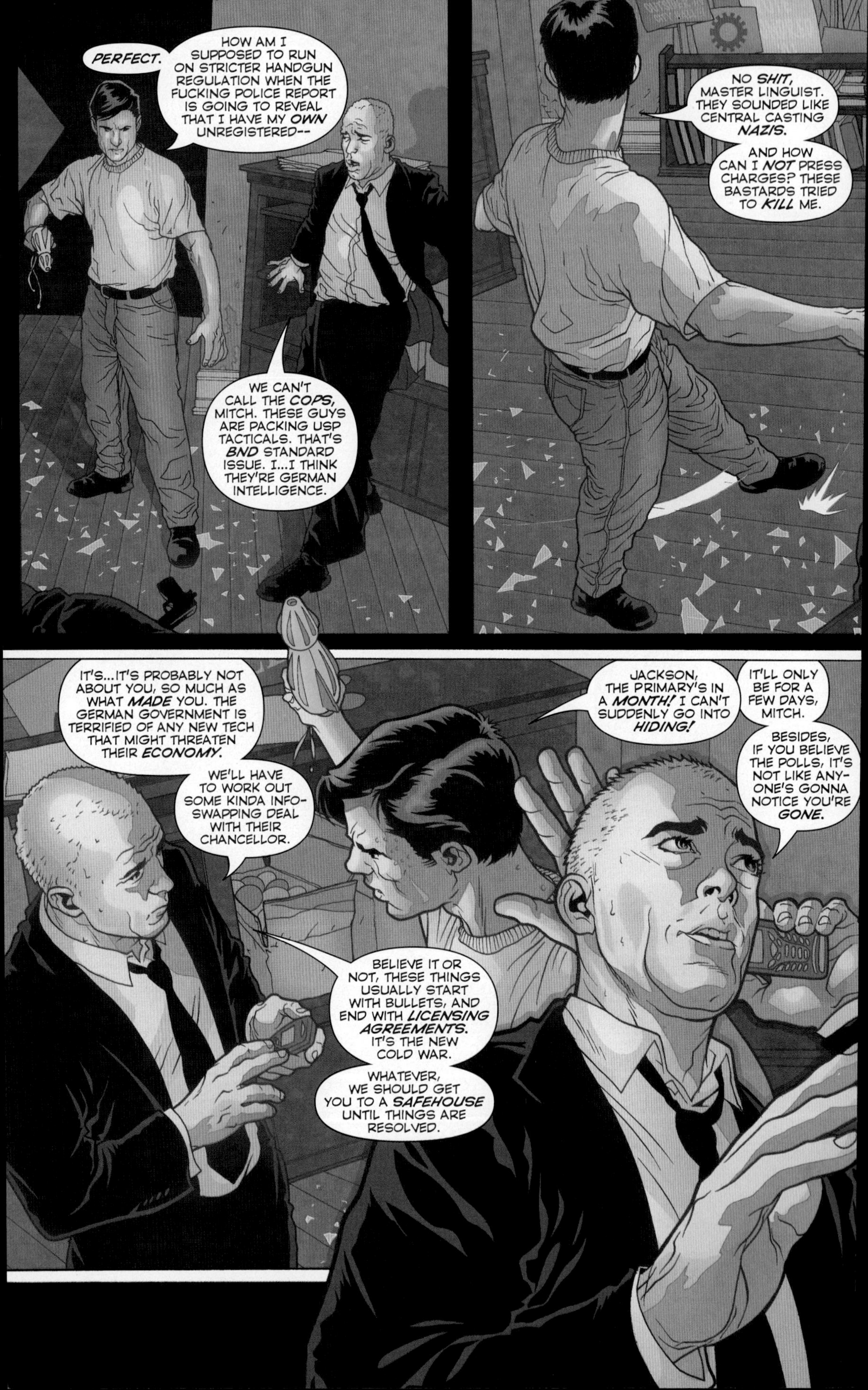
PERFECT.
HOW AM I SUPPOSED TO RUN ON STRICTER HANDGUN REGULATION WHEN THE FUCKING POLICE REPORT IS GOING TO REVEAL THAT I HAVE MY OWN UNREGISTERED--
WE CAN'T CALL THE COPS, MITCH. THESE GUYS ARE PACKING USP TACTICALS. THAT'S BND STANDARD ISSUE. I...I THINK THEY'RE GERMAN INTELLIGENCE.
NO SHIT, MASTER LINGUIST. THEY SOUNDED LIKE CENTRAL CASTING NAZIS.
AND HOW CAN I NOT PRESS CHARGES? THESE BASTARDS TRIED TO KILL ME.
IT'S...IT'S PROBABLY NOT ABOUT YOU, SO MUCH AS WHAT MADE YOU. THE GERMAN GOVERNMENT IS TERRIFIED OF ANY NEW TECH THAT MIGHT THREATEN THEIR ECONOMY.
WE'LL HAVE TO WORK OUT SOME KINDA INFO-SWAPPING DEAL WITH THEIR CHANCELLOR.
BELIEVE IT OR NOT, THESE THINGS USUALLY START WITH BULLETS, AND END WITH LICENSING AGREEMENTS. IT'S THE NEW COLD WAR.
WHATEVER, WE SHOULD GET YOU TO A SAFEHOUSE UNTIL THINGS ARE RESOLVED.
JACKSON, THE PRIMARY'S IN A MONTH! I CAN'T SUDDENLY GO INTO HIDING!
IT'LL ONLY BE FOR A FEW DAYS, MITCH.
BESIDES, IF YOU BELIEVE THE POLLS, IT'S NOT LIKE ANY-ONE'S GONNA NOTICE YOU'RE GONE.

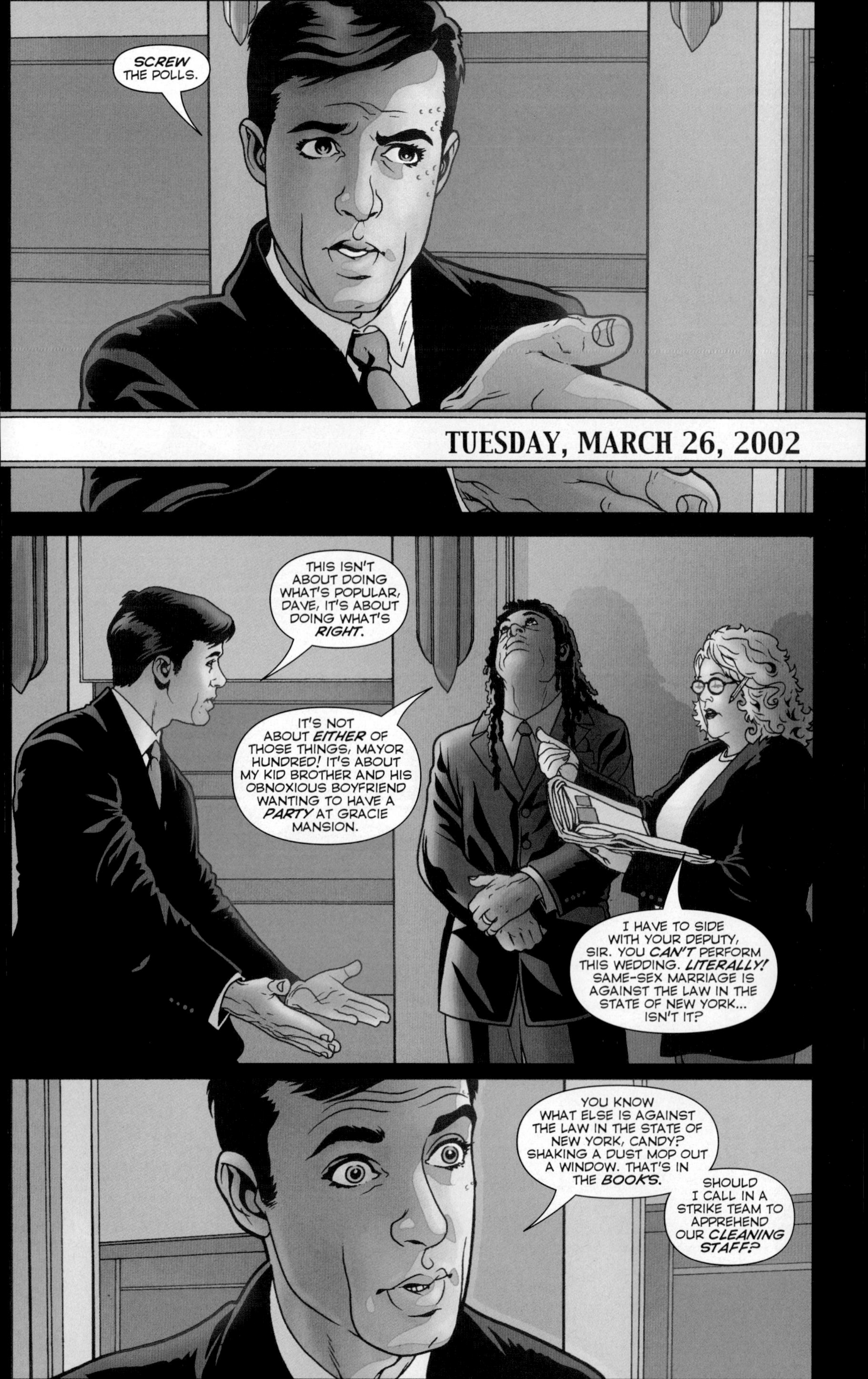
SCREW THE POLLS.
TUESDAY, MARCH 26, 2002
THIS ISN'T ABOUT DOING WHAT'S POPULAR, DAVE, IT'S ABOUT DOING WHAT'S RIGHT.
IT'S NOT ABOUT EITHER OF THOSE THINGS, MAYOR HUNDRED! IT'S ABOUT MY KID BROTHER AND HIS OBNOXIOUS BOYFRIEND WANTING TO HAVE A PARTY AT GRACIE MANSION.
I HAVE TO SIDE WITH YOUR DEPUTY, SIR. YOU CAN'T PERFORM THIS WEDDING. LITERALLY! SAME-SEX MARRIAGE IS AGAINST THE LAW IN THE STATE OF NEW YORK... ISN'T IT?
YOU KNOW WHAT ELSE IS AGAINST THE LAW IN THE STATE OF NEW YORK, CANDY? SHAKING A DUST MOP OUT A WINDOW. THAT'S IN THE BOOKS.
SHOULD I CALL IN A STRIKE TEAM TO APPREHEND OUR CLEANING STAFF?

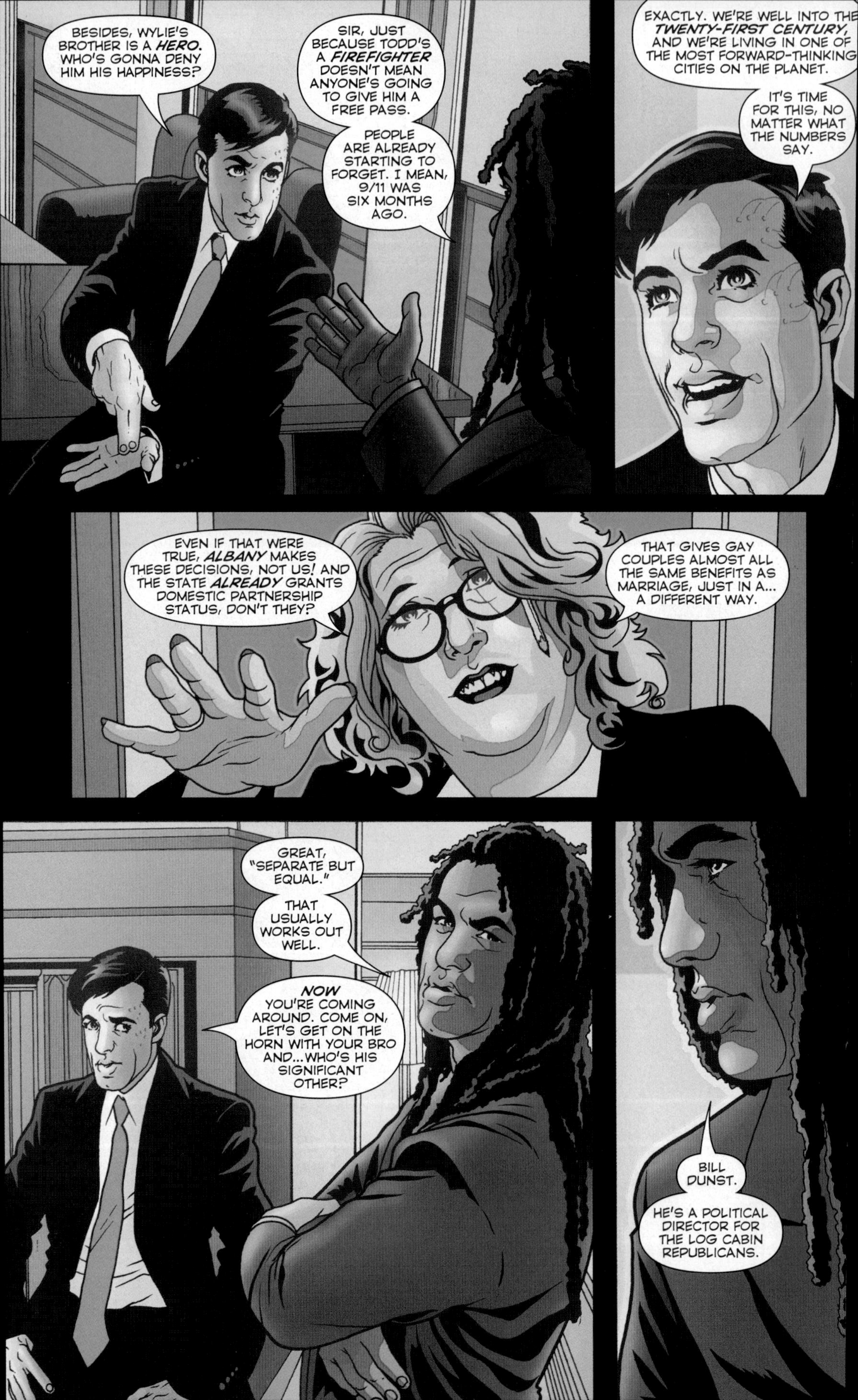
BESIDES, WYLIE'S BROTHER IS A **HERO.** WHO'S GONNA DENY HIM HIS HAPPINESS?
SIR, JUST BECAUSE TODD'S A ***FIREFIGHTER*** DOESN'T MEAN ANYONE'S GOING TO GIVE HIM A FREE PASS.
PEOPLE ARE ALREADY STARTING TO FORGET. I MEAN, 9/11 WAS SIX MONTHS AGO.
EXACTLY. WE'RE WELL INTO THE ***TWENTY-FIRST CENTURY,*** AND WE'RE LIVING IN ONE OF THE MOST FORWARD-THINKING CITIES ON THE PLANET.
IT'S TIME FOR THIS, NO MATTER WHAT THE NUMBERS SAY.
EVEN IF THAT WERE TRUE, ***ALBANY*** MAKES THESE DECISIONS, NOT US! AND THE STATE ***ALREADY*** GRANTS DOMESTIC PARTNERSHIP STATUS, DON'T THEY?
THAT GIVES GAY COUPLES ALMOST ALL THE SAME BENEFITS AS MARRIAGE, JUST IN A... A DIFFERENT WAY.
GREAT, "SEPARATE BUT EQUAL."
THAT USUALLY WORKS OUT WELL.
NOW YOU'RE COMING AROUND. COME ON, LET'S GET ON THE HORN WITH YOUR BRO AND...WHO'S HIS SIGNIFICANT OTHER?
BILL DUNST.
HE'S A POLITICAL DIRECTOR FOR THE LOG CABIN REPUBLICANS.

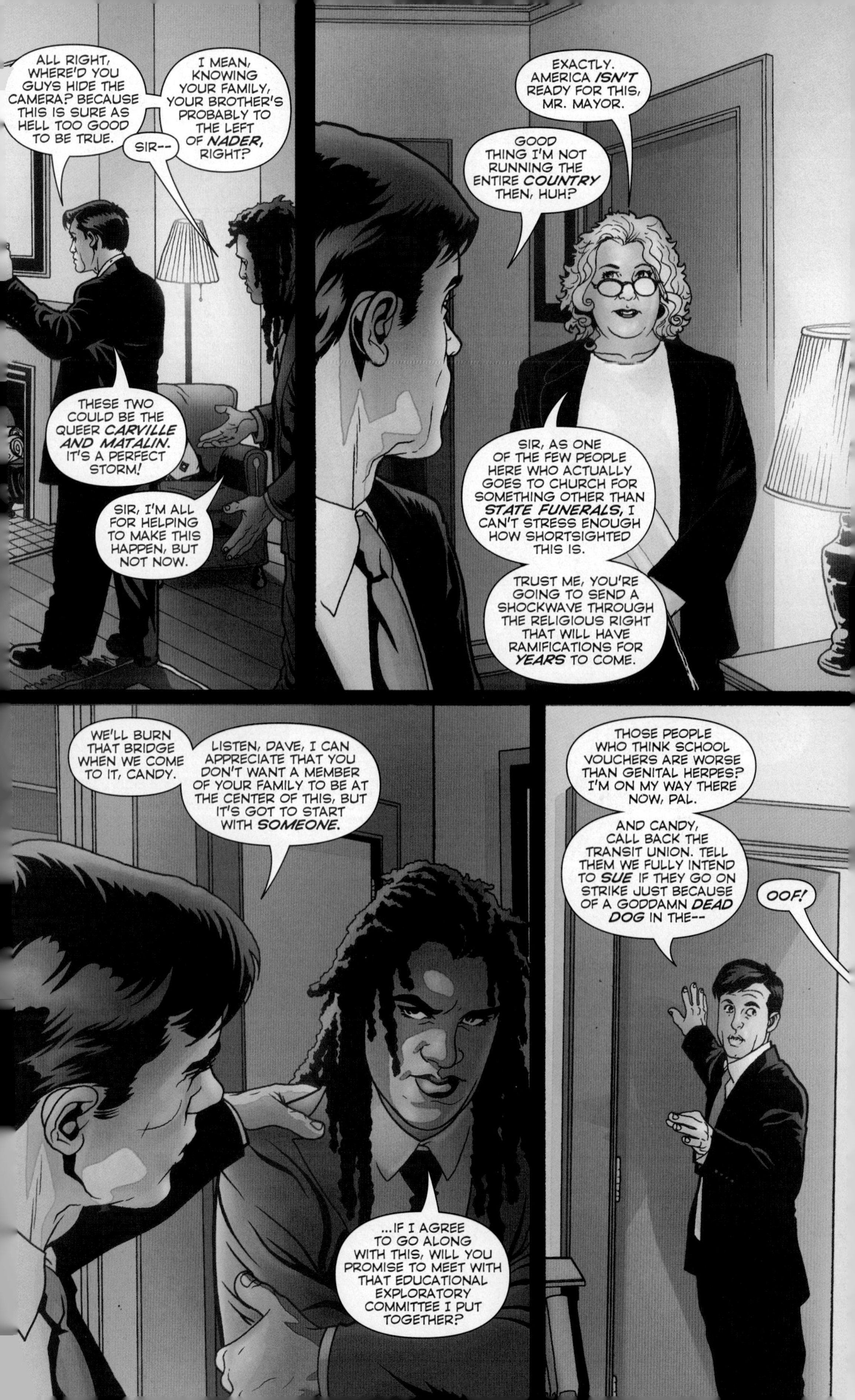
ALL RIGHT, WHERE'D YOU GUYS HIDE THE CAMERA? BECAUSE THIS IS SURE AS HELL TOO GOOD TO BE TRUE.
SIR--
I MEAN, KNOWING YOUR FAMILY, YOUR BROTHER'S PROBABLY TO THE LEFT OF NADER, RIGHT?
THESE TWO COULD BE THE QUEER CARVILLE AND MATALIN. IT'S A PERFECT STORM!
SIR, I'M ALL FOR HELPING TO MAKE THIS HAPPEN, BUT NOT NOW.
EXACTLY. AMERICA ISN'T READY FOR THIS, MR. MAYOR.
GOOD THING I'M NOT RUNNING THE ENTIRE COUNTRY THEN, HUH?
SIR, AS ONE OF THE FEW PEOPLE HERE WHO ACTUALLY GOES TO CHURCH FOR SOMETHING OTHER THAN STATE FUNERALS, I CAN'T STRESS ENOUGH HOW SHORTSIGHTED THIS IS.
TRUST ME, YOU'RE GOING TO SEND A SHOCKWAVE THROUGH THE RELIGIOUS RIGHT THAT WILL HAVE RAMIFICATIONS FOR YEARS TO COME.
WE'LL BURN THAT BRIDGE WHEN WE COME TO IT, CANDY.
LISTEN, DAVE, I CAN APPRECIATE THAT YOU DON'T WANT A MEMBER OF YOUR FAMILY TO BE AT THE CENTER OF THIS, BUT IT'S GOT TO START WITH SOMEONE.
...IF I AGREE TO GO ALONG WITH THIS, WILL YOU PROMISE TO MEET WITH THAT EDUCATIONAL EXPLORATORY COMMITTEE I PUT TOGETHER?
THOSE PEOPLE WHO THINK SCHOOL VOUCHERS ARE WORSE THAN GENITAL HERPES? I'M ON MY WAY THERE NOW, PAL.
AND CANDY, CALL BACK THE TRANSIT UNION. TELL THEM WE FULLY INTEND TO SUE IF THEY GO ON STRIKE JUST BECAUSE OF A GODDAMN DEAD DOG IN THE--
OOF!

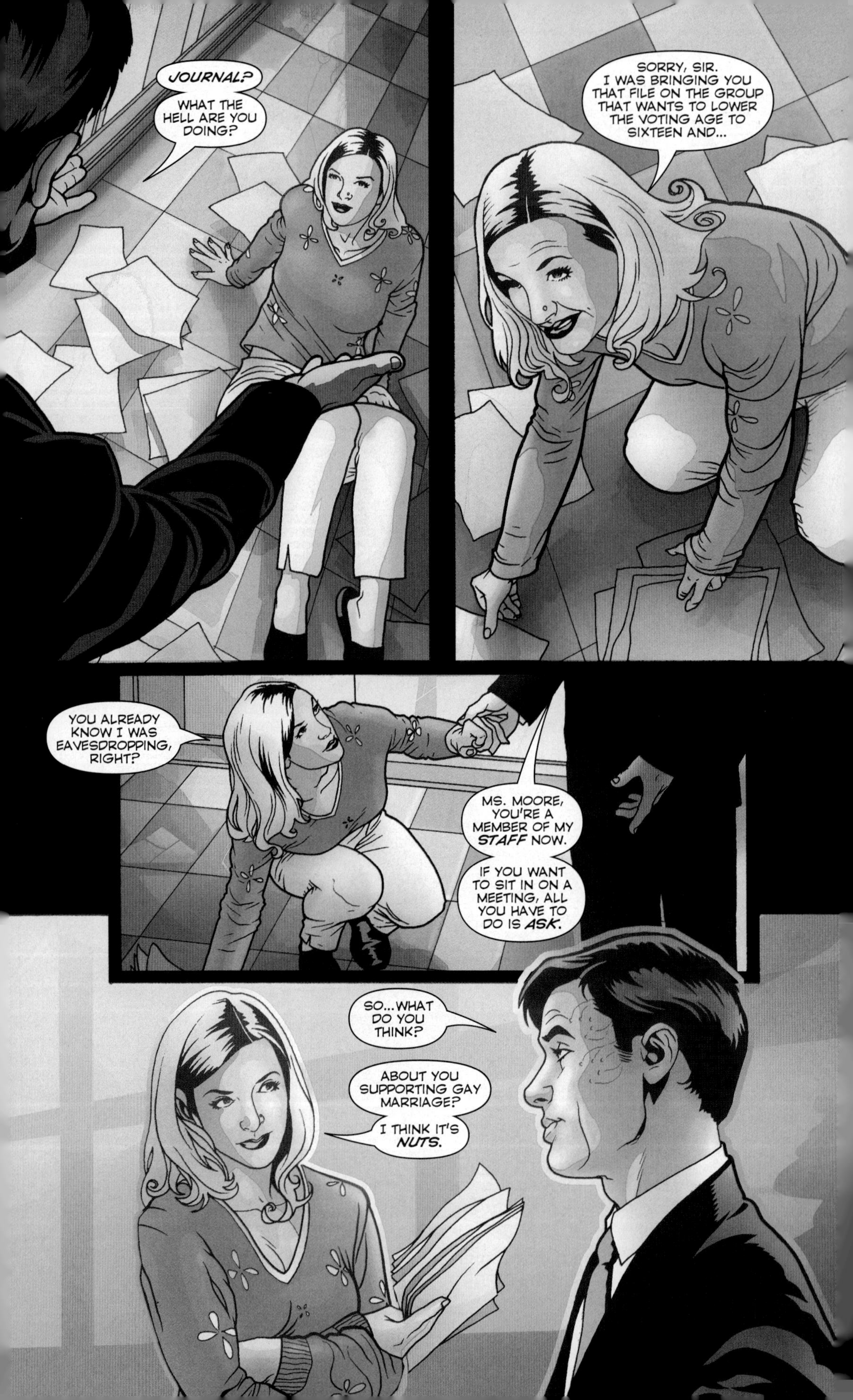
JOURNAL?
WHAT THE HELL ARE YOU DOING?
SORRY, SIR. I WAS BRINGING YOU THAT FILE ON THE GROUP THAT WANTS TO LOWER THE VOTING AGE TO SIXTEEN AND...
YOU ALREADY KNOW I WAS EAVESDROPPING, RIGHT?
MS. MOORE, YOU'RE A MEMBER OF MY STAFF NOW.
IF YOU WANT TO SIT IN ON A MEETING, ALL YOU HAVE TO DO IS ASK.
SO...WHAT DO YOU THINK?
ABOUT YOU SUPPORTING GAY MARRIAGE?
I THINK IT'S NUTS.

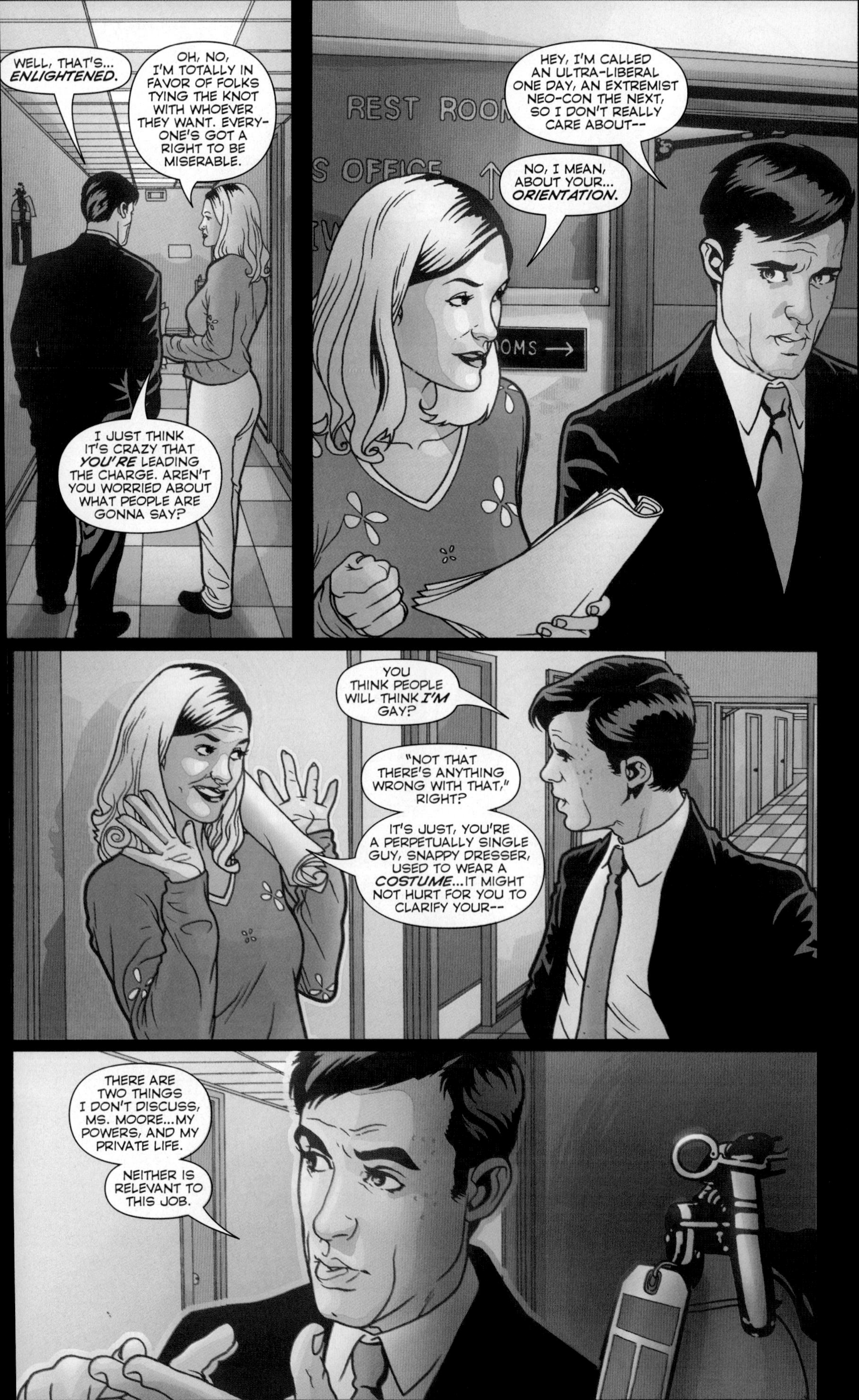
WELL, THAT'S... ENLIGHTENED.
OH, NO, I'M TOTALLY IN FAVOR OF FOLKS TYING THE KNOT WITH WHOEVER THEY WANT. EVERY-ONE'S GOT A RIGHT TO BE MISERABLE.
I JUST THINK IT'S CRAZY THAT YOU'RE LEADING THE CHARGE. AREN'T YOU WORRIED ABOUT WHAT PEOPLE ARE GONNA SAY?
REST ROOM
S OFFICE
OMS →
HEY, I'M CALLED AN ULTRA-LIBERAL ONE DAY, AN EXTREMIST NEO-CON THE NEXT, SO I DON'T REALLY CARE ABOUT--
NO, I MEAN, ABOUT YOUR... ORIENTATION.
YOU THINK PEOPLE WILL THINK I'M GAY?
"NOT THAT THERE'S ANYTHING WRONG WITH THAT," RIGHT?
IT'S JUST, YOU'RE A PERPETUALLY SINGLE GUY, SNAPPY DRESSER, USED TO WEAR A COSTUME...IT MIGHT NOT HURT FOR YOU TO CLARIFY YOUR--
THERE ARE TWO THINGS I DON'T DISCUSS, MS. MOORE...MY POWERS, AND MY PRIVATE LIFE.
NEITHER IS RELEVANT TO THIS JOB.

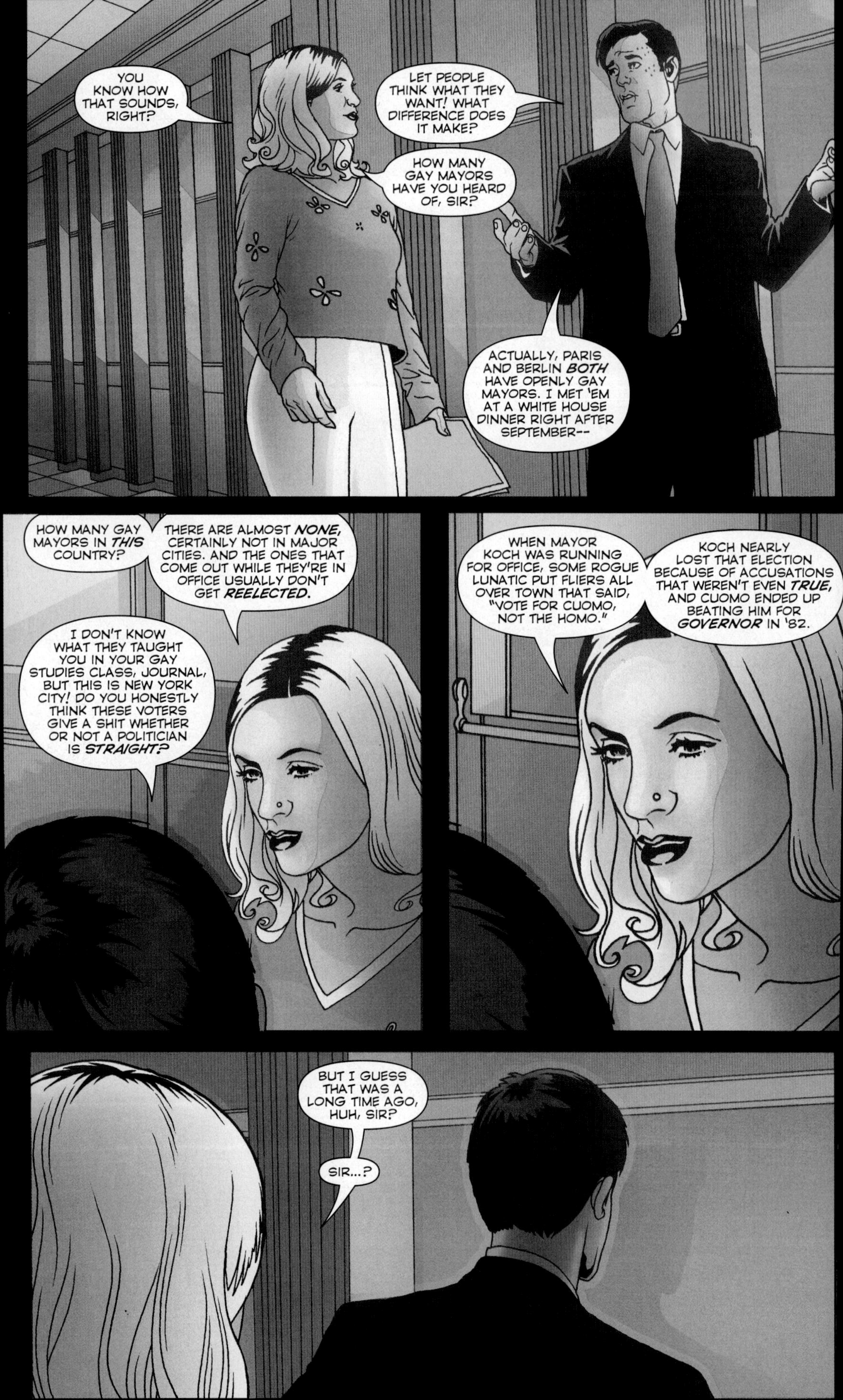
YOU KNOW HOW THAT SOUNDS, RIGHT?
LET PEOPLE THINK WHAT THEY WANT! WHAT DIFFERENCE DOES IT MAKE?
HOW MANY GAY MAYORS HAVE YOU HEARD OF, SIR?
ACTUALLY, PARIS AND BERLIN *BOTH* HAVE OPENLY GAY MAYORS. I MET 'EM AT A WHITE HOUSE DINNER RIGHT AFTER SEPTEMBER--
HOW MANY GAY MAYORS IN *THIS* COUNTRY?
THERE ARE ALMOST *NONE*, CERTAINLY NOT IN MAJOR CITIES. AND THE ONES THAT COME OUT WHILE THEY'RE IN OFFICE USUALLY DON'T GET *REELECTED*.
I DON'T KNOW WHAT THEY TAUGHT YOU IN YOUR GAY STUDIES CLASS, JOURNAL, BUT THIS IS NEW YORK CITY! DO YOU HONESTLY THINK THESE VOTERS GIVE A SHIT WHETHER OR NOT A POLITICIAN IS *STRAIGHT?*
WHEN MAYOR KOCH WAS RUNNING FOR OFFICE, SOME ROGUE LUNATIC PUT FLIERS ALL OVER TOWN THAT SAID, "VOTE FOR CUOMO, NOT THE HOMO."
KOCH NEARLY LOST THAT ELECTION BECAUSE OF ACCUSATIONS THAT WEREN'T EVEN *TRUE*, AND CUOMO ENDED UP BEATING HIM FOR *GOVERNOR* IN '82.
BUT I GUESS THAT WAS A LONG TIME AGO, HUH, SIR?
SIR...?

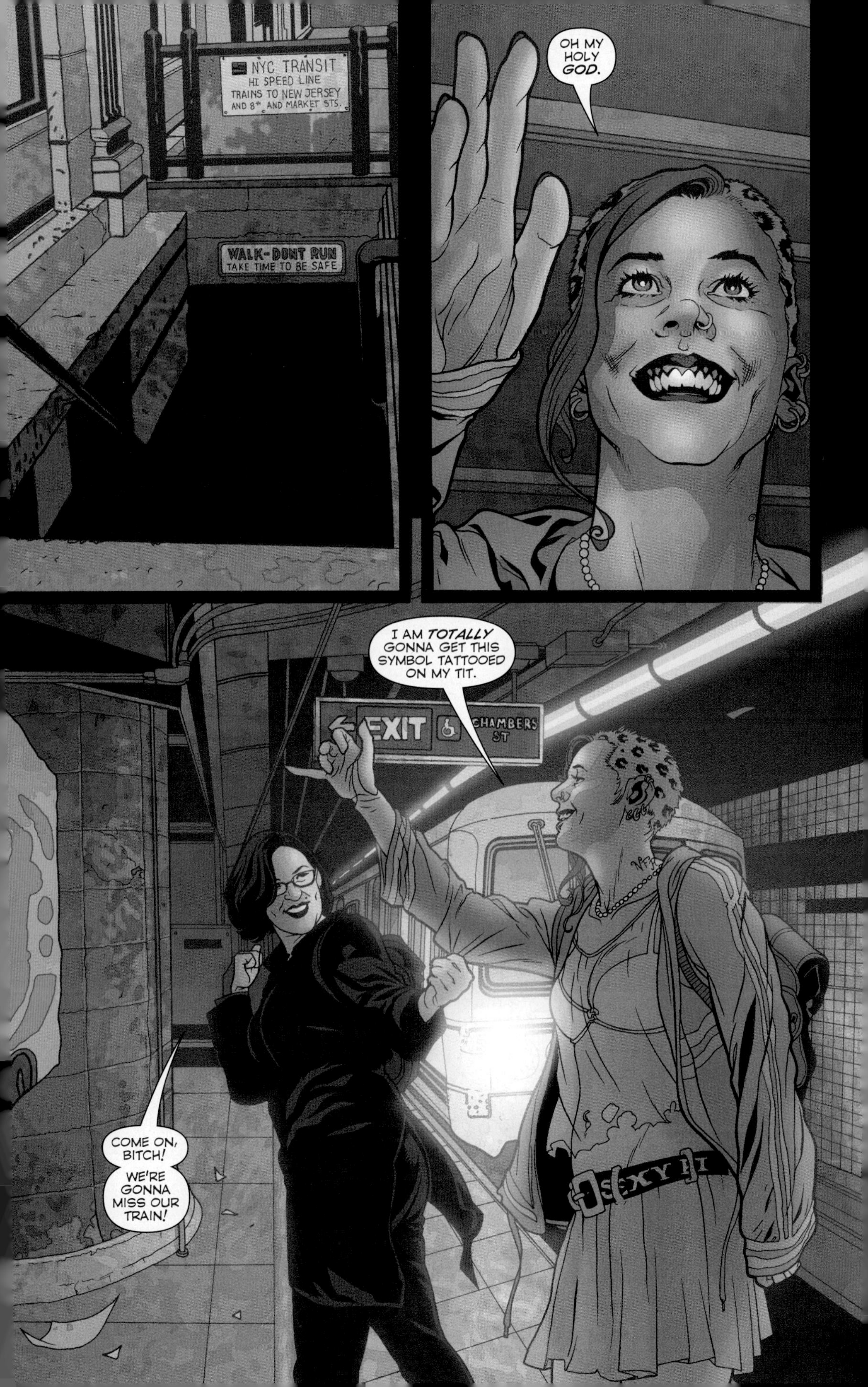
NYC TRANSIT
HI SPEED LINE
TRAINS TO NEW JERSEY
AND 8th AND MARKET STS.
WALK-DONT RUN
TAKE TIME TO BE SAFE
OH MY HOLY *GOD.*
EXIT
CHAMBERS ST
I AM *TOTALLY* GONNA GET THIS SYMBOL TATTOOED ON MY TIT.
COME ON, BITCH!
WE'RE GONNA MISS OUR TRAIN!
SEXY

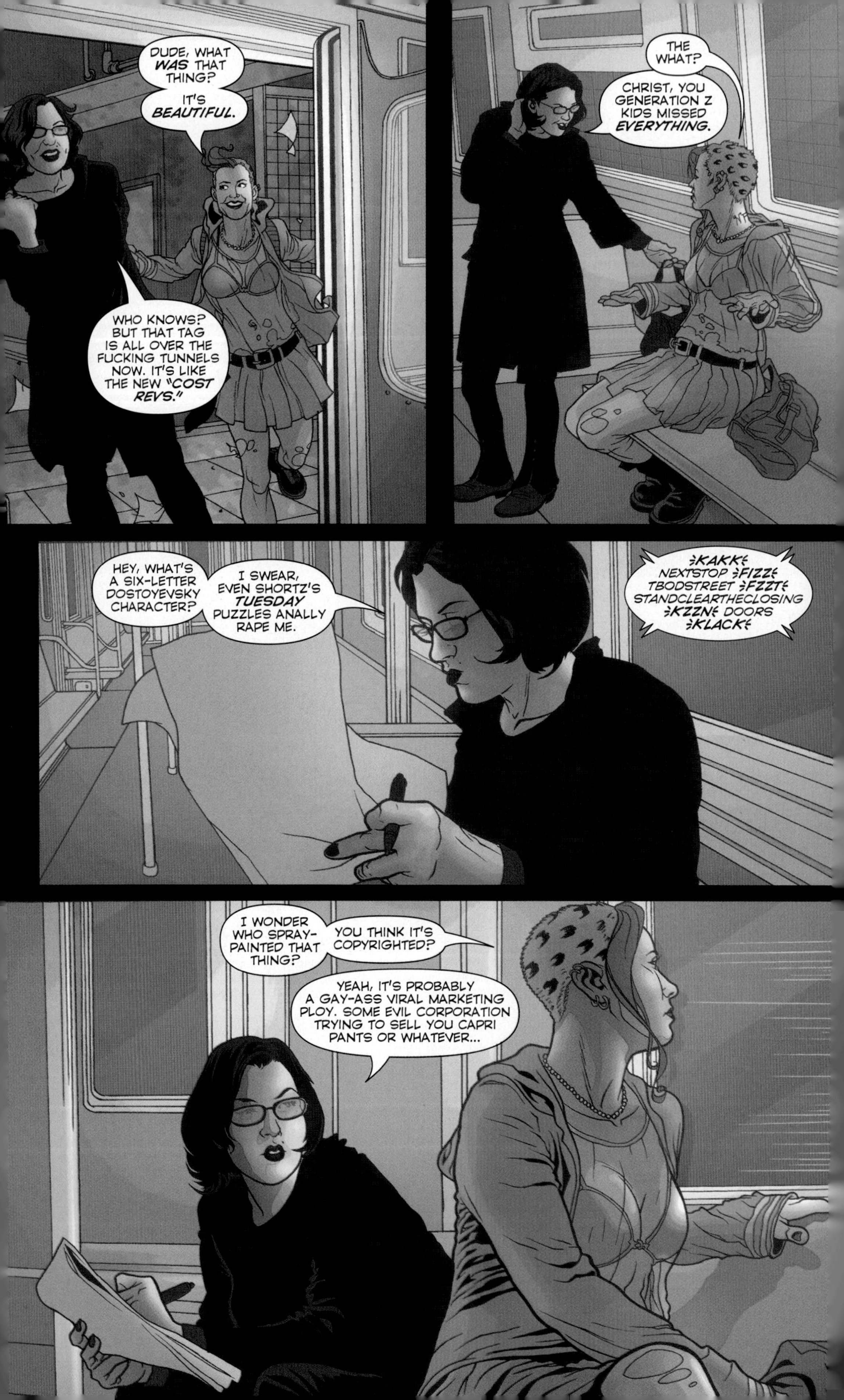
DUDE, WHAT WAS THAT THING?
IT'S BEAUTIFUL.
WHO KNOWS? BUT THAT TAG IS ALL OVER THE FUCKING TUNNELS NOW. IT'S LIKE THE NEW "COST REVS."
THE WHAT?
CHRIST, YOU GENERATION Z KIDS MISSED EVERYTHING.
HEY, WHAT'S A SIX-LETTER DOSTOYEVSKY CHARACTER?
I SWEAR, EVEN SHORTZ'S TUESDAY PUZZLES ANALLY RAPE ME.
KAKK NEXTSTOP FIZZ TBODSTREET FZZT STANDCLEARTHECLOSING KZZN DOORS KLACK
I WONDER WHO SPRAY-PAINTED THAT THING?
YOU THINK IT'S COPYRIGHTED?
YEAH, IT'S PROBABLY A GAY-ASS VIRAL MARKETING PLOY. SOME EVIL CORPORATION TRYING TO SELL YOU CAPRI PANTS OR WHATEVER...

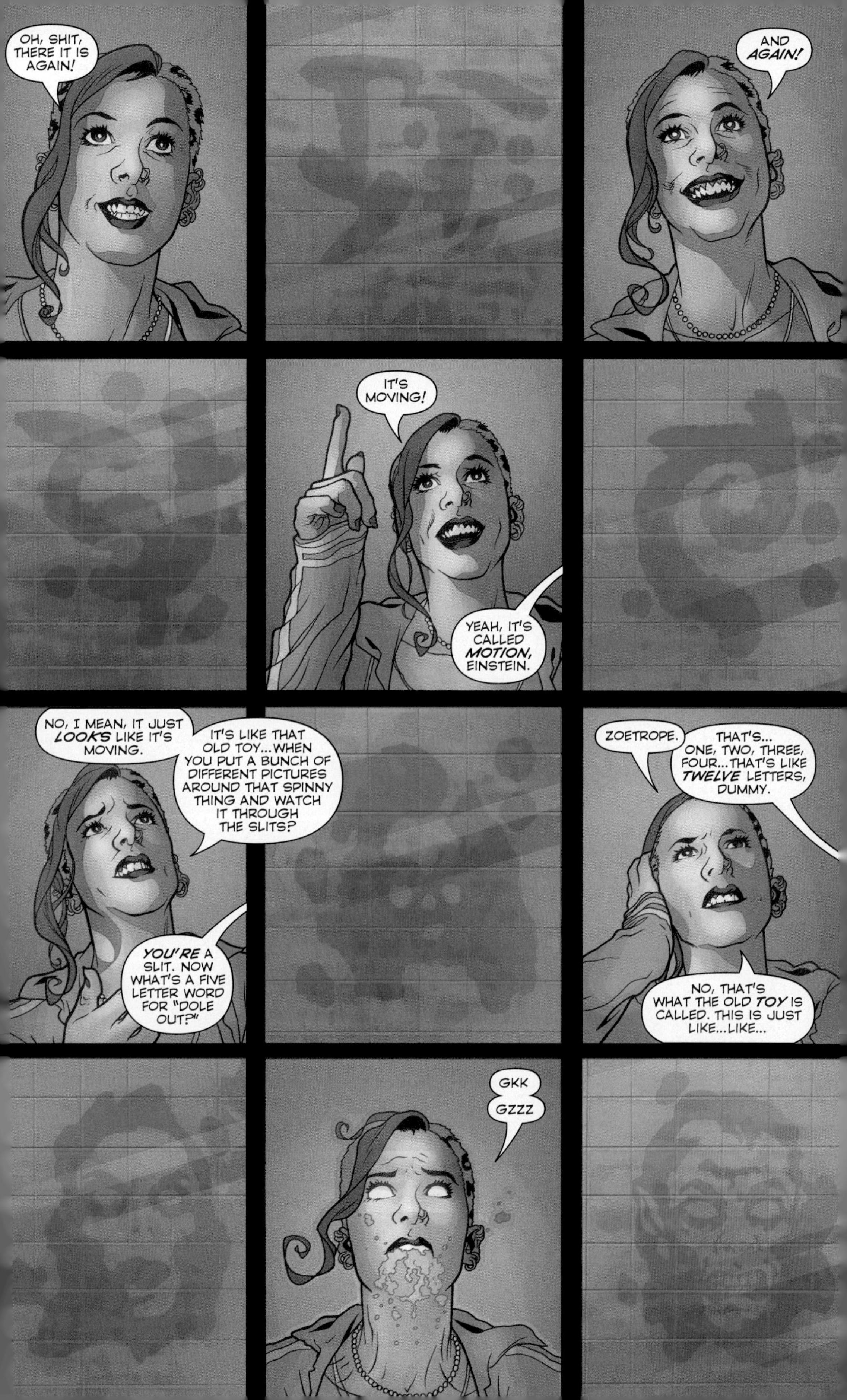

OH, SHIT, THERE IT IS AGAIN!
AND AGAIN!
IT'S MOVING!
YEAH, IT'S CALLED MOTION, EINSTEIN.
NO, I MEAN, IT JUST LOOKS LIKE IT'S MOVING.
IT'S LIKE THAT OLD TOY...WHEN YOU PUT A BUNCH OF DIFFERENT PICTURES AROUND THAT SPINNY THING AND WATCH IT THROUGH THE SLITS?
YOU'RE A SLIT. NOW WHAT'S A FIVE LETTER WORD FOR "DOLE OUT?"
ZOETROPE.
THAT'S... ONE, TWO, THREE, FOUR...THAT'S LIKE TWELVE LETTERS, DUMMY.
NO, THAT'S WHAT THE OLD TOY IS CALLED. THIS IS JUST LIKE...LIKE...
GKK
GZZZ

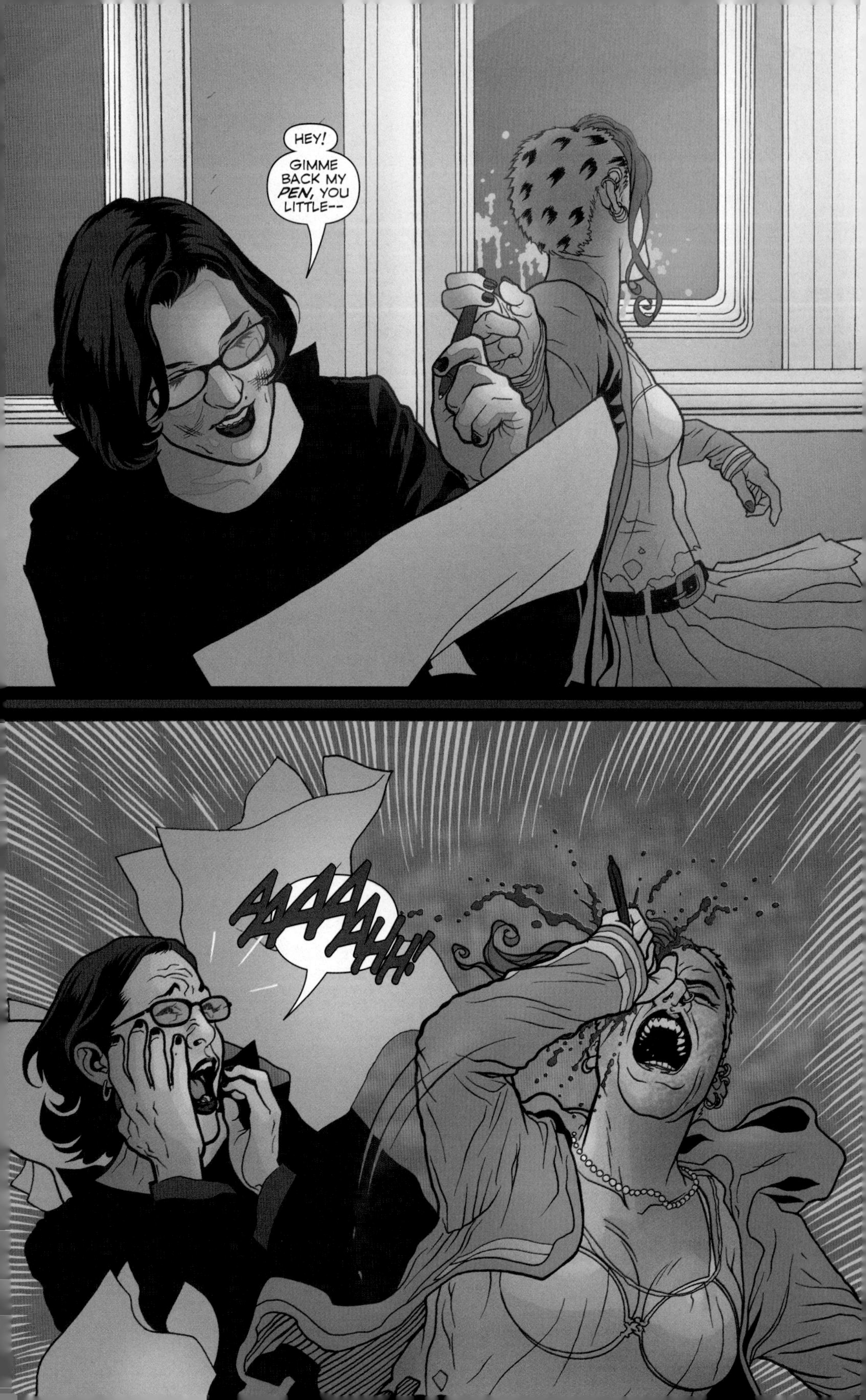
HEY!
GIMME BACK MY PEN, YOU LITTLE--
AAAAAHH!

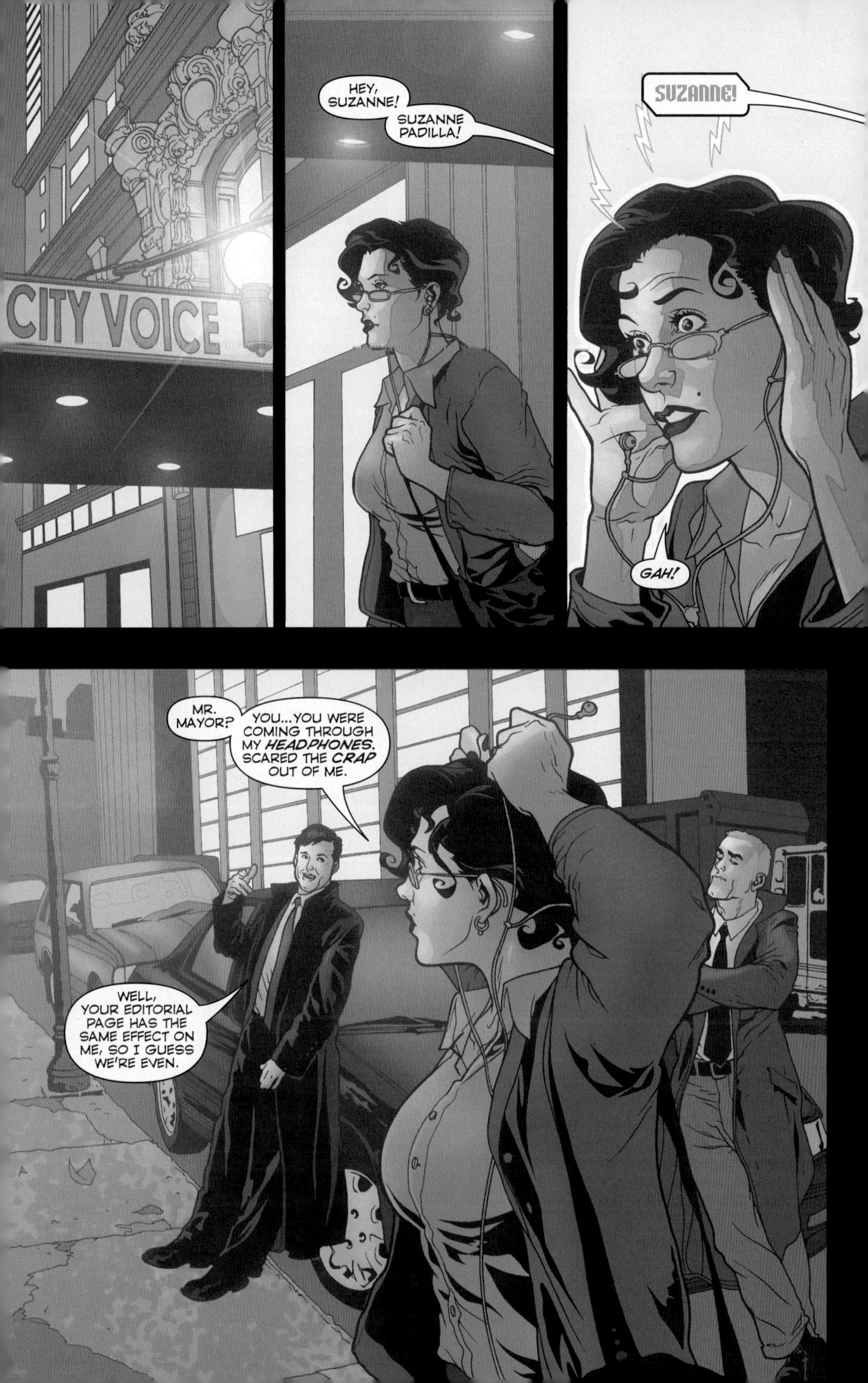
CITY VOICE
HEY, SUZANNE!
SUZANNE PADILLA!
SUZANNE!
GAH!
MR. MAYOR?
YOU...YOU WERE COMING THROUGH MY HEADPHONES. SCARED THE CRAP OUT OF ME.
WELL, YOUR EDITORIAL PAGE HAS THE SAME EFFECT ON ME, SO I GUESS WE'RE EVEN.

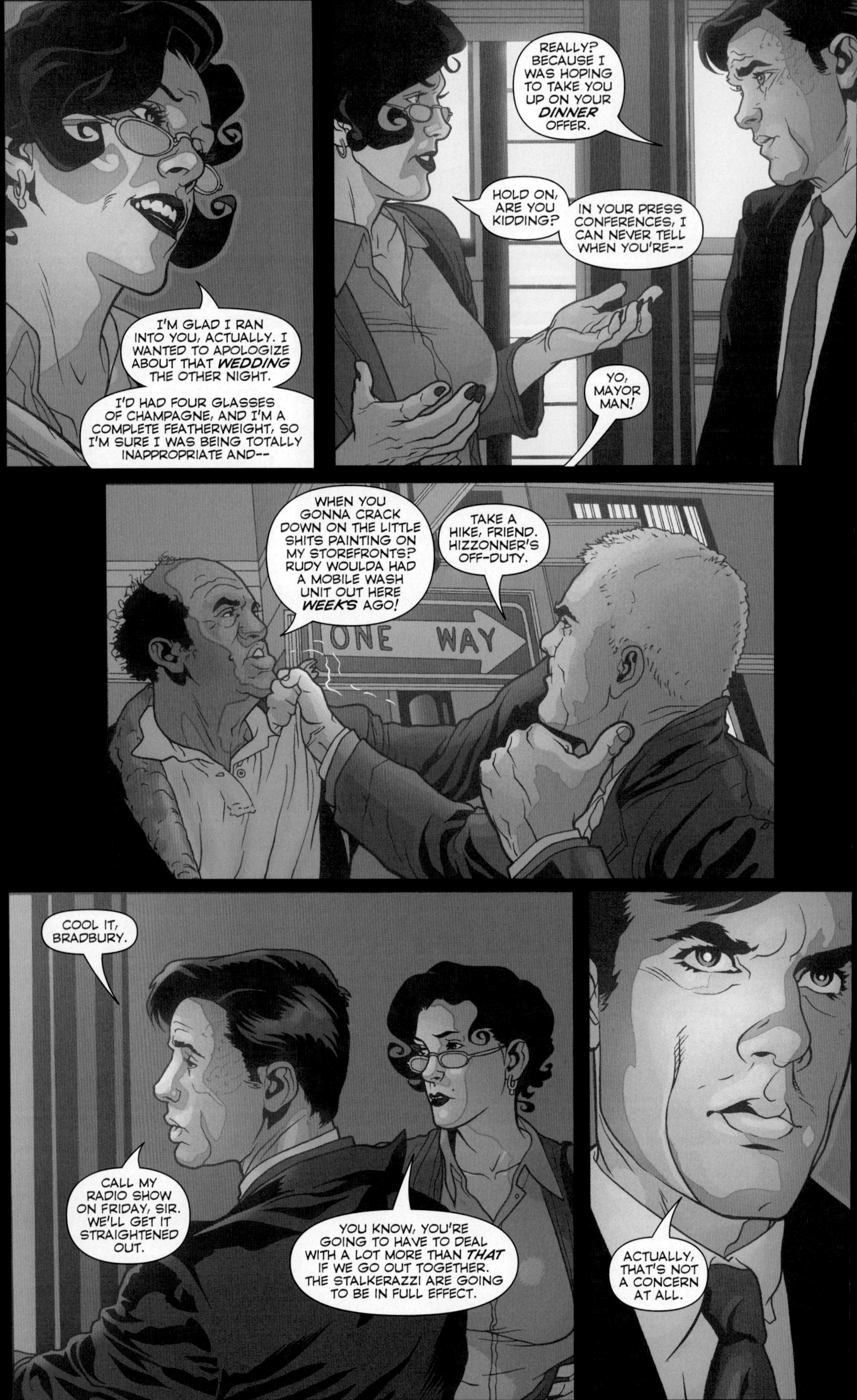
I'M GLAD I RAN INTO YOU, ACTUALLY. I WANTED TO APOLOGIZE ABOUT THAT *WEDDING* THE OTHER NIGHT.
I'D HAD FOUR GLASSES OF CHAMPAGNE, AND I'M A COMPLETE FEATHERWEIGHT, SO I'M SURE I WAS BEING TOTALLY INAPPROPRIATE AND--
REALLY? BECAUSE I WAS HOPING TO TAKE YOU UP ON YOUR *DINNER* OFFER.
HOLD ON, ARE YOU KIDDING?
IN YOUR PRESS CONFERENCES, I CAN NEVER TELL WHEN YOU'RE--
YO, MAYOR MAN!
WHEN YOU GONNA CRACK DOWN ON THE LITTLE SHITS PAINTING ON MY STOREFRONTS? RUDY WOULDA HAD A MOBILE WASH UNIT OUT HERE *WEEKS* AGO!
TAKE A HIKE, FRIEND. HIZZONNER'S OFF-DUTY.
ONE WAY
COOL IT, BRADBURY.
CALL MY RADIO SHOW ON FRIDAY, SIR. WE'LL GET IT STRAIGHTENED OUT.
YOU KNOW, YOU'RE GOING TO HAVE TO DEAL WITH A LOT MORE THAN *THAT* IF WE GO OUT TOGETHER. THE STALKERAZZI ARE GOING TO BE IN FULL EFFECT.
ACTUALLY, THAT'S NOT A CONCERN AT ALL.

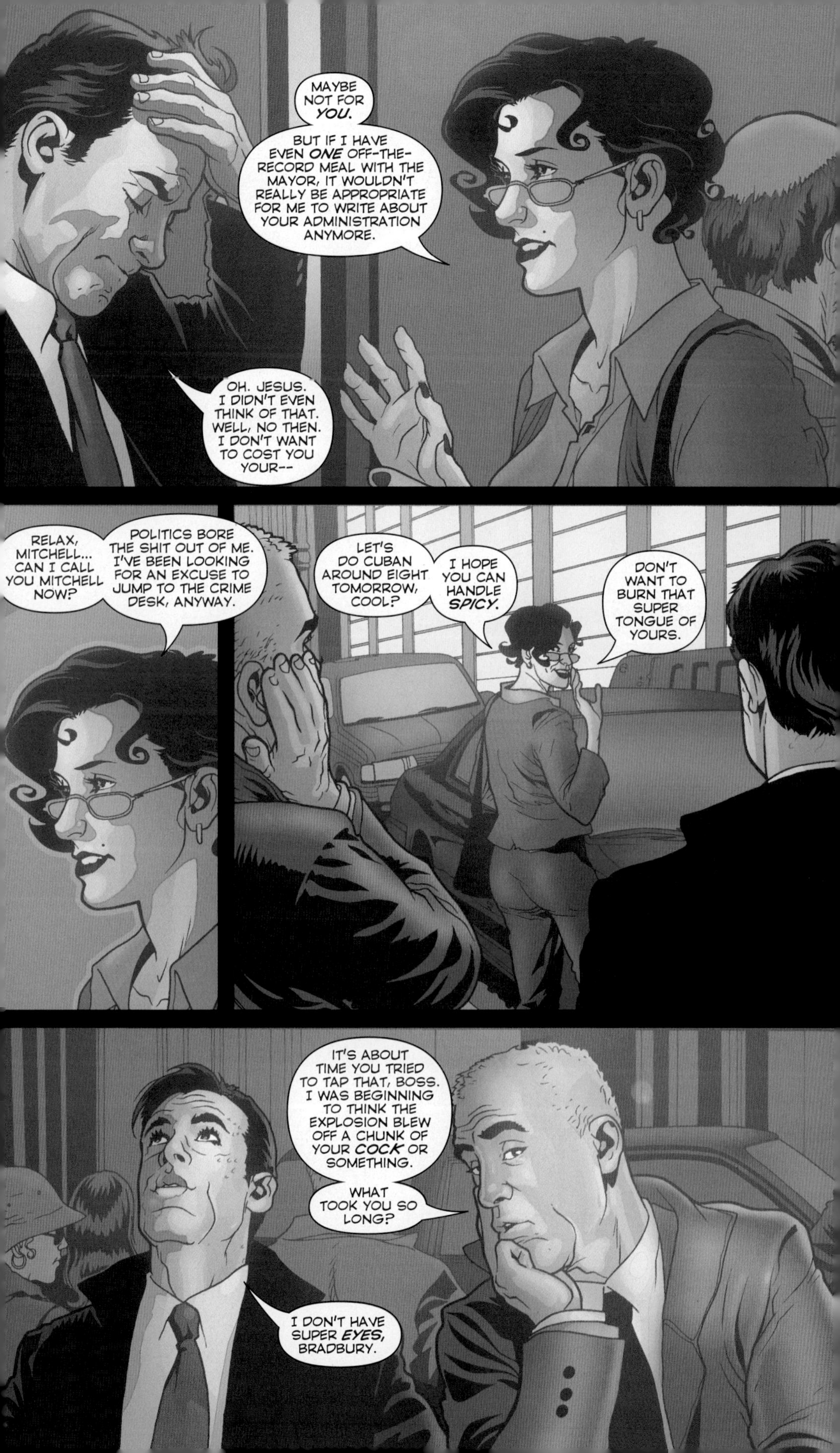
MAYBE NOT FOR YOU.
BUT IF I HAVE EVEN ONE OFF-THE-RECORD MEAL WITH THE MAYOR, IT WOULDN'T REALLY BE APPROPRIATE FOR ME TO WRITE ABOUT YOUR ADMINISTRATION ANYMORE.
OH. JESUS. I DIDN'T EVEN THINK OF THAT. WELL, NO THEN. I DON'T WANT TO COST YOU YOUR--
RELAX, MITCHELL... CAN I CALL YOU MITCHELL NOW?
POLITICS BORE THE SHIT OUT OF ME. I'VE BEEN LOOKING FOR AN EXCUSE TO JUMP TO THE CRIME DESK, ANYWAY.
LET'S DO CUBAN AROUND EIGHT TOMORROW, COOL?
I HOPE YOU CAN HANDLE SPICY.
DON'T WANT TO BURN THAT SUPER TONGUE OF YOURS.
IT'S ABOUT TIME YOU TRIED TO TAP THAT, BOSS. I WAS BEGINNING TO THINK THE EXPLOSION BLEW OFF A CHUNK OF YOUR COCK OR SOMETHING.
WHAT TOOK YOU SO LONG?
I DON'T HAVE SUPER EYES, BRADBURY.

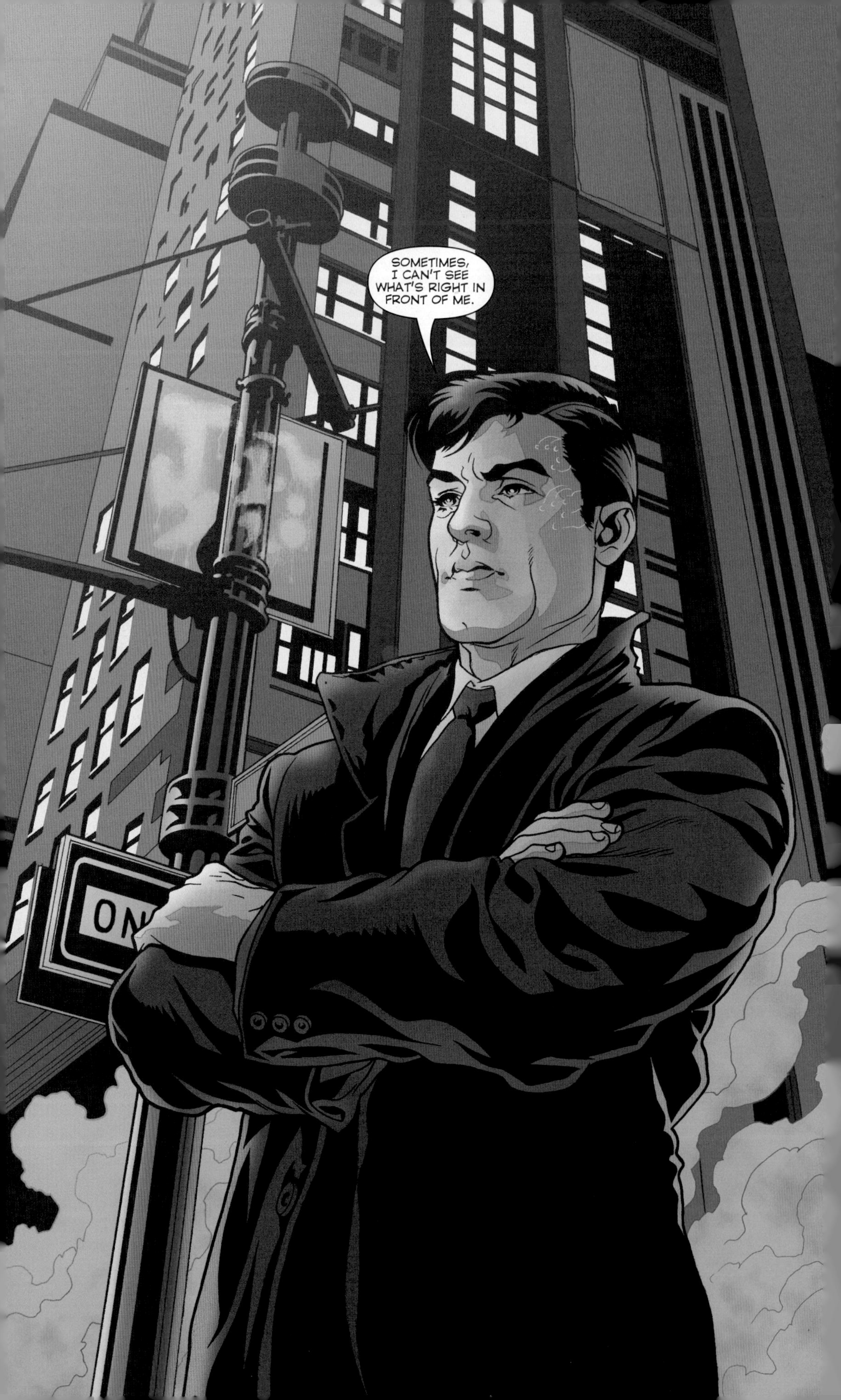
SOMETIMES, I CAN'T SEE WHAT'S RIGHT IN FRONT OF ME.
ON

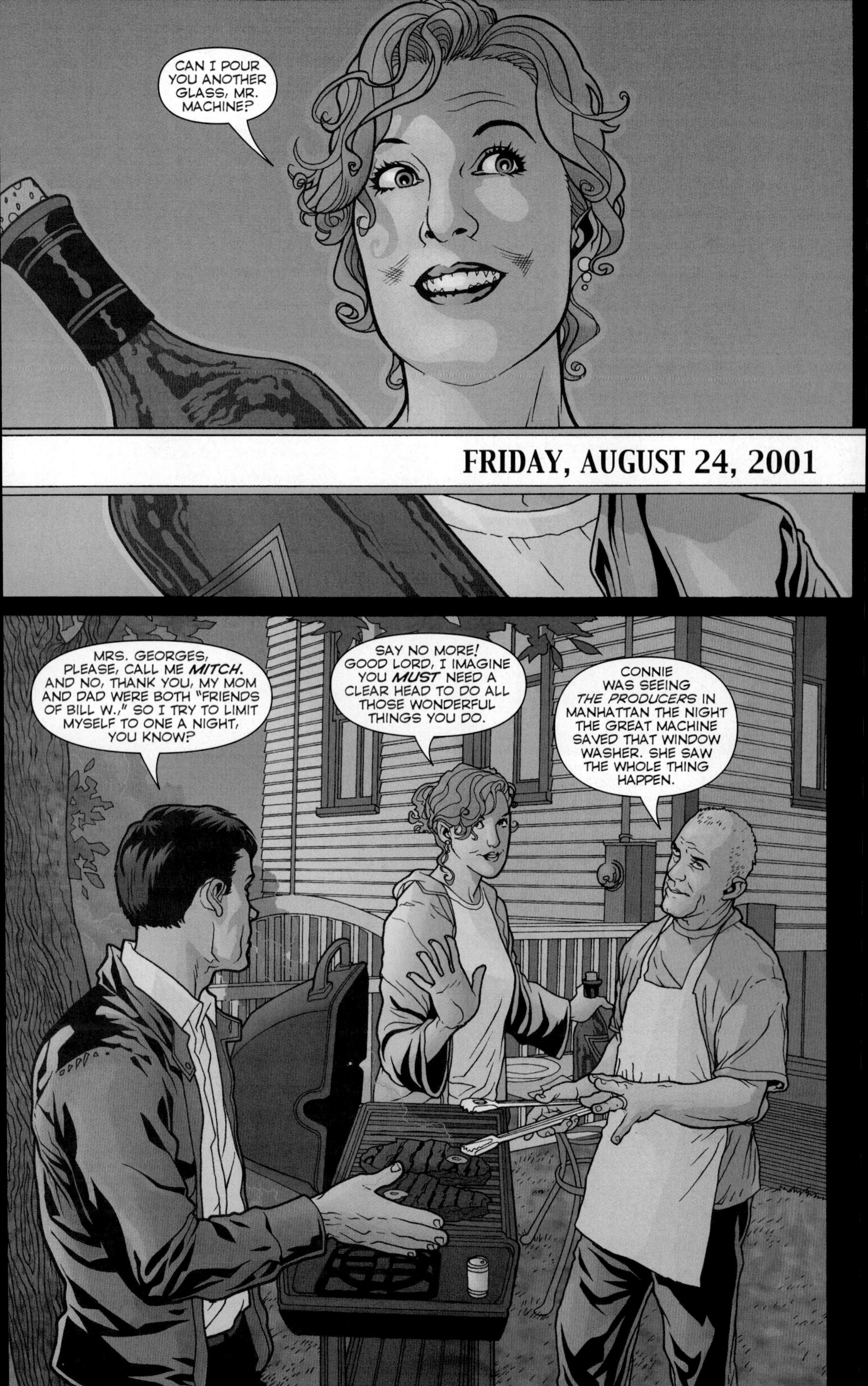
CAN I POUR YOU ANOTHER GLASS, MR. MACHINE?
FRIDAY, AUGUST 24, 2001
MRS. GEORGES, PLEASE, CALL ME *MITCH.* AND NO, THANK YOU, MY MOM AND DAD WERE BOTH "FRIENDS OF BILL W.," SO I TRY TO LIMIT MYSELF TO ONE A NIGHT, YOU KNOW?
SAY NO MORE! GOOD LORD, I IMAGINE YOU *MUST* NEED A CLEAR HEAD TO DO ALL THOSE WONDERFUL THINGS YOU DO.
CONNIE WAS SEEING *THE PRODUCERS* IN MANHATTAN THE NIGHT THE GREAT MACHINE SAVED THAT WINDOW WASHER. SHE SAW THE WHOLE THING HAPPEN.

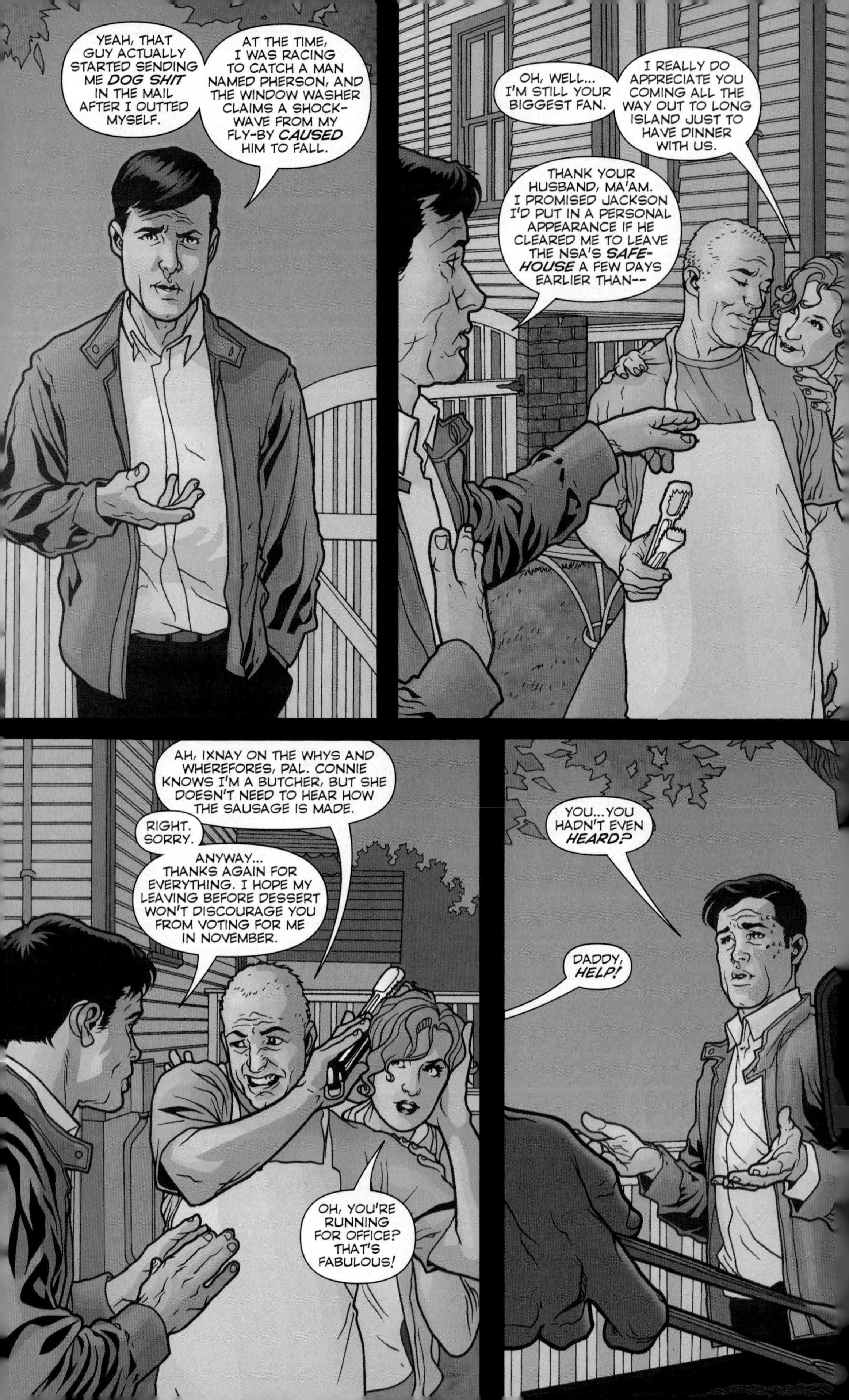
YEAH, THAT GUY ACTUALLY STARTED SENDING ME DOG SHIT IN THE MAIL AFTER I OUTTED MYSELF.
AT THE TIME, I WAS RACING TO CATCH A MAN NAMED PHERSON, AND THE WINDOW WASHER CLAIMS A SHOCK-WAVE FROM MY FLY-BY CAUSED HIM TO FALL.
OH, WELL... I'M STILL YOUR BIGGEST FAN.
I REALLY DO APPRECIATE YOU COMING ALL THE WAY OUT TO LONG ISLAND JUST TO HAVE DINNER WITH US.
THANK YOUR HUSBAND, MA'AM. I PROMISED JACKSON I'D PUT IN A PERSONAL APPEARANCE IF HE CLEARED ME TO LEAVE THE NSA'S SAFE-HOUSE A FEW DAYS EARLIER THAN--
AH, IXNAY ON THE WHYS AND WHEREFORES, PAL. CONNIE KNOWS I'M A BUTCHER, BUT SHE DOESN'T NEED TO HEAR HOW THE SAUSAGE IS MADE.
RIGHT. SORRY.
ANYWAY... THANKS AGAIN FOR EVERYTHING. I HOPE MY LEAVING BEFORE DESSERT WON'T DISCOURAGE YOU FROM VOTING FOR ME IN NOVEMBER.
OH, YOU'RE RUNNING FOR OFFICE? THAT'S FABULOUS!
YOU...YOU HADN'T EVEN HEARD?
DADDY, HELP!

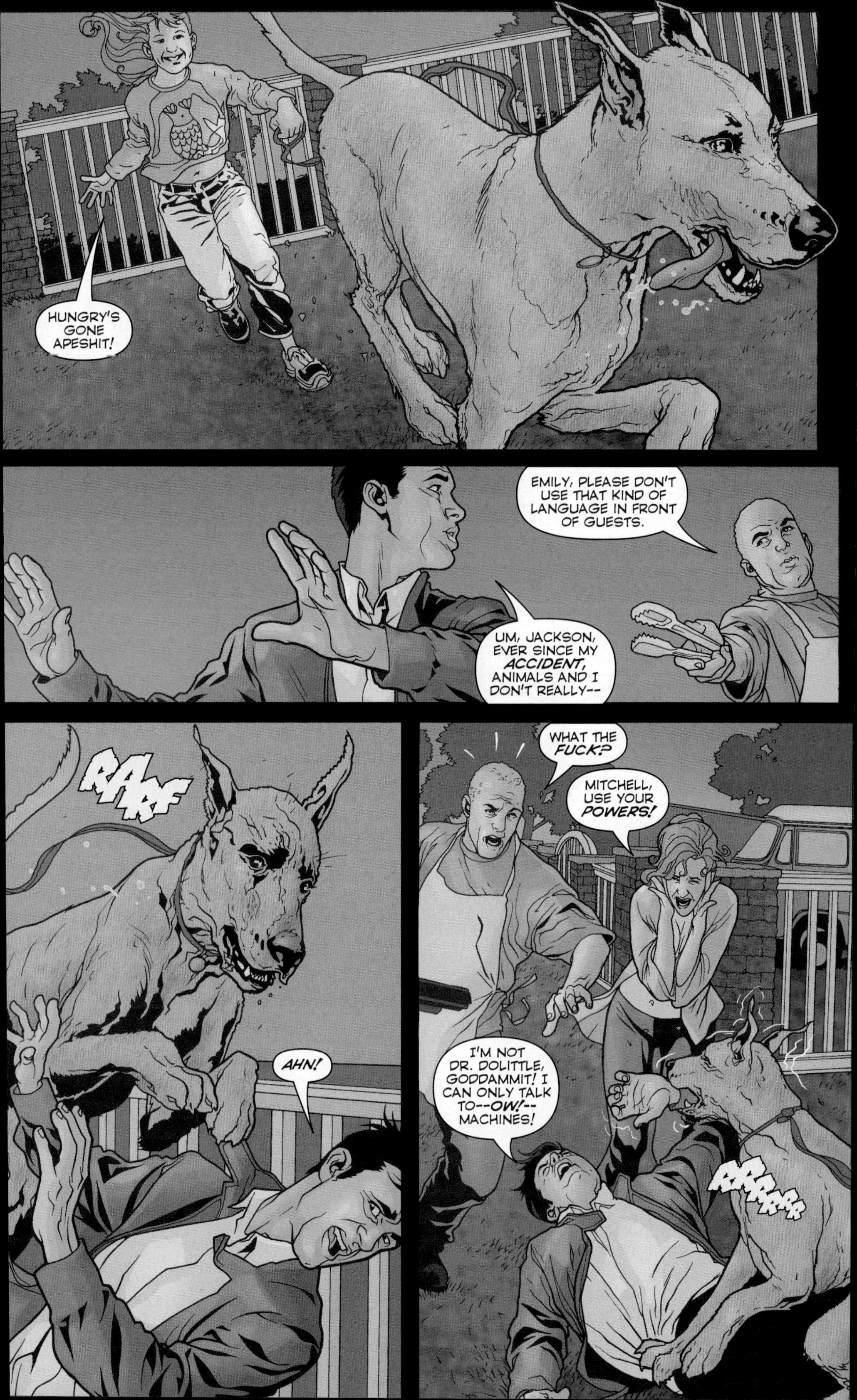
HUNGRY'S GONE APESHIT!
EMILY, PLEASE DON'T USE THAT KIND OF LANGUAGE IN FRONT OF GUESTS.
UM, JACKSON, EVER SINCE MY ACCIDENT, ANIMALS AND I DON'T REALLY--
RARF
AHN!
WHAT THE FUCK?
MITCHELL, USE YOUR POWERS!
I'M NOT DR. DOLITTLE, GODDAMMIT! I CAN ONLY TALK TO--OW!--MACHINES!
RRRRRR

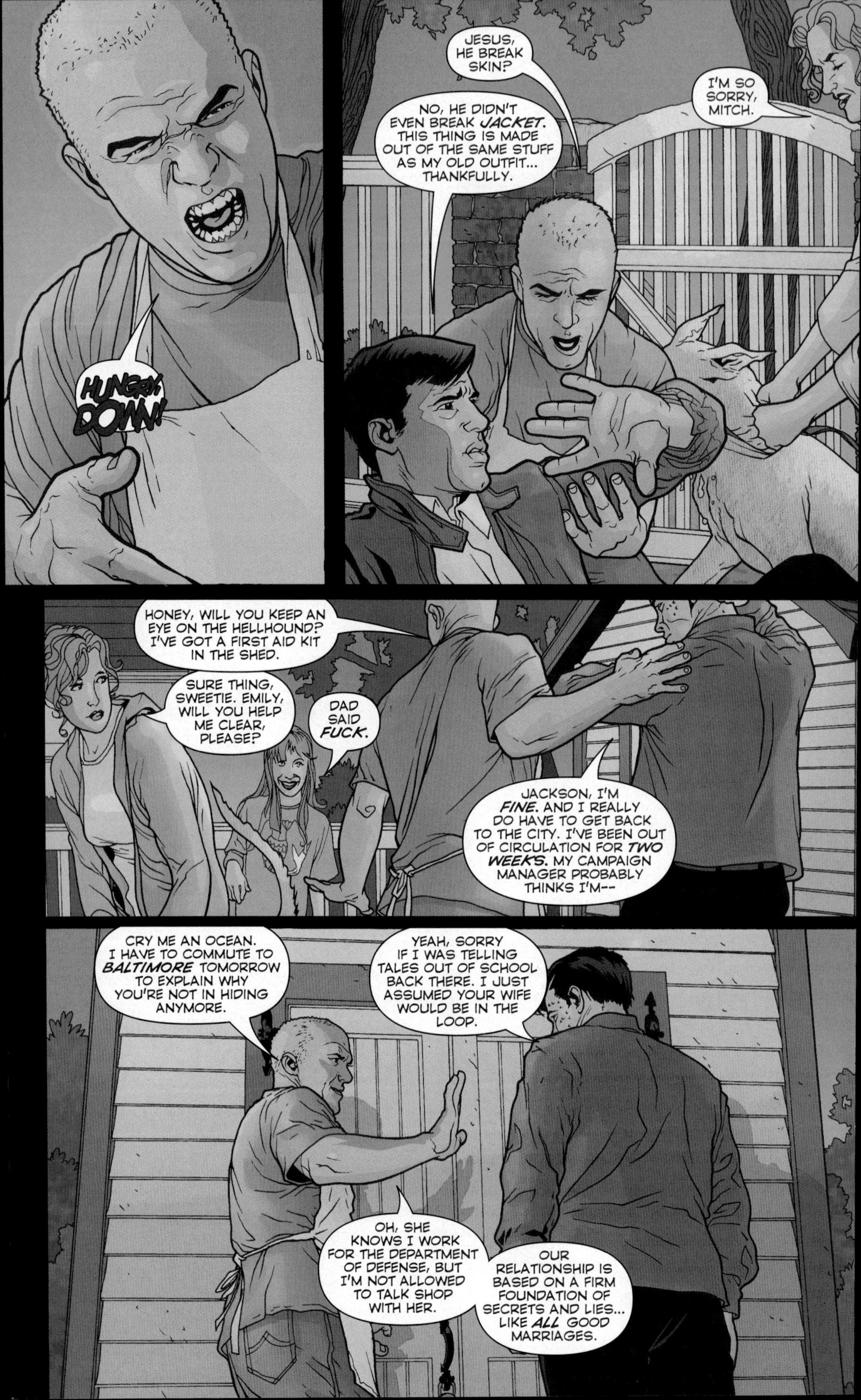
HUNGRY. DOWN!
JESUS, HE BREAK SKIN?
I'M SO SORRY, MITCH.
NO, HE DIDN'T EVEN BREAK JACKET. THIS THING IS MADE OUT OF THE SAME STUFF AS MY OLD OUTFIT... THANKFULLY.
HONEY, WILL YOU KEEP AN EYE ON THE HELLHOUND? I'VE GOT A FIRST AID KIT IN THE SHED.
SURE THING, SWEETIE. EMILY, WILL YOU HELP ME CLEAR, PLEASE?
DAD SAID FUCK.
JACKSON, I'M FINE. AND I REALLY DO HAVE TO GET BACK TO THE CITY. I'VE BEEN OUT OF CIRCULATION FOR TWO WEEKS. MY CAMPAIGN MANAGER PROBABLY THINKS I'M--
CRY ME AN OCEAN. I HAVE TO COMMUTE TO BALTIMORE TOMORROW TO EXPLAIN WHY YOU'RE NOT IN HIDING ANYMORE.
YEAH, SORRY IF I WAS TELLING TALES OUT OF SCHOOL BACK THERE. I JUST ASSUMED YOUR WIFE WOULD BE IN THE LOOP.
OH, SHE KNOWS I WORK FOR THE DEPARTMENT OF DEFENSE, BUT I'M NOT ALLOWED TO TALK SHOP WITH HER.
OUR RELATIONSHIP IS BASED ON A FIRM FOUNDATION OF SECRETS AND LIES... LIKE ALL GOOD MARRIAGES.

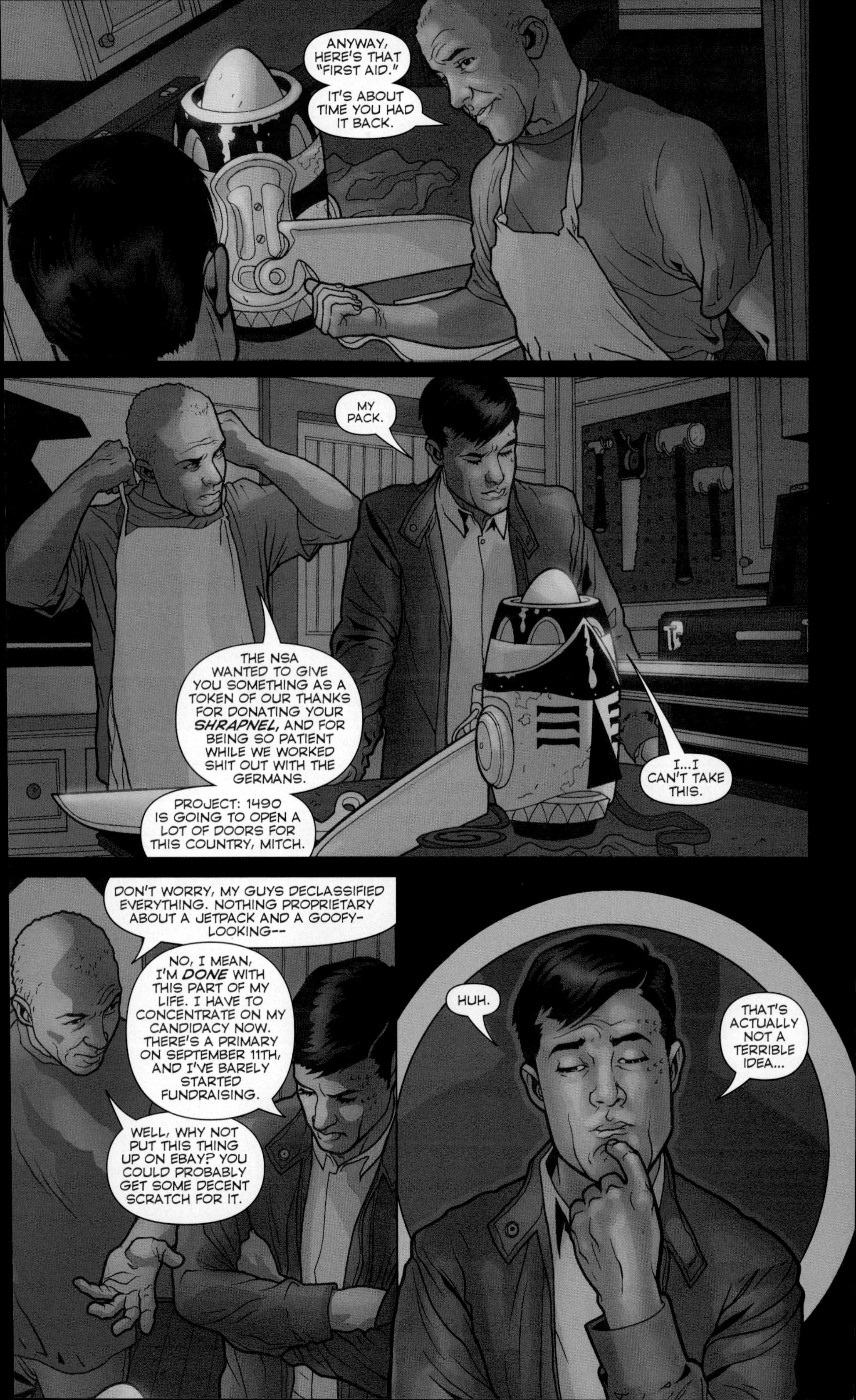
ANYWAY, HERE'S THAT "FIRST AID."
IT'S ABOUT TIME YOU HAD IT BACK.
MY PACK.
THE NSA WANTED TO GIVE YOU SOMETHING AS A TOKEN OF OUR THANKS FOR DONATING YOUR *SHRAPNEL,* AND FOR BEING SO PATIENT WHILE WE WORKED SHIT OUT WITH THE GERMANS.
PROJECT: 1490 IS GOING TO OPEN A LOT OF DOORS FOR THIS COUNTRY, MITCH.
I...I CAN'T TAKE THIS.
DON'T WORRY, MY GUYS DECLASSIFIED EVERYTHING. NOTHING PROPRIETARY ABOUT A JETPACK AND A GOOFY-LOOKING--
NO, I MEAN, I'M *DONE* WITH THIS PART OF MY LIFE. I HAVE TO CONCENTRATE ON MY CANDIDACY NOW. THERE'S A PRIMARY ON SEPTEMBER 11TH, AND I'VE BARELY STARTED FUNDRAISING.
WELL, WHY NOT PUT THIS THING UP ON EBAY? YOU COULD PROBABLY GET SOME DECENT SCRATCH FOR IT.
HUH.
THAT'S ACTUALLY NOT A TERRIBLE IDEA...

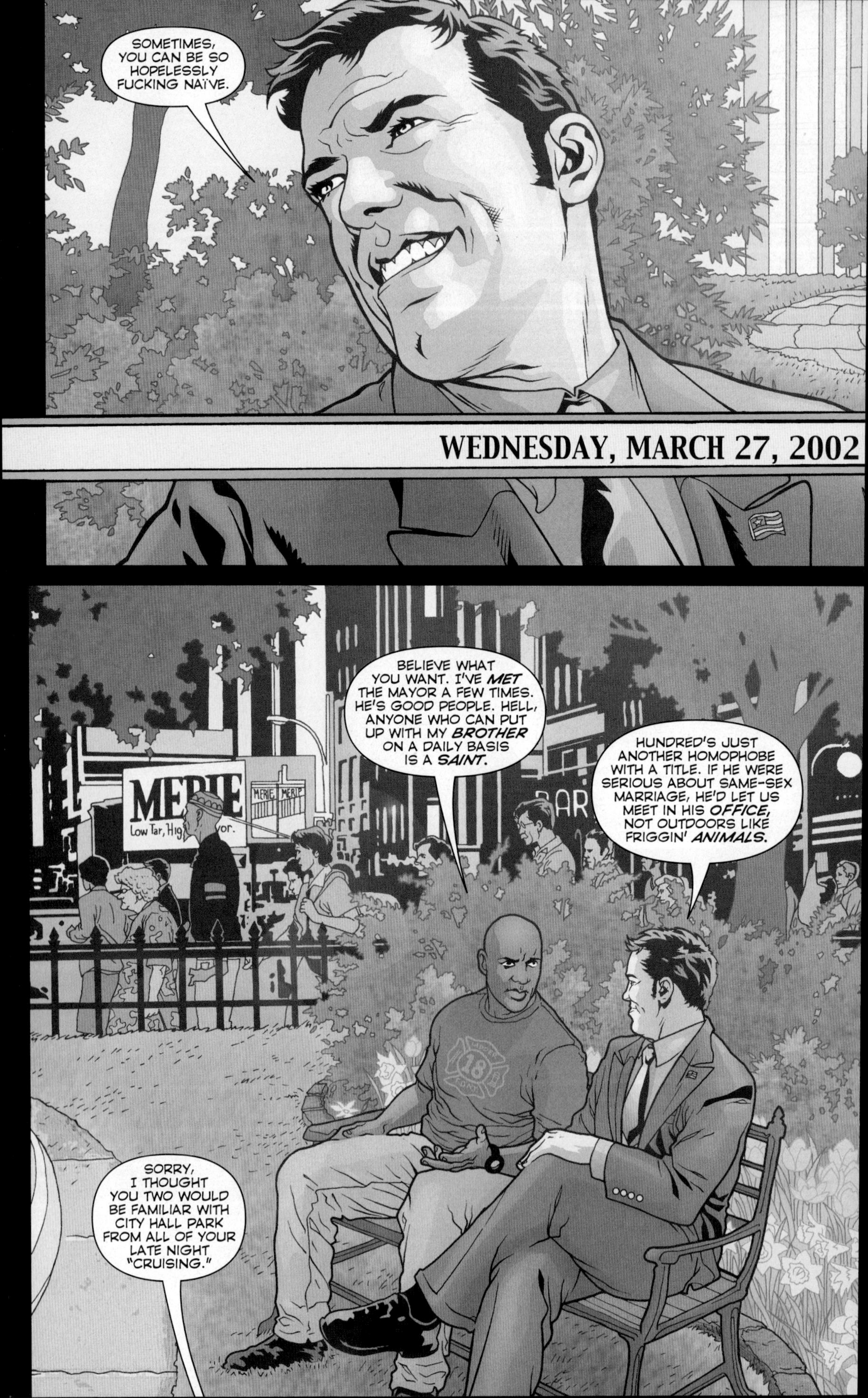
SOMETIMES, YOU CAN BE SO HOPELESSLY FUCKING NAÏVE.
WEDNESDAY, MARCH 27, 2002
BELIEVE WHAT YOU WANT. I'VE MET THE MAYOR A FEW TIMES. HE'S GOOD PEOPLE. HELL, ANYONE WHO CAN PUT UP WITH MY BROTHER ON A DAILY BASIS IS A SAINT.
HUNDRED'S JUST ANOTHER HOMOPHOBE WITH A TITLE. IF HE WERE SERIOUS ABOUT SAME-SEX MARRIAGE, HE'D LET US MEET IN HIS OFFICE, NOT OUTDOORS LIKE FRIGGIN' ANIMALS.
SORRY, I THOUGHT YOU TWO WOULD BE FAMILIAR WITH CITY HALL PARK FROM ALL OF YOUR LATE NIGHT "CRUISING."
MERIE
Low Tar, Hig

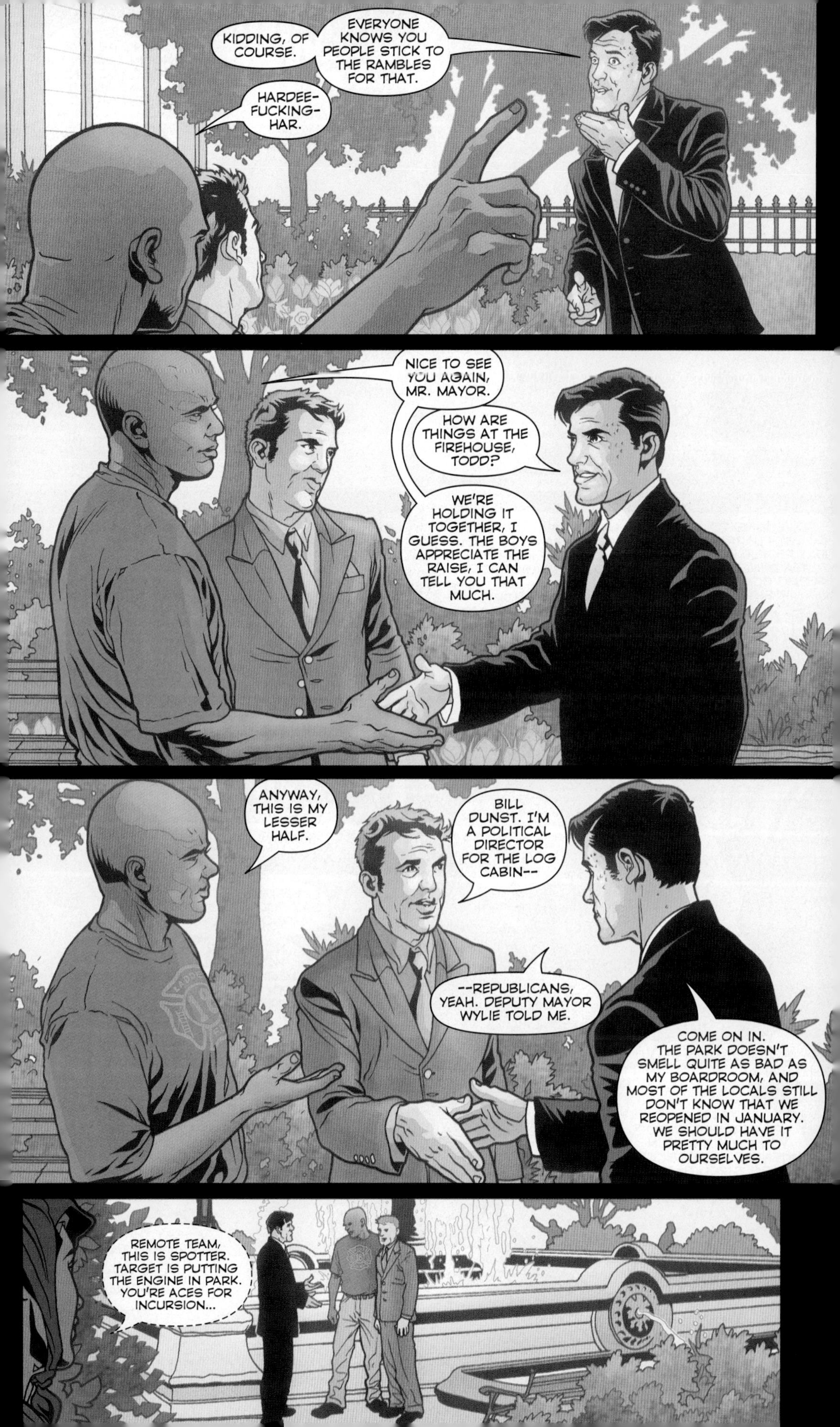
KIDDING, OF COURSE.
EVERYONE KNOWS YOU PEOPLE STICK TO THE RAMBLES FOR THAT.
HARDEE-FUCKING-HAR.
NICE TO SEE YOU AGAIN, MR. MAYOR.
HOW ARE THINGS AT THE FIREHOUSE, TODD?
WE'RE HOLDING IT TOGETHER, I GUESS. THE BOYS APPRECIATE THE RAISE, I CAN TELL YOU THAT MUCH.
ANYWAY, THIS IS MY LESSER HALF.
BILL DUNST. I'M A POLITICAL DIRECTOR FOR THE LOG CABIN--
--REPUBLICANS, YEAH. DEPUTY MAYOR WYLIE TOLD ME.
COME ON IN. THE PARK DOESN'T SMELL QUITE AS BAD AS MY BOARDROOM, AND MOST OF THE LOCALS STILL DON'T KNOW THAT WE REOPENED IN JANUARY. WE SHOULD HAVE IT PRETTY MUCH TO OURSELVES.
REMOTE TEAM, THIS IS SPOTTER. TARGET IS PUTTING THE ENGINE IN PARK. YOU'RE ACES FOR INCURSION...

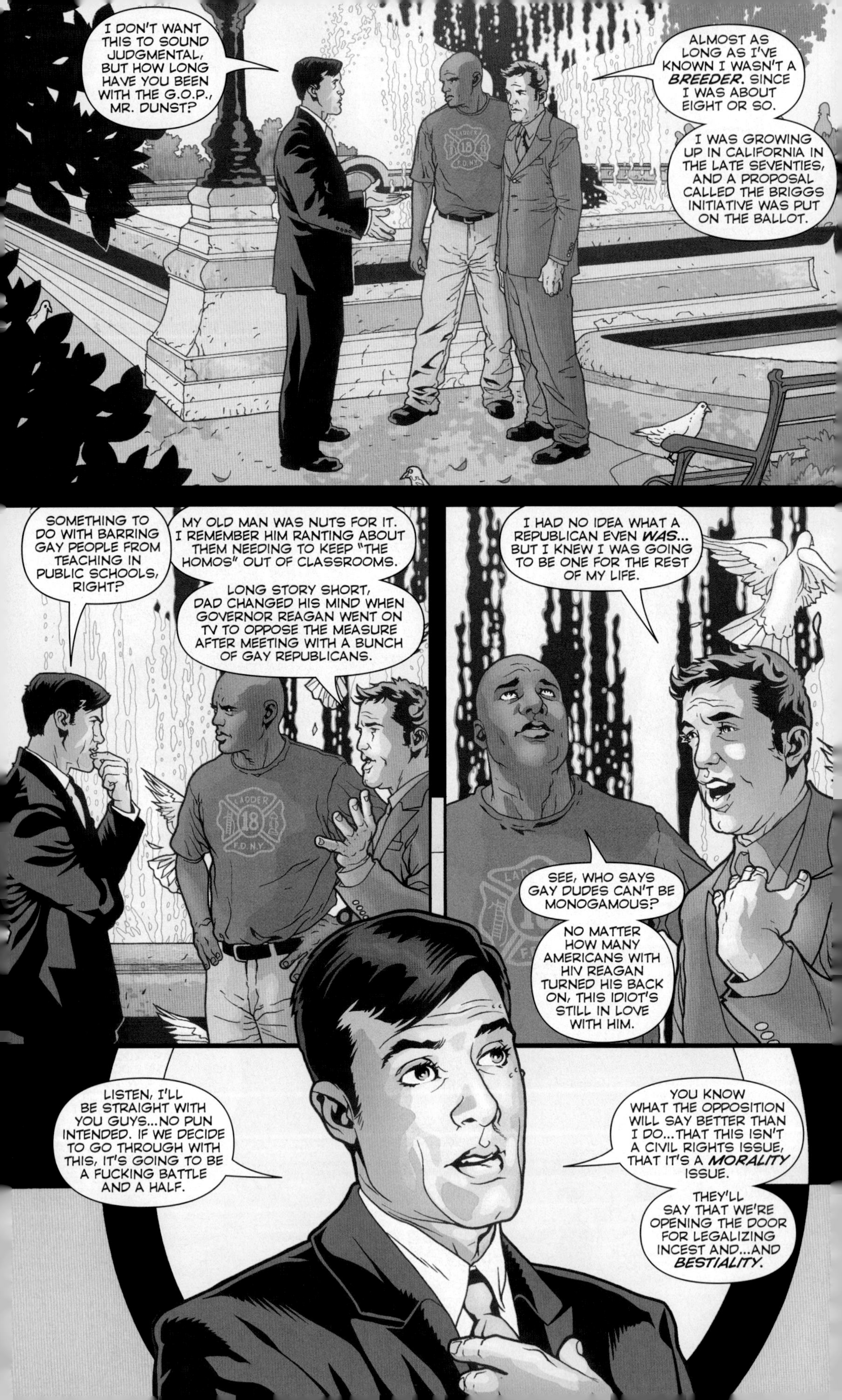
I DON'T WANT THIS TO SOUND JUDGMENTAL, BUT HOW LONG HAVE YOU BEEN WITH THE G.O.P., MR. DUNST?
ALMOST AS LONG AS I'VE KNOWN I WASN'T A ***BREEDER***. SINCE I WAS ABOUT EIGHT OR SO.
I WAS GROWING UP IN CALIFORNIA IN THE LATE SEVENTIES, AND A PROPOSAL CALLED THE BRIGGS INITIATIVE WAS PUT ON THE BALLOT.
LADDER 18 F.D.N.Y.
SOMETHING TO DO WITH BARRING GAY PEOPLE FROM TEACHING IN PUBLIC SCHOOLS, RIGHT?
MY OLD MAN WAS NUTS FOR IT. I REMEMBER HIM RANTING ABOUT THEM NEEDING TO KEEP "THE HOMOS" OUT OF CLASSROOMS.
LONG STORY SHORT, DAD CHANGED HIS MIND WHEN GOVERNOR REAGAN WENT ON TV TO OPPOSE THE MEASURE AFTER MEETING WITH A BUNCH OF GAY REPUBLICANS.
I HAD NO IDEA WHAT A REPUBLICAN EVEN ***WAS***... BUT I KNEW I WAS GOING TO BE ONE FOR THE REST OF MY LIFE.
SEE, WHO SAYS GAY DUDES CAN'T BE MONOGAMOUS?
NO MATTER HOW MANY AMERICANS WITH HIV REAGAN TURNED HIS BACK ON, THIS IDIOT'S STILL IN LOVE WITH HIM.
LISTEN, I'LL BE STRAIGHT WITH YOU GUYS...NO PUN INTENDED. IF WE DECIDE TO GO THROUGH WITH THIS, IT'S GOING TO BE A FUCKING BATTLE AND A HALF.
YOU KNOW WHAT THE OPPOSITION WILL SAY BETTER THAN I DO...THAT THIS ISN'T A CIVIL RIGHTS ISSUE, THAT IT'S A ***MORALITY*** ISSUE.
THEY'LL SAY THAT WE'RE OPENING THE DOOR FOR LEGALIZING INCEST AND...AND ***BESTIALITY***.

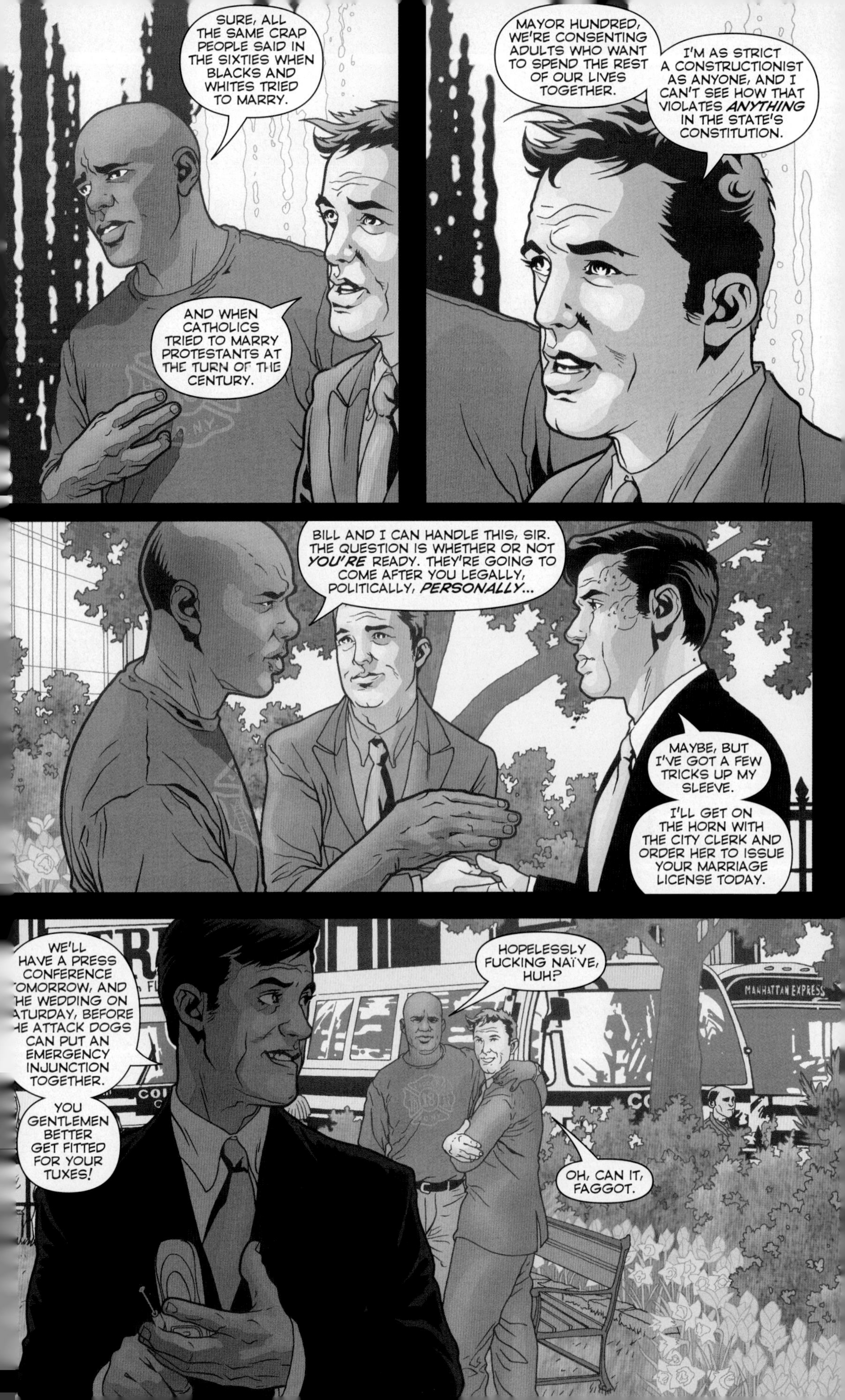
SURE, ALL THE SAME CRAP PEOPLE SAID IN THE SIXTIES WHEN BLACKS AND WHITES TRIED TO MARRY.
AND WHEN CATHOLICS TRIED TO MARRY PROTESTANTS AT THE TURN OF THE CENTURY.
MAYOR HUNDRED, WE'RE CONSENTING ADULTS WHO WANT TO SPEND THE REST OF OUR LIVES TOGETHER.
I'M AS STRICT A CONSTRUCTIONIST AS ANYONE, AND I CAN'T SEE HOW THAT VIOLATES *ANYTHING* IN THE STATE'S CONSTITUTION.
BILL AND I CAN HANDLE THIS, SIR. THE QUESTION IS WHETHER OR NOT *YOU'RE* READY. THEY'RE GOING TO COME AFTER YOU LEGALLY, POLITICALLY, *PERSONALLY*...
MAYBE, BUT I'VE GOT A FEW TRICKS UP MY SLEEVE.
I'LL GET ON THE HORN WITH THE CITY CLERK AND ORDER HER TO ISSUE YOUR MARRIAGE LICENSE TODAY.
WE'LL HAVE A PRESS CONFERENCE TOMORROW, AND THE WEDDING ON SATURDAY, BEFORE THE ATTACK DOGS CAN PUT AN EMERGENCY INJUNCTION TOGETHER.
YOU GENTLEMEN BETTER GET FITTED FOR YOUR TUXES!
HOPELESSLY FUCKING NAÏVE, HUH?
MANHATTAN EXPRESS
OH, CAN IT, FAGGOT.

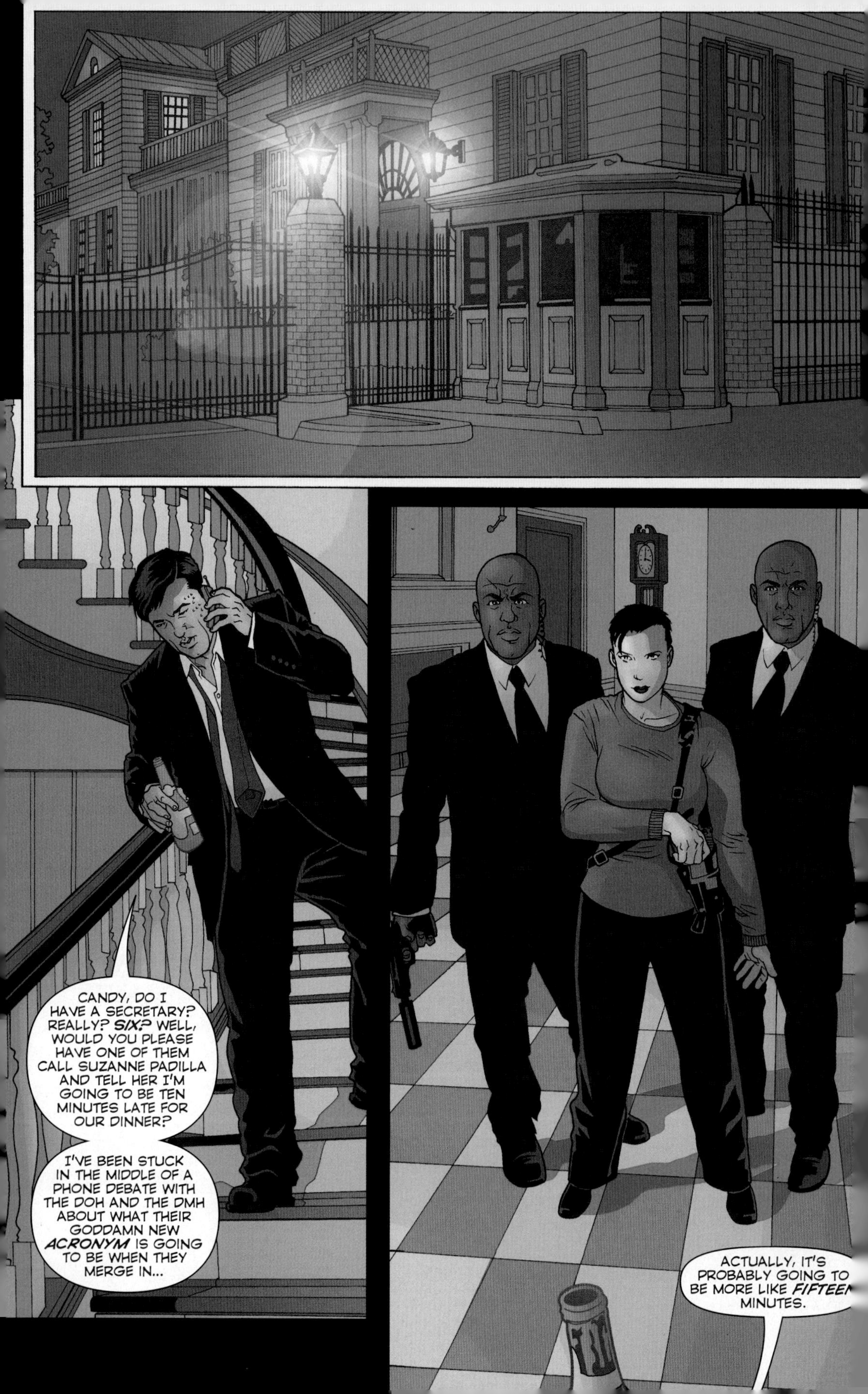
CANDY, DO I HAVE A SECRETARY? REALLY? SIX? WELL, WOULD YOU PLEASE HAVE ONE OF THEM CALL SUZANNE PADILLA AND TELL HER I'M GOING TO BE TEN MINUTES LATE FOR OUR DINNER?
I'VE BEEN STUCK IN THE MIDDLE OF A PHONE DEBATE WITH THE DOH AND THE DMH ABOUT WHAT THEIR GODDAMN NEW ACRONYM IS GOING TO BE WHEN THEY MERGE IN...
ACTUALLY, IT'S PROBABLY GOING TO BE MORE LIKE FIFTEE MINUTES.

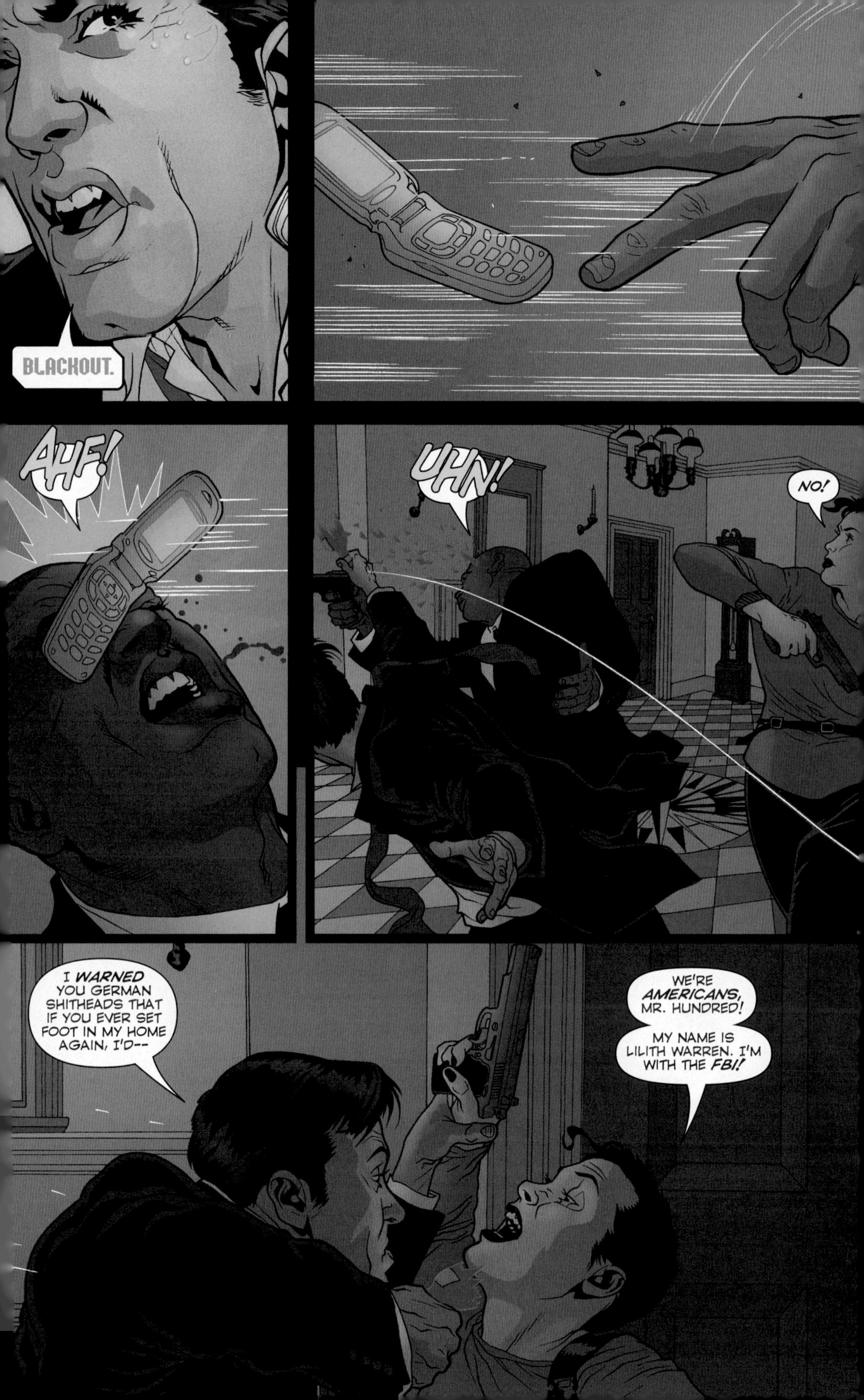
BLACKOUT.
AHF!
UHN!
NO!
I WARNED YOU GERMAN SHITHEADS THAT IF YOU EVER SET FOOT IN MY HOME AGAIN, I'D--
WE'RE AMERICANS, MR. HUNDRED!
MY NAME IS LILITH WARREN. I'M WITH THE FBI!

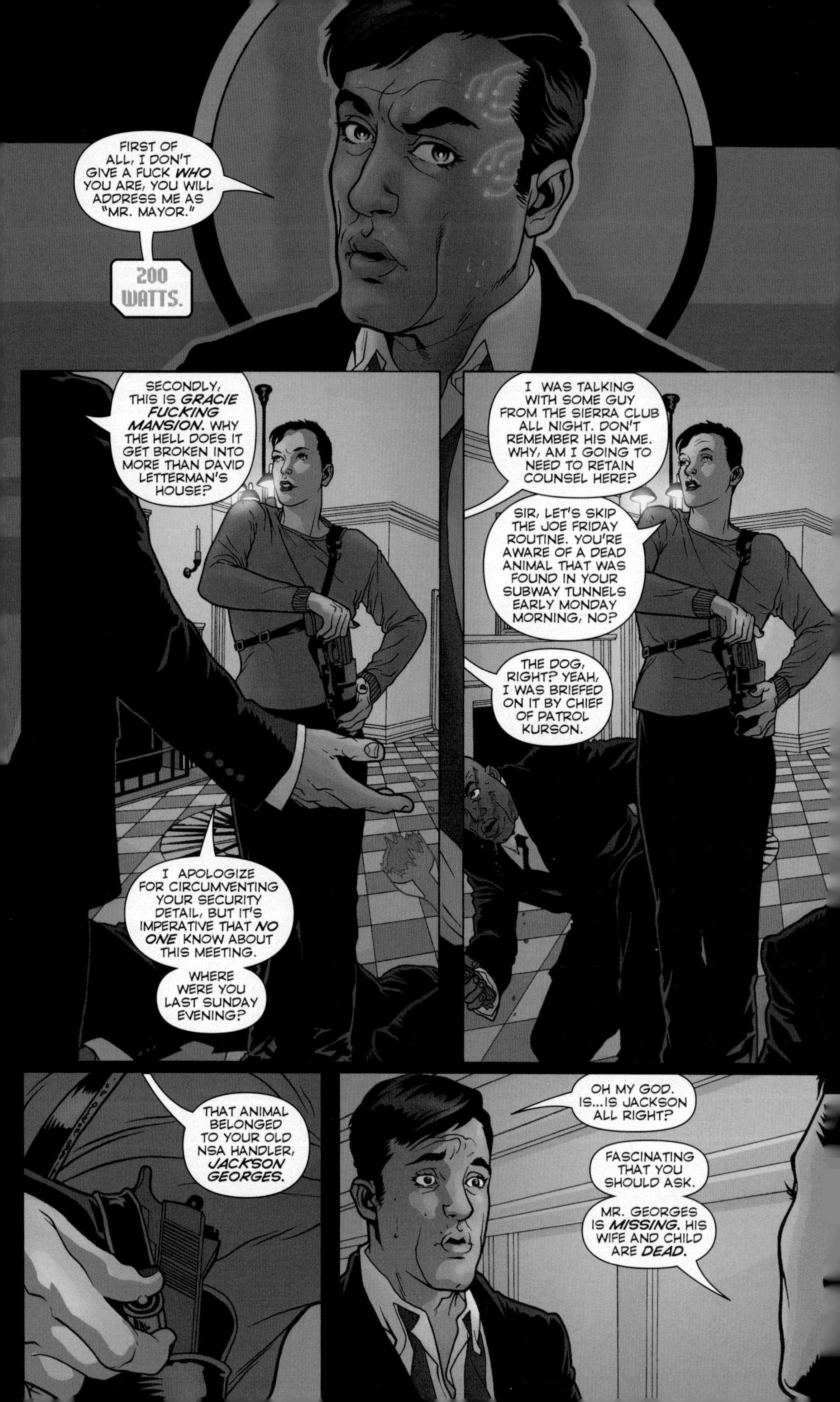

FIRST OF ALL, I DON'T GIVE A FUCK WHO YOU ARE, YOU WILL ADDRESS ME AS "MR. MAYOR."
200 WATTS.
SECONDLY, THIS IS GRACIE FUCKING MANSION. WHY THE HELL DOES IT GET BROKEN INTO MORE THAN DAVID LETTERMAN'S HOUSE?
I APOLOGIZE FOR CIRCUMVENTING YOUR SECURITY DETAIL, BUT IT'S IMPERATIVE THAT NO ONE KNOW ABOUT THIS MEETING.
WHERE WERE YOU LAST SUNDAY EVENING?
I WAS TALKING WITH SOME GUY FROM THE SIERRA CLUB ALL NIGHT. DON'T REMEMBER HIS NAME. WHY, AM I GOING TO NEED TO RETAIN COUNSEL HERE?
SIR, LET'S SKIP THE JOE FRIDAY ROUTINE. YOU'RE AWARE OF A DEAD ANIMAL THAT WAS FOUND IN YOUR SUBWAY TUNNELS EARLY MONDAY MORNING, NO?
THE DOG, RIGHT? YEAH, I WAS BRIEFED ON IT BY CHIEF OF PATROL KURSON.
THAT ANIMAL BELONGED TO YOUR OLD NSA HANDLER, JACKSON GEORGES.
OH MY GOD. IS...IS JACKSON ALL RIGHT?
FASCINATING THAT YOU SHOULD ASK.
MR. GEORGES IS MISSING. HIS WIFE AND CHILD ARE DEAD.

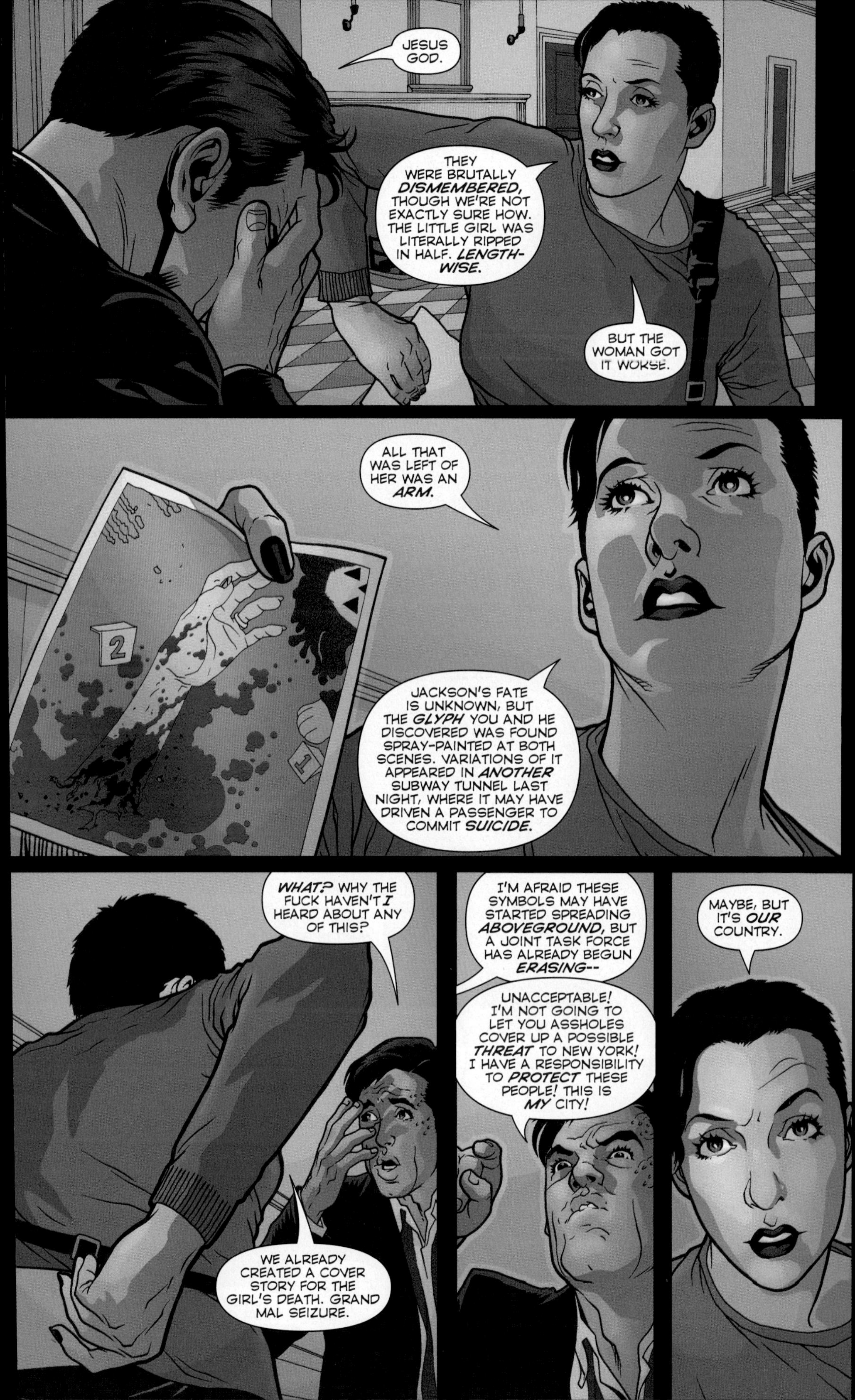

JESUS GOD.
THEY WERE BRUTALLY DISMEMBERED, THOUGH WE'RE NOT EXACTLY SURE HOW. THE LITTLE GIRL WAS LITERALLY RIPPED IN HALF. LENGTH-WISE.
BUT THE WOMAN GOT IT WORSE.
ALL THAT WAS LEFT OF HER WAS AN ARM.
JACKSON'S FATE IS UNKNOWN, BUT THE GLYPH YOU AND HE DISCOVERED WAS FOUND SPRAY-PAINTED AT BOTH SCENES. VARIATIONS OF IT APPEARED IN ANOTHER SUBWAY TUNNEL LAST NIGHT, WHERE IT MAY HAVE DRIVEN A PASSENGER TO COMMIT SUICIDE.
WHAT? WHY THE FUCK HAVEN'T I HEARD ABOUT ANY OF THIS?
WE ALREADY CREATED A COVER STORY FOR THE GIRL'S DEATH. GRAND MAL SEIZURE.
I'M AFRAID THESE SYMBOLS MAY HAVE STARTED SPREADING ABOVEGROUND, BUT A JOINT TASK FORCE HAS ALREADY BEGUN ERASING--
UNACCEPTABLE! I'M NOT GOING TO LET YOU ASSHOLES COVER UP A POSSIBLE THREAT TO NEW YORK! I HAVE A RESPONSIBILITY TO PROTECT THESE PEOPLE! THIS IS MY CITY!
MAYBE, BUT IT'S OUR COUNTRY.

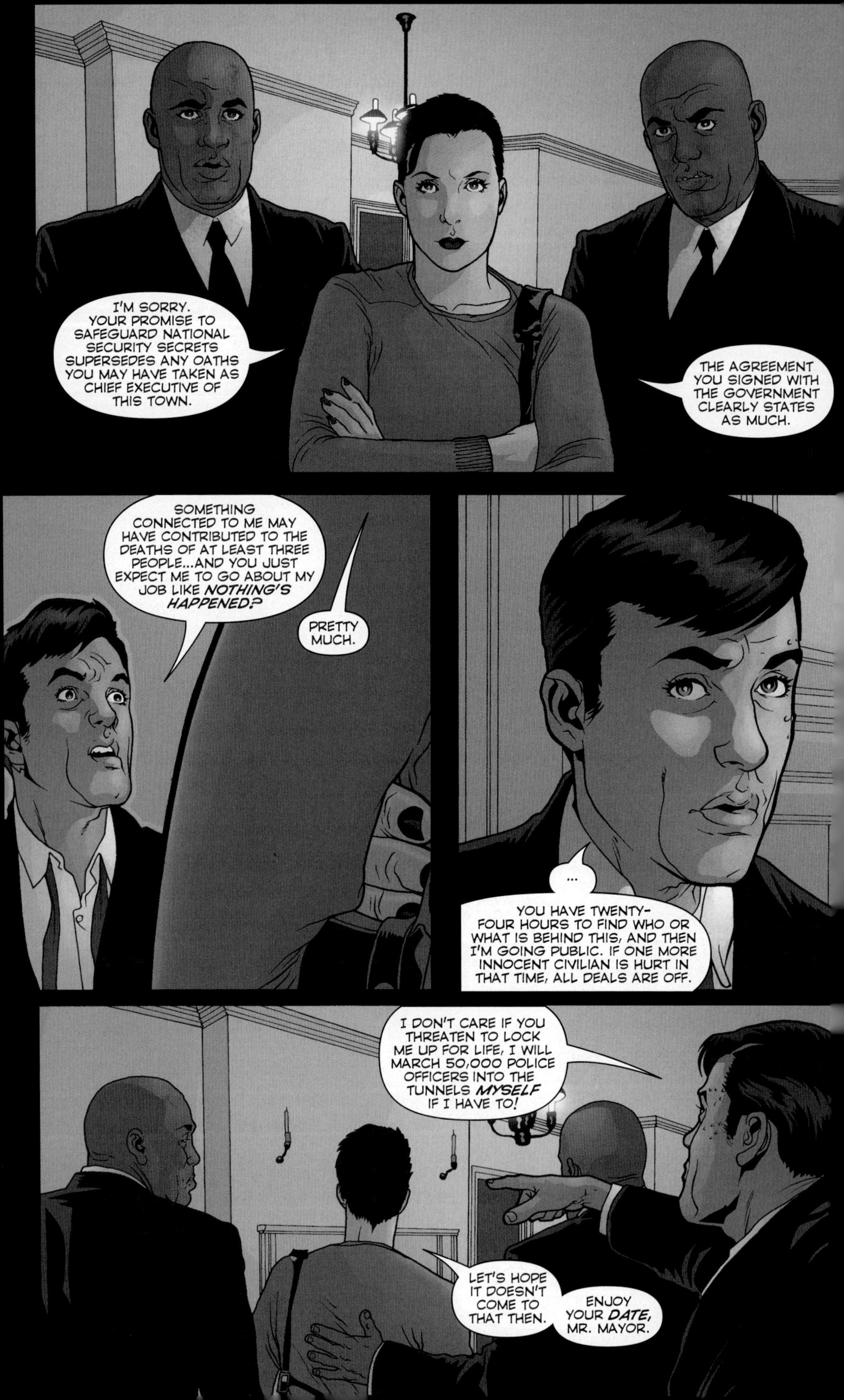
I'M SORRY. YOUR PROMISE TO SAFEGUARD NATIONAL SECURITY SECRETS SUPERSEDES ANY OATHS YOU MAY HAVE TAKEN AS CHIEF EXECUTIVE OF THIS TOWN.
THE AGREEMENT YOU SIGNED WITH THE GOVERNMENT CLEARLY STATES AS MUCH.
SOMETHING CONNECTED TO ME MAY HAVE CONTRIBUTED TO THE DEATHS OF AT LEAST THREE PEOPLE...AND YOU JUST EXPECT ME TO GO ABOUT MY JOB LIKE *NOTHING'S HAPPENED?*
PRETTY MUCH.
...
YOU HAVE TWENTY-FOUR HOURS TO FIND WHO OR WHAT IS BEHIND THIS, AND THEN I'M GOING PUBLIC. IF ONE MORE INNOCENT CIVILIAN IS HURT IN THAT TIME, ALL DEALS ARE OFF.
I DON'T CARE IF YOU THREATEN TO LOCK ME UP FOR LIFE, I WILL MARCH 50,000 POLICE OFFICERS INTO THE TUNNELS *MYSELF* IF I HAVE TO!
LET'S HOPE IT DOESN'T COME TO THAT THEN.
ENJOY YOUR *DATE,* MR. MAYOR.

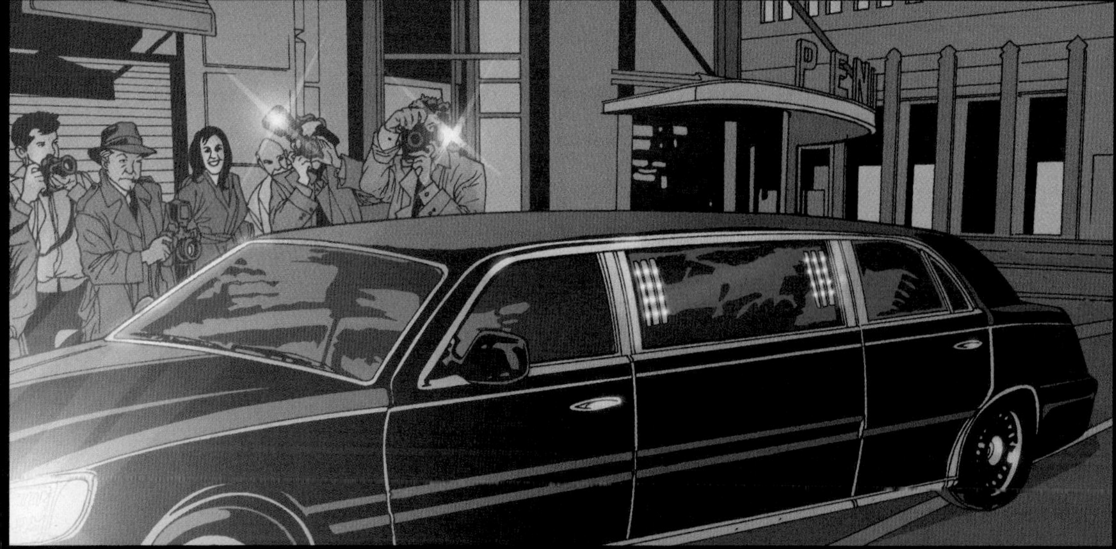
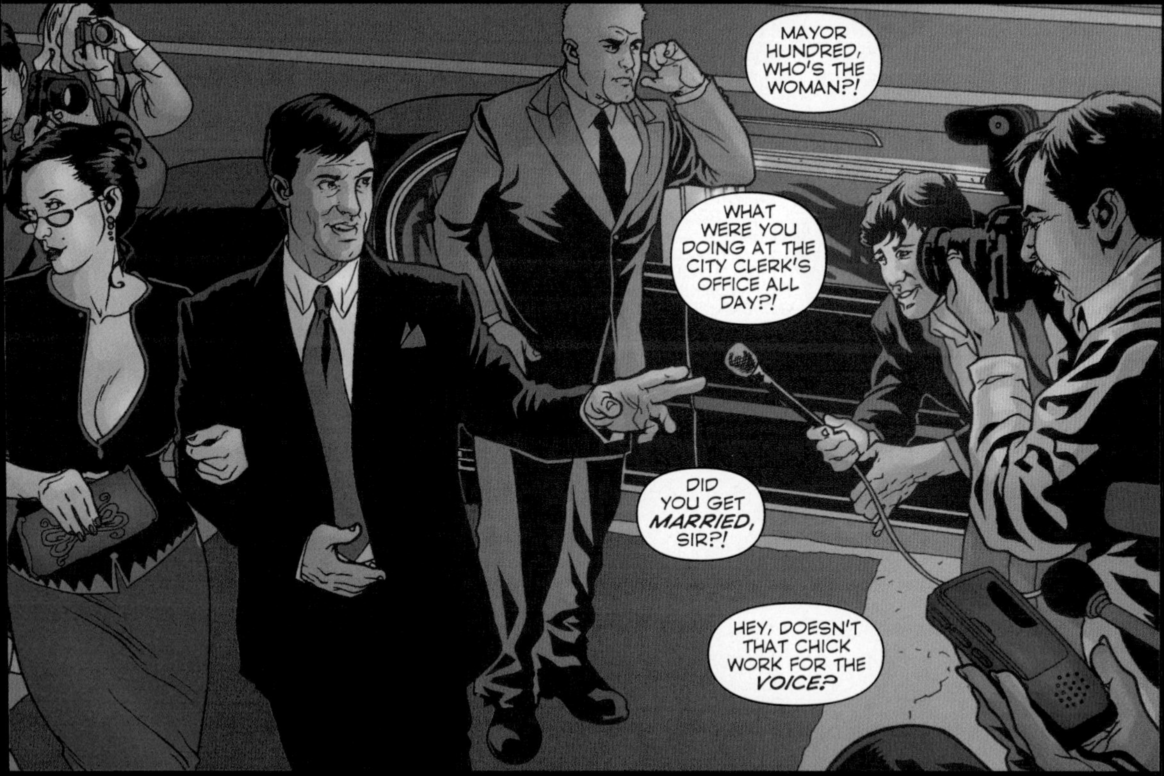
MAYOR HUNDRED, WHO'S THE WOMAN?!
WHAT WERE YOU DOING AT THE CITY CLERK'S OFFICE ALL DAY?!
DID YOU GET *MARRIED*, SIR?!
HEY, DOESN'T THAT CHICK WORK FOR THE *VOICE?*
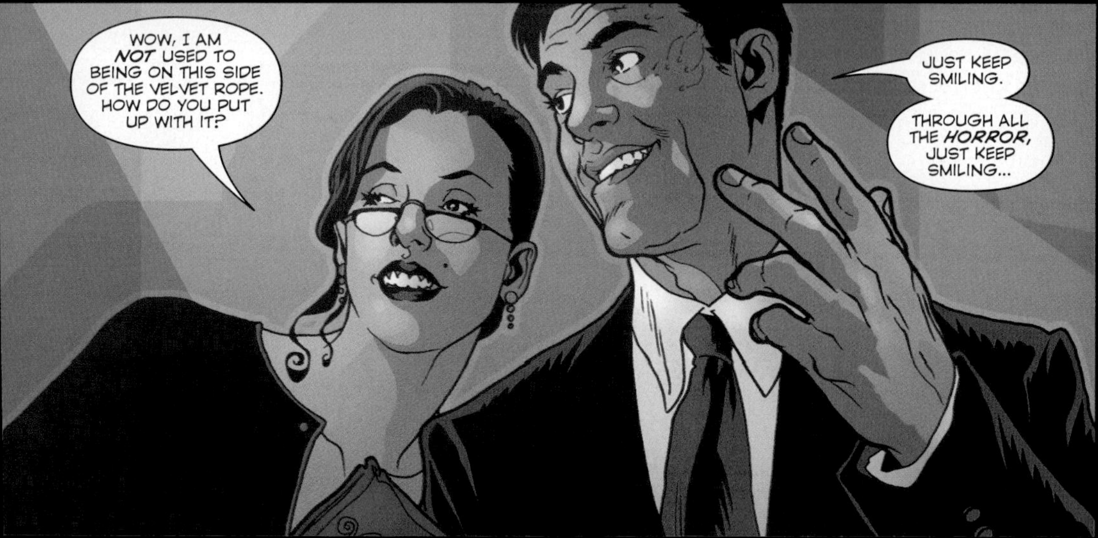
WOW, I AM *NOT* USED TO BEING ON THIS SIDE OF THE VELVET ROPE. HOW DO YOU PUT UP WITH IT?
JUST KEEP SMILING.
THROUGH ALL THE *HORROR*, JUST KEEP SMILING...

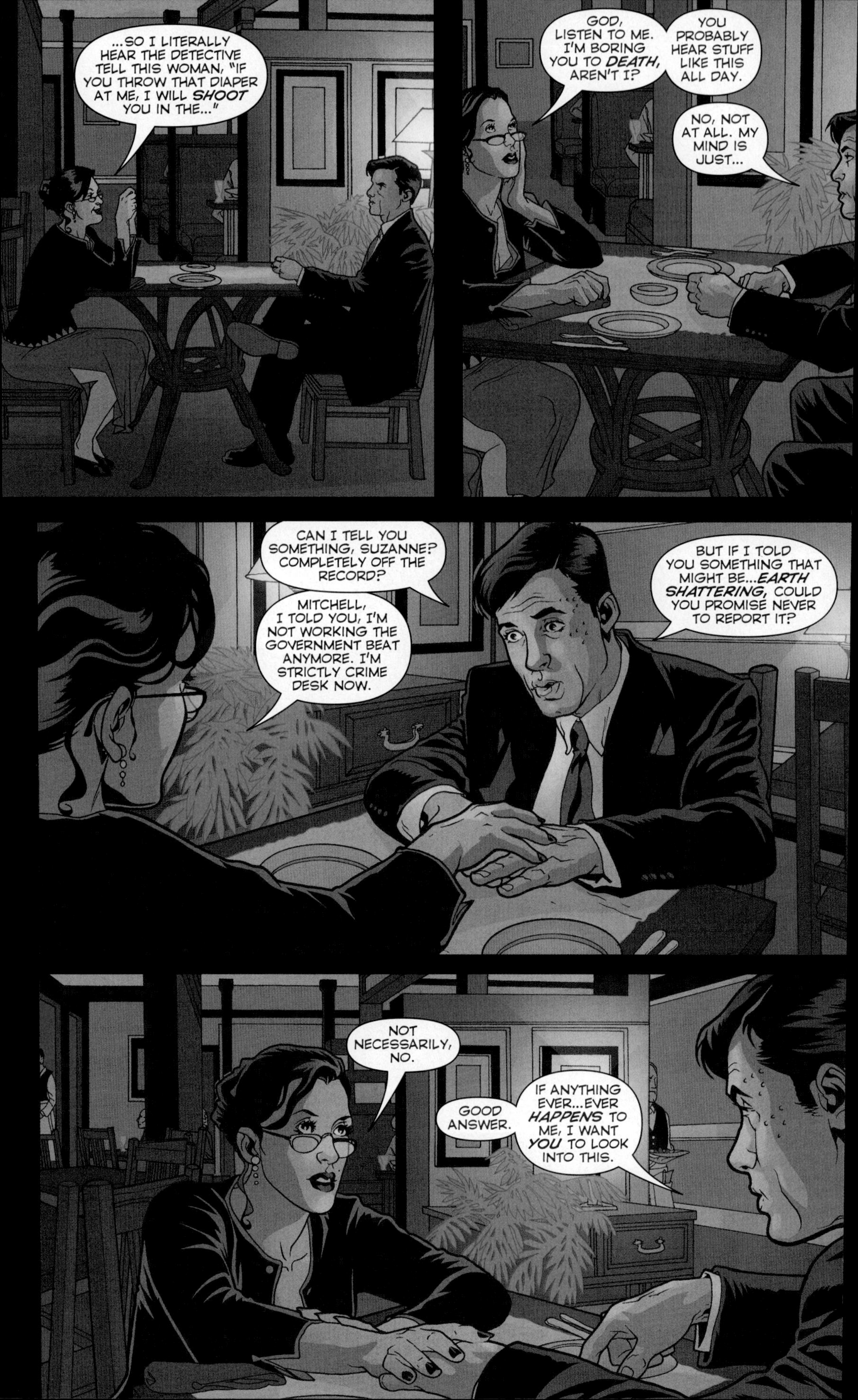
...SO I LITERALLY HEAR THE DETECTIVE TELL THIS WOMAN, "IF YOU THROW THAT DIAPER AT ME, I WILL SHOOT YOU IN THE..."
GOD, LISTEN TO ME. I'M BORING YOU TO DEATH, AREN'T I?
YOU PROBABLY HEAR STUFF LIKE THIS ALL DAY.
NO, NOT AT ALL. MY MIND IS JUST...
CAN I TELL YOU SOMETHING, SUZANNE? COMPLETELY OFF THE RECORD?
MITCHELL, I TOLD YOU, I'M NOT WORKING THE GOVERNMENT BEAT ANYMORE. I'M STRICTLY CRIME DESK NOW.
BUT IF I TOLD YOU SOMETHING THAT MIGHT BE...EARTH SHATTERING, COULD YOU PROMISE NEVER TO REPORT IT?
NOT NECESSARILY, NO.
GOOD ANSWER.
IF ANYTHING EVER...EVER HAPPENS TO ME, I WANT YOU TO LOOK INTO THIS.

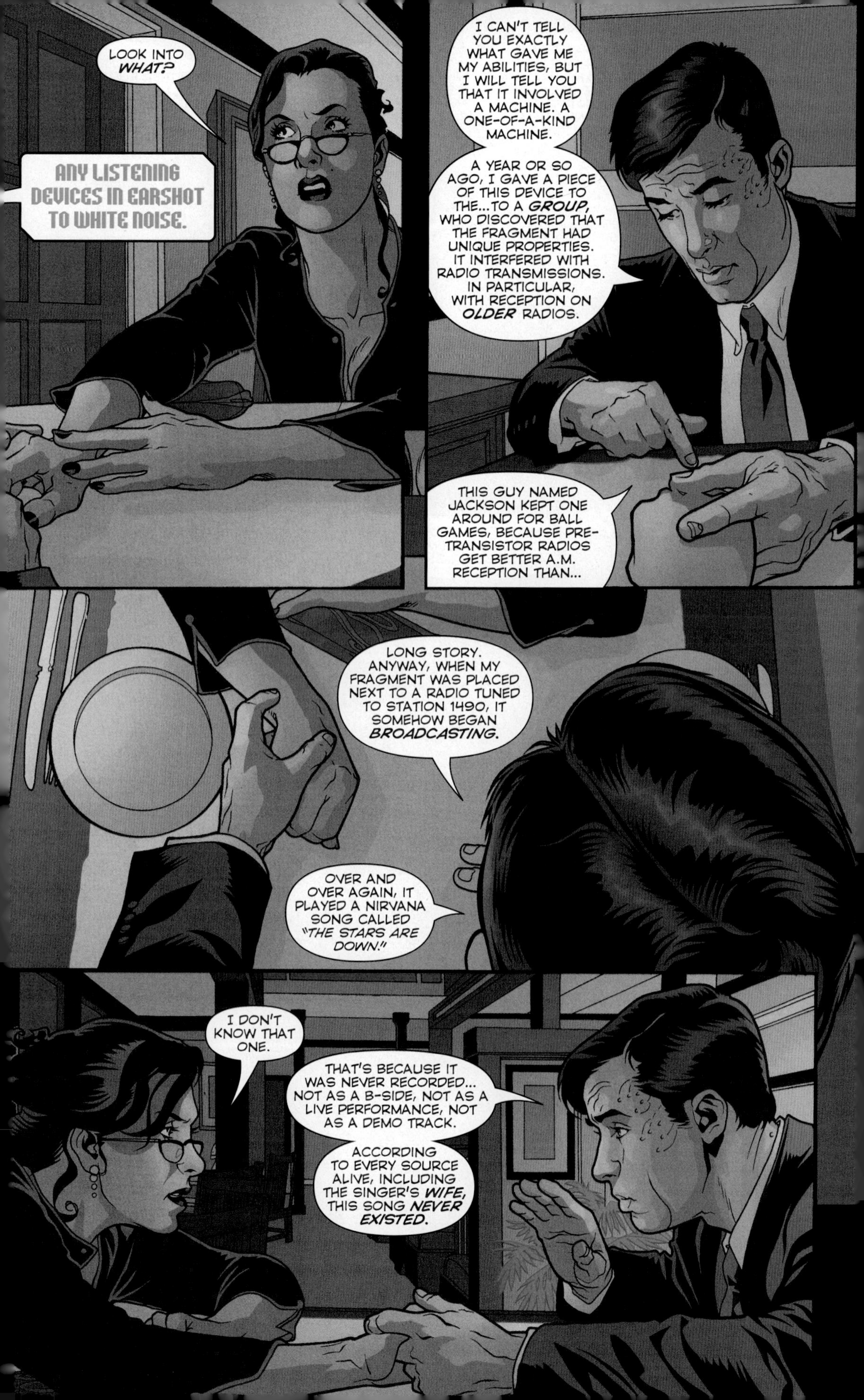
LOOK INTO *WHAT?*
ANY LISTENING DEVICES IN EARSHOT TO WHITE NOISE.
I CAN'T TELL YOU EXACTLY WHAT GAVE ME MY ABILITIES, BUT I WILL TELL YOU THAT IT INVOLVED A MACHINE. A ONE-OF-A-KIND MACHINE.
A YEAR OR SO AGO, I GAVE A PIECE OF THIS DEVICE TO THE...TO A *GROUP*, WHO DISCOVERED THAT THE FRAGMENT HAD UNIQUE PROPERTIES. IT INTERFERED WITH RADIO TRANSMISSIONS. IN PARTICULAR, WITH RECEPTION ON *OLDER* RADIOS.
THIS GUY NAMED JACKSON KEPT ONE AROUND FOR BALL GAMES, BECAUSE PRE-TRANSISTOR RADIOS GET BETTER A.M. RECEPTION THAN...
LONG STORY. ANYWAY, WHEN MY FRAGMENT WAS PLACED NEXT TO A RADIO TUNED TO STATION 1490, IT SOMEHOW BEGAN *BROADCASTING*.
OVER AND OVER AGAIN, IT PLAYED A NIRVANA SONG CALLED *"THE STARS ARE DOWN."*
I DON'T KNOW THAT ONE.
THAT'S BECAUSE IT WAS NEVER RECORDED... NOT AS A B-SIDE, NOT AS A LIVE PERFORMANCE, NOT AS A DEMO TRACK.
ACCORDING TO EVERY SOURCE ALIVE, INCLUDING THE SINGER'S *WIFE*, THIS SONG *NEVER EXISTED*.

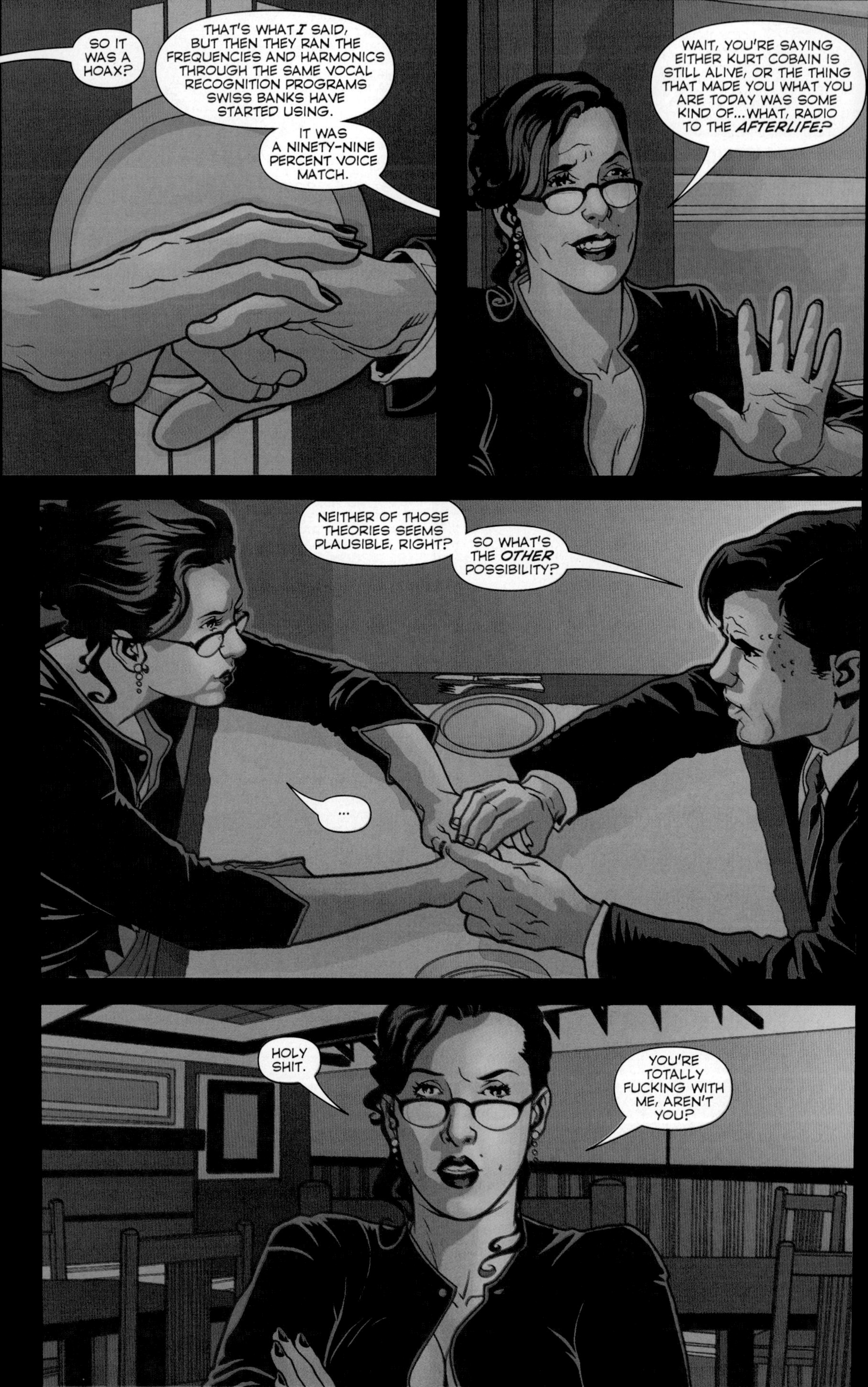
SO IT WAS A HOAX?
THAT'S WHAT I SAID, BUT THEN THEY RAN THE FREQUENCIES AND HARMONICS THROUGH THE SAME VOCAL RECOGNITION PROGRAMS SWISS BANKS HAVE STARTED USING.
IT WAS A NINETY-NINE PERCENT VOICE MATCH.
WAIT, YOU'RE SAYING EITHER KURT COBAIN IS STILL ALIVE, OR THE THING THAT MADE YOU WHAT YOU ARE TODAY WAS SOME KIND OF...WHAT, RADIO TO THE AFTERLIFE?
NEITHER OF THOSE THEORIES SEEMS PLAUSIBLE, RIGHT?
SO WHAT'S THE OTHER POSSIBILITY?
...
HOLY SHIT.
YOU'RE TOTALLY FUCKING WITH ME, AREN'T YOU?

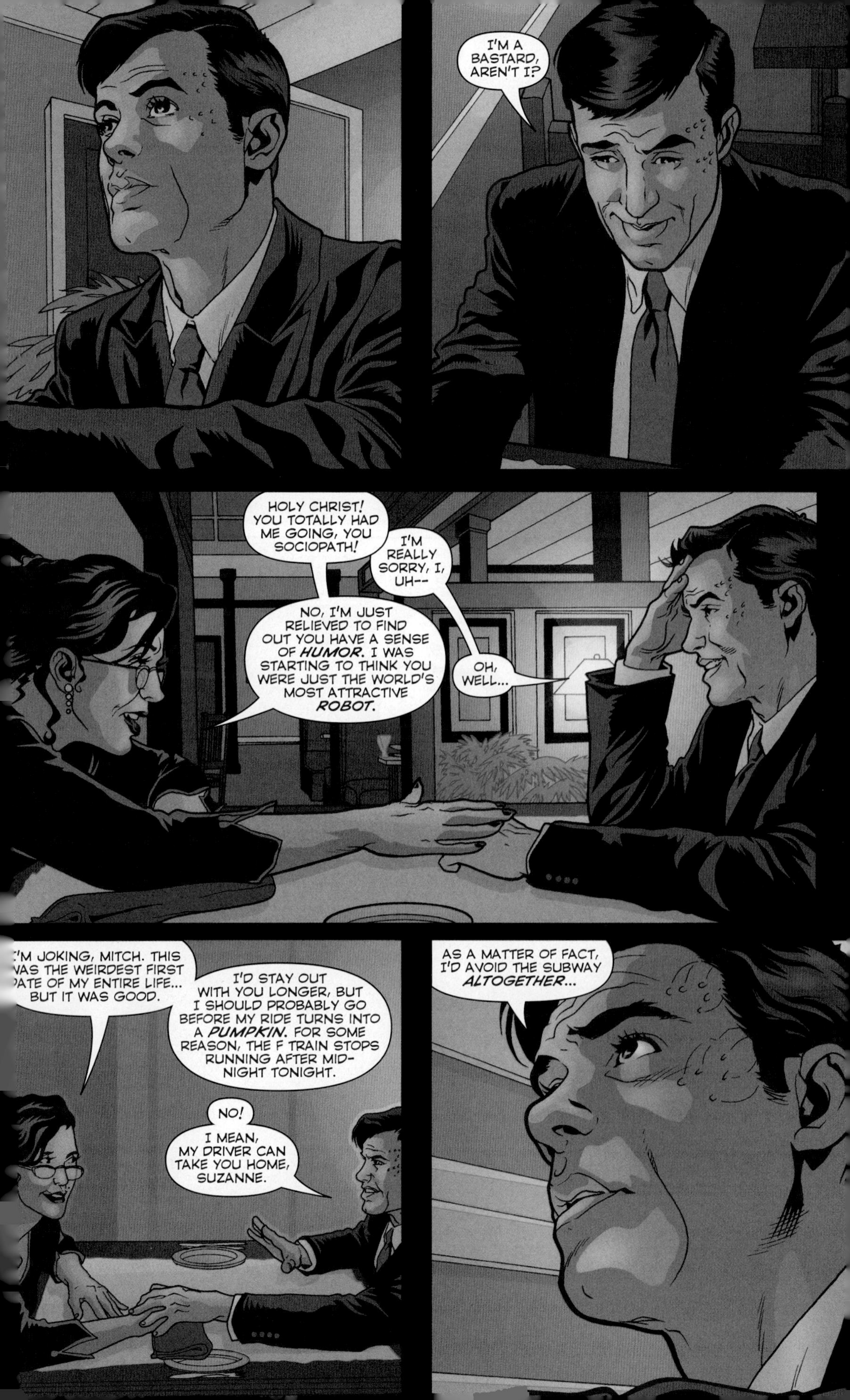
I'M A BASTARD, AREN'T I?
HOLY CHRIST! YOU TOTALLY HAD ME GOING, YOU SOCIOPATH!
I'M REALLY SORRY, I, UH--
NO, I'M JUST RELIEVED TO FIND OUT YOU HAVE A SENSE OF *HUMOR*. I WAS STARTING TO THINK YOU WERE JUST THE WORLD'S MOST ATTRACTIVE *ROBOT*.
OH, WELL...
I'M JOKING, MITCH. THIS WAS THE WEIRDEST FIRST DATE OF MY ENTIRE LIFE... BUT IT WAS GOOD.
I'D STAY OUT WITH YOU LONGER, BUT I SHOULD PROBABLY GO BEFORE MY RIDE TURNS INTO A *PUMPKIN*. FOR SOME REASON, THE F TRAIN STOPS RUNNING AFTER MID-NIGHT TONIGHT.
NO!
I MEAN, MY DRIVER CAN TAKE YOU HOME, SUZANNE.
AS A MATTER OF FACT, I'D AVOID THE SUBWAY *ALTOGETHER*...

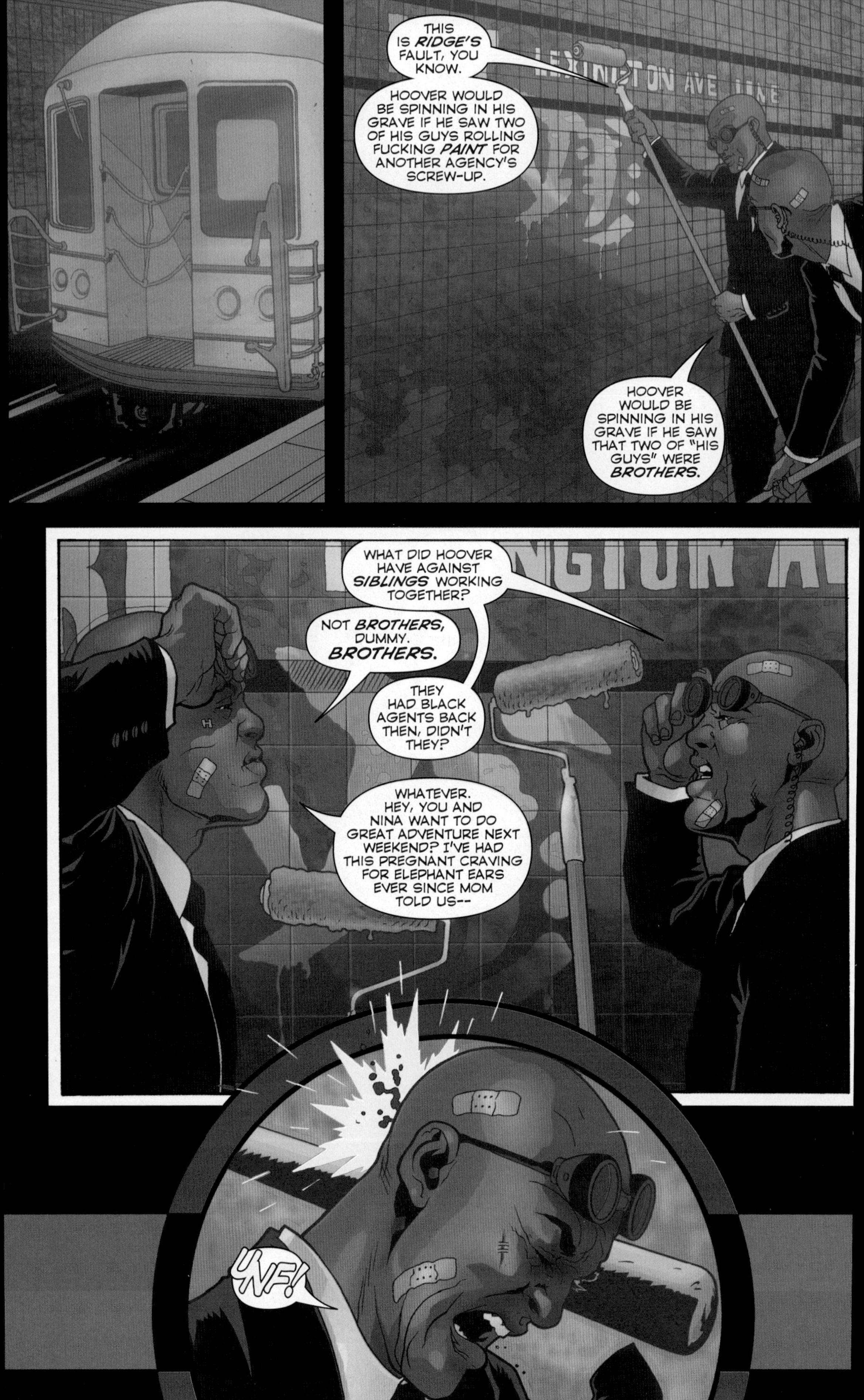
LEXINGTON AVE LINE
THIS IS *RIDGE'S* FAULT, YOU KNOW.
HOOVER WOULD BE SPINNING IN HIS GRAVE IF HE SAW TWO OF HIS GUYS ROLLING FUCKING *PAINT* FOR ANOTHER AGENCY'S SCREW-UP.
HOOVER WOULD BE SPINNING IN HIS GRAVE IF HE SAW THAT TWO OF "HIS GUYS" WERE ***BROTHERS.***
WHAT DID HOOVER HAVE AGAINST *SIBLINGS* WORKING TOGETHER?
NOT ***BROTHERS,*** DUMMY. ***BROTHERS.***
THEY HAD BLACK AGENTS BACK THEN, DIDN'T THEY?
WHATEVER. HEY, YOU AND NINA WANT TO DO GREAT ADVENTURE NEXT WEEKEND? I'VE HAD THIS PREGNANT CRAVING FOR ELEPHANT EARS EVER SINCE MOM TOLD US--
UNF!

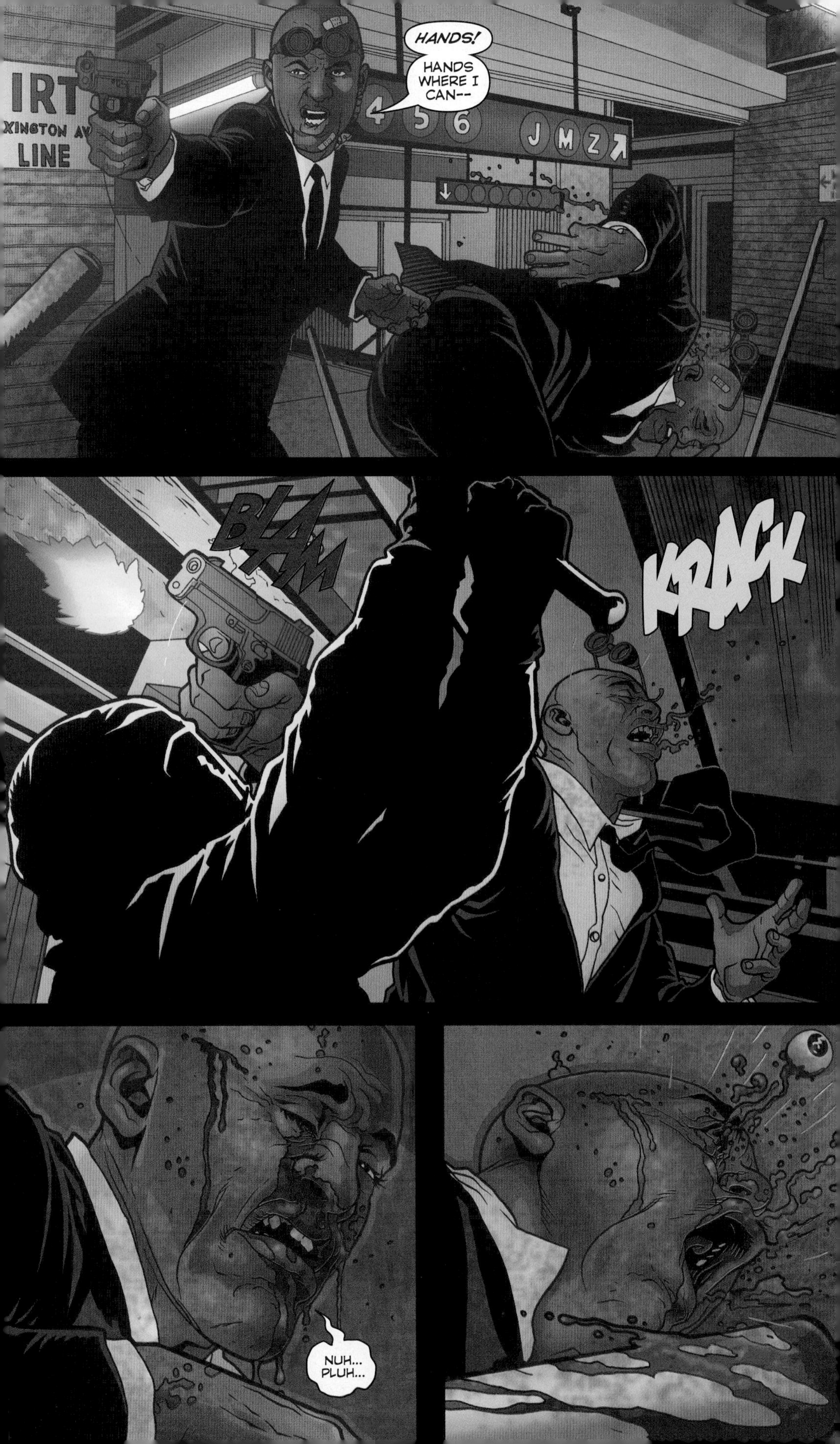
IRT
XINGTON AV
LINE
HANDS!
HANDS WHERE I CAN--
4 5 6
J M Z
BLAM
KRACK
NUH... PLUH...

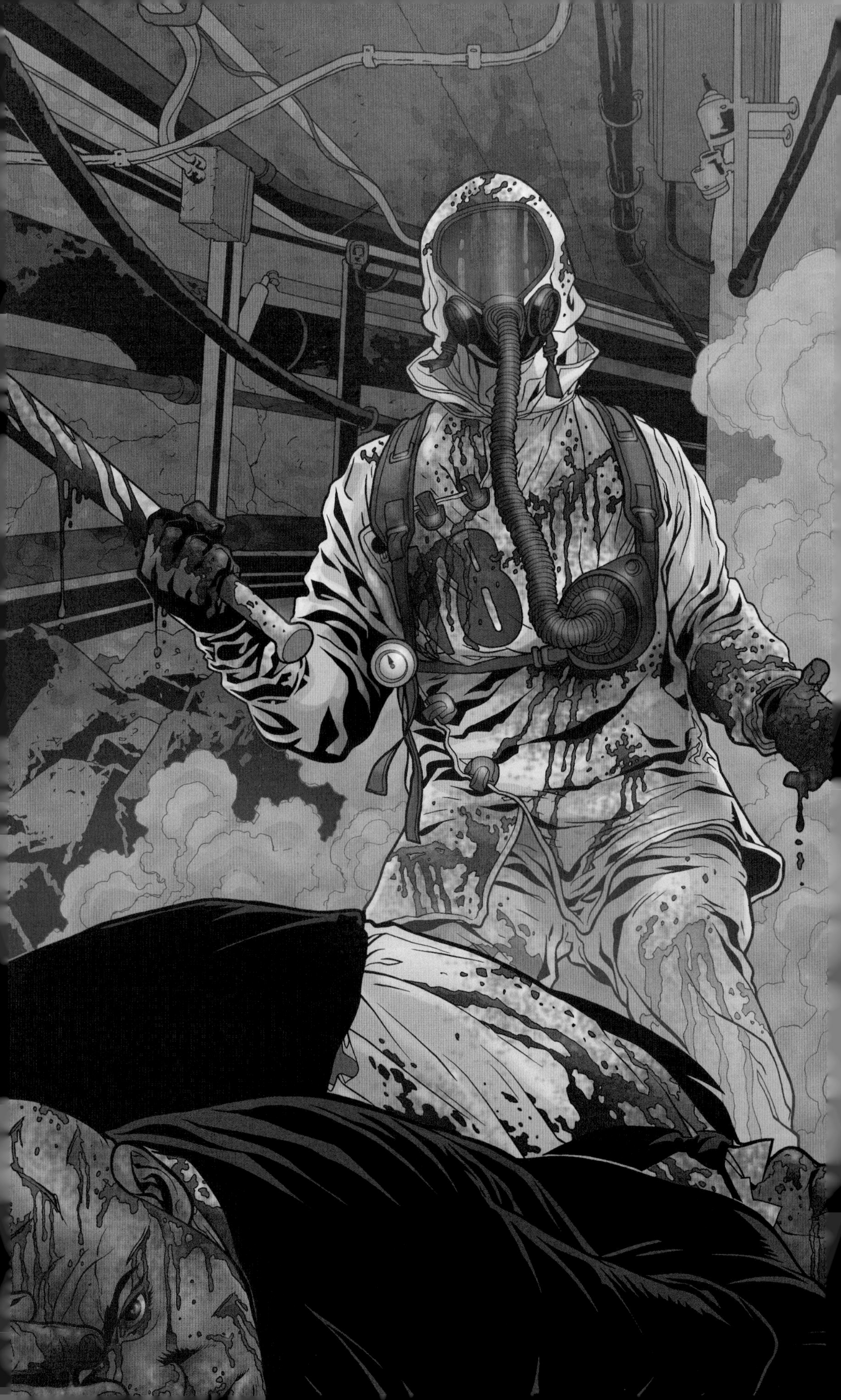

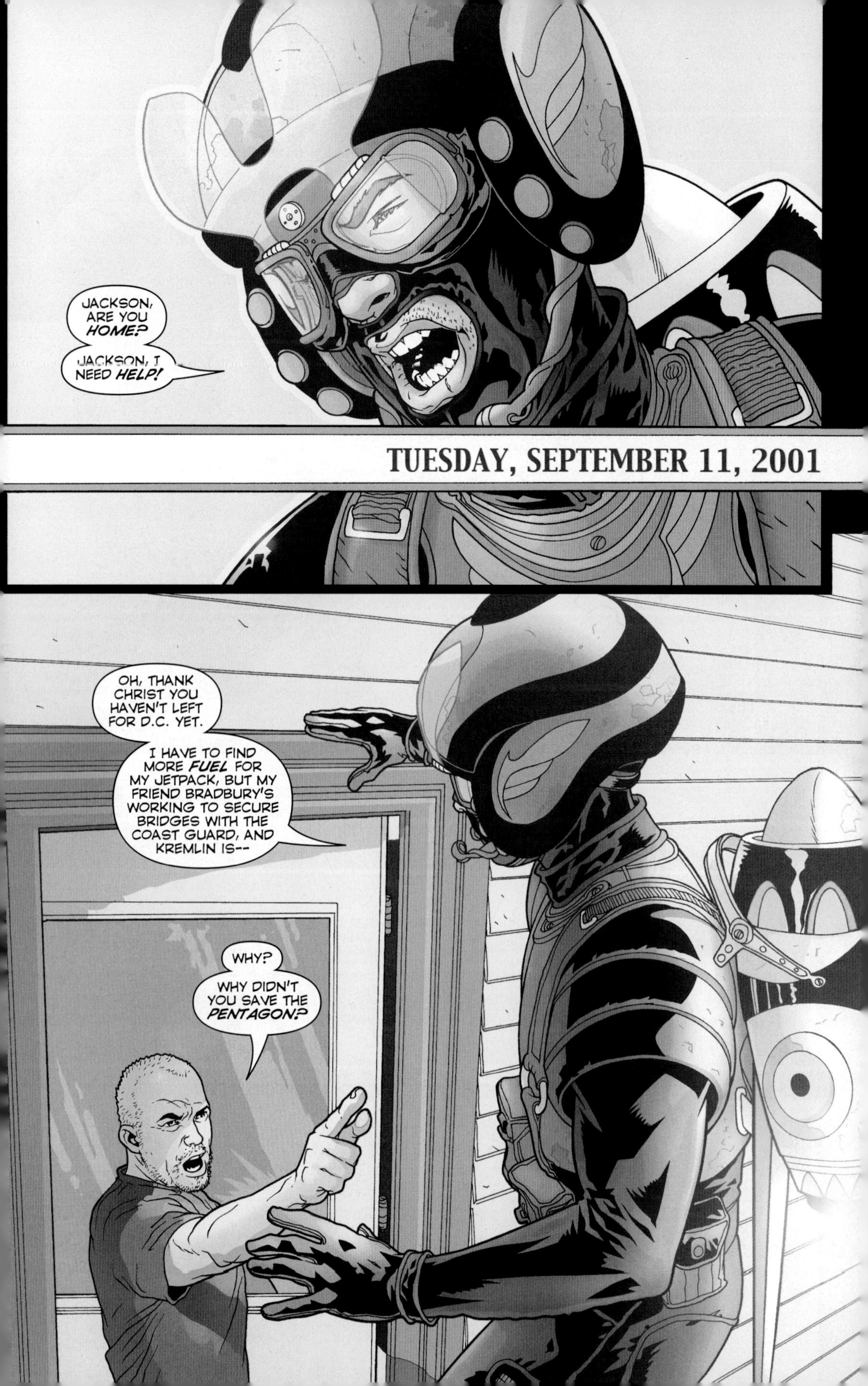
JACKSON, ARE YOU HOME?
JACKSON, I NEED HELP!
TUESDAY, SEPTEMBER 11, 2001
OH, THANK CHRIST YOU HAVEN'T LEFT FOR D.C. YET.
I HAVE TO FIND MORE FUEL FOR MY JETPACK, BUT MY FRIEND BRADBURY'S WORKING TO SECURE BRIDGES WITH THE COAST GUARD, AND KREMLIN IS--
WHY?
WHY DIDN'T YOU SAVE THE PENTAGON?

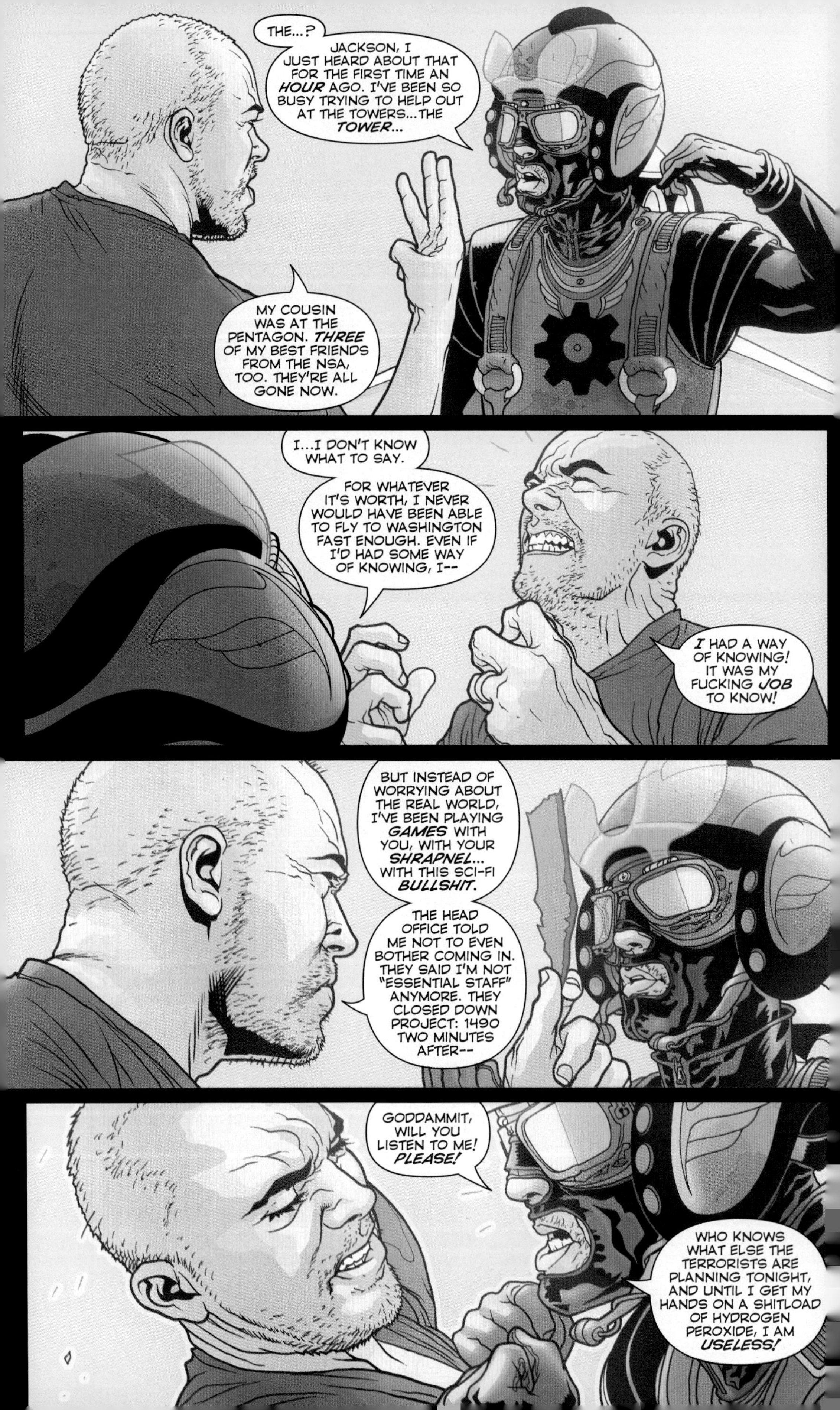
THE...?
JACKSON, I JUST HEARD ABOUT THAT FOR THE FIRST TIME AN *HOUR* AGO. I'VE BEEN SO BUSY TRYING TO HELP OUT AT THE TOWERS...THE *TOWER*...
MY COUSIN WAS AT THE PENTAGON. *THREE* OF MY BEST FRIENDS FROM THE NSA, TOO. THEY'RE ALL GONE NOW.
I...I DON'T KNOW WHAT TO SAY.
FOR WHATEVER IT'S WORTH, I NEVER WOULD HAVE BEEN ABLE TO FLY TO WASHINGTON FAST ENOUGH. EVEN IF I'D HAD SOME WAY OF KNOWING, I--
I HAD A WAY OF KNOWING! IT WAS MY FUCKING *JOB* TO KNOW!
BUT INSTEAD OF WORRYING ABOUT THE REAL WORLD, I'VE BEEN PLAYING *GAMES* WITH YOU, WITH YOUR *SHRAPNEL*... WITH THIS SCI-FI *BULLSHIT*.
THE HEAD OFFICE TOLD ME NOT TO EVEN BOTHER COMING IN. THEY SAID I'M NOT "ESSENTIAL STAFF" ANYMORE. THEY CLOSED DOWN PROJECT: 1490 TWO MINUTES AFTER--
GODDAMMIT, WILL YOU LISTEN TO ME! *PLEASE!*
WHO KNOWS WHAT ELSE THE TERRORISTS ARE PLANNING TONIGHT, AND UNTIL I GET MY HANDS ON A SHITLOAD OF HYDROGEN PEROXIDE, I AM *USELESS!*

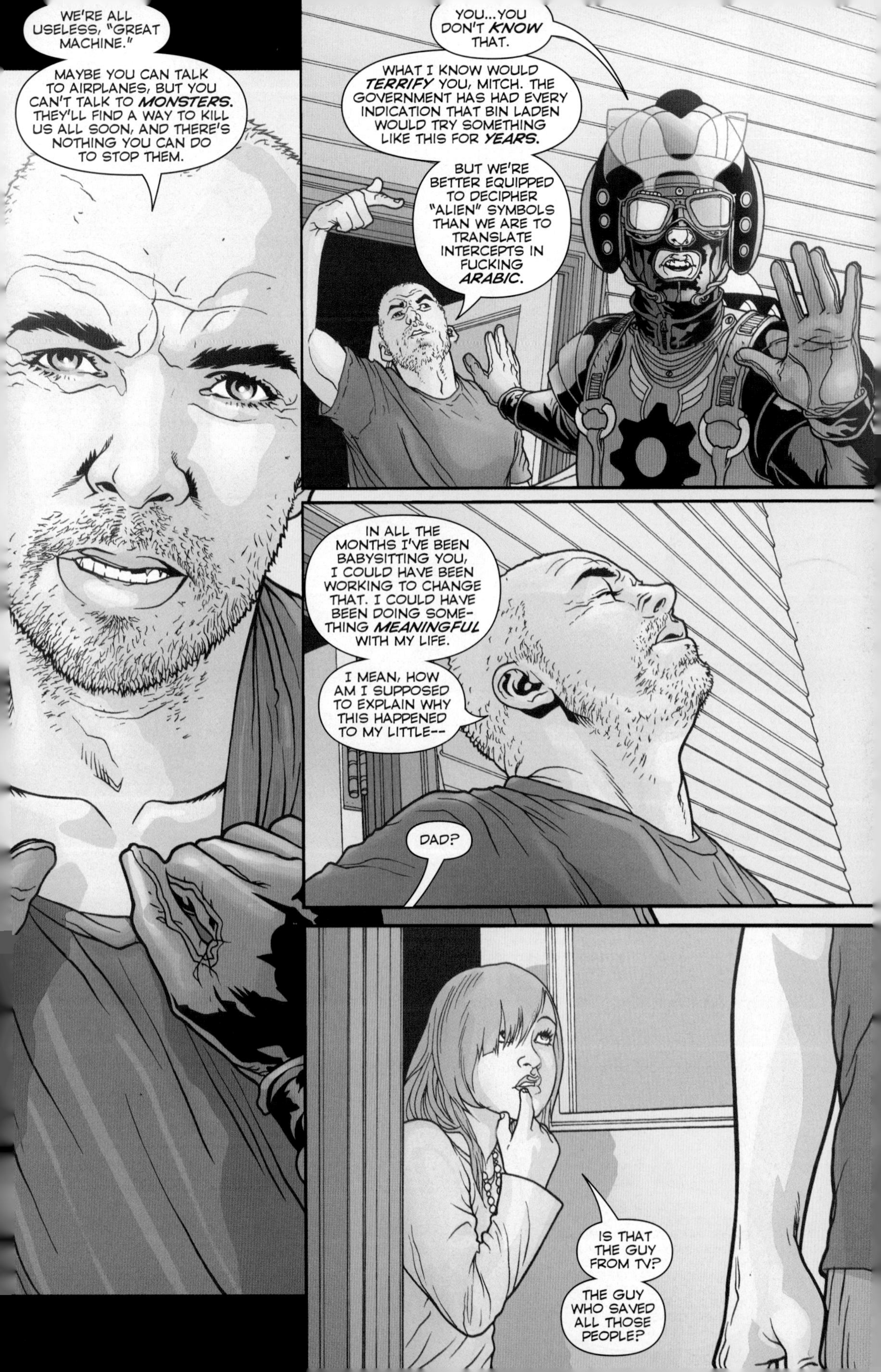

WE'RE ALL USELESS, "GREAT MACHINE."
MAYBE YOU CAN TALK TO AIRPLANES, BUT YOU CAN'T TALK TO MONSTERS. THEY'LL FIND A WAY TO KILL US ALL SOON, AND THERE'S NOTHING YOU CAN DO TO STOP THEM.
YOU...YOU DON'T KNOW THAT.
WHAT I KNOW WOULD TERRIFY YOU, MITCH. THE GOVERNMENT HAS HAD EVERY INDICATION THAT BIN LADEN WOULD TRY SOMETHING LIKE THIS FOR YEARS.
BUT WE'RE BETTER EQUIPPED TO DECIPHER "ALIEN" SYMBOLS THAN WE ARE TO TRANSLATE INTERCEPTS IN FUCKING ARABIC.
IN ALL THE MONTHS I'VE BEEN BABYSITTING YOU, I COULD HAVE BEEN WORKING TO CHANGE THAT. I COULD HAVE BEEN DOING SOMETHING MEANINGFUL WITH MY LIFE.
I MEAN, HOW AM I SUPPOSED TO EXPLAIN WHY THIS HAPPENED TO MY LITTLE--
DAD?
IS THAT THE GUY FROM TV?
THE GUY WHO SAVED ALL THOSE PEOPLE?

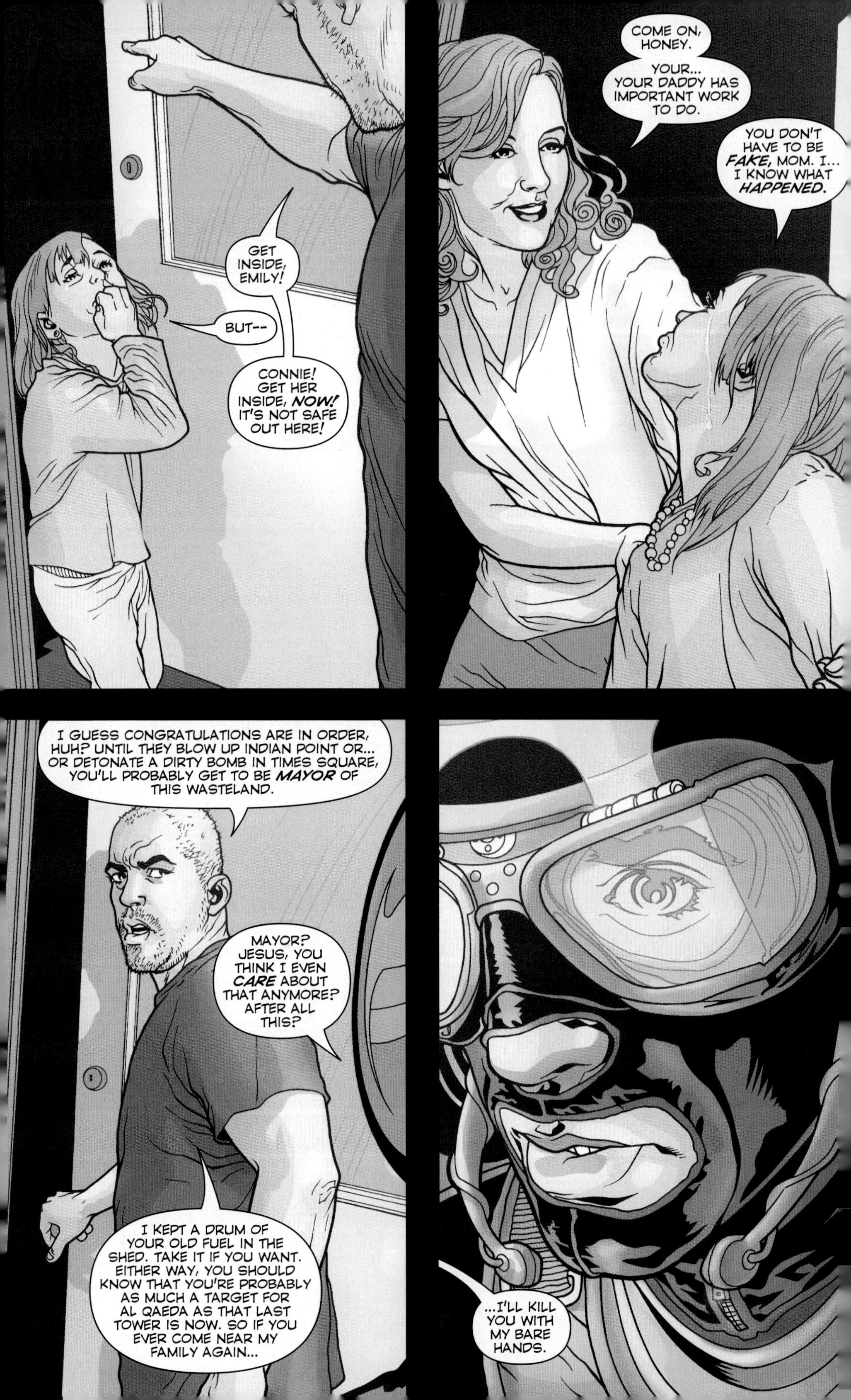
GET INSIDE, EMILY!
BUT--
CONNIE! GET HER INSIDE, NOW! IT'S NOT SAFE OUT HERE!
COME ON, HONEY.
YOUR... YOUR DADDY HAS IMPORTANT WORK TO DO.
YOU DON'T HAVE TO BE FAKE, MOM. I... I KNOW WHAT HAPPENED.
I GUESS CONGRATULATIONS ARE IN ORDER, HUH? UNTIL THEY BLOW UP INDIAN POINT OR... OR DETONATE A DIRTY BOMB IN TIMES SQUARE, YOU'LL PROBABLY GET TO BE MAYOR OF THIS WASTELAND.
MAYOR? JESUS, YOU THINK I EVEN CARE ABOUT THAT ANYMORE? AFTER ALL THIS?
I KEPT A DRUM OF YOUR OLD FUEL IN THE SHED. TAKE IT IF YOU WANT. EITHER WAY, YOU SHOULD KNOW THAT YOU'RE PROBABLY AS MUCH A TARGET FOR AL QAEDA AS THAT LAST TOWER IS NOW. SO IF YOU EVER COME NEAR MY FAMILY AGAIN...
...I'LL KILL YOU WITH MY BARE HANDS.

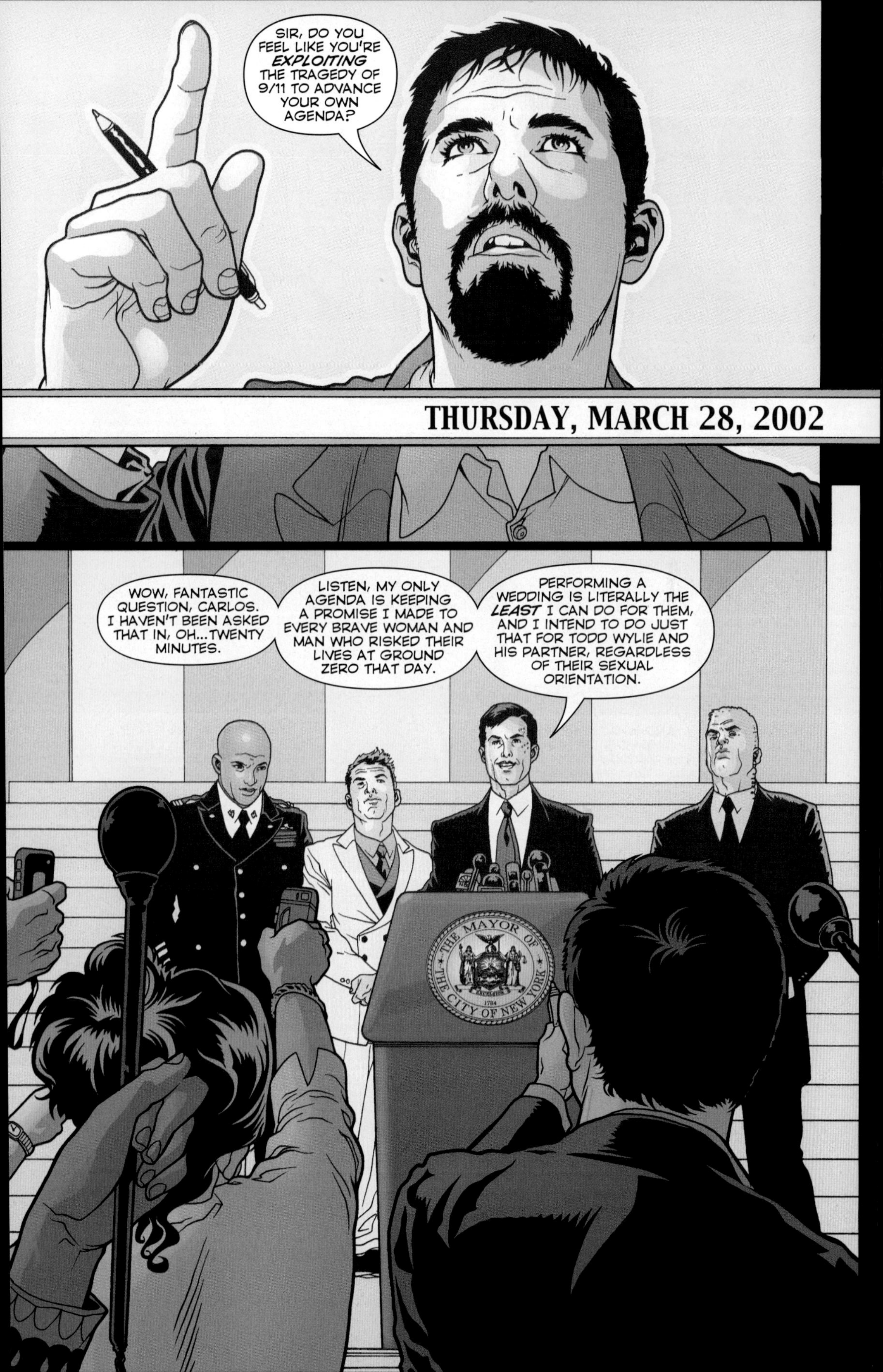

SIR, DO YOU FEEL LIKE YOU'RE *EXPLOITING* THE TRAGEDY OF 9/11 TO ADVANCE YOUR OWN AGENDA?
THURSDAY, MARCH 28, 2002
WOW, FANTASTIC QUESTION, CARLOS. I HAVEN'T BEEN ASKED THAT IN, OH...TWENTY MINUTES.
LISTEN, MY ONLY AGENDA IS KEEPING A PROMISE I MADE TO EVERY BRAVE WOMAN AND MAN WHO RISKED THEIR LIVES AT GROUND ZERO THAT DAY.
PERFORMING A WEDDING IS LITERALLY THE *LEAST* I CAN DO FOR THEM, AND I INTEND TO DO JUST THAT FOR TODD WYLIE AND HIS PARTNER, REGARDLESS OF THEIR SEXUAL ORIENTATION.
THE MAYOR OF THE CITY OF NEW YORK
1784

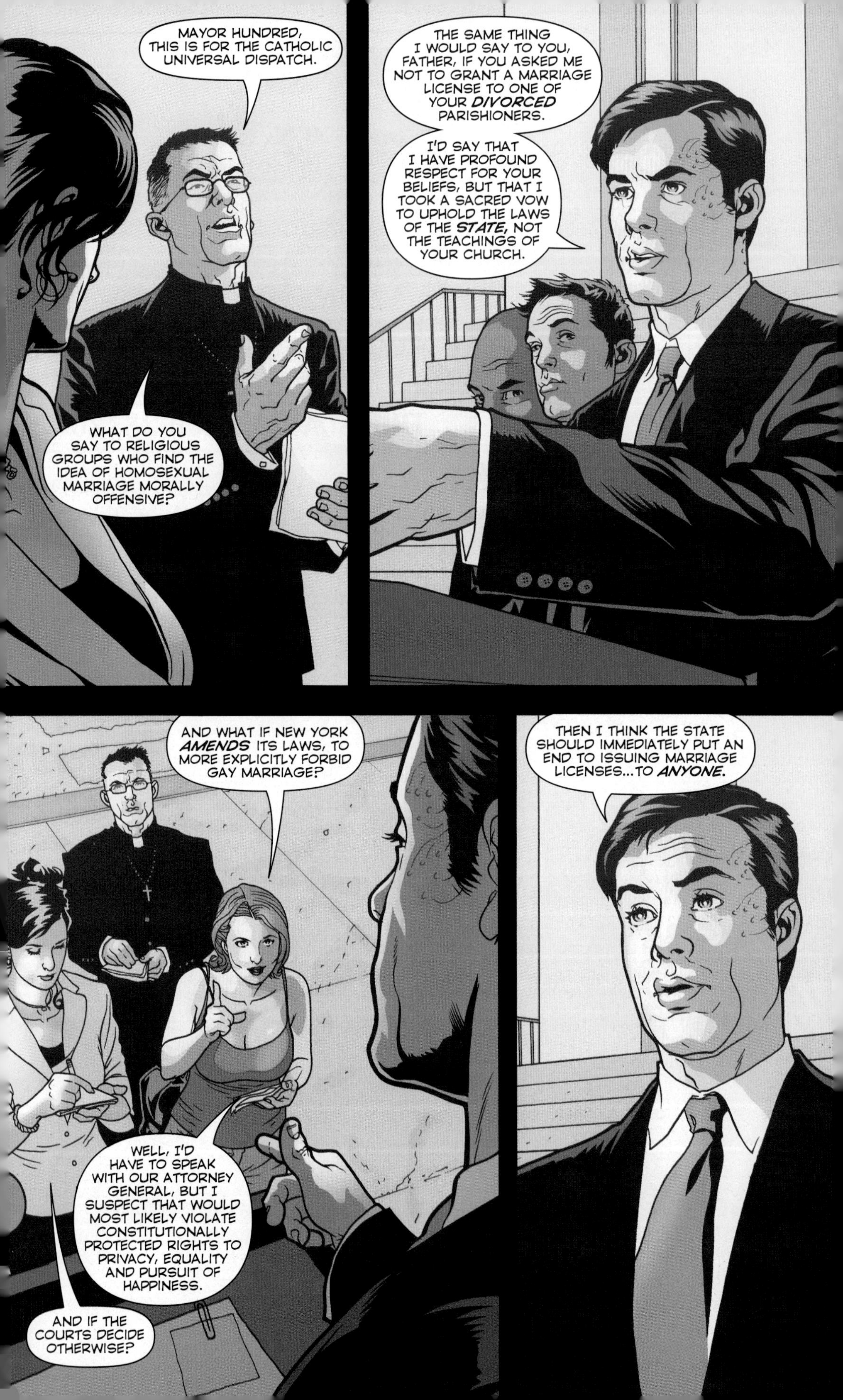
MAYOR HUNDRED, THIS IS FOR THE CATHOLIC UNIVERSAL DISPATCH.
WHAT DO YOU SAY TO RELIGIOUS GROUPS WHO FIND THE IDEA OF HOMOSEXUAL MARRIAGE MORALLY OFFENSIVE?
THE SAME THING I WOULD SAY TO YOU, FATHER, IF YOU ASKED ME NOT TO GRANT A MARRIAGE LICENSE TO ONE OF YOUR *DIVORCED* PARISHIONERS.
I'D SAY THAT I HAVE PROFOUND RESPECT FOR YOUR BELIEFS, BUT THAT I TOOK A SACRED VOW TO UPHOLD THE LAWS OF THE *STATE,* NOT THE TEACHINGS OF YOUR CHURCH.
AND WHAT IF NEW YORK *AMENDS* ITS LAWS, TO MORE EXPLICITLY FORBID GAY MARRIAGE?
WELL, I'D HAVE TO SPEAK WITH OUR ATTORNEY GENERAL, BUT I SUSPECT THAT WOULD MOST LIKELY VIOLATE CONSTITUTIONALLY PROTECTED RIGHTS TO PRIVACY, EQUALITY AND PURSUIT OF HAPPINESS.
AND IF THE COURTS DECIDE OTHERWISE?
THEN I THINK THE STATE SHOULD IMMEDIATELY PUT AN END TO ISSUING MARRIAGE LICENSES...TO *ANYONE.*

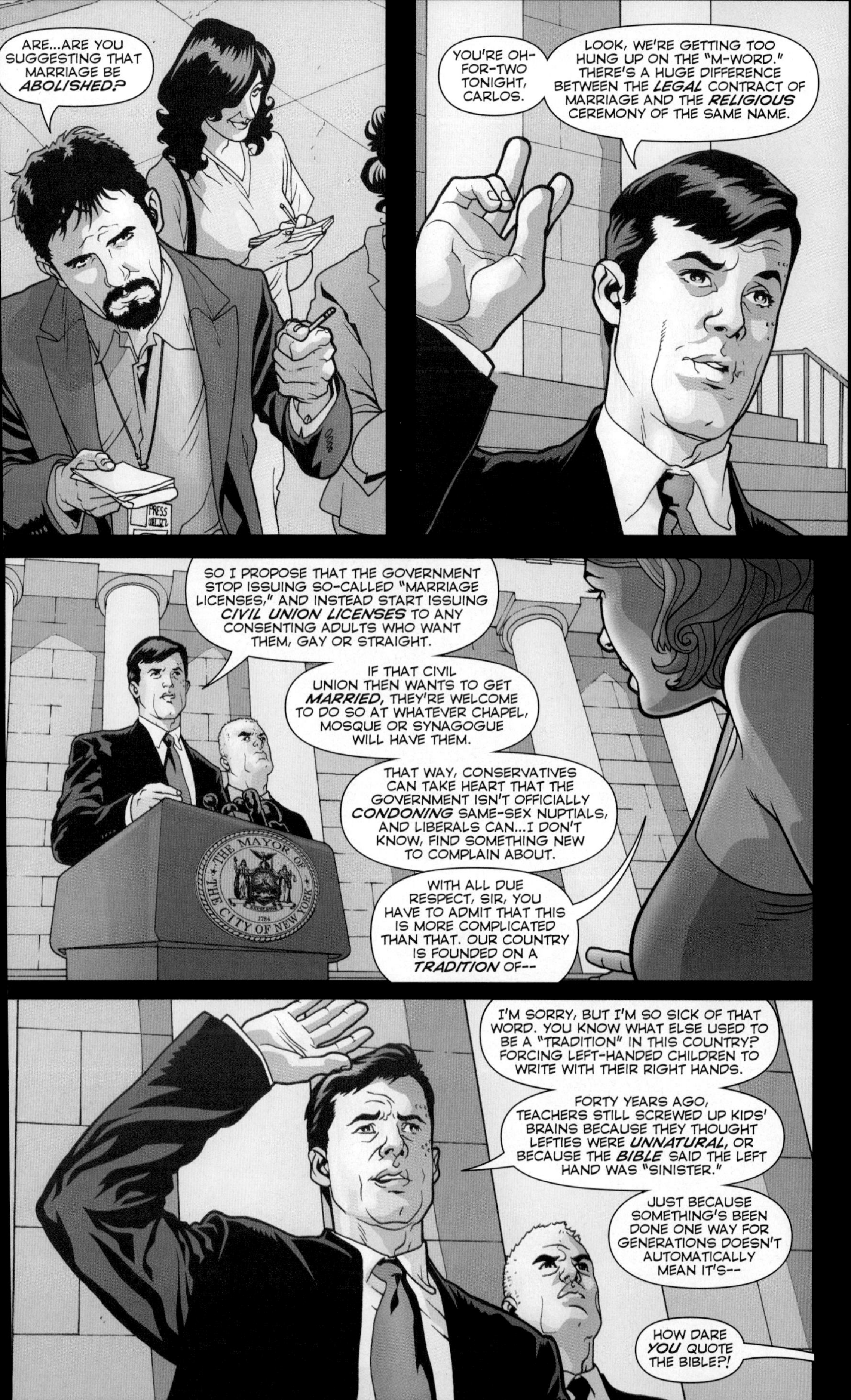
ARE...ARE YOU SUGGESTING THAT MARRIAGE BE ABOLISHED?
YOU'RE OH-FOR-TWO TONIGHT, CARLOS.
LOOK, WE'RE GETTING TOO HUNG UP ON THE "M-WORD." THERE'S A HUGE DIFFERENCE BETWEEN THE LEGAL CONTRACT OF MARRIAGE AND THE RELIGIOUS CEREMONY OF THE SAME NAME.
SO I PROPOSE THAT THE GOVERNMENT STOP ISSUING SO-CALLED "MARRIAGE LICENSES," AND INSTEAD START ISSUING CIVIL UNION LICENSES TO ANY CONSENTING ADULTS WHO WANT THEM, GAY OR STRAIGHT.
IF THAT CIVIL UNION THEN WANTS TO GET MARRIED, THEY'RE WELCOME TO DO SO AT WHATEVER CHAPEL, MOSQUE OR SYNAGOGUE WILL HAVE THEM.
THAT WAY, CONSERVATIVES CAN TAKE HEART THAT THE GOVERNMENT ISN'T OFFICIALLY CONDONING SAME-SEX NUPTIALS, AND LIBERALS CAN...I DON'T KNOW, FIND SOMETHING NEW TO COMPLAIN ABOUT.
THE MAYOR OF THE CITY OF NEW YORK
1784
WITH ALL DUE RESPECT, SIR, YOU HAVE TO ADMIT THAT THIS IS MORE COMPLICATED THAN THAT. OUR COUNTRY IS FOUNDED ON A TRADITION OF--
I'M SORRY, BUT I'M SO SICK OF THAT WORD. YOU KNOW WHAT ELSE USED TO BE A "TRADITION" IN THIS COUNTRY? FORCING LEFT-HANDED CHILDREN TO WRITE WITH THEIR RIGHT HANDS.
FORTY YEARS AGO, TEACHERS STILL SCREWED UP KIDS' BRAINS BECAUSE THEY THOUGHT LEFTIES WERE UNNATURAL, OR BECAUSE THE BIBLE SAID THE LEFT HAND WAS "SINISTER."
JUST BECAUSE SOMETHING'S BEEN DONE ONE WAY FOR GENERATIONS DOESN'T AUTOMATICALLY MEAN IT'S--
HOW DARE YOU QUOTE THE BIBLE?!

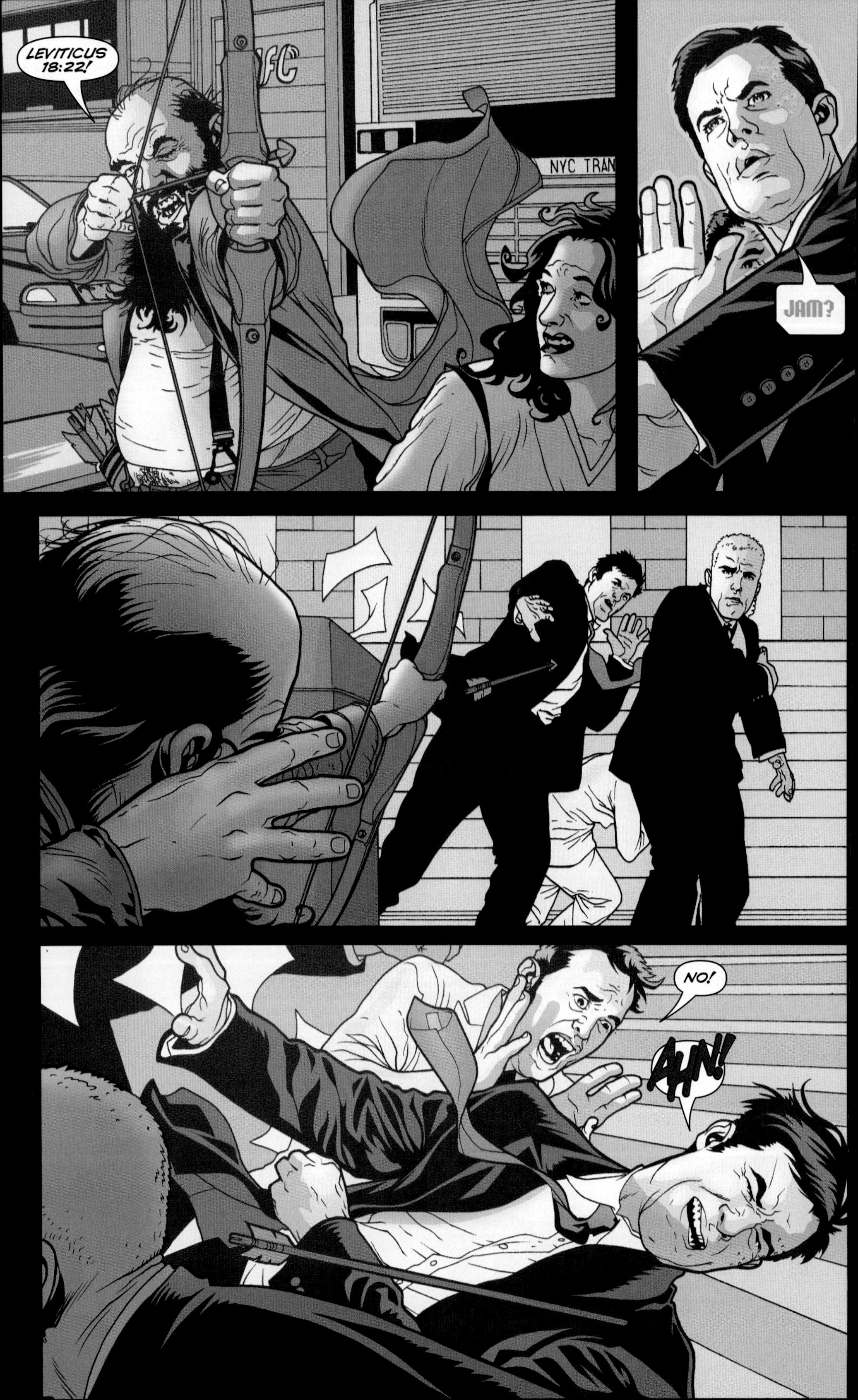
LEVITICUS 18:22!
NYC TRAN
JAM?
NO!
AHN!

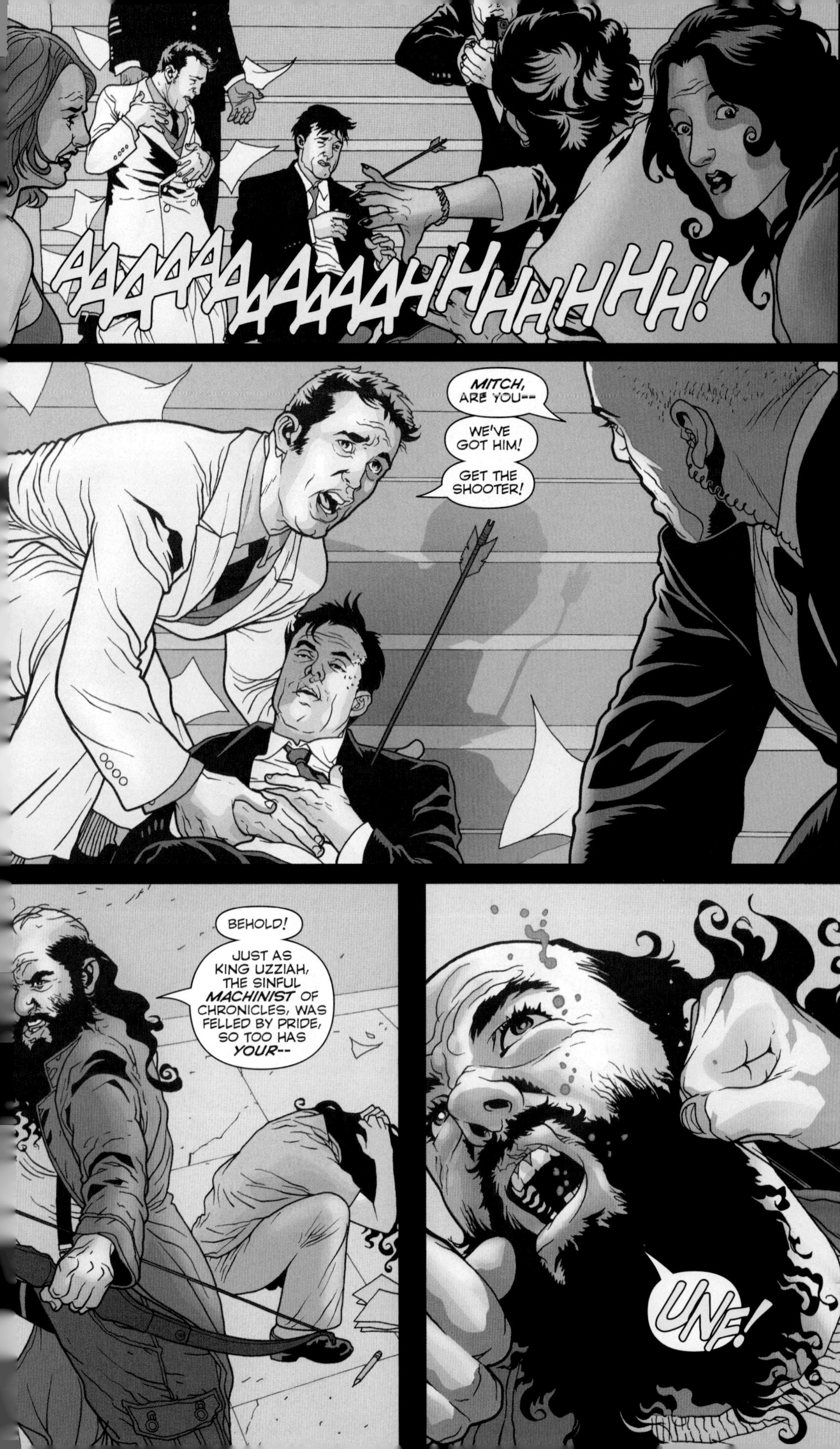
AAAAAAAAAAAHHHHHHH!
MITCH, ARE YOU--
WE'VE GOT HIM!
GET THE SHOOTER!
BEHOLD!
JUST AS KING UZZIAH, THE SINFUL MACHINIST OF CHRONICLES, WAS FELLED BY PRIDE, SO TOO HAS YOUR--
UNF!

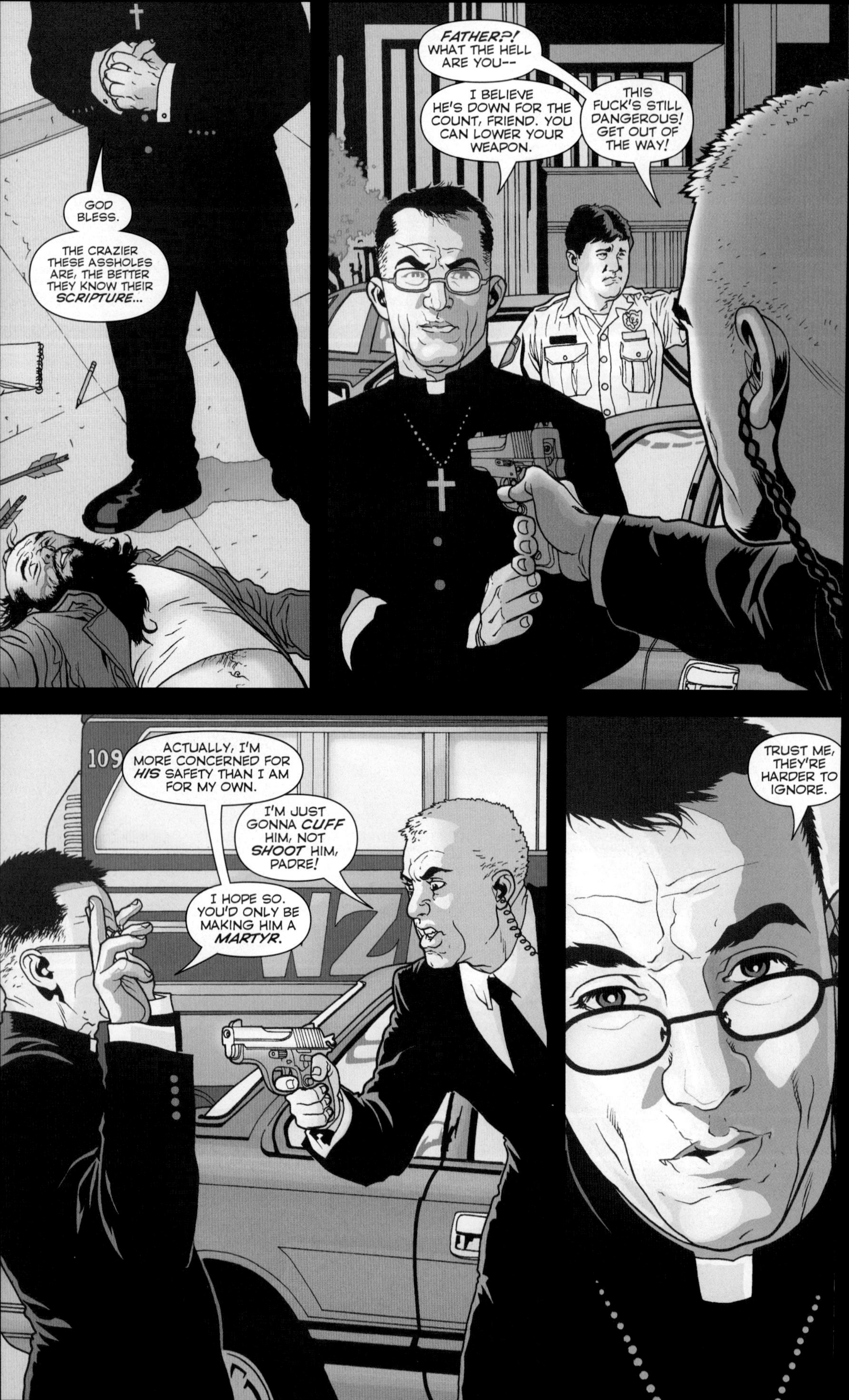
GOD BLESS.
THE CRAZIER THESE ASSHOLES ARE, THE BETTER THEY KNOW THEIR SCRIPTURE...
FATHER?! WHAT THE HELL ARE YOU--
I BELIEVE HE'S DOWN FOR THE COUNT, FRIEND. YOU CAN LOWER YOUR WEAPON.
THIS FUCK'S STILL DANGEROUS! GET OUT OF THE WAY!
109
ACTUALLY, I'M MORE CONCERNED FOR HIS SAFETY THAN I AM FOR MY OWN.
I'M JUST GONNA CUFF HIM, NOT SHOOT HIM, PADRE!
I HOPE SO. YOU'D ONLY BE MAKING HIM A MARTYR.
TRUST ME, THEY'RE HARDER TO IGNORE.

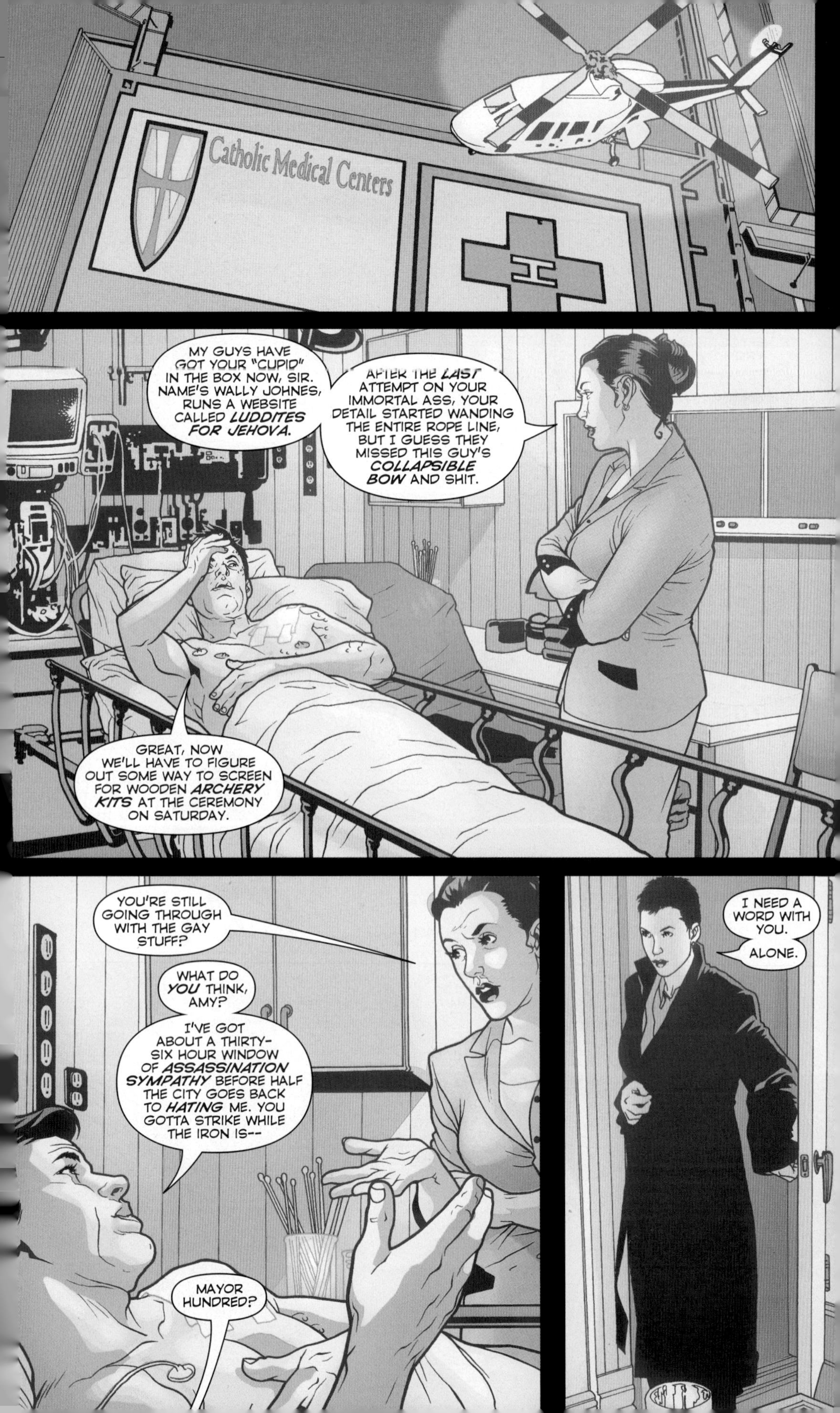

Catholic Medical Centers
MY GUYS HAVE GOT YOUR "CUPID" IN THE BOX NOW, SIR. NAME'S WALLY JOHNES, RUNS A WEBSITE CALLED LUDDITES FOR JEHOVA.
AFTER THE LAST ATTEMPT ON YOUR IMMORTAL ASS, YOUR DETAIL STARTED WANDING THE ENTIRE ROPE LINE, BUT I GUESS THEY MISSED THIS GUY'S COLLAPSIBLE BOW AND SHIT.
GREAT, NOW WE'LL HAVE TO FIGURE OUT SOME WAY TO SCREEN FOR WOODEN ARCHERY KITS AT THE CEREMONY ON SATURDAY.
YOU'RE STILL GOING THROUGH WITH THE GAY STUFF?
WHAT DO YOU THINK, AMY?
I'VE GOT ABOUT A THIRTY-SIX HOUR WINDOW OF ASSASSINATION SYMPATHY BEFORE HALF THE CITY GOES BACK TO HATING ME. YOU GOTTA STRIKE WHILE THE IRON IS--
I NEED A WORD WITH YOU.
ALONE.
MAYOR HUNDRED?

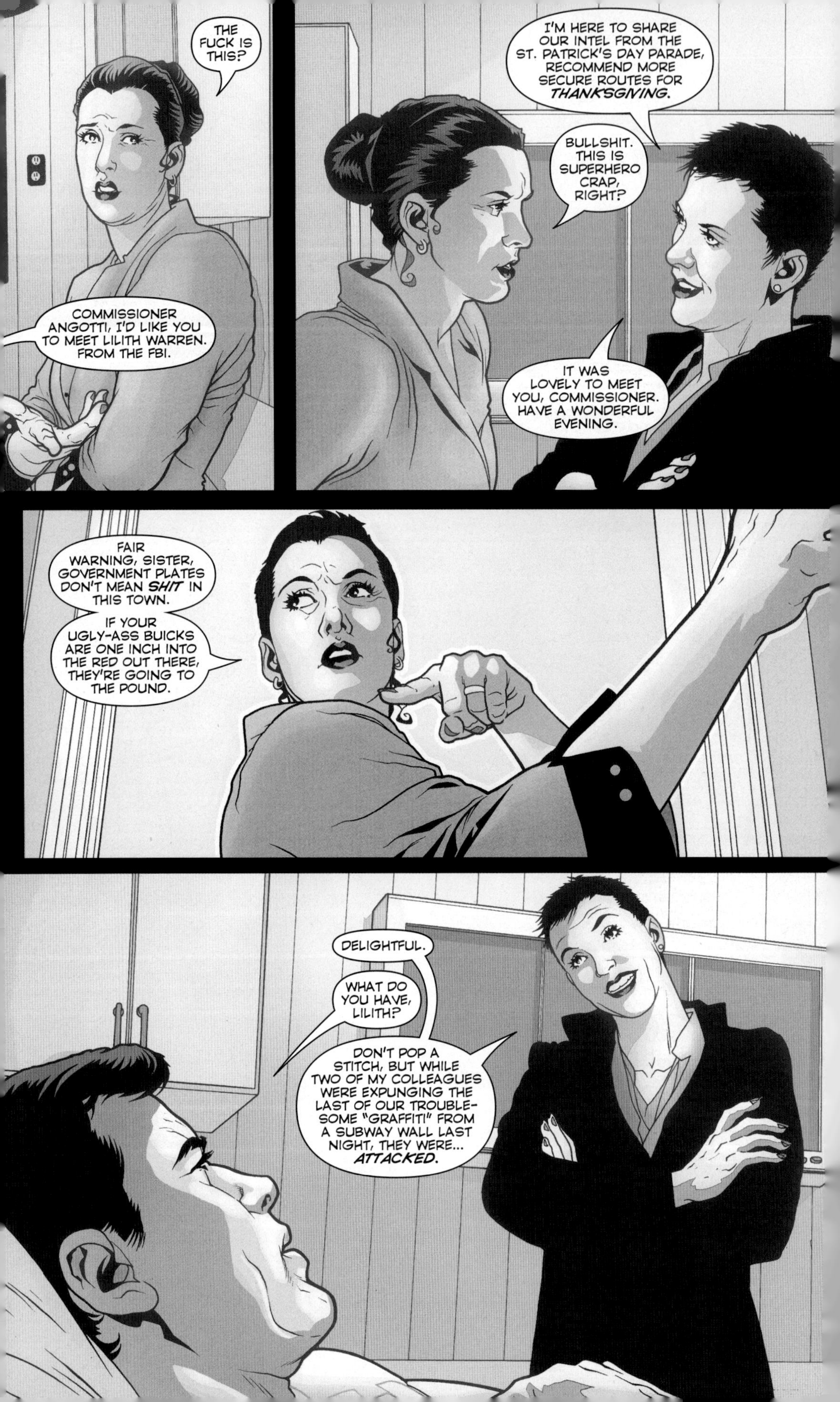
THE FUCK IS THIS?
COMMISSIONER ANGOTTI, I'D LIKE YOU TO MEET LILITH WARREN. FROM THE FBI.
I'M HERE TO SHARE OUR INTEL FROM THE ST. PATRICK'S DAY PARADE, RECOMMEND MORE SECURE ROUTES FOR *THANKSGIVING*.
BULLSHIT. THIS IS SUPERHERO CRAP, RIGHT?
IT WAS LOVELY TO MEET YOU, COMMISSIONER. HAVE A WONDERFUL EVENING.
FAIR WARNING, SISTER, GOVERNMENT PLATES DON'T MEAN *SHIT* IN THIS TOWN.
IF YOUR UGLY-ASS BUICKS ARE ONE INCH INTO THE RED OUT THERE, THEY'RE GOING TO THE POUND.
DELIGHTFUL.
WHAT DO YOU HAVE, LILITH?
DON'T POP A STITCH, BUT WHILE TWO OF MY COLLEAGUES WERE EXPUNGING THE LAST OF OUR TROUBLE-SOME "GRAFFITI" FROM A SUBWAY WALL LAST NIGHT, THEY WERE... *ATTACKED*.

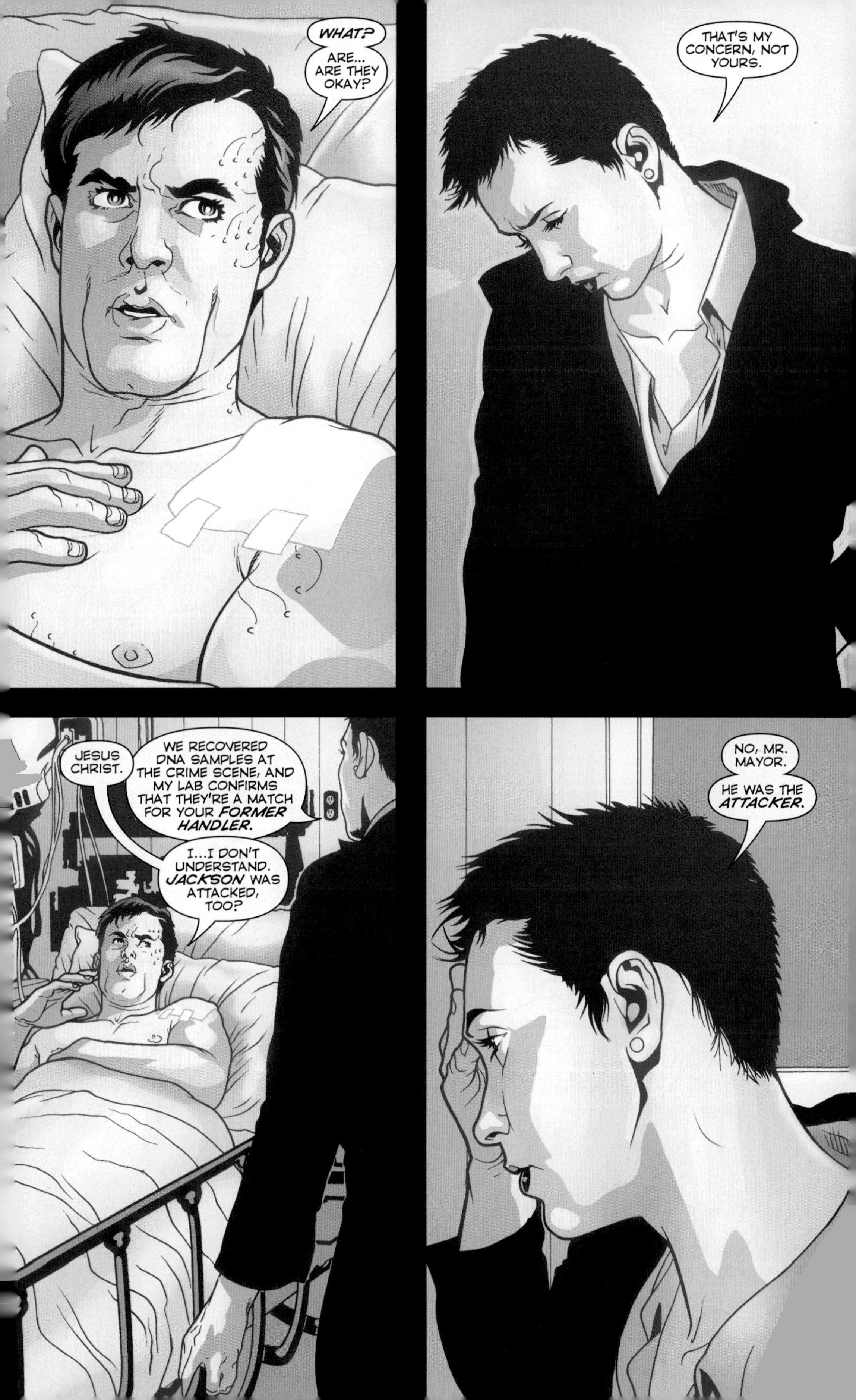
WHAT? ARE... ARE THEY OKAY?
THAT'S MY CONCERN, NOT YOURS.
WE RECOVERED DNA SAMPLES AT THE CRIME SCENE, AND MY LAB CONFIRMS THAT THEY'RE A MATCH FOR YOUR FORMER HANDLER.
JESUS CHRIST.
I...I DON'T UNDERSTAND. JACKSON WAS ATTACKED, TOO?
NO, MR. MAYOR.
HE WAS THE ATTACKER.

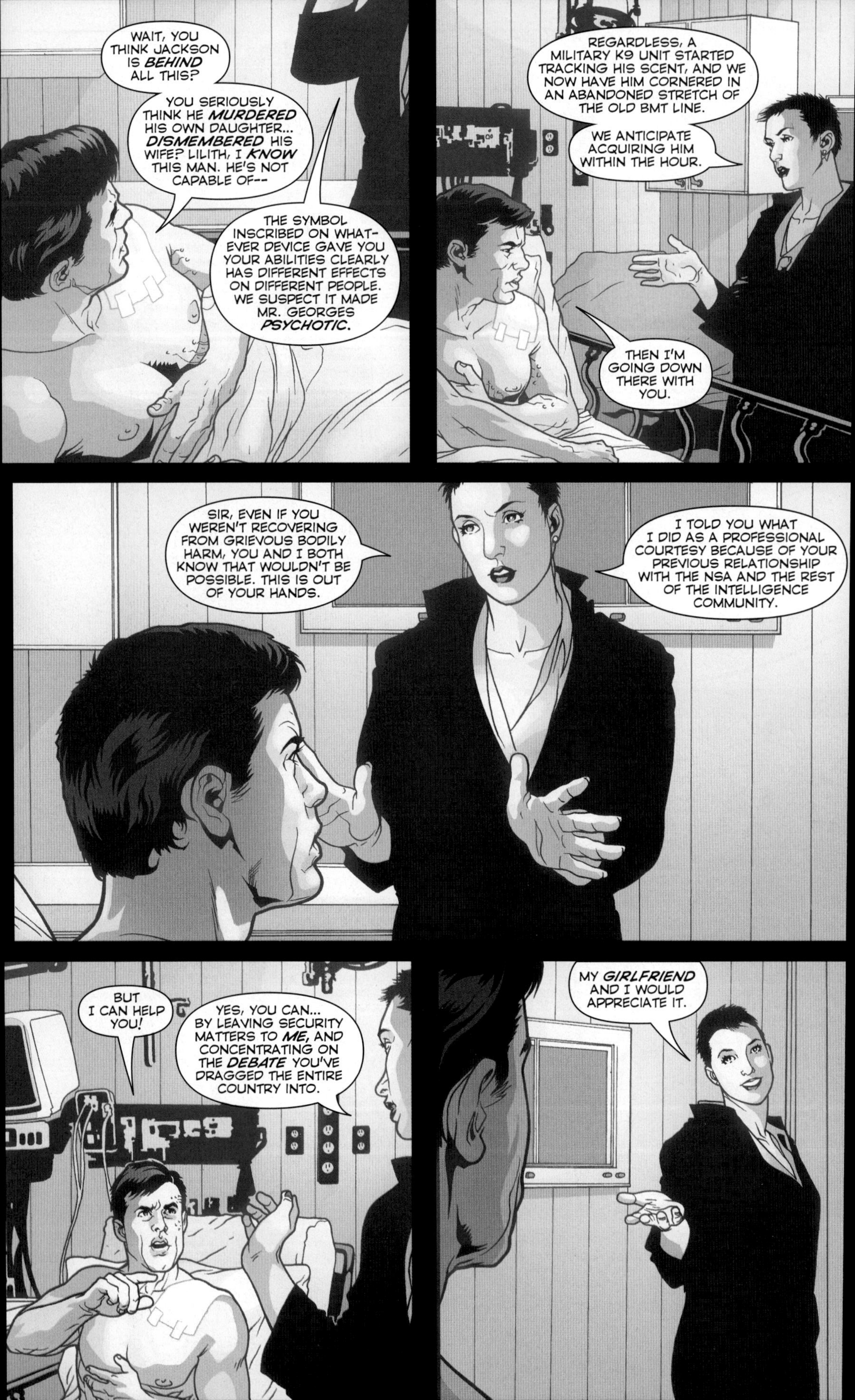

WAIT, YOU THINK JACKSON IS BEHIND ALL THIS?
YOU SERIOUSLY THINK HE MURDERED HIS OWN DAUGHTER... DISMEMBERED HIS WIFE? LILITH, I KNOW THIS MAN. HE'S NOT CAPABLE OF--
THE SYMBOL INSCRIBED ON WHAT-EVER DEVICE GAVE YOU YOUR ABILITIES CLEARLY HAS DIFFERENT EFFECTS ON DIFFERENT PEOPLE. WE SUSPECT IT MADE MR. GEORGES PSYCHOTIC.
REGARDLESS, A MILITARY K9 UNIT STARTED TRACKING HIS SCENT, AND WE NOW HAVE HIM CORNERED IN AN ABANDONED STRETCH OF THE OLD BMT LINE.
WE ANTICIPATE ACQUIRING HIM WITHIN THE HOUR.
THEN I'M GOING DOWN THERE WITH YOU.
SIR, EVEN IF YOU WEREN'T RECOVERING FROM GRIEVOUS BODILY HARM, YOU AND I BOTH KNOW THAT WOULDN'T BE POSSIBLE. THIS IS OUT OF YOUR HANDS.
I TOLD YOU WHAT I DID AS A PROFESSIONAL COURTESY BECAUSE OF YOUR PREVIOUS RELATIONSHIP WITH THE NSA AND THE REST OF THE INTELLIGENCE COMMUNITY.
BUT I CAN HELP YOU!
YES, YOU CAN... BY LEAVING SECURITY MATTERS TO ME, AND CONCENTRATING ON THE DEBATE YOU'VE DRAGGED THE ENTIRE COUNTRY INTO.
MY GIRLFRIEND AND I WOULD APPRECIATE IT.

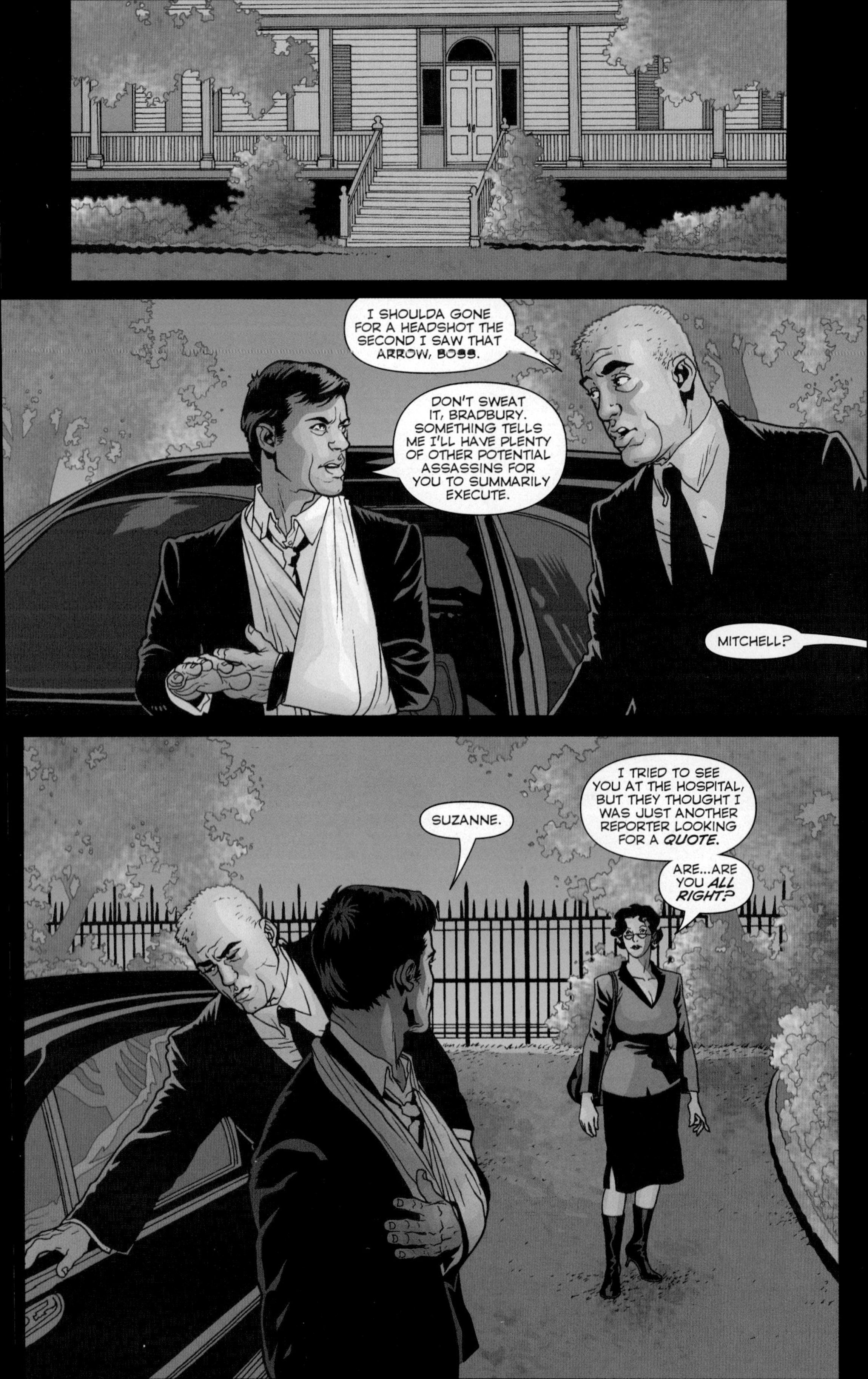
I SHOULDA GONE FOR A HEADSHOT THE SECOND I SAW THAT ARROW, BOSS.
DON'T SWEAT IT, BRADBURY. SOMETHING TELLS ME I'LL HAVE PLENTY OF OTHER POTENTIAL ASSASSINS FOR YOU TO SUMMARILY EXECUTE.
MITCHELL?
SUZANNE.
I TRIED TO SEE YOU AT THE HOSPITAL, BUT THEY THOUGHT I WAS JUST ANOTHER REPORTER LOOKING FOR A *QUOTE*.
ARE...ARE YOU *ALL RIGHT?*

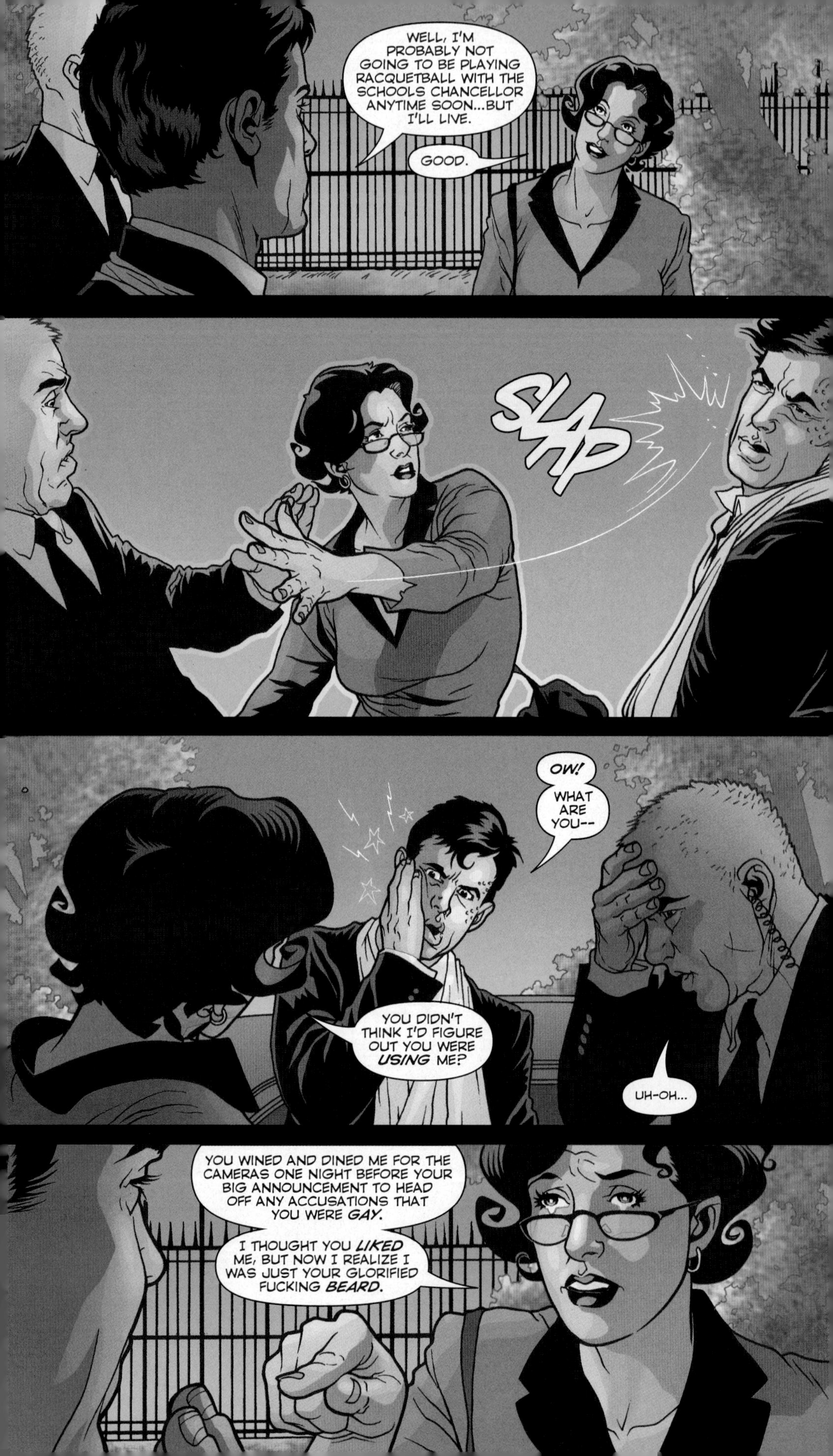
WELL, I'M PROBABLY NOT GOING TO BE PLAYING RACQUETBALL WITH THE SCHOOLS CHANCELLOR ANYTIME SOON...BUT I'LL LIVE.
GOOD.
SLAP
OW!
WHAT ARE YOU--
YOU DIDN'T THINK I'D FIGURE OUT YOU WERE *USING* ME?
UH-OH...
YOU WINED AND DINED ME FOR THE CAMERAS ONE NIGHT BEFORE YOUR BIG ANNOUNCEMENT TO HEAD OFF ANY ACCUSATIONS THAT YOU WERE *GAY*.
I THOUGHT YOU *LIKED* ME, BUT NOW I REALIZE I WAS JUST YOUR GLORIFIED FUCKING *BEARD*.

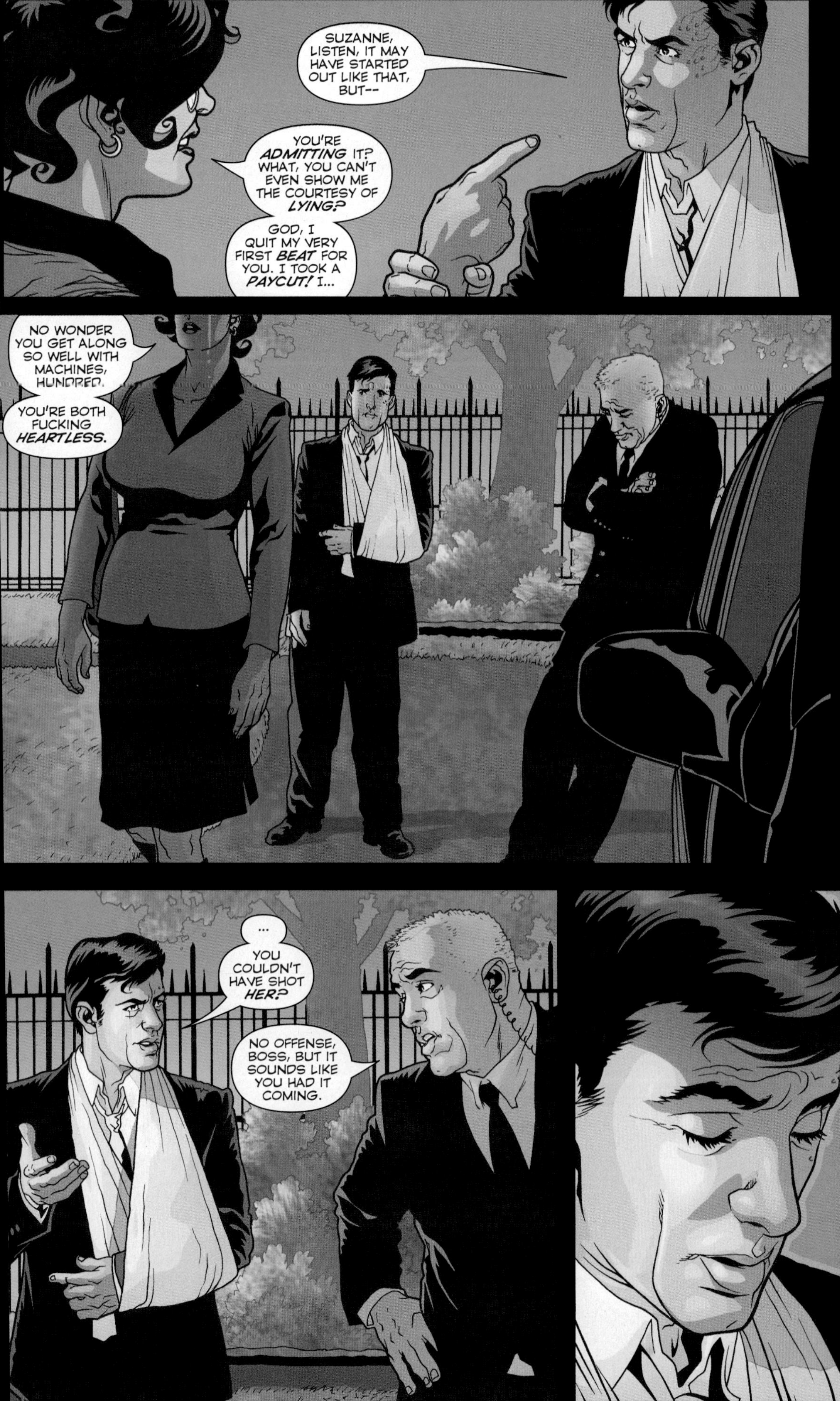
SUZANNE, LISTEN, IT MAY HAVE STARTED OUT LIKE THAT, BUT--
YOU'RE *ADMITTING* IT? WHAT, YOU CAN'T EVEN SHOW ME THE COURTESY OF *LYING?*
GOD, I QUIT MY VERY FIRST *BEAT* FOR YOU. I TOOK A *PAYCUT!* I...
NO WONDER YOU GET ALONG SO WELL WITH MACHINES, HUNDRED.
YOU'RE BOTH FUCKING *HEARTLESS*.
...
YOU COULDN'T HAVE SHOT *HER?*
NO OFFENSE, BOSS, BUT IT SOUNDS LIKE YOU HAD IT COMING.

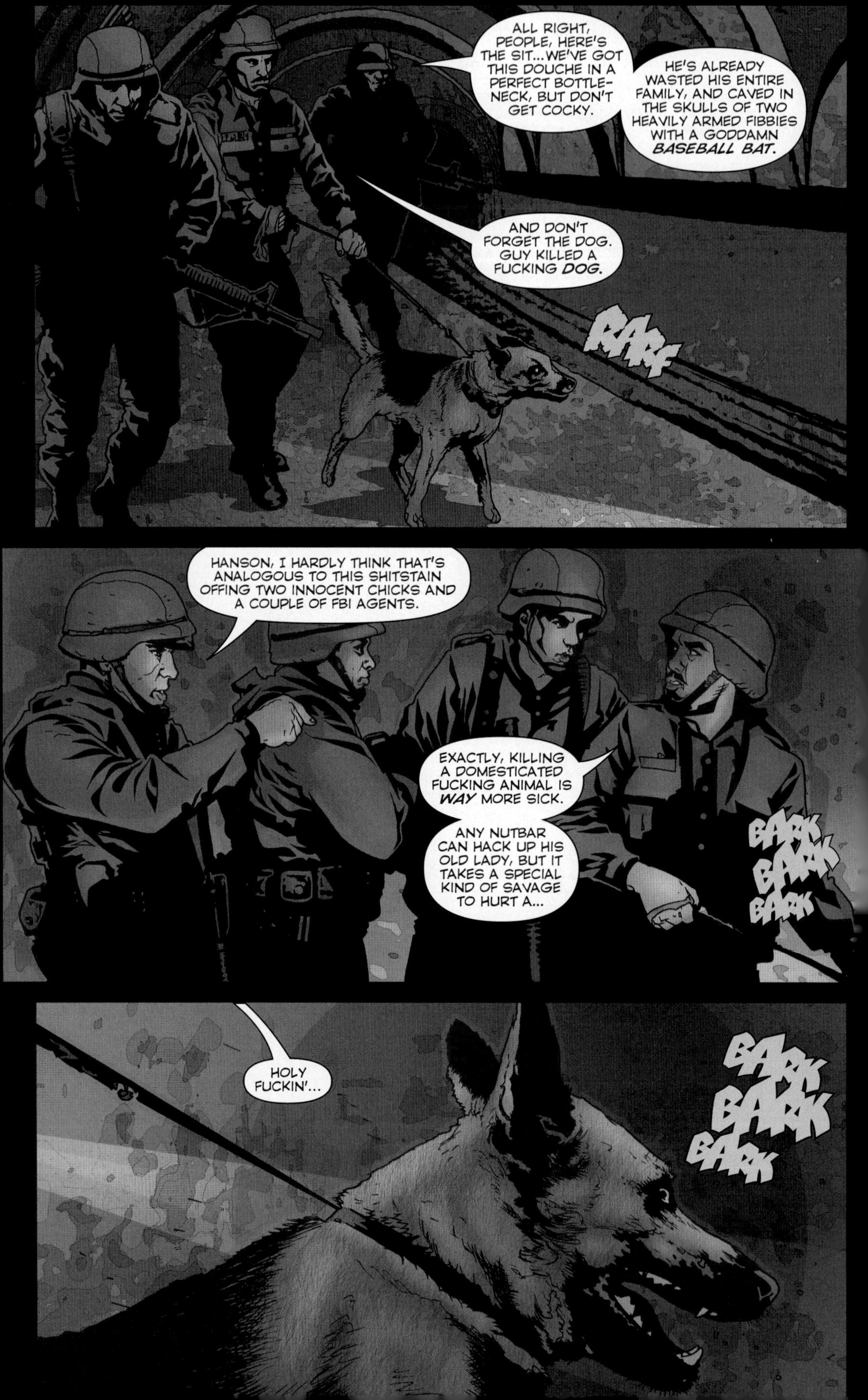
ALL RIGHT, PEOPLE, HERE'S THE SIT... WE'VE GOT THIS DOUCHE IN A PERFECT BOTTLE-NECK, BUT DON'T GET COCKY.
HE'S ALREADY WASTED HIS ENTIRE FAMILY, AND CAVED IN THE SKULLS OF TWO HEAVILY ARMED FIBBIES WITH A GODDAMN *BASEBALL BAT*.
AND DON'T FORGET THE DOG. GUY KILLED A FUCKING *DOG*.
RARF
HANSON, I HARDLY THINK THAT'S ANALOGOUS TO THIS SHITSTAIN OFFING TWO INNOCENT CHICKS AND A COUPLE OF FBI AGENTS.
EXACTLY, KILLING A DOMESTICATED FUCKING ANIMAL IS *WAY* MORE SICK.
ANY NUTBAR CAN HACK UP HIS OLD LADY, BUT IT TAKES A SPECIAL KIND OF SAVAGE TO HURT A...
BARK BARK BARK
HOLY FUCKIN'...
BARK BARK BARK

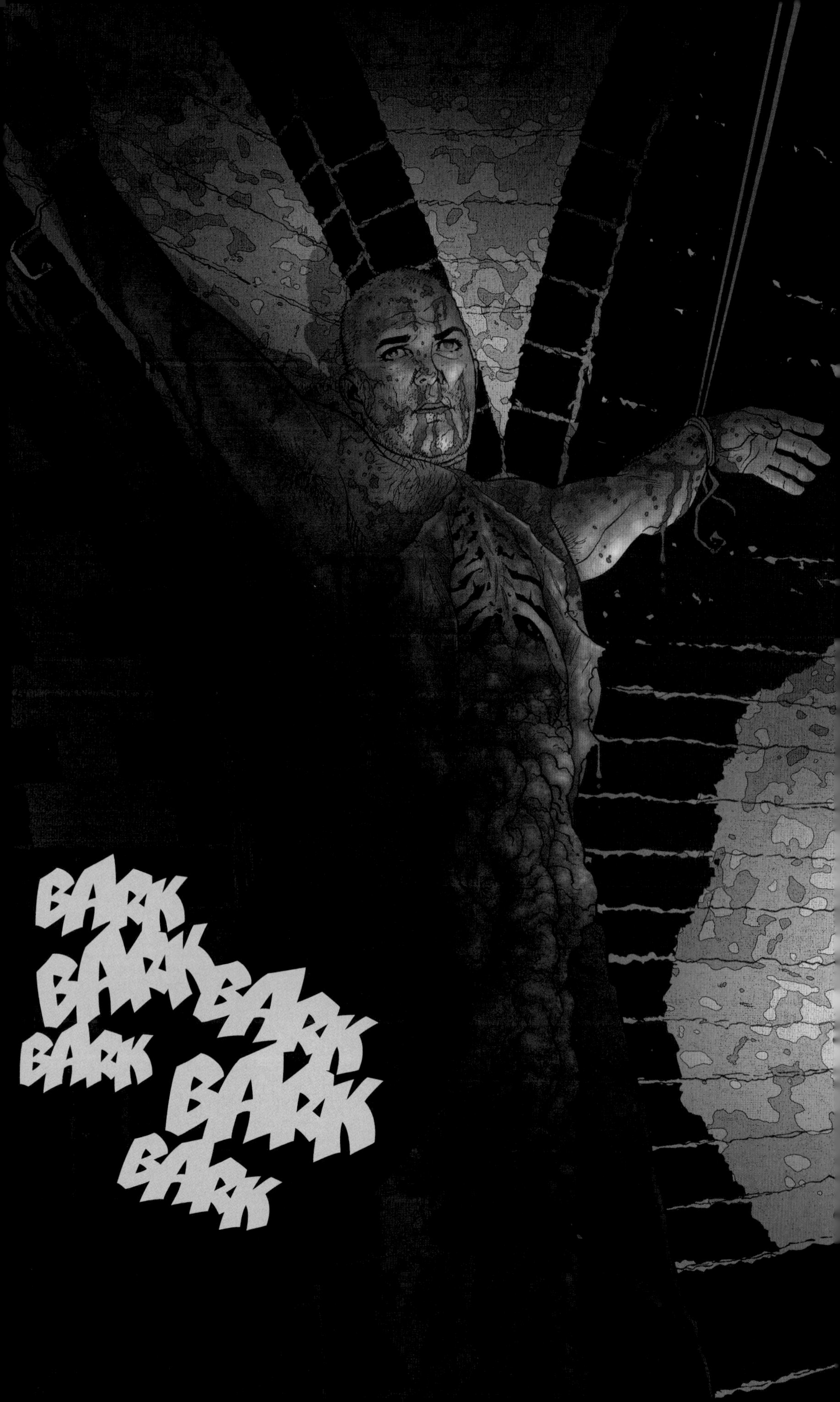
BARK
BARK
BARK
BARK
BARK
BARK

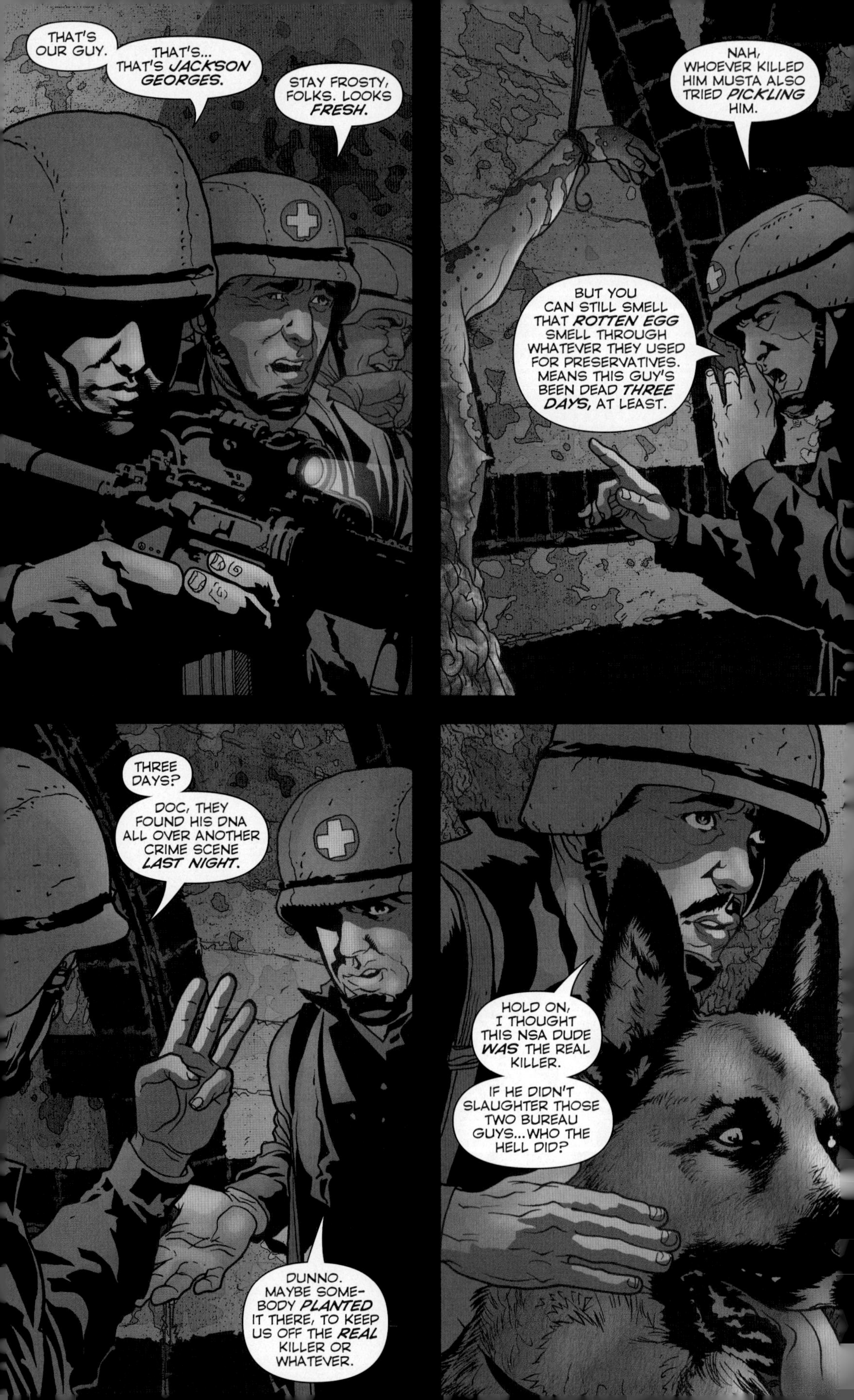
THAT'S OUR GUY.
THAT'S... THAT'S JACKSON GEORGES.
STAY FROSTY, FOLKS. LOOKS FRESH.
NAH, WHOEVER KILLED HIM MUSTA ALSO TRIED PICKLING HIM.
BUT YOU CAN STILL SMELL THAT ROTTEN EGG SMELL THROUGH WHATEVER THEY USED FOR PRESERVATIVES. MEANS THIS GUY'S BEEN DEAD THREE DAYS, AT LEAST.
THREE DAYS?
DOC, THEY FOUND HIS DNA ALL OVER ANOTHER CRIME SCENE LAST NIGHT.
DUNNO. MAYBE SOMEBODY PLANTED IT THERE, TO KEEP US OFF THE REAL KILLER OR WHATEVER.
HOLD ON, I THOUGHT THIS NSA DUDE WAS THE REAL KILLER.
IF HE DIDN'T SLAUGHTER THOSE TWO BUREAU GUYS...WHO THE HELL DID?

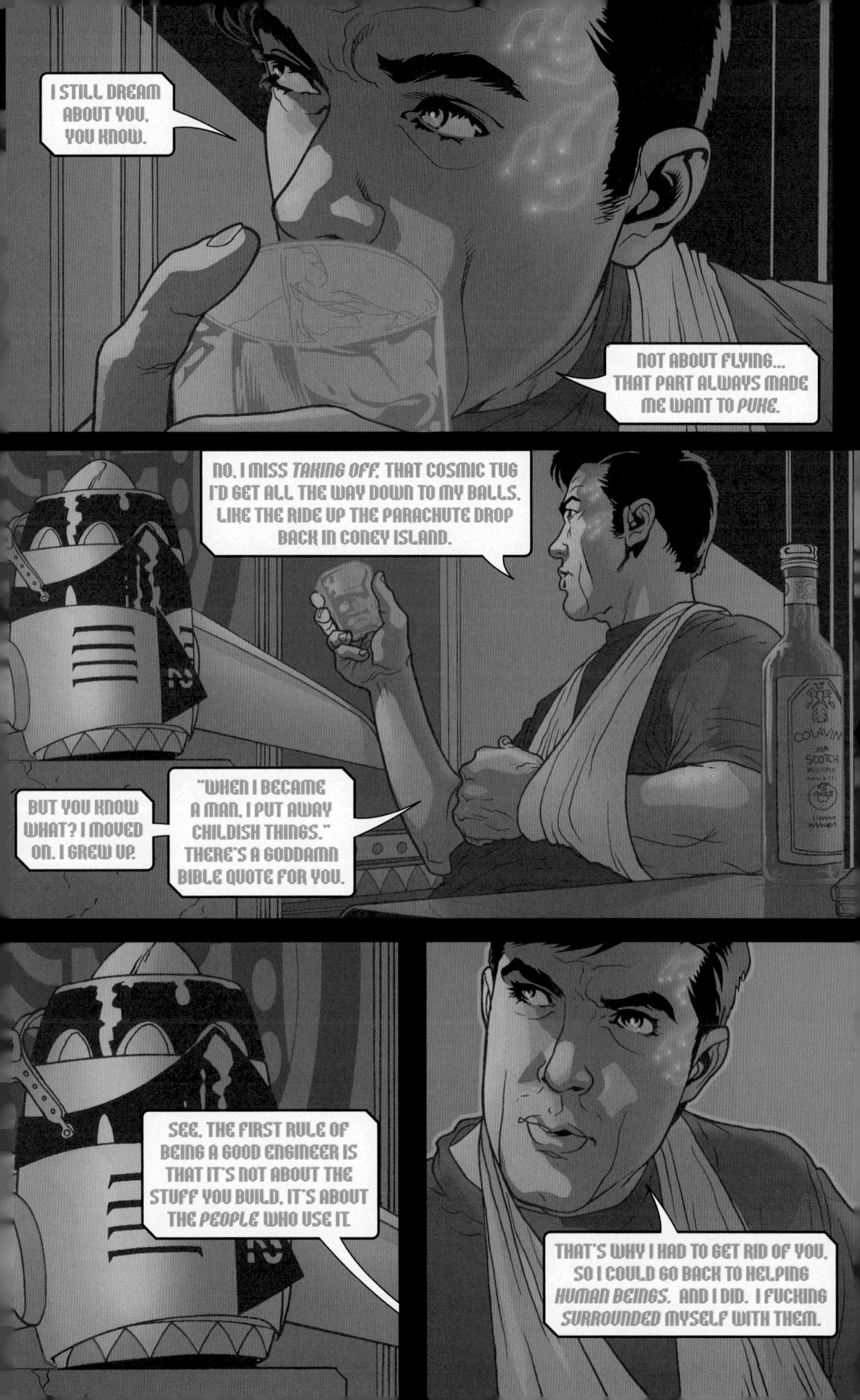
I STILL DREAM ABOUT YOU, YOU KNOW.
NOT ABOUT FLYING... THAT PART ALWAYS MADE ME WANT TO PUKE.
NO, I MISS TAKING OFF. THAT COSMIC TUG I'D GET ALL THE WAY DOWN TO MY BALLS. LIKE THE RIDE UP THE PARACHUTE DROP BACK IN CONEY ISLAND.
BUT YOU KNOW WHAT? I MOVED ON. I GREW UP.
"WHEN I BECAME A MAN, I PUT AWAY CHILDISH THINGS." THERE'S A GODDAMN BIBLE QUOTE FOR YOU.
COLAVIN SCOTCH
SEE, THE FIRST RULE OF BEING A GOOD ENGINEER IS THAT IT'S NOT ABOUT THE STUFF YOU BUILD, IT'S ABOUT THE PEOPLE WHO USE IT.
THAT'S WHY I HAD TO GET RID OF YOU, SO I COULD GO BACK TO HELPING HUMAN BEINGS. AND I DID. I FUCKING SURROUNDED MYSELF WITH THEM.

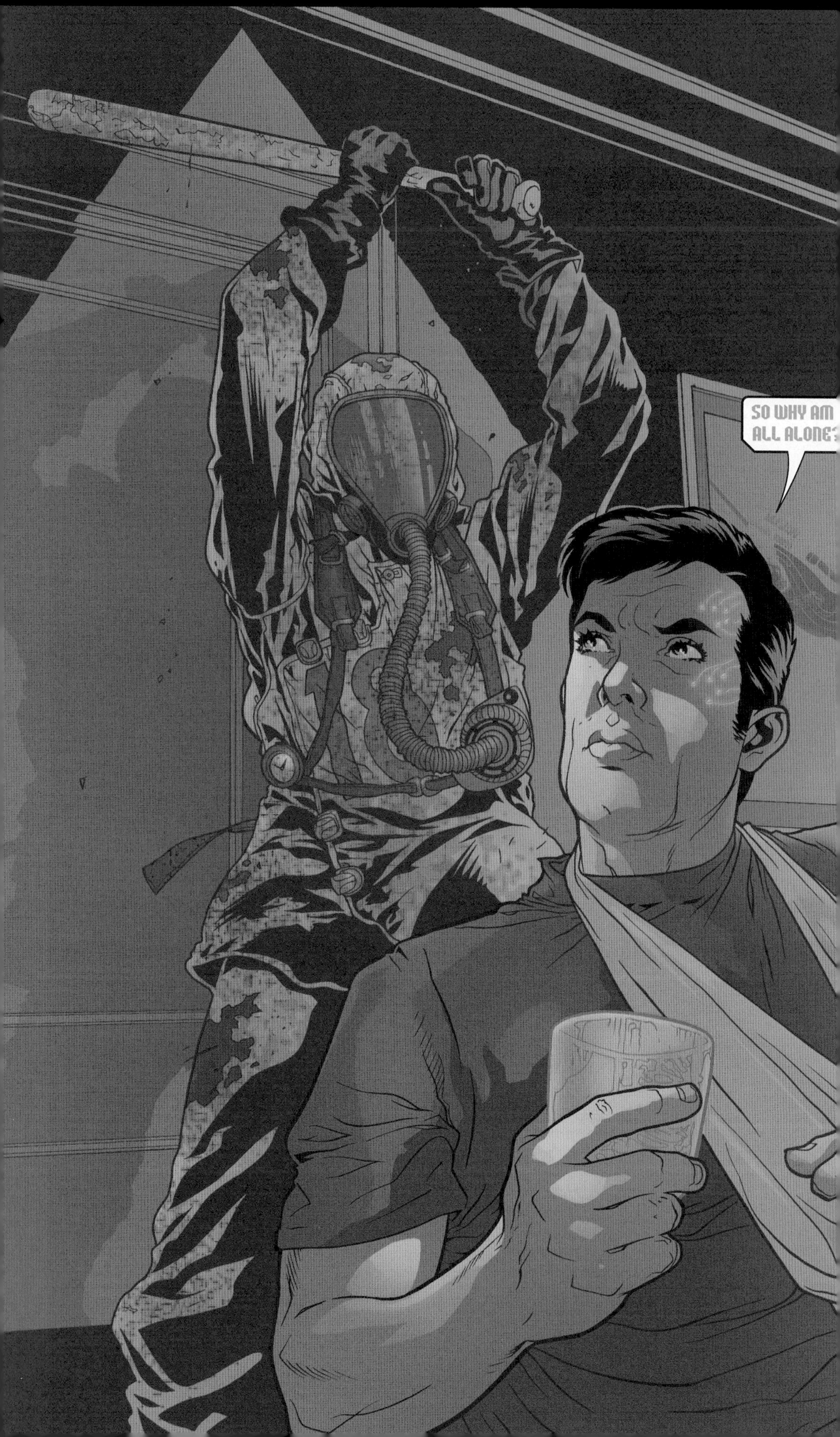
SO WHY AM
ALL ALONE?

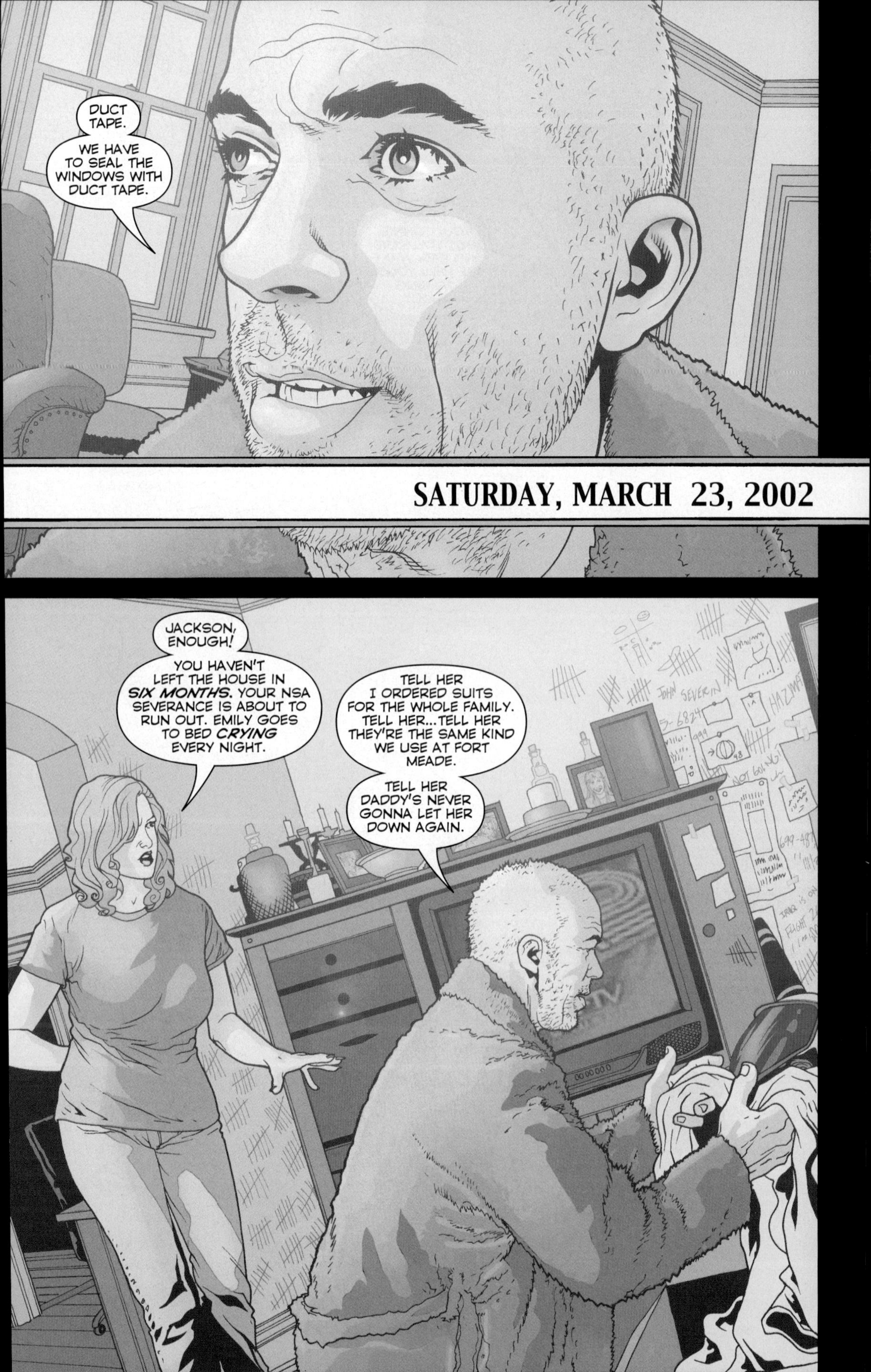
DUCT TAPE.
WE HAVE TO SEAL THE WINDOWS WITH DUCT TAPE.
SATURDAY, MARCH 23, 2002
JACKSON, ENOUGH!
YOU HAVEN'T LEFT THE HOUSE IN SIX MONTHS. YOUR NSA SEVERANCE IS ABOUT TO RUN OUT. EMILY GOES TO BED CRYING EVERY NIGHT.
TELL HER I ORDERED SUITS FOR THE WHOLE FAMILY. TELL HER...TELL HER THEY'RE THE SAME KIND WE USE AT FORT MEADE.
TELL HER DADDY'S NEVER GONNA LET HER DOWN AGAIN.

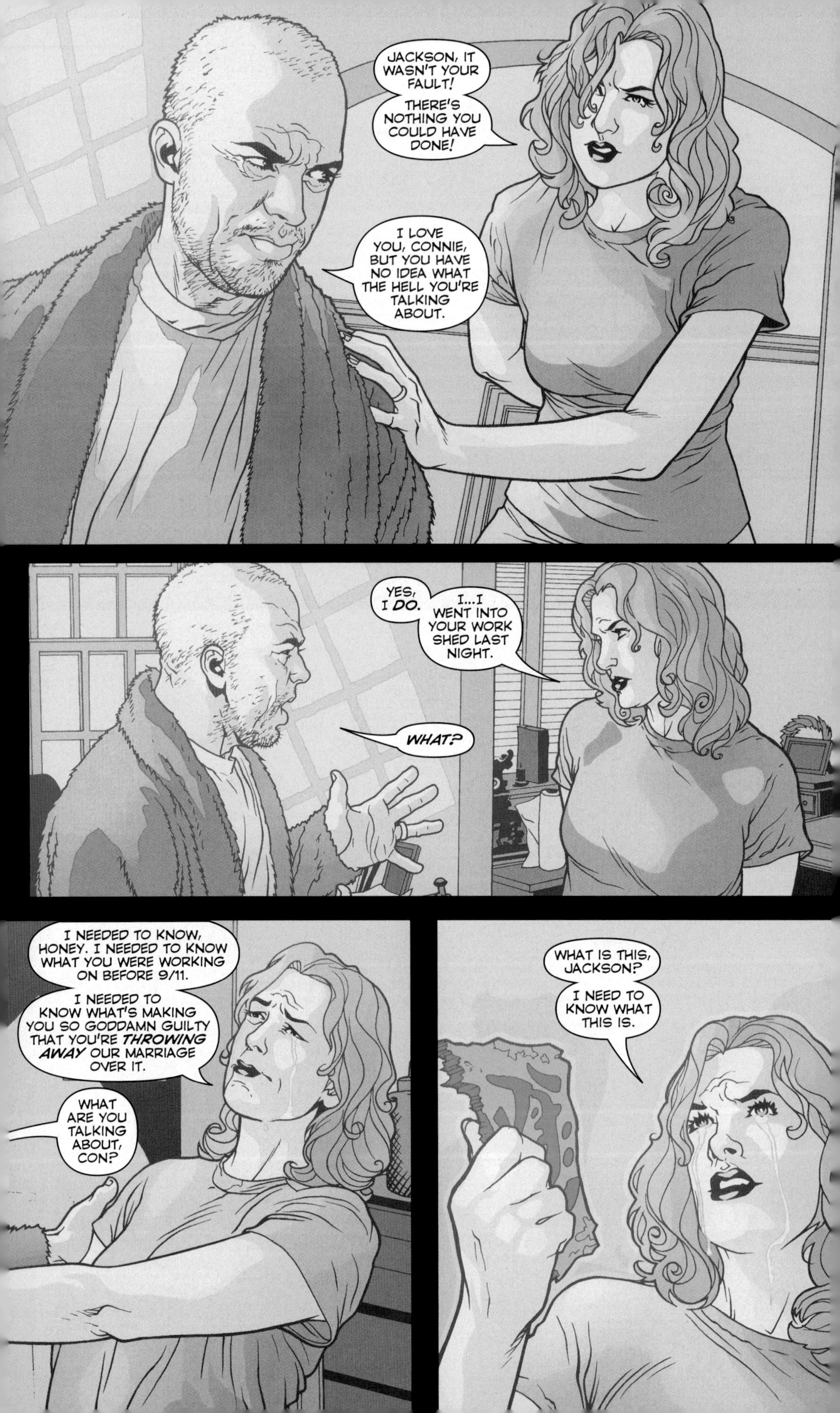
JACKSON, IT WASN'T YOUR FAULT!
THERE'S NOTHING YOU COULD HAVE DONE!
I LOVE YOU, CONNIE, BUT YOU HAVE NO IDEA WHAT THE HELL YOU'RE TALKING ABOUT.
YES, I *DO*.
I...I WENT INTO YOUR WORK SHED LAST NIGHT.
WHAT?
I NEEDED TO KNOW, HONEY. I NEEDED TO KNOW WHAT YOU WERE WORKING ON BEFORE 9/11.
I NEEDED TO KNOW WHAT'S MAKING YOU SO GODDAMN GUILTY THAT YOU'RE *THROWING AWAY* OUR MARRIAGE OVER IT.
WHAT ARE YOU TALKING ABOUT, CON?
WHAT IS THIS, JACKSON?
I NEED TO KNOW WHAT THIS IS.

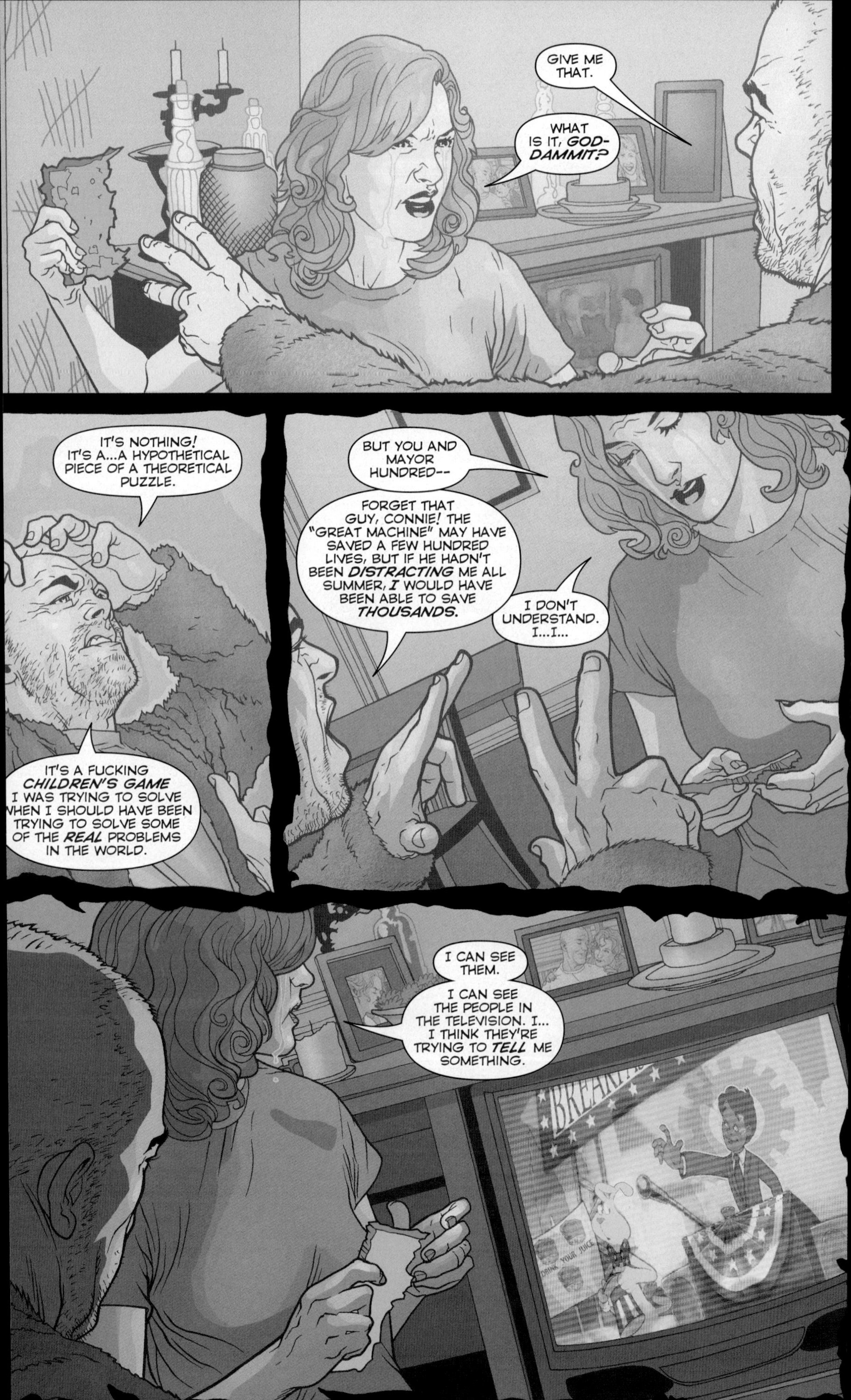
GIVE ME THAT.
WHAT IS IT, GOD-DAMMIT?
IT'S NOTHING! IT'S A...A HYPOTHETICAL PIECE OF A THEORETICAL PUZZLE.
IT'S A FUCKING CHILDREN'S GAME I WAS TRYING TO SOLVE WHEN I SHOULD HAVE BEEN TRYING TO SOLVE SOME OF THE REAL PROBLEMS IN THE WORLD.
BUT YOU AND MAYOR HUNDRED--
FORGET THAT GUY, CONNIE! THE "GREAT MACHINE" MAY HAVE SAVED A FEW HUNDRED LIVES, BUT IF HE HADN'T BEEN DISTRACTING ME ALL SUMMER, I WOULD HAVE BEEN ABLE TO SAVE THOUSANDS.
I DON'T UNDERSTAND. I...I...
I CAN SEE THEM.
I CAN SEE THE PEOPLE IN THE TELEVISION. I... I THINK THEY'RE TRYING TO TELL ME SOMETHING.
DRINK YOUR JUICE

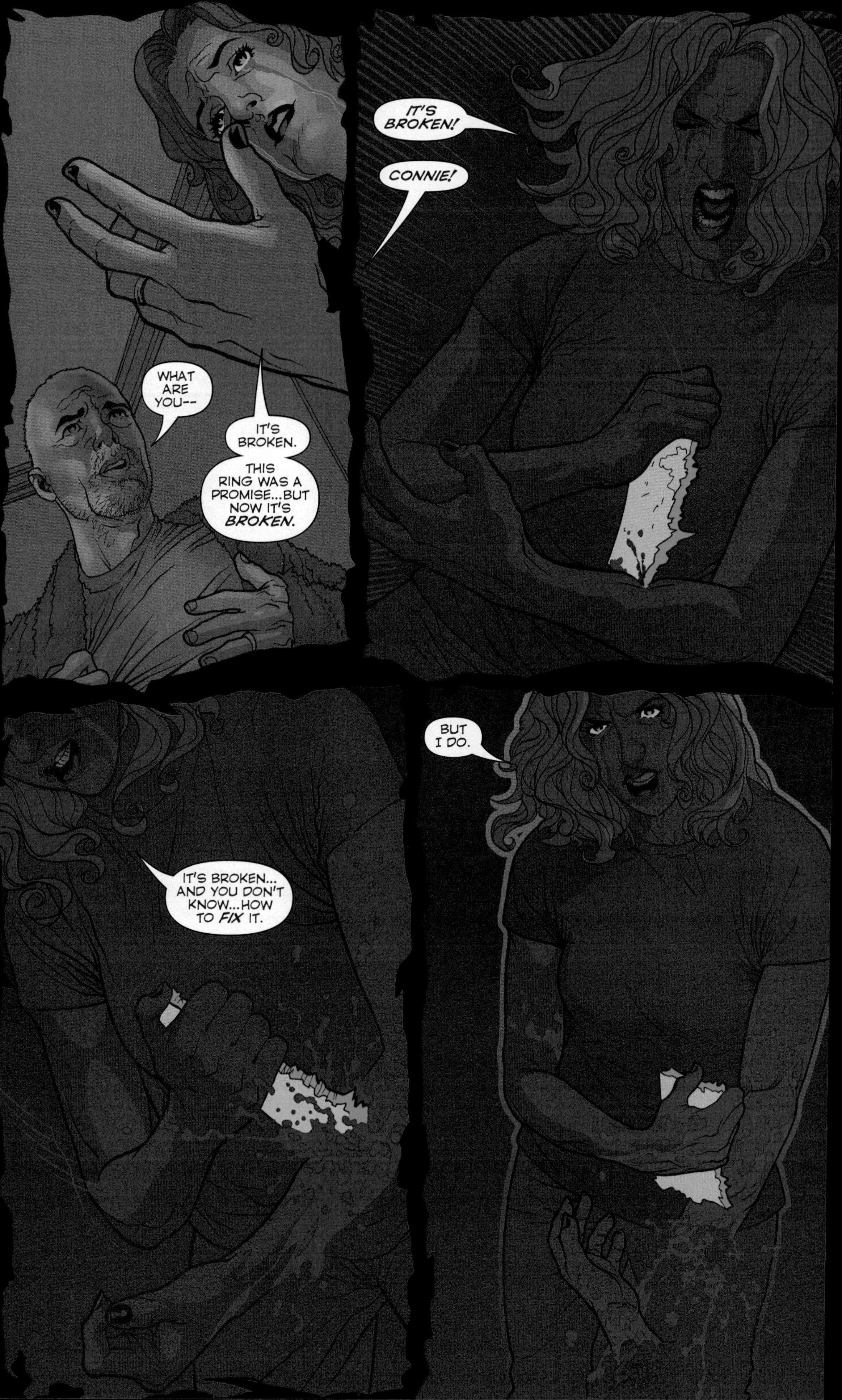
WHAT ARE YOU--
IT'S BROKEN.
THIS RING WAS A PROMISE...BUT NOW IT'S *BROKEN*.
IT'S BROKEN!
CONNIE!
IT'S BROKEN... AND YOU DON'T KNOW...HOW TO *FIX* IT.
BUT I DO.

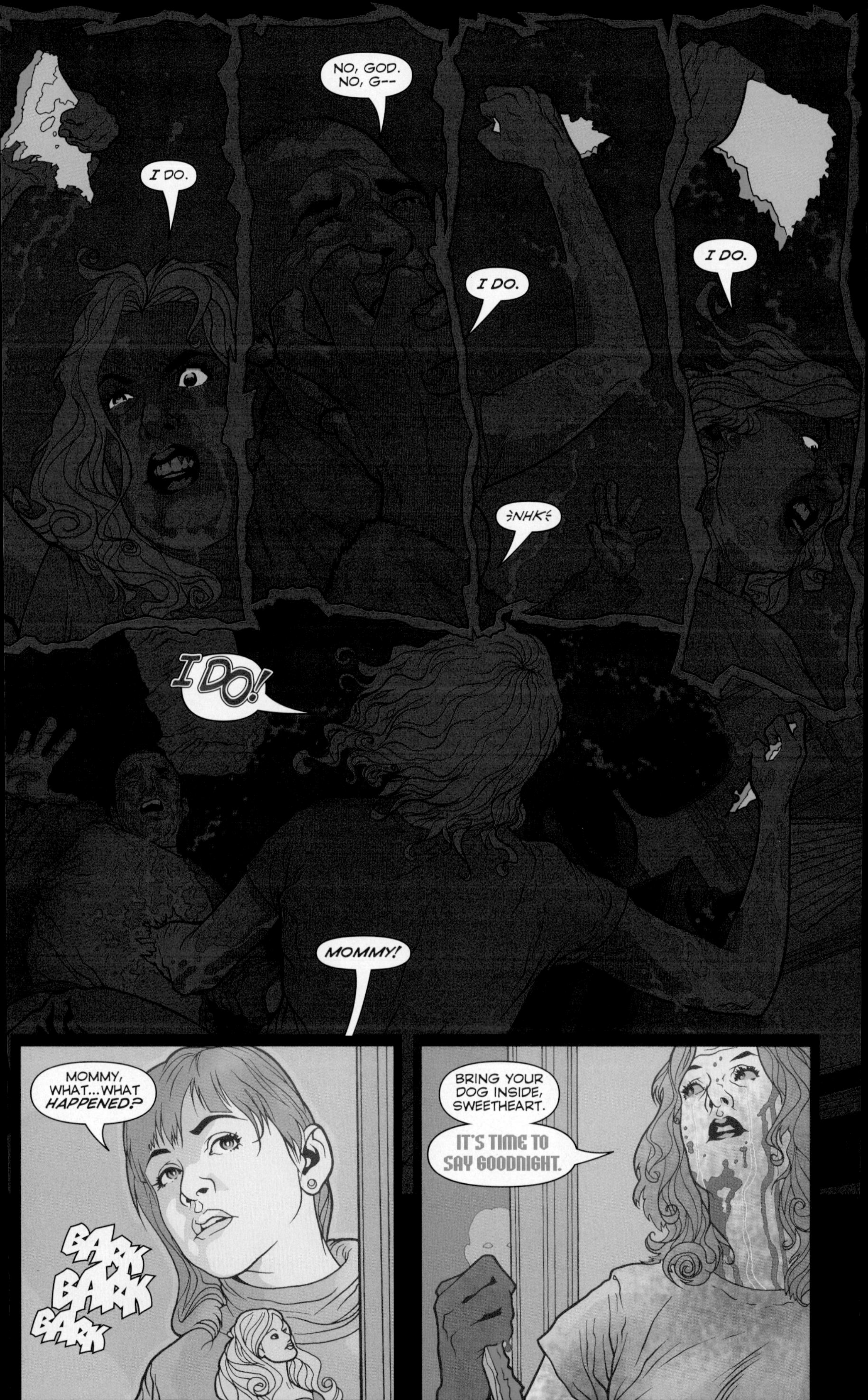
I DO.
NO, GOD.
NO, G--
I DO.
NHK
I DO.
I DO!
MOMMY!
MOMMY, WHAT...WHAT HAPPENED?
BARK BARK BARK
BRING YOUR DOG INSIDE, SWEETHEART.
IT'S TIME TO SAY GOODNIGHT.

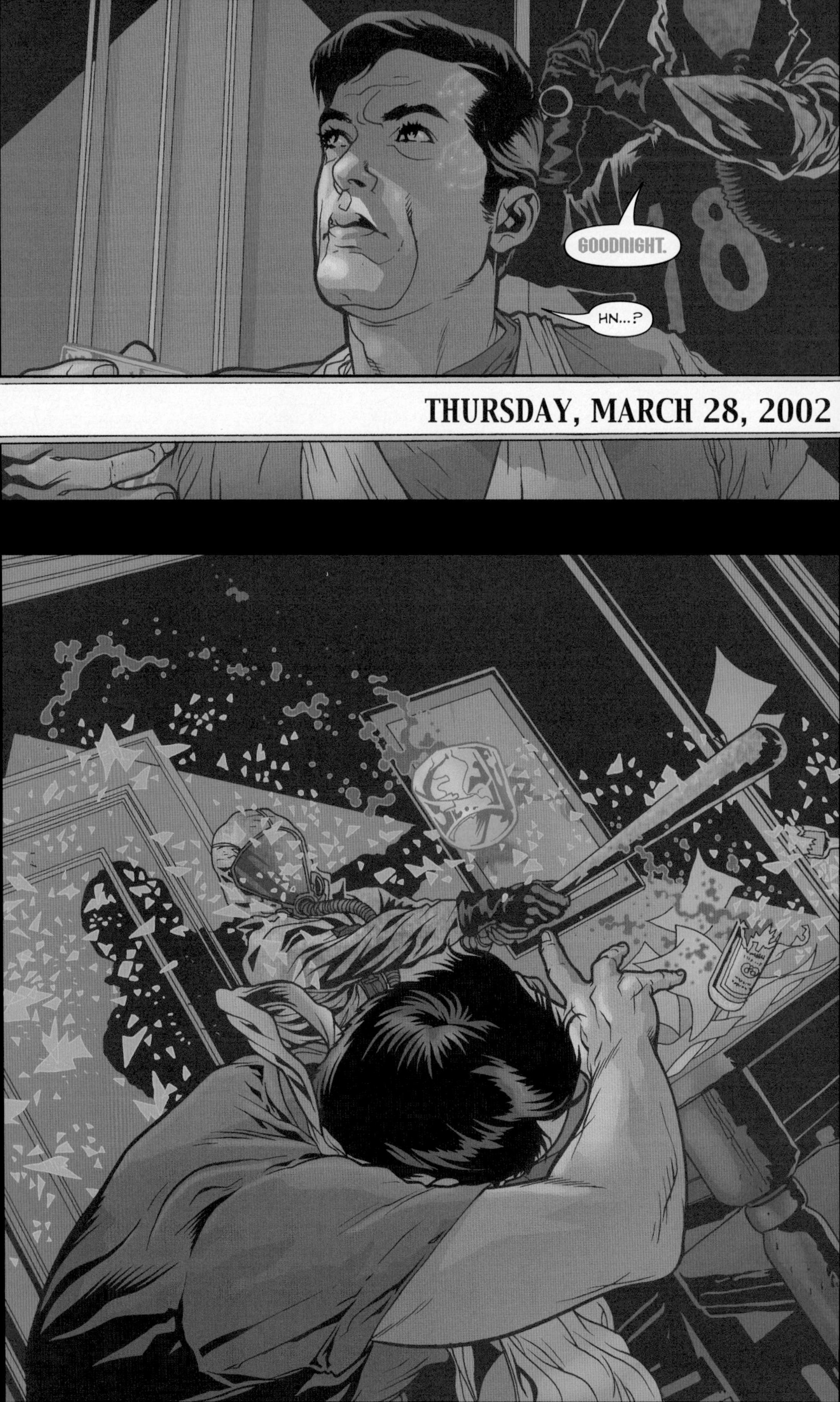
GOODNIGHT.
HN...?
THURSDAY, MARCH 28, 2002

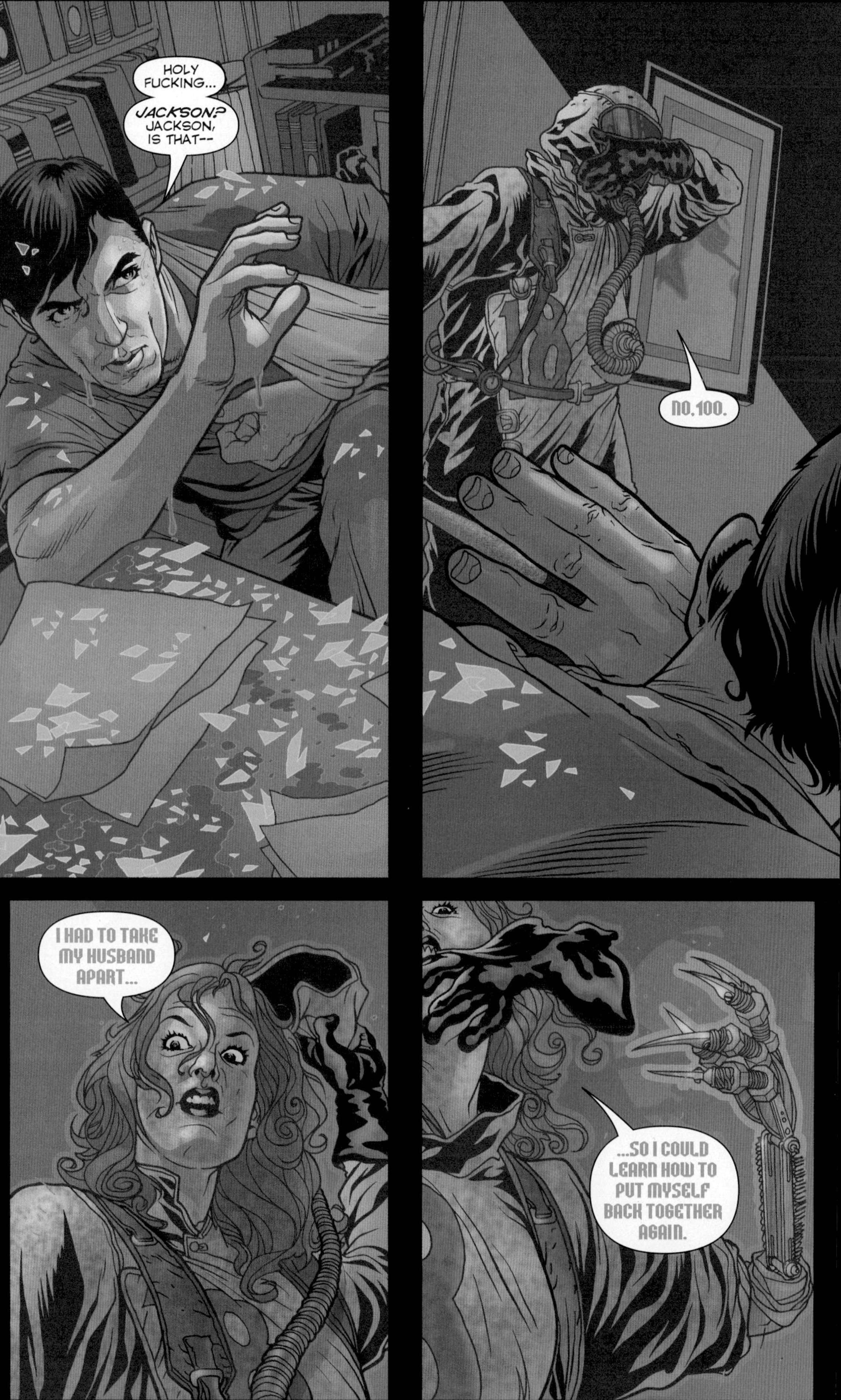
HOLY FUCKING... JACKSON? JACKSON, IS THAT--
NO. 100.
I HAD TO TAKE MY HUSBAND APART...
...SO I COULD LEARN HOW TO PUT MYSELF BACK TOGETHER AGAIN.

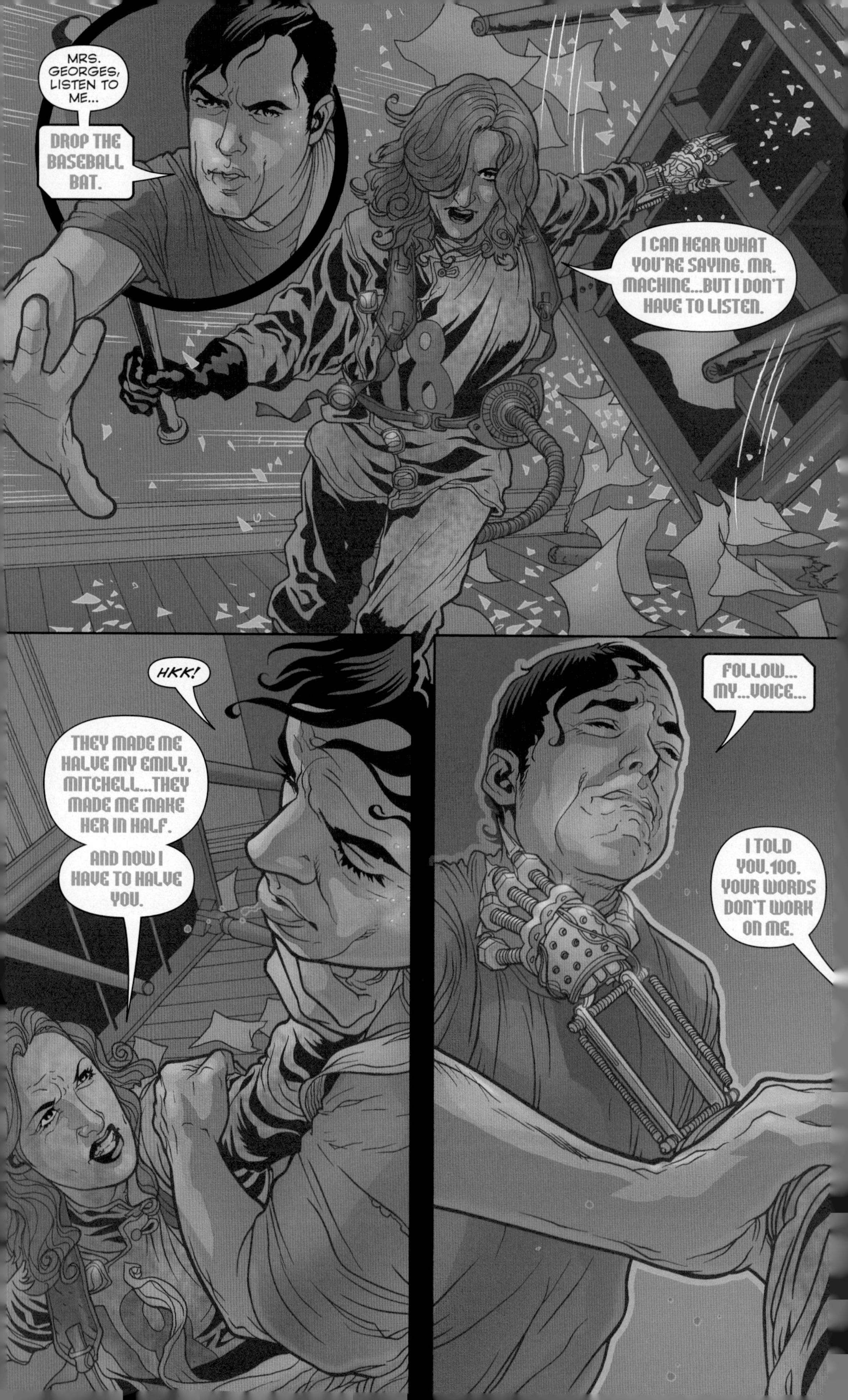
MRS. GEORGES, LISTEN TO ME...
DROP THE BASEBALL BAT.
I CAN HEAR WHAT YOU'RE SAYING, MR. MACHINE...BUT I DON'T HAVE TO LISTEN.
HKK!
THEY MADE ME HALVE MY EMILY, MITCHELL...THEY MADE ME MAKE HER IN HALF.
AND NOW I HAVE TO HALVE YOU.
FOLLOW... MY...VOICE...
I TOLD YOU, TOO. YOUR WORDS DON'T WORK ON ME.

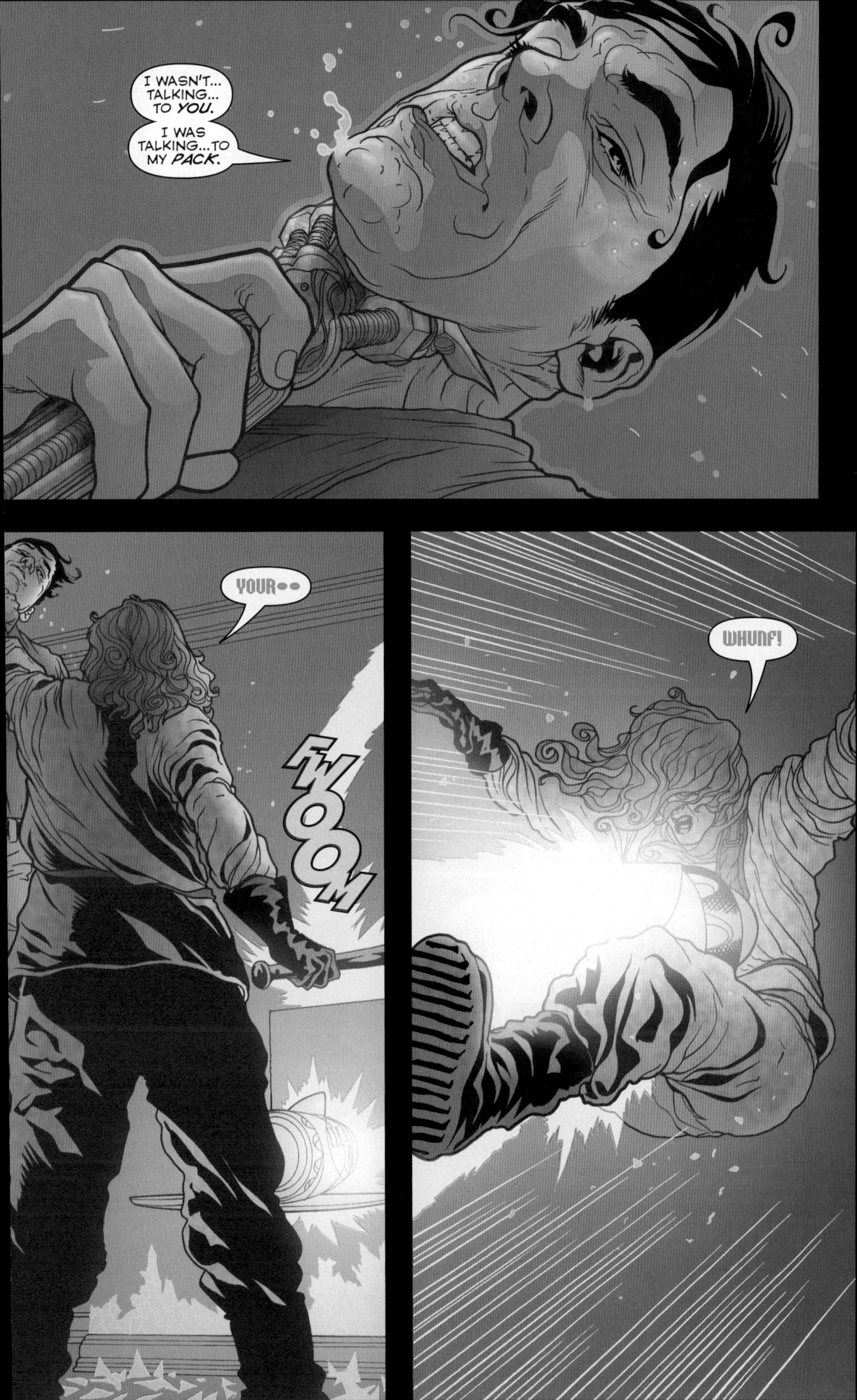
I WASN'T... TALKING... TO YOU.
I WAS TALKING...TO MY PACK.
YOUR--
FWOOOM
WHUNF!

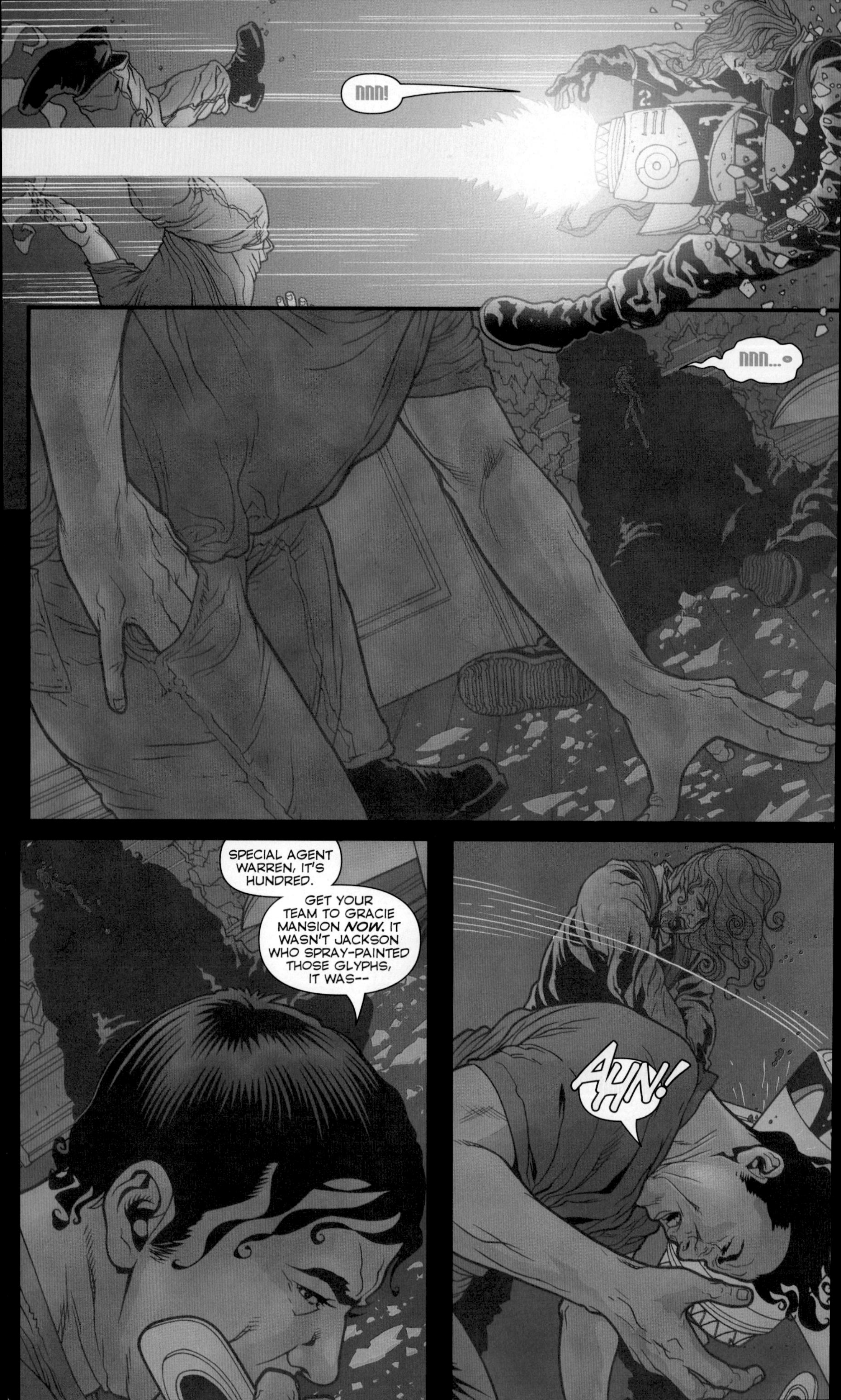

NNN!
NNN...
SPECIAL AGENT WARREN, IT'S HUNDRED.
GET YOUR TEAM TO GRACIE MANSION *NOW.* IT WASN'T JACKSON WHO SPRAY-PAINTED THOSE GLYPHS, IT WAS--
AUN!

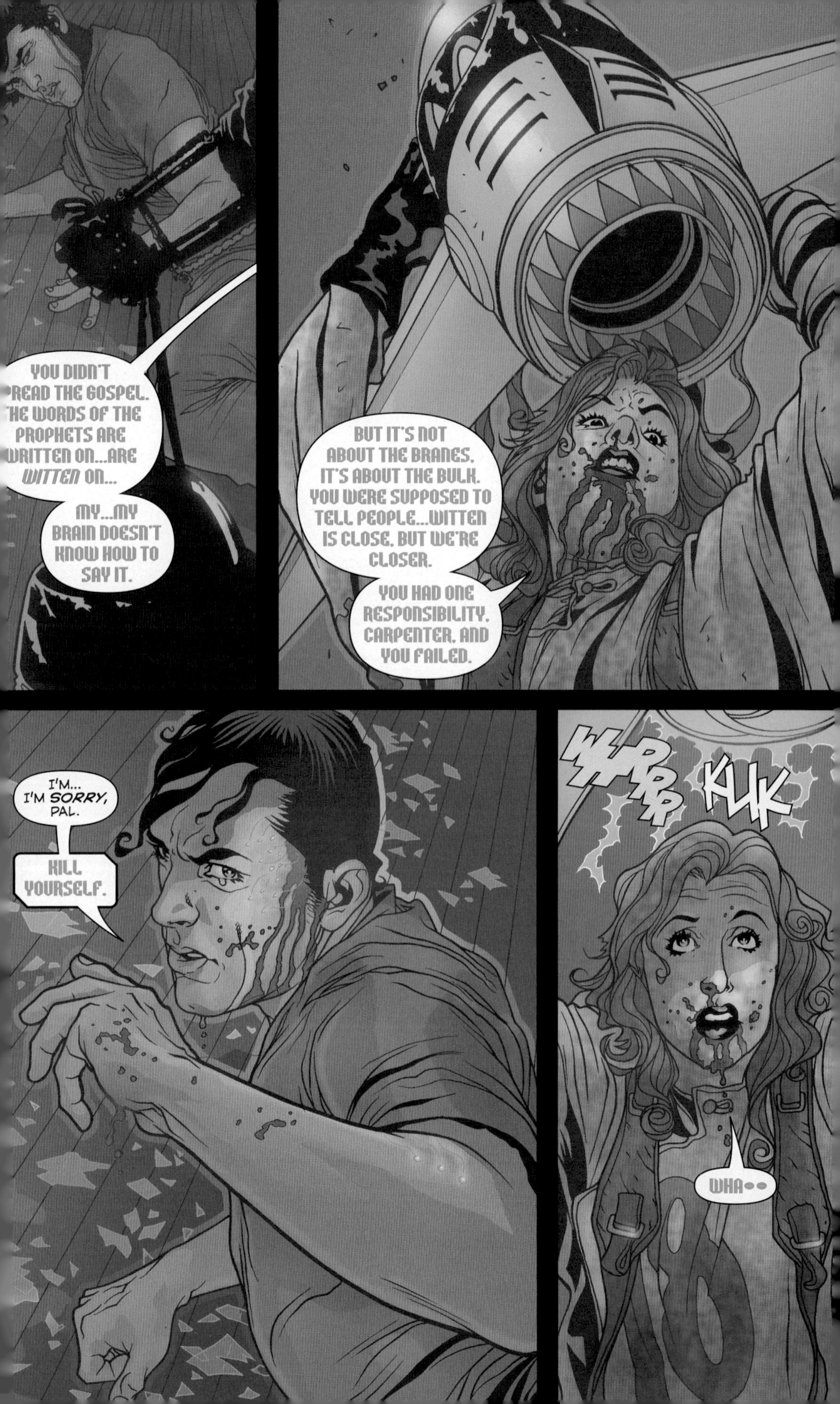
YOU DIDN'T READ THE GOSPEL. THE WORDS OF THE PROPHETS ARE WRITTEN ON...ARE WITTEN ON...
MY...MY BRAIN DOESN'T KNOW HOW TO SAY IT.
BUT IT'S NOT ABOUT THE BRANES. IT'S ABOUT THE BULK. YOU WERE SUPPOSED TO TELL PEOPLE...WITTEN IS CLOSE, BUT WE'RE CLOSER.
YOU HAD ONE RESPONSIBILITY, CARPENTER, AND YOU FAILED.
I'M... I'M SORRY, PAL.
KILL YOURSELF.
WRRR KLIK
WHA..

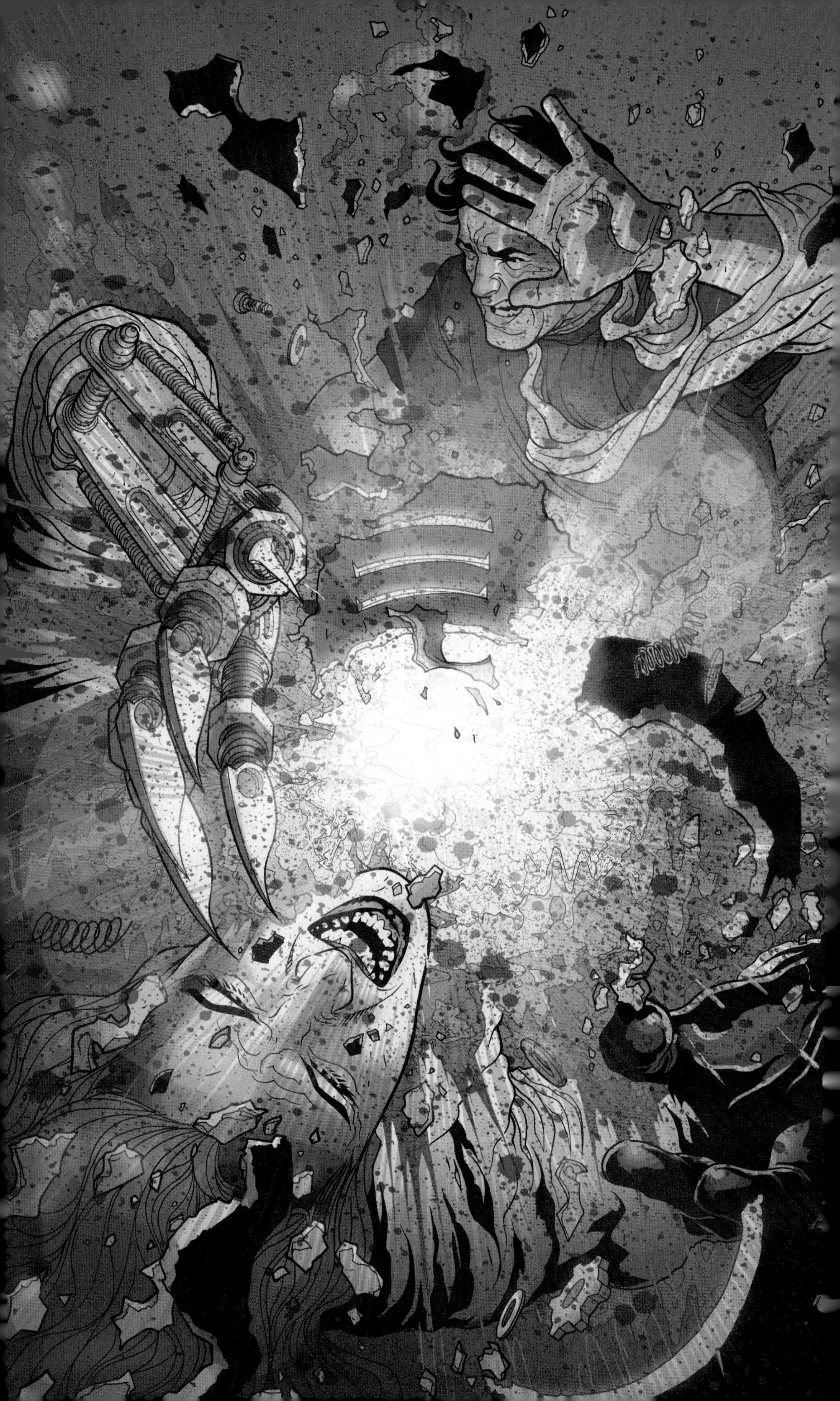

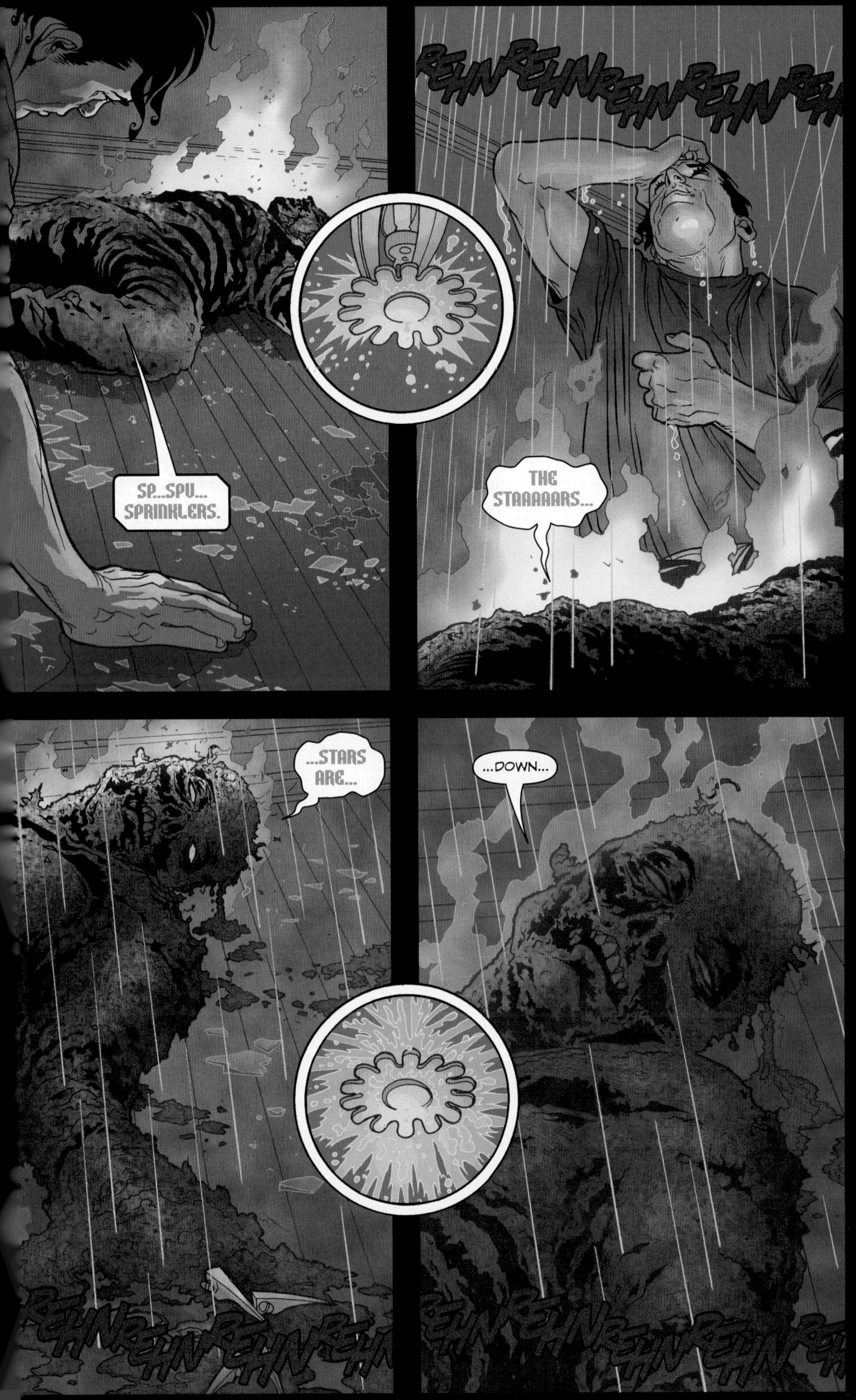

SP...SPU... SPRINKLERS.
REHNREHNREHNREHNREH
THE STAAAAARS...
...STARS ARE...
...DOWN...
REHNREHNREHNREHNREHNREHN

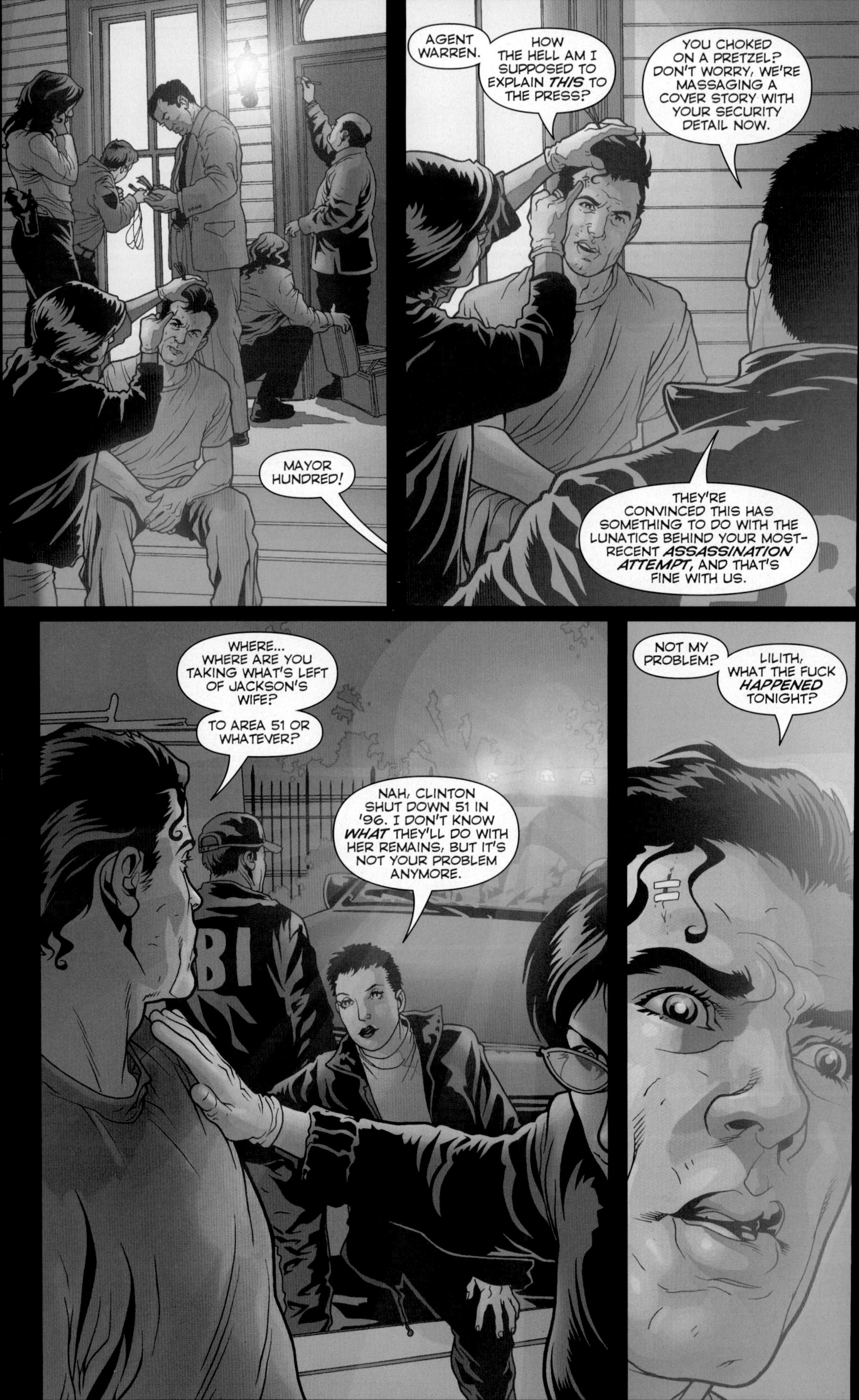
MAYOR HUNDRED!
AGENT WARREN.
HOW THE HELL AM I SUPPOSED TO EXPLAIN THIS TO THE PRESS?
YOU CHOKED ON A PRETZEL? DON'T WORRY, WE'RE MASSAGING A COVER STORY WITH YOUR SECURITY DETAIL NOW.
THEY'RE CONVINCED THIS HAS SOMETHING TO DO WITH THE LUNATICS BEHIND YOUR MOST-RECENT ASSASSINATION ATTEMPT, AND THAT'S FINE WITH US.
WHERE... WHERE ARE YOU TAKING WHAT'S LEFT OF JACKSON'S WIFE?
TO AREA 51 OR WHATEVER?
NAH, CLINTON SHUT DOWN 51 IN '96. I DON'T KNOW WHAT THEY'LL DO WITH HER REMAINS, BUT IT'S NOT YOUR PROBLEM ANYMORE.
NOT MY PROBLEM?
LILITH, WHAT THE FUCK HAPPENED TONIGHT?
FBI

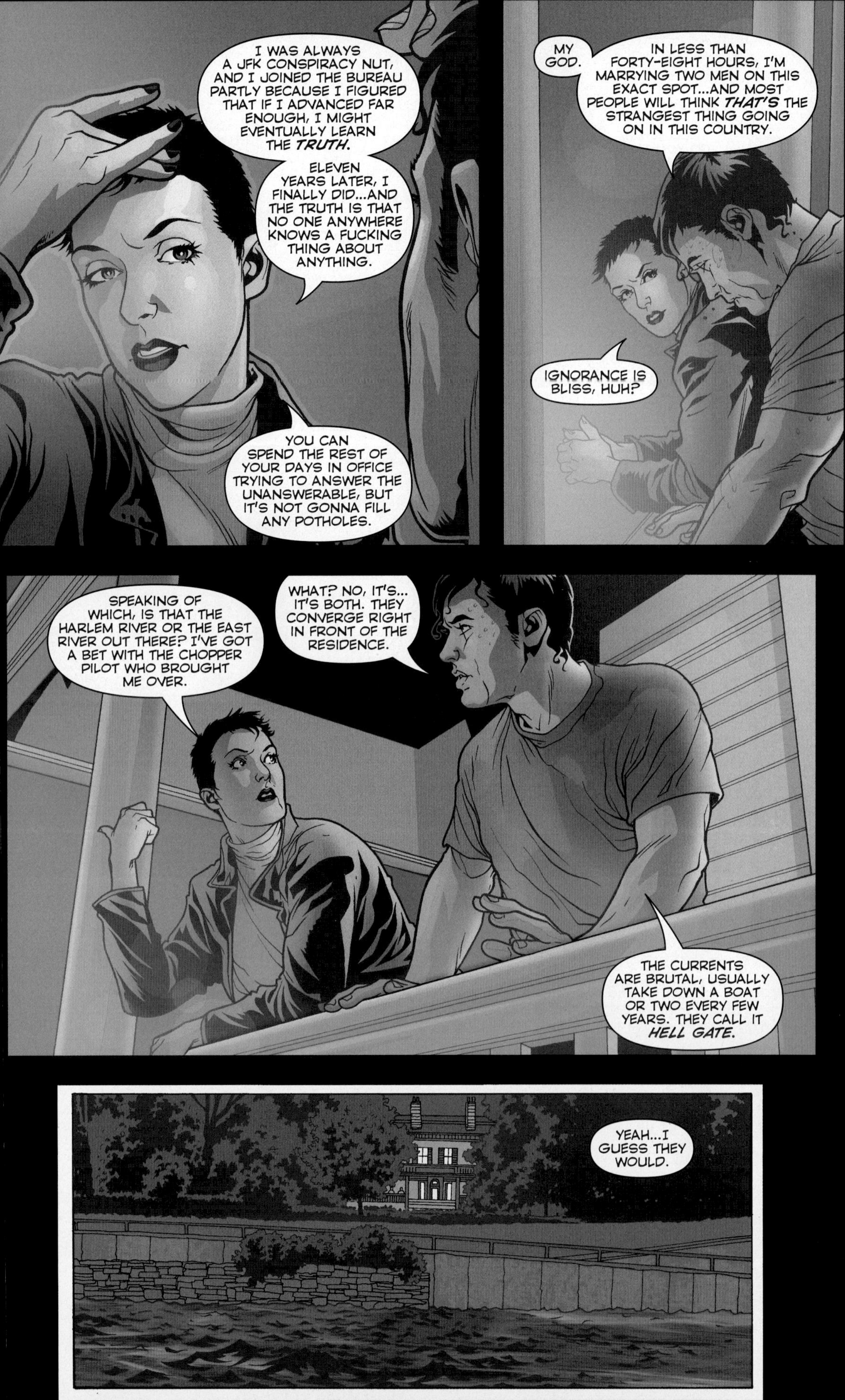
I WAS ALWAYS A JFK CONSPIRACY NUT, AND I JOINED THE BUREAU PARTLY BECAUSE I FIGURED THAT IF I ADVANCED FAR ENOUGH, I MIGHT EVENTUALLY LEARN THE TRUTH.
ELEVEN YEARS LATER, I FINALLY DID...AND THE TRUTH IS THAT NO ONE ANYWHERE KNOWS A FUCKING THING ABOUT ANYTHING.
YOU CAN SPEND THE REST OF YOUR DAYS IN OFFICE TRYING TO ANSWER THE UNANSWERABLE, BUT IT'S NOT GONNA FILL ANY POTHOLES.
MY GOD.
IN LESS THAN FORTY-EIGHT HOURS, I'M MARRYING TWO MEN ON THIS EXACT SPOT...AND MOST PEOPLE WILL THINK THAT'S THE STRANGEST THING GOING ON IN THIS COUNTRY.
IGNORANCE IS BLISS, HUH?
SPEAKING OF WHICH, IS THAT THE HARLEM RIVER OR THE EAST RIVER OUT THERE? I'VE GOT A BET WITH THE CHOPPER PILOT WHO BROUGHT ME OVER.
WHAT? NO, IT'S... IT'S BOTH. THEY CONVERGE RIGHT IN FRONT OF THE RESIDENCE.
THE CURRENTS ARE BRUTAL, USUALLY TAKE DOWN A BOAT OR TWO EVERY FEW YEARS. THEY CALL IT HELL GATE.
YEAH...I GUESS THEY WOULD.

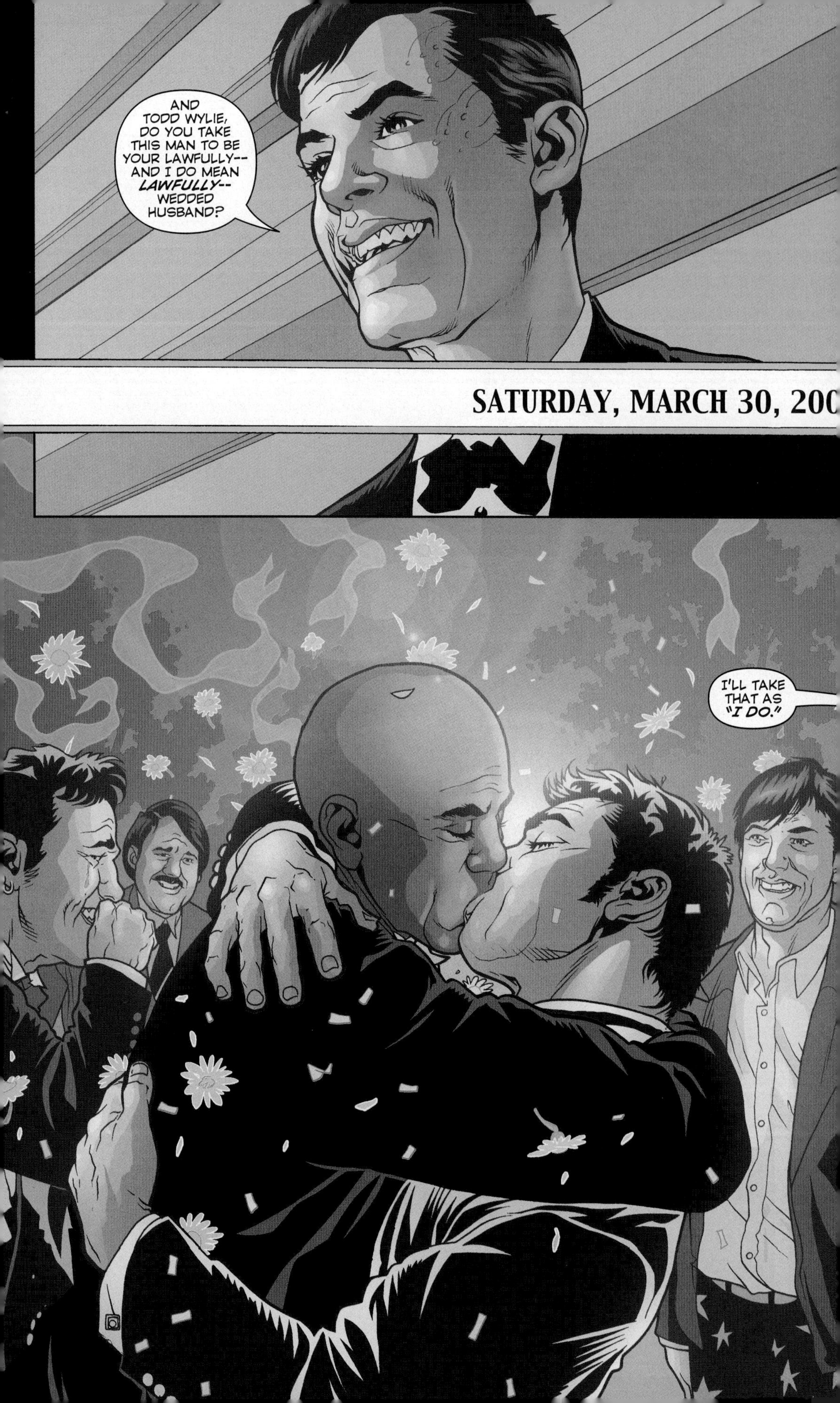
AND TODD WYLIE, DO YOU TAKE THIS MAN TO BE YOUR LAWFULLY-- AND I DO MEAN *LAWFULLY*-- WEDDED HUSBAND?
SATURDAY, MARCH 30, 200
I'LL TAKE THAT AS *"I DO."*

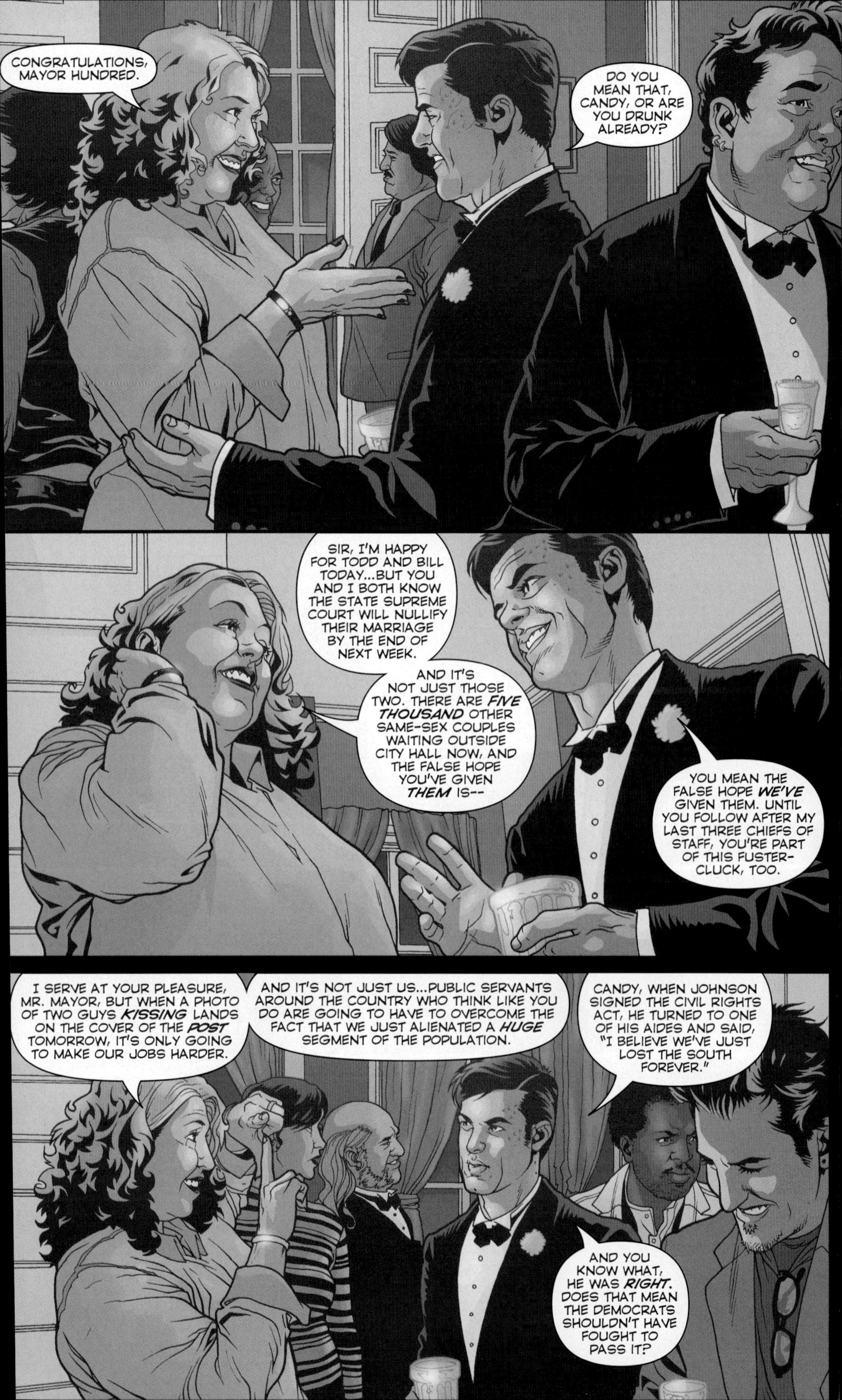
CONGRATULATIONS, MAYOR HUNDRED.
DO YOU MEAN THAT, CANDY, OR ARE YOU DRUNK ALREADY?
SIR, I'M HAPPY FOR TODD AND BILL TODAY...BUT YOU AND I BOTH KNOW THE STATE SUPREME COURT WILL NULLIFY THEIR MARRIAGE BY THE END OF NEXT WEEK.
AND IT'S NOT JUST THOSE TWO. THERE ARE *FIVE THOUSAND* OTHER SAME-SEX COUPLES WAITING OUTSIDE CITY HALL NOW, AND THE FALSE HOPE YOU'VE GIVEN *THEM* IS--
YOU MEAN THE FALSE HOPE *WE'VE* GIVEN THEM. UNTIL YOU FOLLOW AFTER MY LAST THREE CHIEFS OF STAFF, YOU'RE PART OF THIS FUSTER-CLUCK, TOO.
I SERVE AT YOUR PLEASURE, MR. MAYOR, BUT WHEN A PHOTO OF TWO GUYS *KISSING* LANDS ON THE COVER OF THE *POST* TOMORROW, IT'S ONLY GOING TO MAKE OUR JOBS HARDER.
AND IT'S NOT JUST US...PUBLIC SERVANTS AROUND THE COUNTRY WHO THINK LIKE YOU DO ARE GOING TO HAVE TO OVERCOME THE FACT THAT WE JUST ALIENATED A *HUGE* SEGMENT OF THE POPULATION.
CANDY, WHEN JOHNSON SIGNED THE CIVIL RIGHTS ACT, HE TURNED TO ONE OF HIS AIDES AND SAID, "I BELIEVE WE'VE JUST LOST THE SOUTH FOREVER."
AND YOU KNOW WHAT, HE WAS *RIGHT*. DOES THAT MEAN THE DEMOCRATS SHOULDN'T HAVE FOUGHT TO PASS IT?

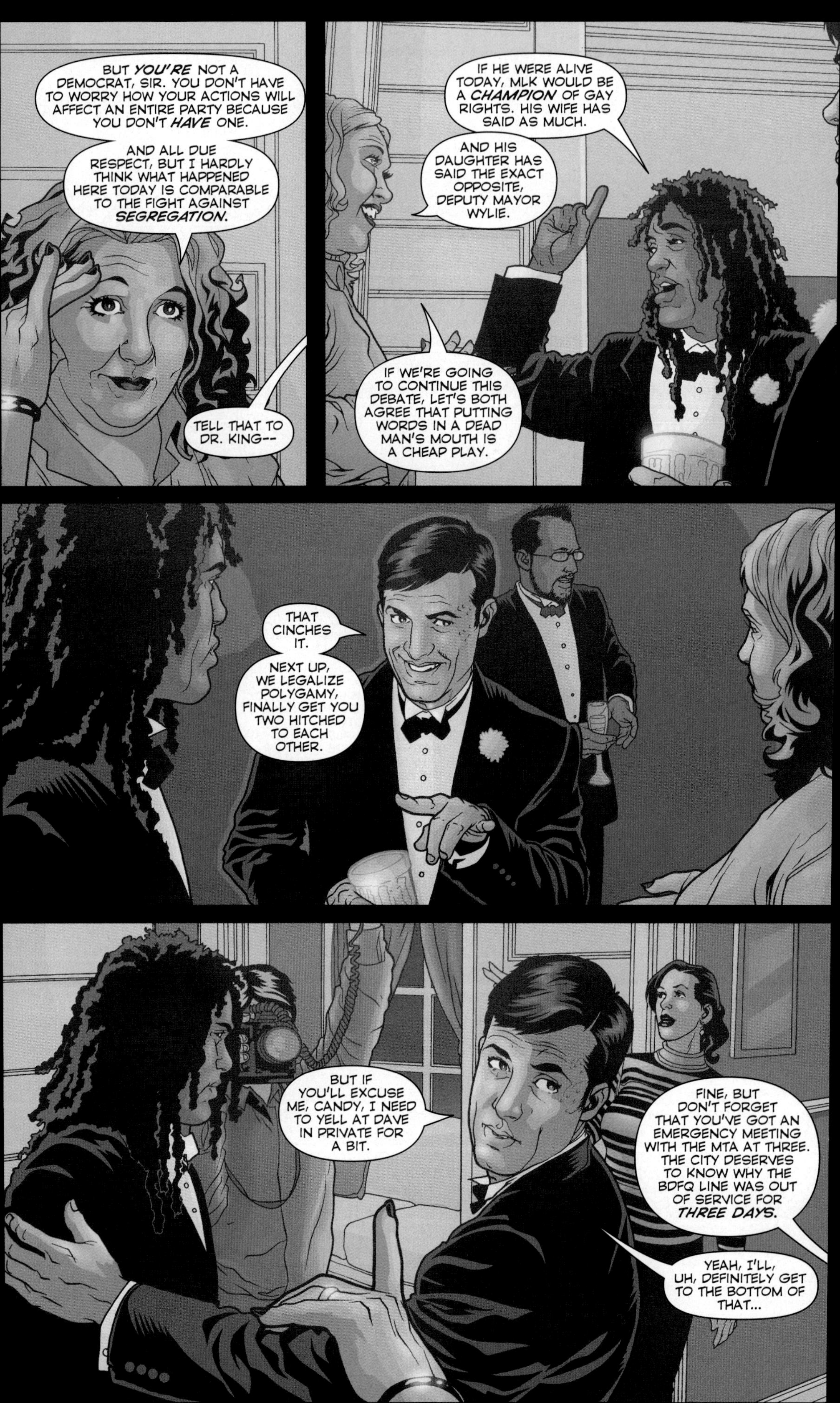
BUT *YOU'RE* NOT A DEMOCRAT, SIR. YOU DON'T HAVE TO WORRY HOW YOUR ACTIONS WILL AFFECT AN ENTIRE PARTY BECAUSE YOU DON'T *HAVE* ONE.
AND ALL DUE RESPECT, BUT I HARDLY THINK WHAT HAPPENED HERE TODAY IS COMPARABLE TO THE FIGHT AGAINST *SEGREGATION*.
TELL THAT TO DR. KING--
IF HE WERE ALIVE TODAY, MLK WOULD BE A *CHAMPION* OF GAY RIGHTS. HIS WIFE HAS SAID AS MUCH.
AND HIS DAUGHTER HAS SAID THE EXACT OPPOSITE, DEPUTY MAYOR WYLIE.
IF WE'RE GOING TO CONTINUE THIS DEBATE, LET'S BOTH AGREE THAT PUTTING WORDS IN A DEAD MAN'S MOUTH IS A CHEAP PLAY.
THAT CINCHES IT.
NEXT UP, WE LEGALIZE POLYGAMY, FINALLY GET YOU TWO HITCHED TO EACH OTHER.
BUT IF YOU'LL EXCUSE ME, CANDY, I NEED TO YELL AT DAVE IN PRIVATE FOR A BIT.
FINE, BUT DON'T FORGET THAT YOU'VE GOT AN EMERGENCY MEETING WITH THE MTA AT THREE. THE CITY DESERVES TO KNOW WHY THE BDFQ LINE WAS OUT OF SERVICE FOR *THREE DAYS*.
YEAH, I'LL, UH, DEFINITELY GET TO THE BOTTOM OF THAT...

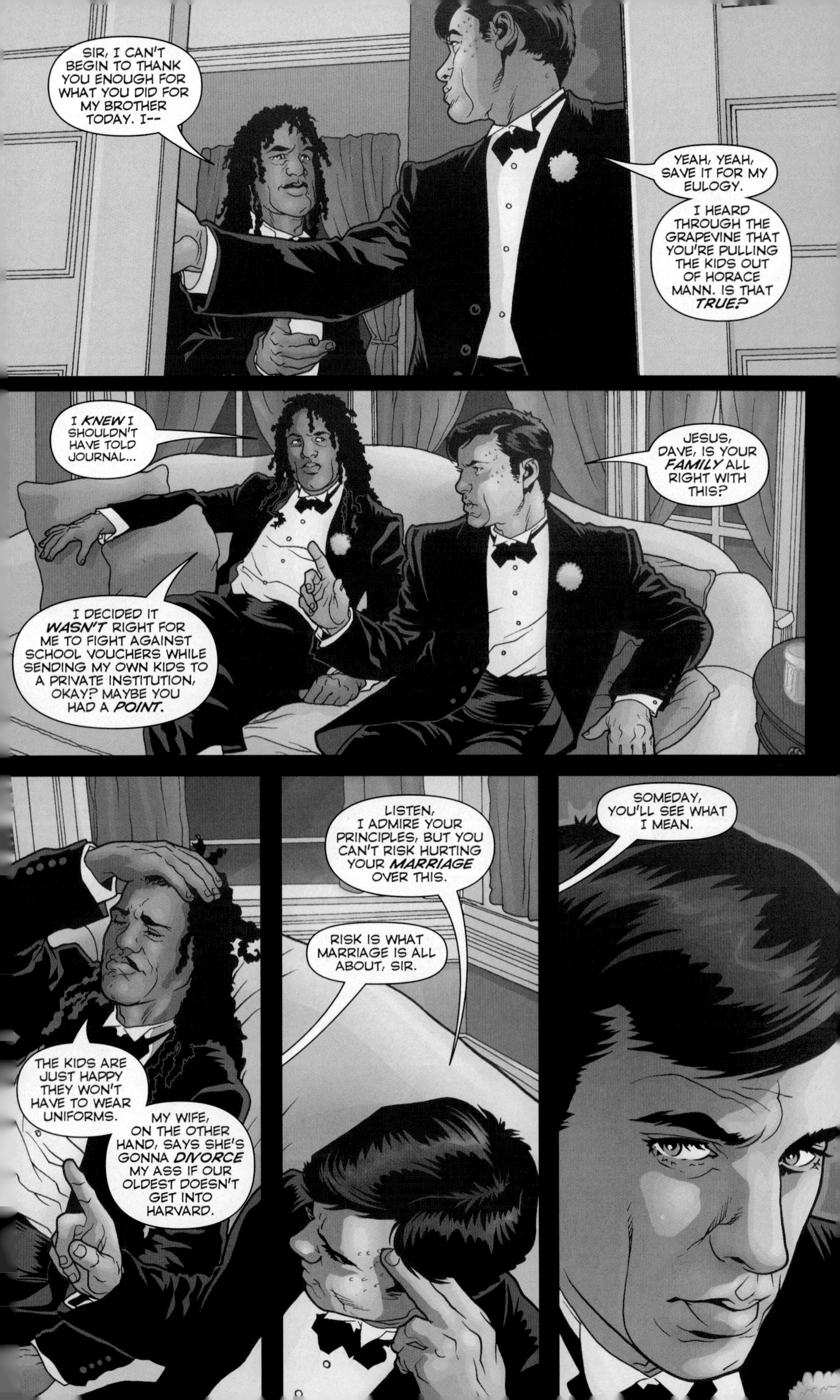

SIR, I CAN'T BEGIN TO THANK YOU ENOUGH FOR WHAT YOU DID FOR MY BROTHER TODAY. I--
YEAH, YEAH, SAVE IT FOR MY EULOGY.
I HEARD THROUGH THE GRAPEVINE THAT YOU'RE PULLING THE KIDS OUT OF HORACE MANN. IS THAT TRUE?
I KNEW I SHOULDN'T HAVE TOLD JOURNAL...
JESUS, DAVE, IS YOUR FAMILY ALL RIGHT WITH THIS?
I DECIDED IT WASN'T RIGHT FOR ME TO FIGHT AGAINST SCHOOL VOUCHERS WHILE SENDING MY OWN KIDS TO A PRIVATE INSTITUTION, OKAY? MAYBE YOU HAD A POINT.
THE KIDS ARE JUST HAPPY THEY WON'T HAVE TO WEAR UNIFORMS.
MY WIFE, ON THE OTHER HAND, SAYS SHE'S GONNA DIVORCE MY ASS IF OUR OLDEST DOESN'T GET INTO HARVARD.
LISTEN, I ADMIRE YOUR PRINCIPLES, BUT YOU CAN'T RISK HURTING YOUR MARRIAGE OVER THIS.
RISK IS WHAT MARRIAGE IS ALL ABOUT, SIR.
SOMEDAY, YOU'LL SEE WHAT I MEAN.

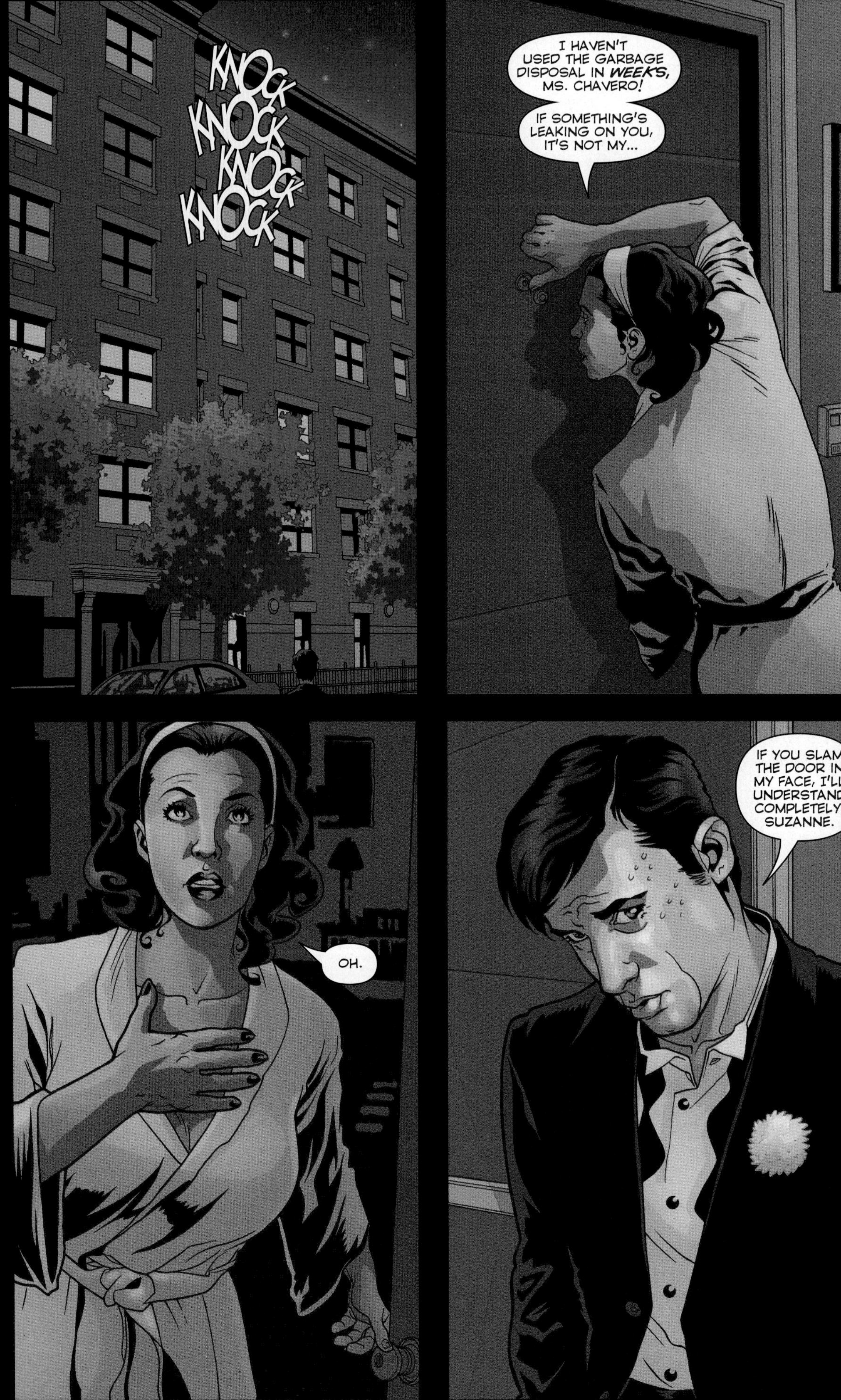
KNOCK KNOCK KNOCK KNOCK
I HAVEN'T USED THE GARBAGE DISPOSAL IN *WEEKS,* MS. CHAVERO!
IF SOMETHING'S LEAKING ON YOU, IT'S NOT MY...
OH.
IF YOU SLAM THE DOOR IN MY FACE, I'LL UNDERSTAND COMPLETELY, SUZANNE.

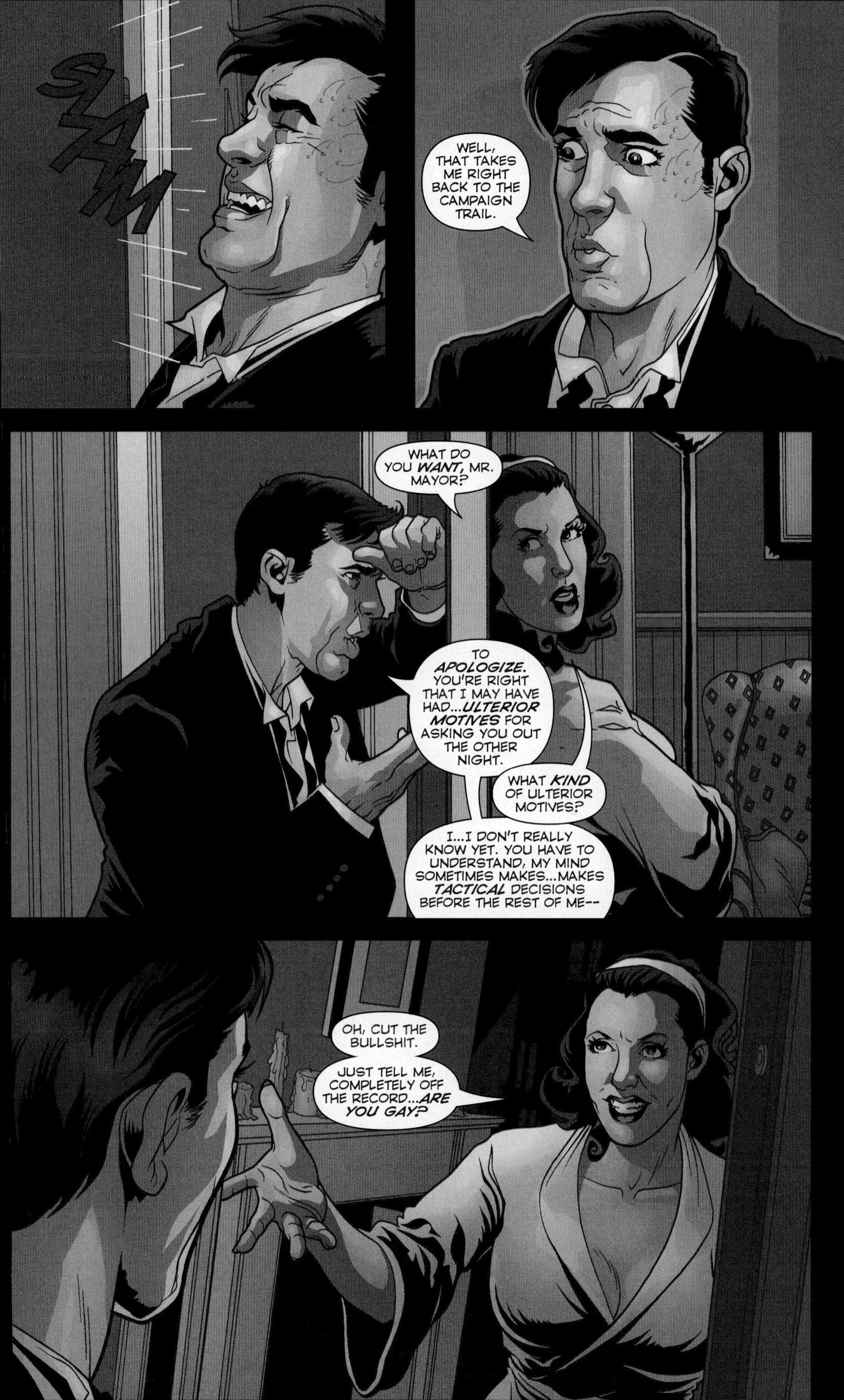
SLAM
WELL, THAT TAKES ME RIGHT BACK TO THE CAMPAIGN TRAIL.
WHAT DO YOU *WANT*, MR. MAYOR?
TO *APOLOGIZE*. YOU'RE RIGHT THAT I MAY HAVE HAD...*ULTERIOR MOTIVES* FOR ASKING YOU OUT THE OTHER NIGHT.
WHAT *KIND* OF ULTERIOR MOTIVES?
I...I DON'T REALLY KNOW YET. YOU HAVE TO UNDERSTAND, MY MIND SOMETIMES MAKES...MAKES *TACTICAL* DECISIONS BEFORE THE REST OF ME--
OH, CUT THE BULLSHIT.
JUST TELL ME, COMPLETELY OFF THE RECORD...*ARE YOU GAY?*

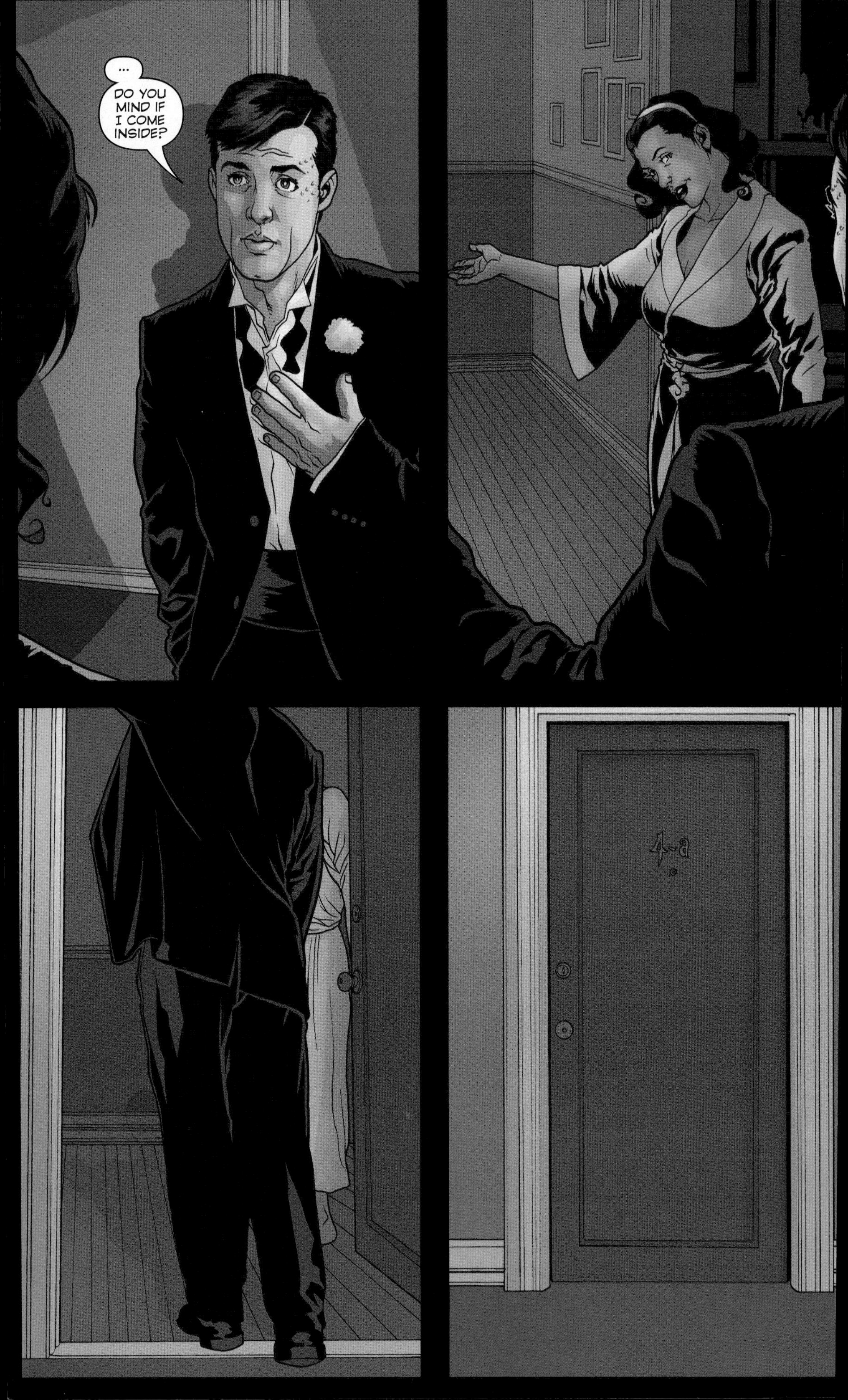
...
DO YOU MIND IF I COME INSIDE?
4-a

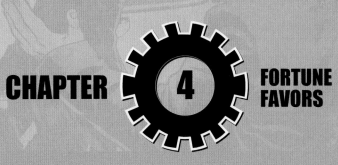

CHAPTER 4 FORTUNE FAVORS

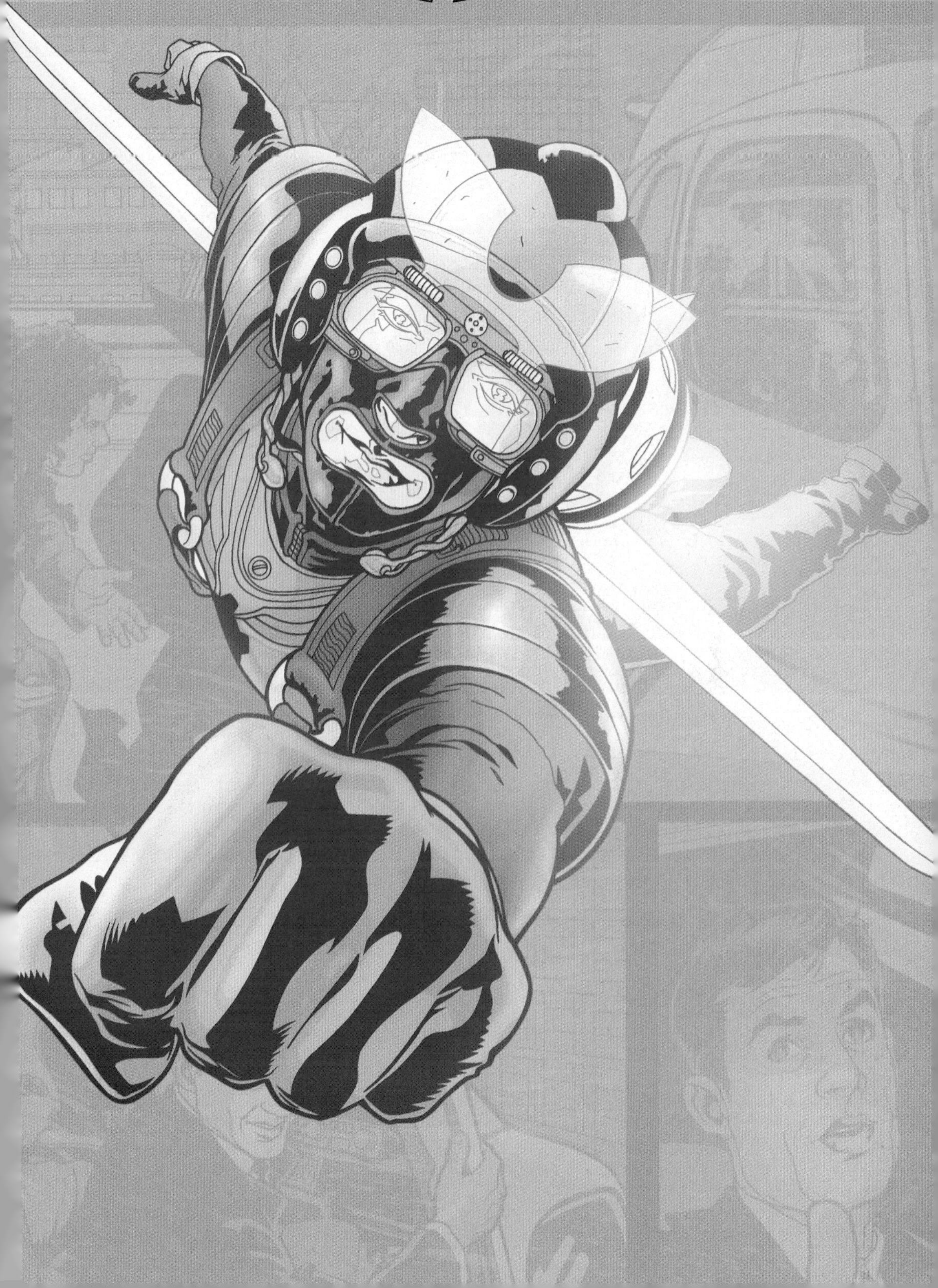

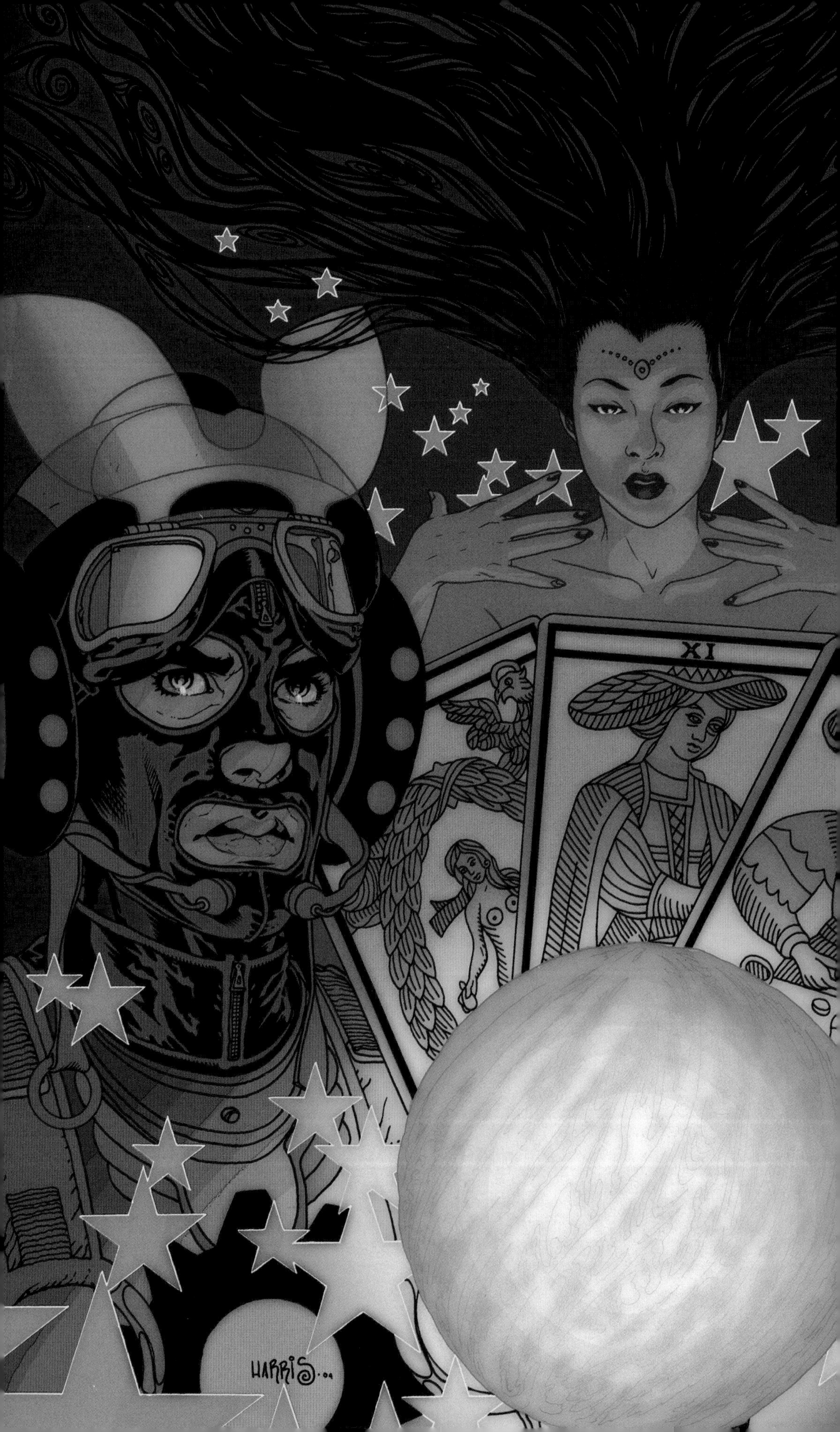
XI
HARRIS .04

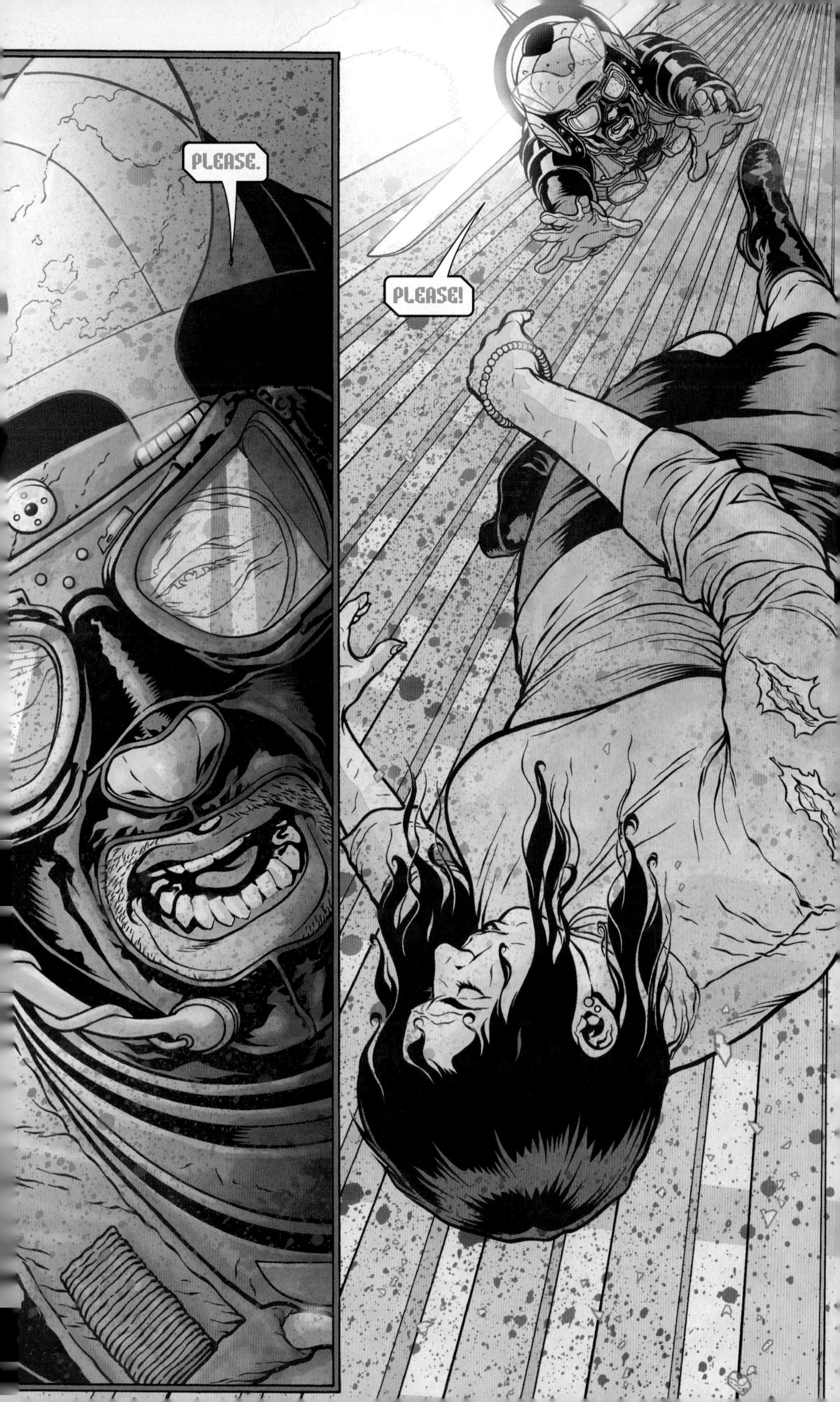
PLEASE.
PLEASE!

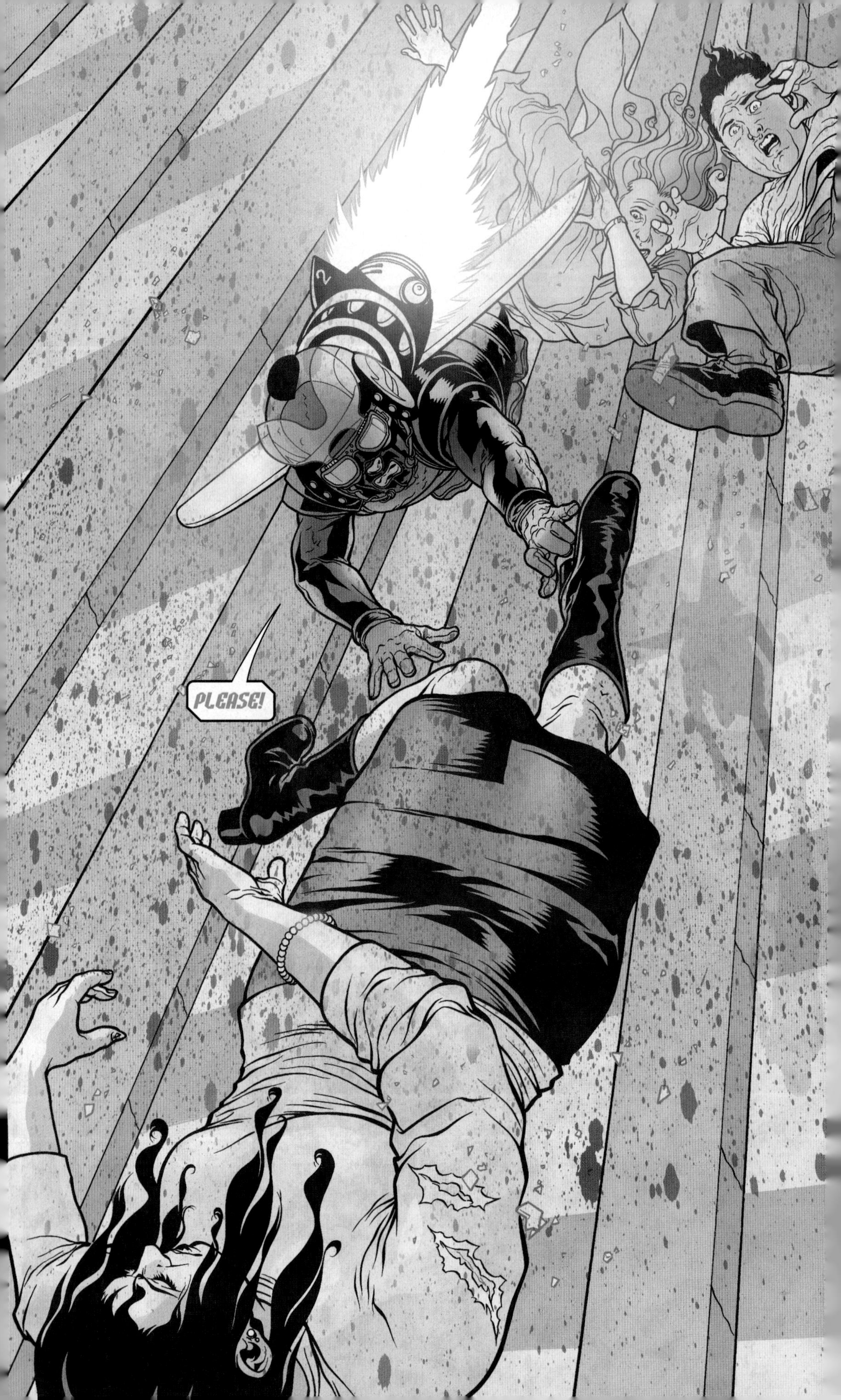
PLEASE!

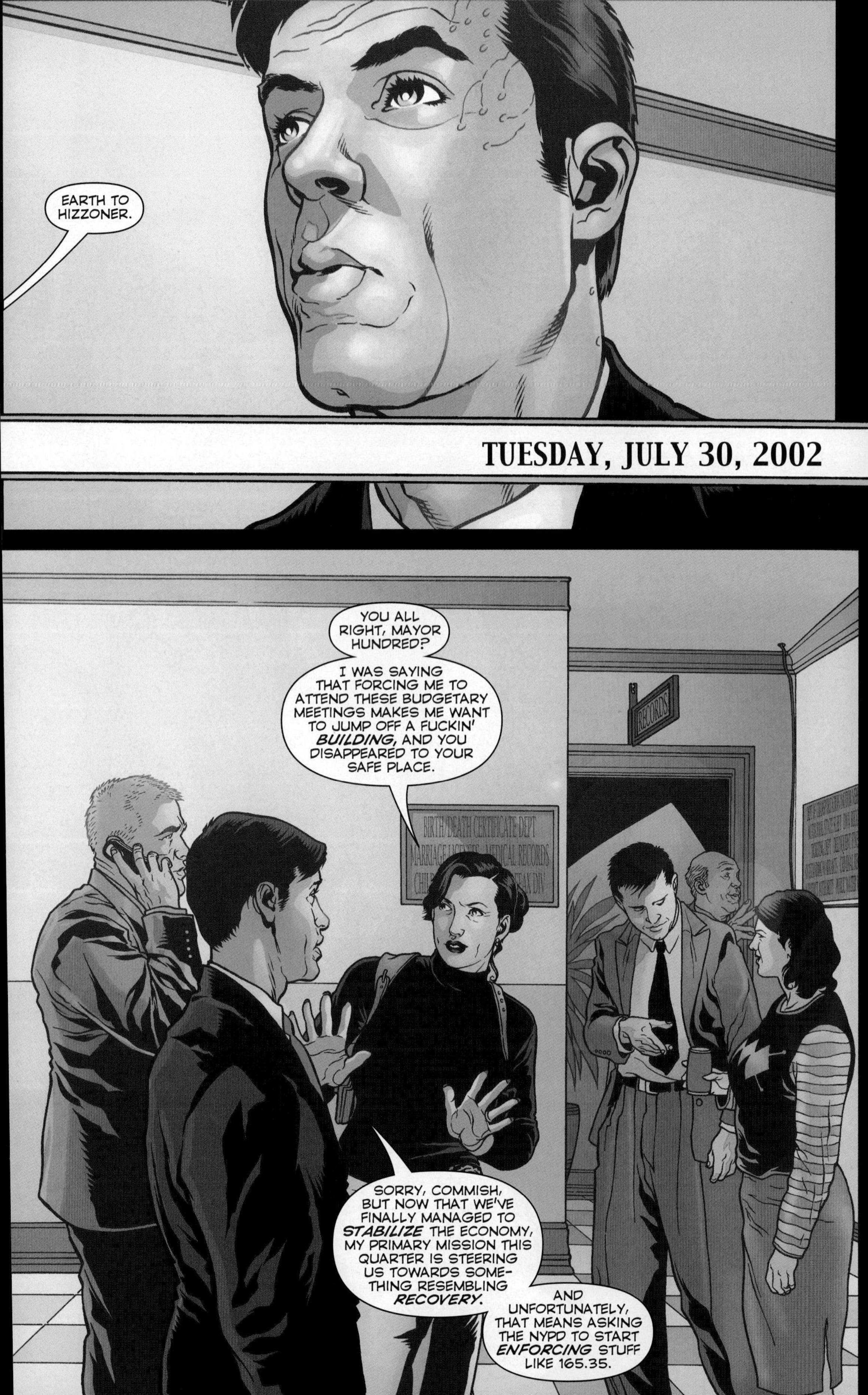
EARTH TO HIZZONER.
TUESDAY, JULY 30, 2002
YOU ALL RIGHT, MAYOR HUNDRED?
I WAS SAYING THAT FORCING ME TO ATTEND THESE BUDGETARY MEETINGS MAKES ME WANT TO JUMP OFF A FUCKIN' *BUILDING,* AND YOU DISAPPEARED TO YOUR SAFE PLACE.
RECORDS
BIRTH/DEATH CERTIFICATE DEPT
SORRY, COMMISH, BUT NOW THAT WE'VE FINALLY MANAGED TO *STABILIZE* THE ECONOMY, MY PRIMARY MISSION THIS QUARTER IS STEERING US TOWARDS SOMETHING RESEMBLING *RECOVERY.*
AND UNFORTUNATELY, THAT MEANS ASKING THE NYPD TO START *ENFORCING* STUFF LIKE 165.35.

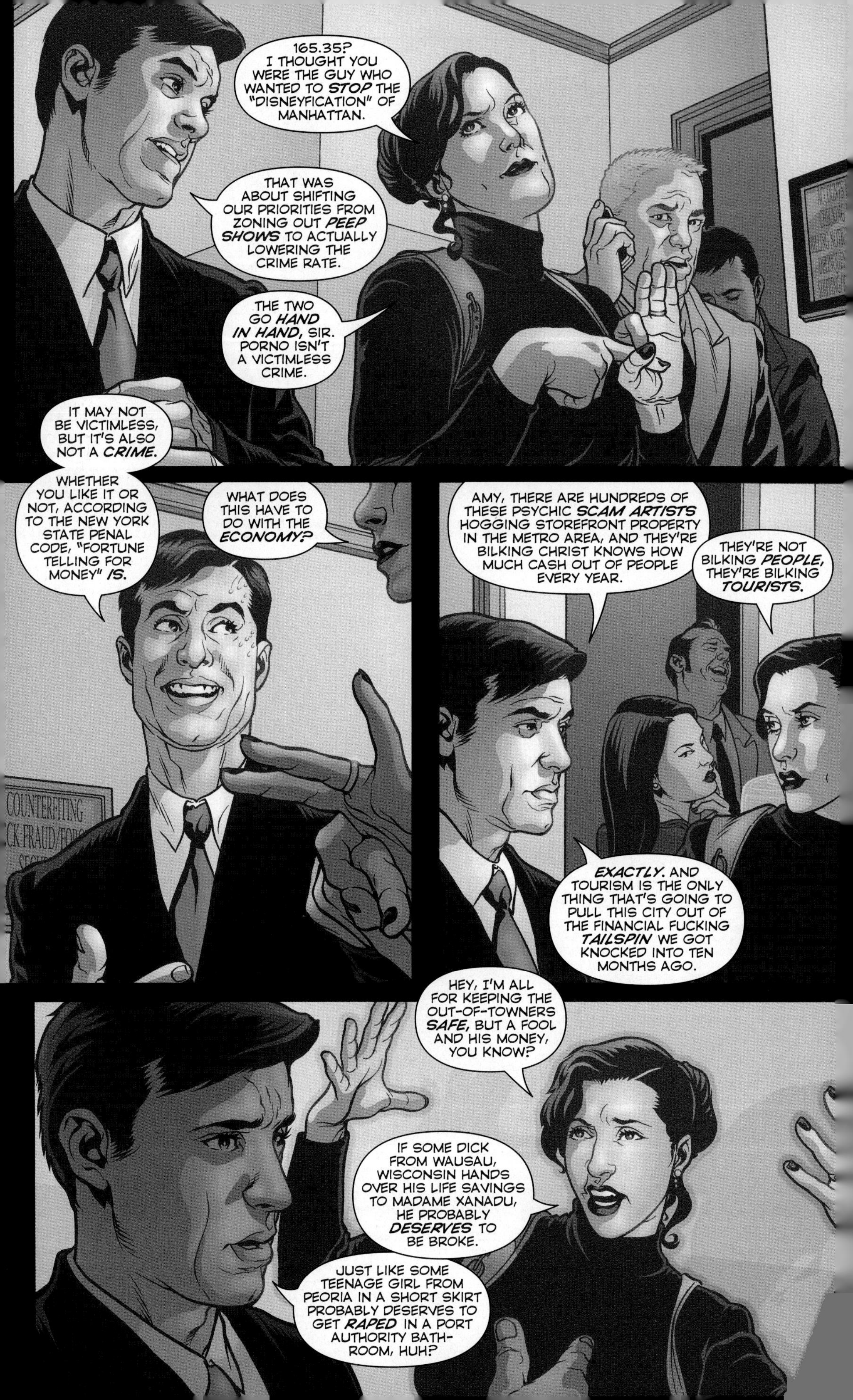
165.35? I THOUGHT YOU WERE THE GUY WHO WANTED TO STOP THE "DISNEYFICATION" OF MANHATTAN.
THAT WAS ABOUT SHIFTING OUR PRIORITIES FROM ZONING OUT PEEP SHOWS TO ACTUALLY LOWERING THE CRIME RATE.
THE TWO GO HAND IN HAND, SIR. PORNO ISN'T A VICTIMLESS CRIME.
IT MAY NOT BE VICTIMLESS, BUT IT'S ALSO NOT A CRIME.
WHETHER YOU LIKE IT OR NOT, ACCORDING TO THE NEW YORK STATE PENAL CODE, "FORTUNE TELLING FOR MONEY" IS.
WHAT DOES THIS HAVE TO DO WITH THE ECONOMY?
COUNTERFEITING
AMY, THERE ARE HUNDREDS OF THESE PSYCHIC SCAM ARTISTS HOGGING STOREFRONT PROPERTY IN THE METRO AREA, AND THEY'RE BILKING CHRIST KNOWS HOW MUCH CASH OUT OF PEOPLE EVERY YEAR.
THEY'RE NOT BILKING PEOPLE, THEY'RE BILKING TOURISTS.
EXACTLY. AND TOURISM IS THE ONLY THING THAT'S GOING TO PULL THIS CITY OUT OF THE FINANCIAL FUCKING TAILSPIN WE GOT KNOCKED INTO TEN MONTHS AGO.
HEY, I'M ALL FOR KEEPING THE OUT-OF-TOWNERS SAFE, BUT A FOOL AND HIS MONEY, YOU KNOW?
IF SOME DICK FROM WAUSAU, WISCONSIN HANDS OVER HIS LIFE SAVINGS TO MADAME XANADU, HE PROBABLY DESERVES TO BE BROKE.
JUST LIKE SOME TEENAGE GIRL FROM PEORIA IN A SHORT SKIRT PROBABLY DESERVES TO GET RAPED IN A PORT AUTHORITY BATHROOM, HUH?

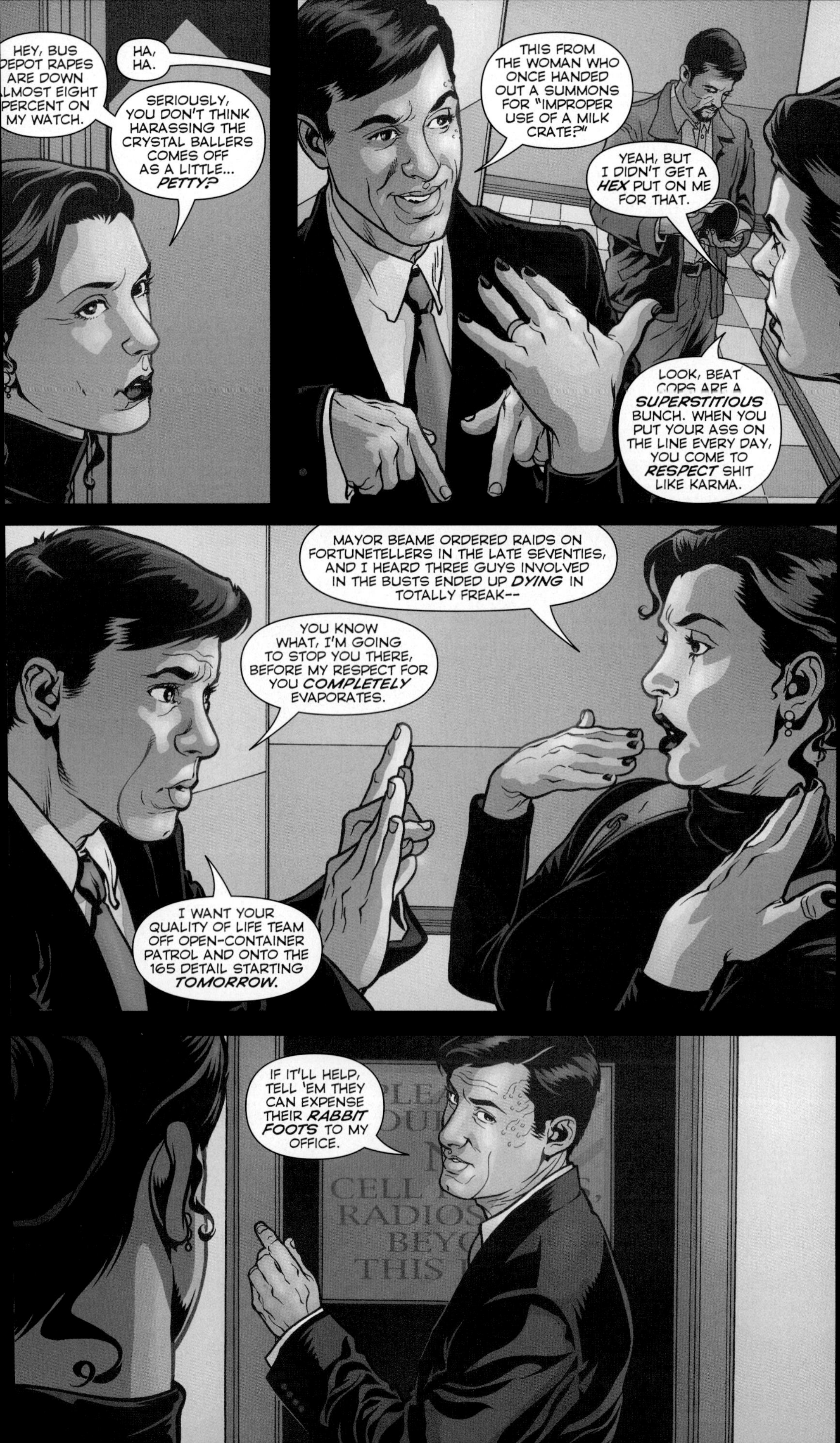

HEY, BUS DEPOT RAPES ARE DOWN ALMOST EIGHT PERCENT ON MY WATCH.
HA, HA.
SERIOUSLY, YOU DON'T THINK HARASSING THE CRYSTAL BALLERS COMES OFF AS A LITTLE... *PETTY?*
THIS FROM THE WOMAN WHO ONCE HANDED OUT A SUMMONS FOR "IMPROPER USE OF A MILK CRATE?"
YEAH, BUT I DIDN'T GET A *HEX* PUT ON ME FOR THAT.
LOOK, BEAT COPS ARE A *SUPERSTITIOUS* BUNCH. WHEN YOU PUT YOUR ASS ON THE LINE EVERY DAY, YOU COME TO *RESPECT* SHIT LIKE KARMA.
MAYOR BEAME ORDERED RAIDS ON FORTUNETELLERS IN THE LATE SEVENTIES, AND I HEARD THREE GUYS INVOLVED IN THE BUSTS ENDED UP *DYING* IN TOTALLY FREAK--
YOU KNOW WHAT, I'M GOING TO STOP YOU THERE, BEFORE MY RESPECT FOR YOU *COMPLETELY* EVAPORATES.
I WANT YOUR QUALITY OF LIFE TEAM OFF OPEN-CONTAINER PATROL AND ONTO THE 165 DETAIL STARTING *TOMORROW.*
IF IT'LL HELP, TELL 'EM THEY CAN EXPENSE THEIR *RABBIT FOOTS* TO MY OFFICE.

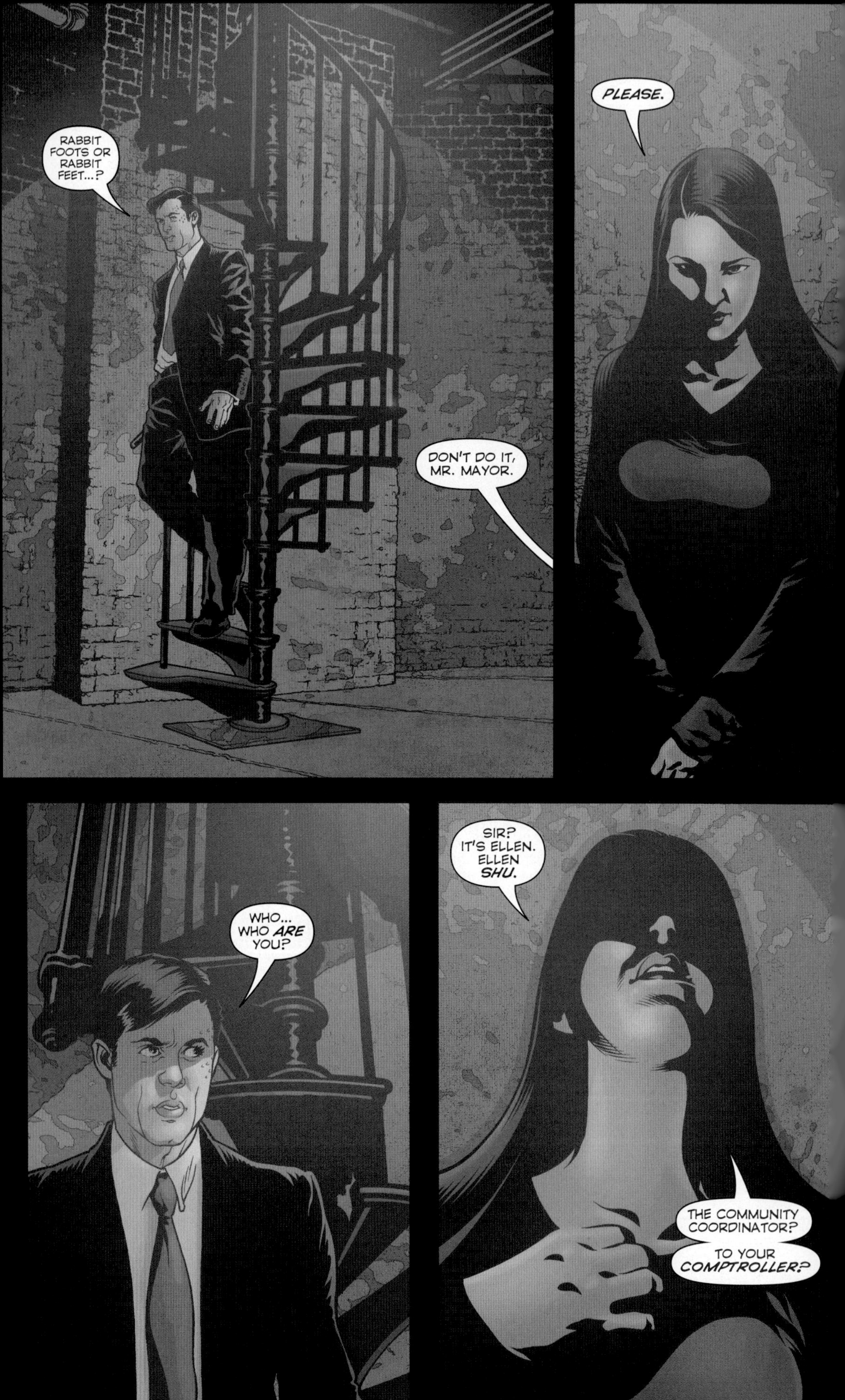
RABBIT FOOTS OR RABBIT FEET...?
DON'T DO IT, MR. MAYOR.
PLEASE.
WHO... WHO ARE YOU?
SIR? IT'S ELLEN. ELLEN SHU.
THE COMMUNITY COORDINATOR?
TO YOUR COMPTROLLER?

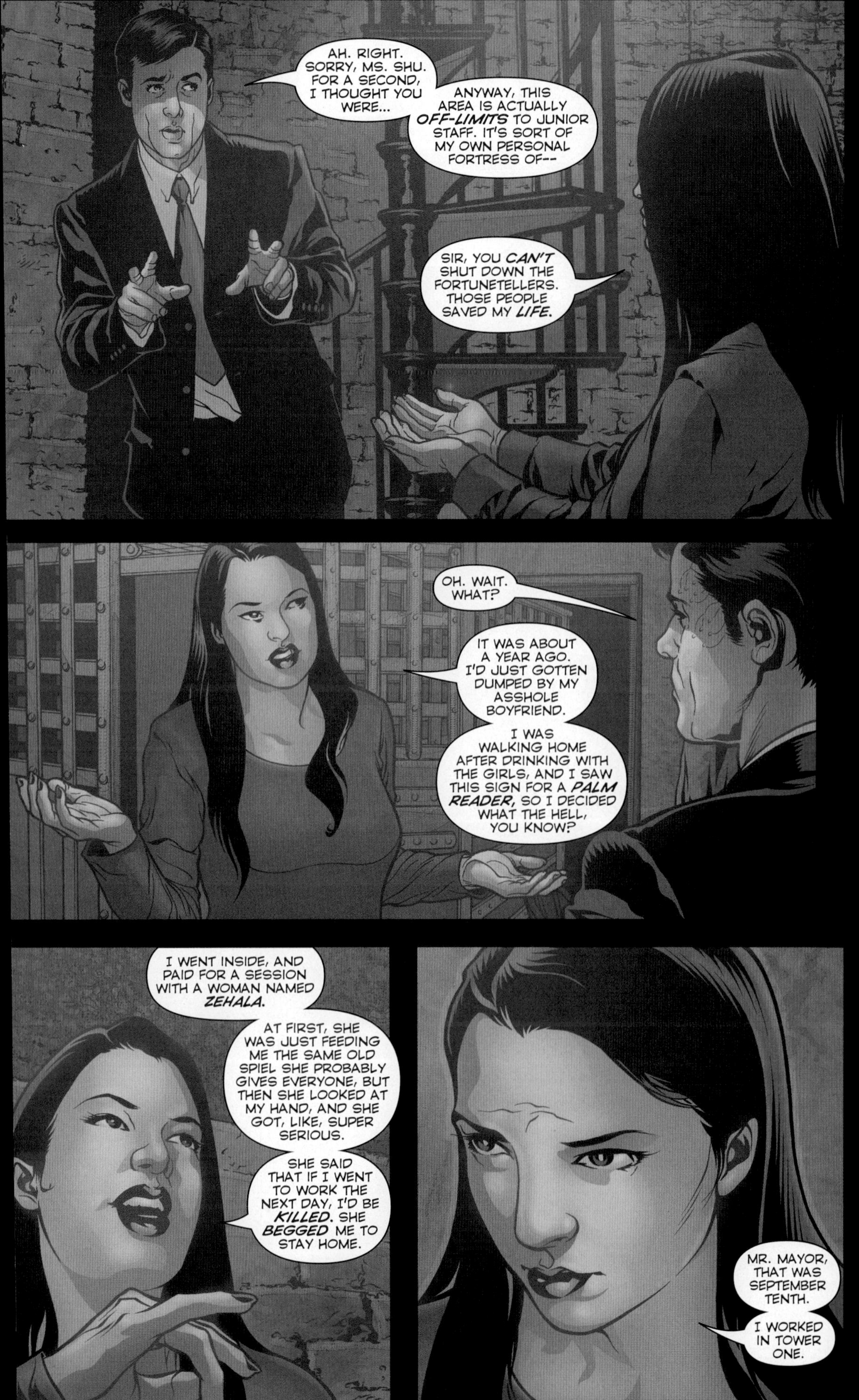
AH. RIGHT. SORRY, MS. SHU. FOR A SECOND, I THOUGHT YOU WERE...
ANYWAY, THIS AREA IS ACTUALLY OFF-LIMITS TO JUNIOR STAFF. IT'S SORT OF MY OWN PERSONAL FORTRESS OF--
SIR, YOU CAN'T SHUT DOWN THE FORTUNETELLERS. THOSE PEOPLE SAVED MY LIFE.
OH. WAIT. WHAT?
IT WAS ABOUT A YEAR AGO. I'D JUST GOTTEN DUMPED BY MY ASSHOLE BOYFRIEND.
I WAS WALKING HOME AFTER DRINKING WITH THE GIRLS, AND I SAW THIS SIGN FOR A PALM READER, SO I DECIDED WHAT THE HELL, YOU KNOW?
I WENT INSIDE, AND PAID FOR A SESSION WITH A WOMAN NAMED ZEHALA.
AT FIRST, SHE WAS JUST FEEDING ME THE SAME OLD SPIEL SHE PROBABLY GIVES EVERYONE, BUT THEN SHE LOOKED AT MY HAND, AND SHE GOT, LIKE, SUPER SERIOUS.
SHE SAID THAT IF I WENT TO WORK THE NEXT DAY, I'D BE KILLED. SHE BEGGED ME TO STAY HOME.
MR. MAYOR, THAT WAS SEPTEMBER TENTH.
I WORKED IN TOWER ONE.

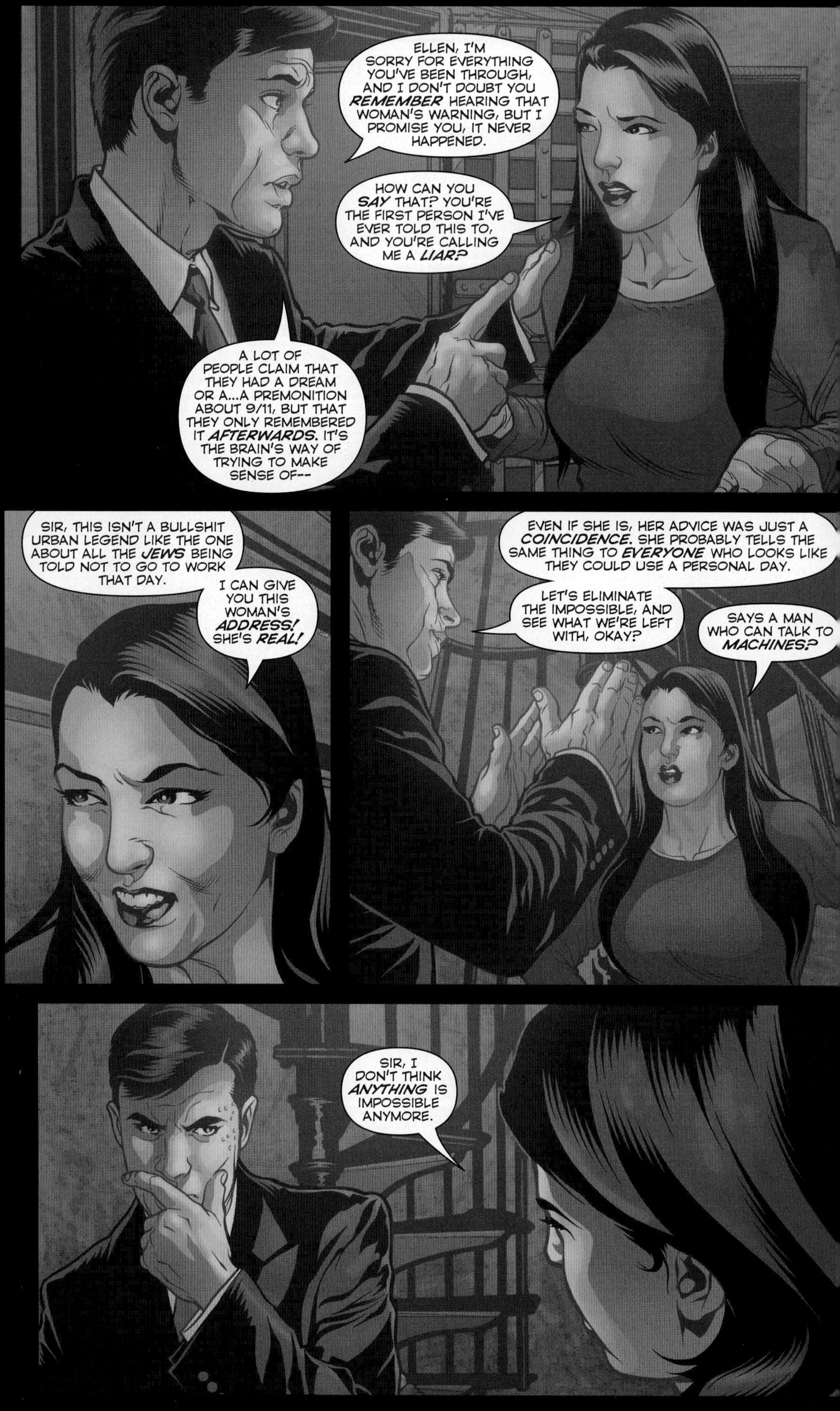
ELLEN, I'M SORRY FOR EVERYTHING YOU'VE BEEN THROUGH, AND I DON'T DOUBT YOU REMEMBER HEARING THAT WOMAN'S WARNING, BUT I PROMISE YOU, IT NEVER HAPPENED.
HOW CAN YOU SAY THAT? YOU'RE THE FIRST PERSON I'VE EVER TOLD THIS TO, AND YOU'RE CALLING ME A LIAR?
A LOT OF PEOPLE CLAIM THAT THEY HAD A DREAM OR A...A PREMONITION ABOUT 9/11, BUT THAT THEY ONLY REMEMBERED IT AFTERWARDS. IT'S THE BRAIN'S WAY OF TRYING TO MAKE SENSE OF--
SIR, THIS ISN'T A BULLSHIT URBAN LEGEND LIKE THE ONE ABOUT ALL THE JEWS BEING TOLD NOT TO GO TO WORK THAT DAY.
I CAN GIVE YOU THIS WOMAN'S ADDRESS! SHE'S REAL!
EVEN IF SHE IS, HER ADVICE WAS JUST A COINCIDENCE. SHE PROBABLY TELLS THE SAME THING TO EVERYONE WHO LOOKS LIKE THEY COULD USE A PERSONAL DAY.
LET'S ELIMINATE THE IMPOSSIBLE, AND SEE WHAT WE'RE LEFT WITH, OKAY?
SAYS A MAN WHO CAN TALK TO MACHINES?
SIR, I DON'T THINK ANYTHING IS IMPOSSIBLE ANYMORE.

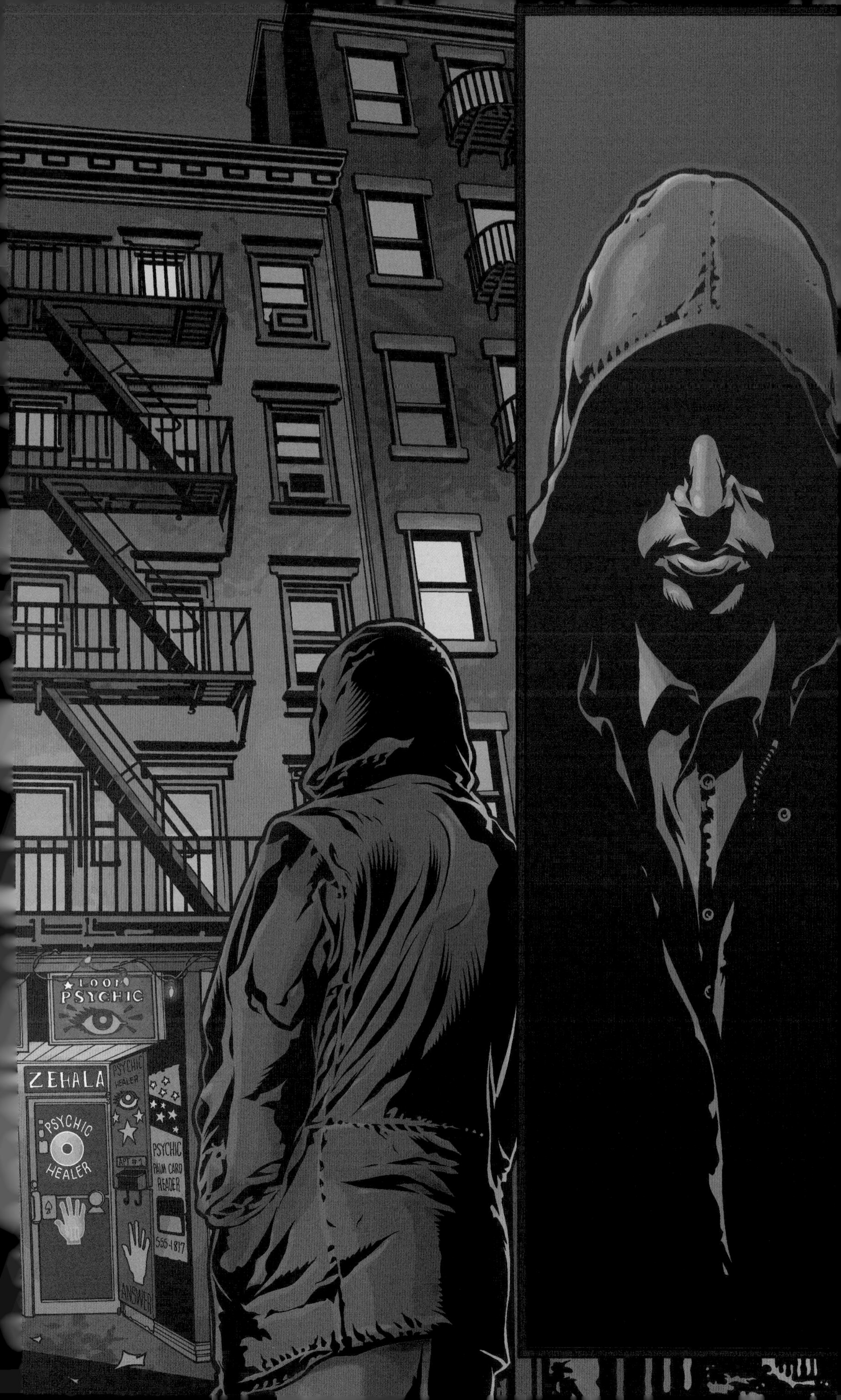
PSYCHIC
ZEHALA
PSYCHIC HEALER
PSYCHIC HEALER
APT #1
ANSWER
PSYCHIC PALM CARD READER
555-1817

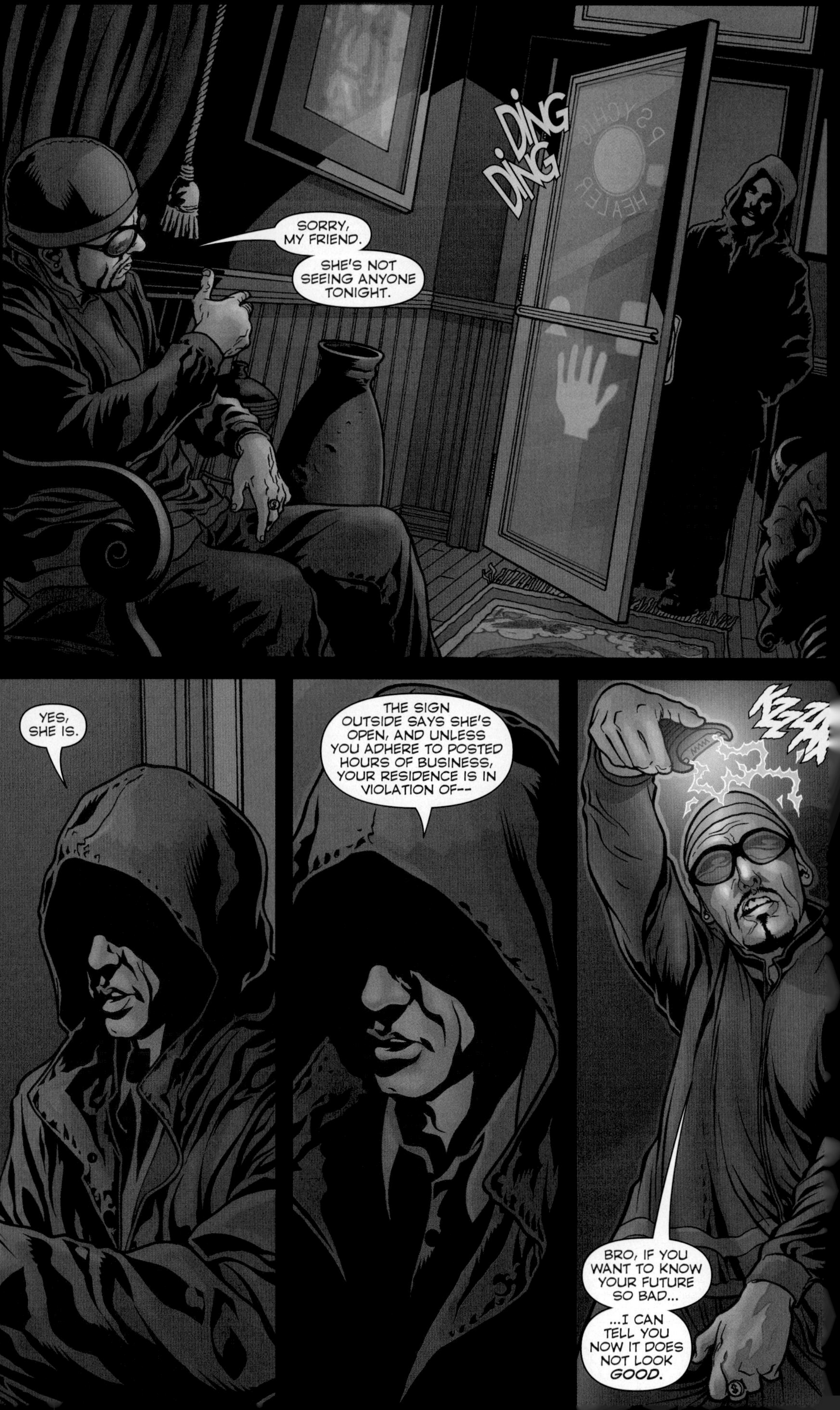
DING DING
PSYCHIC HEALER
SORRY, MY FRIEND.
SHE'S NOT SEEING ANYONE TONIGHT.
YES, SHE IS.
THE SIGN OUTSIDE SAYS SHE'S OPEN, AND UNLESS YOU ADHERE TO POSTED HOURS OF BUSINESS, YOUR RESIDENCE IS IN VIOLATION OF--
BRO, IF YOU WANT TO KNOW YOUR FUTURE SO BAD...
...I CAN TELL YOU NOW IT DOES NOT LOOK GOOD.

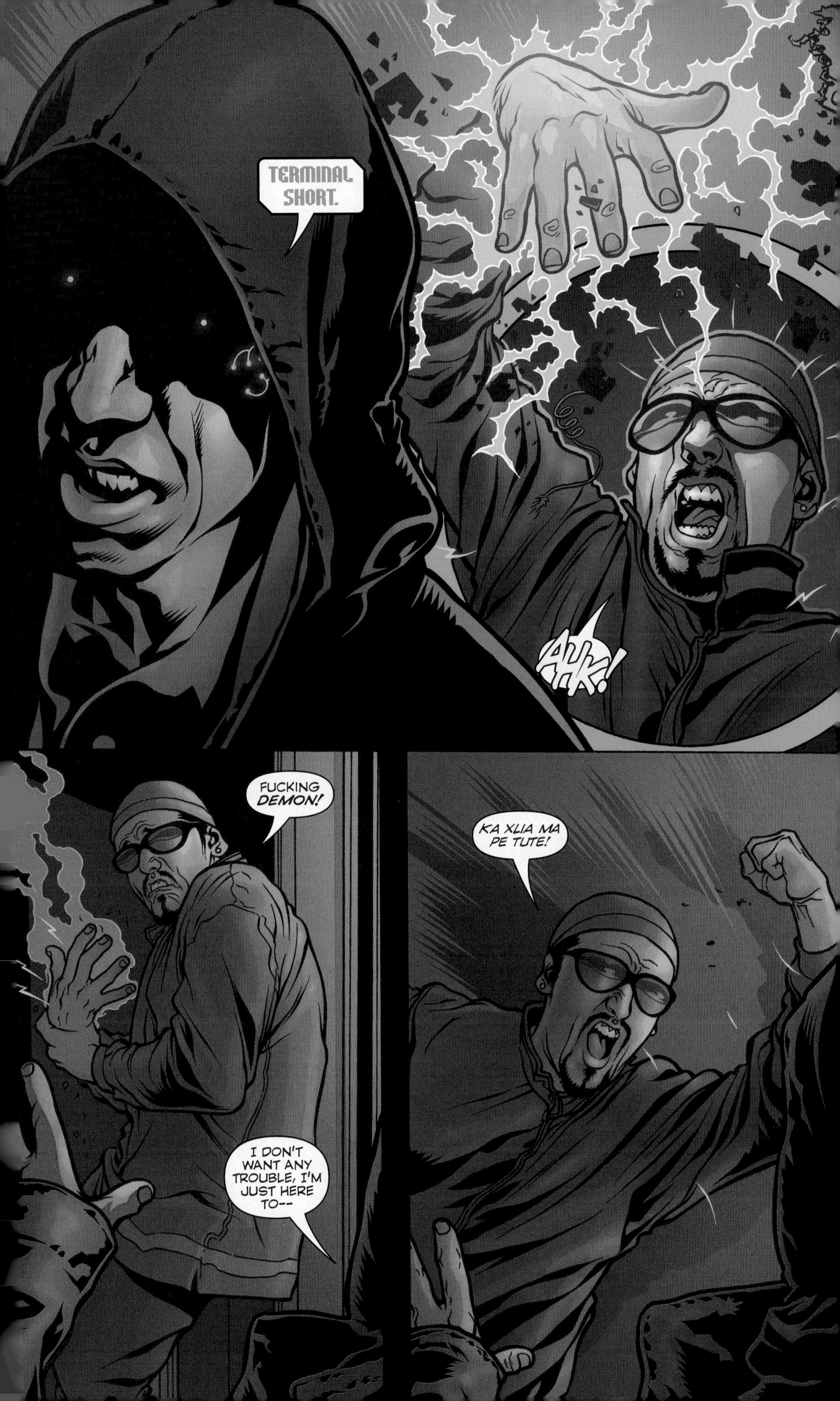
TERMINAL SHORT.
AHK!
FUCKING *DEMON!*
I DON'T WANT ANY TROUBLE, I'M JUST HERE TO--
KA XLIA MA PE TUTE!

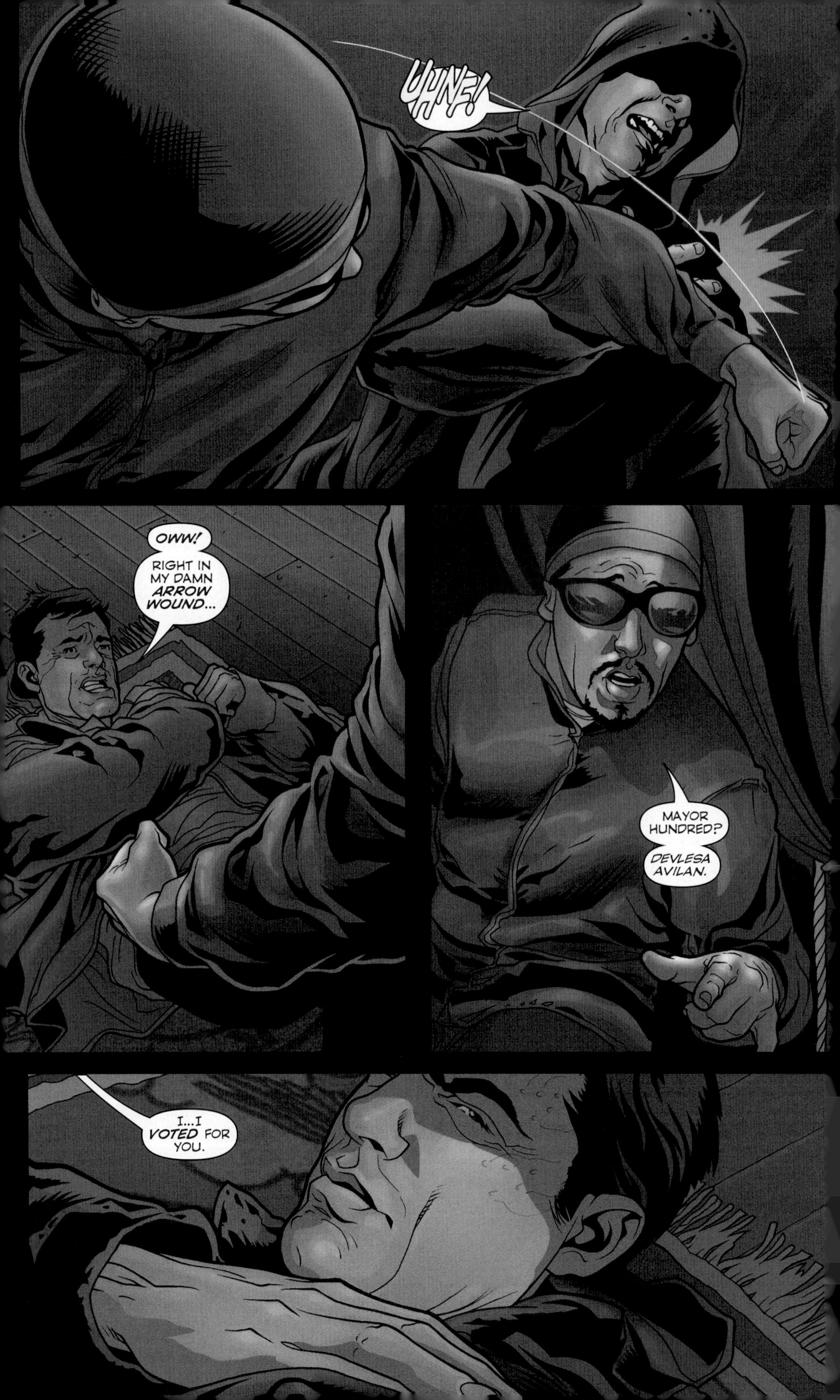
UHNF!
OWW!
RIGHT IN MY DAMN *ARROW WOUND*...
MAYOR HUNDRED?
DEVLESA AVILAN.
I...I *VOTED* FOR YOU.

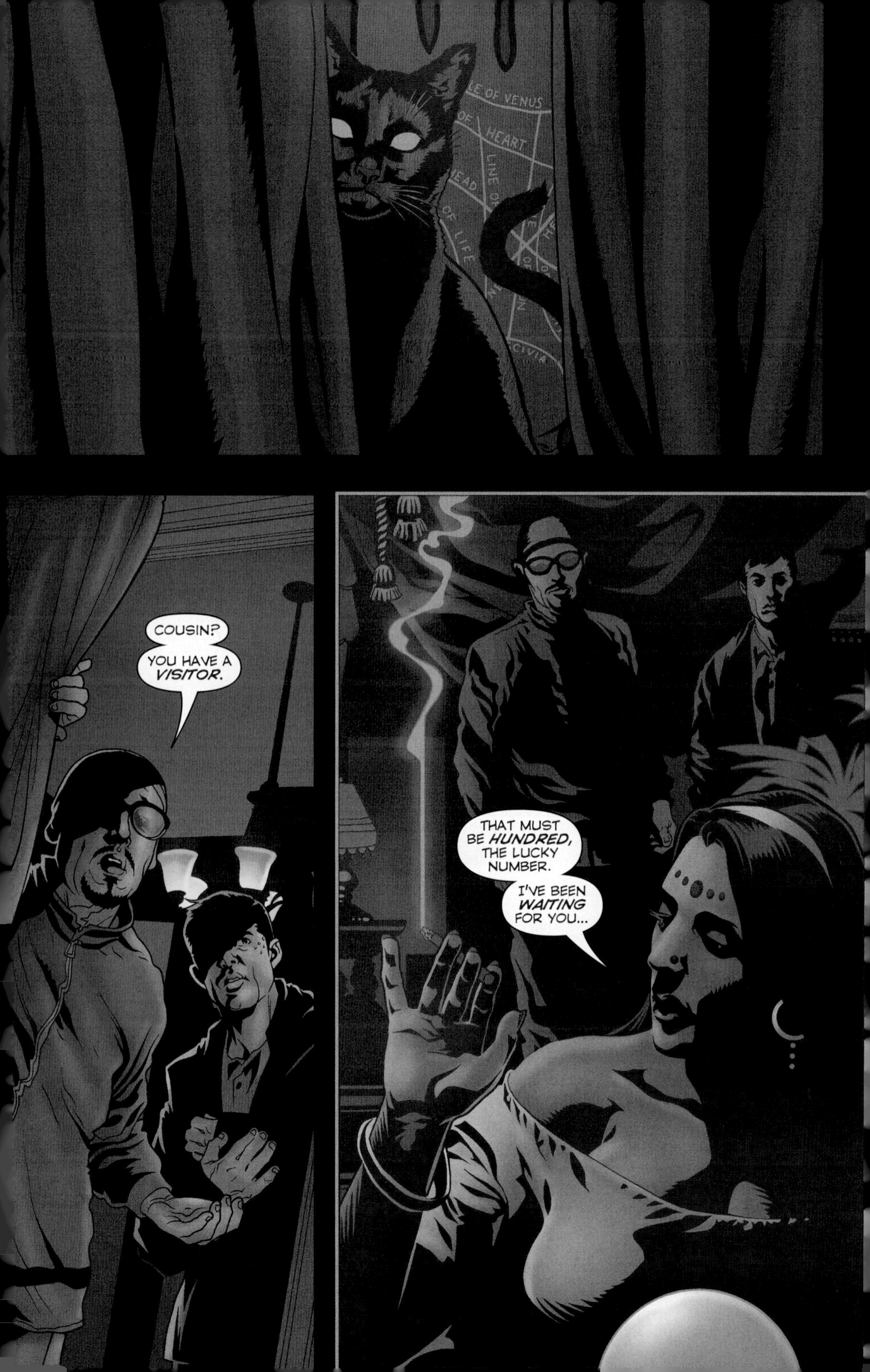
COUSIN?
YOU HAVE A *VISITOR*.
THAT MUST BE *HUNDRED*, THE LUCKY NUMBER.
I'VE BEEN *WAITING* FOR YOU...

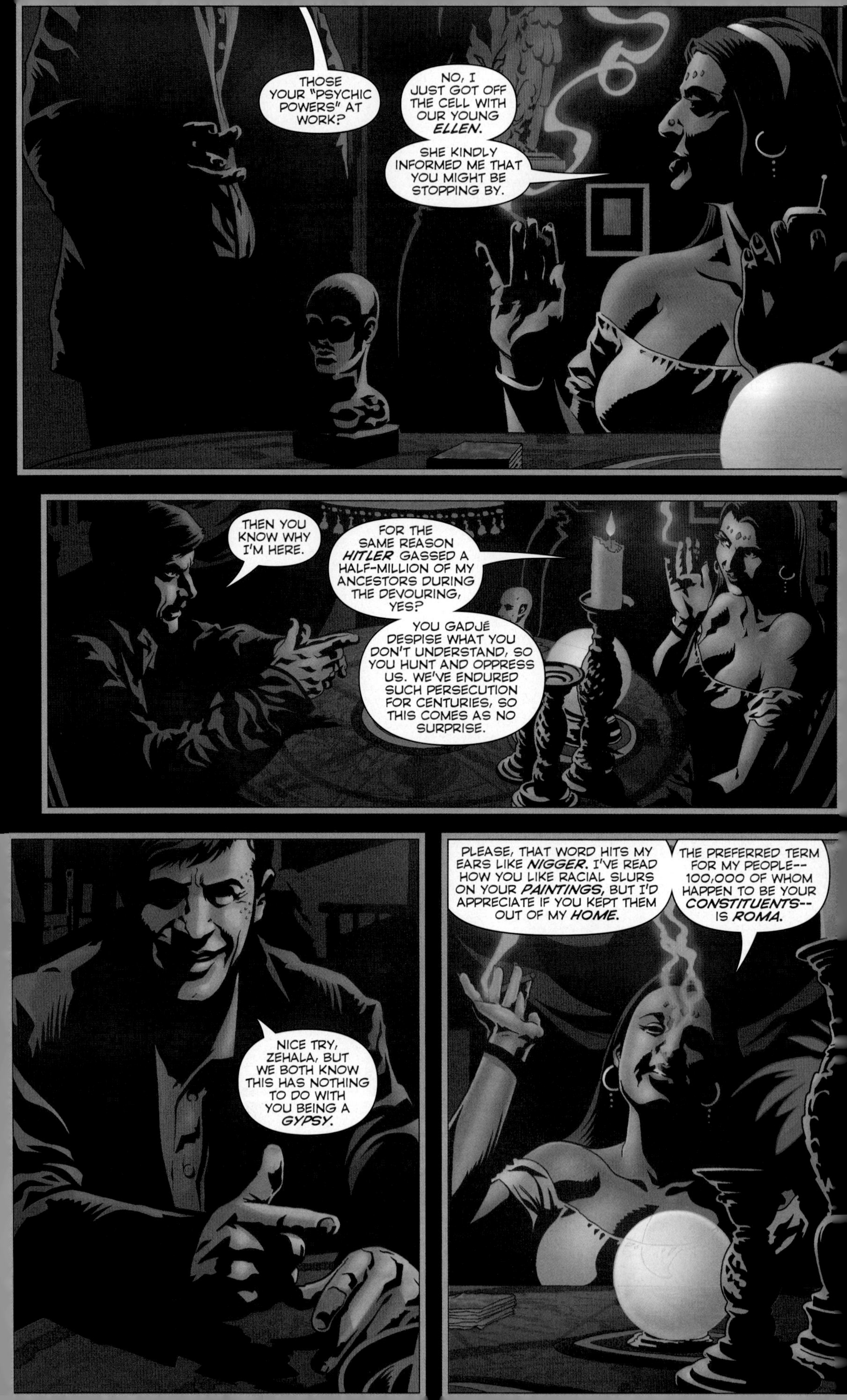
THOSE YOUR "PSYCHIC POWERS" AT WORK?
NO, I JUST GOT OFF THE CELL WITH OUR YOUNG *ELLEN*.
SHE KINDLY INFORMED ME THAT YOU MIGHT BE STOPPING BY.
THEN YOU KNOW WHY I'M HERE.
FOR THE SAME REASON *HITLER* GASSED A HALF-MILLION OF MY ANCESTORS DURING THE DEVOURING, YES?
YOU GADJÉ DESPISE WHAT YOU DON'T UNDERSTAND, SO YOU HUNT AND OPPRESS US. WE'VE ENDURED SUCH PERSECUTION FOR CENTURIES, SO THIS COMES AS NO SURPRISE.
NICE TRY, ZEHALA, BUT WE BOTH KNOW THIS HAS NOTHING TO DO WITH YOU BEING A *GYPSY*.
PLEASE, THAT WORD HITS MY EARS LIKE *NIGGER*. I'VE READ HOW YOU LIKE RACIAL SLURS ON YOUR *PAINTINGS*, BUT I'D APPRECIATE IF YOU KEPT THEM OUT OF MY *HOME*.
THE PREFERRED TERM FOR MY PEOPLE-- 100,000 OF WHOM HAPPEN TO BE YOUR *CONSTITUENTS*-- IS *ROMA*.

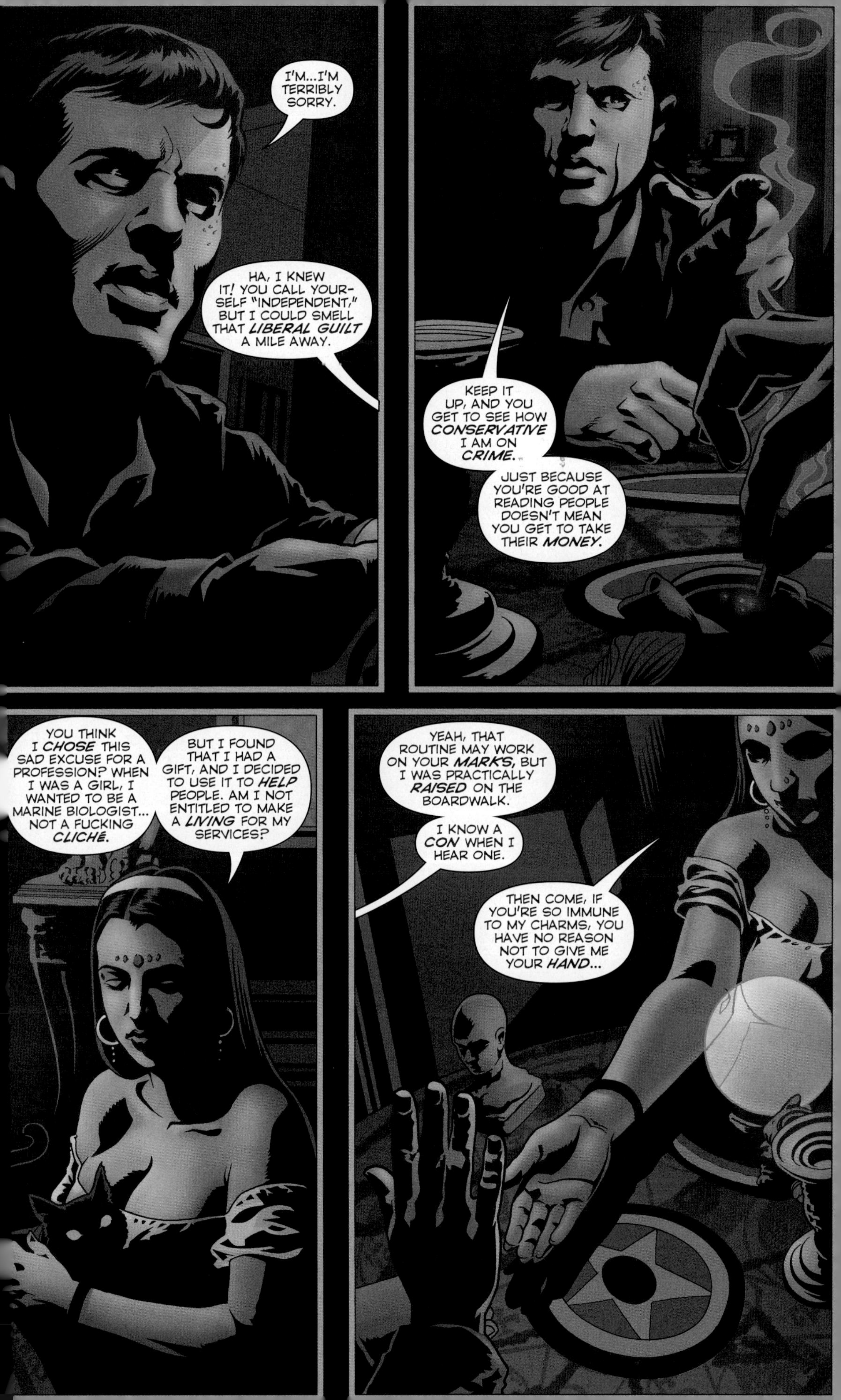

I'M...I'M TERRIBLY SORRY.
HA, I KNEW IT! YOU CALL YOUR-SELF "INDEPENDENT," BUT I COULD SMELL THAT LIBERAL GUILT A MILE AWAY.
KEEP IT UP, AND YOU GET TO SEE HOW CONSERVATIVE I AM ON CRIME.
JUST BECAUSE YOU'RE GOOD AT READING PEOPLE DOESN'T MEAN YOU GET TO TAKE THEIR MONEY.
YOU THINK I CHOSE THIS SAD EXCUSE FOR A PROFESSION? WHEN I WAS A GIRL, I WANTED TO BE A MARINE BIOLOGIST... NOT A FUCKING CLICHÉ.
BUT I FOUND THAT I HAD A GIFT, AND I DECIDED TO USE IT TO HELP PEOPLE. AM I NOT ENTITLED TO MAKE A LIVING FOR MY SERVICES?
YEAH, THAT ROUTINE MAY WORK ON YOUR MARKS, BUT I WAS PRACTICALLY RAISED ON THE BOARDWALK.
I KNOW A CON WHEN I HEAR ONE.
THEN COME, IF YOU'RE SO IMMUNE TO MY CHARMS, YOU HAVE NO REASON NOT TO GIVE ME YOUR HAND...

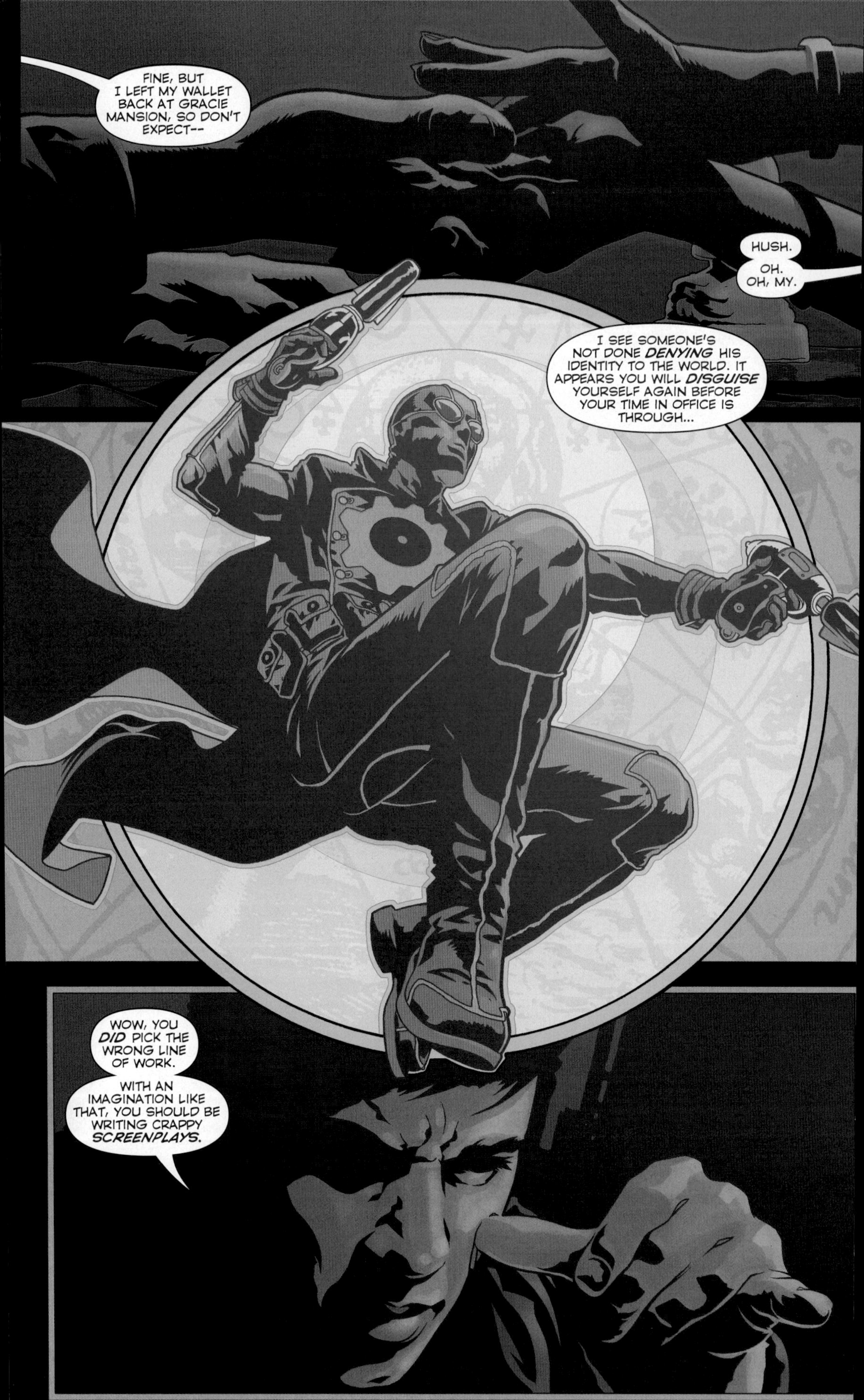

FINE, BUT I LEFT MY WALLET BACK AT GRACIE MANSION, SO DON'T EXPECT--
HUSH.
OH. OH, MY.
I SEE SOMEONE'S NOT DONE *DENYING* HIS IDENTITY TO THE WORLD. IT APPEARS YOU WILL *DISGUISE* YOURSELF AGAIN BEFORE YOUR TIME IN OFFICE IS THROUGH...
WOW, YOU *DID* PICK THE WRONG LINE OF WORK.
WITH AN IMAGINATION LIKE THAT, YOU SHOULD BE WRITING CRAPPY *SCREENPLAYS*.

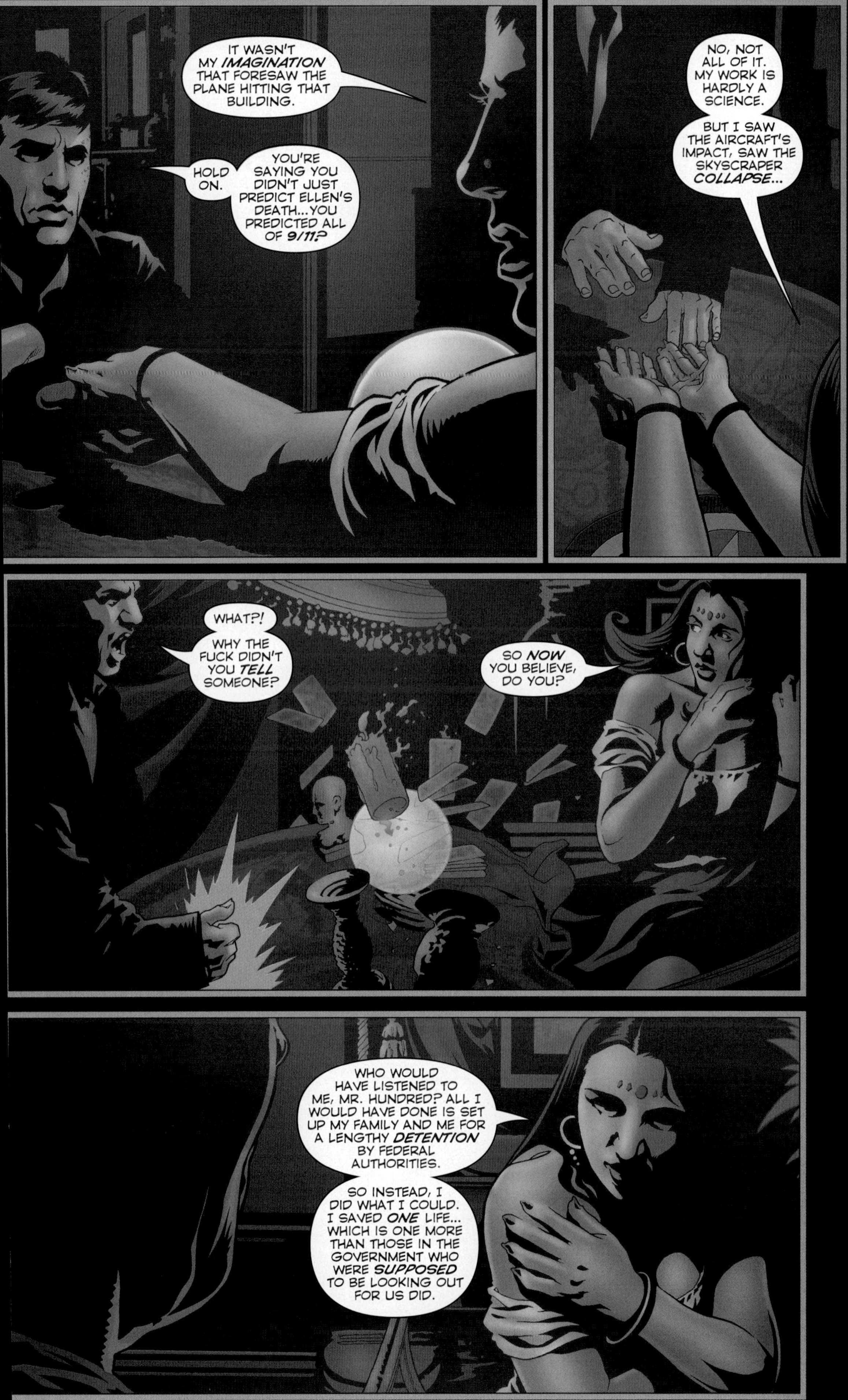
IT WASN'T MY IMAGINATION THAT FORESAW THE PLANE HITTING THAT BUILDING.
HOLD ON.
YOU'RE SAYING YOU DIDN'T JUST PREDICT ELLEN'S DEATH...YOU PREDICTED ALL OF 9/11?
NO, NOT ALL OF IT. MY WORK IS HARDLY A SCIENCE.
BUT I SAW THE AIRCRAFT'S IMPACT, SAW THE SKYSCRAPER COLLAPSE...
WHAT?!
WHY THE FUCK DIDN'T YOU TELL SOMEONE?
SO NOW YOU BELIEVE, DO YOU?
WHO WOULD HAVE LISTENED TO ME, MR. HUNDRED? ALL I WOULD HAVE DONE IS SET UP MY FAMILY AND ME FOR A LENGTHY DETENTION BY FEDERAL AUTHORITIES.
SO INSTEAD, I DID WHAT I COULD. I SAVED ONE LIFE... WHICH IS ONE MORE THAN THOSE IN THE GOVERNMENT WHO WERE SUPPOSED TO BE LOOKING OUT FOR US DID.

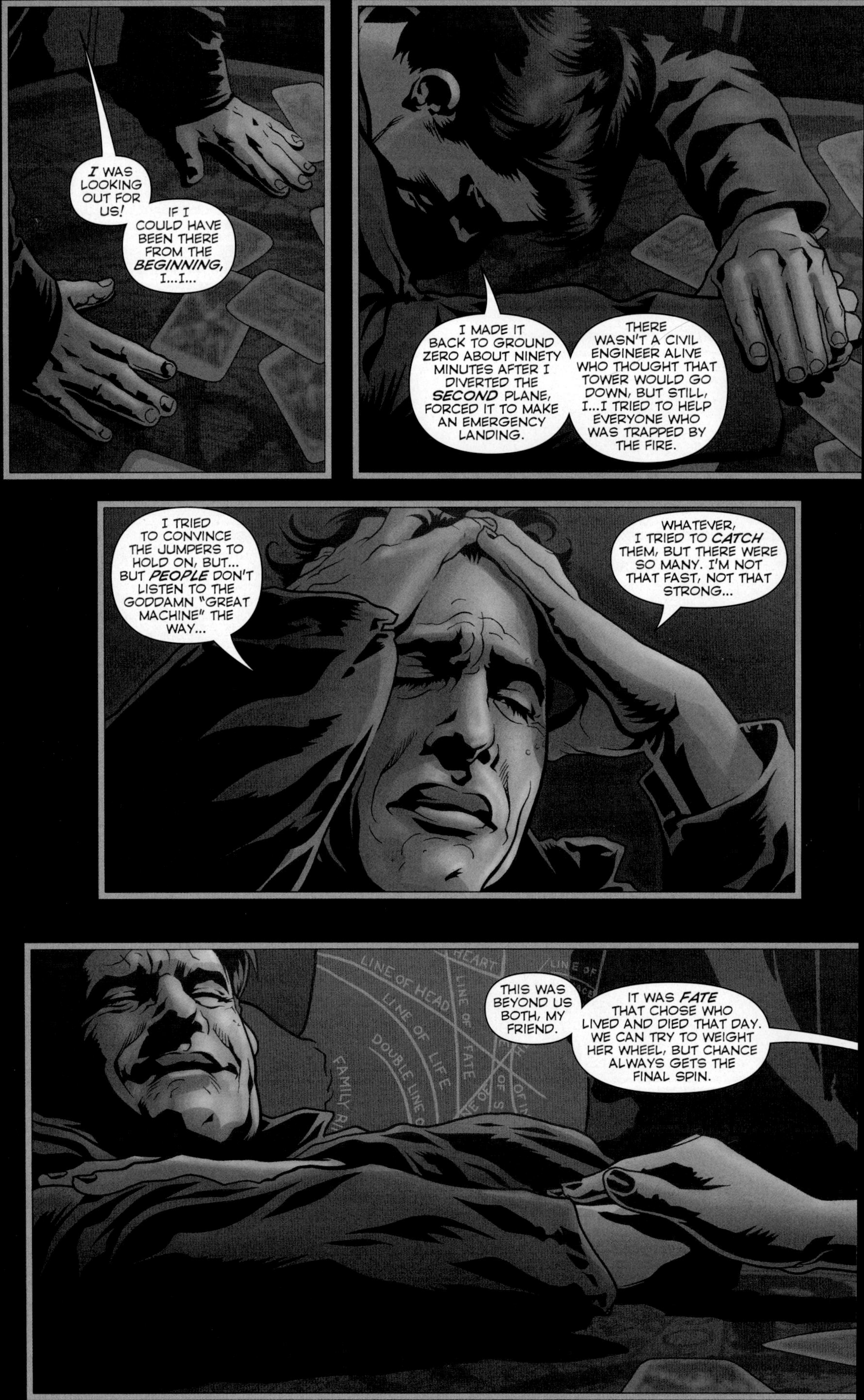
I WAS LOOKING OUT FOR US!
IF I COULD HAVE BEEN THERE FROM THE BEGINNING, I...I...
I MADE IT BACK TO GROUND ZERO ABOUT NINETY MINUTES AFTER I DIVERTED THE SECOND PLANE, FORCED IT TO MAKE AN EMERGENCY LANDING.
THERE WASN'T A CIVIL ENGINEER ALIVE WHO THOUGHT THAT TOWER WOULD GO DOWN, BUT STILL, I...I TRIED TO HELP EVERYONE WHO WAS TRAPPED BY THE FIRE.
I TRIED TO CONVINCE THE JUMPERS TO HOLD ON, BUT... BUT PEOPLE DON'T LISTEN TO THE GODDAMN "GREAT MACHINE" THE WAY...
WHATEVER, I TRIED TO CATCH THEM, BUT THERE WERE SO MANY. I'M NOT THAT FAST, NOT THAT STRONG...
LINE OF HEAD
LINE OF LIFE
THIS WAS BEYOND US BOTH, MY FRIEND.
IT WAS FATE THAT CHOSE WHO LIVED AND DIED THAT DAY. WE CAN TRY TO WEIGHT HER WHEEL, BUT CHANCE ALWAYS GETS THE FINAL SPIN.

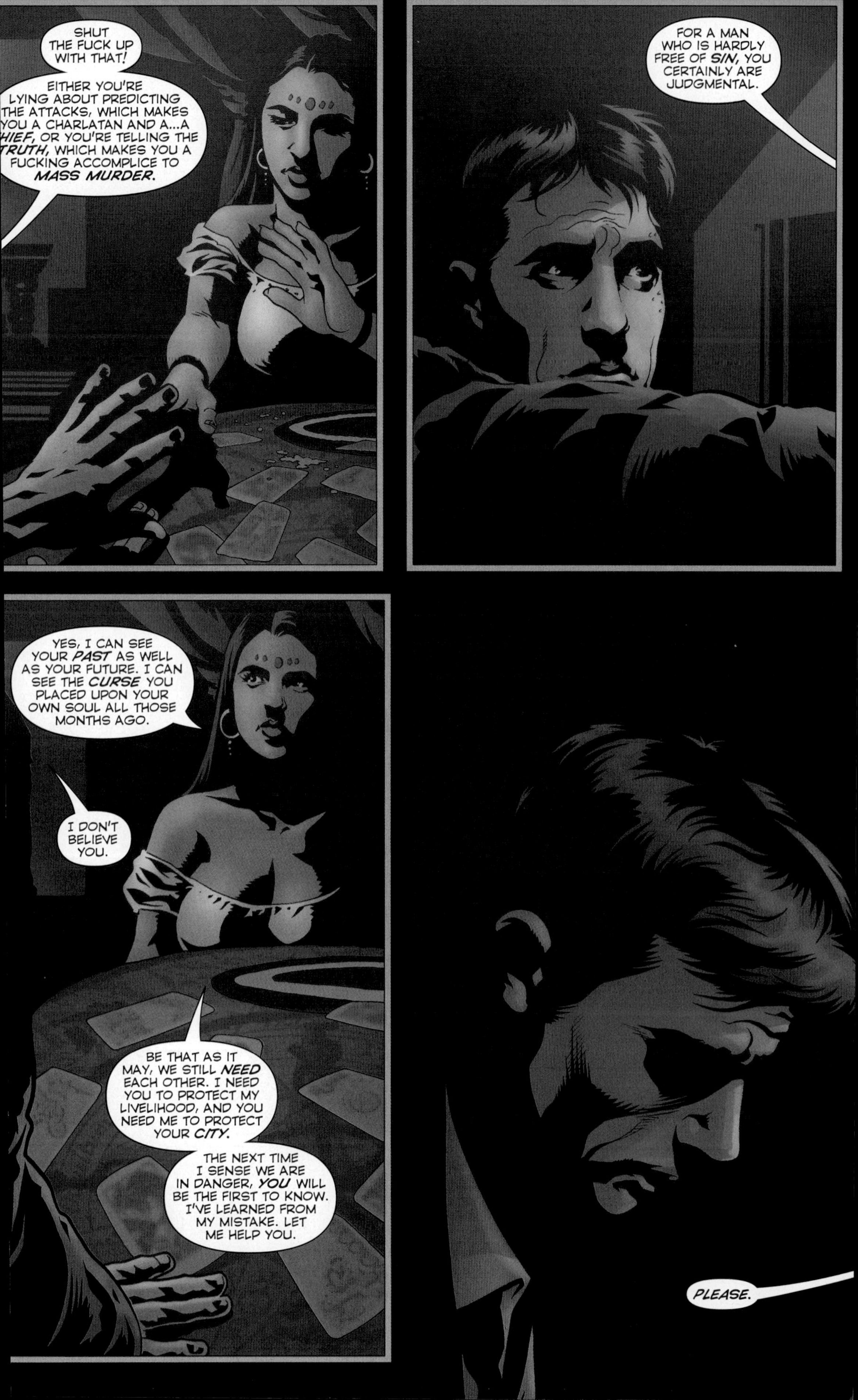
SHUT THE FUCK UP WITH THAT!
EITHER YOU'RE LYING ABOUT PREDICTING THE ATTACKS, WHICH MAKES YOU A CHARLATAN AND A...A HIEF, OR YOU'RE TELLING THE TRUTH, WHICH MAKES YOU A FUCKING ACCOMPLICE TO MASS MURDER.
FOR A MAN WHO IS HARDLY FREE OF SIN, YOU CERTAINLY ARE JUDGMENTAL.
YES, I CAN SEE YOUR PAST AS WELL AS YOUR FUTURE. I CAN SEE THE CURSE YOU PLACED UPON YOUR OWN SOUL ALL THOSE MONTHS AGO.
I DON'T BELIEVE YOU.
BE THAT AS IT MAY, WE STILL NEED EACH OTHER. I NEED YOU TO PROTECT MY LIVELIHOOD, AND YOU NEED ME TO PROTECT YOUR CITY.
THE NEXT TIME I SENSE WE ARE IN DANGER, YOU WILL BE THE FIRST TO KNOW. I'VE LEARNED FROM MY MISTAKE. LET ME HELP YOU.
PLEASE.

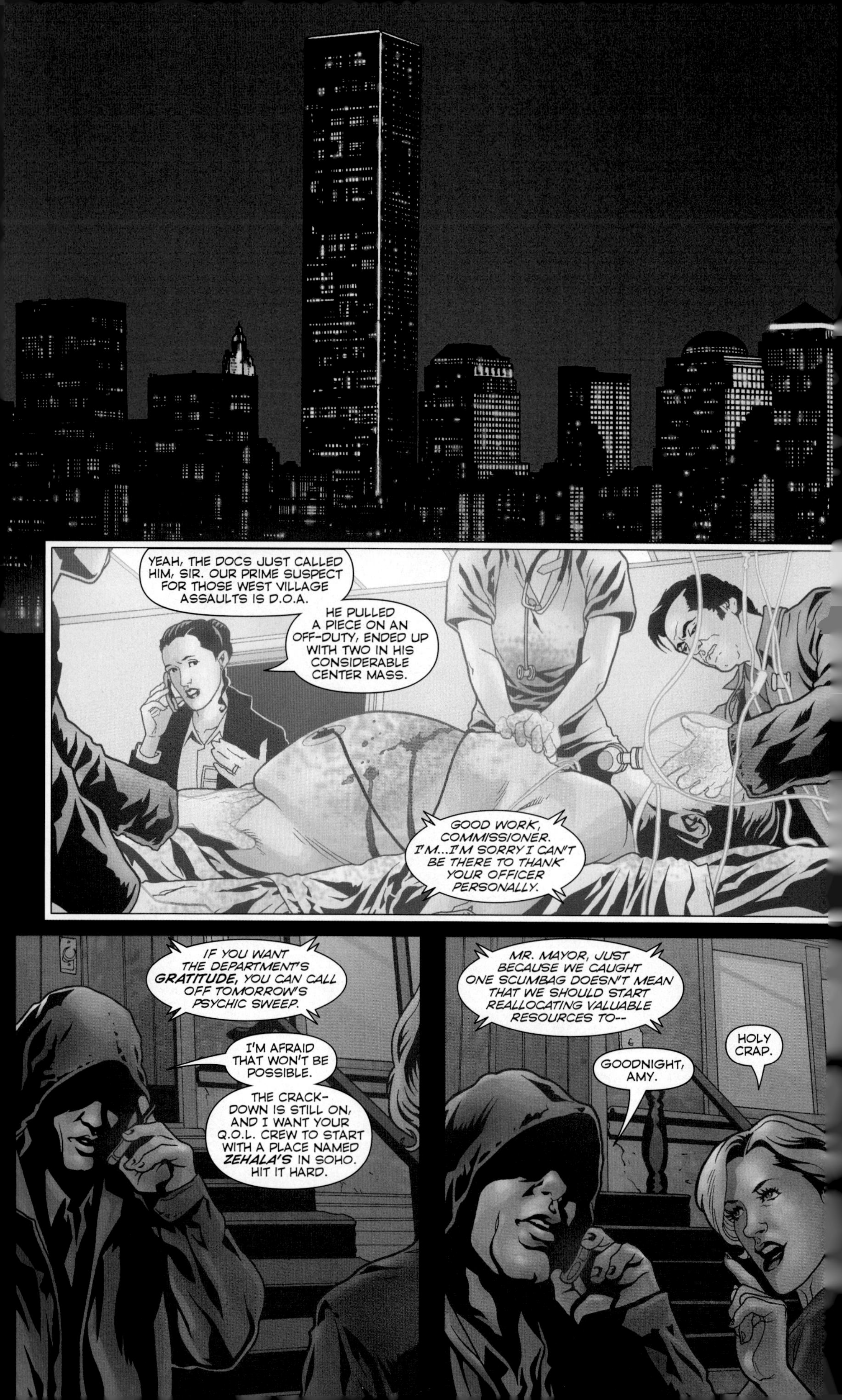
YEAH, THE DOCS JUST CALLED HIM, SIR. OUR PRIME SUSPECT FOR THOSE WEST VILLAGE ASSAULTS IS D.O.A.
HE PULLED A PIECE ON AN OFF-DUTY, ENDED UP WITH TWO IN HIS CONSIDERABLE CENTER MASS.
GOOD WORK, COMMISSIONER. I'M...I'M SORRY I CAN'T BE THERE TO THANK YOUR OFFICER PERSONALLY.
IF YOU WANT THE DEPARTMENT'S GRATITUDE, YOU CAN CALL OFF TOMORROW'S PSYCHIC SWEEP.
I'M AFRAID THAT WON'T BE POSSIBLE.
THE CRACK-DOWN IS STILL ON, AND I WANT YOUR Q.O.L. CREW TO START WITH A PLACE NAMED ZEHALA'S IN SOHO. HIT IT HARD.
MR. MAYOR, JUST BECAUSE WE CAUGHT ONE SCUMBAG DOESN'T MEAN THAT WE SHOULD START REALLOCATING VALUABLE RESOURCES TO--
GOODNIGHT, AMY.
HOLY CRAP.

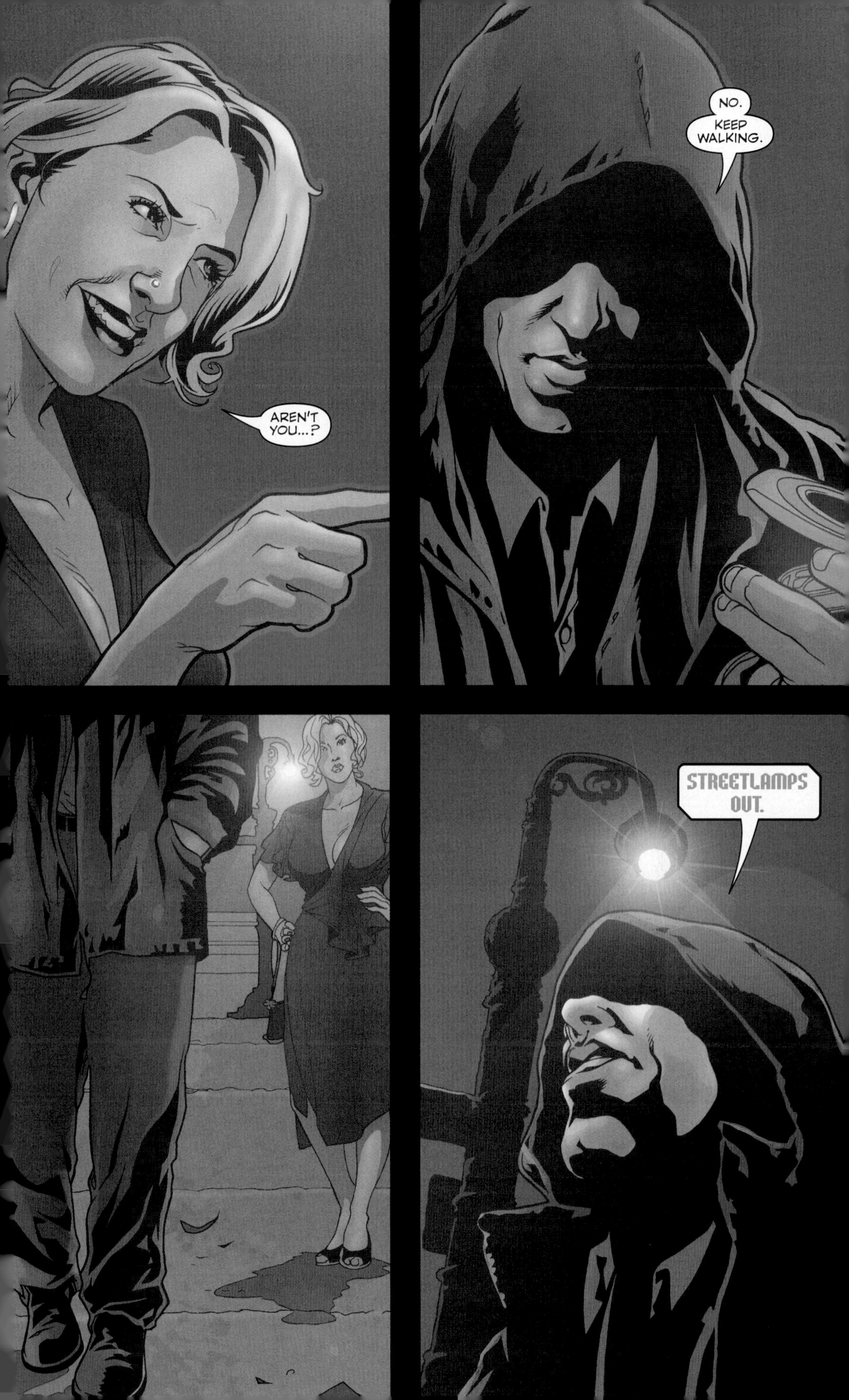
AREN'T YOU...?
NO. KEEP WALKING.
STREETLAMPS OUT.

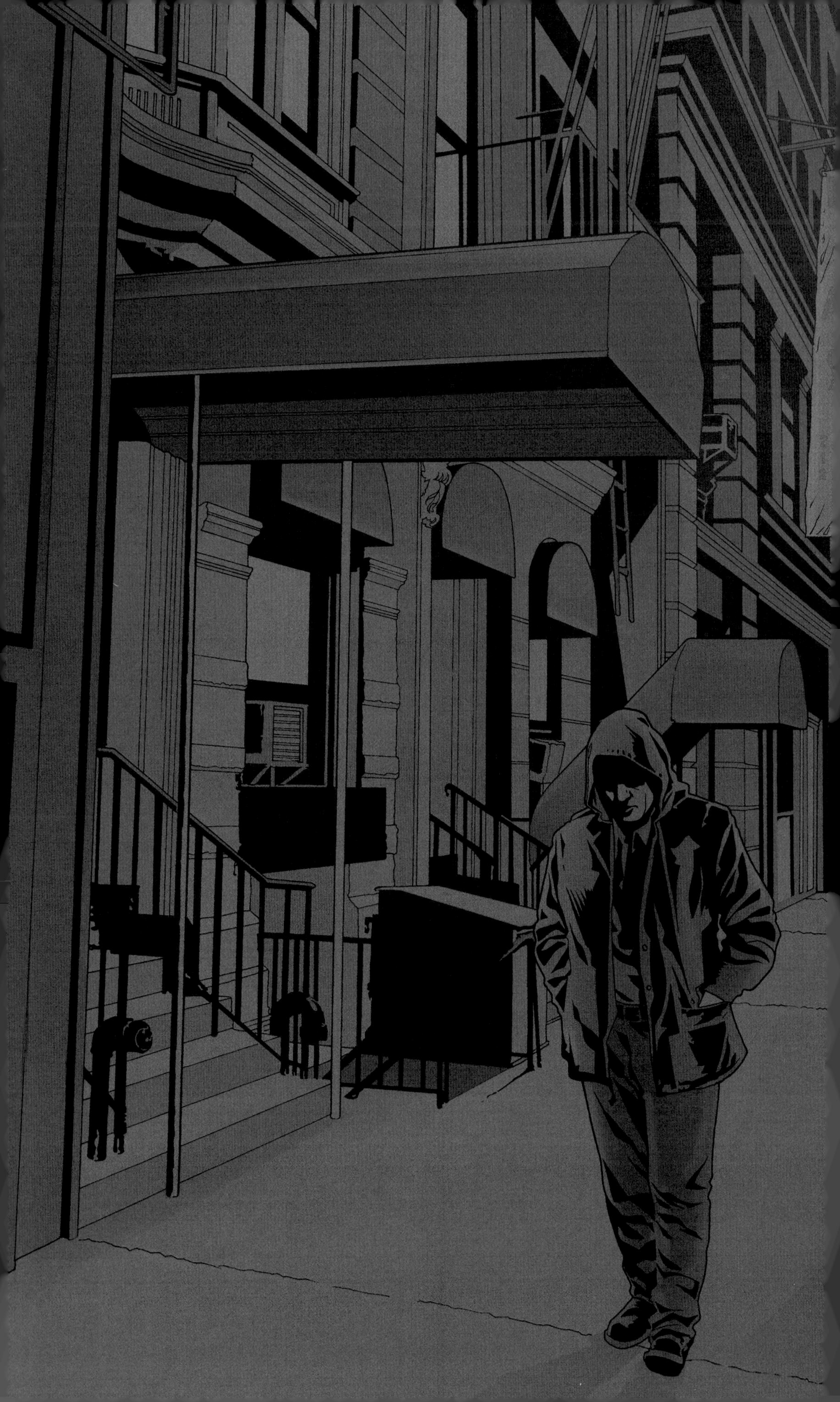

A NOTE FROM THE EDITOR:

What follows is Brian's original proposal for EX MACHINA. It features the character descriptions and plot summaries for the opening two arcs of the book (including some of the original character designs from Tony). Obviously, some of the details have changed from the original outline to what you just finished reading, and the tweaks reflect the ever-evolving development of the series. Enjoy!

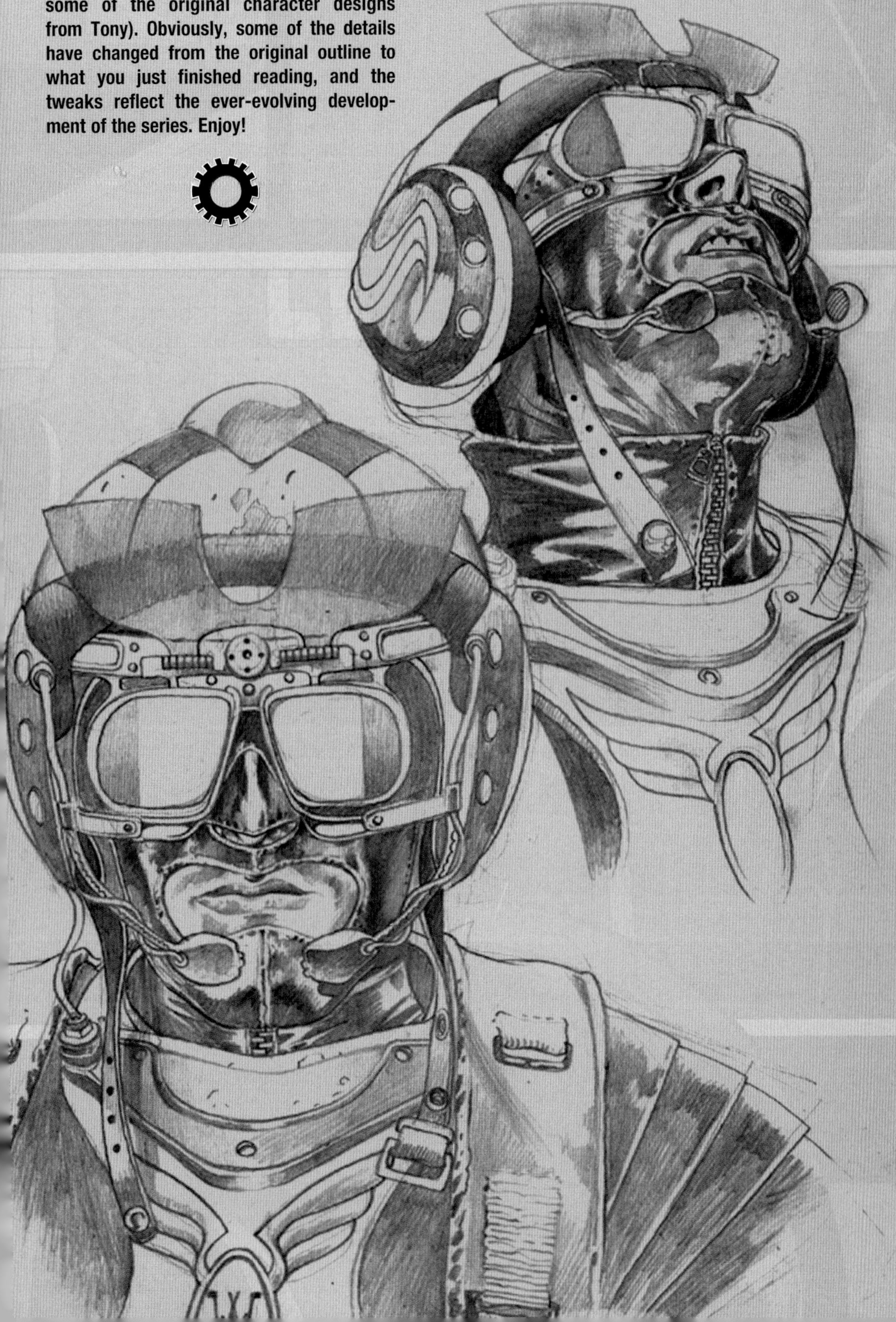

PROPOSAL

EX MACHINA - An Overview
by Brian K. Vaughan / Four Pages Total

EX MACHINA
An overview of the all-new
Homage Comics ongoing series
Prepared for Ben Abernathy & Co.
October 14, 2002

"One of the penalties for refusing to participate in politics is that you end up being governed by your inferiors."
-Plato

Tired of risking his life merely to help maintain the status quo, Mitchell "The Great Machine" Hundred retires from masked crimefighting and runs for Mayor of New York City…eventually winning by a landslide.

And while Mitch is able to do more good as mayor than he ever was as a superhero, he now has to overcome sex scandals, assassination attempts, and a $5 billion deficit.

***The West Wing* meets *Unbreakable* in a fast-paced political thriller "recommended for citizens of voting age."**

WINGMAN-
BIGGS
PLATES
SIMPLIFY DECO
SMOKES A PIPE
MAMBE A WING ON SIDES OF HIS
BACK SHEILD.
COOL BELT AT STUDIO
THUMB + FOREFINGER EXPOSED FOR BETTER DEXTERITY
MAMBE HE'S HALF JAPANESE
MOM JAPANESE
DAD WHITE
WEARS A MASK TO HIDE THAT (WAR TIME & ALL)

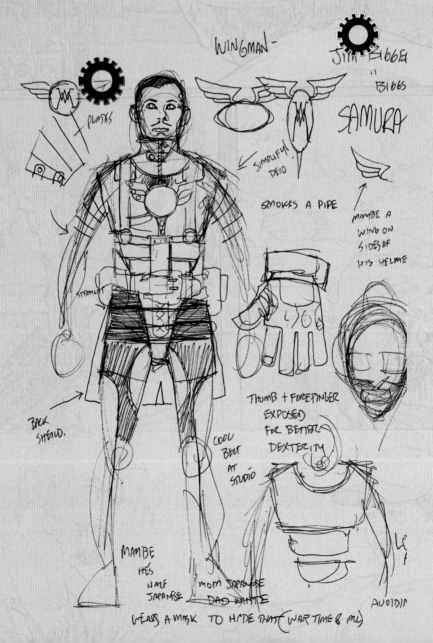

THE PREMISE

Surviving a mysterious accident, civil engineer and Brooklyn-native Mitchell Hundred gained incredible powers, including the ability to telepathically control all earthly technology.

Donning a mask and calling himself "The Great Machine," Mitchell had limited success as a costumed crimefighter. But once he revealed his identity to the world, he was able to parlay his notoriety into a burgeoning political career.

An Independent candidate for Mayor of New York City, Mitchell makes countless enemies in the Republican and Democratic parties when he's eventually elected. These adversaries (in addition to a jealous governor and a bloodthirsty media) prove to be much more dangerous than any of the villains Mitchell faced as the Machine.

With the help of a dedicated staff and a few eccentric companions, New York City's youngest mayor hopes to usher in an era of unity, growth and progress. But if he's going to succeed, Mitch will have to protect a dark secret that could ruin his career. Because when the masks come off… a few heroes still have something to hide.

On September 11th, even New Yorkers who hated Rudy Giuliani's politics (like me) had to be impressed by his brave, calm, compassionate response to the tragedy. For the first time in ages, a politician was seen as a hero. Never has there been a better time for a series like EX MACHINA, a parable about the power, fame, honor, and disgrace that come with serving the public in the 21st Century.

THE CHARACTERS

The Honorable Mayor Hundred - Born and raised in Brooklyn's Coney Island, Mitchell Hundred is a thirteenth-generation American. (His colonial ancestors renamed themselves after Brandywine Hundred, the division of Delaware where they first lived.)

Abandoned by his father and raised by his mother, Mitchell was an only child who spent much of his youth reading DC Comics. A talented artist, he wanted to draw superheroes like Batman and Superman for a living, but his mom encouraged him to pursue the more lucrative world of architecture. Eventually graduating from NYU, the young man went on to become one of the city's premier civil engineers.

After a strange onsite accident, fragments of a seemingly alien engine were grafted to Mitchell's face and body. These fragments somehow granted him the ability to telepathically "communicate" with technology (a bit like Aquaman communicates with marine life). Though he has difficulty commanding simple/compound machines like semi-automatic weapons and typewriters, Mitchell has almost full dominion over complex machinery like cars and computers.

Hoping to use these newfound abilities to serve the public (like the fictional heroes of his youth), Mitchell donned a cape and mask and became the world's first real superhero. Calling himself "the Great Machine" (how his hero Thomas Jefferson once described American society), he set out to fight crime in New York City. Unfortunately, despite a few successes, Mitchell usually ended up getting in the way of authorities, and doing more harm than good.

Gaining notoriety more as a spectacle than a champion, the Great Machine realized he could at least use his newfound celebrity to promote his deeply held political beliefs. Eventually revealing his true identity to the public, Mitchell announced that he would be running for Mayor of New York City.

A young, inexperienced Independent, Mitchell knew that he stood little chance of defeating the Republican and Democratic candidates, but he hoped to introduce important new ideas into the debate.

But when Mitchell used his powers to help stop a terrorist attack just before Election Day, grateful New Yorkers rushed to the polls and elected him Mayor... perhaps the most shocking political win since Jesse Ventura became governor.

Our story begins after Mitchell Hundred's been in office for a little over a month. The honeymoon is almost over, and New Yorkers want to know what their Mayor plans to do about rising crime rates, falling test scores, and an economy in jeopardy. The former civil engineer has an ambitious blueprint to rebuild the Big Apple, but he also has a lot of enemies.

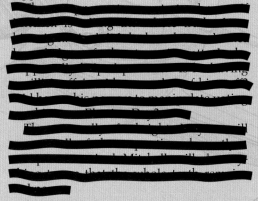

Deputy Mayor Wylie - As Deputy Mayor of Operations, Dave Wylie is Mitchell's right-hand man. This middle-aged African-American Democrat is a career politician, and while he admires his boss's idealism, he's always trying to temper it with the cynical realism that comes from years of experience in local government. A devoted family man and father of three, Wylie is obsessed with repairing the city's profoundly troubled school system.

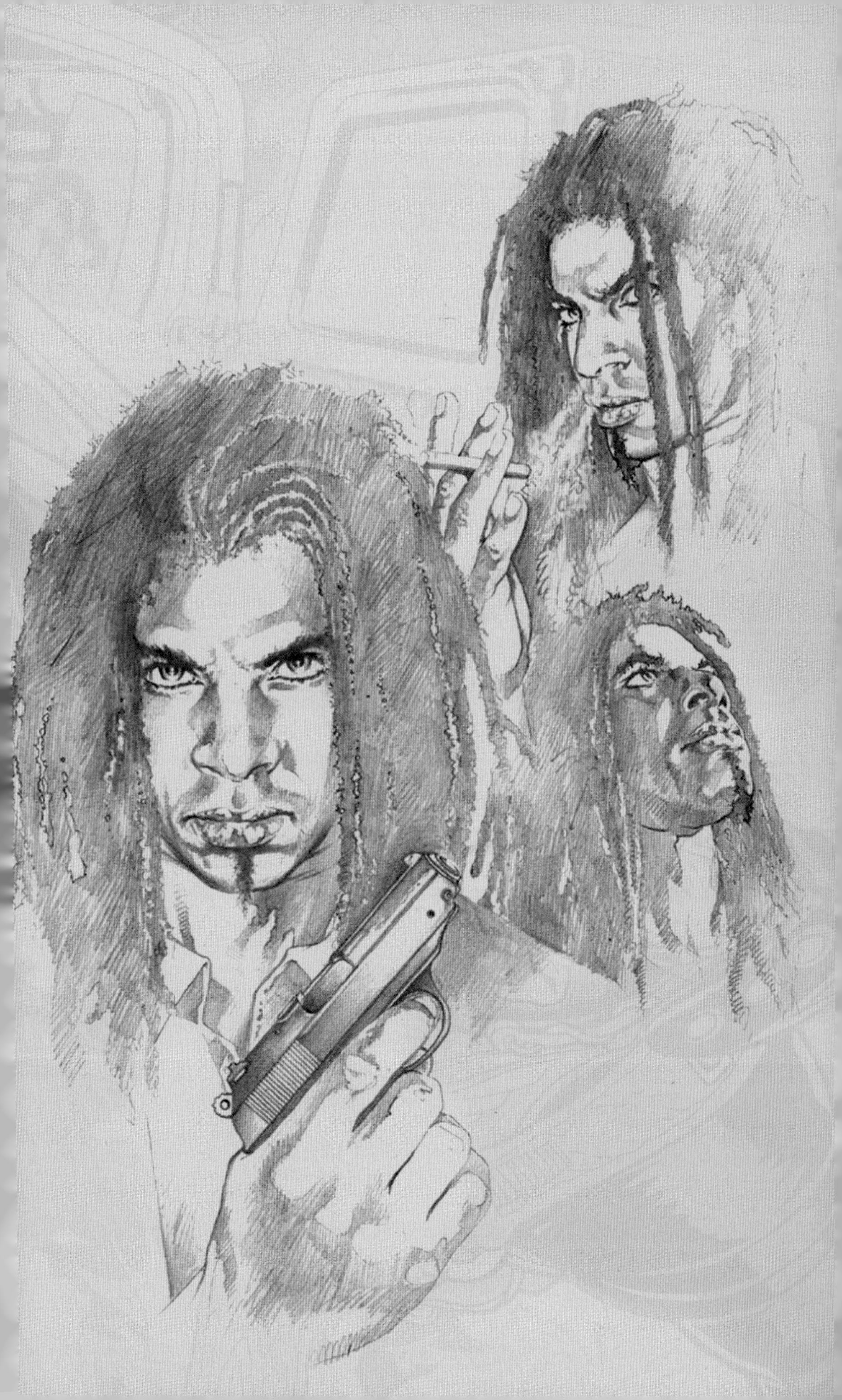

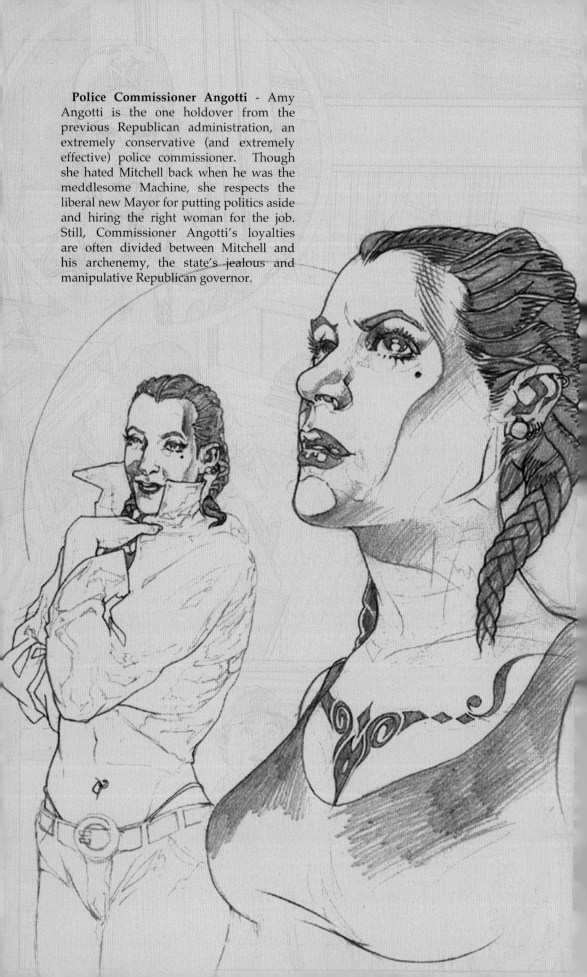

Police Commissioner Angotti - Amy Angotti is the one holdover from the previous Republican administration, an extremely conservative (and extremely effective) police commissioner. Though she hated Mitchell back when he was the meddlesome Machine, she respects the liberal new Mayor for putting politics aside and hiring the right woman for the job. Still, Commissioner Angotti's loyalties are often divided between Mitchell and his archenemy, the state's jealous and manipulative Republican governor.

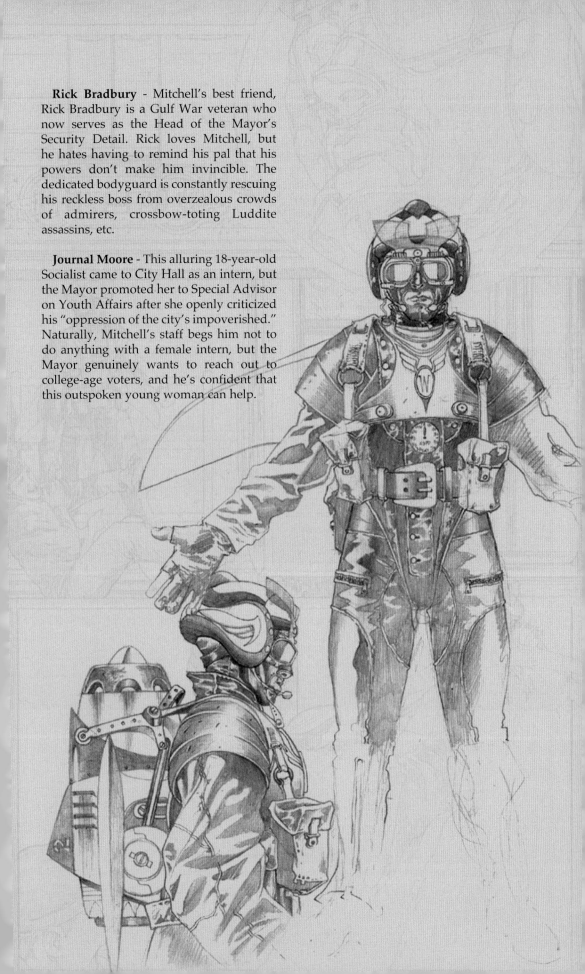

Rick Bradbury - Mitchell's best friend, Rick Bradbury is a Gulf War veteran who now serves as the Head of the Mayor's Security Detail. Rick loves Mitchell, but he hates having to remind his pal that his powers don't make him invincible. The dedicated bodyguard is constantly rescuing his reckless boss from overzealous crowds of admirers, crossbow-toting Luddite assassins, etc.

Journal Moore - This alluring 18-year-old Socialist came to City Hall as an intern, but the Mayor promoted her to Special Advisor on Youth Affairs after she openly criticized his "oppression of the city's impoverished." Naturally, Mitchell's staff begs him not to do anything with a female intern, but the Mayor genuinely wants to reach out to college-age voters, and he's confident that this outspoken young woman can help.

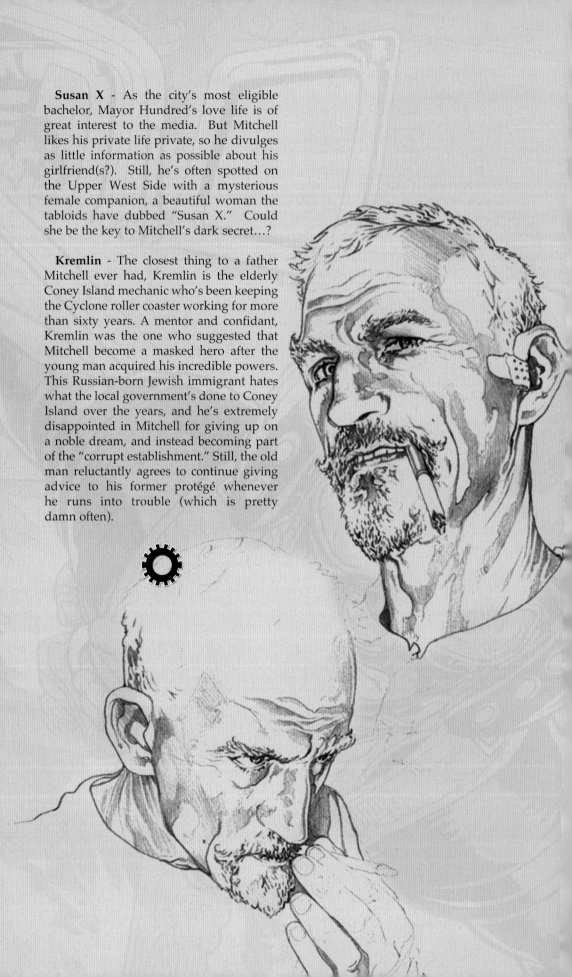

Susan X - As the city's most eligible bachelor, Mayor Hundred's love life is of great interest to the media. But Mitchell likes his private life private, so he divulges as little information as possible about his girlfriend(s?). Still, he's often spotted on the Upper West Side with a mysterious female companion, a beautiful woman the tabloids have dubbed "Susan X." Could she be the key to Mitchell's dark secret...?

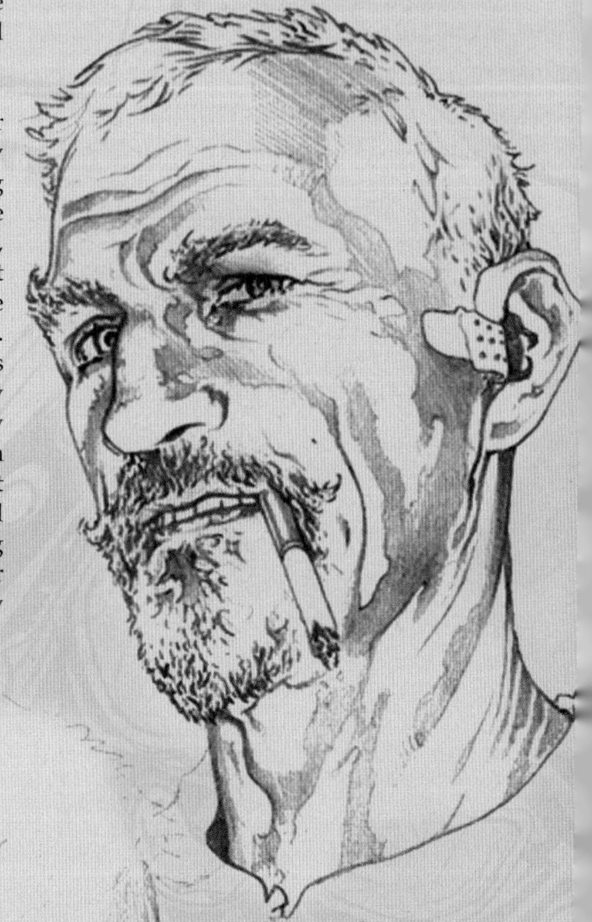

Kremlin - The closest thing to a father Mitchell ever had, Kremlin is the elderly Coney Island mechanic who's been keeping the Cyclone roller coaster working for more than sixty years. A mentor and confidant, Kremlin was the one who suggested that Mitchell become a masked hero after the young man acquired his incredible powers. This Russian-born Jewish immigrant hates what the local government's done to Coney Island over the years, and he's extremely disappointed in Mitchell for giving up on a noble dream, and instead becoming part of the "corrupt establishment." Still, the old man reluctantly agrees to continue giving advice to his former protégé whenever he runs into trouble (which is pretty damn often).

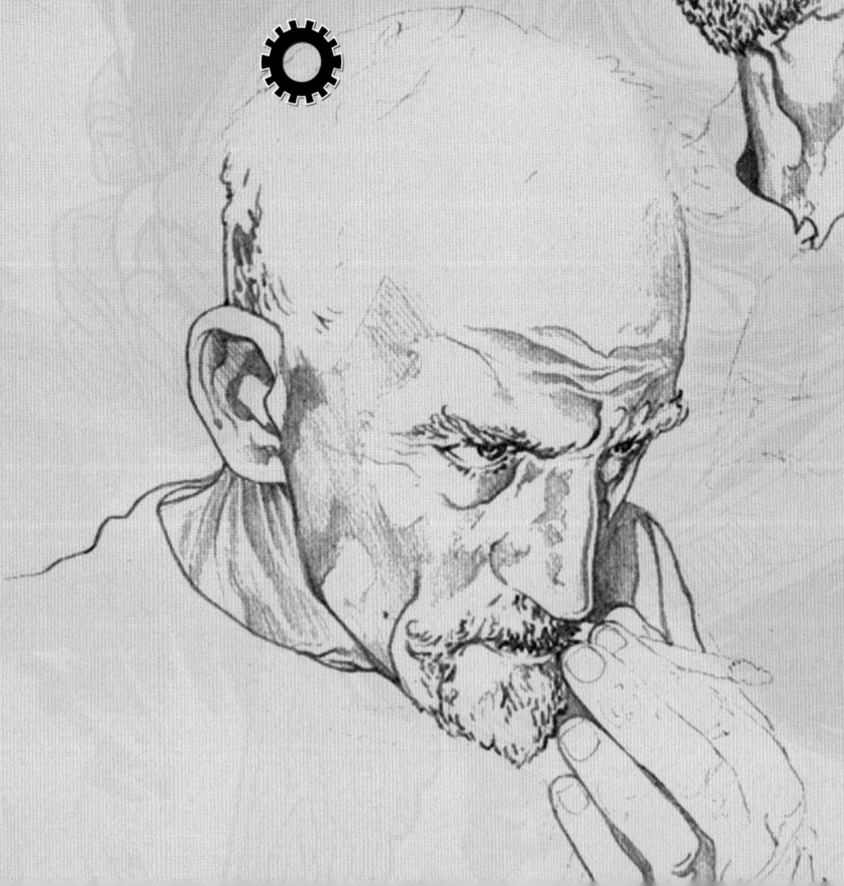

THE STORIES

Each five-issue arc of EX MACHINA will comprise three parallel storylines. The "A-Plot" will usually be an action-packed thriller containing some aspect of sci-fi, horror, super-heroism, etc. The "B-Plot" will be a political drama dealing with more down-to-earth, real world issues. And the "C-Plot" will involve our "soap opera" elements, the ongoing romance and intrigue that will hopefully bring readers back month after month. Obviously, these storylines will occasionally intersect, and while some plot points may bleed over from one arc to the next, each complete arc will generally be a self-contained (and TPB-ready!) adventure, providing new readers with a perfect jumping-on point every five issues.

Anyway, here are my very tentative plans for our first two arcs:

"State of Emergency" (Issues #1-#5): During New York's worst blizzard since the Christmas storm of 1947, unknown gunmen begin killing snowplow divers. When the surviving drivers refuse to show up for work and clear the congested roads, the new Mayor and his administration must use all of their resources to find the killers and avert a citywide shutdown (without help from the governor, who refuses to activate the National Guard). Mitchell fears that these executions may be mob related, but when they turn out to be the work of a violent gang of teenagers (they're trying to keep city schools closed all winter), the situation becomes even more complicated.

Meanwhile, the Mayor must also deal with the fallout of the previous administration's "welfare reform," which forced many of the city's unemployed and under-employed into grievous poverty. Mitchell desperately searches for novel ways to create jobs and provide for single mothers.

To make matters worse, the former superhero is forced to contend with a blackmailing tabloid reporter who's some-how learned Mitchell's dark secret. Mayor Hundred could easily use his new powers to kill this pacemaker-wearing journalist… but will he?

"Tag" (Issues #6-#10): Dealing with graffiti is an important rite of passage for every leader of New York City, but no one's ever had it quite as rough as Mayor Hundred. Strange spray-painted "glyphs" begin appearing all over the five boroughs, occult symbols that cause serious seizures in anyone who looks at them. And as quickly as the markings are removed, others soon appear. After a fatal glyph-related bus accident kills three people, many citizens refuse to leave their homes. As the police hunt for the taggers behind these crimes, the Mayor searches for a possible "antidote." Could these symbols be related to the accident that gave Mitchell his powers?

Elsewhere, in one of the city's countless art museums, minority groups begin pro-testing new paintings that they consider racist. Because the offensive installation is technically funded by tax dollars, Mitchell must decide between his most loyal constituents and his own fierce dedication to the First Amendment.

Finally, Mayor Hundred faces the ramifications of last arc's blackmailing storyline, while he also tries to make sense of his increasingly complicated love life.

VERTIGO

"A seriously funny, nuanced fable...Grade A."
—Entertainment Weekly

"Complete and utter comic gold."
—Publishers Weekly (starred review)

"Funny and scary...an utterly believable critique of society. A+."
—The Washington Post

"The year's best movie is a comic book: Brian K. Vaughan's 'Y: The Last Man'." —National Public Radio All Things Considered

Y: THE LAST MAN

BRIAN K. VAUGHAN & PIA GUERRA

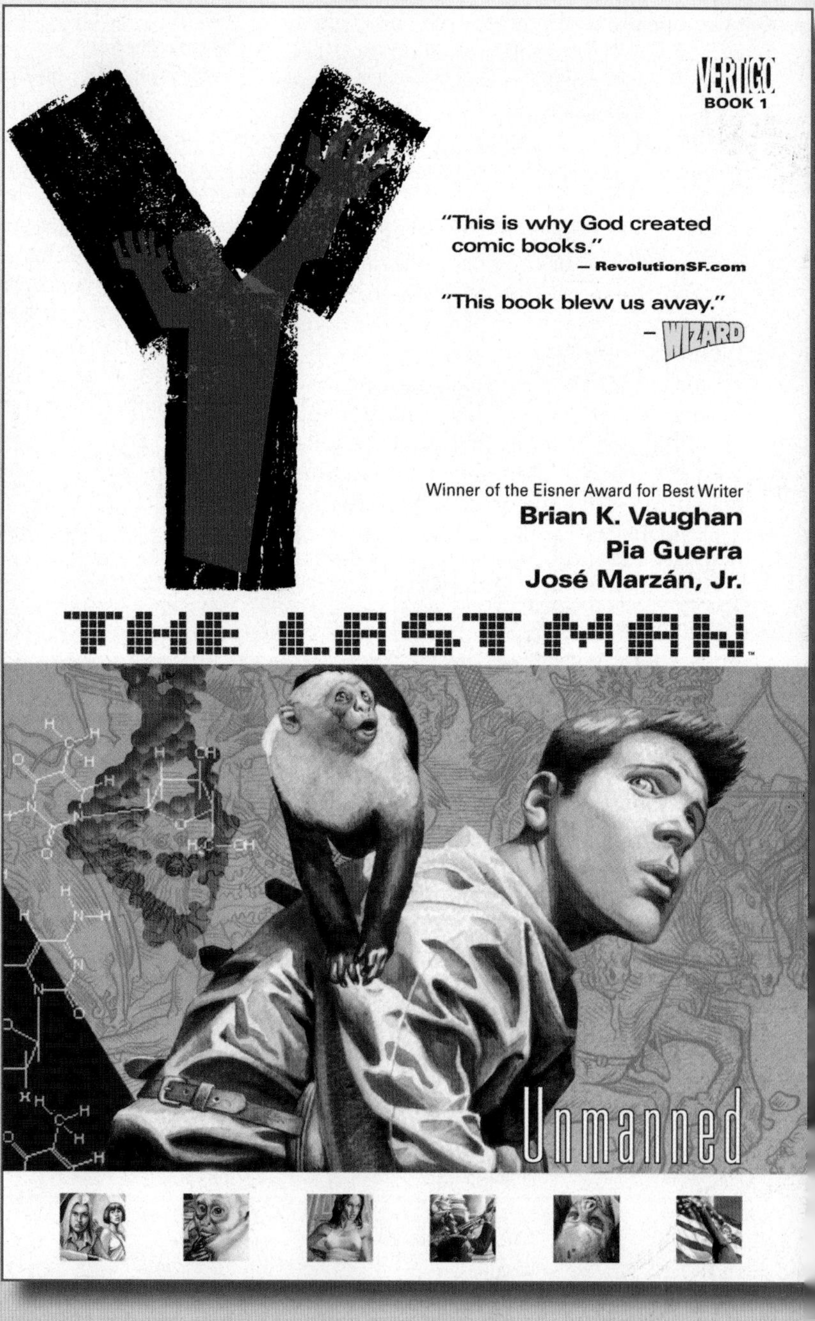
VERTIGO
BOOK 1
"This is why God created comic books."
— RevolutionSF.com
"This book blew us away."
— WIZARD
Winner of the Eisner Award for Best Writer
Brian K. Vaughan
Pia Guerra
José Marzán, Jr.
THE LAST MAN
Unmanned

Y: THE LAST MAN VOL. 10: WHYS AND WHEREFORES

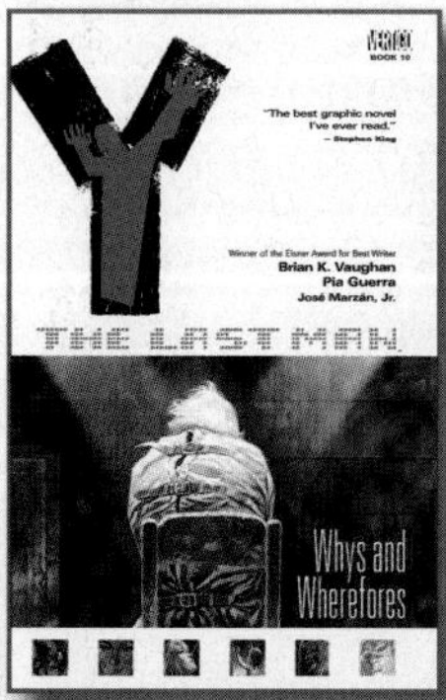
THE LAST MAN
Whys and Wherefores

Read the Complete Series!

Y: THE LAST MAN VOL. 1: UNMANNED

Y: THE LAST MAN VOL. 2: CYCLES

Y: THE LAST MAN VOL. 3: ONE SMALL STEP

Y: THE LAST MAN VOL. 4: SAFEWORD

Y: THE LAST MAN VOL. 5: RING OF TRUTH

Y: THE LAST MAN VOL. 6: GIRL ON GIRL

Y: THE LAST MAN VOL. 7: PAPER DOLLS

Y: THE LAST MAN VOL. 8: KIMONO DRAGONS

Y: THE LAST MAN VOL. 9: MOTHERLAND

Y: THE LAST MAN VOL. 10: WHYS AND WHEREFORES

Y: THE LAST MAN: THE DELUXE EDITION BOOK ONE

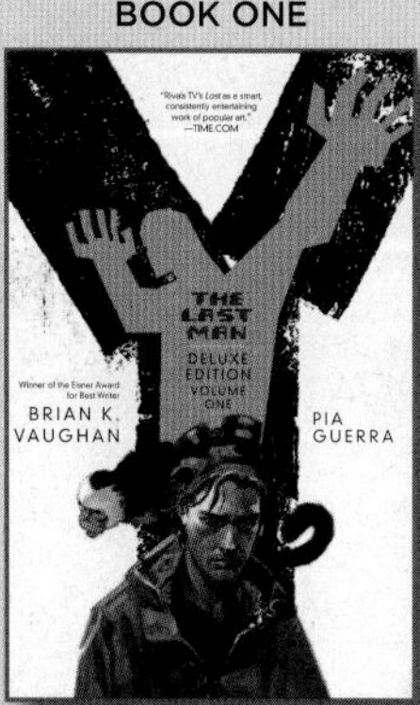
THE LAST MAN
DELUXE EDITION VOLUME ONE
BRIAN K. VAUGHAN
PIA GUERRA

ALSO AVAILABLE AS DELUXE HARDCOVER IN A 5 VOLUME SERIES